MW00805378

LIFE AND DEATH IN THE COMIC BOOK TRENCHES

ENTIRE CONTENTS ARE COPYRIGHT BRANDON GRAHAM.
EXCEPT FOR REVIEW PURPOSES, NO PORTION OF THIS PUBLICATION
MAY BE REPRODUCED WITHOUT THE PRIOR WRITTEN CONSENT OF
BRANDON GRAHAM. PRINTED IN CANADA. SEPTEMBER 2004 DUDE.
ESCALATOR IS PUBLISHED BY ALTERNATIVE COMICS - 503 NW 37TH
AVENUE, GAINESVILLE, FL 32609-2204. PHONE: (352) 373-6336.
EMAIL: JMASON@INDYWORLD.COM
VISIT: WWW.INDYWORLD.COM/ALTCOMICS
ISBN: 1-891867-81-4

OSCAVA

IT BEGAN
RIGHT HERE AND
CONTINUED TO
GAIN MOMENTUM

RED LIGHTS
FOLLOWED BY
YELLOW LIGHTS
FOLLOWED BY
GREEN.

GREEN IS
GO.

T.P. WITH ALOE TASTES NASTY.
YUK.

FOR
JESSICA,
FOR EVERYTHING.

cherry
grape
CHILD OF COLD.

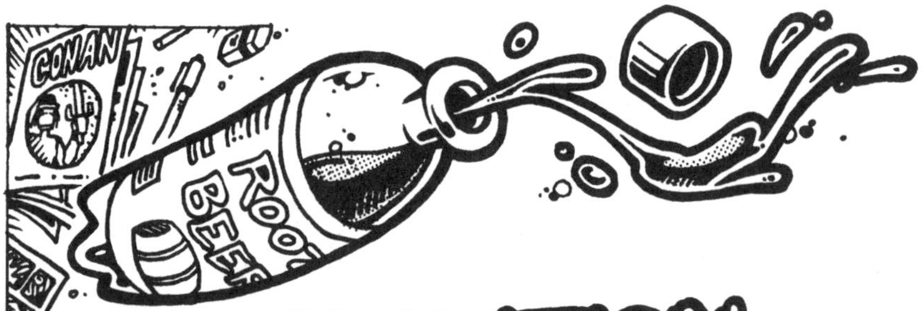
CONAN

INTRODUCTION

- BY DAVID LINDER

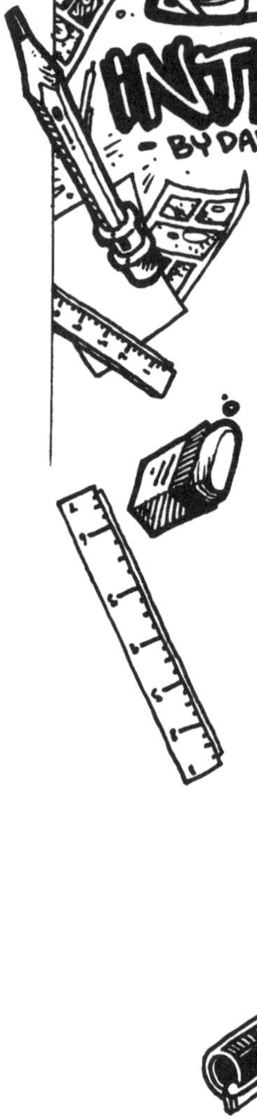

IN THE I.O.U. STORY IN THIS BOOK, BRANDON TALKS ABOUT HIS CHRISTMAS IN '01. '02 WAS A GOOD TIME AS WELL, AND SINCE I WAS THERE, I'LL TELL YOU ABOUT IT. ME AND BRANDON WERE SNOWED IN, DRAWING AND DRINKING INSTANT COCOA. WE DIDN'T HAVE ANY SNOW GEAR, SO WE PUT PLASTIC GROCERY BAGS OVER OUR SNEAKERS AND WRAPPED THEM IN DUCT TAPE. IT WORKED GREAT. IT WAS LIKE AFTER NINE PM, GUSTING AND HOWLING WIND, AND BRANDON WAS ADAMANT THAT WE HAD TO GO TO THIS BODEGA THAT HE KNEW OF, UP IN THE BRONX. THEY HAD A 2 FOR A DOLLAR COMIC BOOK BIN. IF YOU WERE LUCKY, YOU MIGHT FIND SOME ⇨

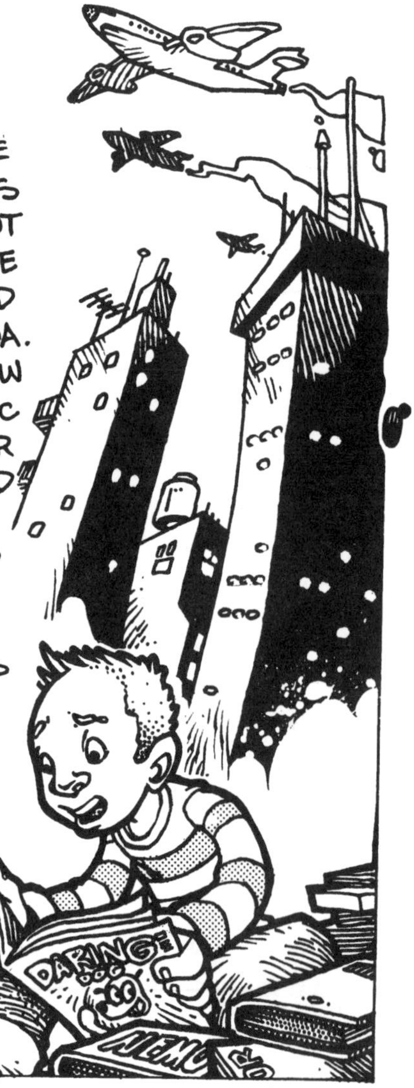
DARING

↪UNDERGROUND COMICS FROM THE EARLY 90'S. NERD GOLD. WHATEVER. WE HIKED UP TO THE HARLEM RIVER, AND CROSSED THE BRIDGE. EVERYTHING WAS LIT WITH THAT SPOOKY BLUE LIGHT THAT YOU ONLY SEE ON THE NIGHT OF A SNOWSTORM. THERE WERE FAT MARSHMALLOWY SNOW DRIFTS BY THE ROAD, AND BIG POLAR ICE CHUNKS FLOATING IN THE RIVER.
WE SLOGGED INTO THE BODEGA, AND DUG THROUGH THE COMICS, BUT I GEUSS THEY DIDN'T HAVE WHATEVER OBSCURE OLD ISSUE IT WAS THAT BRANDON WANTED, SO WE MOVED ON. IN THE PARK WE SAW A FLOCK OF GEESE. THEY WERE ALL HUNKERED DOWN IN ANKLE DEEP WATER, WEATHERING THE STORM. BRANDON SAID THEY LOOKED LIKE AN EN-TRENCHED ARMY PLATOON.
"SEE THAT BIG ONE STANDING APART FROM THE OTHERS? HE'S THE SARGENT."

"ARE YOU PANSIES COLD YET?! DO YOU WANT YOUR MOMMIES?!!

YOU'RE IN THE ARMY!! THIS IS WAR!!"
I LIKED THE SIMILIE, AND I THINK IT'S A GOOD EXAMPLE OF HOW BRANDON'S REALITY IS COLORED BY OLD PULP AND GRAPHIC NOVELS. BOOKS THAT MIGHT BE MINDLESS ENTERTAIN-MENT TO MOST ARE THE CORNERSTONES OF HIS PHILOSOPHY.

COMICS MEAN A LOT TO BRANDON. NOTHING MAKES HIM MORE UPSET THAN ASSEMBLY-LINE PRODUCTION TEAMS WHO TAKE SPONTAN-EITY OUT OF THE DRAWING PROCESS. WHOEVER SAID THAT 'GOOD' ART CAN'T BE FUN TO LOOK AT, OR THAT A 'GOOD' BOOK SHOULDN'T BE FUN TO READ? BRANDON WILL FIND THOSE PEOPLE SOME DAY, AND PEE IN THEIR SHOES.

SOMEONE ONCE CALLED A GREAT BALL PLAYER A GENIUS. THE PLAYER RESPONDED:

"GENIUS? NO WAY, DO YOU KNOW HOW MUCH I PRACTICE?"

WORD. IF YOU REALLY WANT TO DO SOME-THING, YOU'VE GOTTA LIVE IT. AND I THINK BRANDON IS A PRETTY GOOD EXAMPLE OF SOMEONE WHO'S DOING THAT.

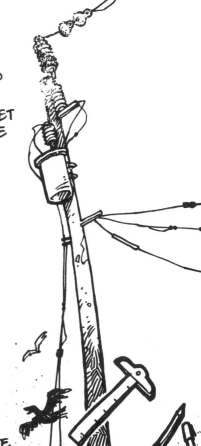

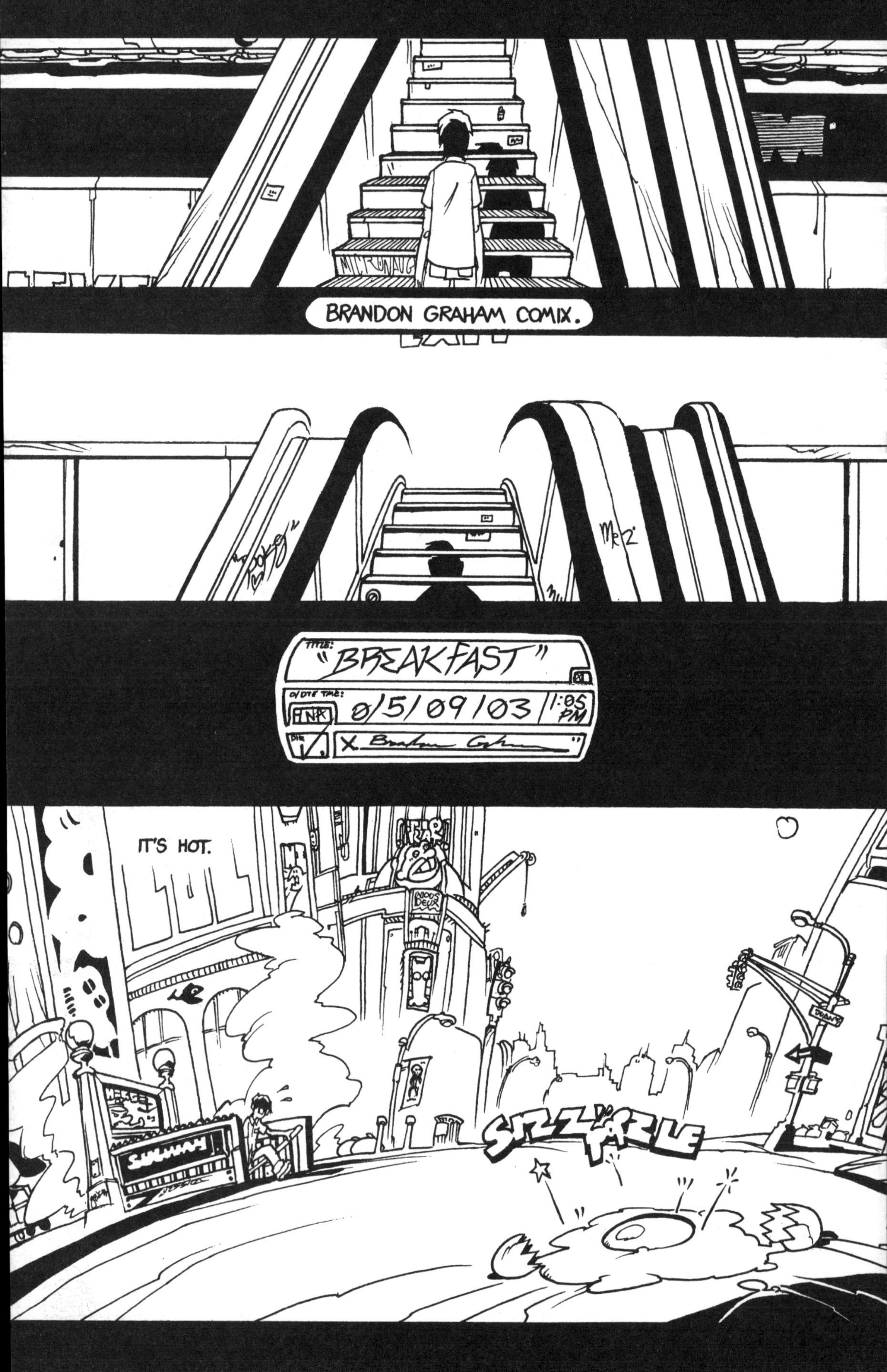
BRANDON GRAHAM COMIX.
TITLE:
"BREAKFAST"
D/DTE TIME:
0/5/09/03
1:05 PM
IT'S HOT.

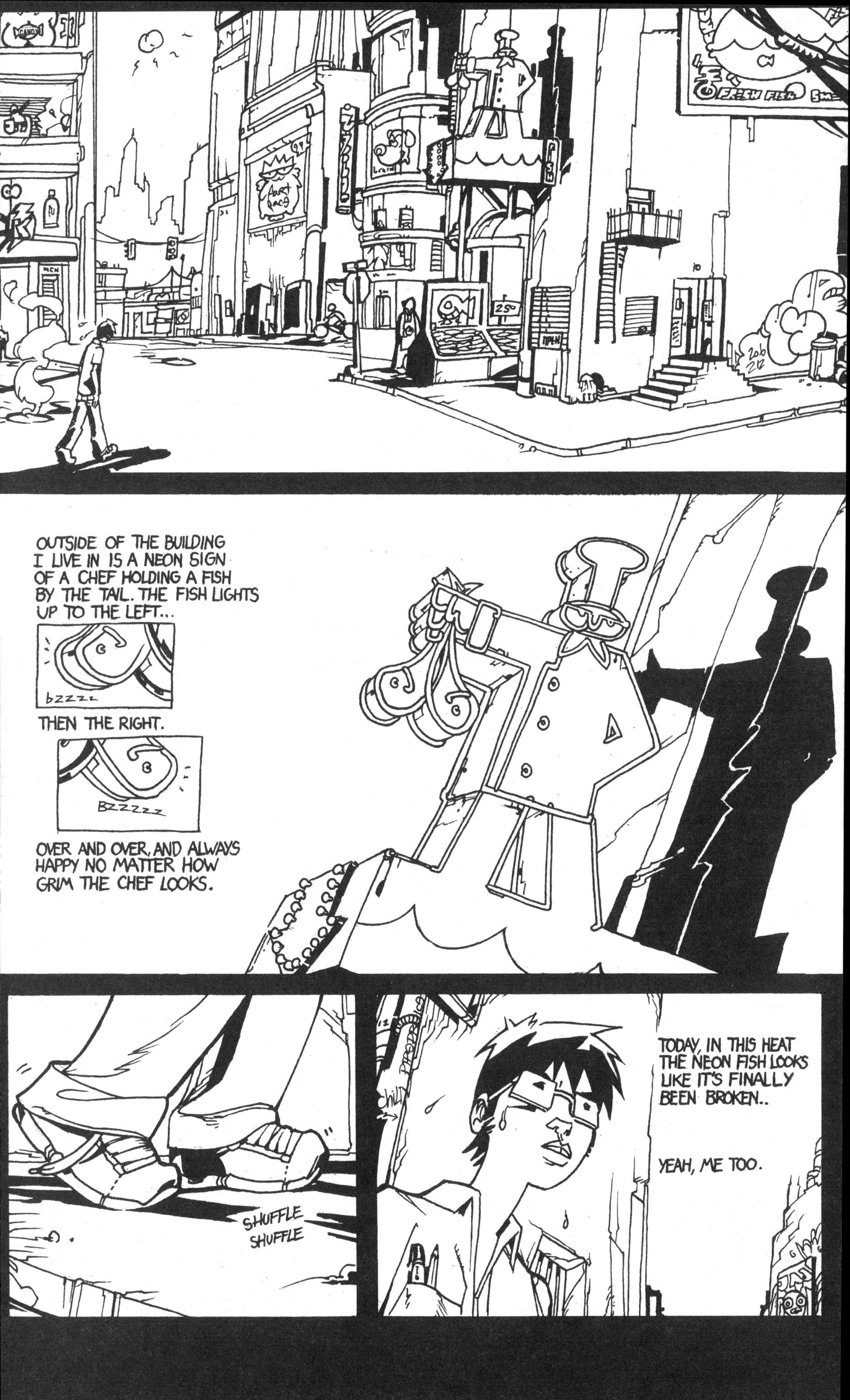
FRESH FISH
OUTSIDE OF THE BUILDING I LIVE IN IS A NEON SIGN OF A CHEF HOLDING A FISH BY THE TAIL. THE FISH LIGHTS UP TO THE LEFT...
bzzzz
THEN THE RIGHT.
BZZZZZ
OVER AND OVER, AND ALWAYS HAPPY NO MATTER HOW GRIM THE CHEF LOOKS.
SHUFFLE
SHUFFLE
TODAY, IN THIS HEAT THE NEON FISH LOOKS LIKE IT'S FINALLY BEEN BROKEN..
YEAH, ME TOO.

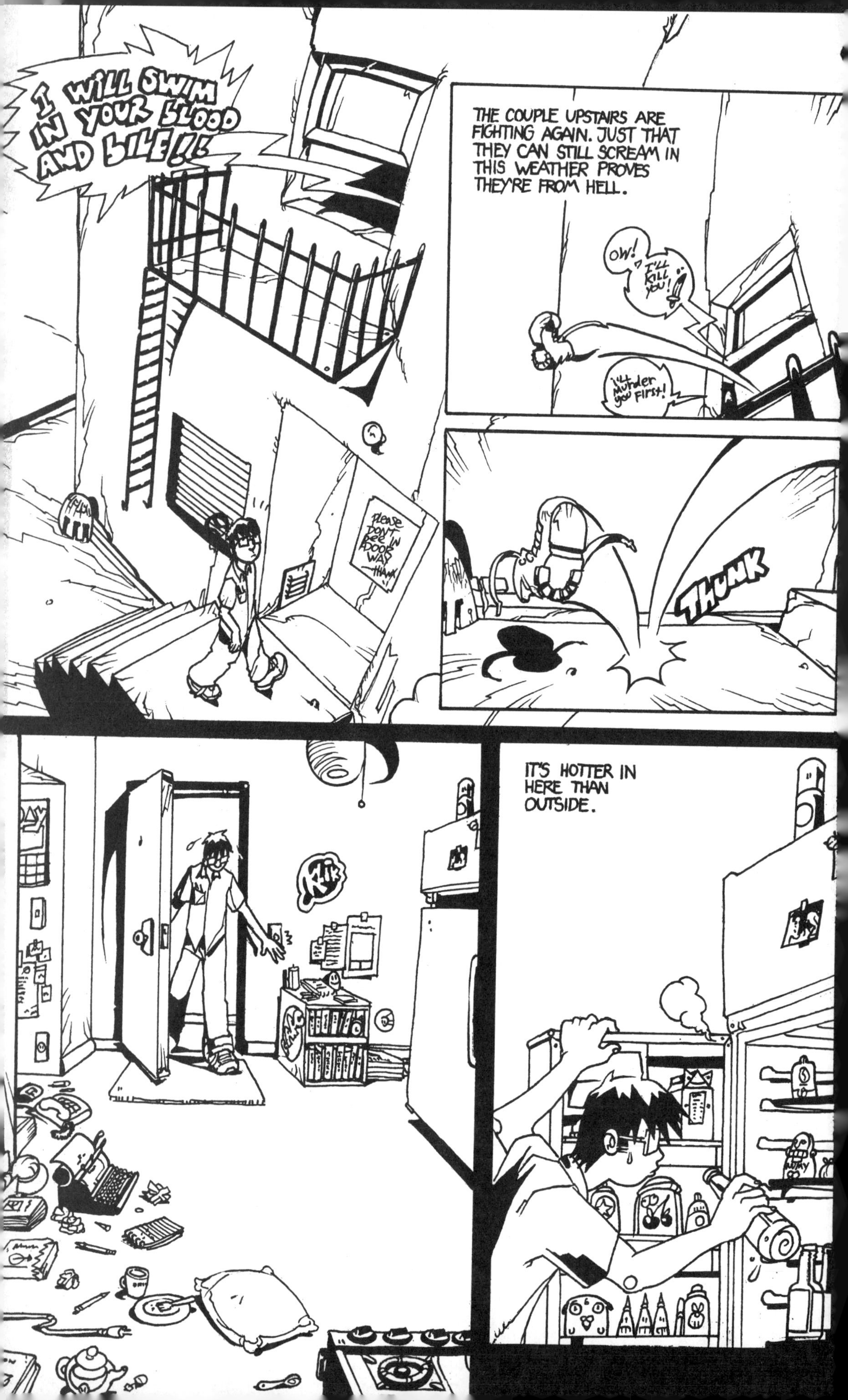
I WILL SWIM IN YOUR BLOOD AND BILE!!!
THE COUPLE UPSTAIRS ARE FIGHTING AGAIN. JUST THAT THEY CAN STILL SCREAM IN THIS WEATHER PROVES THEY'RE FROM HELL.
OW!
I'LL KILL YOU!
I'll Murder you First!
Please DON'T Bee IN A DOOR WAY
THANK
THUNK
KLIK
IT'S HOTTER IN HERE THAN OUTSIDE.

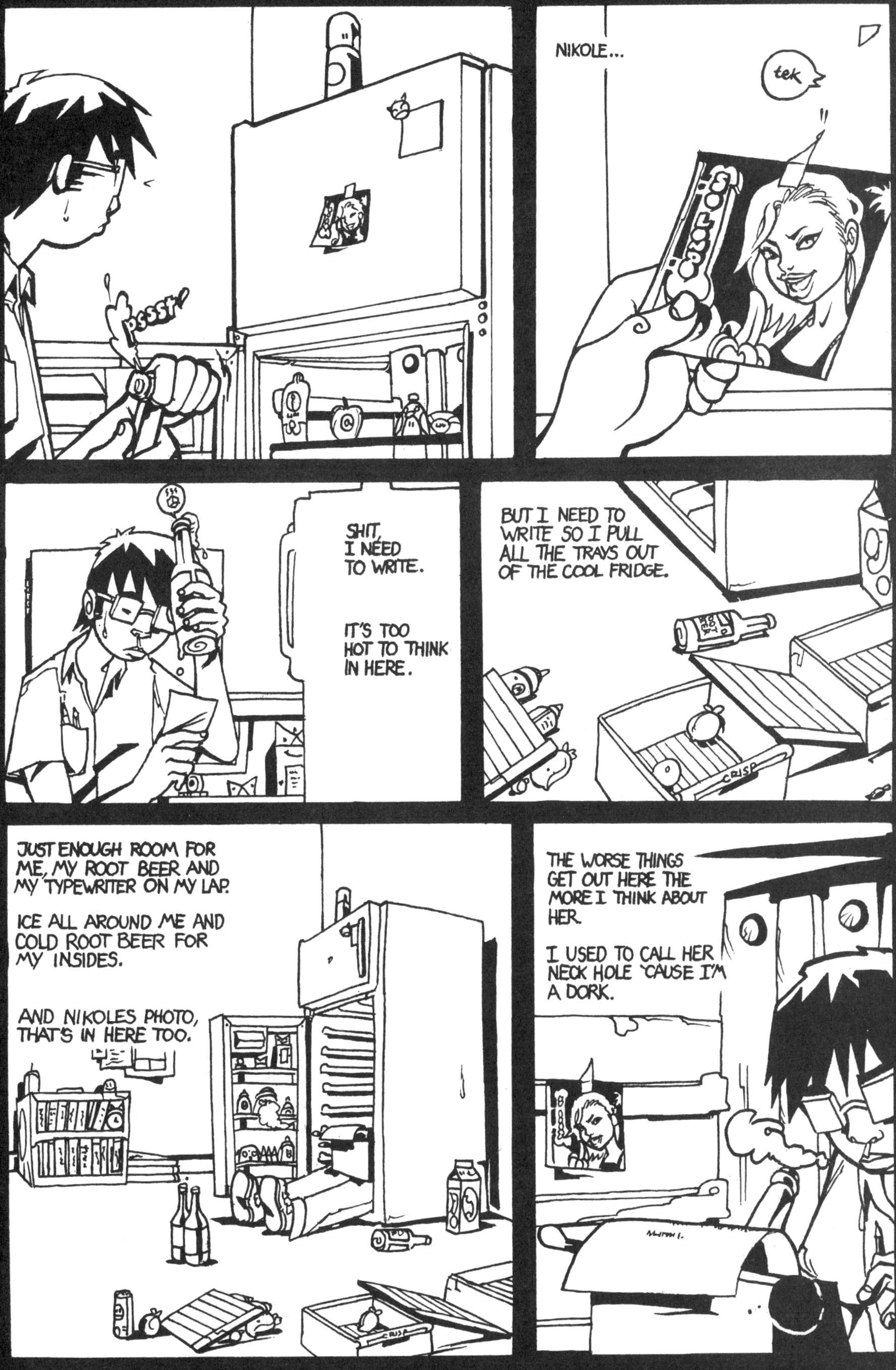
pssst!
NIKOLE...
tek
SHIT, I NEED TO WRITE.
IT'S TOO HOT TO THINK IN HERE.
BUT I NEED TO WRITE SO I PULL ALL THE TRAYS OUT OF THE COOL FRIDGE.
CRISP
JUST ENOUGH ROOM FOR ME, MY ROOT BEER AND MY TYPEWRITER ON MY LAP.
ICE ALL AROUND ME AND COLD ROOT BEER FOR MY INSIDES.
AND NIKOLES PHOTO, THAT'S IN HERE TOO.
THE WORSE THINGS GET OUT HERE THE MORE I THINK ABOUT HER.
I USED TO CALL HER NECK HOLE 'CAUSE I'M A DORK.

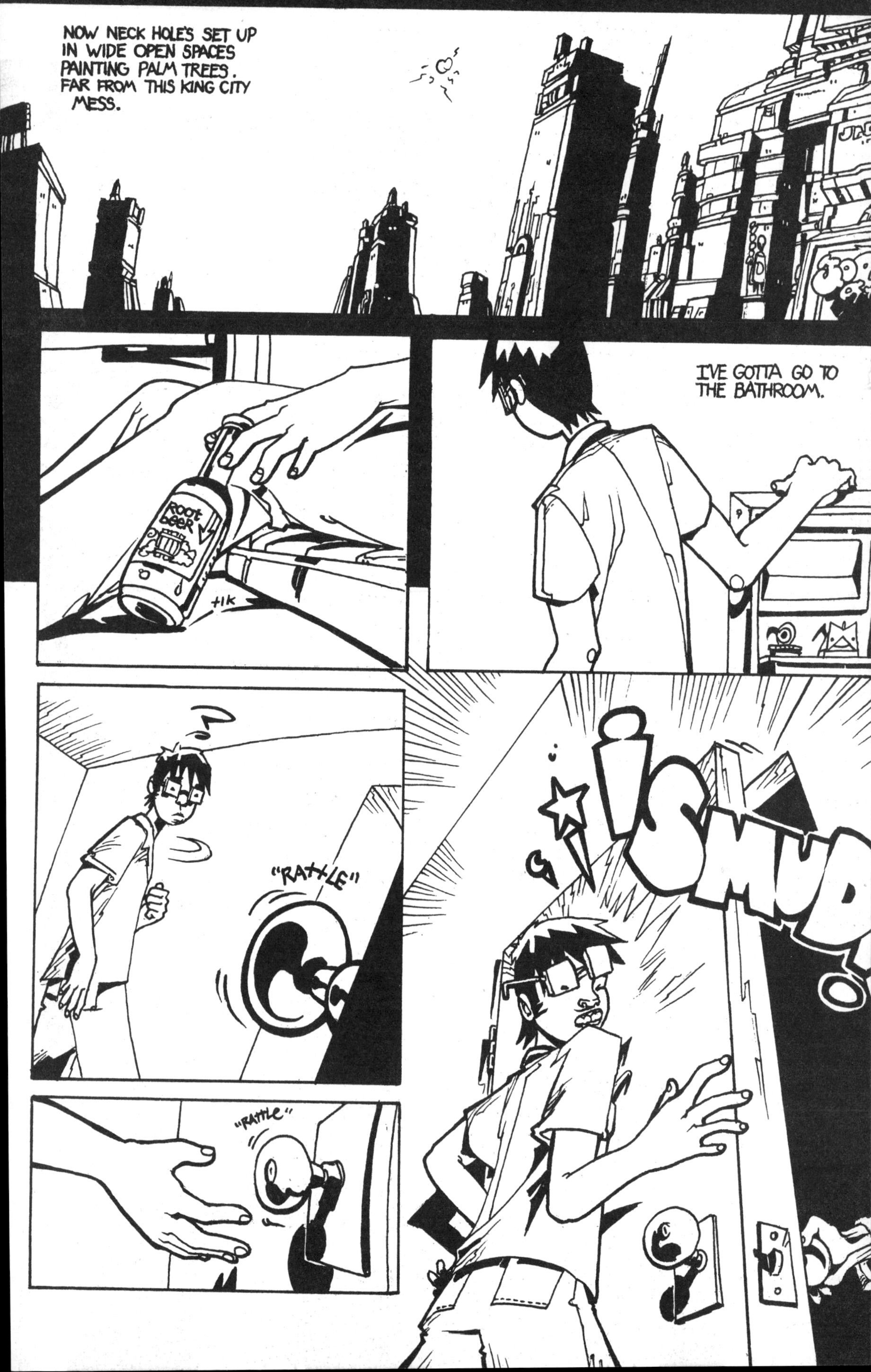
NOW NECK HOLE'S SET UP IN WIDE OPEN SPACES PAINTING PALM TREES. FAR FROM THIS KING CITY MESS.
ROOT BEER
TIK
I'VE GOTTA GO TO THE BATHROOM.
"RATTLE"
"RATTLE"
SMUD

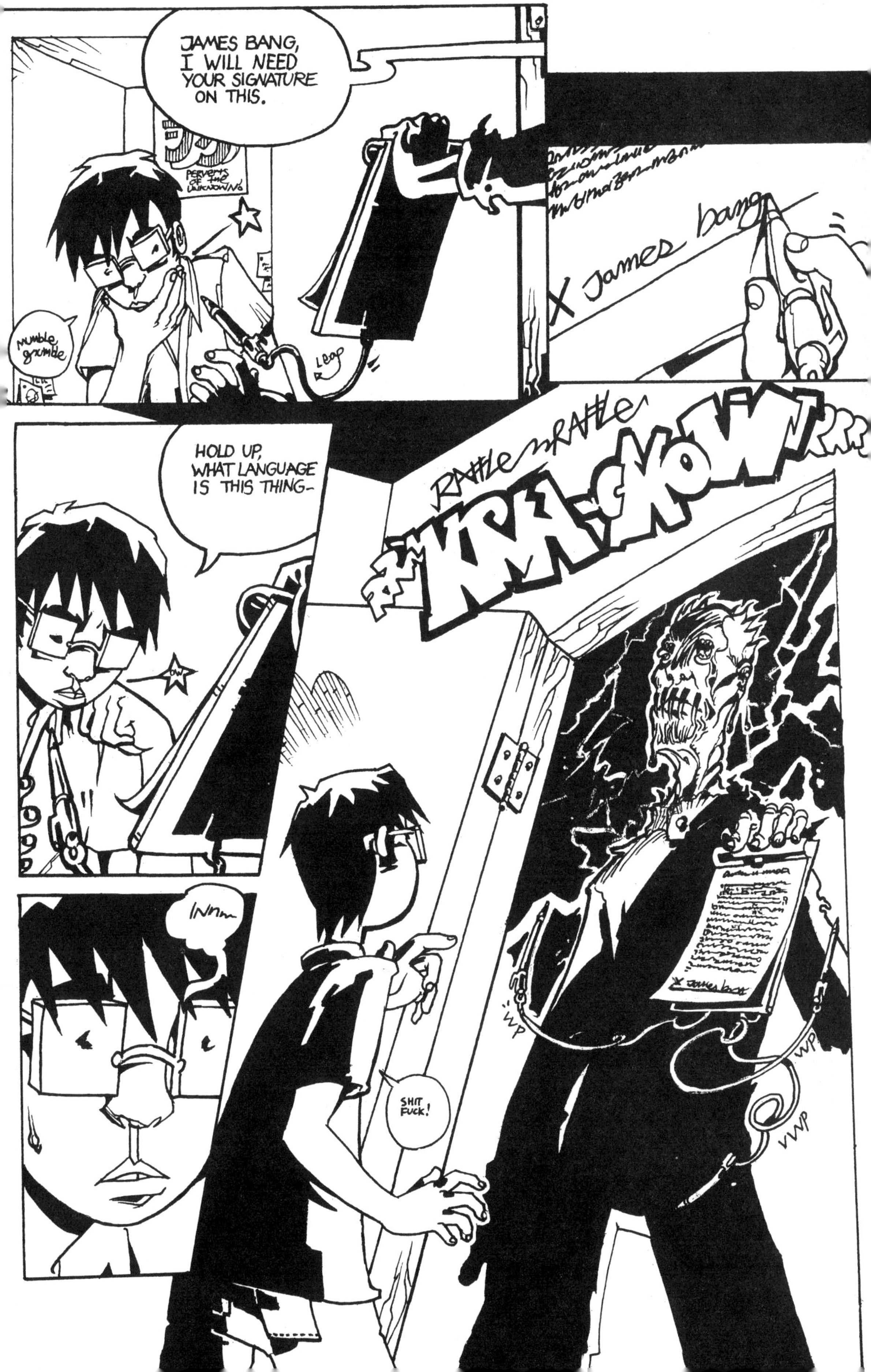
JAMES BANG, I WILL NEED YOUR SIGNATURE ON THIS.
mumble, grumble
LEAP
X james bang
HOLD UP, WHAT LANGUAGE IS THIS THING-
OW
RATTLE RATTLE
KRA-CHOW
Innn
SHIT FUCK!
WP
WP
VWP

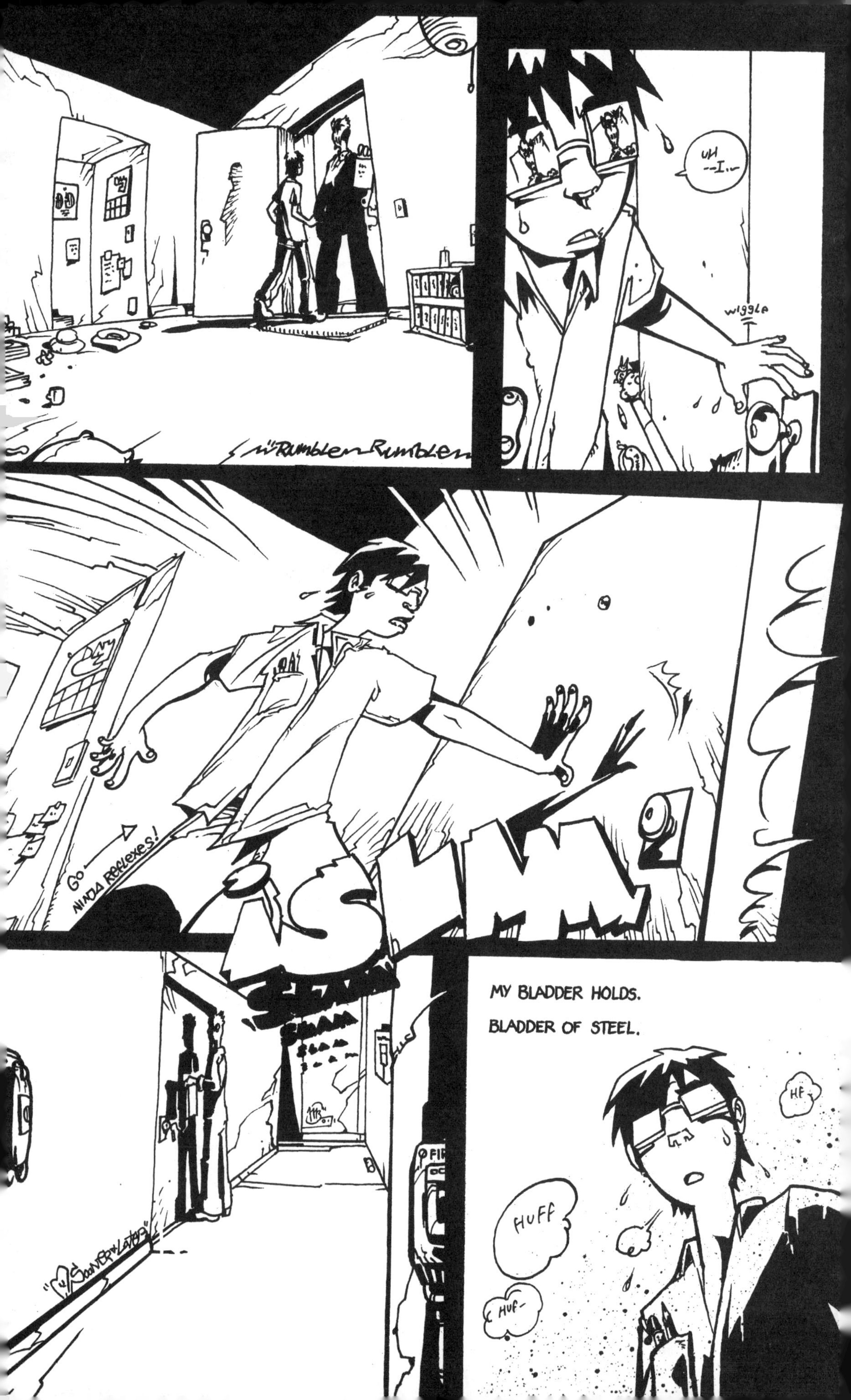
Rumble Rumble
UH --I..
wiggle
GO NINJA REFLEXES!
SLAM
MY BLADDER HOLDS.
BLADDER OF STEEL.
HF
HUFF
HUF-

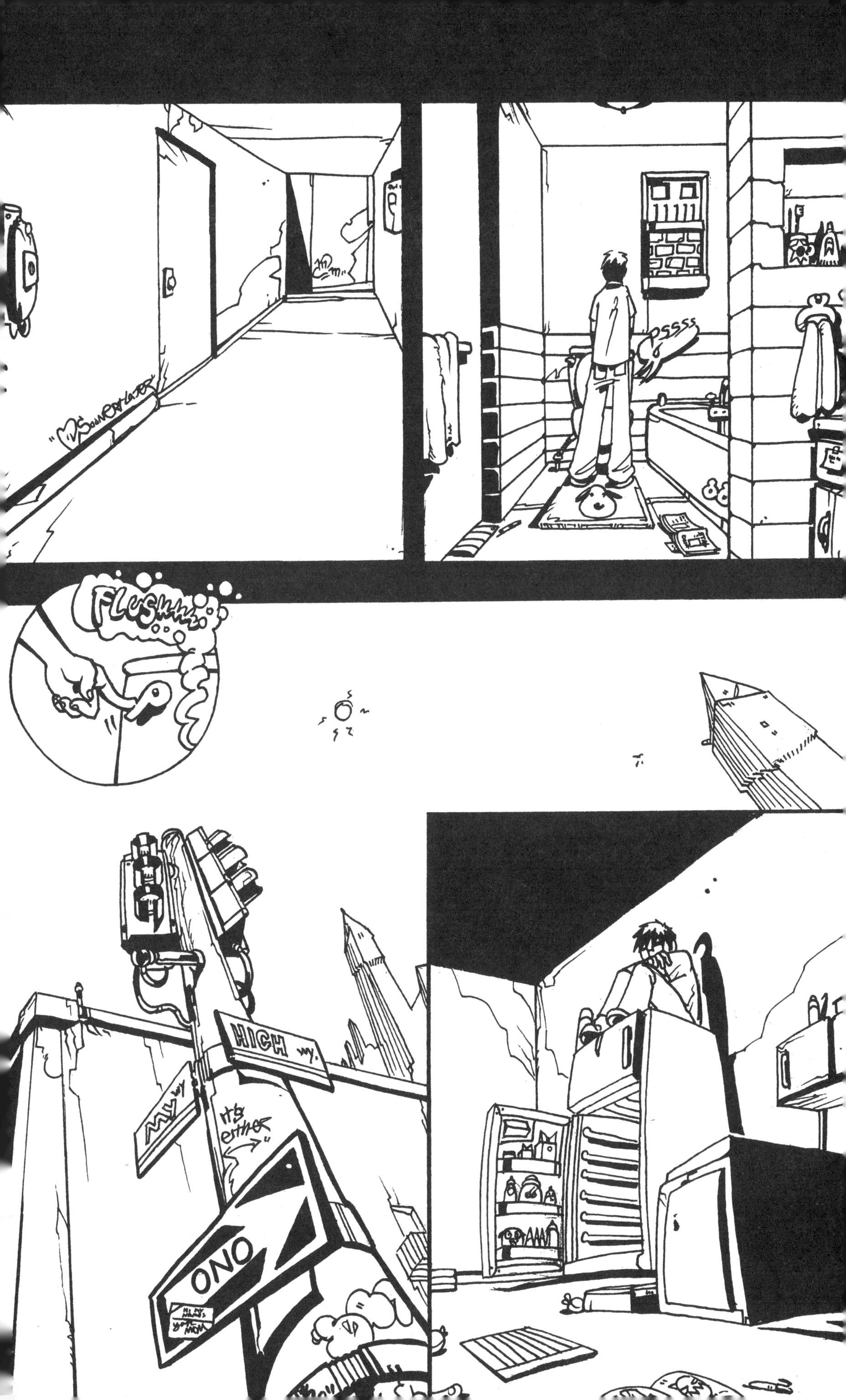
"Soon or later"
PSSSS
FLUSHHH
HIGH way
MY way
It's either
ONO

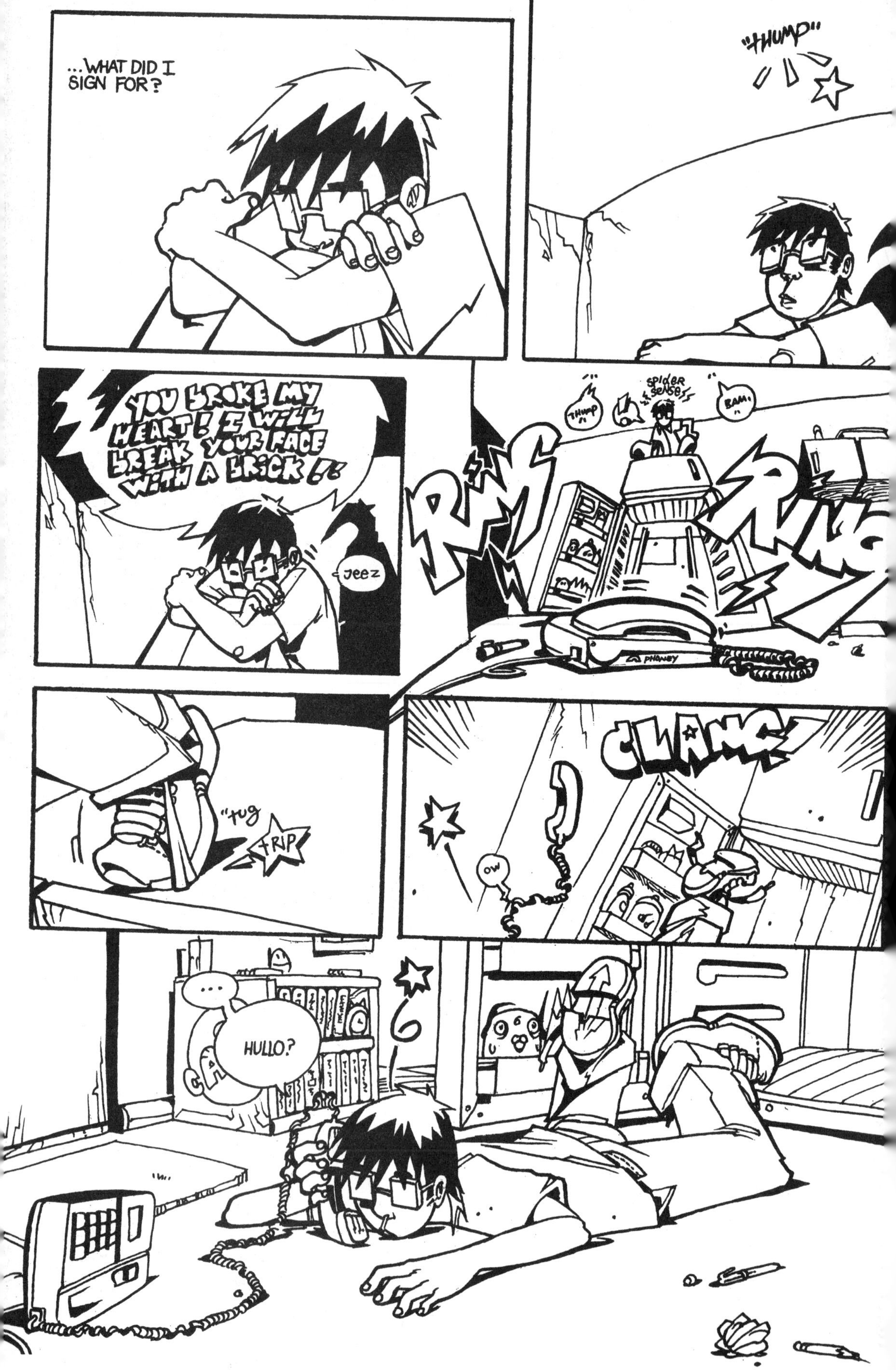
...WHAT DID I SIGN FOR?
"THUMP"
YOU BROKE MY HEART! I WILL BREAK YOUR FACE WITH A BRICK!!
JEEZ
THUMP
SPIDER SENSES
BAM
RING
RING
PHONEY
TUG
TRIP
CLANG
OW
...
HULLO?

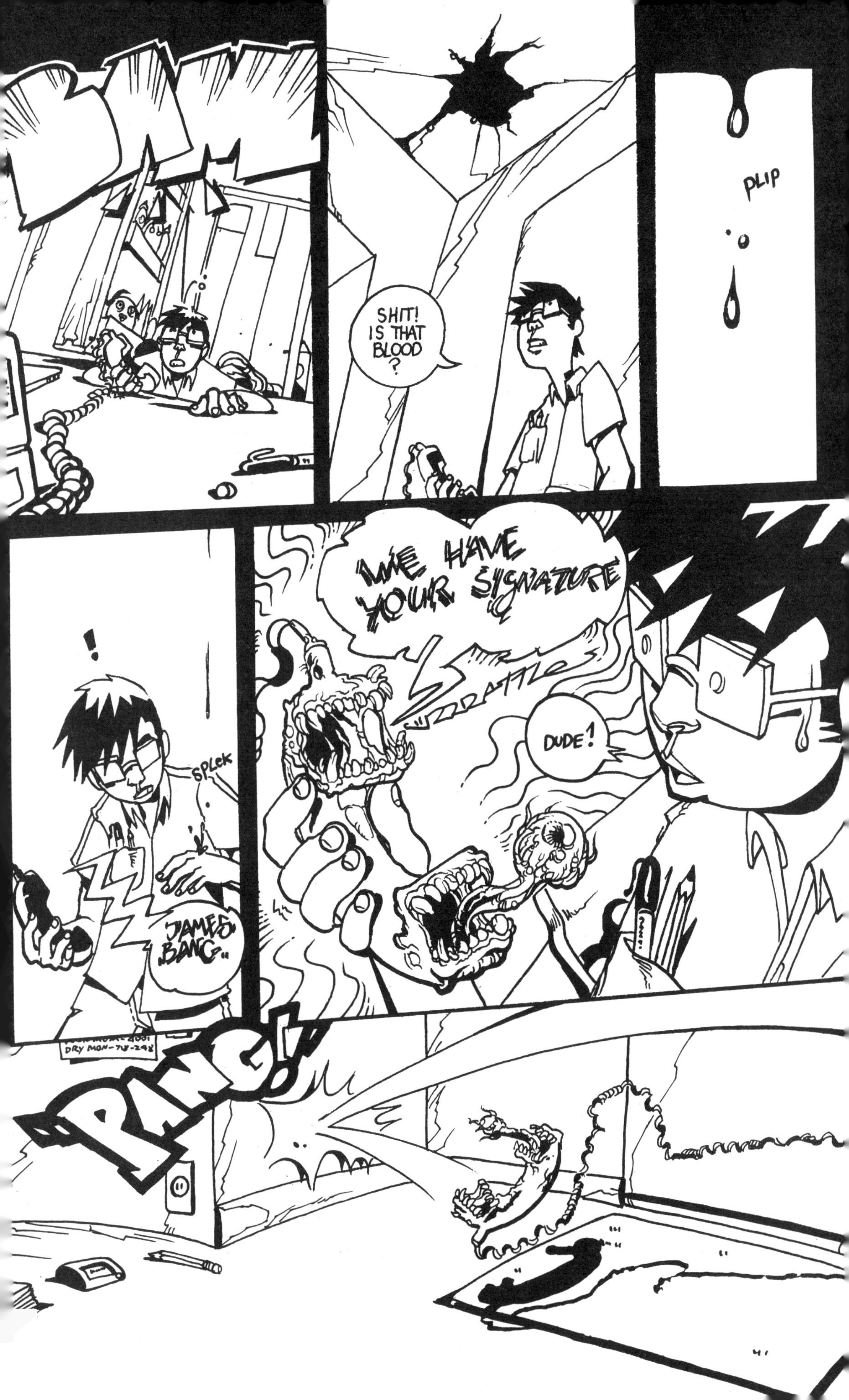
SHIT! IS THAT BLOOD?
PLIP
!
SPLEK
JAMES BANG
WE HAVE YOUR SIGNATURE
ZZRATTLE
DUDE!
PANG!

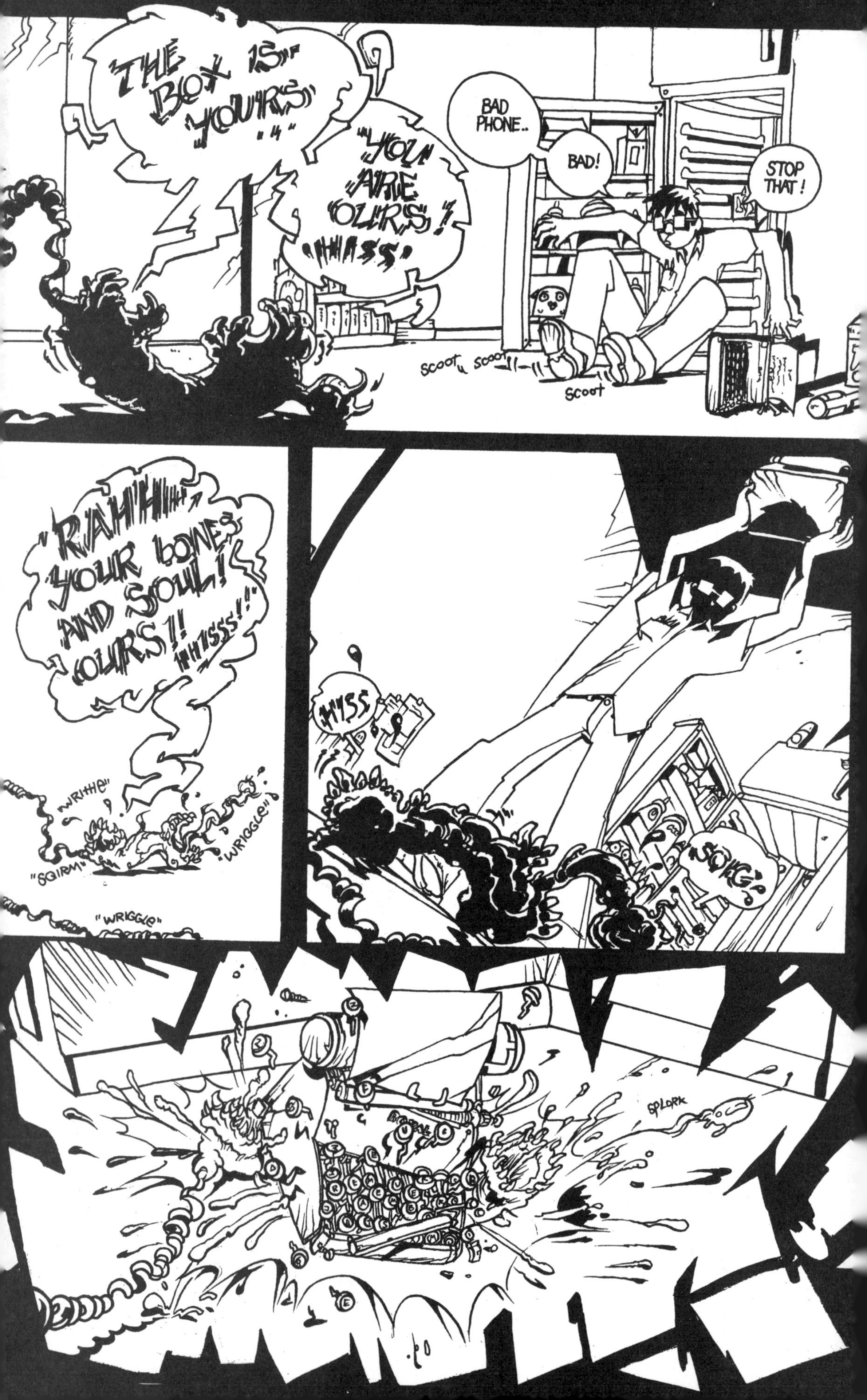

"THE BOX IS YOURS" "
"YOU ARE OURS"! "HISS"
BAD PHONE..
BAD!
STOP THAT!
SCOOT
SCOOT
SCOOT
"RAHH" YOUR BONES AND SOUL! "OURS!! "HISSS!!"
"WRITHE"
"SQIRM"
"WRIGGLE"
"WRIGGLE"
HISS
SQIG
SPLORK

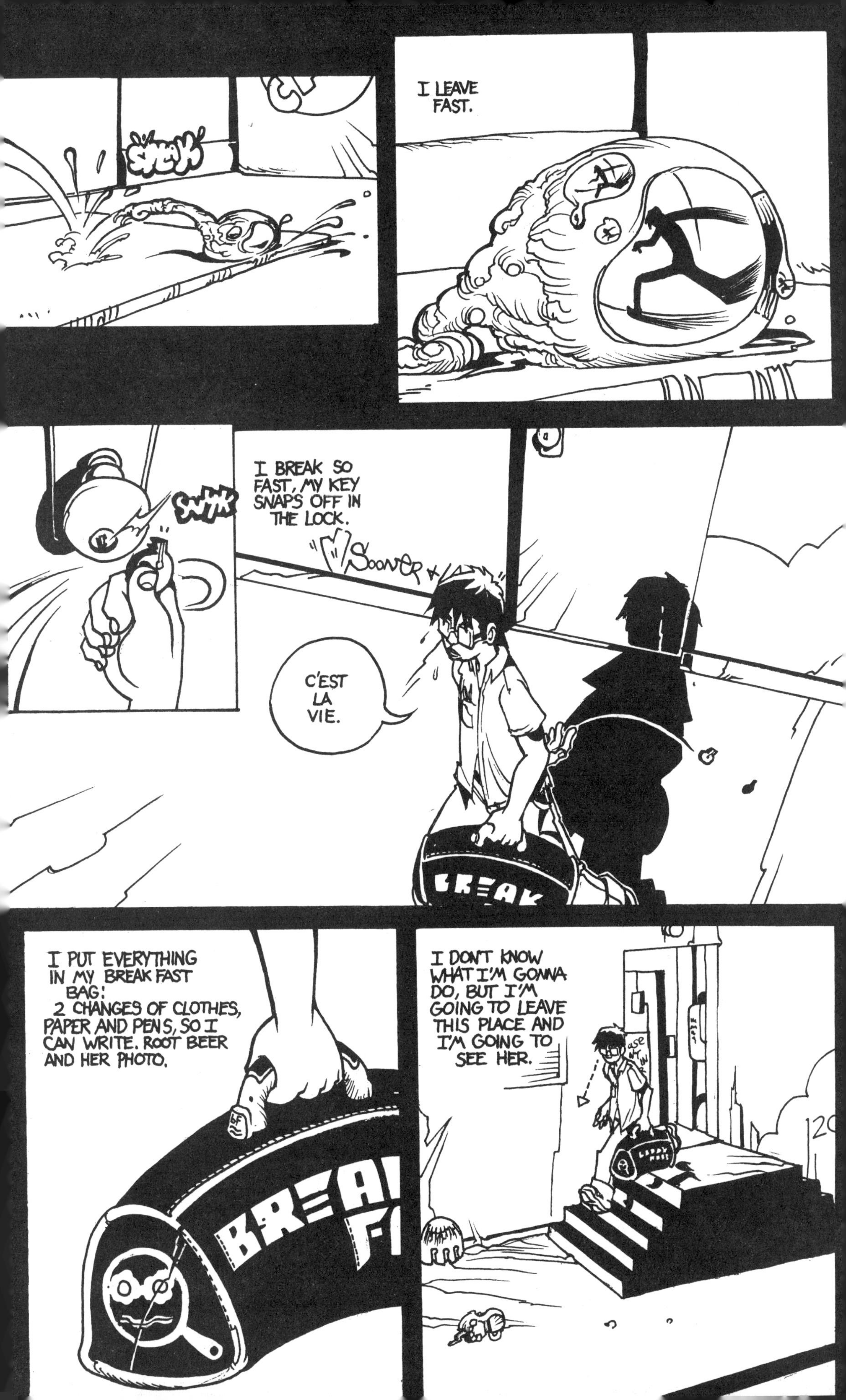
SPLASH
I LEAVE FAST.
I BREAK SO FAST, MY KEY SNAPS OFF IN THE LOCK.
SWIK
Sooner
C'EST LA VIE.
BREAK
I PUT EVERYTHING IN MY BREAK FAST BAG:
2 CHANGES OF CLOTHES, PAPER AND PENS, SO I CAN WRITE. ROOT BEER AND HER PHOTO.
BREA
I DON'T KNOW WHAT I'M GONNA DO, BUT I'M GOING TO LEAVE THIS PLACE AND I'M GOING TO SEE HER.

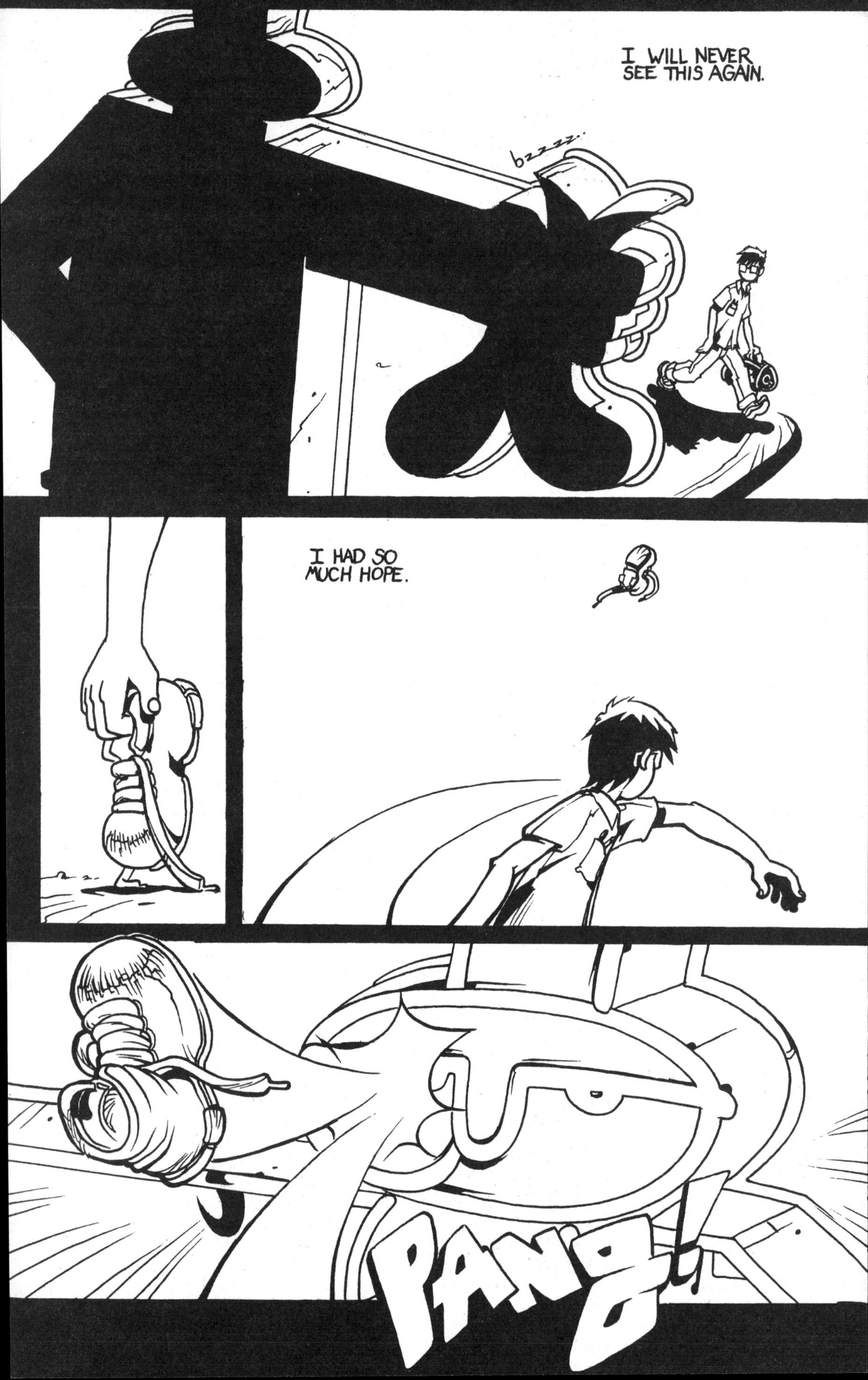
I WILL NEVER SEE THIS AGAIN.
bzzzzz..
I HAD SO MUCH HOPE.
PANG!!

I WON'T MISS THIS PLACE

AND NO CITY EVER CRIES WHEN YOU LEAVE IT.

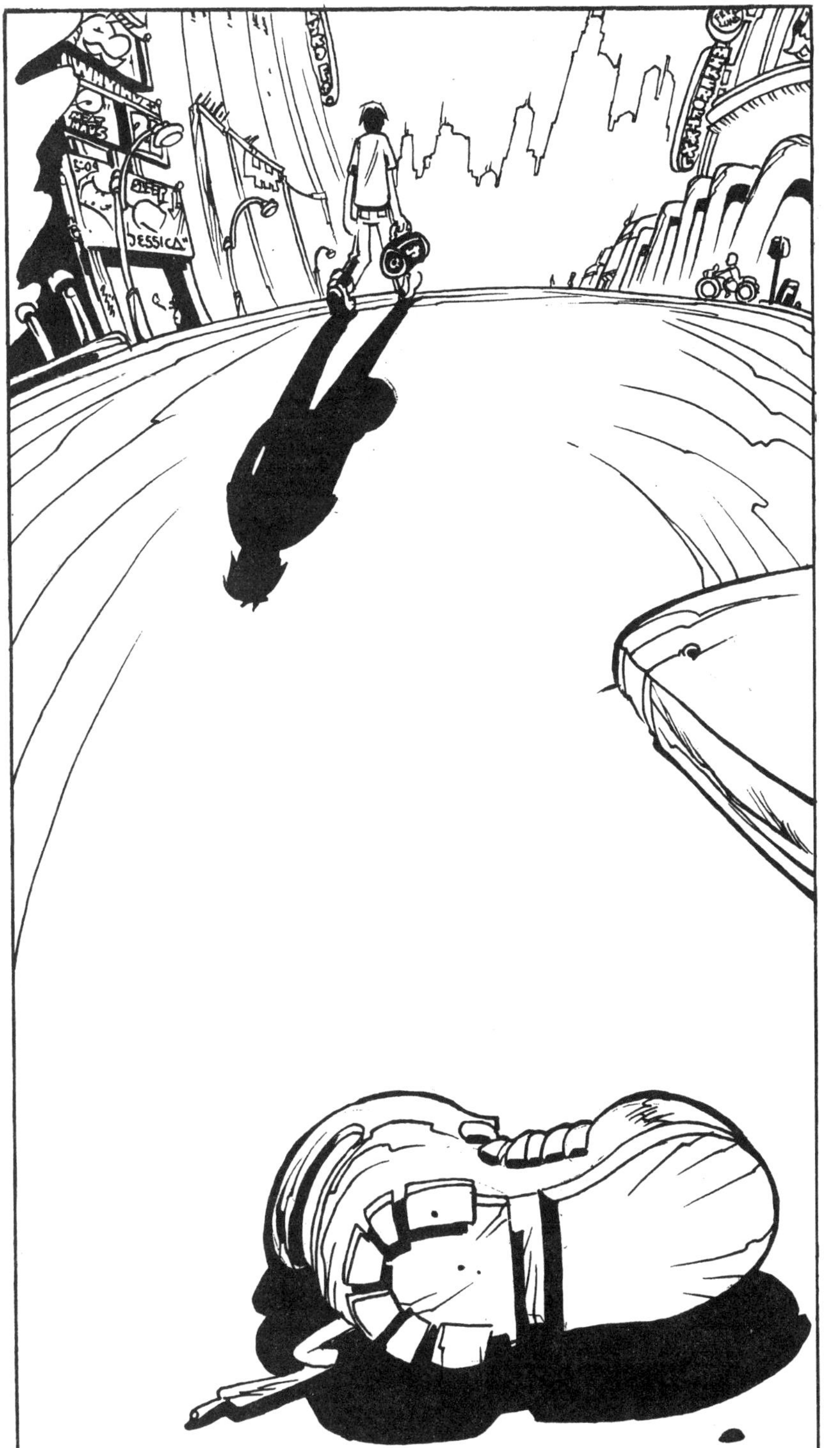
JESSICA

INTO THE SUNSET.

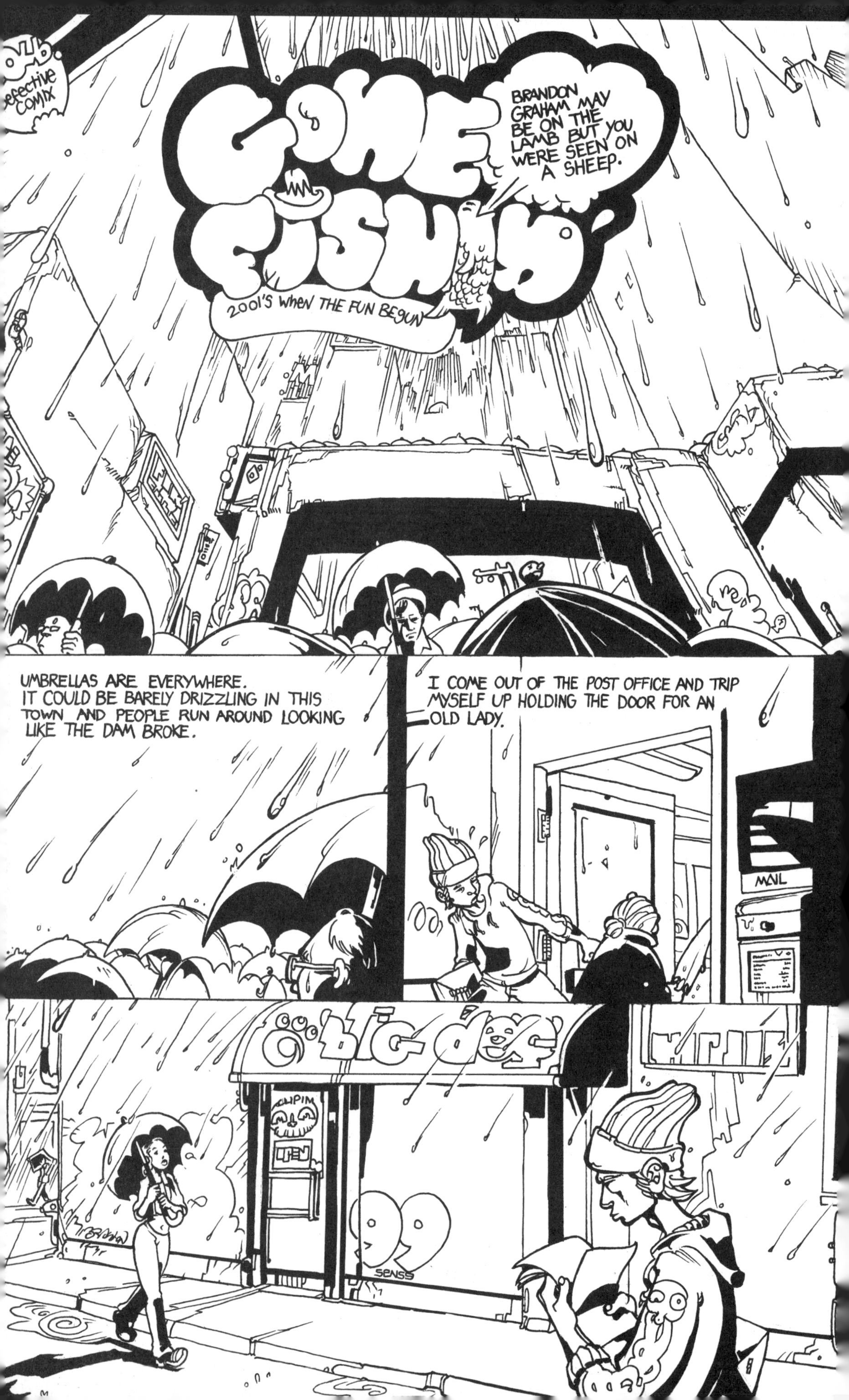
GONE FISHIN
BRANDON GRAHAM MAY BE ON THE LAMB BUT YOU WERE SEEN ON A SHEEP.
2001'S when THE FUN BEGUN
UMBRELLAS ARE EVERYWHERE. IT COULD BE BARELY DRIZZLING IN THIS TOWN AND PEOPLE RUN AROUND LOOKING LIKE THE DAM BROKE.
I COME OUT OF THE POST OFFICE AND TRIP MYSELF UP HOLDING THE DOOR FOR AN OLD LADY.
MAIL
big dog

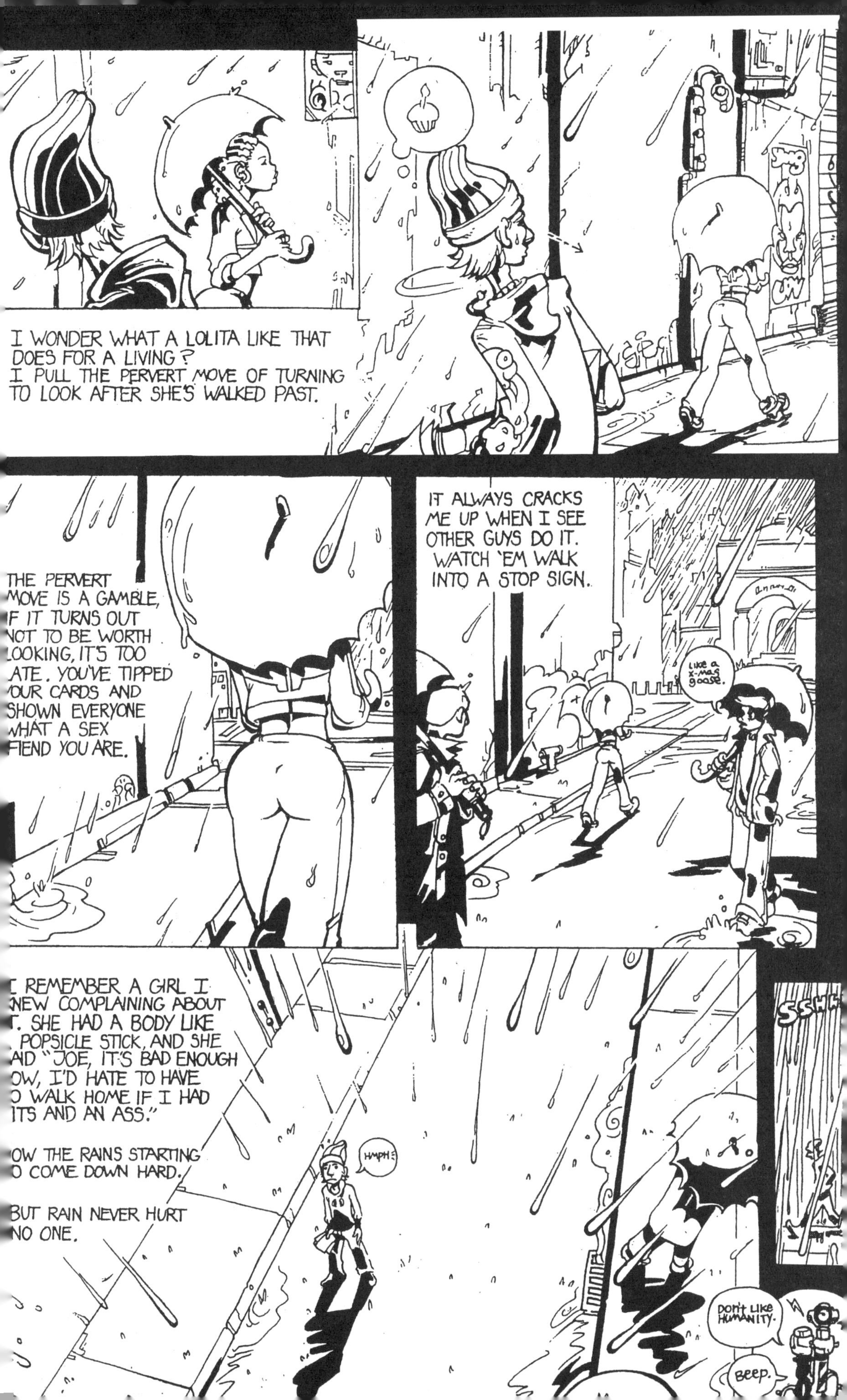
I WONDER WHAT A LOLITA LIKE THAT DOES FOR A LIVING?
I PULL THE PERVERT MOVE OF TURNING TO LOOK AFTER SHE'S WALKED PAST.
THE PERVERT MOVE IS A GAMBLE, IF IT TURNS OUT NOT TO BE WORTH LOOKING, IT'S TOO LATE. YOU'VE TIPPED YOUR CARDS AND SHOWN EVERYONE WHAT A SEX FIEND YOU ARE.
IT ALWAYS CRACKS ME UP WHEN I SEE OTHER GUYS DO IT. WATCH 'EM WALK INTO A STOP SIGN.
Like a x-mas goose.
I REMEMBER A GIRL I KNEW COMPLAINING ABOUT IT. SHE HAD A BODY LIKE A POPSICLE STICK, AND SHE SAID "JOE, IT'S BAD ENOUGH NOW, I'D HATE TO HAVE TO WALK HOME IF I HAD TITS AND AN ASS."
NOW THE RAINS STARTING TO COME DOWN HARD.
BUT RAIN NEVER HURT NO ONE.
HMPH
Don't like HUMANITY.
Beep.

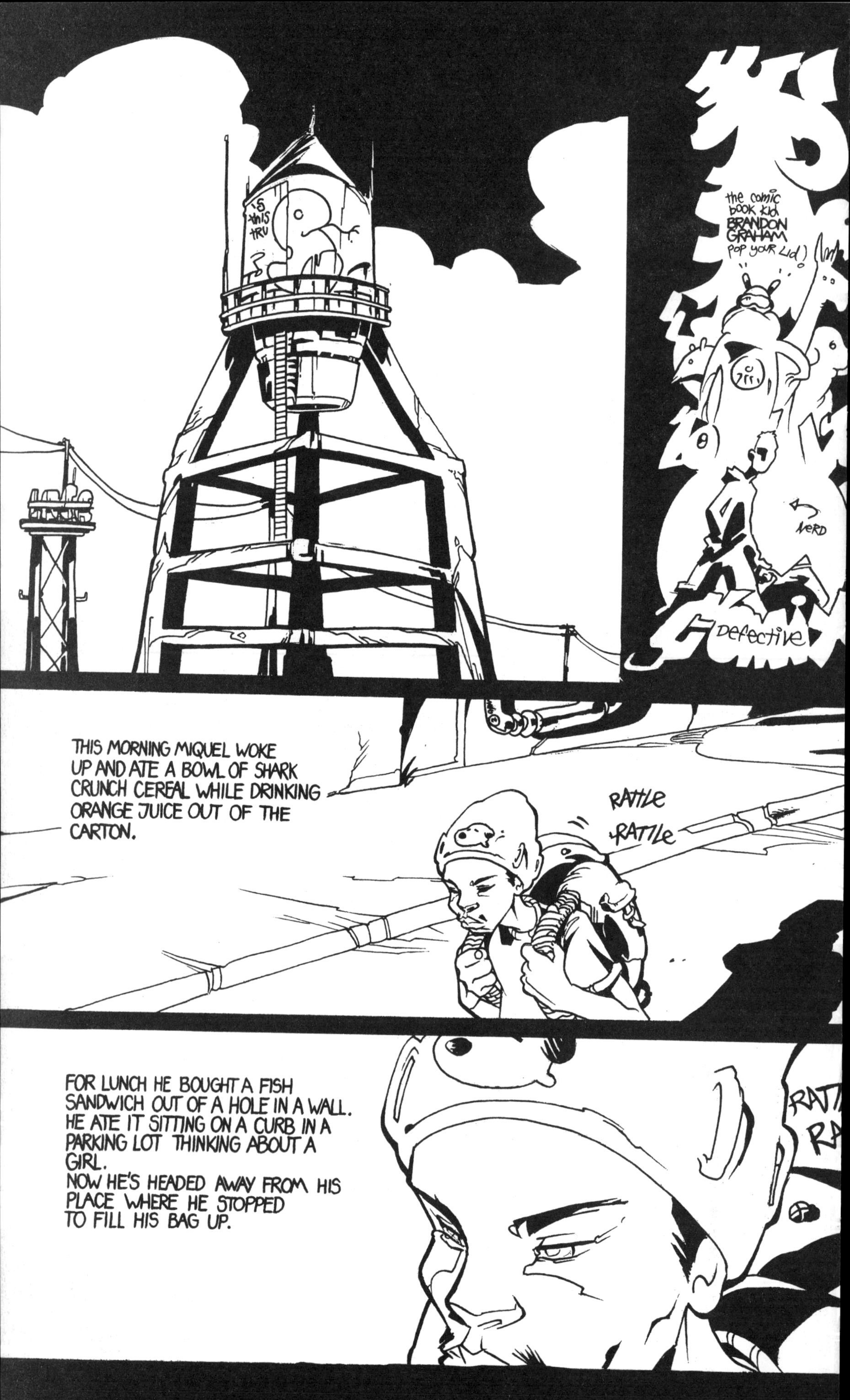
'S this TRU
the comic book kid BRANDON GRAHAM pop your Lid!
NERD
Defective
THIS MORNING MIQUEL WOKE UP AND ATE A BOWL OF SHARK CRUNCH CEREAL WHILE DRINKING ORANGE JUICE OUT OF THE CARTON.
RATTLE
RATTLE
FOR LUNCH HE BOUGHT A FISH SANDWICH OUT OF A HOLE IN A WALL. HE ATE IT SITTING ON A CURB IN A PARKING LOT THINKING ABOUT A GIRL.
NOW HE'S HEADED AWAY FROM HIS PLACE WHERE HE STOPPED TO FILL HIS BAG UP.

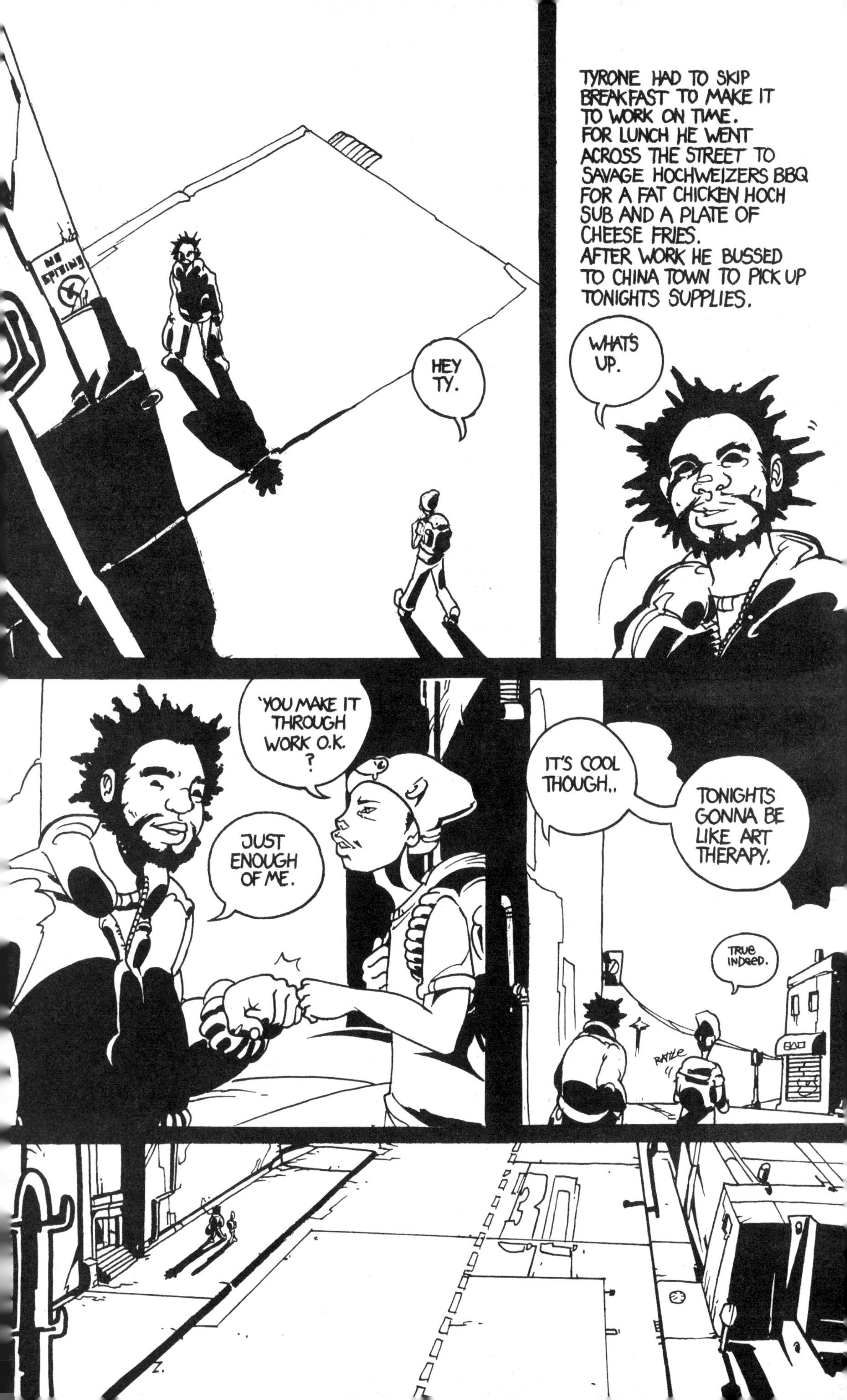
TYRONE HAD TO SKIP BREAKFAST TO MAKE IT TO WORK ON TIME. FOR LUNCH HE WENT ACROSS THE STREET TO SAVAGE HOCHWEIZERS BBQ FOR A FAT CHICKEN HOCH SUB AND A PLATE OF CHEESE FRIES. AFTER WORK HE BUSSED TO CHINA TOWN TO PICK UP TONIGHTS SUPPLIES.
HEY TY.
WHAT'S UP.
'YOU MAKE IT THROUGH WORK O.K. ?
JUST ENOUGH OF ME.
IT'S COOL THOUGH..
TONIGHTS GONNA BE LIKE ART THERAPY.
TRUE INDEED.
RATTLE

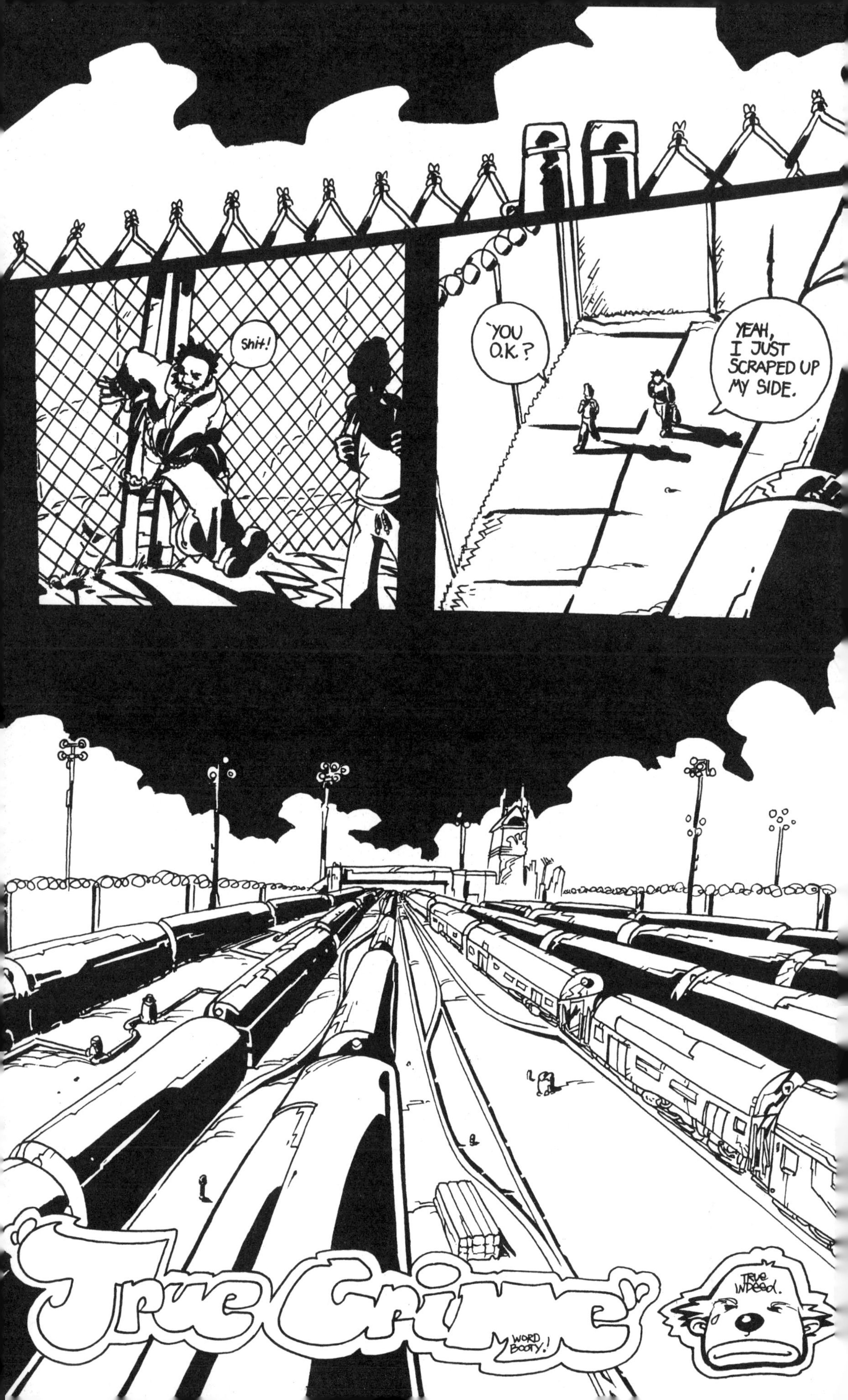

Shit!
YOU O.K.?
YEAH, I JUST SCRAPED UP MY SIDE.
True Crime
WORD BOOTY!
TRUE INDEED.

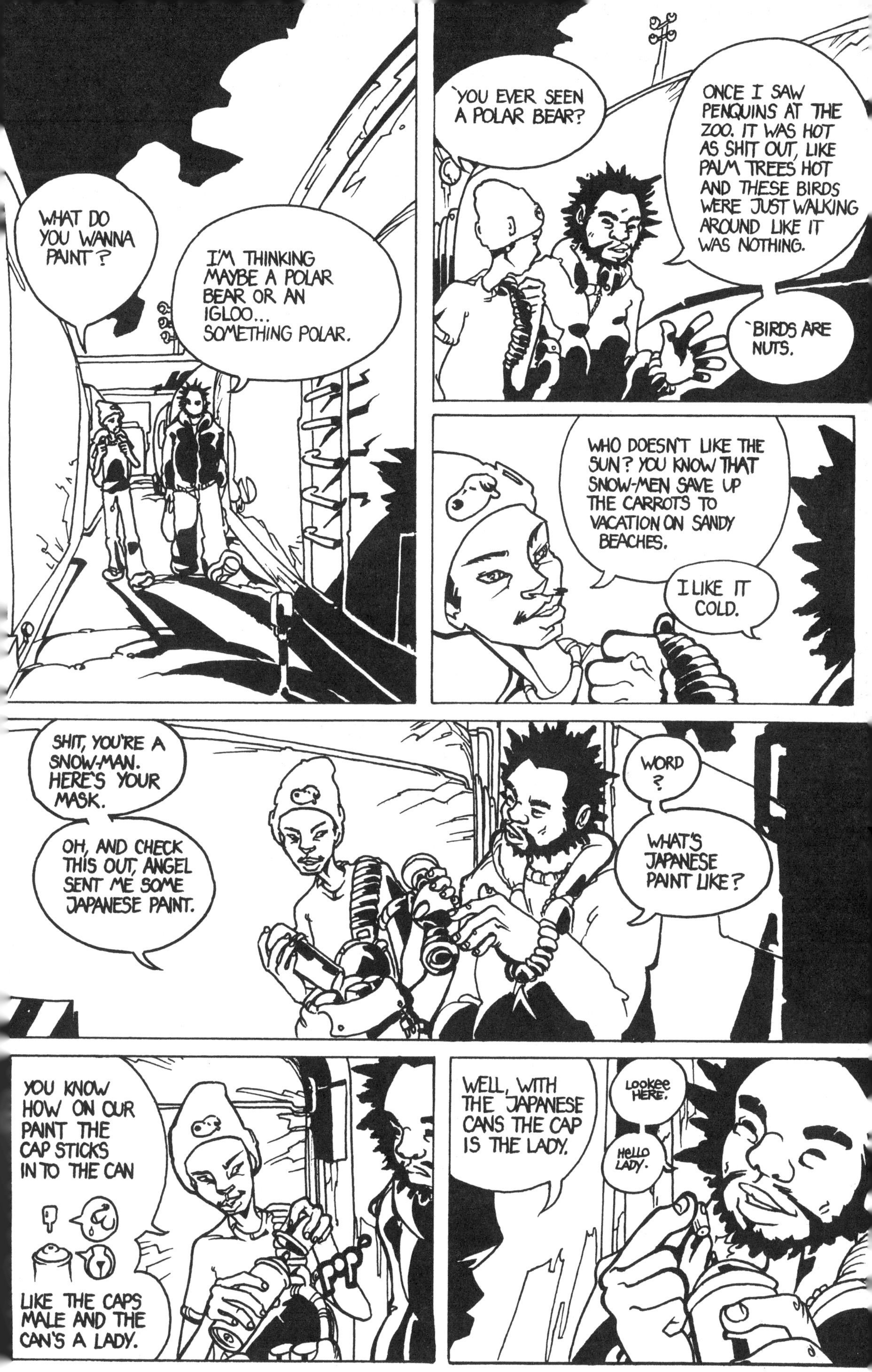
WHAT DO YOU WANNA PAINT?
I'M THINKING MAYBE A POLAR BEAR OR AN IGLOO... SOMETHING POLAR.
`YOU EVER SEEN A POLAR BEAR?
ONCE I SAW PENQUINS AT THE ZOO. IT WAS HOT AS SHIT OUT, LIKE PALM TREES HOT AND THESE BIRDS WERE JUST WALKING AROUND LIKE IT WAS NOTHING.
`BIRDS ARE NUTS.
WHO DOESN'T LIKE THE SUN? YOU KNOW THAT SNOW-MEN SAVE UP THE CARROTS TO VACATION ON SANDY BEACHES.
I LIKE IT COLD.
SHIT, YOU'RE A SNOW-MAN. HERE'S YOUR MASK.
OH, AND CHECK THIS OUT, ANGEL SENT ME SOME JAPANESE PAINT.
WORD?
WHAT'S JAPANESE PAINT LIKE?
YOU KNOW HOW ON OUR PAINT THE CAP STICKS IN TO THE CAN
LIKE THE CAPS MALE AND THE CAN'S A LADY.
WELL, WITH THE JAPANESE CANS THE CAP IS THE LADY.
Lookee HERE.
Hello LADY.

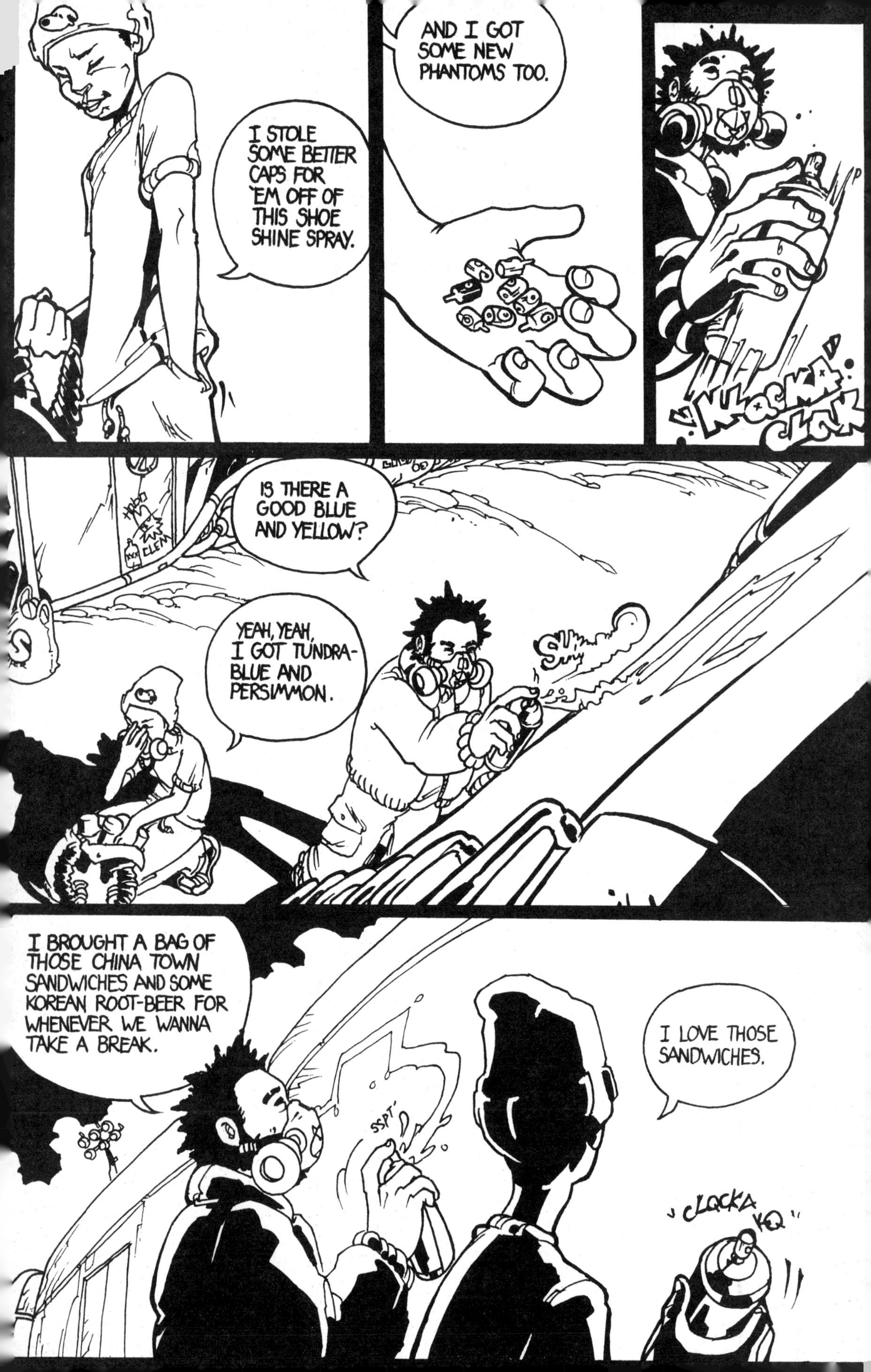
I STOLE SOME BETTER CAPS FOR 'EM OFF OF THIS SHOE SHINE SPRAY.
AND I GOT SOME NEW PHANTOMS TOO.
KLOCKA CLOCK
IS THERE A GOOD BLUE AND YELLOW?
YEAH, YEAH, I GOT TUNDRA-BLUE AND PERSIMMON.
I BROUGHT A BAG OF THOSE CHINA TOWN SANDWICHES AND SOME KOREAN ROOT-BEER FOR WHENEVER WE WANNA TAKE A BREAK.
SSPT
I LOVE THOSE SANDWICHES.
CLOCKA KQ

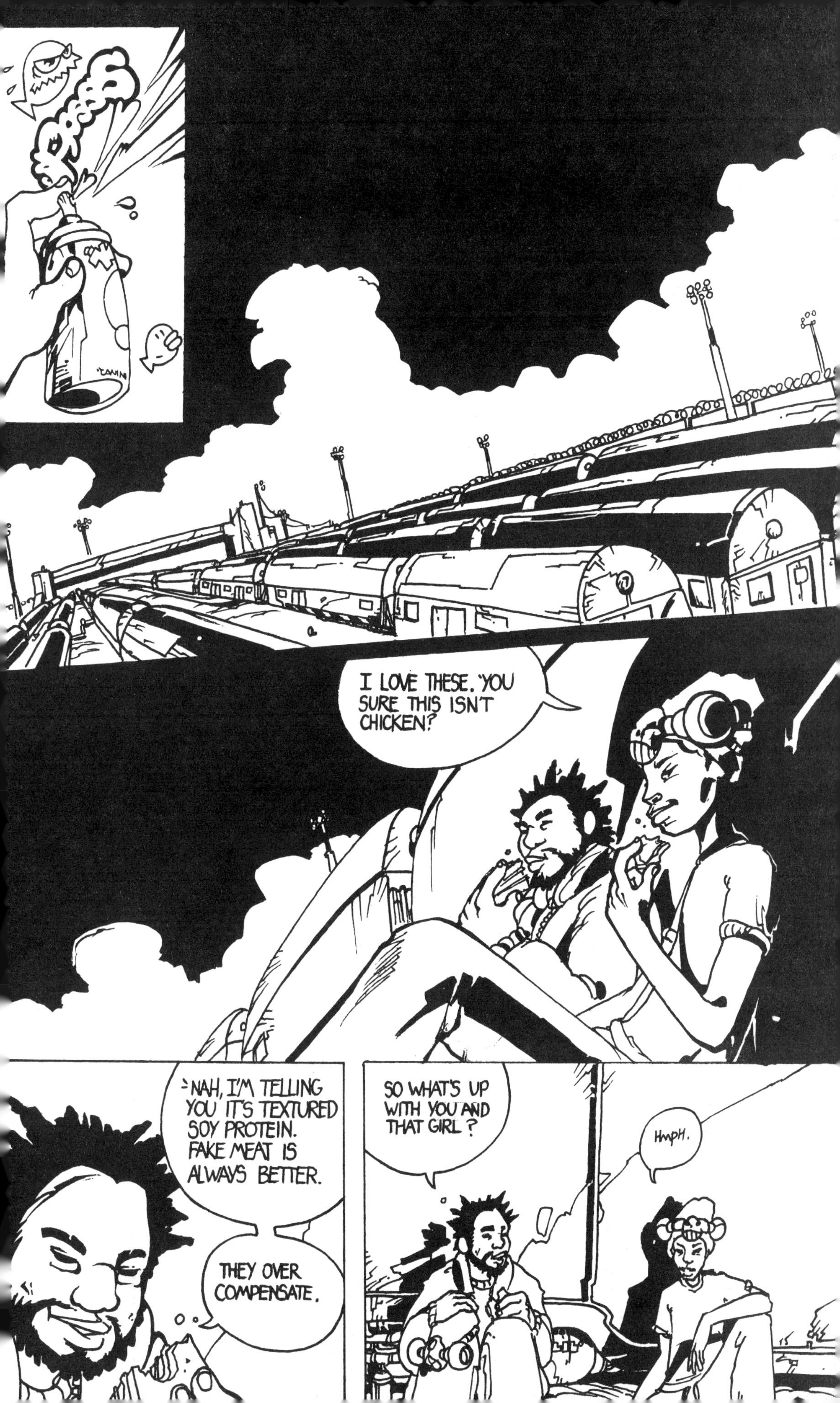
I LOVE THESE. YOU SURE THIS ISN'T CHICKEN?
NAH, I'M TELLING YOU IT'S TEXTURED SOY PROTEIN. FAKE MEAT IS ALWAYS BETTER.
THEY OVER COMPENSATE.
SO WHAT'S UP WITH YOU AND THAT GIRL?
HMPH.

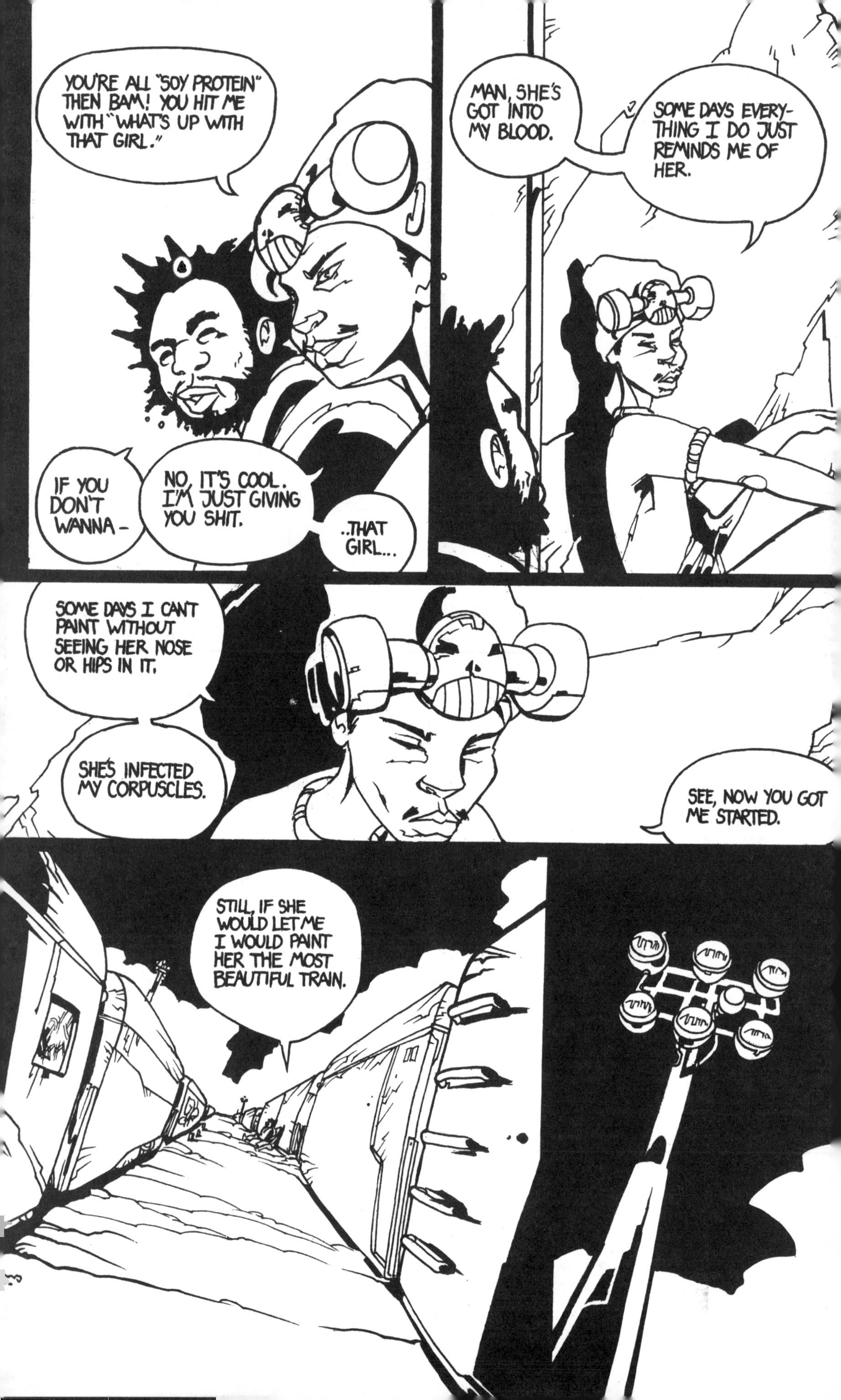
YOU'RE ALL "SOY PROTEIN" THEN BAM! YOU HIT ME WITH "WHAT'S UP WITH THAT GIRL."
IF YOU DON'T WANNA-
NO, IT'S COOL. I'M JUST GIVING YOU SHIT.
..THAT GIRL...
MAN, SHE'S GOT INTO MY BLOOD.
SOME DAYS EVERYTHING I DO JUST REMINDS ME OF HER.
SOME DAYS I CANT PAINT WITHOUT SEEING HER NOSE OR HIPS IN IT.
SHE'S INFECTED MY CORPUSCLES.
SEE, NOW YOU GOT ME STARTED.
STILL, IF SHE WOULD LET ME I WOULD PAINT HER THE MOST BEAUTIFUL TRAIN.

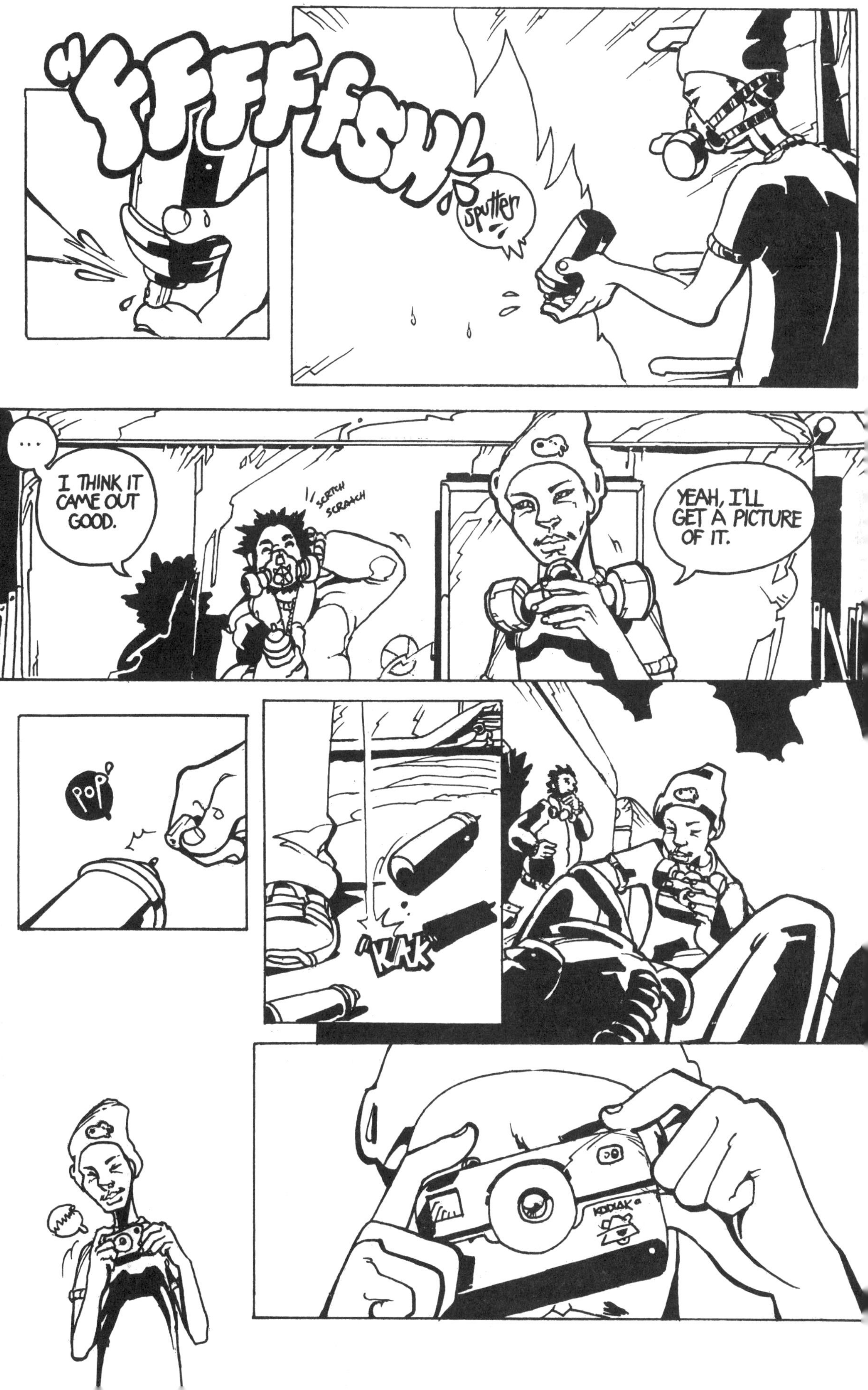
"FFFFSH!"
sputter
...
I THINK IT CAME OUT GOOD.
SCRTCH SCRATCH
YEAH, I'LL GET A PICTURE OF IT.
POP!
'KLAK
KODAK

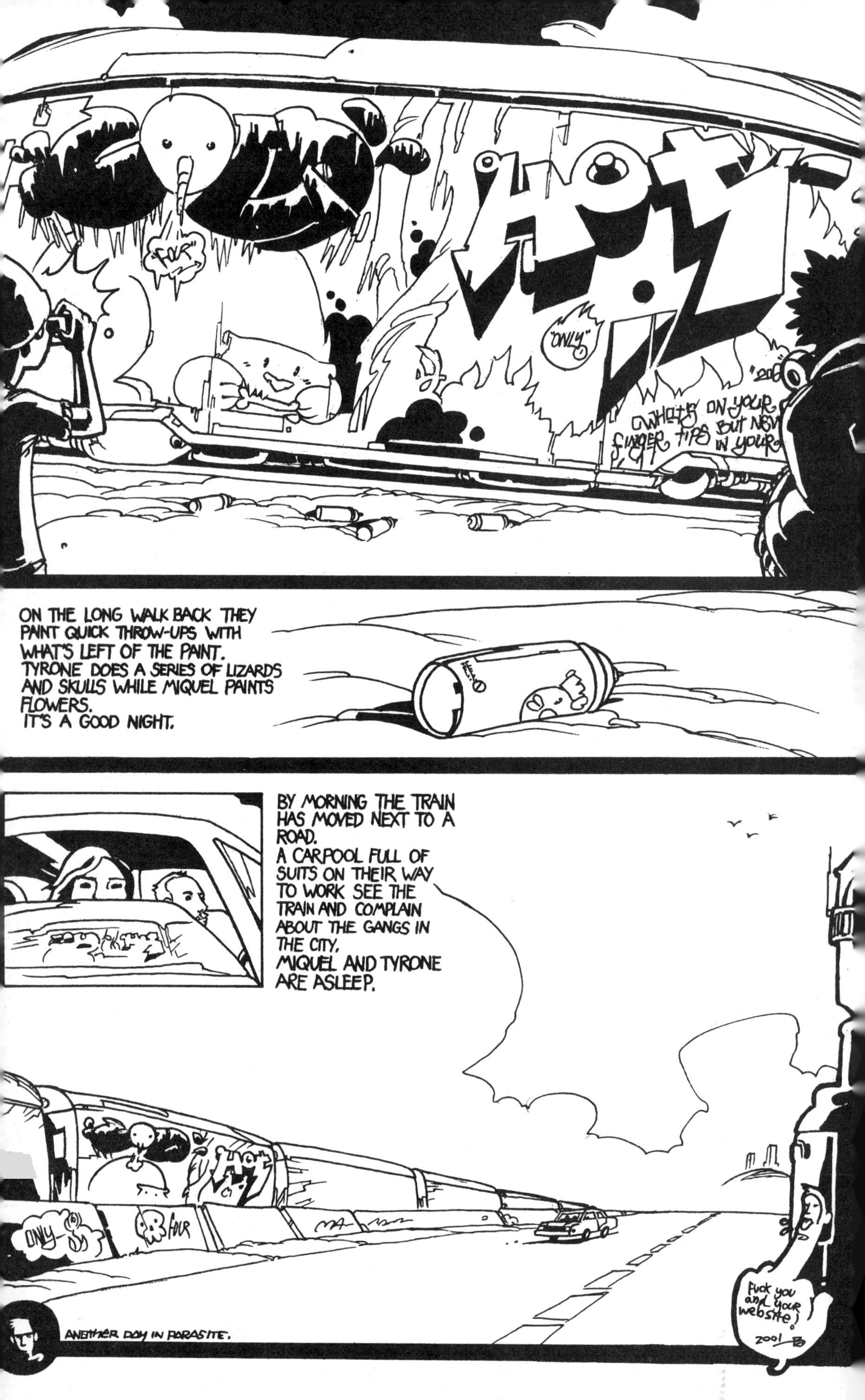

FOUR
ONLY
ON THE LONG WALK BACK THEY PAINT QUICK THROW-UPS WITH WHAT'S LEFT OF THE PAINT. TYRONE DOES A SERIES OF LIZARDS AND SKULLS WHILE MIQUEL PAINTS FLOWERS.
IT'S A GOOD NIGHT.
BY MORNING THE TRAIN HAS MOVED NEXT TO A ROAD.
A CARPOOL FULL OF SUITS ON THEIR WAY TO WORK SEE THE TRAIN AND COMPLAIN ABOUT THE GANGS IN THE CITY.
MIQUEL AND TYRONE ARE ASLEEP.
ONLY
FOUR
Fuck you and your website!
2001
ANOTHER DAY IN PARASITE.

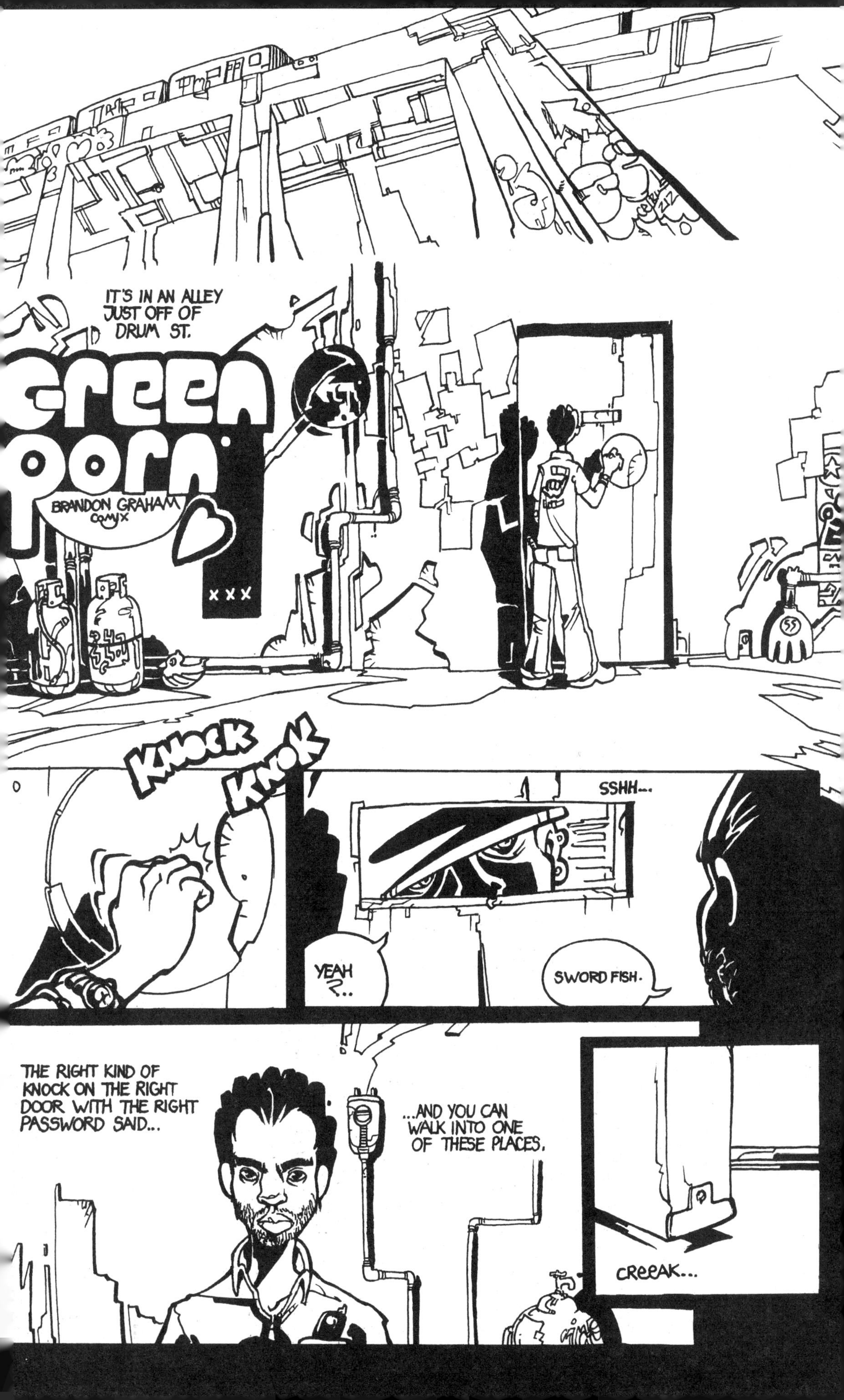
IT'S IN AN ALLEY JUST OFF OF DRUM ST.
Green porn
BRANDON GRAHAM COMIX
XXX
KNOCK KNOCK
SSHH...
YEAH ?...
SWORD FISH.
THE RIGHT KIND OF KNOCK ON THE RIGHT DOOR WITH THE RIGHT PASSWORD SAID...
...AND YOU CAN WALK INTO ONE OF THESE PLACES.
CREEAK...

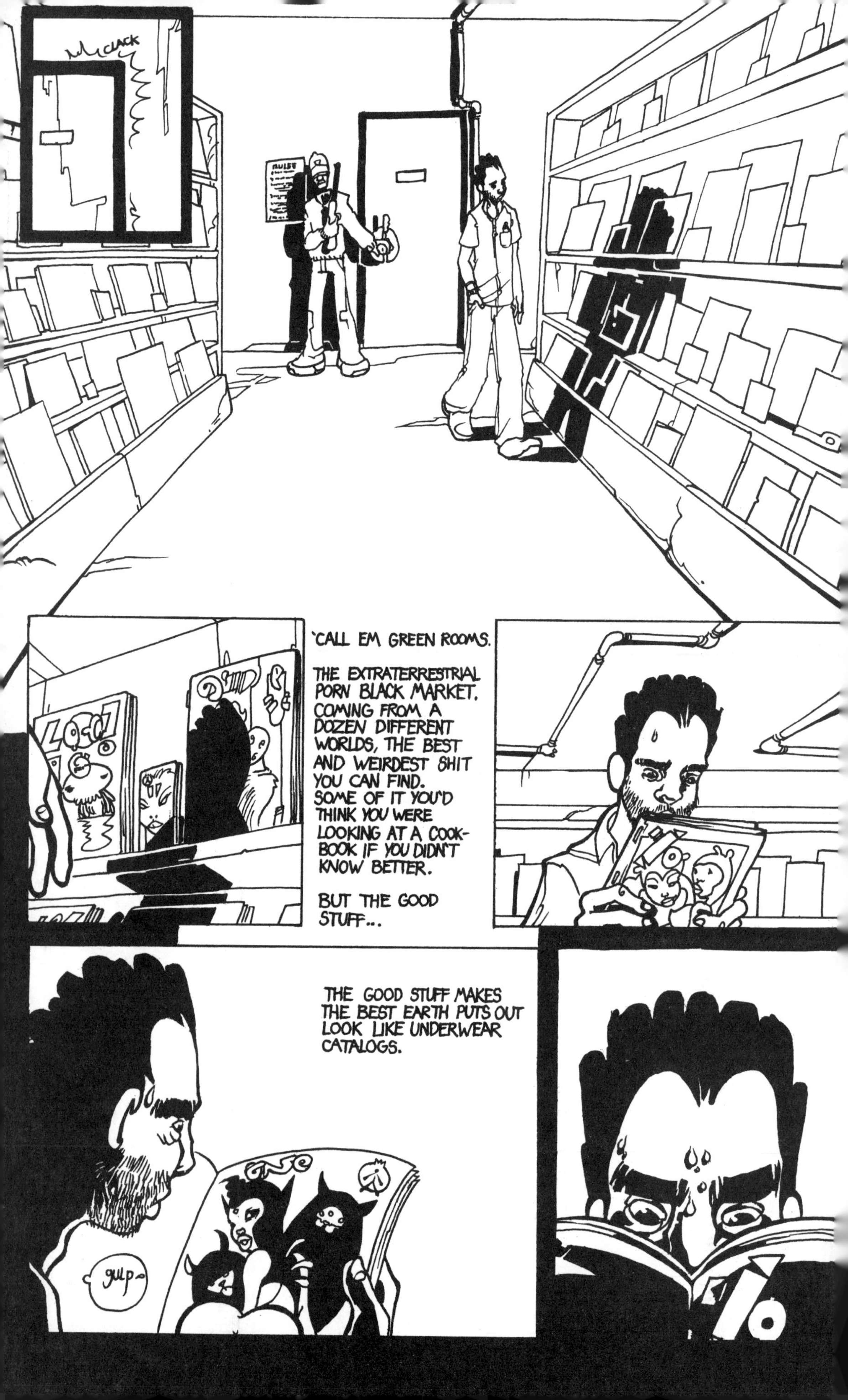

CLACK
RULES
'CALL EM GREEN ROOMS.
THE EXTRATERRESTRIAL PORN BLACK MARKET. COMING FROM A DOZEN DIFFERENT WORLDS, THE BEST AND WEIRDEST SHIT YOU CAN FIND. SOME OF IT YOU'D THINK YOU WERE LOOKING AT A COOK-BOOK IF YOU DIDN'T KNOW BETTER.
BUT THE GOOD STUFF...
THE GOOD STUFF MAKES THE BEST EARTH PUTS OUT LOOK LIKE UNDERWEAR CATALOGS.
gulp

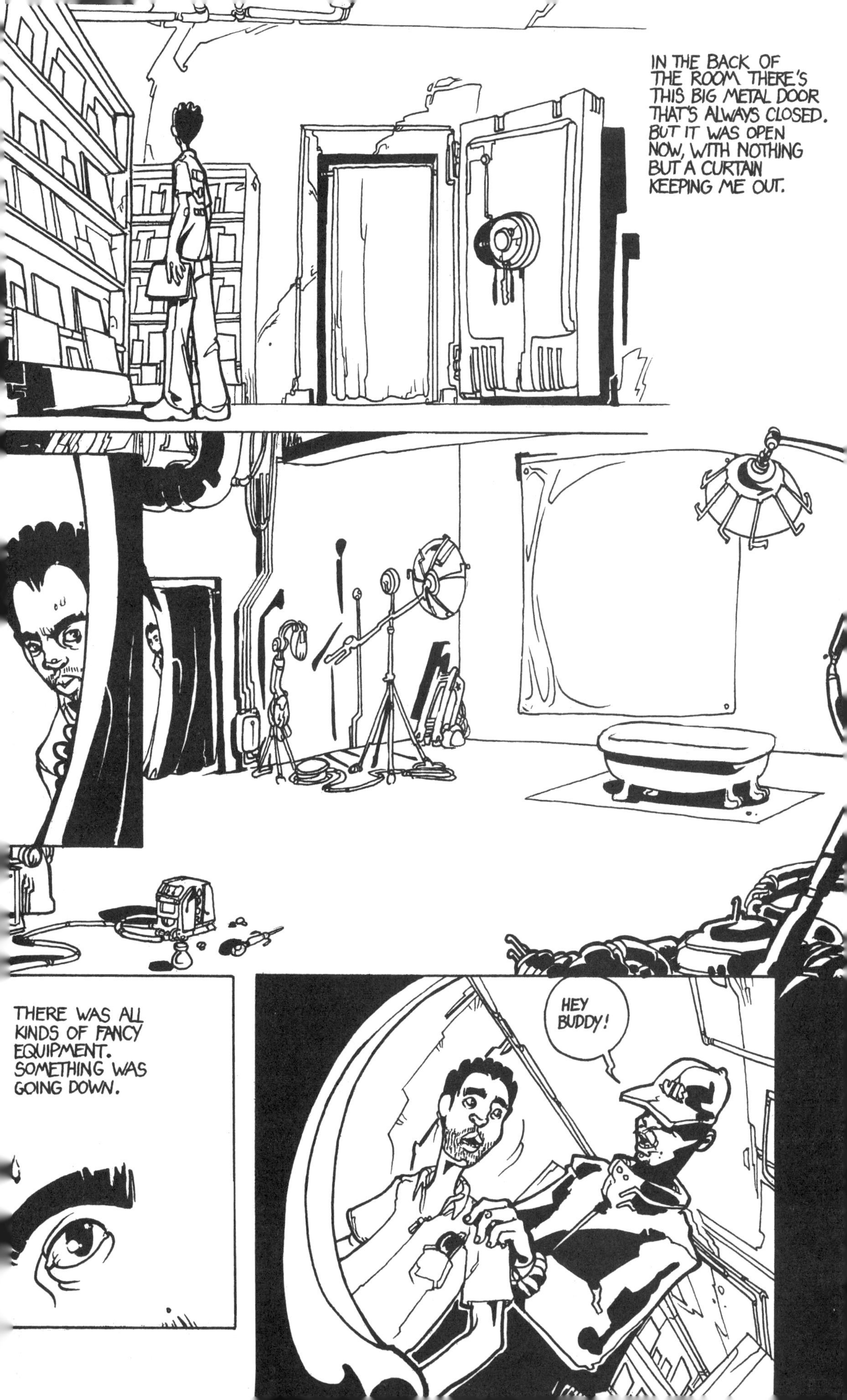
IN THE BACK OF THE ROOM THERE'S THIS BIG METAL DOOR THAT'S ALWAYS CLOSED. BUT IT WAS OPEN NOW, WITH NOTHING BUT A CURTAIN KEEPING ME OUT.
THERE WAS ALL KINDS OF FANCY EQUIPMENT. SOMETHING WAS GOING DOWN.
HEY BUDDY!

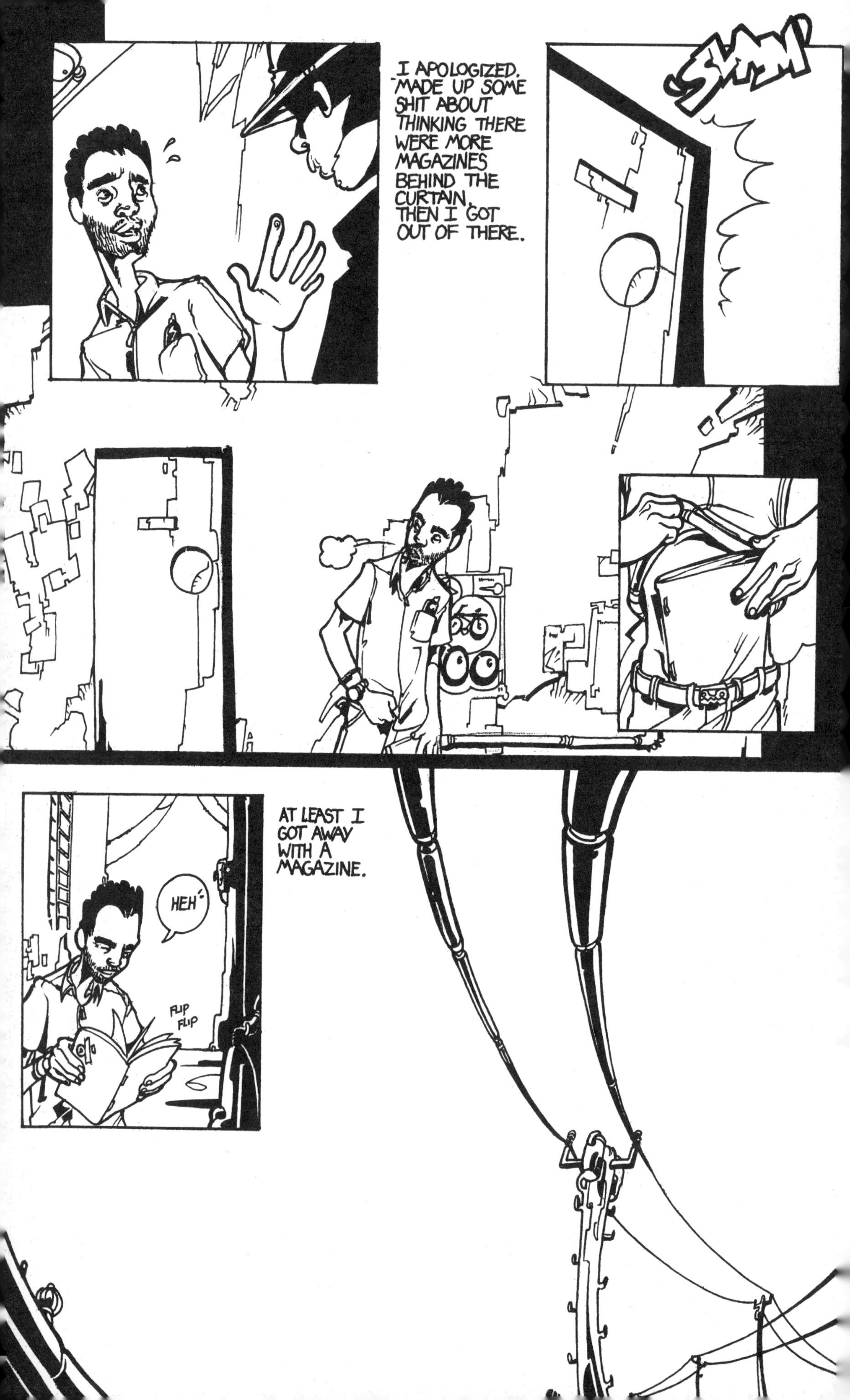
I APOLOGIZED. MADE UP SOME SHIT ABOUT THINKING THERE WERE MORE MAGAZINES BEHIND THE CURTAIN, THEN I GOT OUT OF THERE.
SLAM
AT LEAST I GOT AWAY WITH A MAGAZINE.
HEH
FLIP FLIP

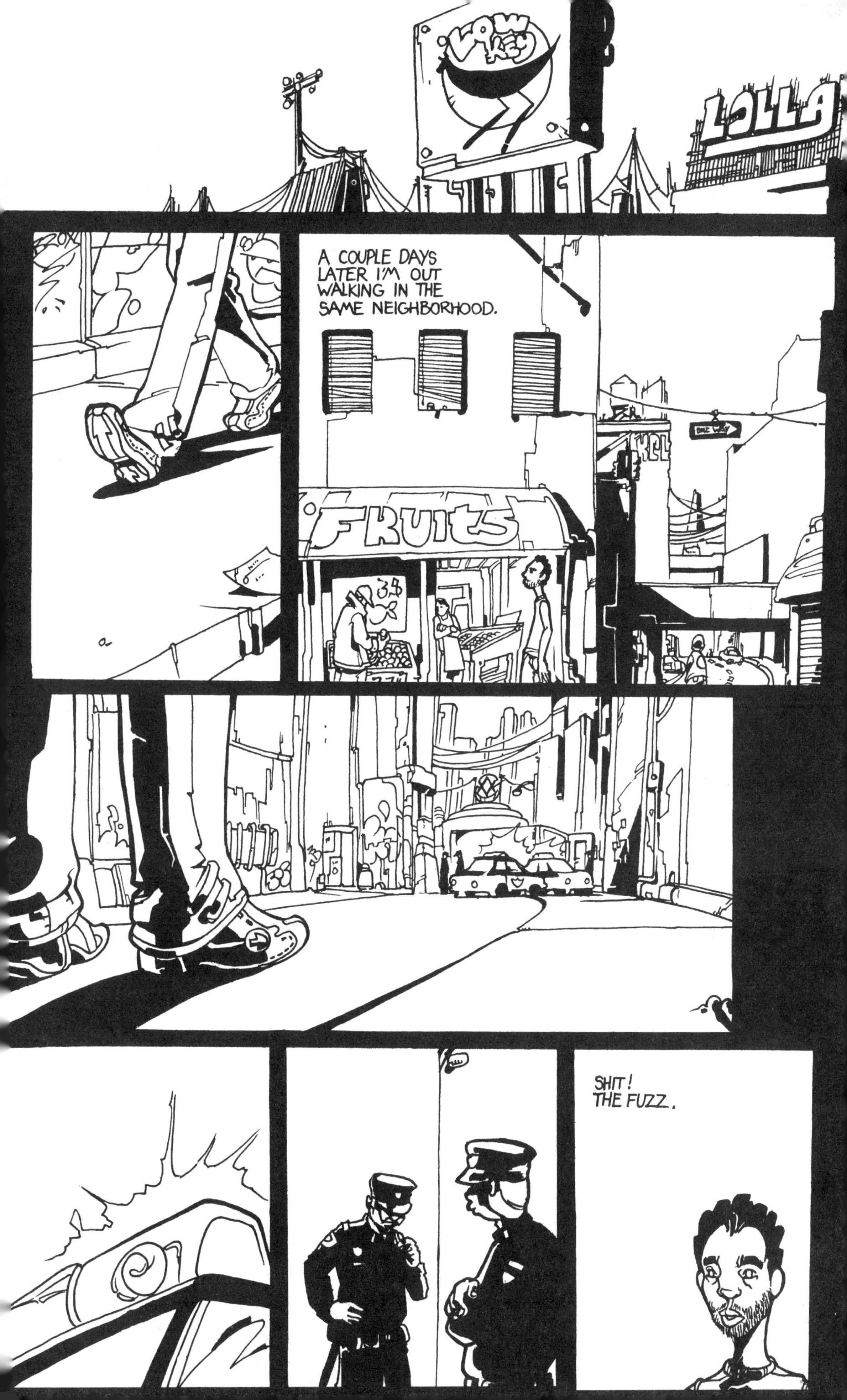
LOW KEY
LOLLA
A COUPLE DAYS LATER I'M OUT WALKING IN THE SAME NEIGHBORHOOD.
FRUITS
ONE WAY
SHIT! THE FUZZ.

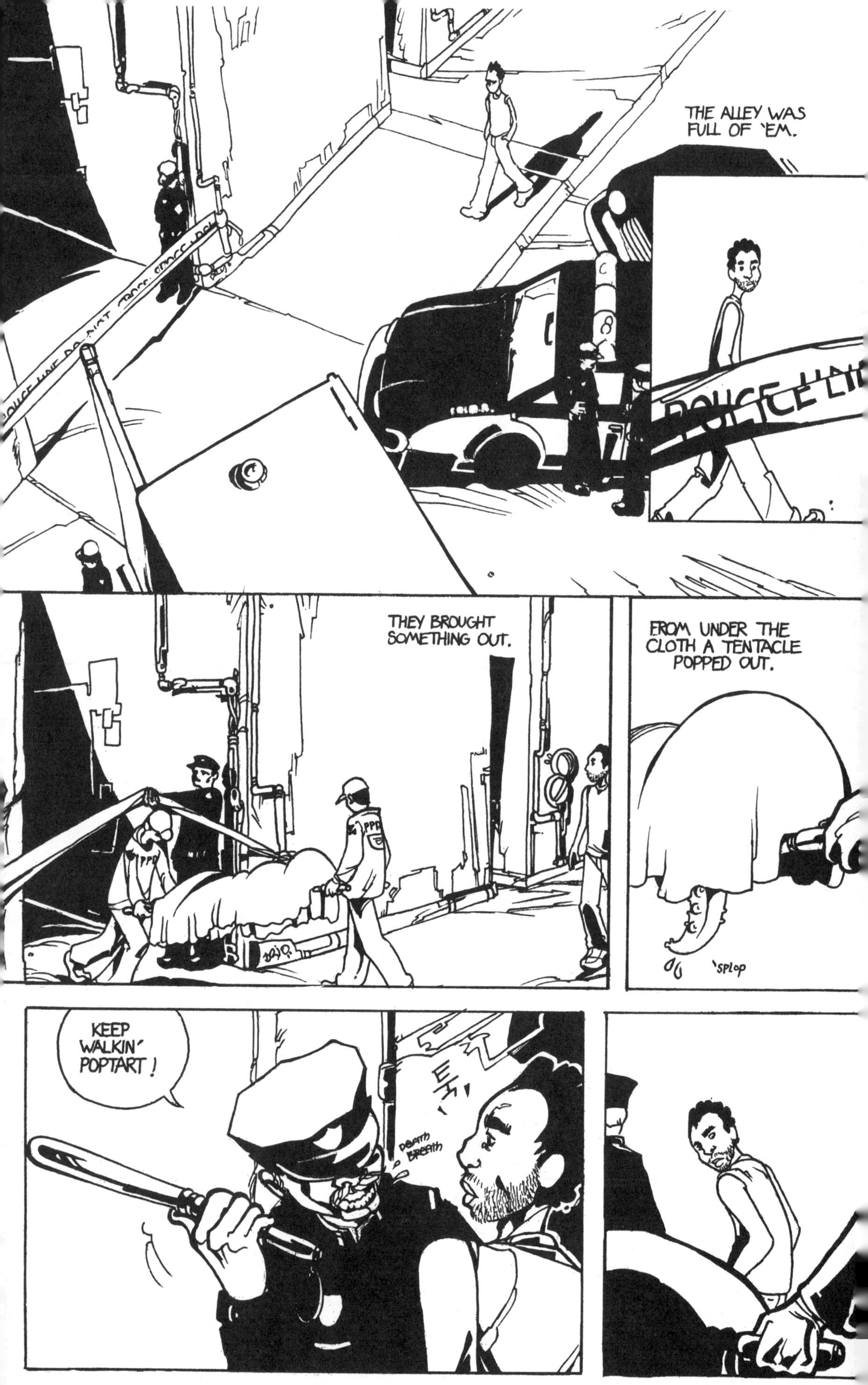
THE ALLEY WAS FULL OF 'EM.
THEY BROUGHT SOMETHING OUT.
FROM UNDER THE CLOTH A TENTACLE POPPED OUT.
'SPLOP
KEEP WALKIN' POPTART!
Death Breath

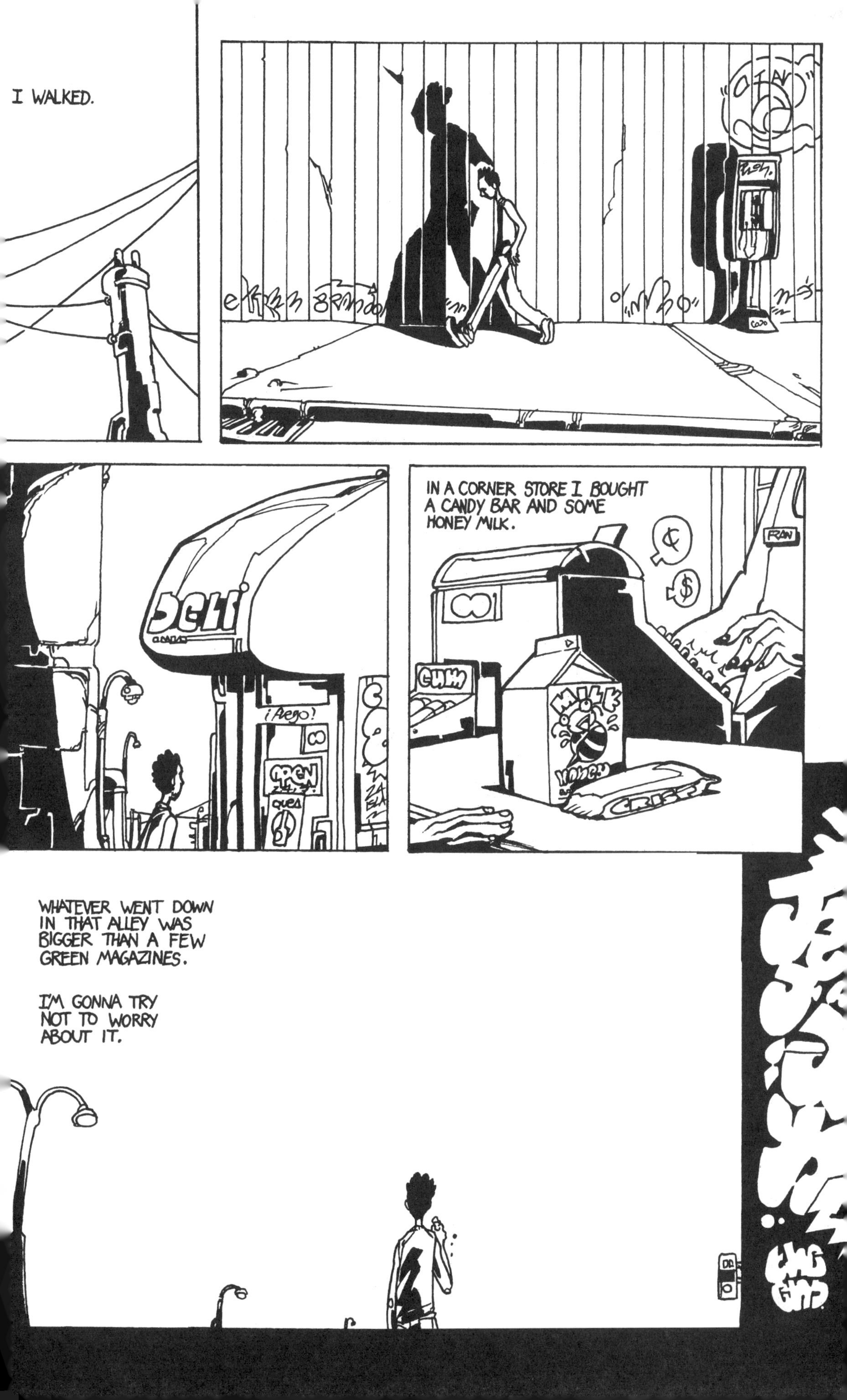
I WALKED.
DELI
¡Fuego!
OPEN
IN A CORNER STORE I BOUGHT A CANDY BAR AND SOME HONEY MILK.
GUM
MILK
WHATEVER WENT DOWN IN THAT ALLEY WAS BIGGER THAN A FEW GREEN MAGAZINES.
I'M GONNA TRY NOT TO WORRY ABOUT IT.

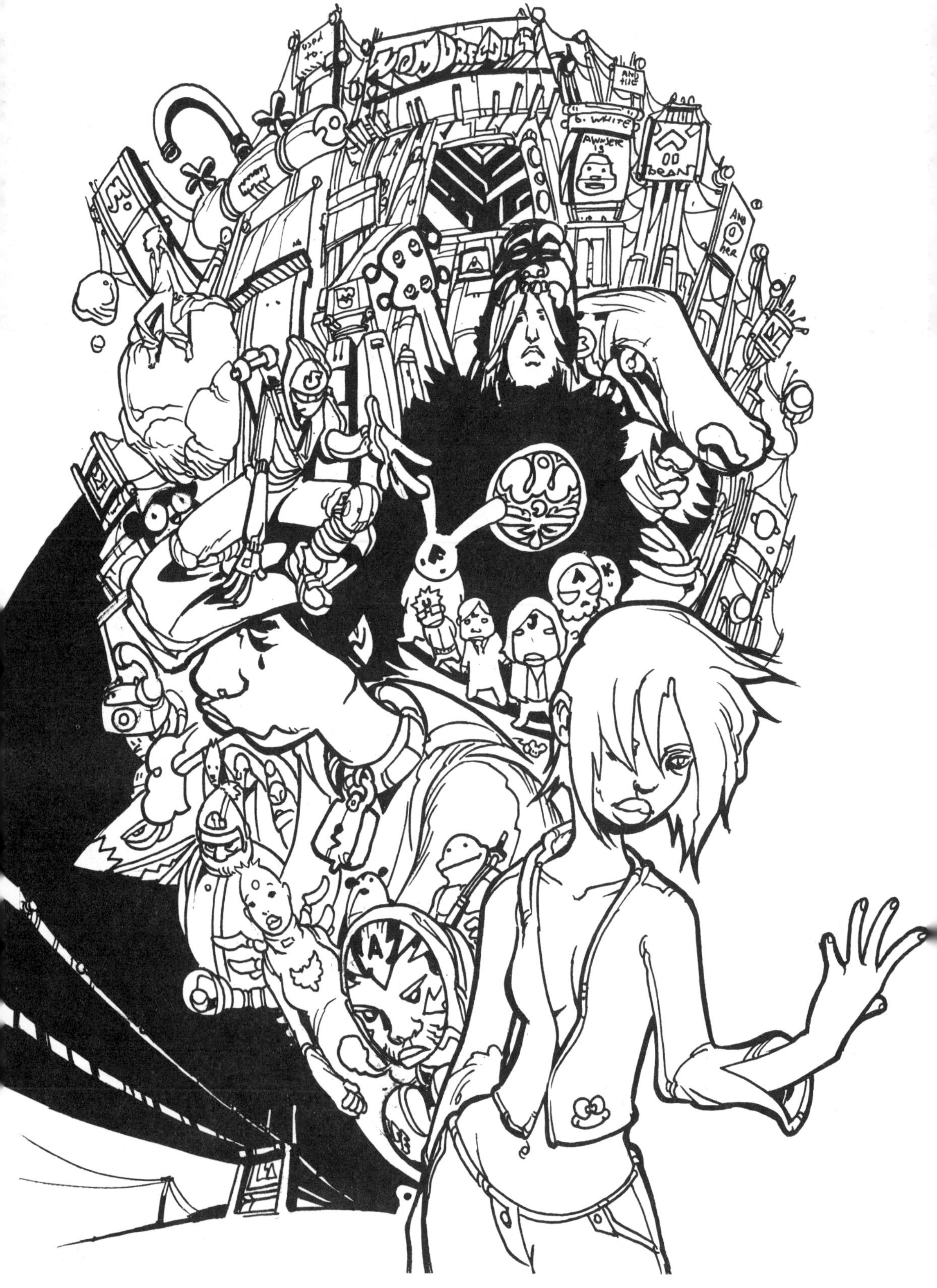
used to.
AND the
b. WHITE
AWNSER IS
AND her

BREAKFAST— I DID THIS TO TRY TO SELL A SIX ISSUE SERIES. THE STORY WAS ABOUT A GUY WHOSE SKELETON HAS A MAP ON IT CONNECTING HELL TO EARTH. THE THING THAT SHOWS UP AT HIS DOOR IN THIS IS A POSSESSED U.P.S. DELIVERY MAN, EVERY ORIFICE IN HIS BODY HAS A DIFFERENT DEMON IN IT AND WOULD SPEAK WITH ITS OWN VOICE. I WAS GOING TO SHOW THIS WITH DIFFERENT STYLES OF WORD BALLOONS. THE NEON SIGN WITH THE FISH IS BASED OFF OF A SIGN IN DOWNTOWN SEATTLE.

WHEN I DREW THIS I WOULD START EVERYDAY WARMING UP BY REDRAWING PANELS OUT OF KOREAN COMICS I'D CHECKED OUT FROM THE LIBRARY. I WAS NEWLY LIVING IN NEW YORK AND IT SEEMED HARSH, I WOULD HAVE DAYDREAMS OF MOVING SOMEPLACE WITH PALM TREES AND WALKING AROUND IN HAWAIIAN SHIRTS AND LOOSE FITTING TAN PANTS.

GONE FISHIN'— ONE WEEKEND I WAS DETERMINED TO DO A NEW STORY BUT I COULDN'T DECIDE WHAT TO DRAW UNTIL I HAD TO GO TO THE POST OFFICE. WHEN I GOT BACK I JUST DREW WHAT HAPPENED.

TRUE CRIME— WHEN I WAS IN MY LATE TEENS AND EARLY 20's, I WAS INTO THE GRAFFITI SCENE IN SEATTLE. THERE WAS SO MUCH ENTHUSIASM ABOUT JUST MAKING GOOD FUN ART. WE WOULD HAVE "ART BATTLES," GET A BUNCH OF PEOPLE TOGETHER DRAWING THE SAME THING COMPARING PICTURES AT THE END. THINGS LIKE OPTIMUS PRIME, WITH ONE PICTURE OF HIM SELLING STOLEN T.V.'S OUT OF THE BACK OF HIS TRAILER AND ANOTHER OF HIM AS AN OLD ROBOT IN A ROCKING CHAIR. WE'D GO OUT PASTEING UP COMICS IN THE RAIN WITH A SOLUTION MADE OUT OF POWDERED MILK, THAT BONDED SO STRONG THAT A BUS SHELTER WINDOW GOT BROKEN WHEN THEY TRIED TO SCRAPE IT OFF. I HAVE SO MANY GOOD MEMORIES FROM THAT TIME. I TRIED TO SHOW HOW IT FELT IN THIS STORY.

I KEPT MY PAL DAVID ON THE PHONE THE WHOLE TIME I WAS FIGURING OUT THE PAGES. HE WAS AN IMMENSE HELP. HE SHOWED ME WHERE TO GET THE GOOD KOREAN ROOT BEER AND TOLD ME ALL ABOUT JAPANESE SPRAY PAINT.

I WENT OUT WITH A POLAROID AND TOOK REFERENCE PHOTOS OF A TRAIN YARD. I HAD A HARD TIME GETTING THE RIGHT SHOTS, SO I TOOK A BUNCH OF SHOTS. ON THE WALK HOME I PASSED A GAS STATION WHERE THEY WERE WORKING ON ONE OF THE PUMPS. ITS FRONT WAS OPEN WITH ALL OF ITS HOSES AND WING NUTS EXPOSED. THE BEST KIND OF ART REFERENCE, COMPLICATED ACCURATE SHIT. I TRIED TO TAKE A PICTURE, BUT I WAS OUT OF FILM. SO SAD.

GREEN PORN— I HAD A BOOK REVIEW I'D TORN OUT OF A MAGAZINE TAPED ABOVE MY DESK. THE BOOK WAS SOME GRITTY SOUTH AMERICAN STORY WITH A PHOTO OF ITS GRIZZLIED AUTHOR CHOMPING ON A CIGAR. I NEVER READ THE BOOK BUT I TRIED TO MAKE THIS FEEL LIKE I THOUGHT IT MIGHT. THE HONEY-MILK HE BUYS AT THE END WAS SOMETHING I'D THOUGHT WOULD MAKE IT MORE SOUTH AMERICAN, I PROBABLY SHOULD'VE WRITTEN IT IN SPANISH.

ORIGINALLY, THIS WAS ONLY 4 PAGES. BUT, WHEN I CALLED THE EDITOR I WAS DRAWING IT TO SHOW HE WAS TOO BUSY TO SEE ME, SO MORE PAGES GOT ADDED. I HAVE A BEAT UP, COVERLESS COLLECTION OF BUKOWSKI STORIES. READING IT HELPED ME FREE UP HOW I WRITE. I LIKE HOW HE ENDS HIS STUFF WITHOUT TRICKS OR BIG REVELATIONS, THEY JUST END SMOOTHLY, AND LIFE KEEPS GOING.

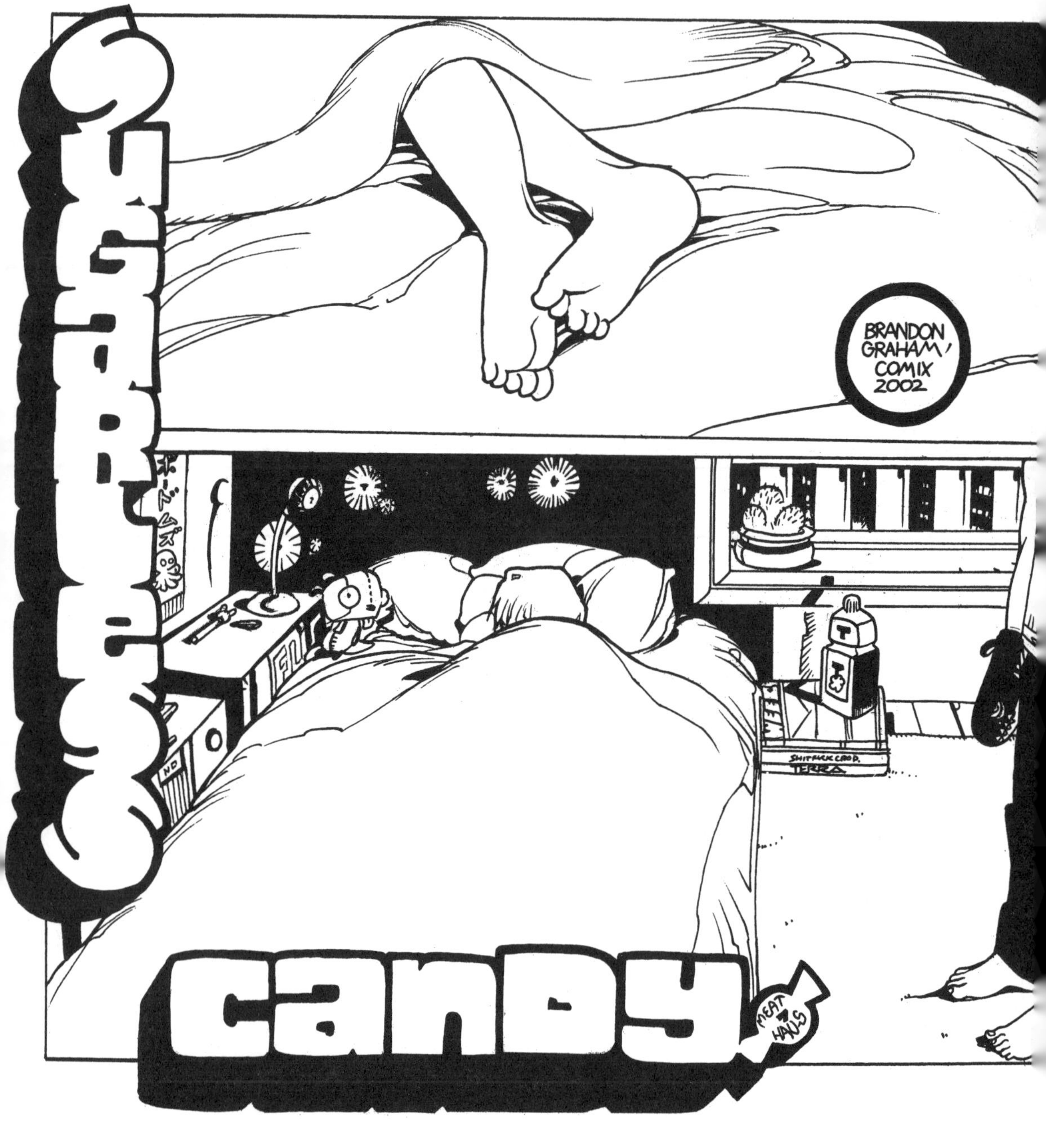
BRANDON GRAHAM' COMIX 2002
ボードムズ
canDy
MEAT HAUS
TERRA

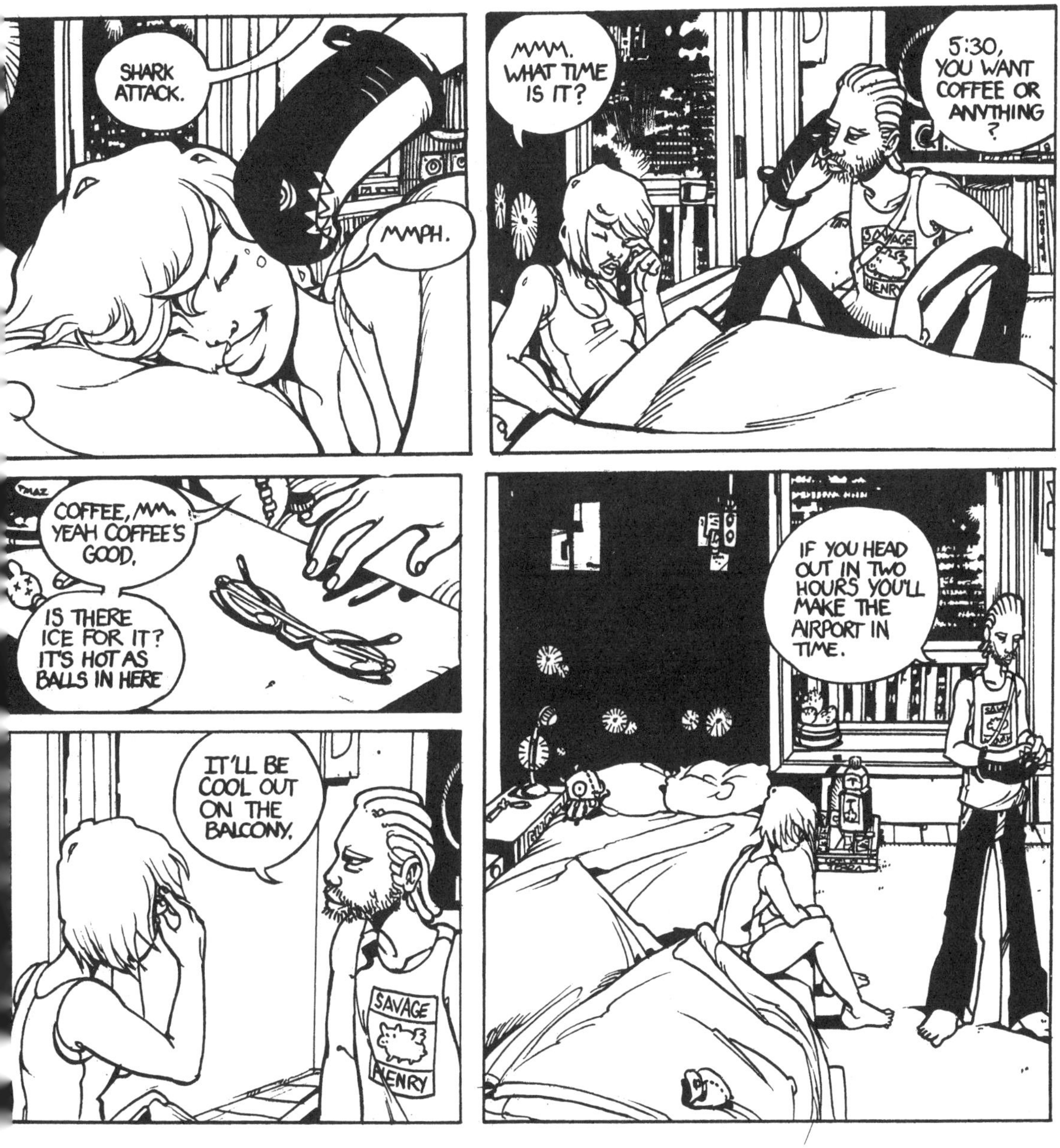
SHARK ATTACK.
MMPH.
MMM. WHAT TIME IS IT?
5:30, YOU WANT COFFEE OR ANYTHING?
COFFEE, MM. YEAH COFFEE'S GOOD.
IS THERE ICE FOR IT? IT'S HOT AS BALLS IN HERE
IT'LL BE COOL OUT ON THE BALCONY.
IF YOU HEAD OUT IN TWO HOURS YOU'LL MAKE THE AIRPORT IN TIME.
SAVAGE HENRY

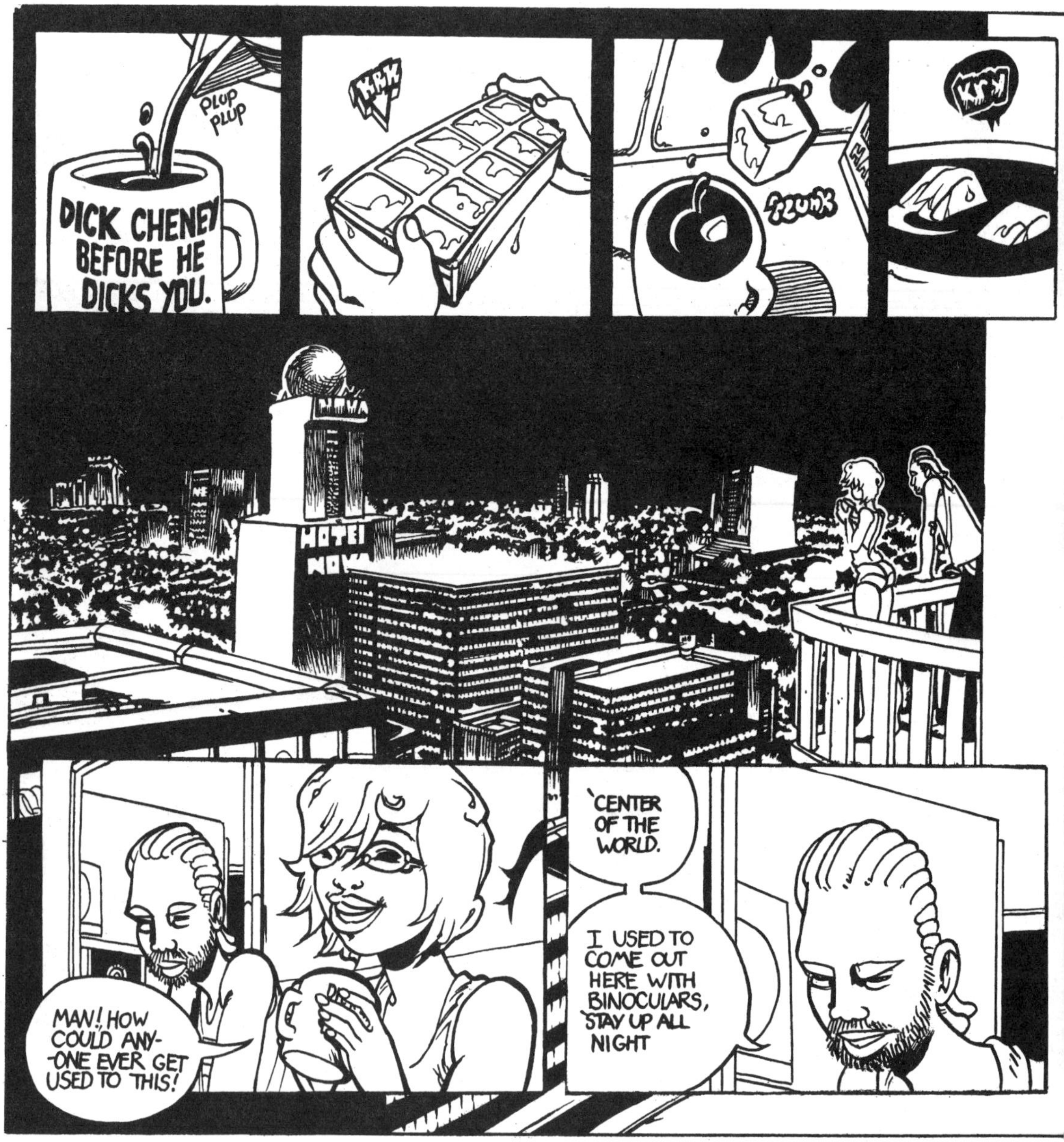
PLUP PLUP
DICK CHENEY BEFORE HE DICKS YOU.
KRK
FLUNK
KSH
NOVA
HOTEL NOVA
MAN! HOW COULD ANY-ONE EVER GET USED TO THIS!
CENTER OF THE WORLD.
I USED TO COME OUT HERE WITH BINOCULARS, STAY UP ALL NIGHT

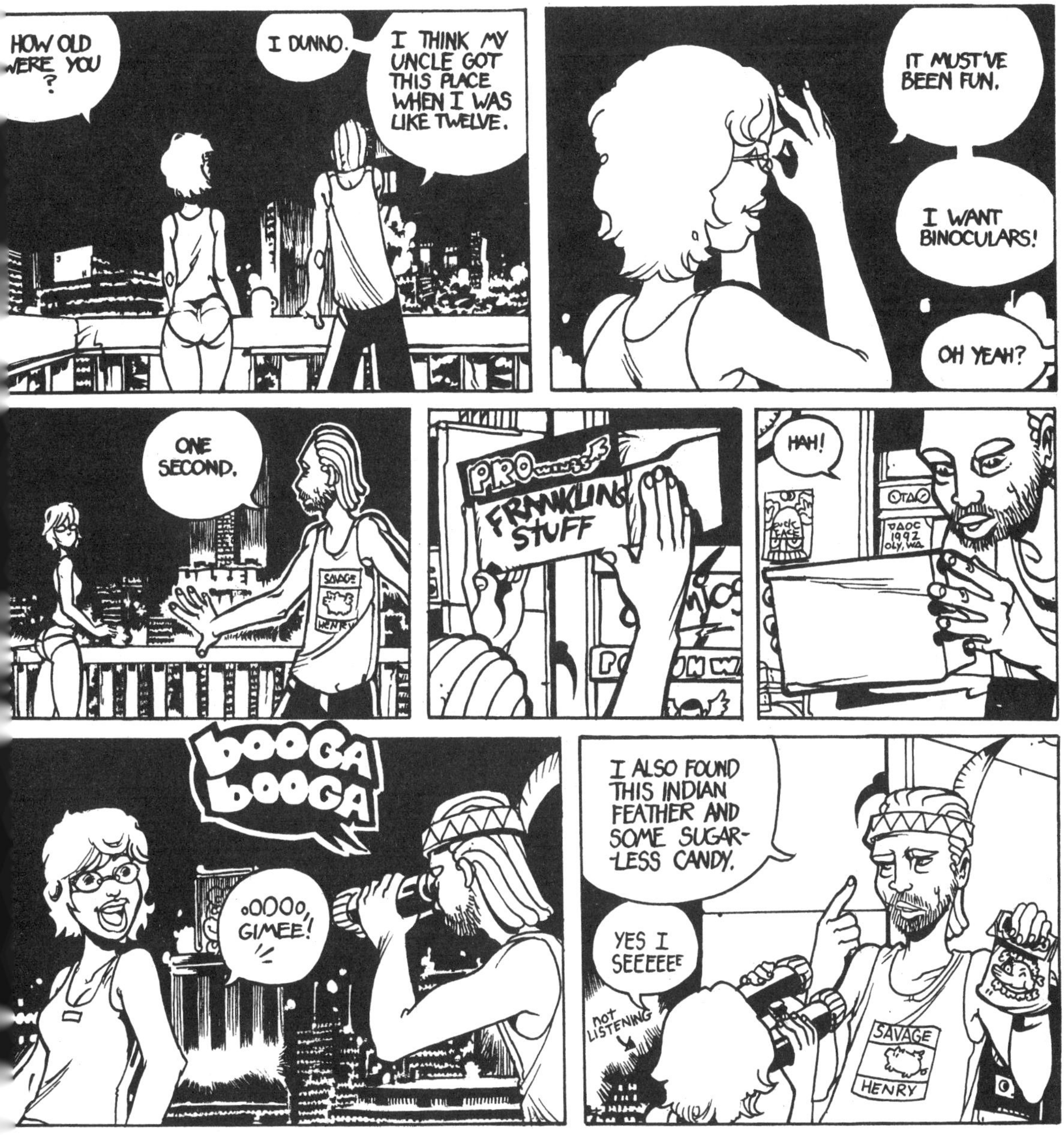
HOW OLD WERE YOU ?
I DUNNO.
I THINK MY UNCLE GOT THIS PLACE WHEN I WAS LIKE TWELVE.
IT MUST'VE BEEN FUN.
I WANT BINOCULARS!
OH YEAH?
ONE SECOND.
SAVAGE HENRY
PRO
FRANKLINS STUFF
HAH!
1992 OLY, WA
booga booga
oOOOo, GIMEE!
I ALSO FOUND THIS INDIAN FEATHER AND SOME SUGAR-LESS CANDY.
YES I SEEEEEE
not LISTENING
SAVAGE HENRY

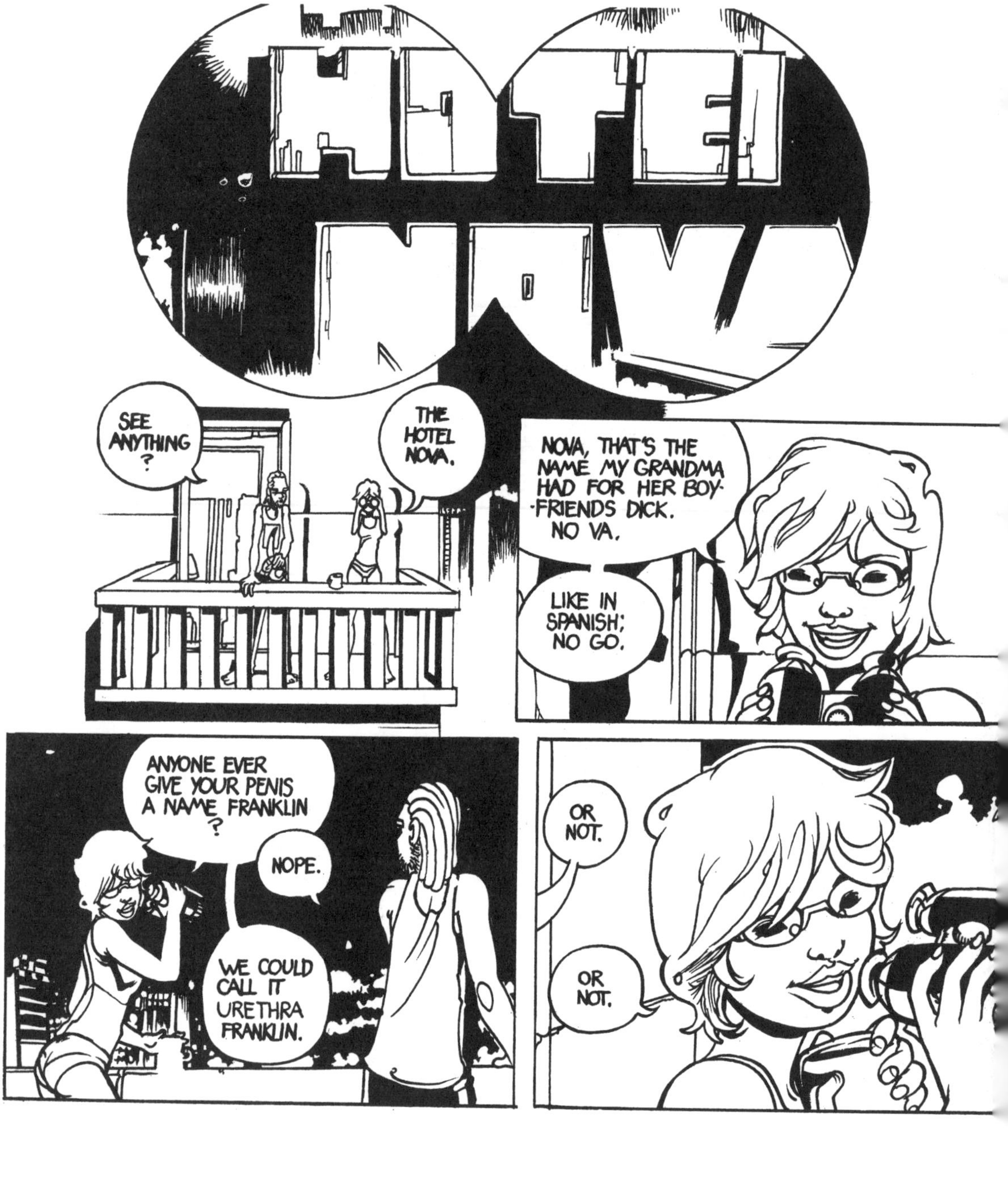

HOTEL NOV
SEE ANYTHING?
THE HOTEL NOVA.
NOVA, THAT'S THE NAME MY GRANDMA HAD FOR HER BOY-FRIENDS DICK. NO VA.
LIKE IN SPANISH; NO GO.
ANYONE EVER GIVE YOUR PENIS A NAME FRANKLIN?
NOPE.
WE COULD CALL IT URETHRA FRANKLIN.
OR NOT.
OR NOT.

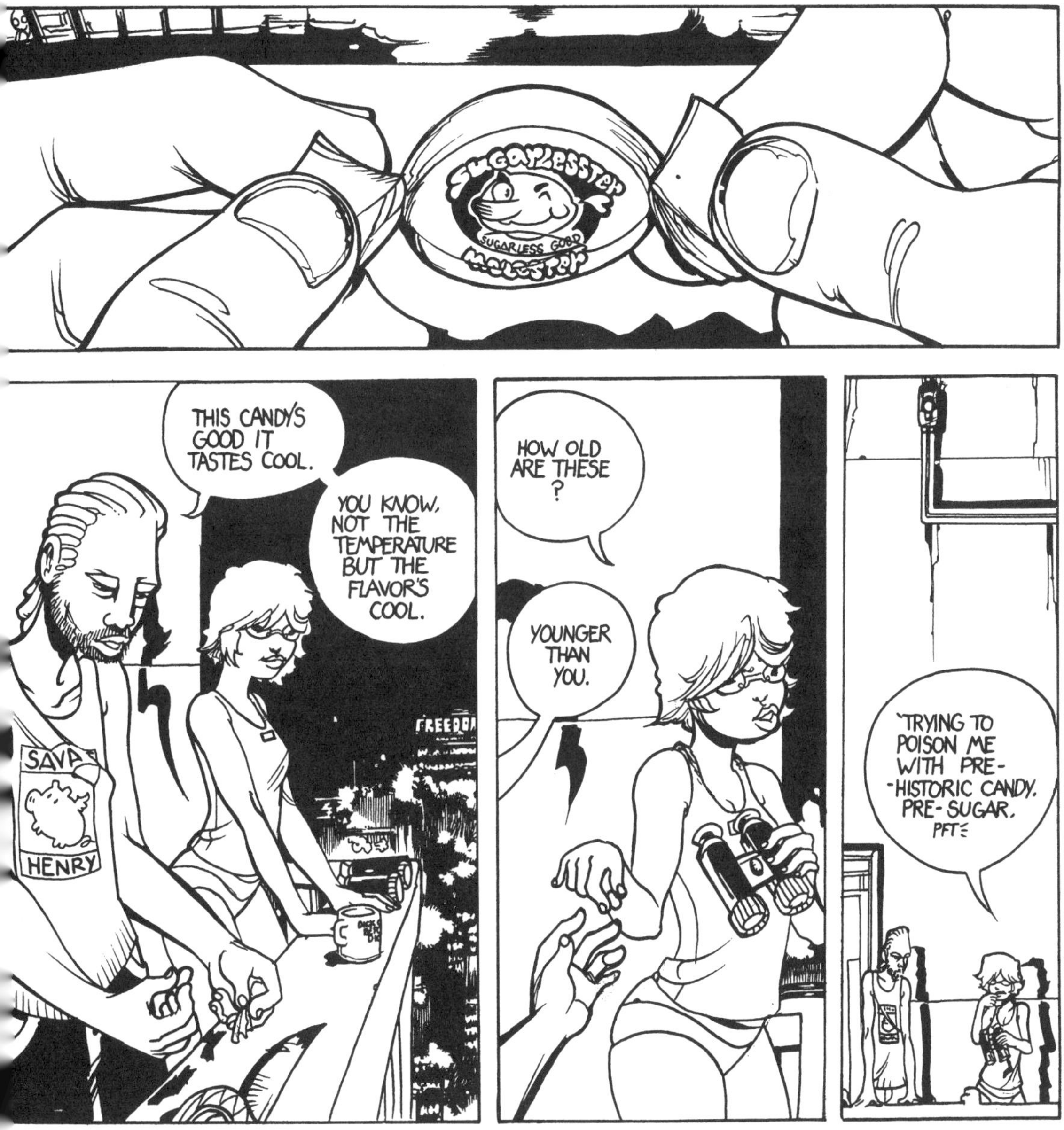

SUGARLESS GOOD
THIS CANDY'S GOOD IT TASTES COOL.
YOU KNOW, NOT THE TEMPERATURE BUT THE FLAVOR'S COOL.
HOW OLD ARE THESE ?
YOUNGER THAN YOU.
`TRYING TO POISON ME WITH PRE- -HISTORIC CANDY. PRE-SUGAR.
PFT

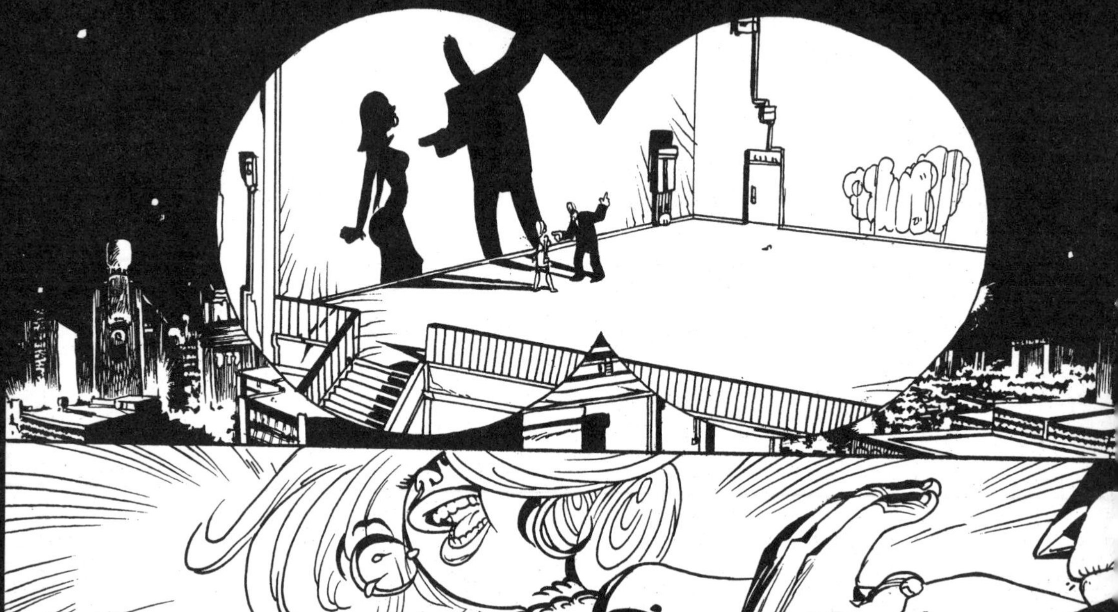
FUCK NUTS!
YOU DROPPED YOUR CANDY.
I JUST SAW...
SOME GIRL JUST GOT HIT ON THAT ROOF OVER THERE!

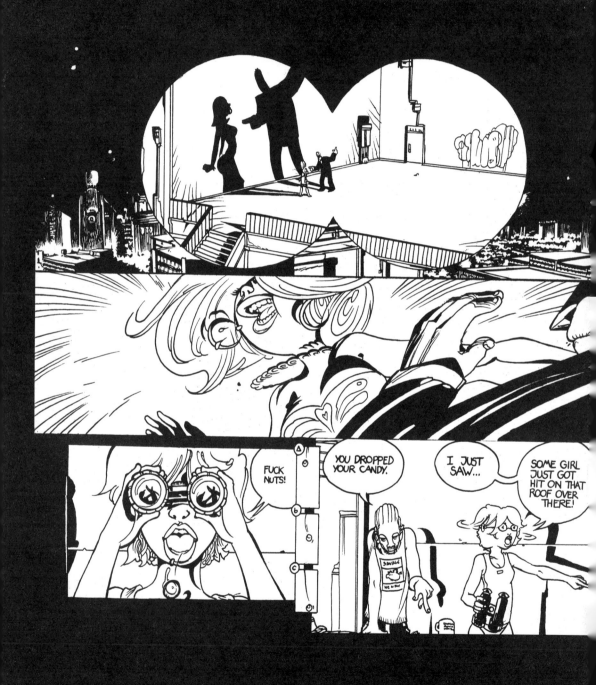

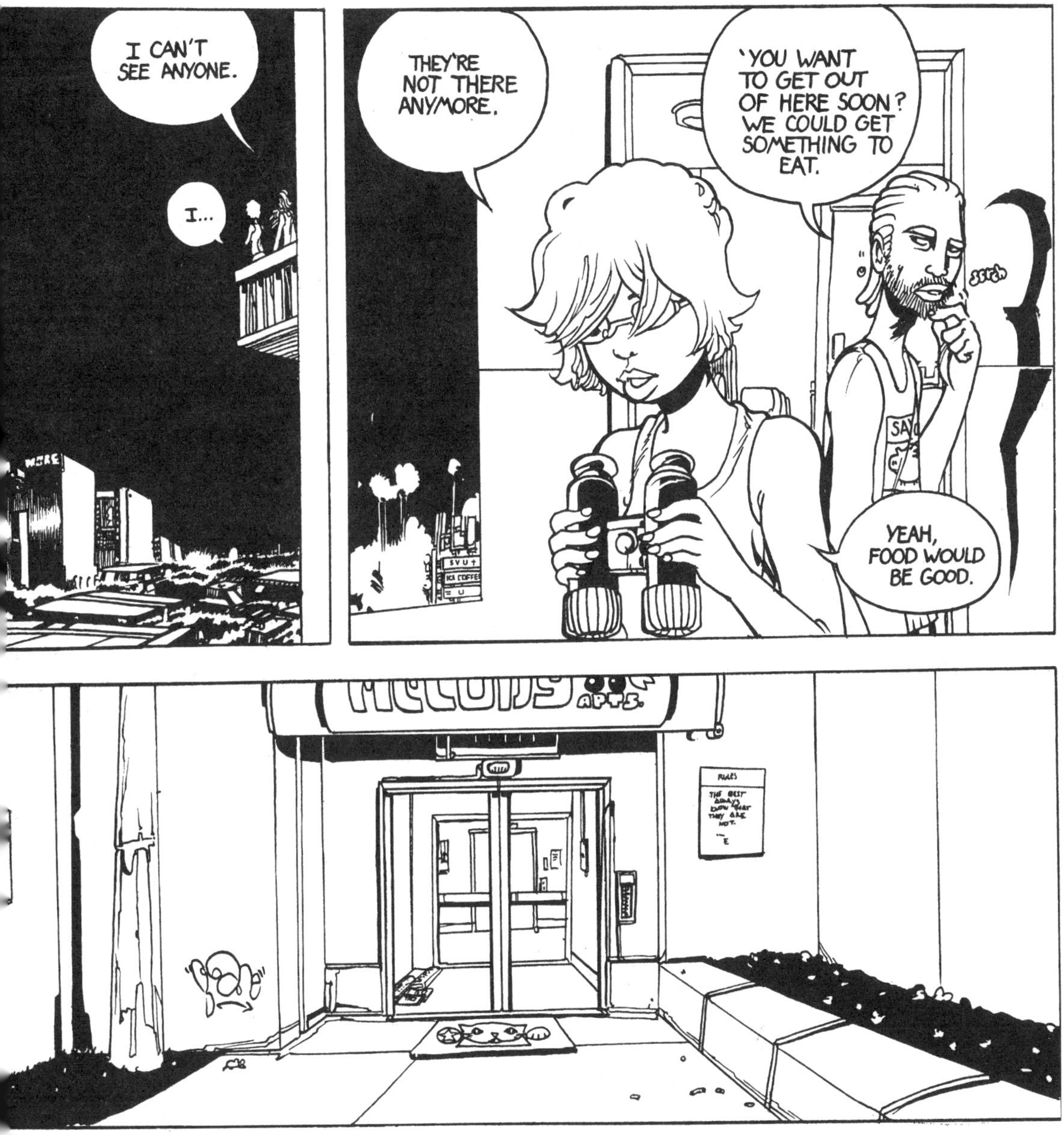
I CAN'T SEE ANYONE.
I...
THEY'RE NOT THERE ANYMORE.
'YOU WANT TO GET OUT OF HERE SOON? WE COULD GET SOMETHING TO EAT.
scrch
YEAH, FOOD WOULD BE GOOD.
APTS.
RULES
THE BEST ALWAYS KNOW THAT THEY ARE NOT.
— E

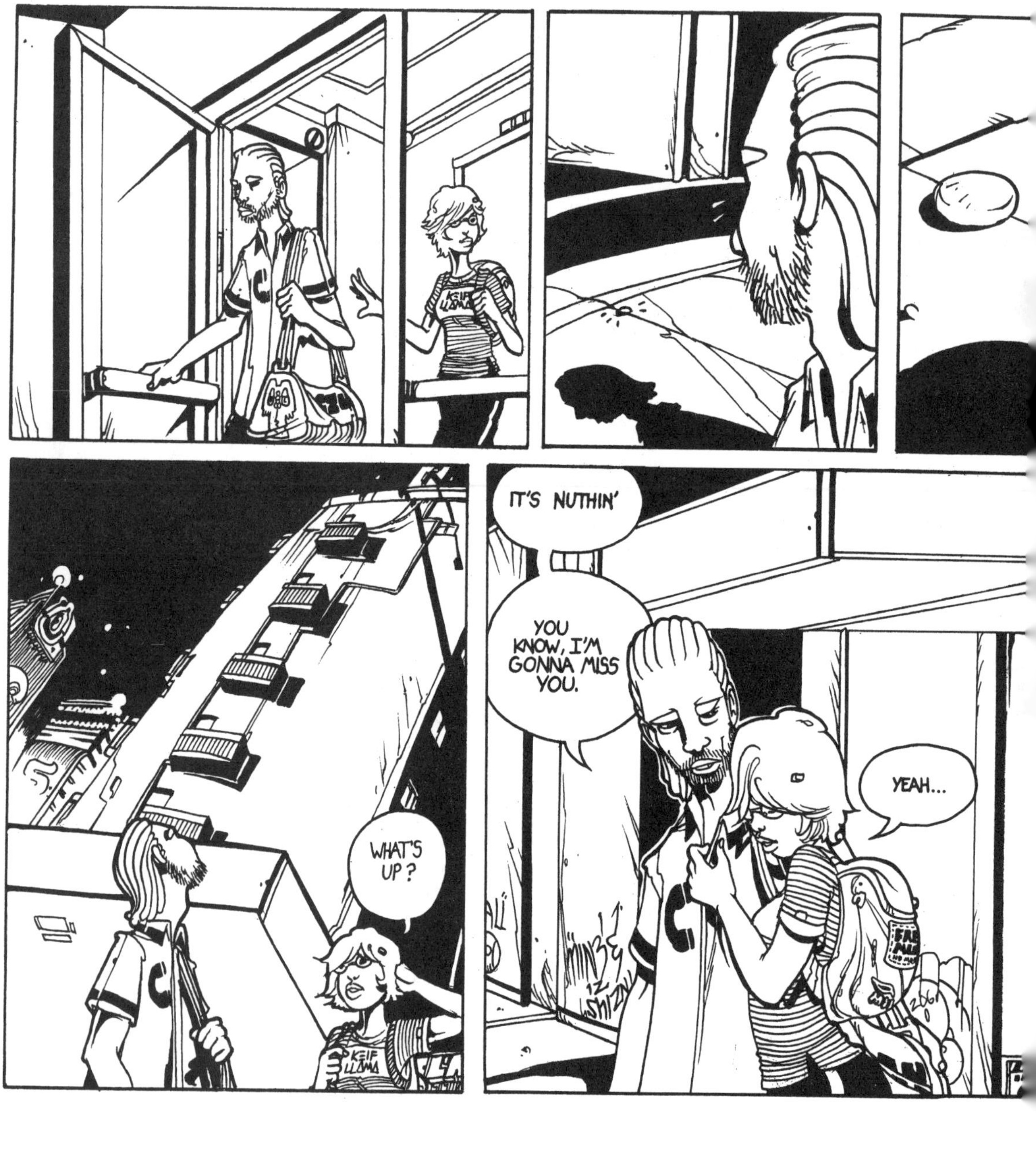
WHAT'S UP?
IT'S NUTHIN'
YOU KNOW, I'M GONNA MISS YOU.
YEAH...

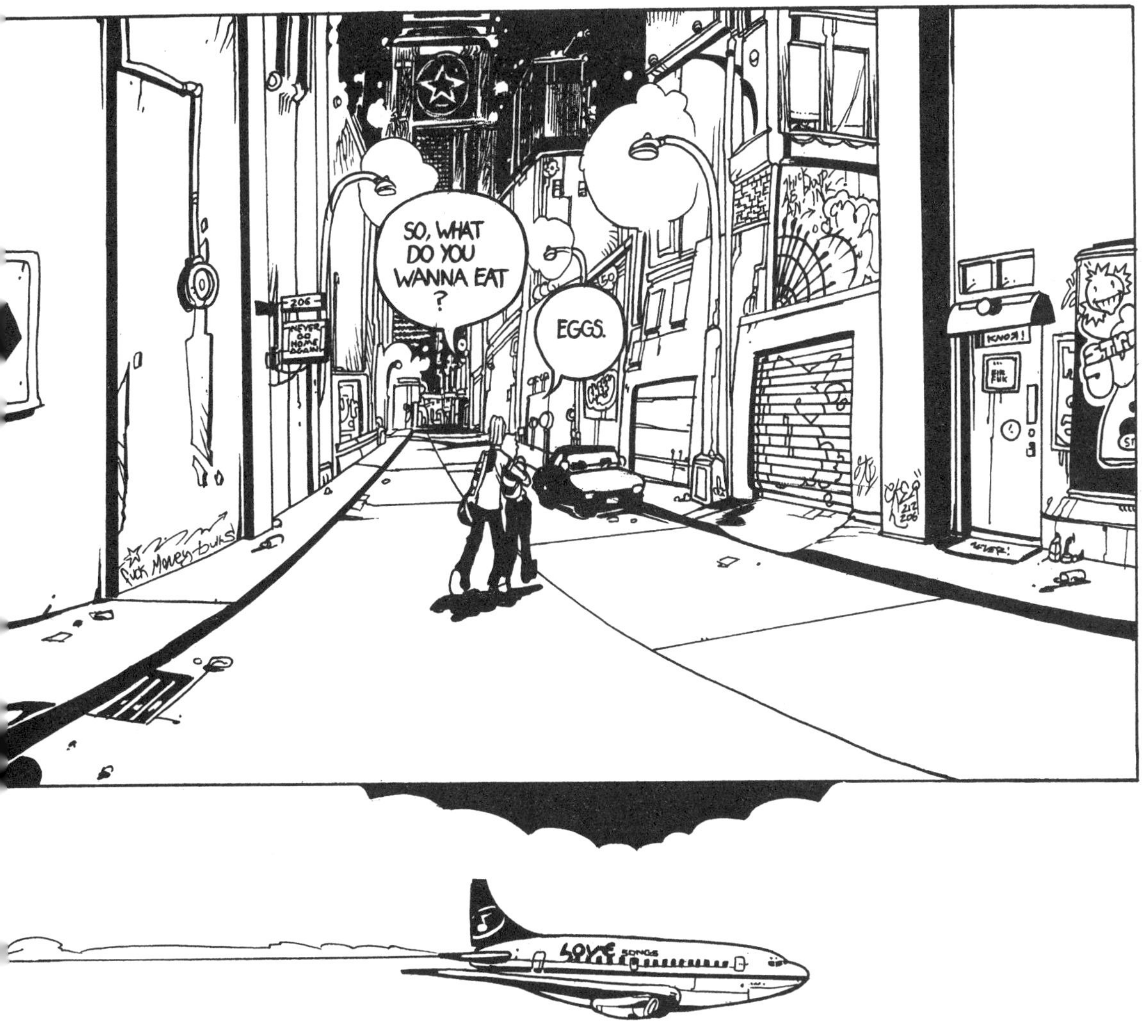
SO, WHAT DO YOU WANNA EAT ?
EGGS.
LOVE SONGS

eggs

T H E E N D

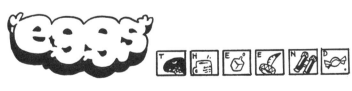

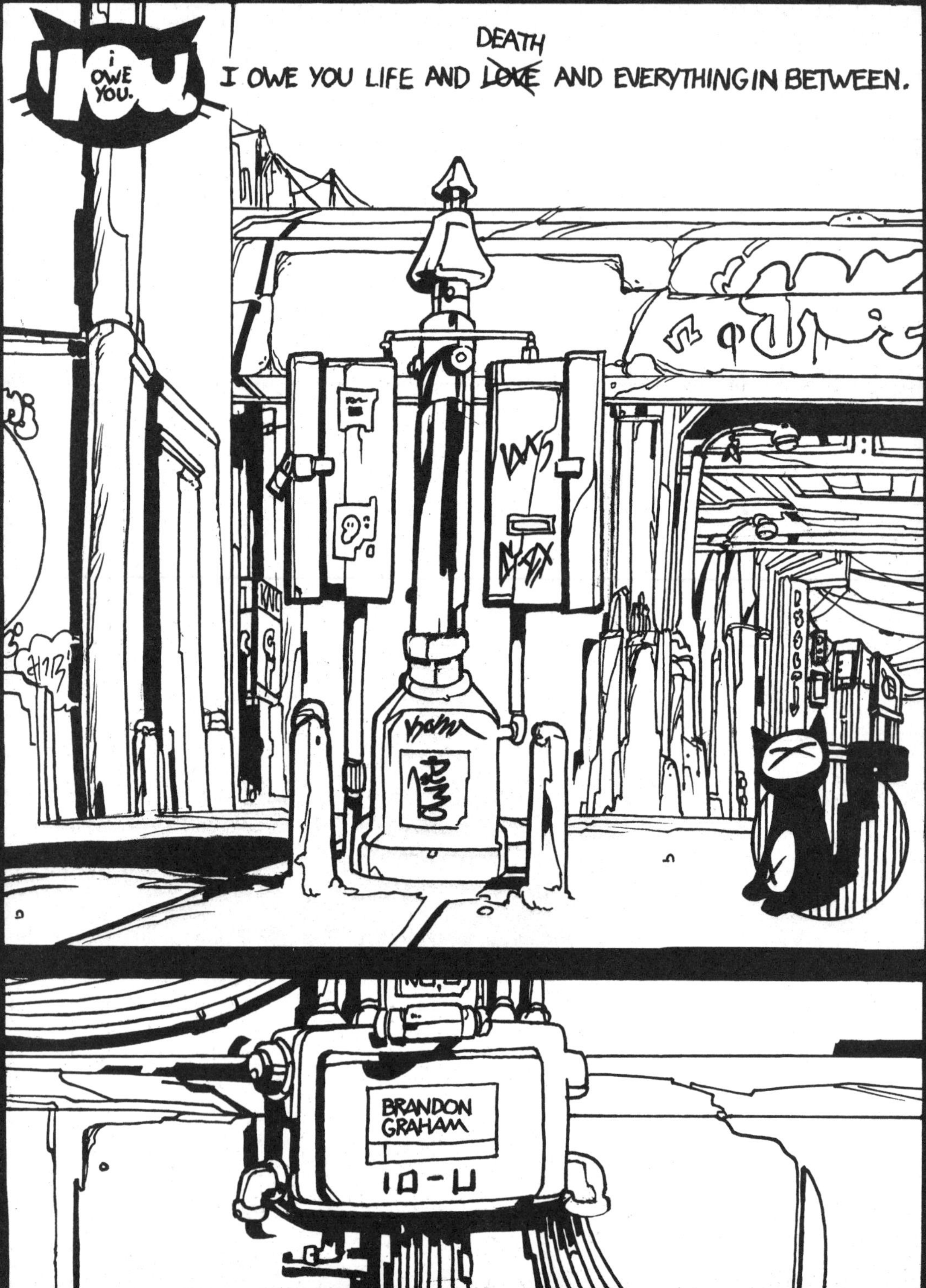
i OWE YOU.
DEATH
I OWE YOU LIFE AND ~~LOVE~~ AND EVERYTHING IN BETWEEN.
BRANDON GRAHAM
10-U

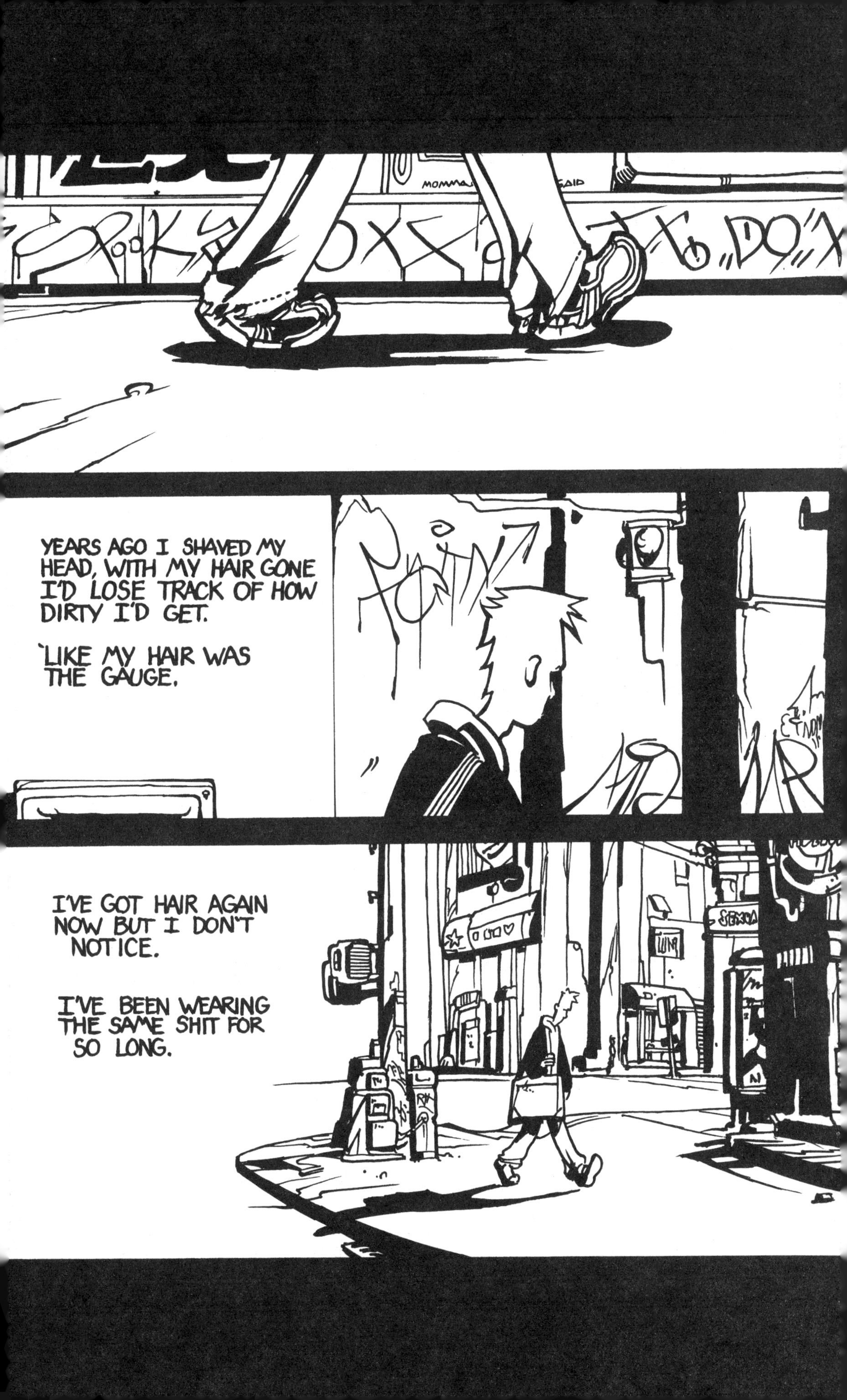
YEARS AGO I SHAVED MY HEAD, WITH MY HAIR GONE I'D LOSE TRACK OF HOW DIRTY I'D GET.
`LIKE MY HAIR WAS THE GAUGE.
I'VE GOT HAIR AGAIN NOW BUT I DON'T NOTICE.
I'VE BEEN WEARING THE SAME SHIT FOR SO LONG.

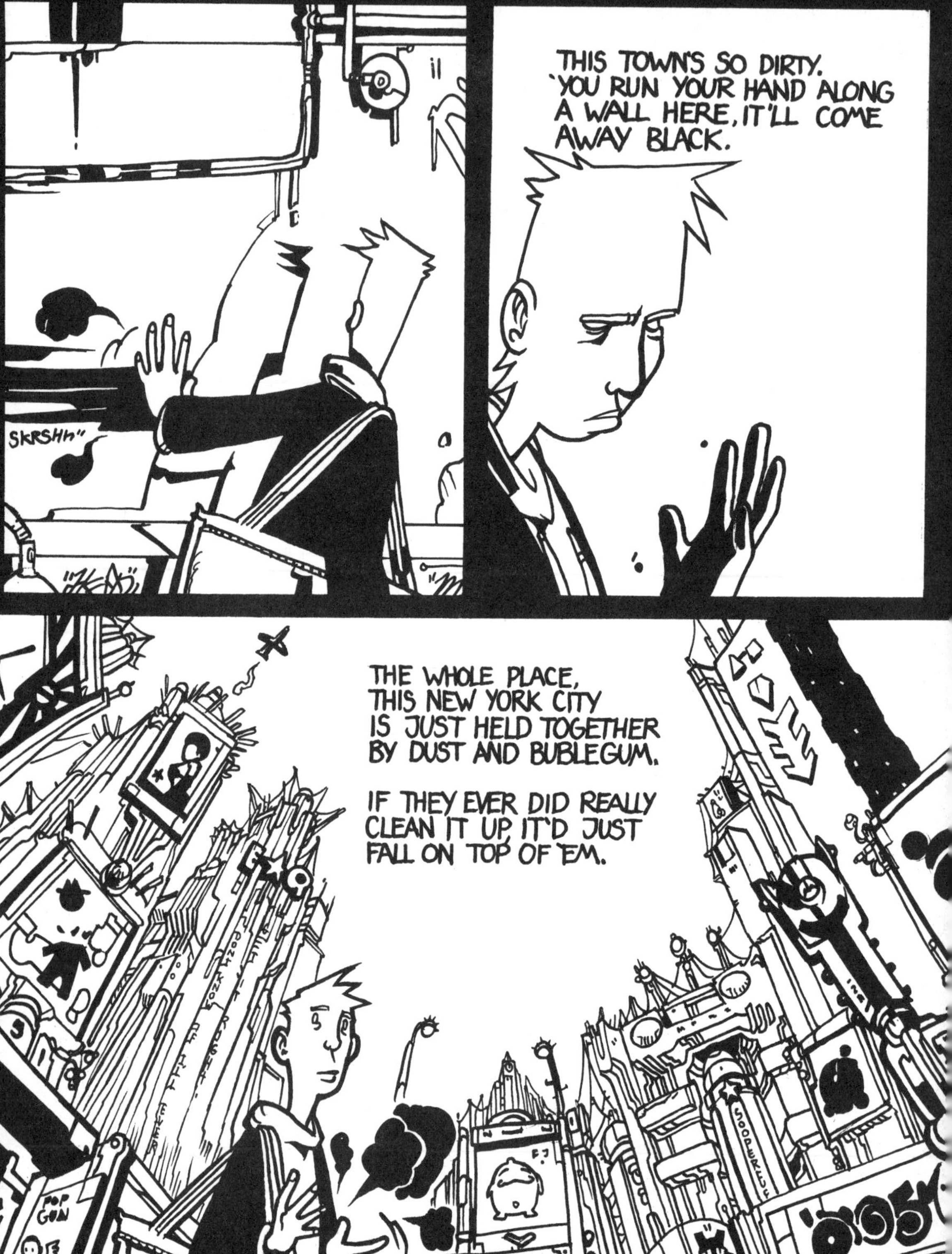
SKRSHh"
THIS TOWN'S SO DIRTY. YOU RUN YOUR HAND ALONG A WALL HERE, IT'LL COME AWAY BLACK.
THE WHOLE PLACE, THIS NEW YORK CITY IS JUST HELD TOGETHER BY DUST AND BUBLEGUM.
IF THEY EVER DID REALLY CLEAN IT UP, IT'D JUST FALL ON TOP OF 'EM.
POP GUN
FIRST

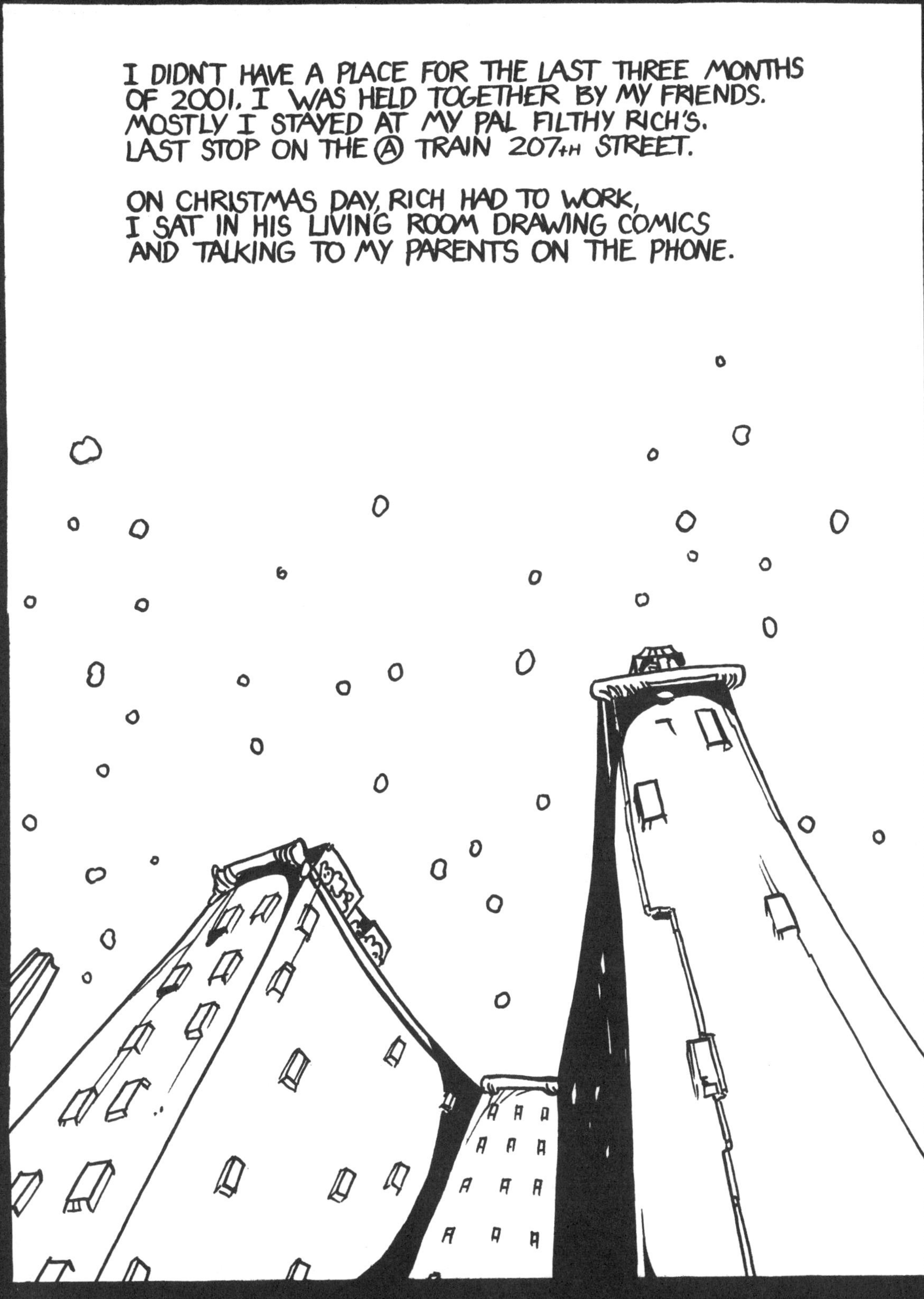
I DIDN'T HAVE A PLACE FOR THE LAST THREE MONTHS OF 2001. I WAS HELD TOGETHER BY MY FRIENDS. MOSTLY I STAYED AT MY PAL FILTHY RICH'S. LAST STOP ON THE Ⓐ TRAIN 207TH STREET.
ON CHRISTMAS DAY, RICH HAD TO WORK, I SAT IN HIS LIVING ROOM DRAWING COMICS AND TALKING TO MY PARENTS ON THE PHONE.

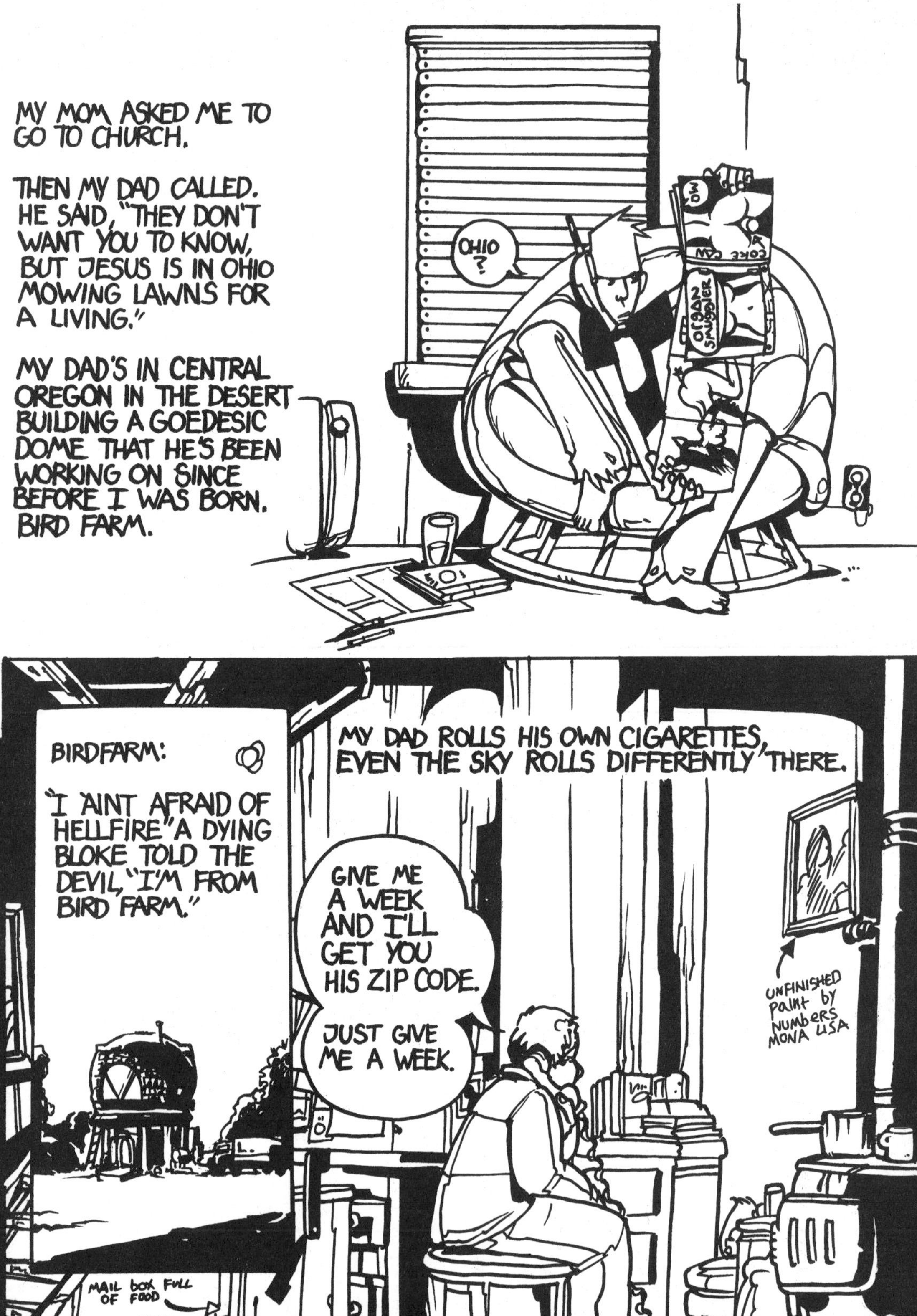
MY MOM ASKED ME TO GO TO CHURCH.
THEN MY DAD CALLED. HE SAID, "THEY DON'T WANT YOU TO KNOW, BUT JESUS IS IN OHIO MOWING LAWNS FOR A LIVING."
MY DAD'S IN CENTRAL OREGON IN THE DESERT BUILDING A GOEDESIC DOME THAT HE'S BEEN WORKING ON SINCE BEFORE I WAS BORN. BIRD FARM.
OHIO ?
COKE CAN
BIRDFARM:
"I AINT AFRAID OF HELLFIRE" A DYING BLOKE TOLD THE DEVIL, "I'M FROM BIRD FARM."
MY DAD ROLLS HIS OWN CIGARETTES, EVEN THE SKY ROLLS DIFFERENTLY THERE.
GIVE ME A WEEK AND I'LL GET YOU HIS ZIP CODE.
JUST GIVE ME A WEEK.
UNFINISHED Paint by Numbers MONA LISA
MAIL BOX FULL OF FOOD

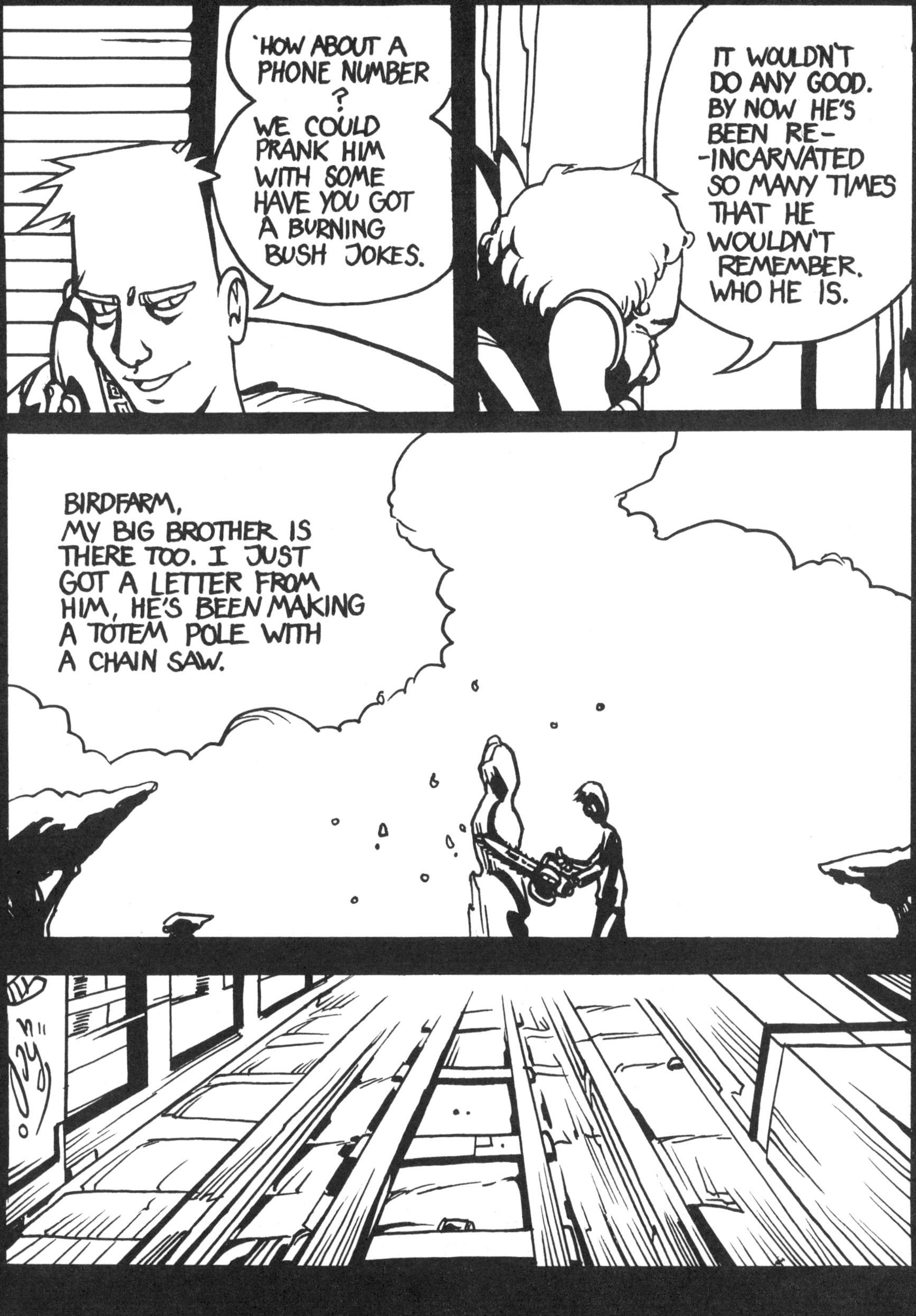

`HOW ABOUT A PHONE NUMBER ? WE COULD PRANK HIM WITH SOME HAVE YOU GOT A BURNING BUSH JOKES.
IT WOULDN'T DO ANY GOOD. BY NOW HE'S BEEN RE--INCARNATED SO MANY TIMES THAT HE WOULDN'T REMEMBER. WHO HE IS.
BIRDFARM, MY BIG BROTHER IS THERE TOO. I JUST GOT A LETTER FROM HIM, HE'S BEEN MAKING A TOTEM POLE WITH A CHAIN SAW.

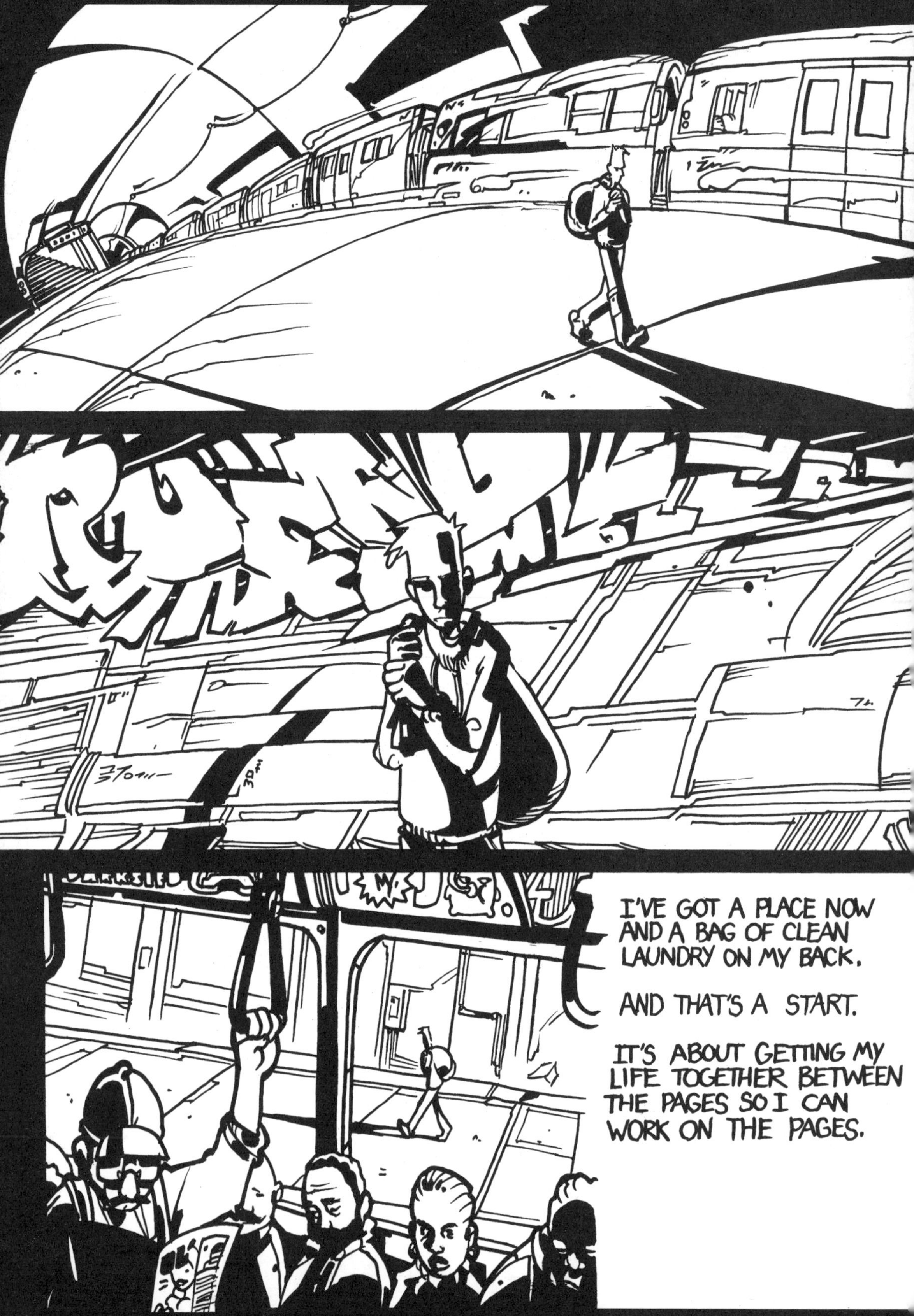
I'VE GOT A PLACE NOW
AND A BAG OF CLEAN
LAUNDRY ON MY BACK.
AND THAT'S A START.
IT'S ABOUT GETTING MY
LIFE TOGETHER BETWEEN
THE PAGES SO I CAN
WORK ON THE PAGES.

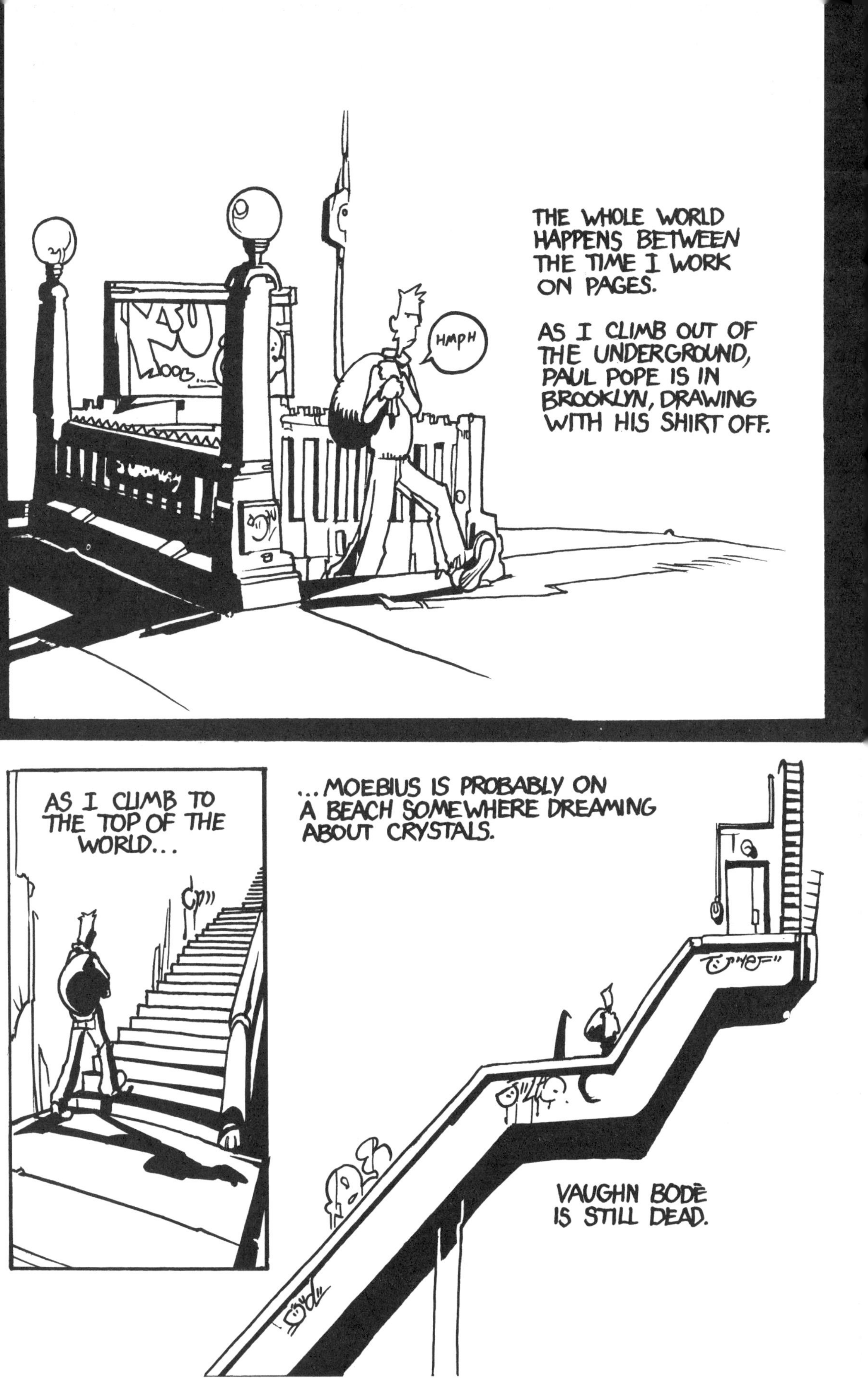
THE WHOLE WORLD HAPPENS BETWEEN THE TIME I WORK ON PAGES.
AS I CLIMB OUT OF THE UNDERGROUND, PAUL POPE IS IN BROOKLYN, DRAWING WITH HIS SHIRT OFF.
HMPH
AS I CLIMB TO THE TOP OF THE WORLD...
...MOEBIUS IS PROBABLY ON A BEACH SOMEWHERE DREAMING ABOUT CRYSTALS.
VAUGHN BODÈ IS STILL DEAD.

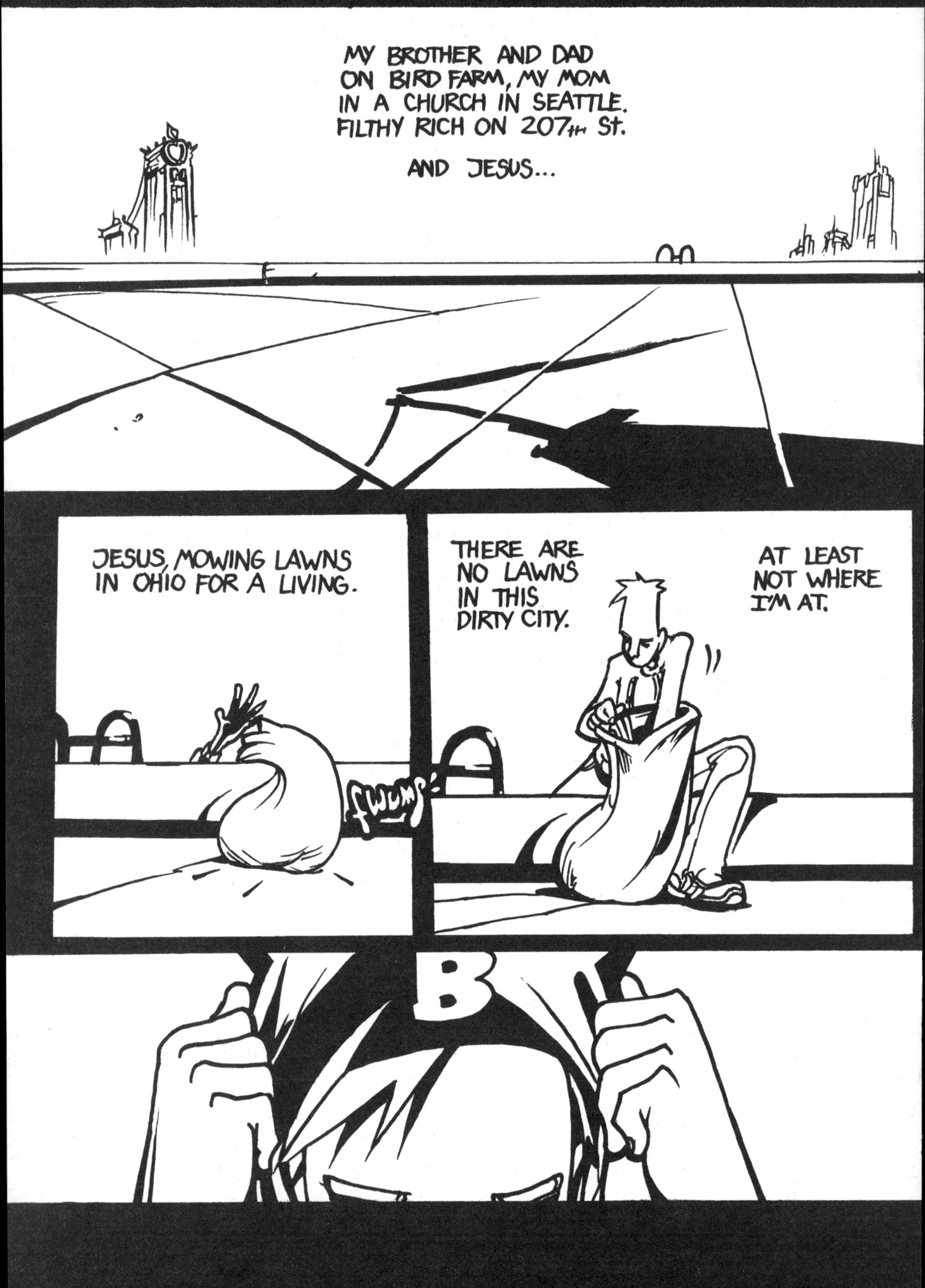
MY BROTHER AND DAD ON BIRD FARM, MY MOM IN A CHURCH IN SEATTLE. FILTHY RICH ON 207th St.
AND JESUS...
JESUS, MOWING LAWNS IN OHIO FOR A LIVING.
FWUMP
THERE ARE NO LAWNS IN THIS DIRTY CITY.
AT LEAST NOT WHERE I'M AT.
B

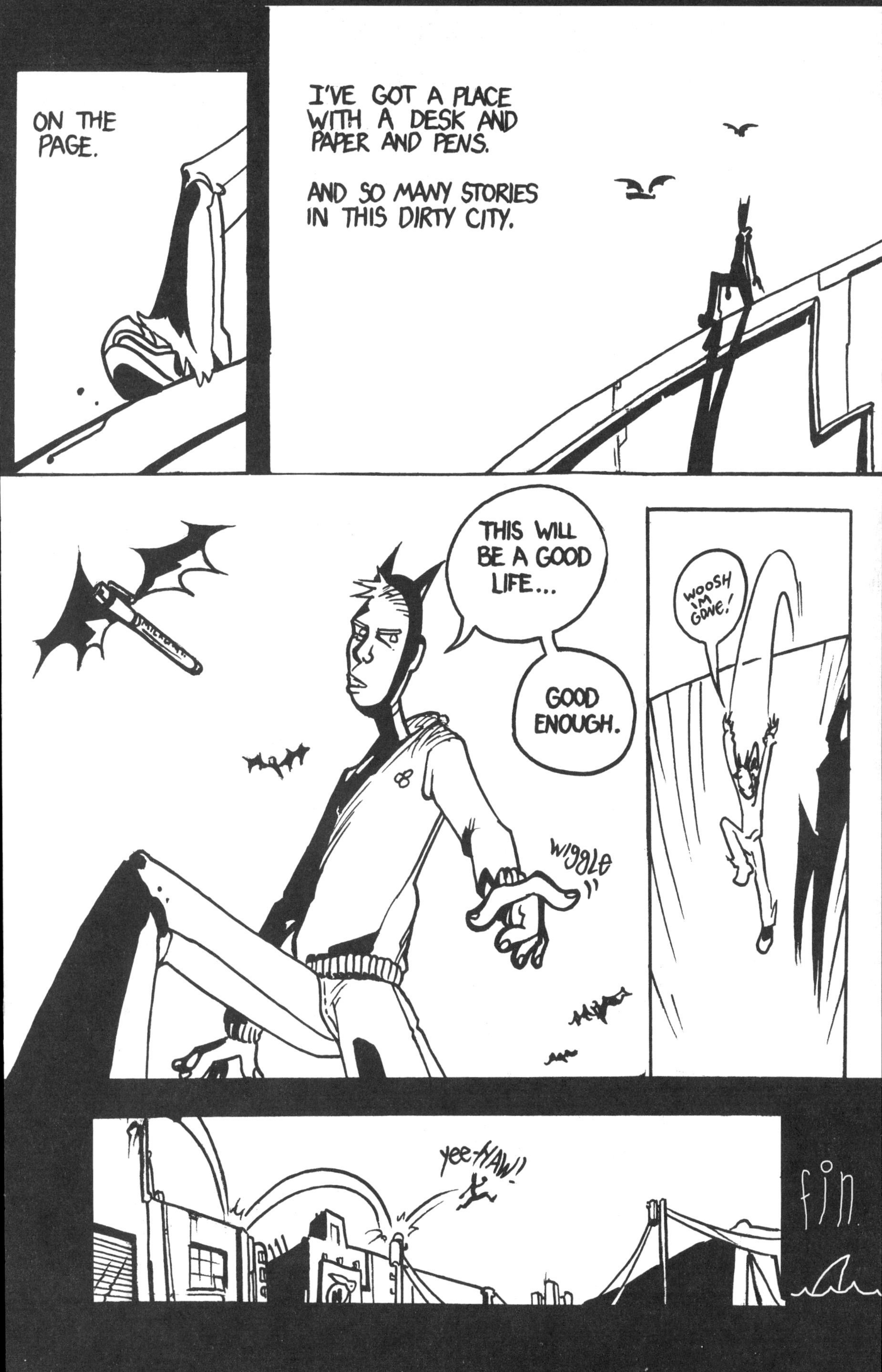
ON THE PAGE.
I'VE GOT A PLACE WITH A DESK AND PAPER AND PENS.
AND SO MANY STORIES IN THIS DIRTY CITY.
THIS WILL BE A GOOD LIFE...
GOOD ENOUGH.
wiggle
WOOSH I'M GONE!
yee-HAW!
fin.

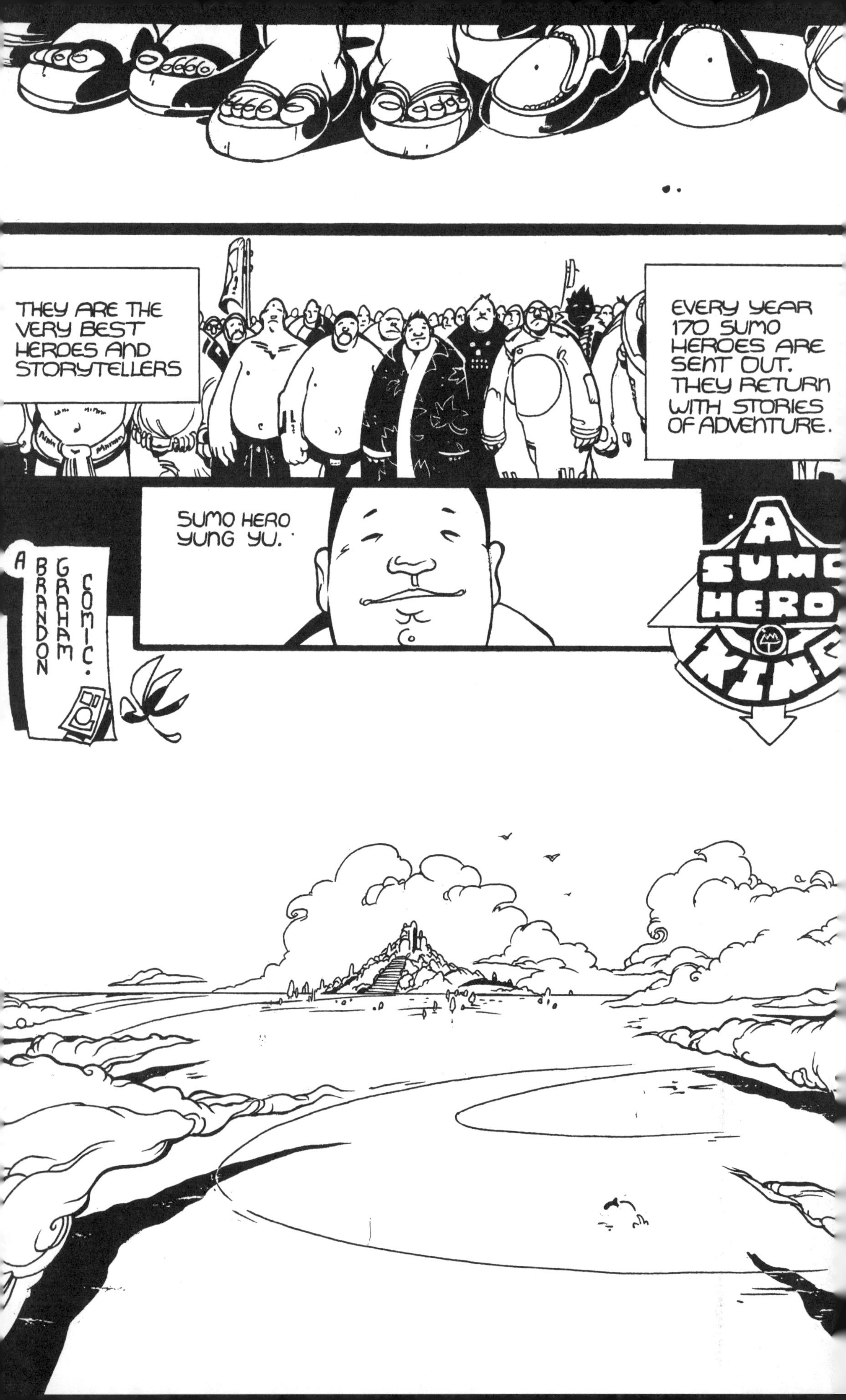
THEY ARE THE VERY BEST HEROES AND STORYTELLERS
EVERY YEAR 170 SUMO HEROES ARE SENT OUT. THEY RETURN WITH STORIES OF ADVENTURE.
SUMO HERO YUNG YU.
A BRANDON GRAHAM COMIC.
A SUMO HERO KING

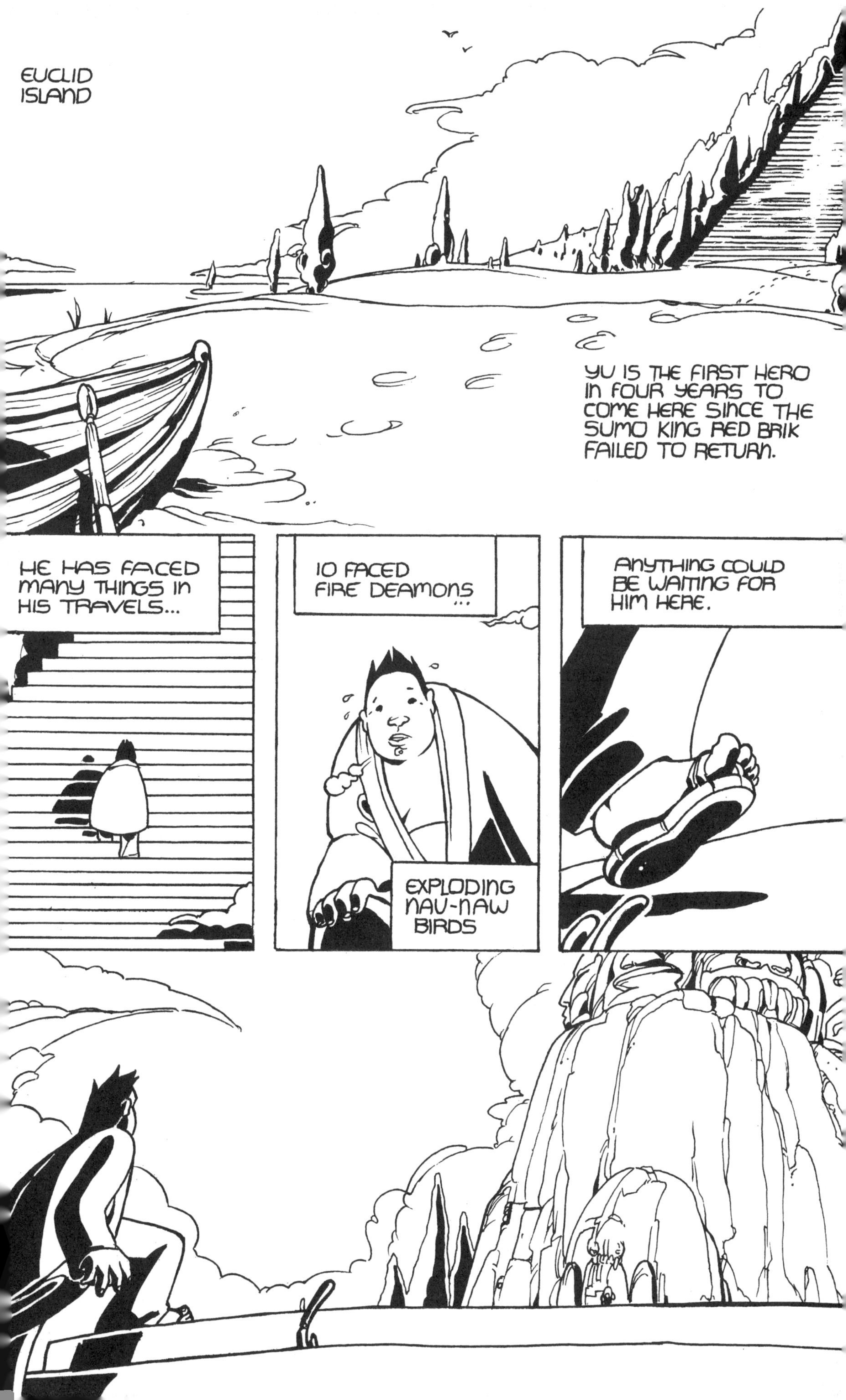
EUCLID
ISLAND
YU IS THE FIRST HERO IN FOUR YEARS TO COME HERE SINCE THE SUMO KING RED BRIK FAILED TO RETURN.
HE HAS FACED MANY THINGS IN HIS TRAVELS...
10 FACED FIRE DEAMONS...
EXPLODING NAU-NAW BIRDS
ANYTHING COULD BE WAITING FOR HIM HERE.

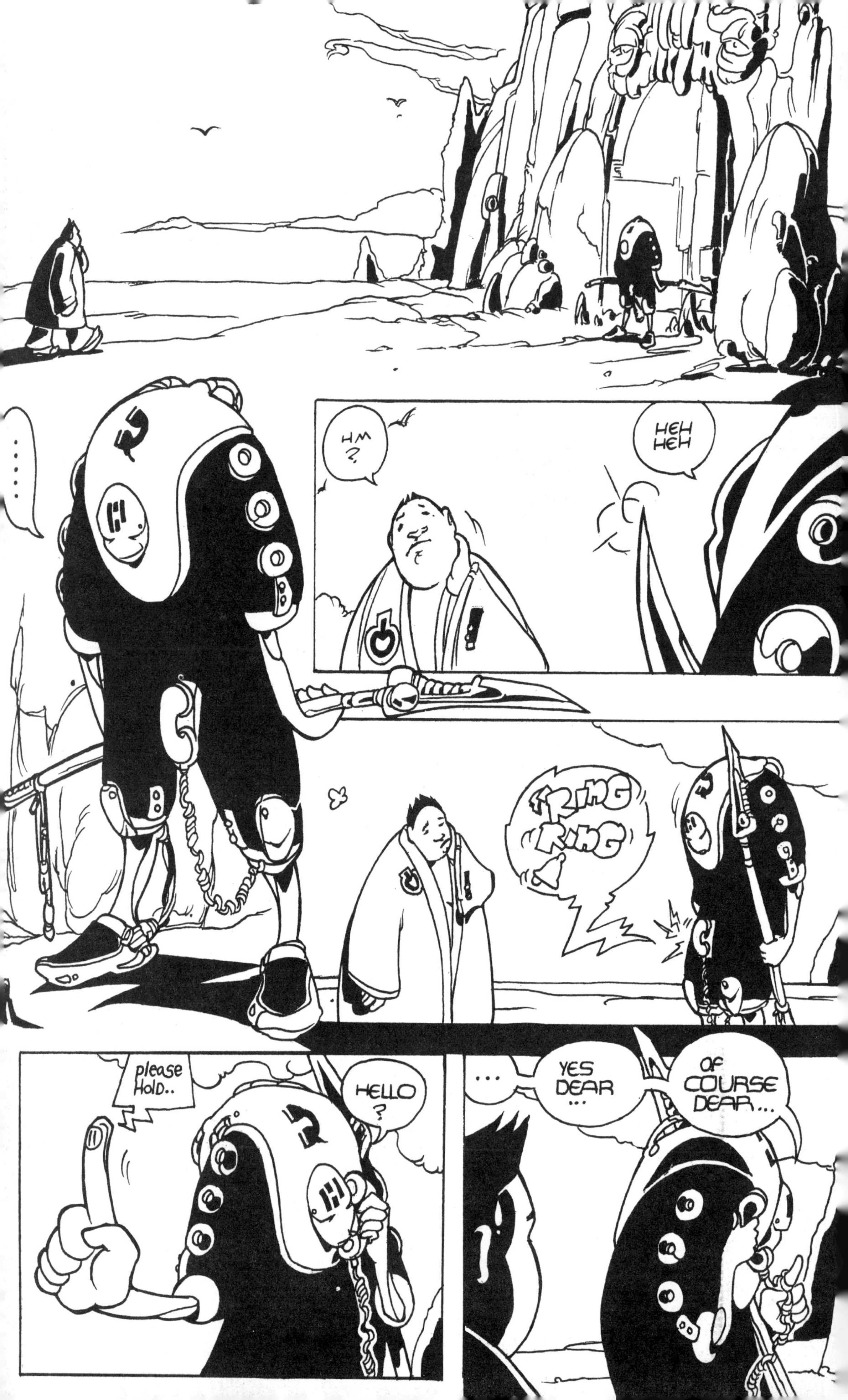

HM ?
HEH HEH
. . . . . .
RING RING
please Hold..
HELLO ?
...
YES DEAR ...
OF COURSE DEAR...

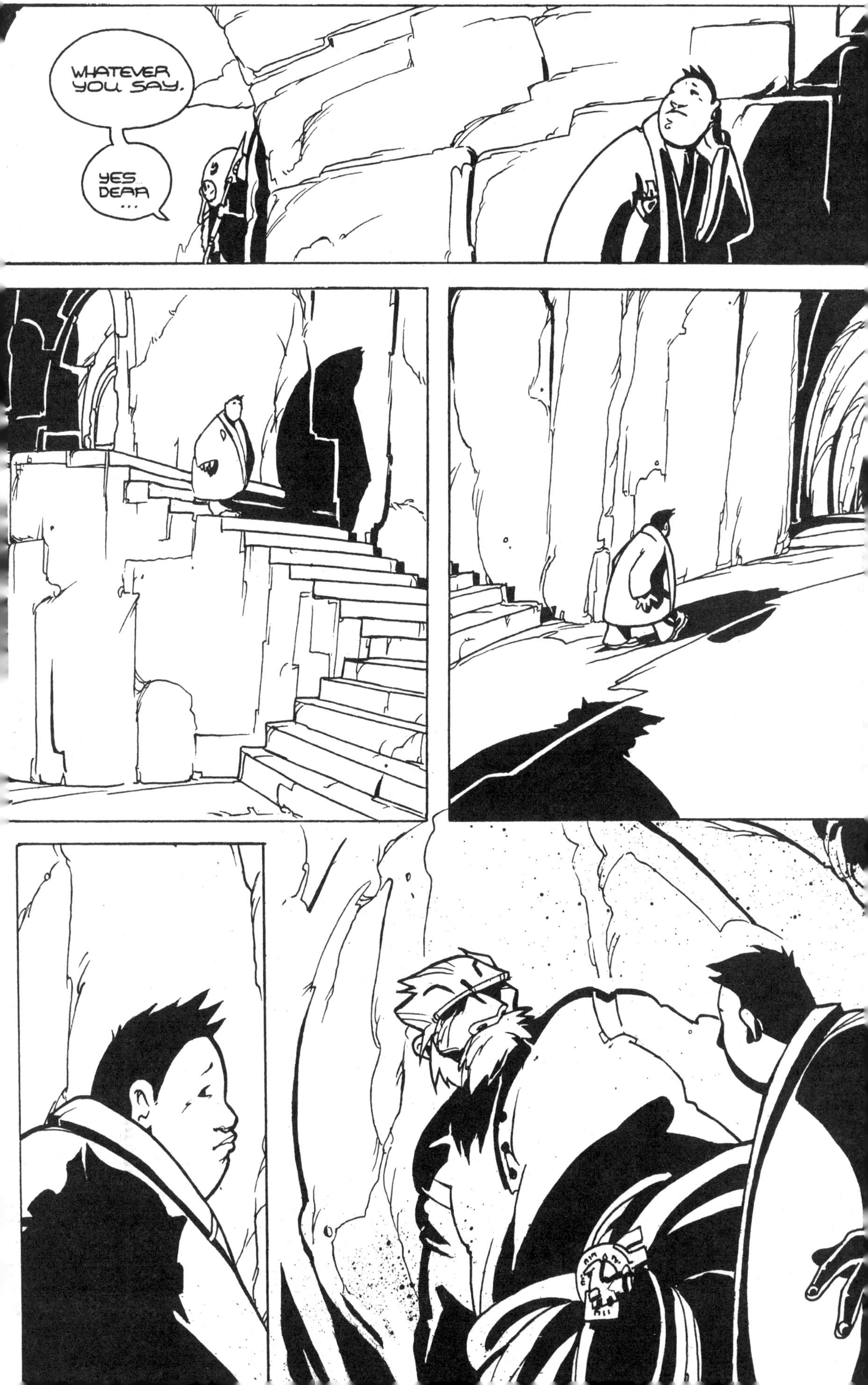
WHATEVER YOU SAY.
YES DEAR ...

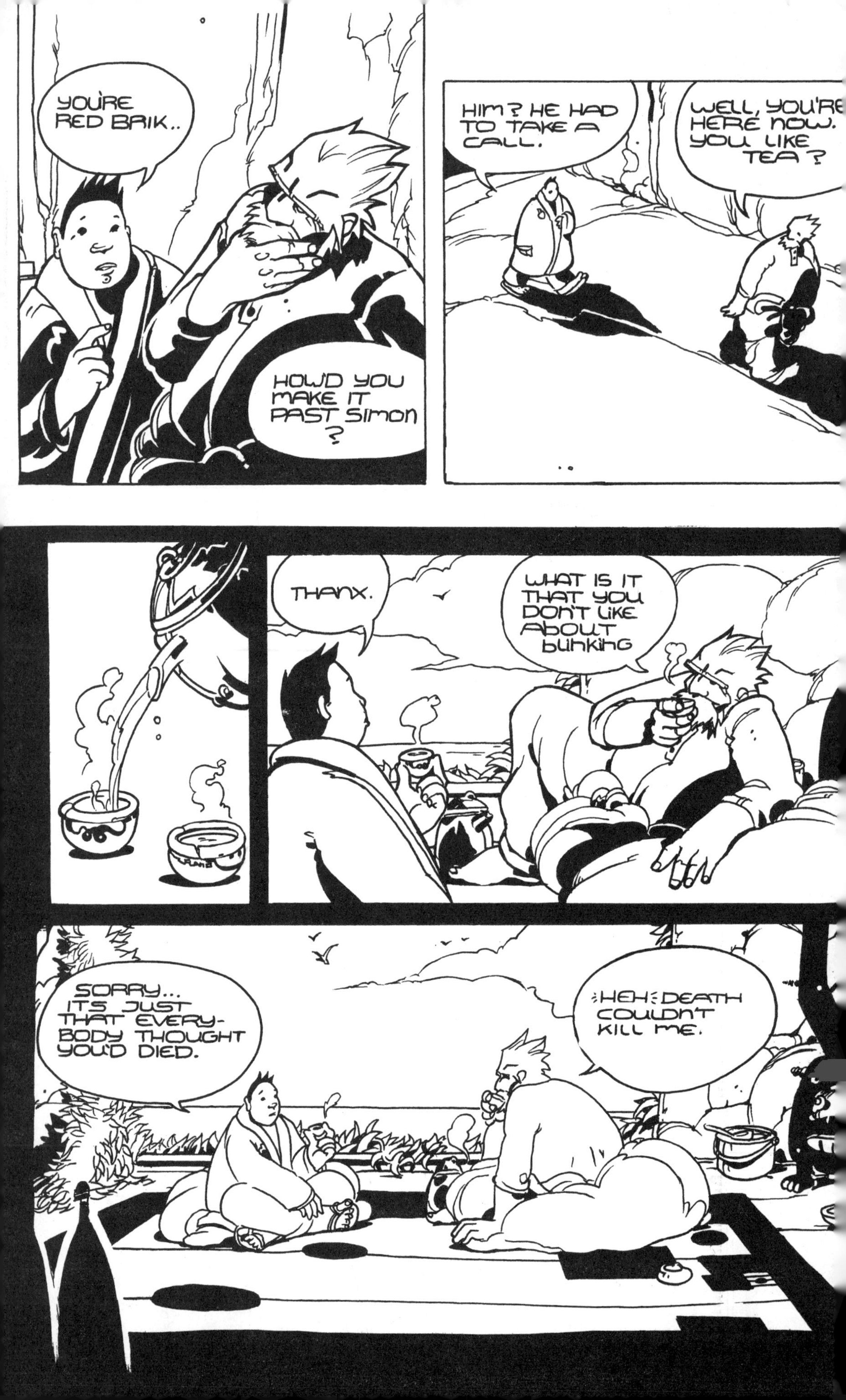
YOU'RE RED BRIK..
HOW'D YOU MAKE IT PAST SIMON ?
HIM? HE HAD TO TAKE A CALL.
WELL, YOU'RE HERE NOW. YOU LIKE TEA ?
THANX.
WHAT IS IT THAT YOU DON'T LIKE ABOUT BUNKING
SORRY... ITS JUST THAT EVERY-BODY THOUGHT YOU'D DIED.
:HEH: DEATH COULDN'T KILL ME.

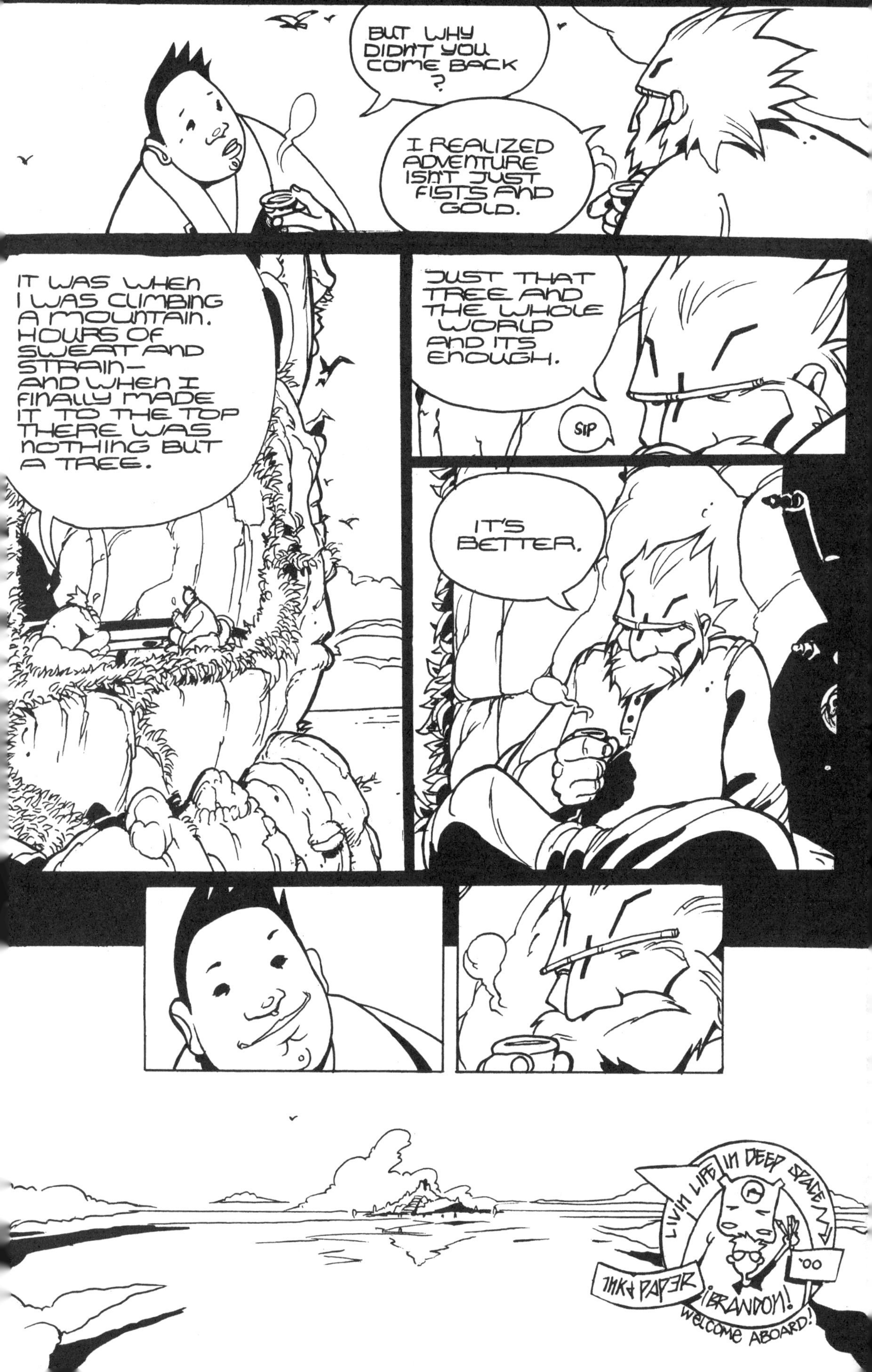
BUT WHY DIDN'T YOU COME BACK ?
I REALIZED ADVENTURE ISN'T JUST FISTS AND GOLD.
IT WAS WHEN I WAS CLIMBING A MOUNTAIN. HOURS OF SWEAT AND STRAIN– AND WHEN I FINALLY MADE IT TO THE TOP THERE WAS NOTHING BUT A TREE.
JUST THAT TREE AND THE WHOLE WORLD AND ITS ENOUGH.
SIP
IT'S BETTER.
LIVIN' LIFE IN DEEP SPACE
INK & PAPER
'00
¡BRANDON!
WELCOME ABOARD!

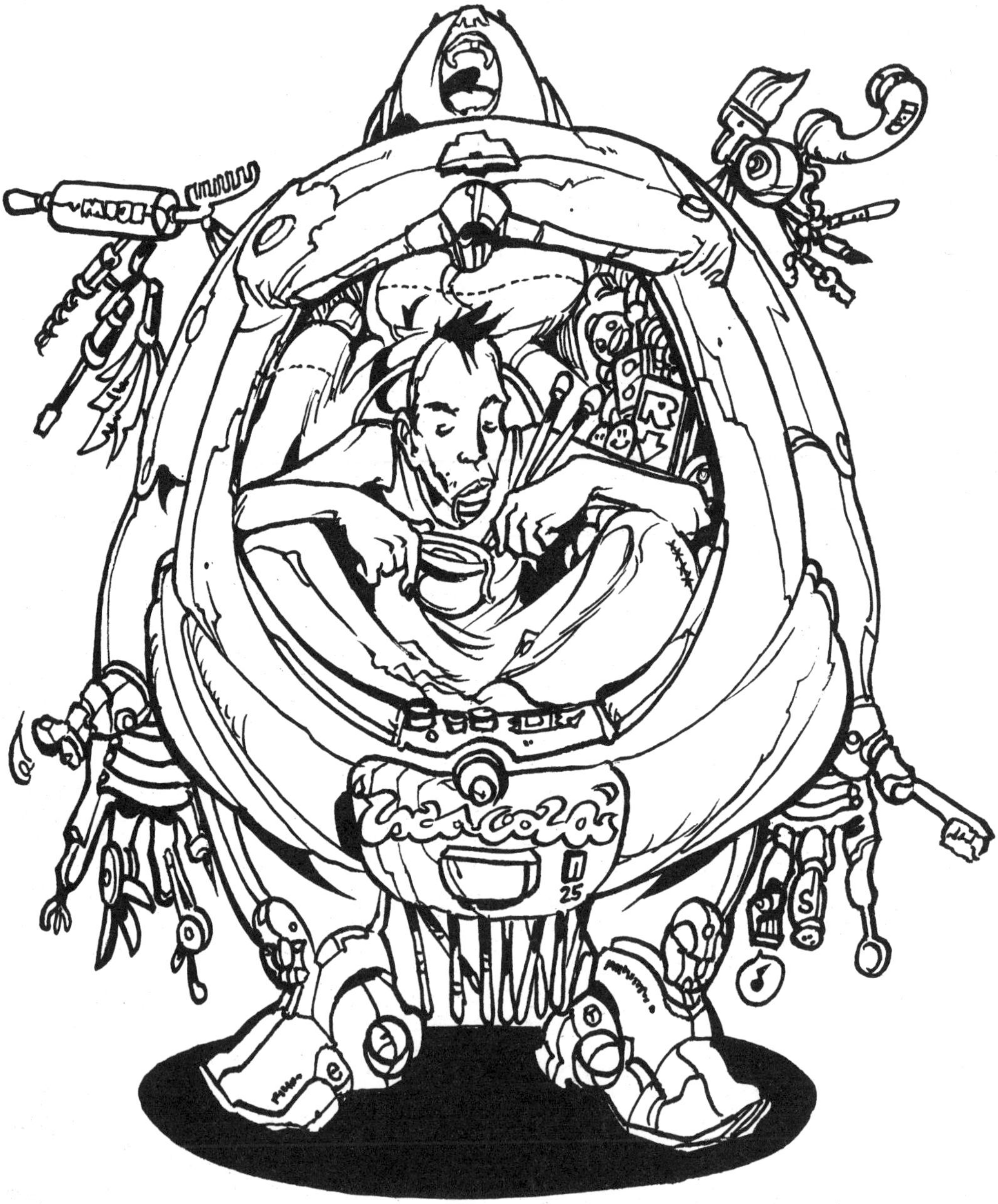

SUGARLESS CANDY- I DID THIS FOR #7 OF THE MEATHAUS ANTHOLOGY. (THE LOVE SONGS ISSUE) THE BOOK WAS SQUARE AND CAME WITH A RECORD WITH A COUPLE OF SONGS BY SOME OF THE MH ARTISTS. I HAD A BOOK OF JAPANESE APARTMENTS I USED TO DESIGN THE ROOM. I GOT THE PAPER CIRCLES ABOVE THE BED OUT OF IT. THERE WAS GOING TO BE A RECORD PLAYER ON THE OTHER SIDE OF THE ROOM, I WAS GOING TO HAVE THEM TALK ABOUT MUSIC BEFORE THEY WENT OUTSIDE.

UP AT FILTHY RICH'S PLACE WHERE I DID THIS, YOU CAN SEE A COUPLE APARTMENT BUILDINGS ACROSS THE WATER IN THE BRONX. I WROTE THIS THINKING ABOUT WHAT MIGHT GO ON IN ALL THOSE WINDOWS. I WAS TRYING TO DO A STORY ABOUT NOTHING. BY THAT I MEAN NO FANTASTIC ELEMENTS, NO BIG DRAMA. IT'S KIND OF GOING AWAY FROM THE SCIENCE FICTION COMICS I'VE DONE MOST OF MY LIFE. I REALIZED THAT THE FRAMEWORK OF A STORY ISN'T VERY IMPORTANT TO ME, JUST HOW IT'S EXECUTED.

IOU- THIS WAS MY FIRST TRY AT AN AUTOBIOGRAPHICAL STORY, AT LEAST A STRAIGHTFORWARD ONE DRAWING MYSELF. I HAD A HELL OF A TIME WITH IT. REALITY IS SO MUCH HARDER TO WRANGLE THAN THE USUAL MIX OF REAL AND FICTION I'M USED TO. I'M ALWAYS FASCINATED WITH HOW OTHER COMIC ARTISTS LIVE THEIR LIVES. EVERY ARTIST HAS TO LEARN COMICS ON THEIR OWN SO EVERYONE HAS THEIR OWN TRICKS AND TICKS.

RIGHT AFTER I FINISHED THIS I MET A GUY AT A COMIC PARTY WHO WAS PUTTING TOGETHER A BOOK OF PHOTOS OF COMIC ARTISTS. THERE WAS ONE OF MOEBIUS STANDING ON A BEACH.

A SUMO HERO KING— I THINK THIS WAS WHEN I FIRST STARTED THINKING ABOUT HOW I WANTED TO STRUCTURE MY COMICS. IT FEELS KIND OF CRUDE NOW.

I HAD A CELL PHONE THAT I COULDN'T STAND. I'VE BEEN ACCUSED OF SPENDING HALF MY LIFE TALKING ON THE PHONE BUT I HATED NOT BEING ABLE TO ESCAPE IT. EVENTUALLY I THREW THE PHONE IN FRONT OF A 7 TRAIN. THEN AFTER IT PASSED, I JUMPED DOWN ON TO THE TRACKS TO COLLECT THE PIECES. I THINK DAVID TOOK THEM TO BUILD A TOY ROBOT OUT OF.

SURVIVE— THIS IS A STORY ABOUT NOTHING IN A TOTALLY DIFFERENT SENSE. IT WAS DRAWN IN A FANCY HOTEL ROOM OVERLOOKING CENTRAL PARK. MY GIRLFRIEND GOT PUT UP THERE BY HER JOB. I SPENT THE WHOLE TIME IN THE ROOM WATCHING CABLE, EATING FREE FOOD AND DRAWING. EVERY TIME I'D LEAVE THE ROOM THE HOTEL STAFF WOULD ASK ME WHAT I WAS DOING THERE SO I STARTED WEARING THE HOTEL ROBE OUT. THEY LEFT ME ALONE AFTER THAT.

I NEVER SAW A TRADITIONAL PLAD SKIRT CATHOLIC SCHOOL GIRL UNTIL I MOVED TO NEW YORK. I REMEMBER WONDERING WHY THE LITTLE GIRLS WERE DRESSED LIKE STRIPPERS.

DEVIL AND THE DEEP— I DID A VERSION OF THIS STORY IN COLOR WITH MARKERS AND WATER COLORS. THIS AND SURVIVE WERE DONE FOR HEAVY METAL MAGAZINE. I MIGHT HAVE BEEN TOO CAUGHT UP IN THE HEAVY METAL STYLE, THIS DOESN'T FEEL THAT PERSONAL. BUT I HAD A LOT OF FUN DRAWING IT.

IN COLOR, THE SIBERIA GIRL IS BLUE WHICH MIGHT EXPLAIN WHY SHE DOSEN'T NEED TO WEAR PANTS. IN THE ARCTIC COLD.— CONAN STYLE.

EAT HERE GET GAS— ONCE ON A CROSS COUNTRY DRIVE, I STOPPED AT THE WORLDS LARGEST TRUCK STOP. ON THE WAY, I WAS REALLY EXCITED. I EXPECTED TO SEE DUDES WITH SCARS SMASHING BOTTLES OVER EACH OTHERS HEADS AND TOOTHLESS HOOKERS. DRY GULCH ADVENTURE. UNFORTUNATLY IT TURNED OUT TO BE A BIG DINER.

FOR SOME REASON I WAS TRYING TO GET THE HUMAN TRUCK DRIVER TO LOOK LIKE COREY FELDMAN BUT TOUGHENED BY THE SPACE LANES. THE WAITRESSES NAME TAG IS THE TITLE CHARACTERS NAME FROM THE GREAT MATT HOWARTH COMIC "KEIF LLAMA: XENOTECH. I THINK THE LEAVES UNDER THE SPLUTZ ARE THE SAME KIND OF LEAVES THAT THE ETCH- DUO FOLDS IN IEONIUM BLUE.

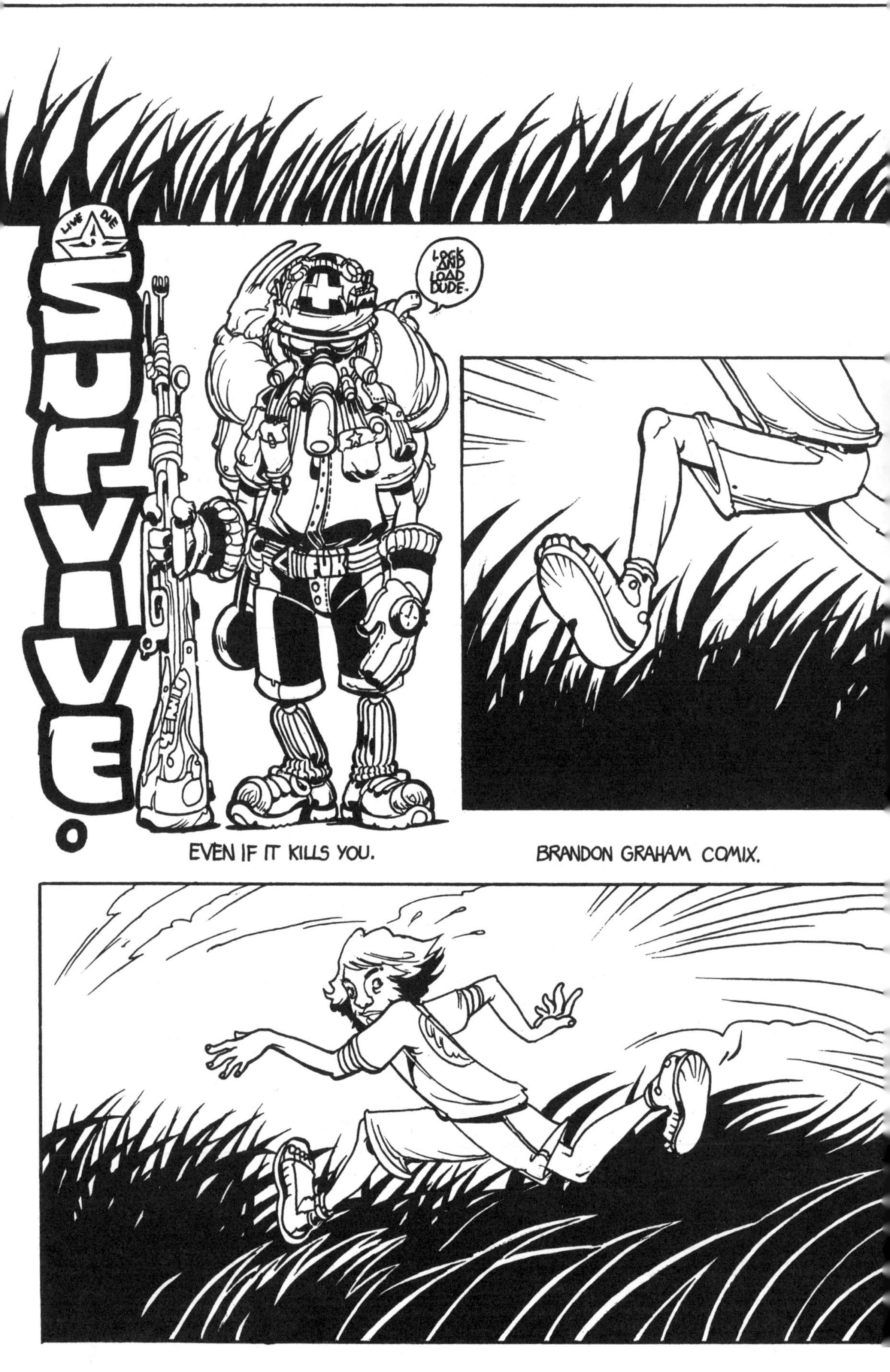
LIVE DIE
SURVIVE.
LOCK AND LOAD DUDE.
FUK
EVEN IF IT KILLS YOU.
BRANDON GRAHAM COMIX.

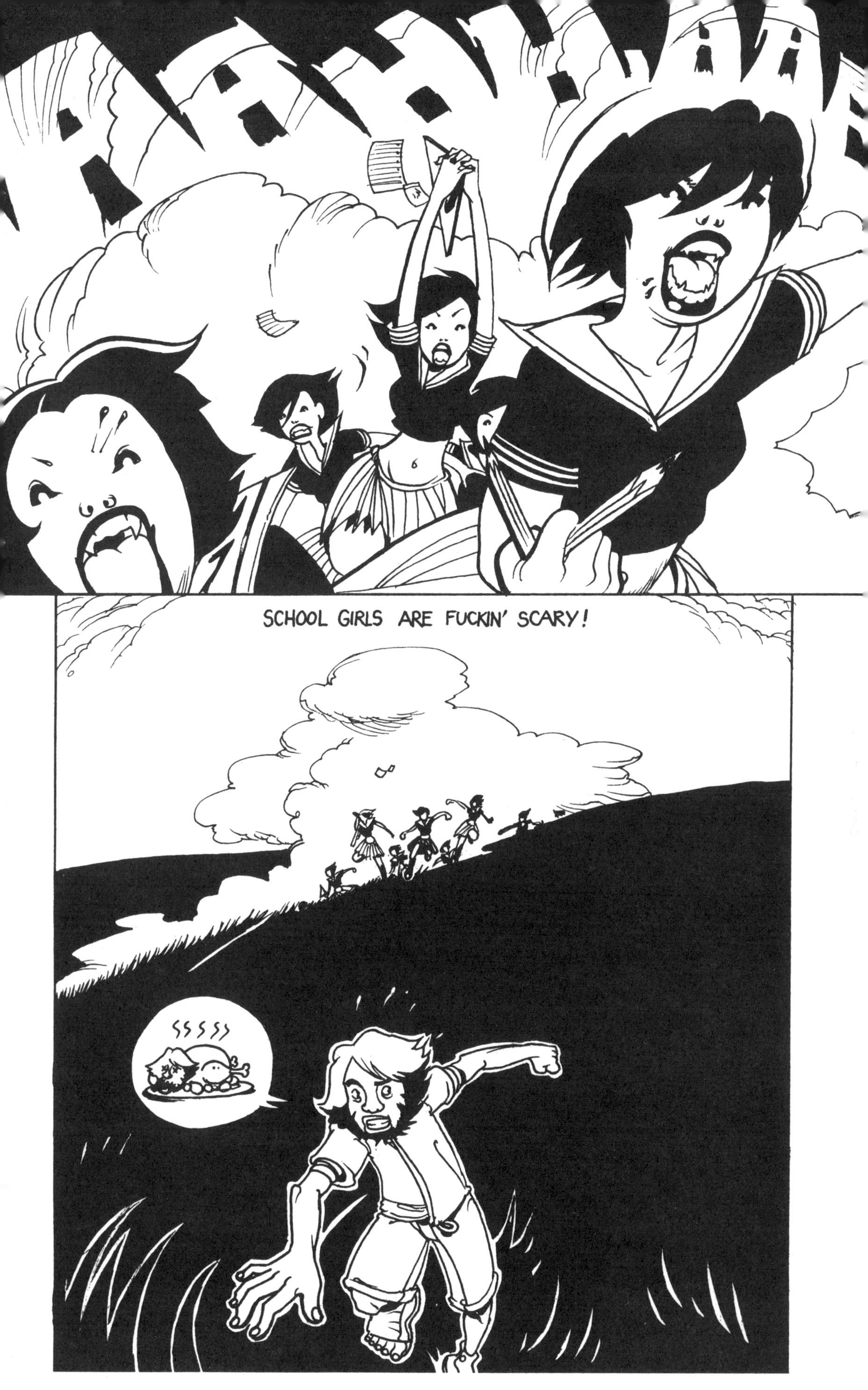
SCHOOL GIRLS ARE FUCKIN' SCARY!

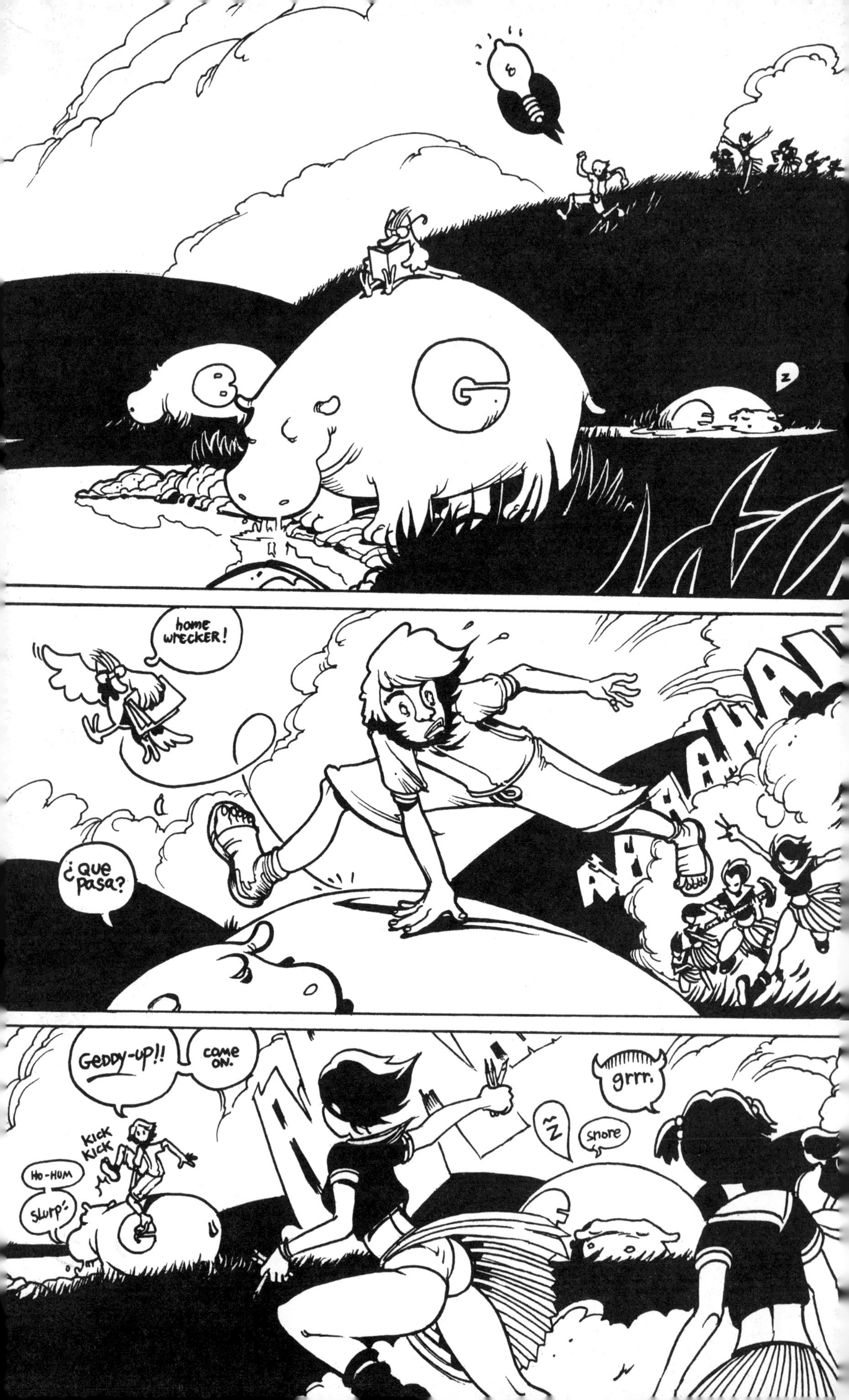
home wrecker!
¿que pasa?
Geddy-up!!
come on.
grrr.
snore
KICK KICK
Ho-HUM
slurp

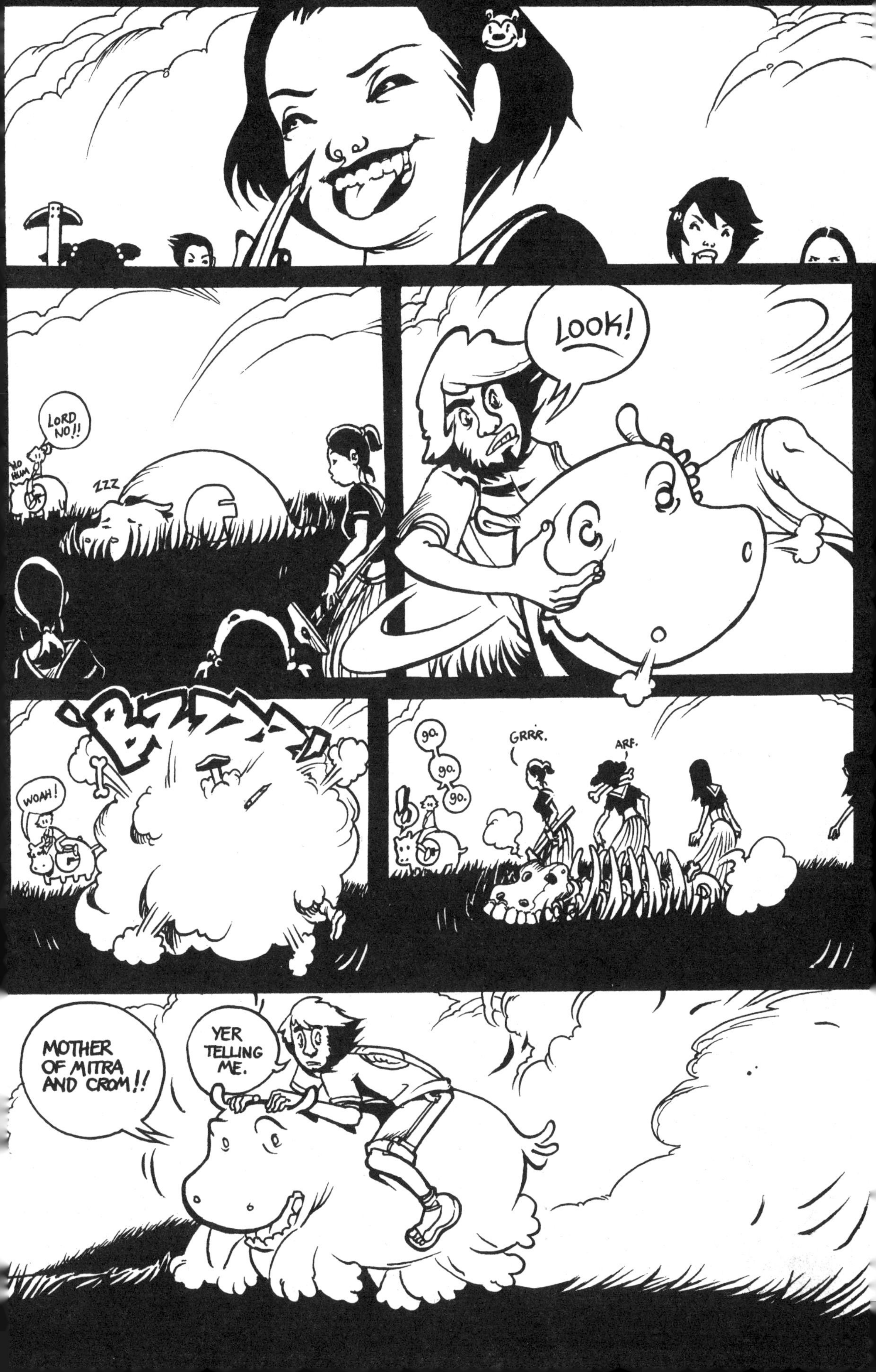
LORD NO!!
HO HUM
ZZZ
LOOK!
WOAH!
go.
go.
go.
GRRR.
ARF.
MOTHER OF MITRA AND CROM!!
YER TELLING ME.

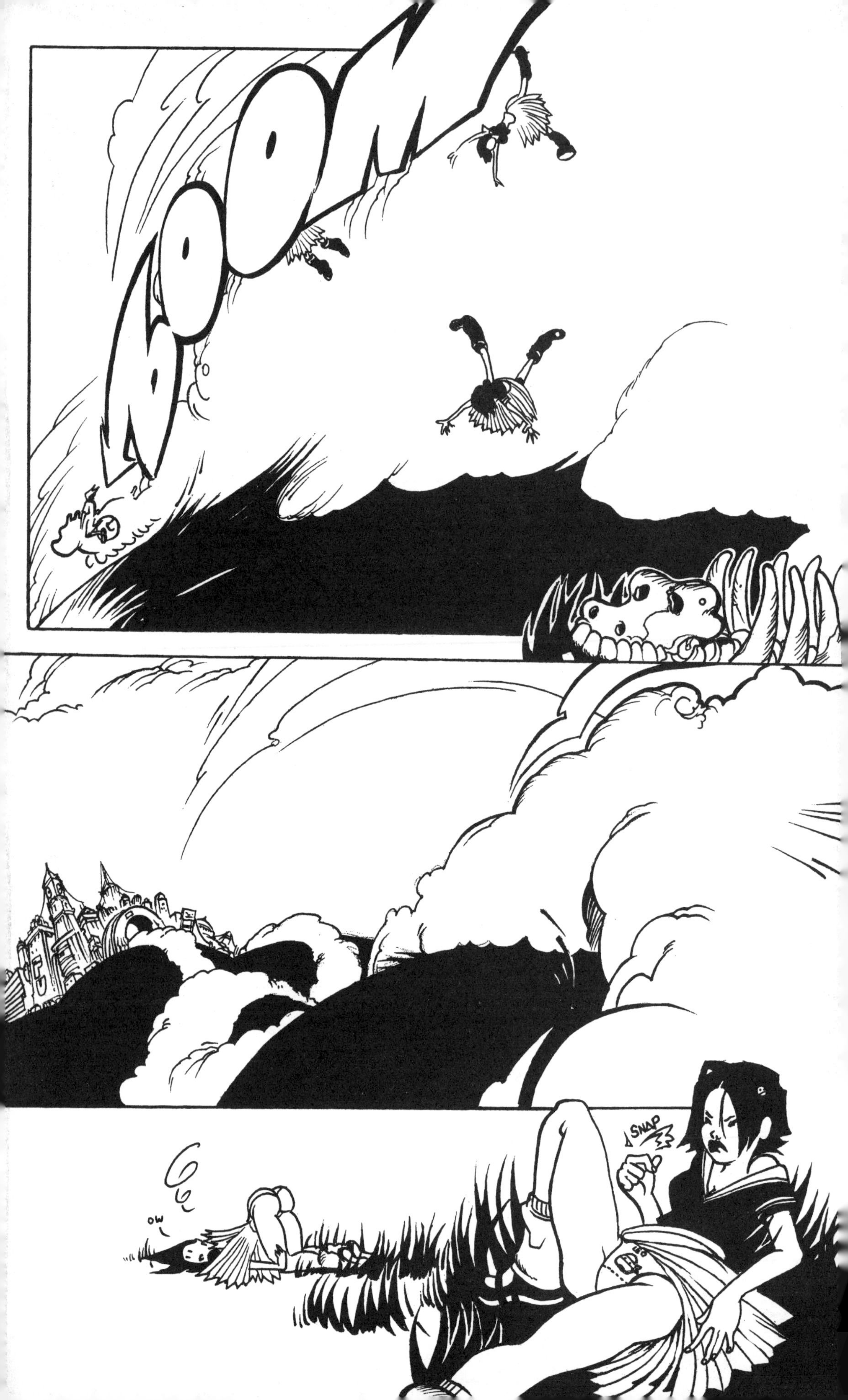

ZOOM
SNAP
OW

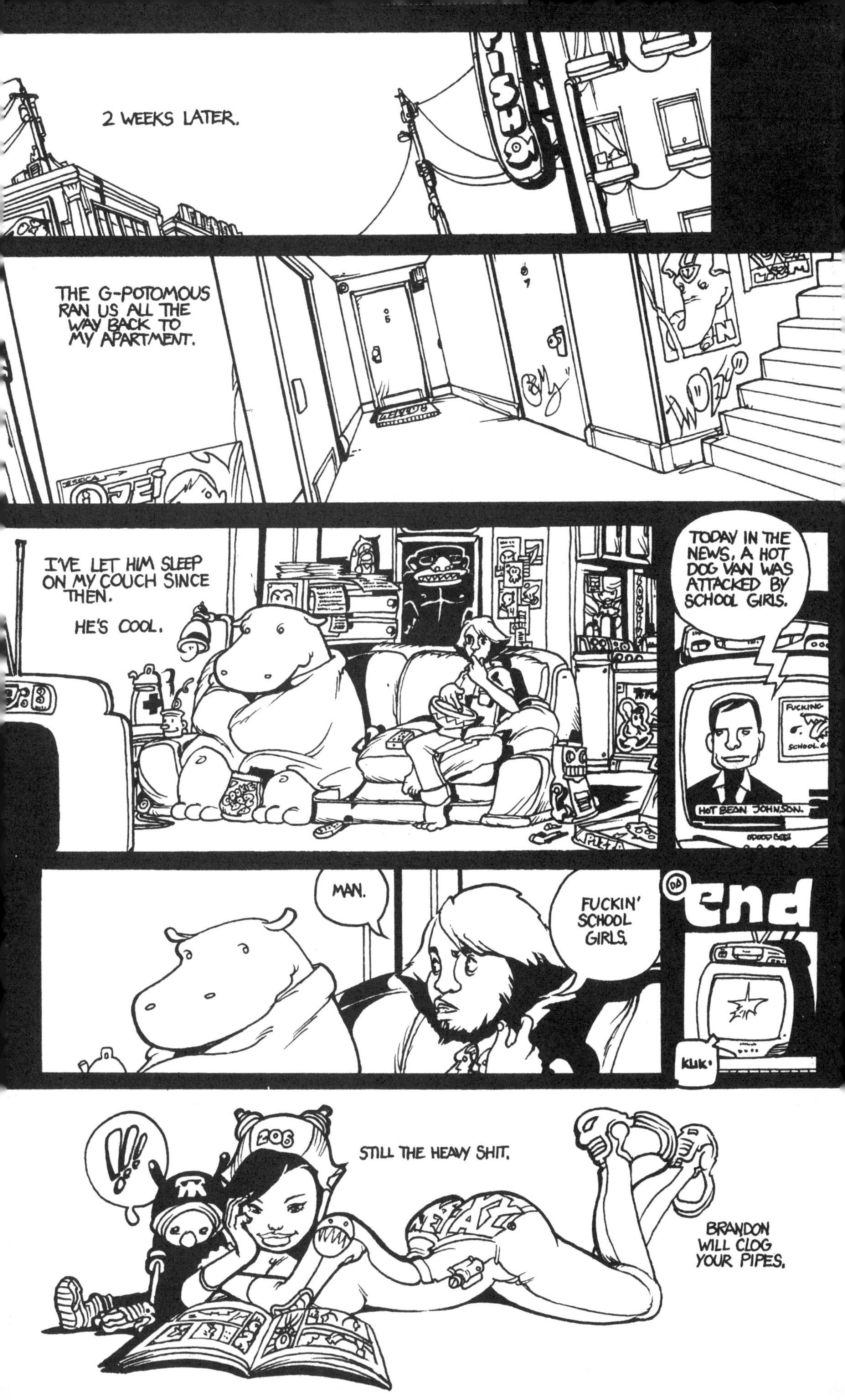

2 WEEKS LATER.
THE G-POTOMOUS RAN US ALL THE WAY BACK TO MY APARTMENT.
JESSICA
I'VE LET HIM SLEEP ON MY COUCH SINCE THEN.
HE'S COOL.
TODAY IN THE NEWS, A HOT DOG VAN WAS ATTACKED BY SCHOOL GIRLS.
HOT BEAN JOHNSON.
MAN.
FUCKIN' SCHOOL GIRLS.
end
KLIK·
206
STILL THE HEAVY SHIT.
BRANDON WILL CLOG YOUR PIPES.

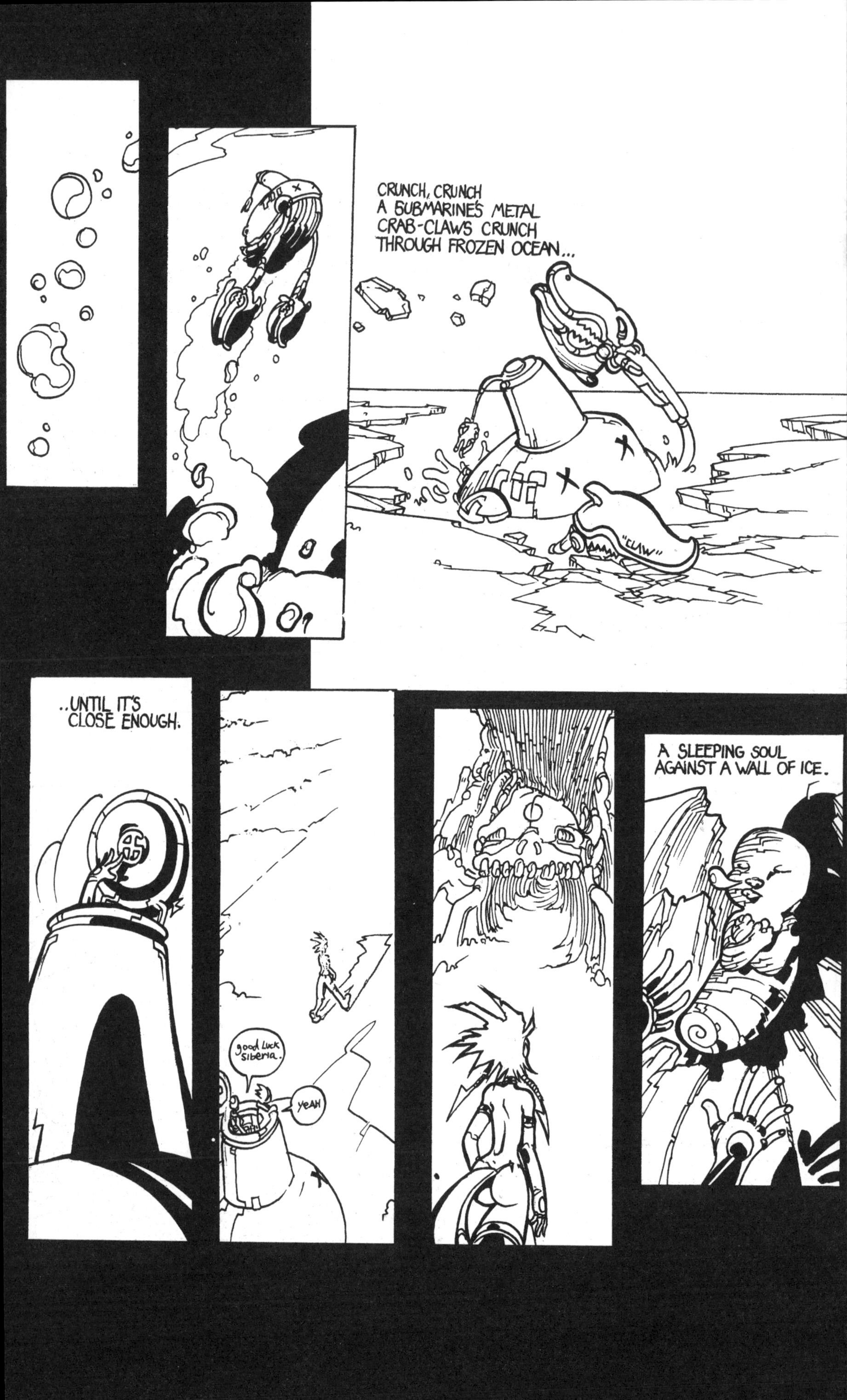
CRUNCH, CRUNCH
A SUBMARINE'S METAL
CRAB-CLAWS CRUNCH
THROUGH FROZEN OCEAN...
"CLAW"
..UNTIL IT'S
CLOSE ENOUGH.
good Luck
siberia.
yeah
A SLEEPING SOUL
AGAINST A WALL OF ICE.

Devil & The Deep

ON THE SHORE WHERE FROZEN OCEAN MEETS FROZEN LAND SITS A ROTTED OUT TEMPLE BUILT INTO THE BONES OF A GIANT.
IT IS NEST TO UBA-OBA, THE SOUL EATER, A NASTY PIG-SHIT OF A DEMON - A DESTROYER OF LIFE AND LOVE.

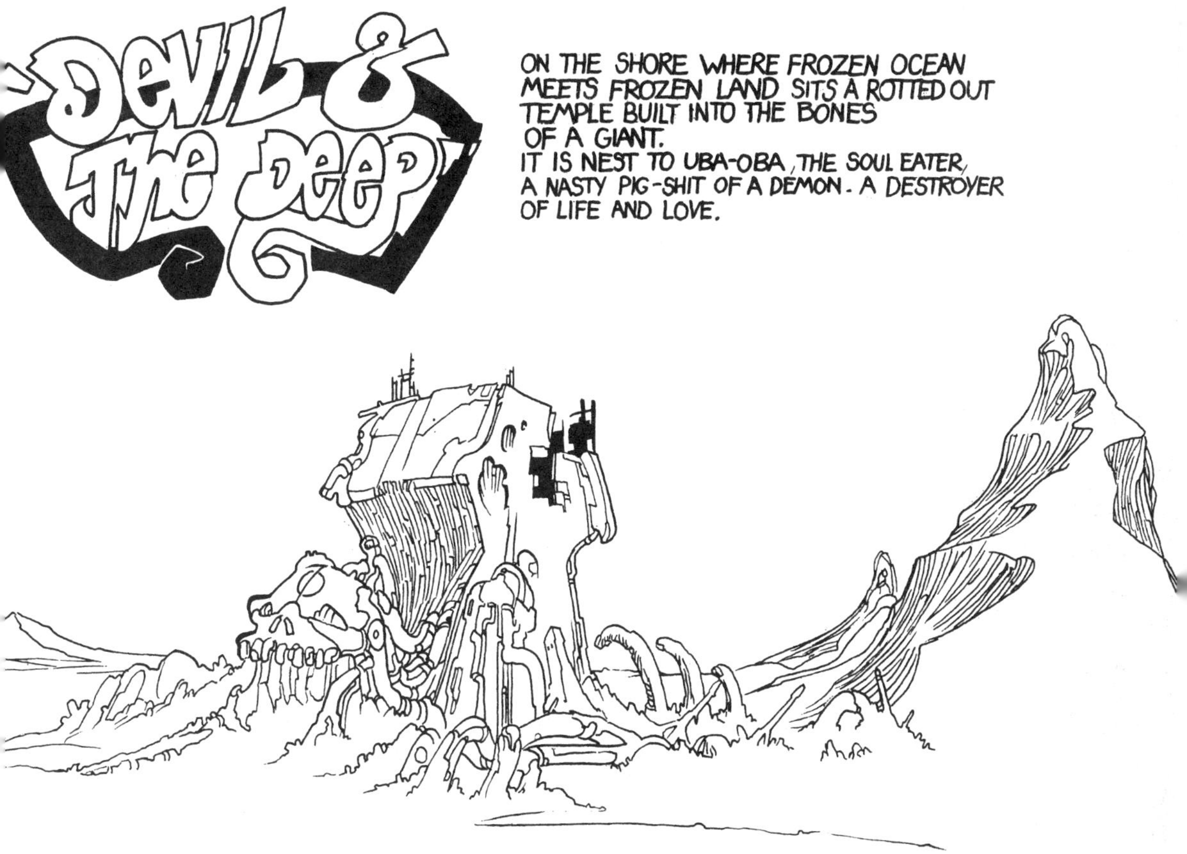

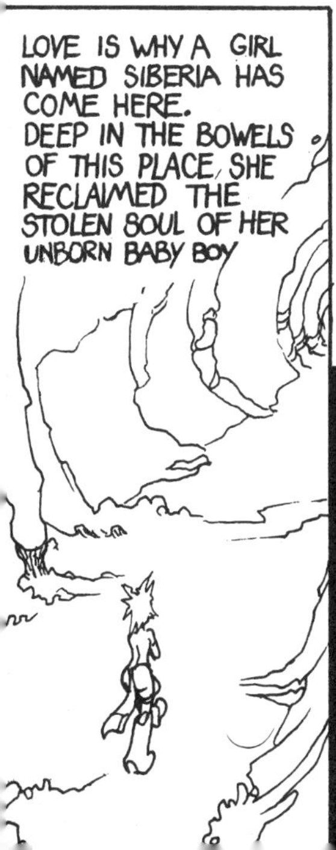
LOVE IS WHY A GIRL NAMED SIBERIA HAS COME HERE.
DEEP IN THE BOWELS OF THIS PLACE, SHE RECLAIMED THE STOLEN SOUL OF HER UNBORN BABY BOY

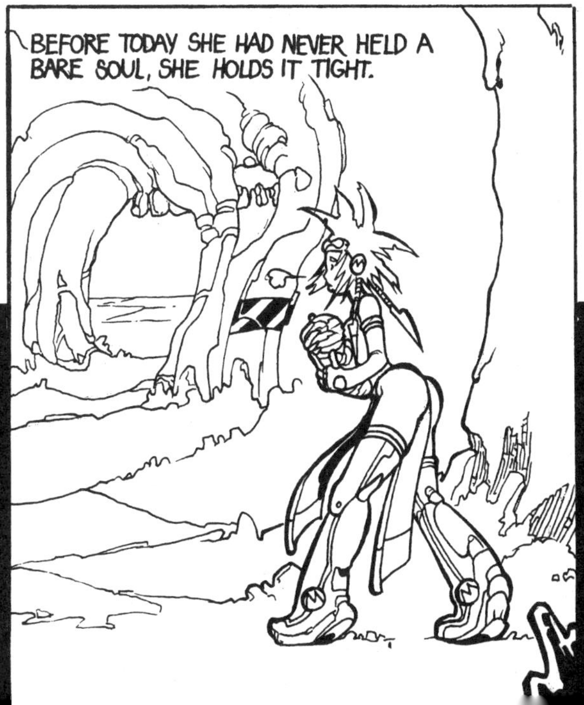
BEFORE TODAY SHE HAD NEVER HELD A BARE SOUL, SHE HOLDS IT TIGHT.

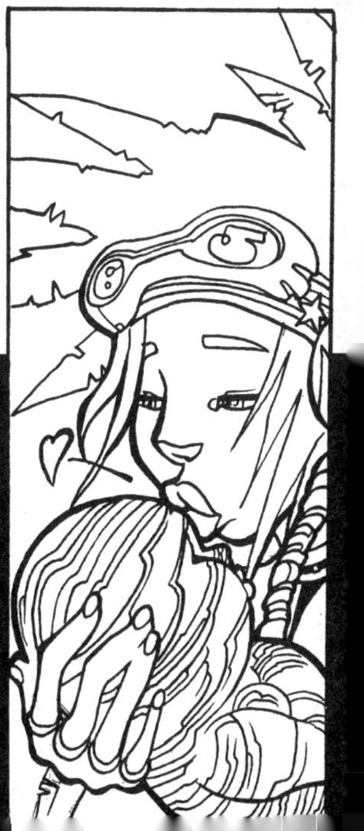

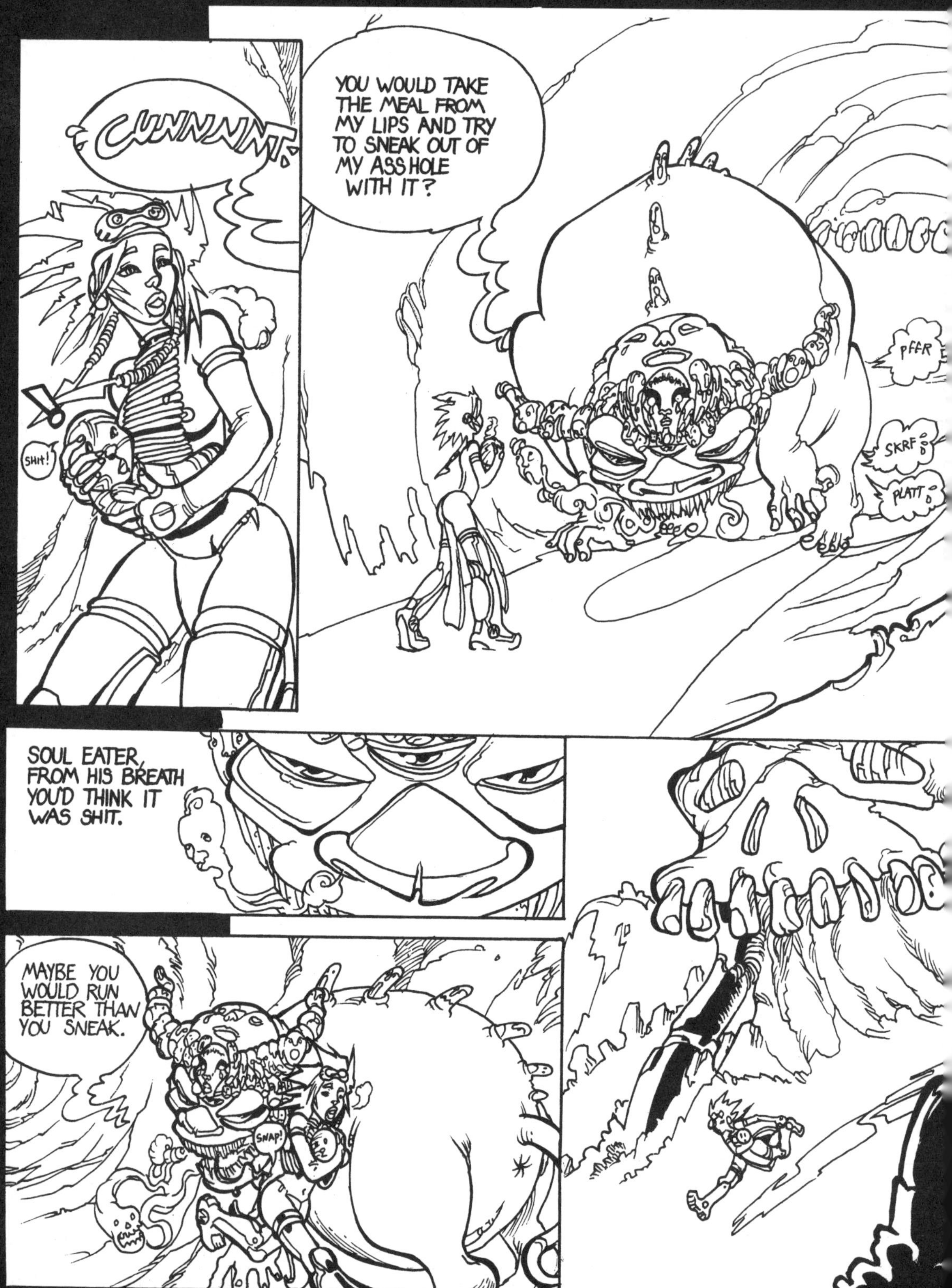
CUNNNNT.
SHIT!
YOU WOULD TAKE THE MEAL FROM MY LIPS AND TRY TO SNEAK OUT OF MY ASSHOLE WITH IT?
PFFR
SKRF
PLATT
SOUL EATER, FROM HIS BREATH YOU'D THINK IT WAS SHIT.
MAYBE YOU WOULD RUN BETTER THAN YOU SNEAK.
SNAP!

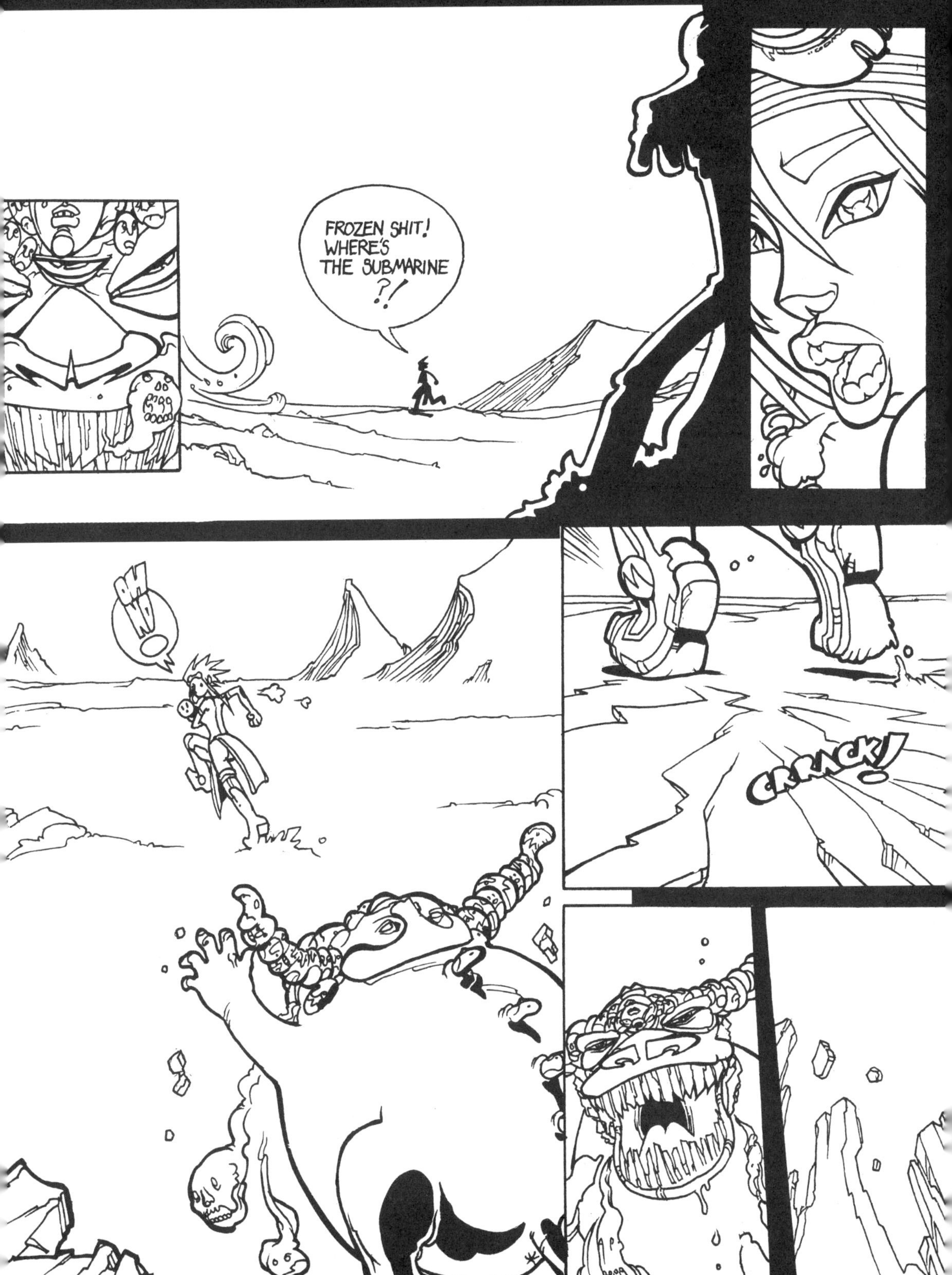
FROZEN SHIT! WHERE'S THE SUBMARINE ?!
OH NO!
CRRACK!

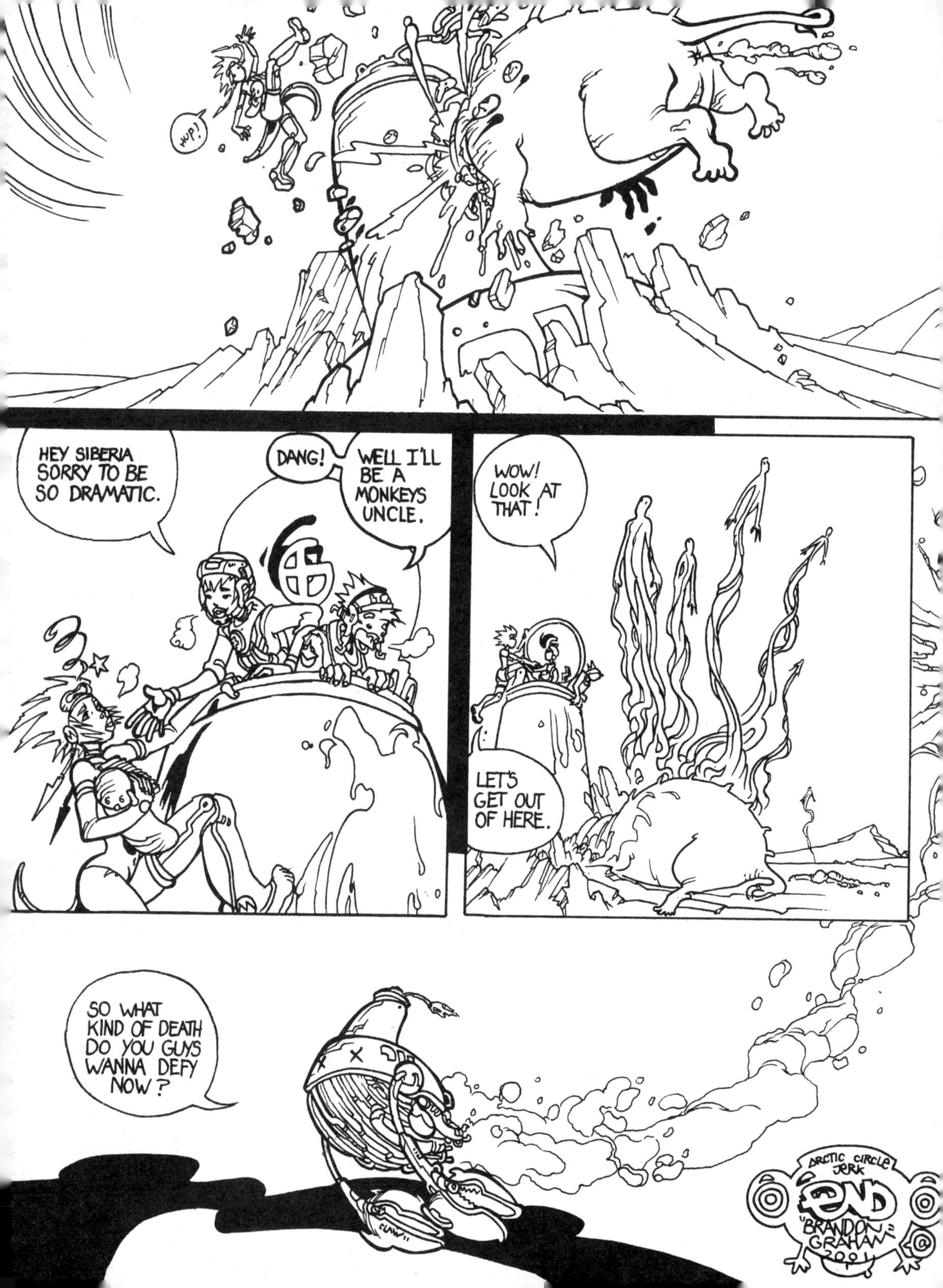
HUP!
HEY SIBERIA SORRY TO BE SO DRAMATIC.
DANG!
WELL I'LL BE A MONKEYS UNCLE.
WOW! LOOK AT THAT!
LET'S GET OUT OF HERE.
SO WHAT KIND OF DEATH DO YOU GUYS WANNA DEFY NOW?
"CLAW"
ARCTIC CIRCLE JERK
END
"BRANDON" GRAHAM
2001

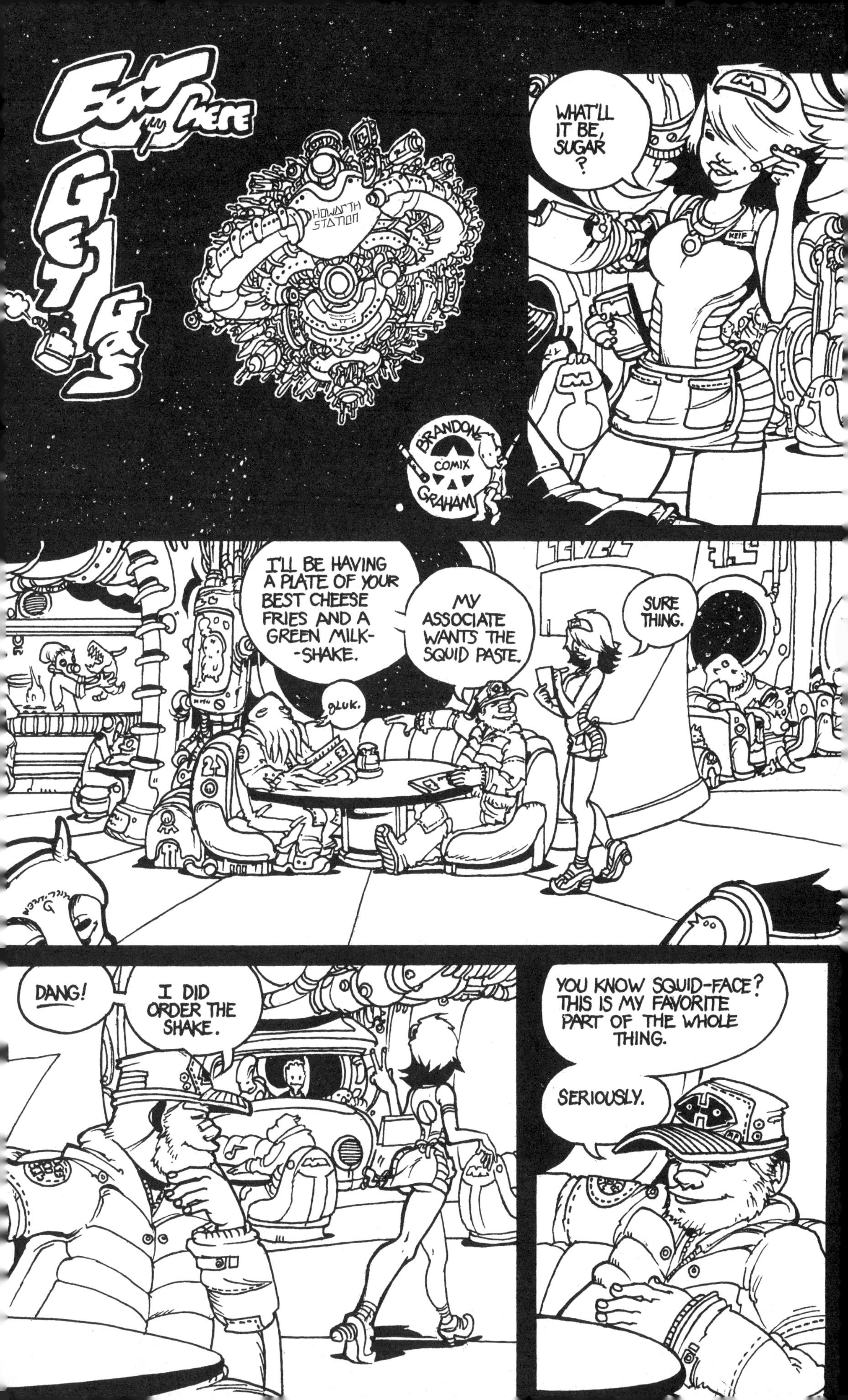

EAT HERE GET GAS
HOWARTH STATION
BRANDON GRAHAM COMIX
WHAT'LL IT BE, SUGAR ?
KEIF
I'LL BE HAVING A PLATE OF YOUR BEST CHEESE FRIES AND A GREEN MILK-SHAKE.
MY ASSOCIATE WANTS THE SQUID PASTE.
SURE THING.
GLUK.
DANG!
I DID ORDER THE SHAKE.
YOU KNOW SQUID-FACE? THIS IS MY FAVORITE PART OF THE WHOLE THING.
SERIOUSLY.

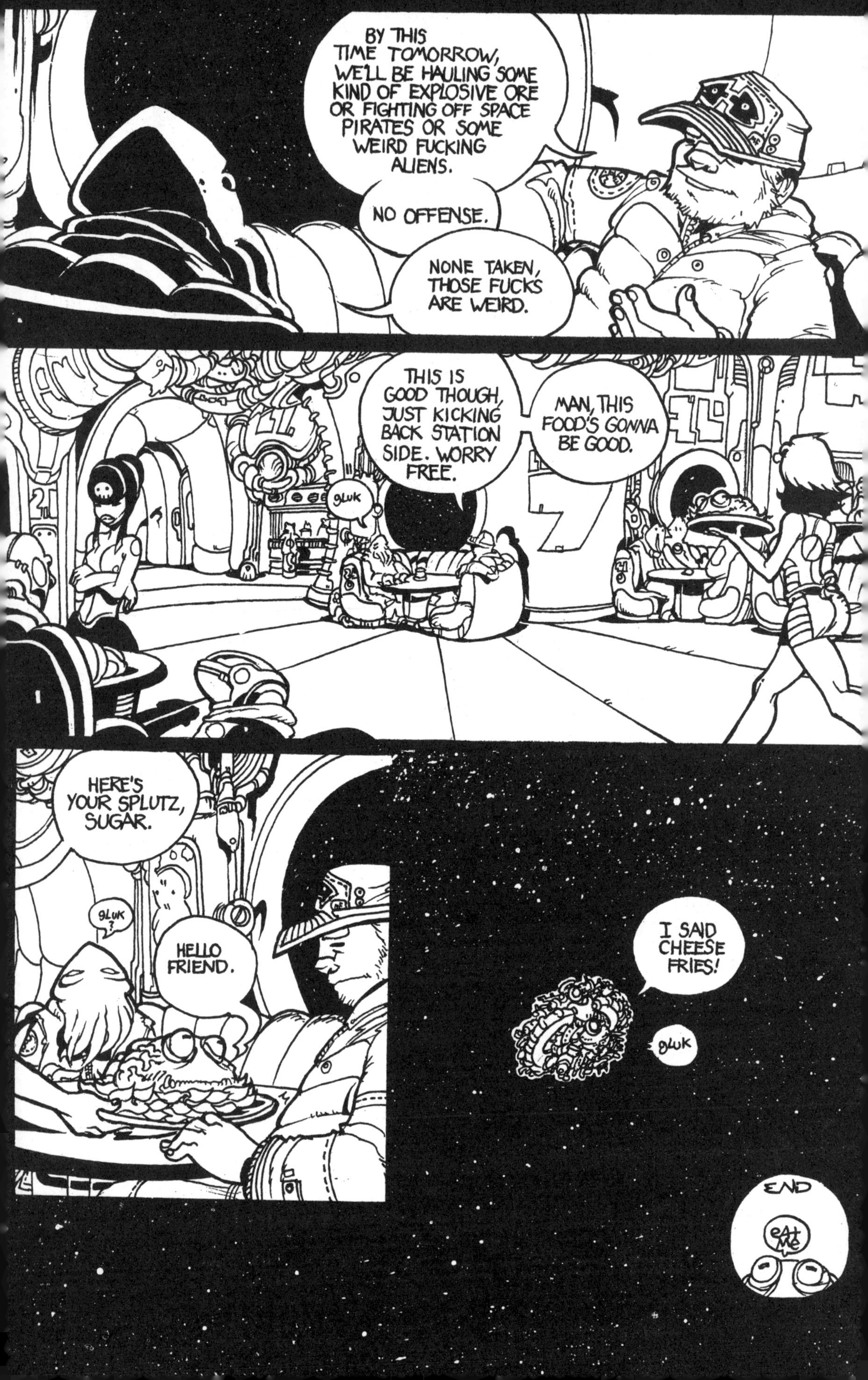
BY THIS TIME TOMORROW, WE'LL BE HAULING SOME KIND OF EXPLOSIVE ORE OR FIGHTING OFF SPACE PIRATES OR SOME WEIRD FUCKING ALIENS.
NO OFFENSE.
NONE TAKEN, THOSE FUCKS ARE WEIRD.
THIS IS GOOD THOUGH, JUST KICKING BACK STATION SIDE. WORRY FREE.
MAN, THIS FOOD'S GONNA BE GOOD.
GLUK
HERE'S YOUR SPLUTZ, SUGAR.
GLUK?
HELLO FRIEND.
I SAID CHEESE FRIES!
GLUK
END
eat me

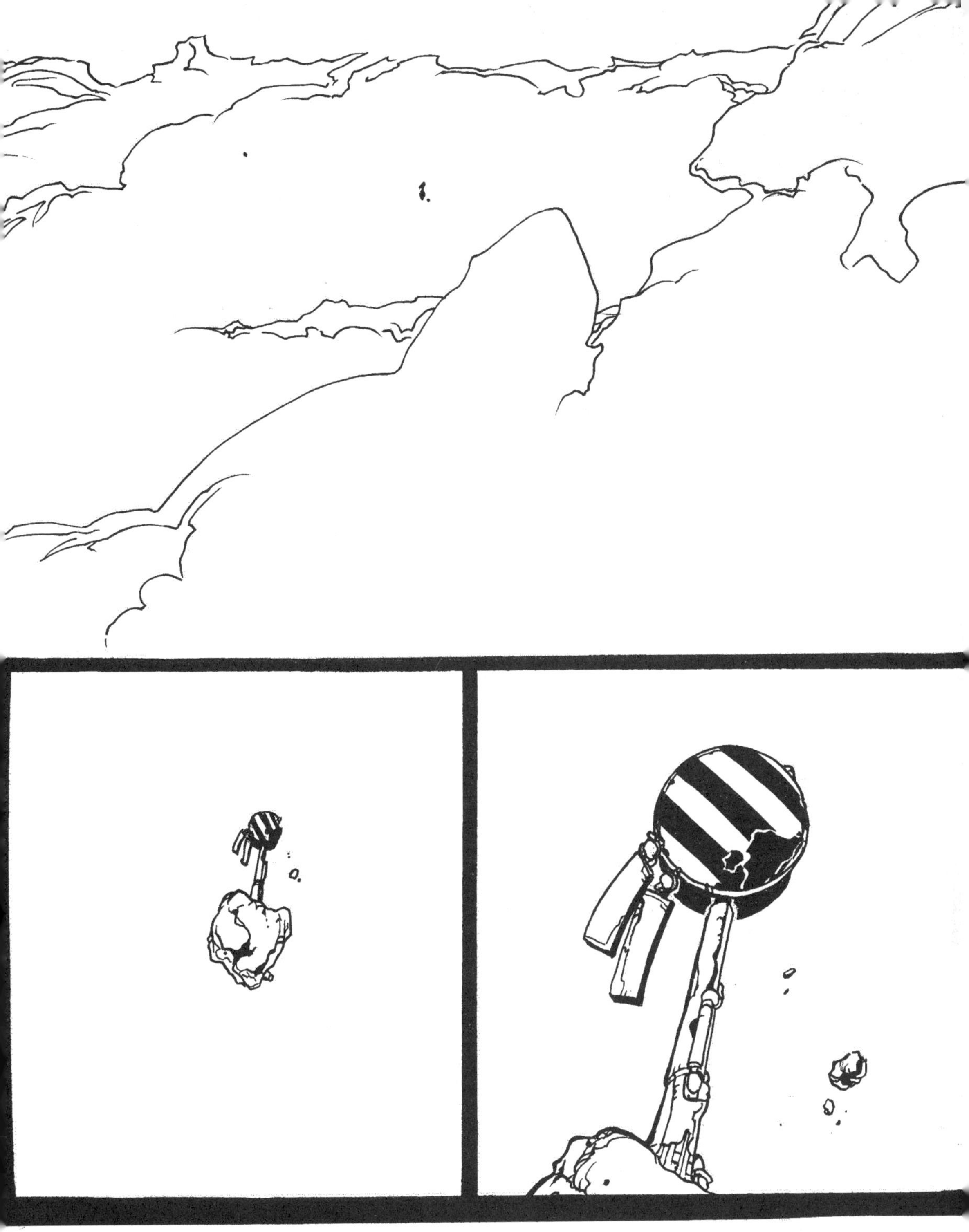

A
BRANDON
GRAHAM
COMIC.

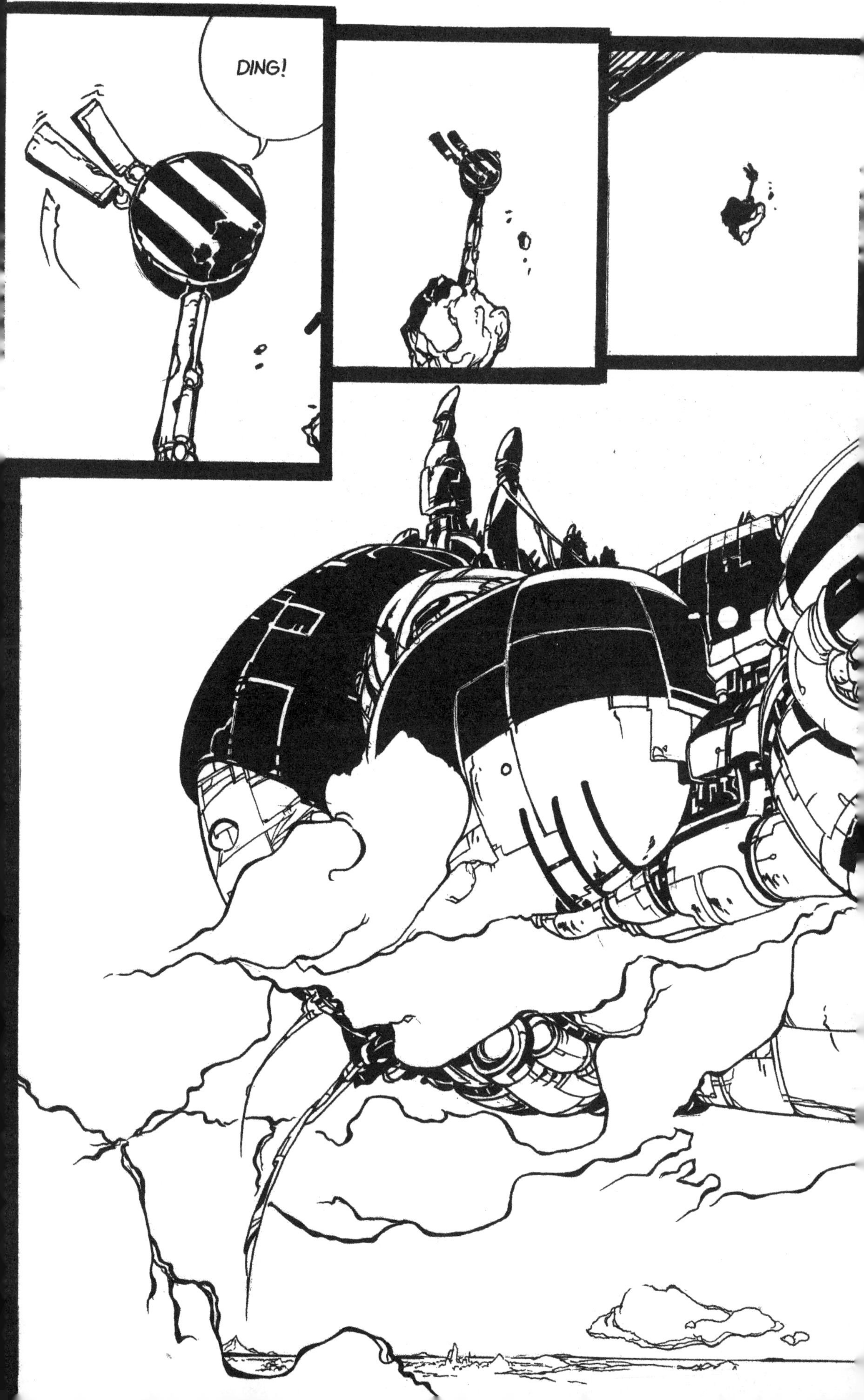
DING!

IFONIUM BLUE
CHAPTER ONE

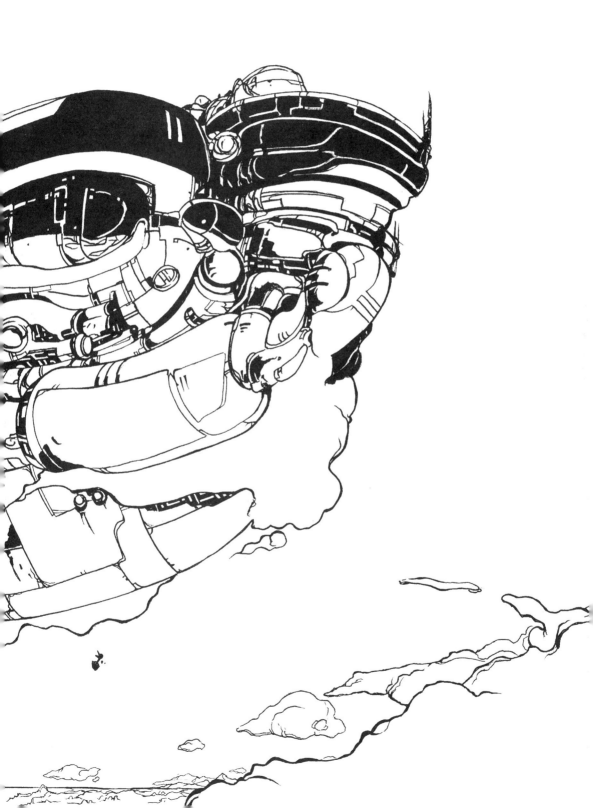

THE OLD
FOURTEEN
LINE

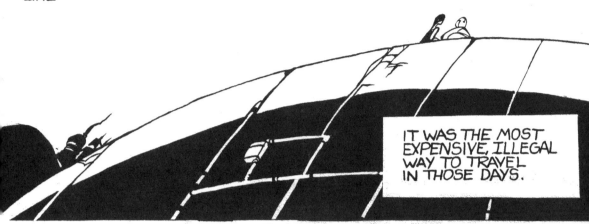

IT WAS THE MOST EXPENSIVE, ILLEGAL WAY TO TRAVEL IN THOSE DAYS.

I SPENT MY DAYS SERVING DRINKS.

SURE, THE PAY WAS GOOD, BUT THE REAL REASON I STAYED ABOARD WAS THE ENTERTAINMENT.

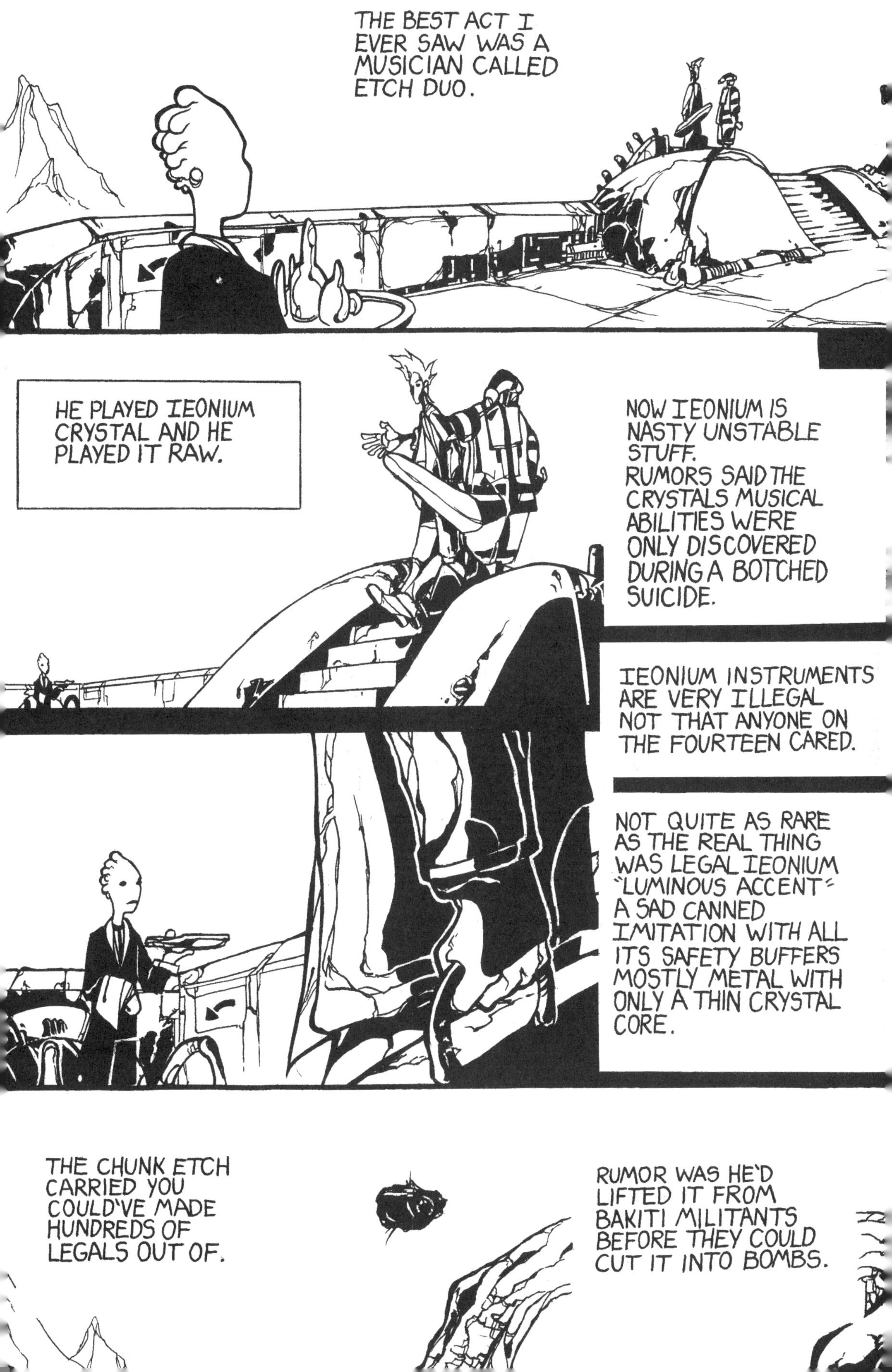
THE BEST ACT I EVER SAW WAS A MUSICIAN CALLED ETCH DUO.
HE PLAYED IEONIUM CRYSTAL AND HE PLAYED IT RAW.
NOW IEONIUM IS NASTY UNSTABLE STUFF. RUMORS SAID THE CRYSTALS MUSICAL ABILITIES WERE ONLY DISCOVERED DURING A BOTCHED SUICIDE.
IEONIUM INSTRUMENTS ARE VERY ILLEGAL NOT THAT ANYONE ON THE FOURTEEN CARED.
NOT QUITE AS RARE AS THE REAL THING WAS LEGAL IEONIUM "LUMINOUS ACCENT" A SAD CANNED IMITATION WITH ALL ITS SAFETY BUFFERS MOSTLY METAL WITH ONLY A THIN CRYSTAL CORE.
THE CHUNK ETCH CARRIED YOU COULD'VE MADE HUNDREDS OF LEGALS OUT OF.
RUMOR WAS HE'D LIFTED IT FROM BAKITI MILITANTS BEFORE THEY COULD CUT IT INTO BOMBS.

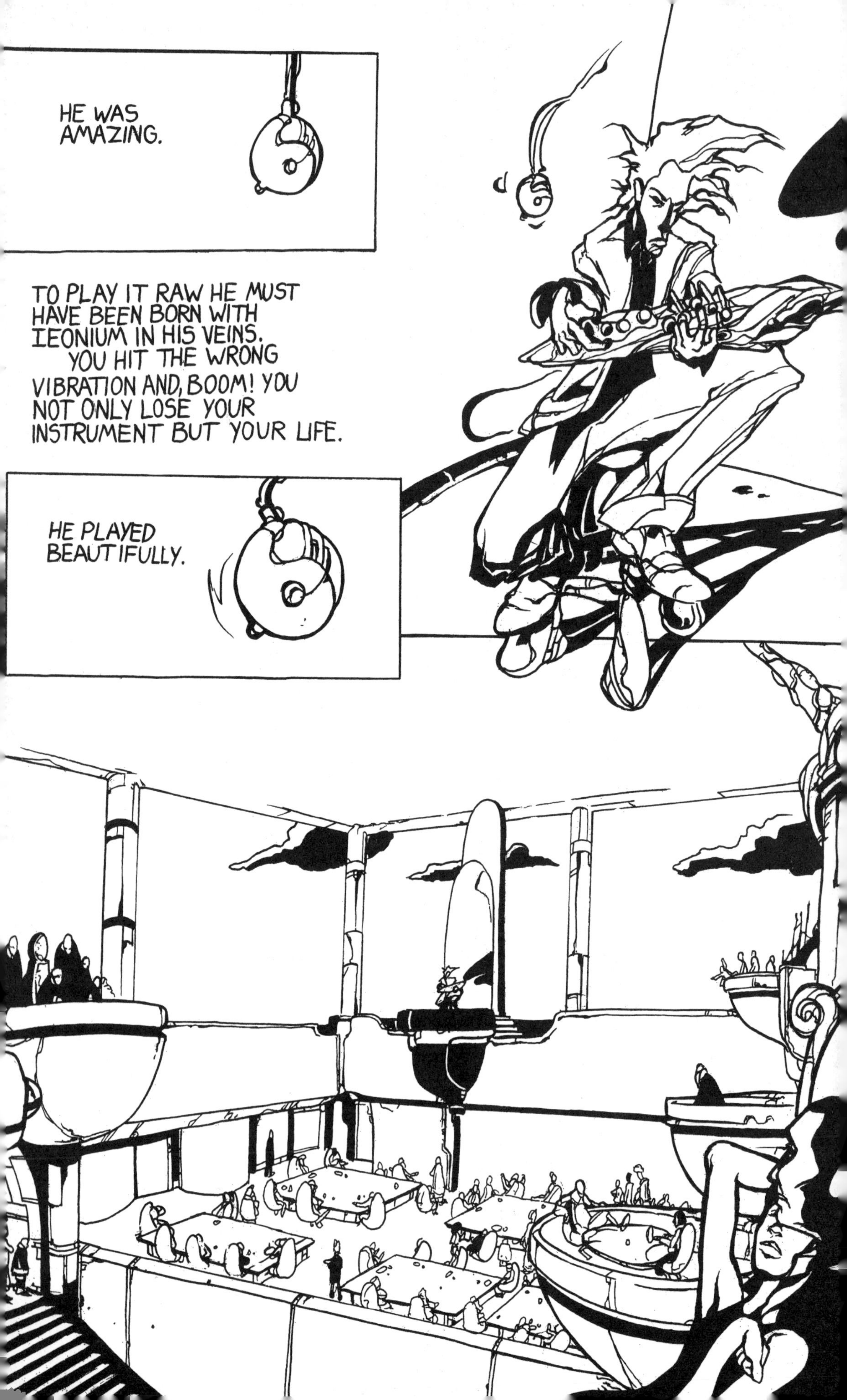
HE WAS AMAZING.
TO PLAY IT RAW HE MUST HAVE BEEN BORN WITH IEONIUM IN HIS VEINS.
YOU HIT THE WRONG VIBRATION AND, BOOM! YOU NOT ONLY LOSE YOUR INSTRUMENT BUT YOUR LIFE.
HE PLAYED BEAUTIFULLY.

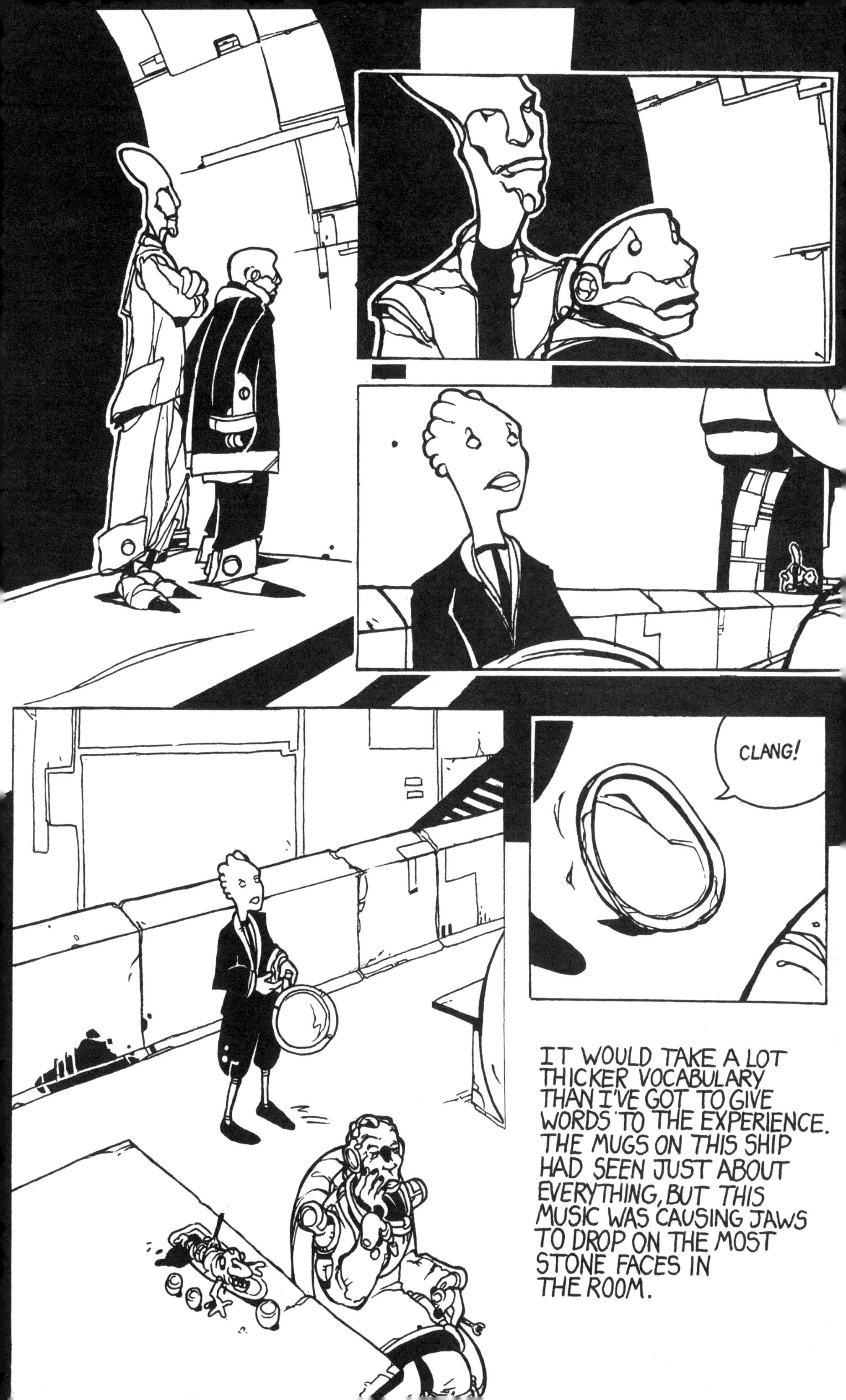
CLANG!
IT WOULD TAKE A LOT THICKER VOCABULARY THAN I'VE GOT TO GIVE WORDS TO THE EXPERIENCE. THE MUGS ON THIS SHIP HAD SEEN JUST ABOUT EVERYTHING, BUT THIS MUSIC WAS CAUSING JAWS TO DROP ON THE MOST STONE FACES IN THE ROOM.

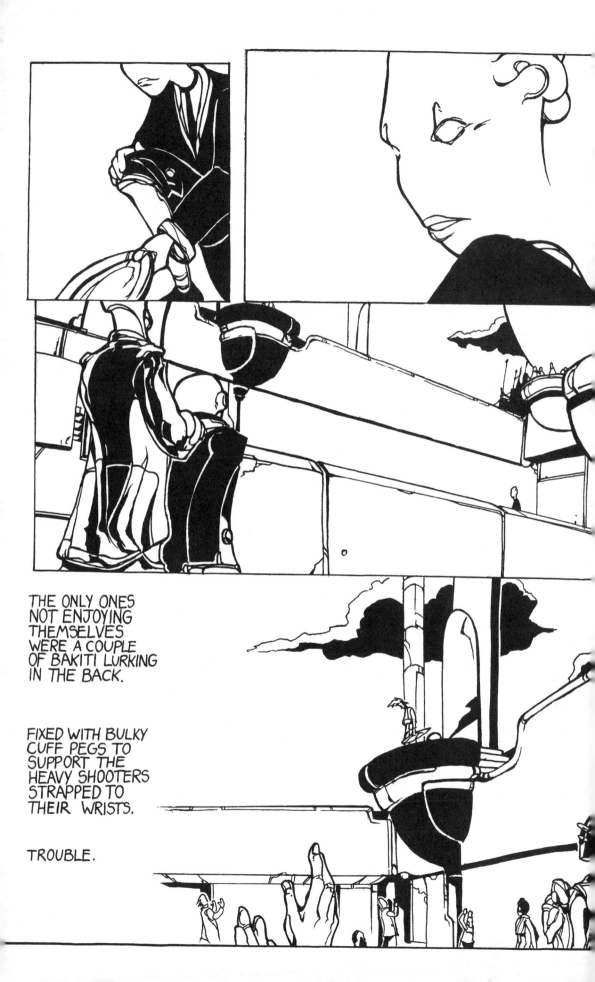

THE ONLY ONES NOT ENJOYING THEMSELVES WERE A COUPLE OF BAKITI LURKING IN THE BACK.

FIXED WITH BULKY CUFF PEGS TO SUPPORT THE HEAVY SHOOTERS STRAPPED TO THEIR WRISTS.

TROUBLE.

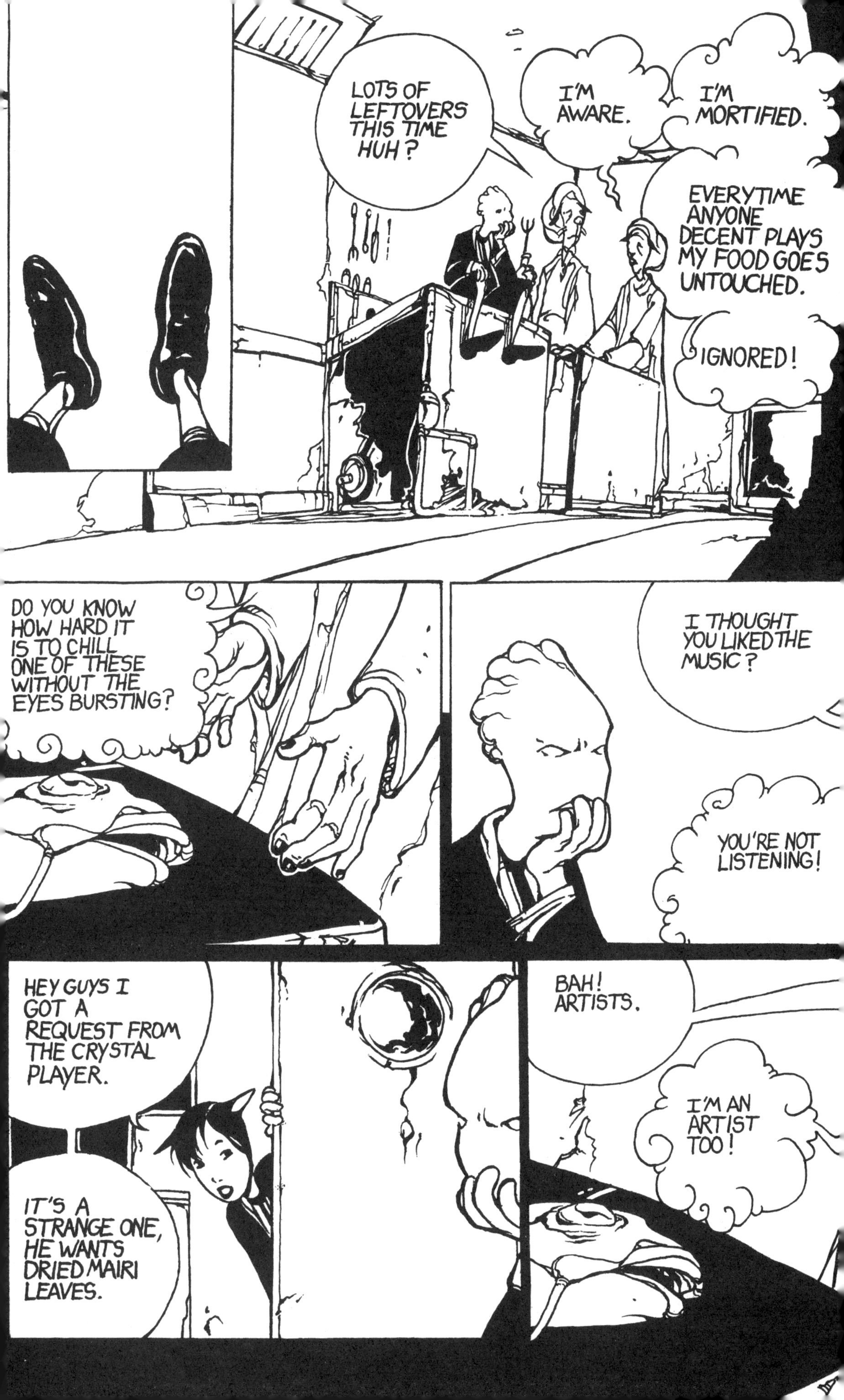
LOTS OF LEFTOVERS THIS TIME HUH?
I'M AWARE.
I'M MORTIFIED.
EVERYTIME ANYONE DECENT PLAYS MY FOOD GOES UNTOUCHED.
IGNORED!
DO YOU KNOW HOW HARD IT IS TO CHILL ONE OF THESE WITHOUT THE EYES BURSTING?
I THOUGHT YOU LIKED THE MUSIC?
YOU'RE NOT LISTENING!
HEY GUYS I GOT A REQUEST FROM THE CRYSTAL PLAYER.
IT'S A STRANGE ONE, HE WANTS DRIED MAIRI LEAVES.
BAH! ARTISTS.
I'M AN ARTIST TOO!

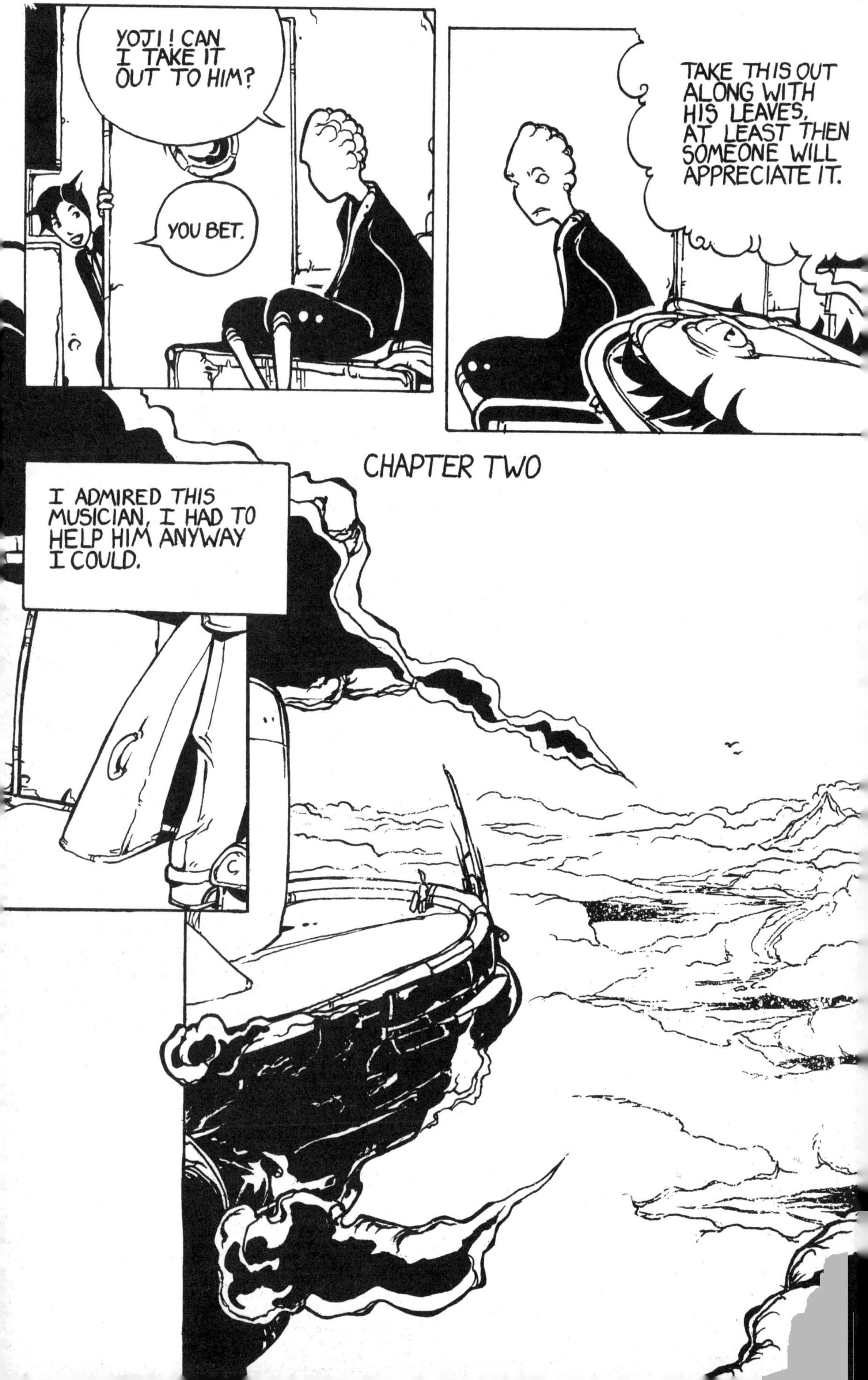
YOJI! CAN I TAKE IT OUT TO HIM?
YOU BET.
TAKE THIS OUT ALONG WITH HIS LEAVES, AT LEAST THEN SOMEONE WILL APPRECIATE IT.
CHAPTER TWO
I ADMIRED THIS MUSICIAN, I HAD TO HELP HIM ANYWAY I COULD.

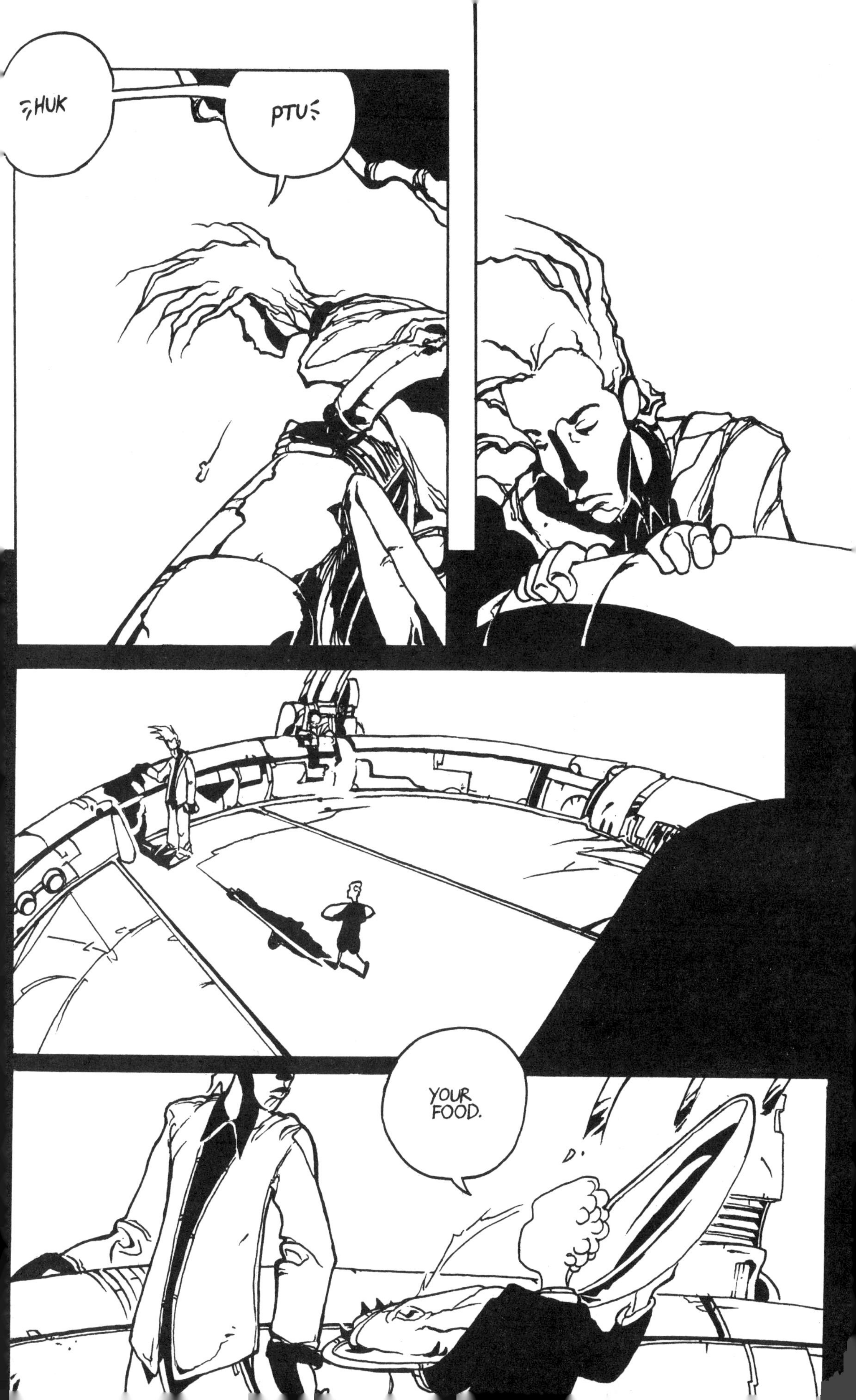
HUK
PTU
YOUR FOOD.

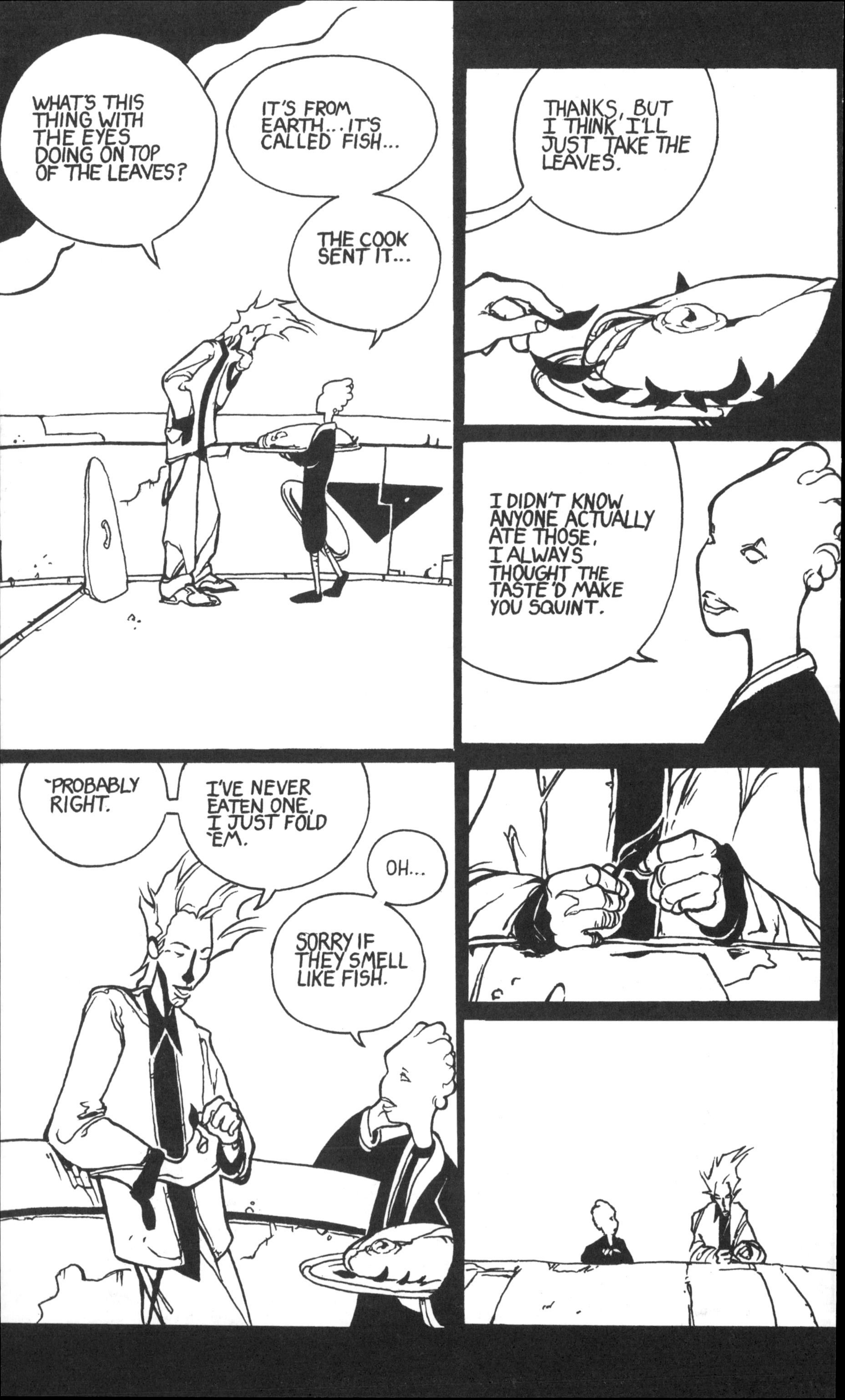
WHAT'S THIS THING WITH THE EYES DOING ON TOP OF THE LEAVES?
IT'S FROM EARTH... IT'S CALLED FISH...
THE COOK SENT IT...
THANKS, BUT I THINK I'LL JUST TAKE THE LEAVES.
I DIDN'T KNOW ANYONE ACTUALLY ATE THOSE, I ALWAYS THOUGHT THE TASTE'D MAKE YOU SQUINT.
'PROBABLY RIGHT.
I'VE NEVER EATEN ONE, I JUST FOLD 'EM.
OH...
SORRY IF THEY SMELL LIKE FISH.

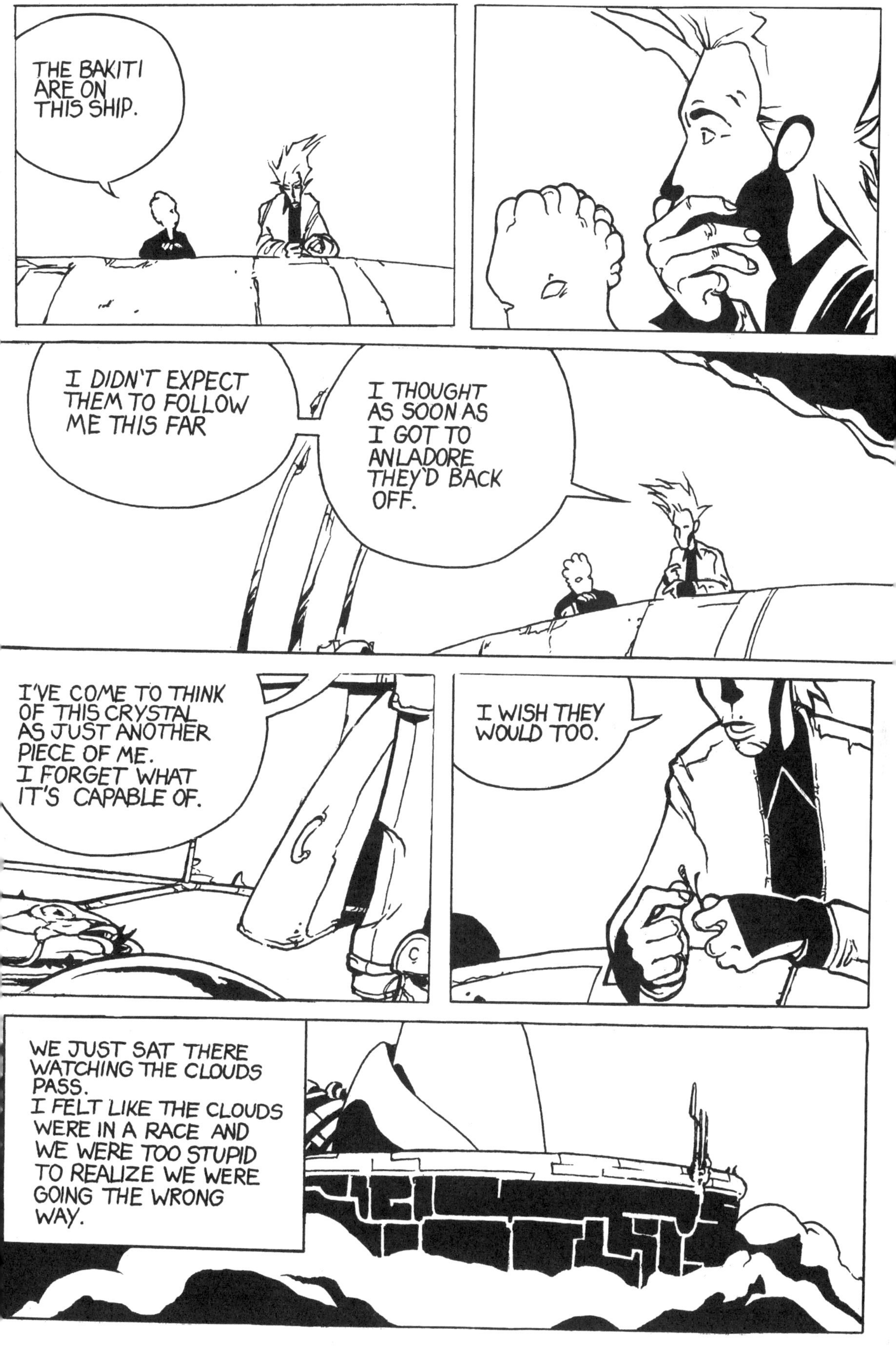
THE BAKITI ARE ON THIS SHIP.
I DIDN'T EXPECT THEM TO FOLLOW ME THIS FAR
I THOUGHT AS SOON AS I GOT TO ANLADORE THEY'D BACK OFF.
I'VE COME TO THINK OF THIS CRYSTAL AS JUST ANOTHER PIECE OF ME. I FORGET WHAT IT'S CAPABLE OF.
I WISH THEY WOULD TOO.
WE JUST SAT THERE WATCHING THE CLOUDS PASS. I FELT LIKE THE CLOUDS WERE IN A RACE AND WE WERE TOO STUPID TO REALIZE WE WERE GOING THE WRONG WAY.

I WAS THINKING ABOUT MY POPS AND THE WAY HE USED TO TAKE US TO HOP SHIPS WITH HIM.

THEN IT CLICKED.

I KNOW A WAY OFF.

WHAT?!

A WAY OFF THIS SHIP!

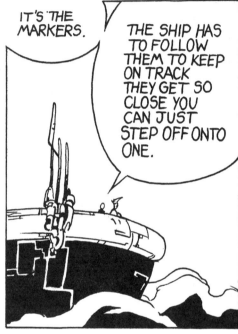

IT'S THE MARKERS.

THE SHIP HAS TO FOLLOW THEM TO KEEP ON TRACK THEY GET SO CLOSE YOU CAN JUST STEP OFF ONTO ONE.

AND WE'RE JUST ABOUT TO COME INTO A SWARM OF 'EM!

ETCH-DUO WAS THRILLED.

HEH!

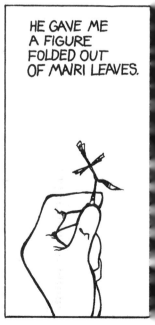

HE GAVE ME A FIGURE FOLDED OUT OF MAIRI LEAVES.

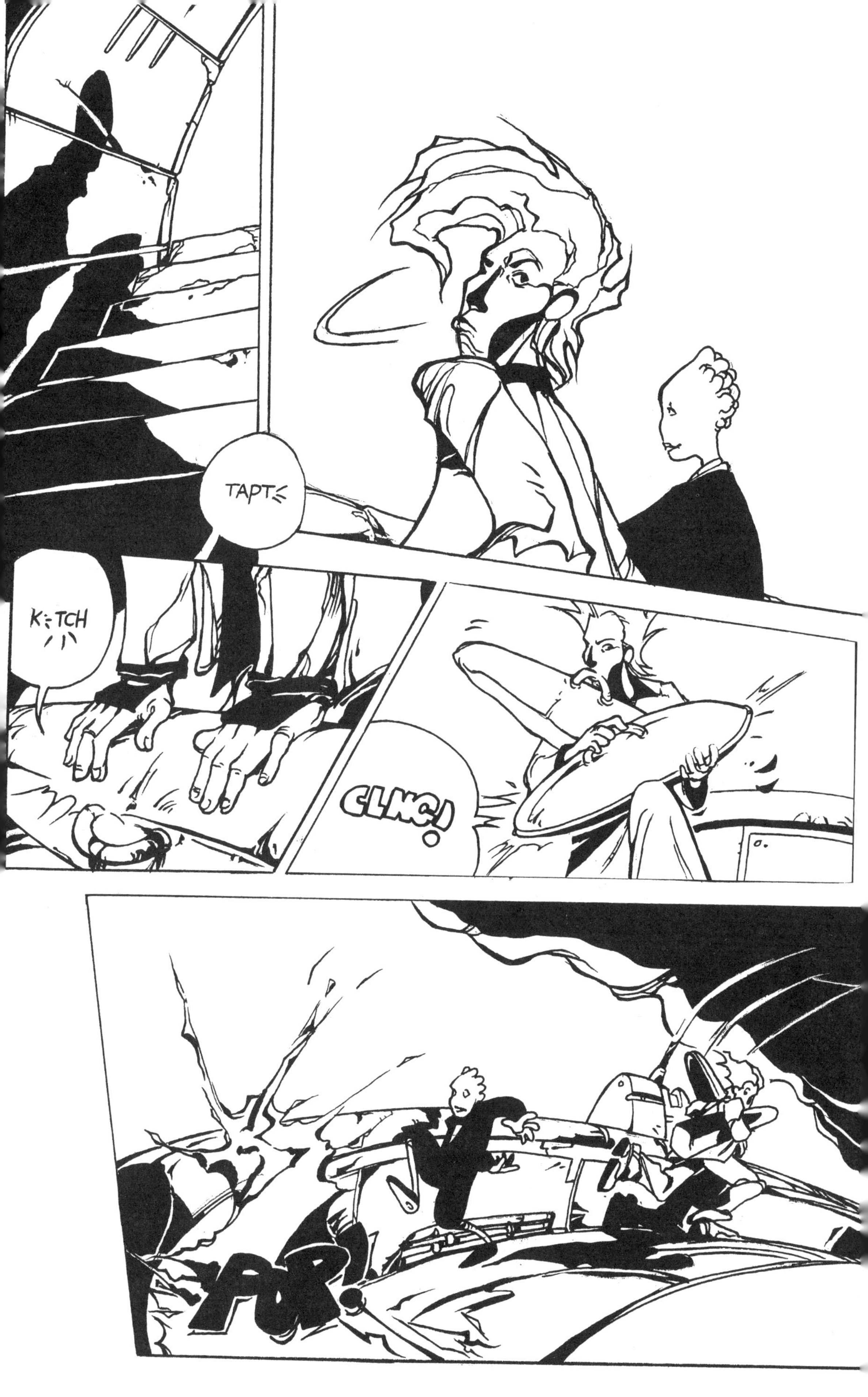
TAPT
K-TCH
CLNG!
POP!

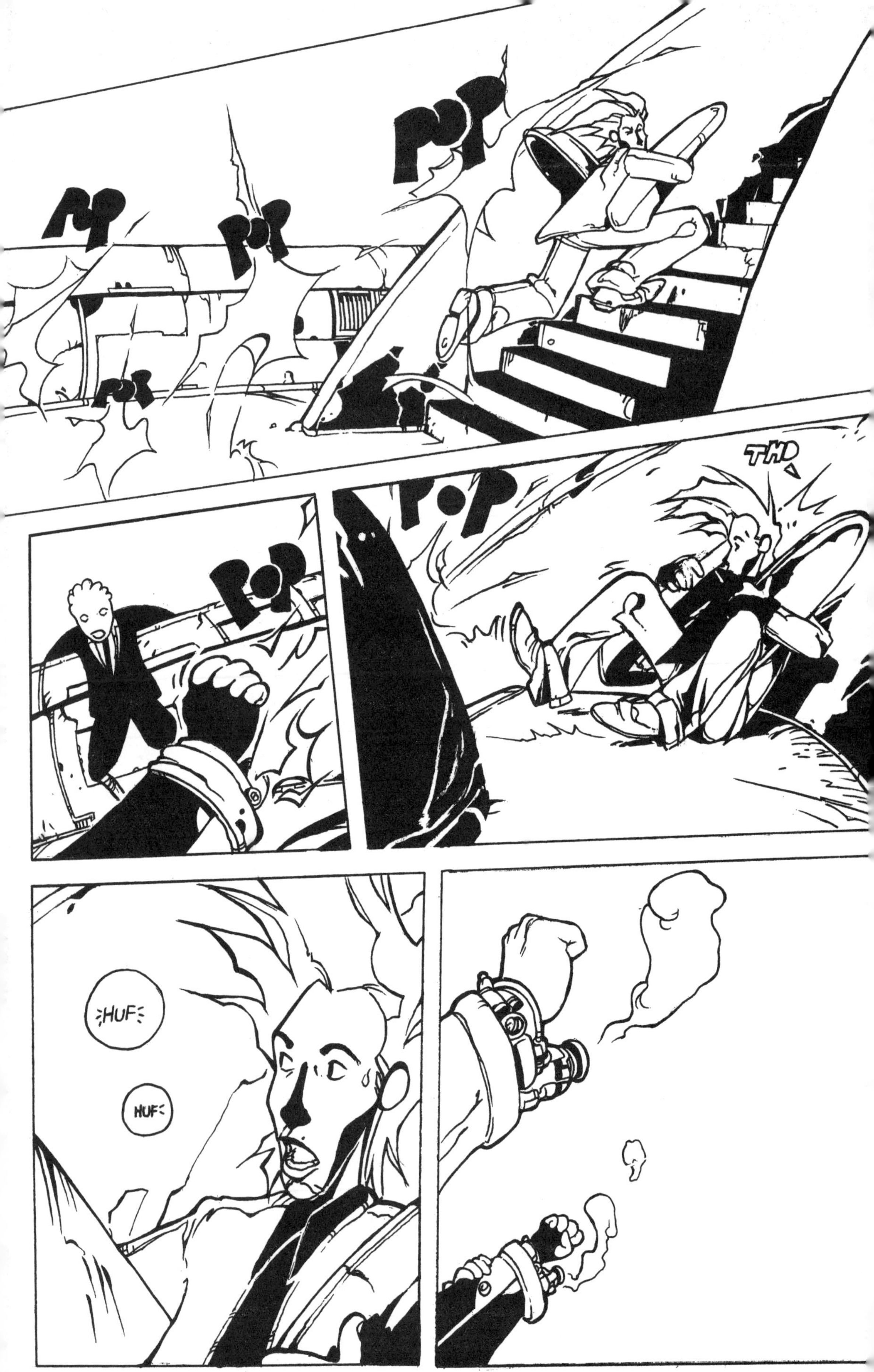
POP
POP
POP
POP
POP
POP
THD
HUF
HUF

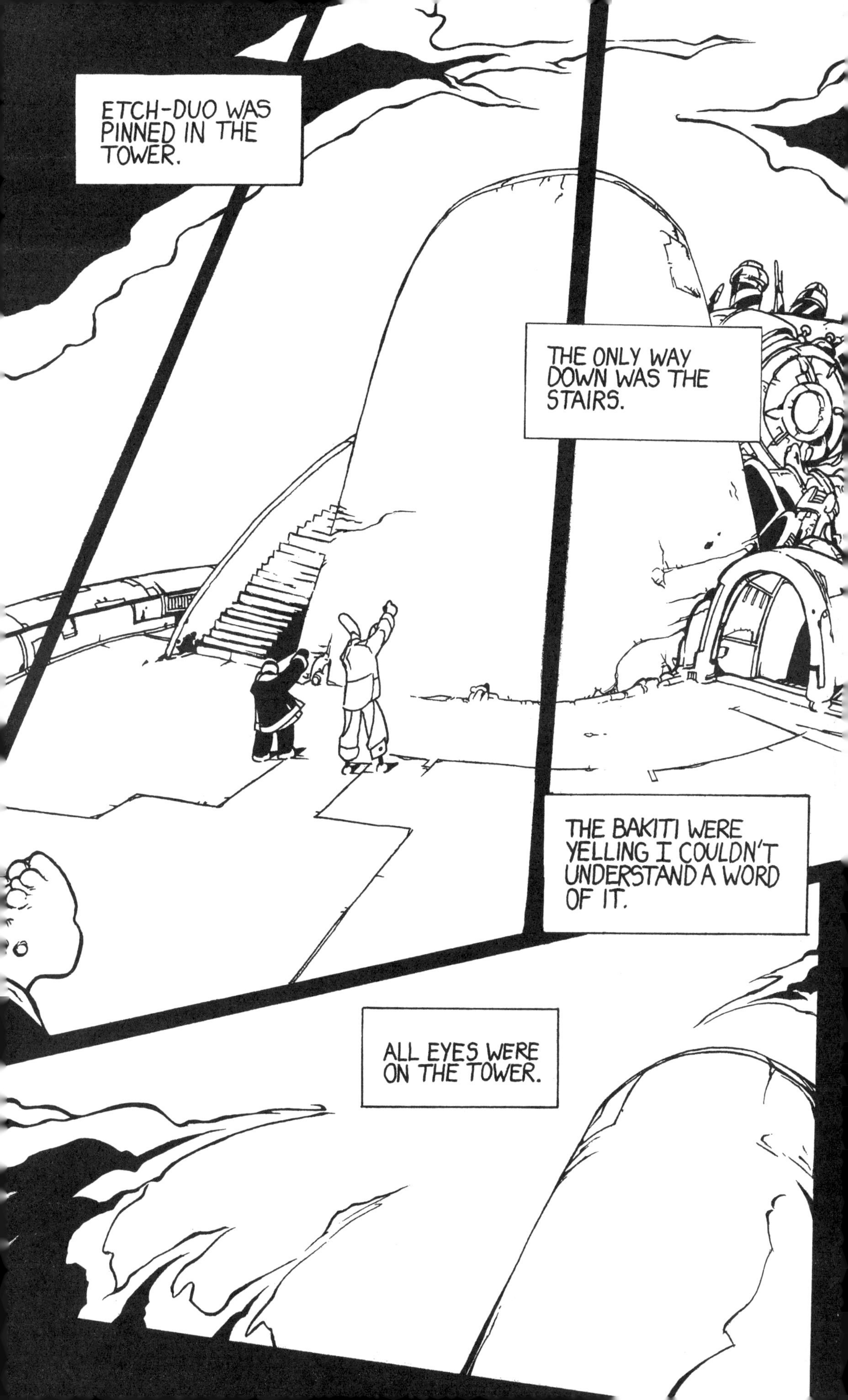
ETCH-DUO WAS PINNED IN THE TOWER.
THE ONLY WAY DOWN WAS THE STAIRS.
THE BAKITI WERE YELLING I COULDN'T UNDERSTAND A WORD OF IT.
ALL EYES WERE ON THE TOWER.

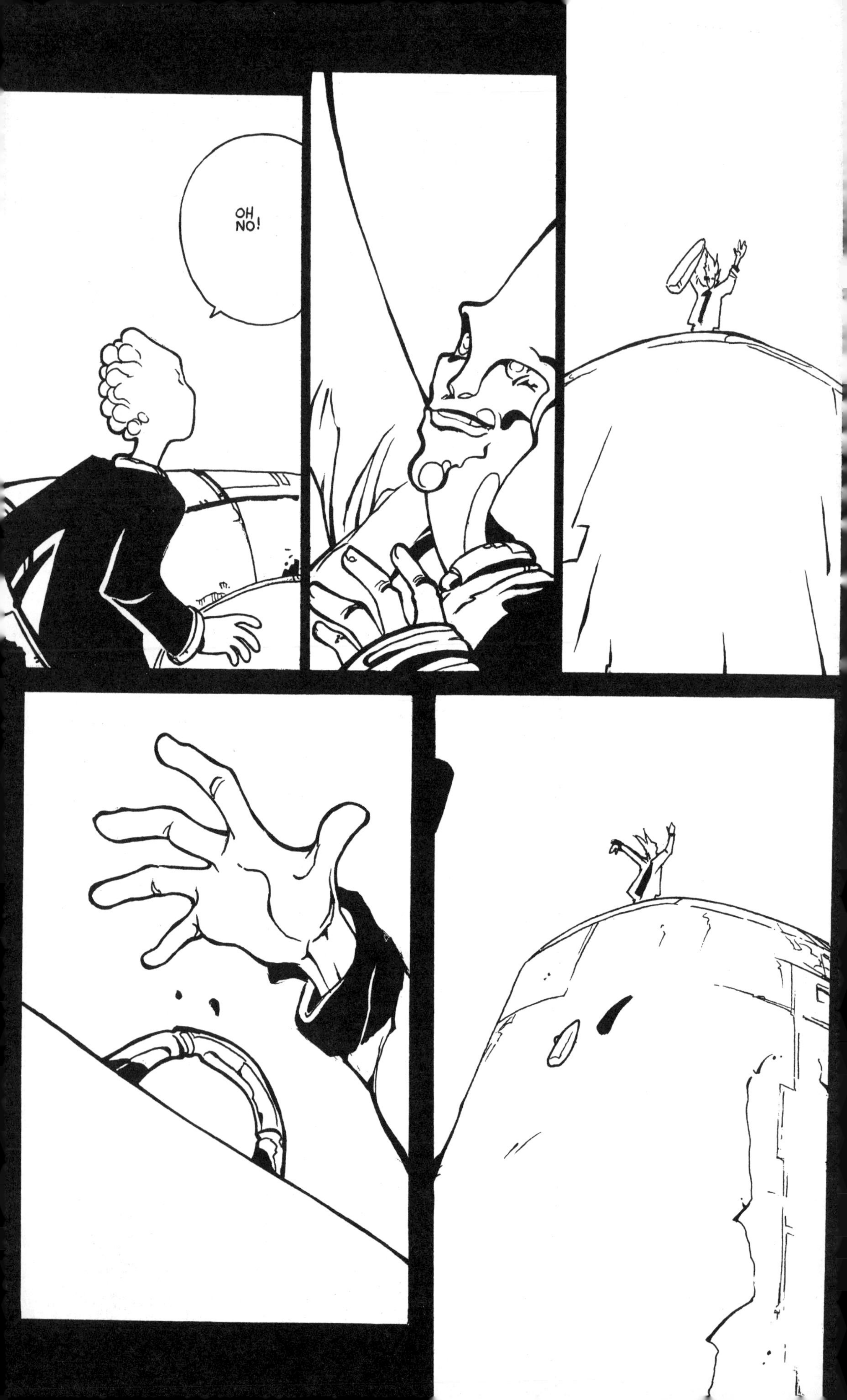
OH NO!

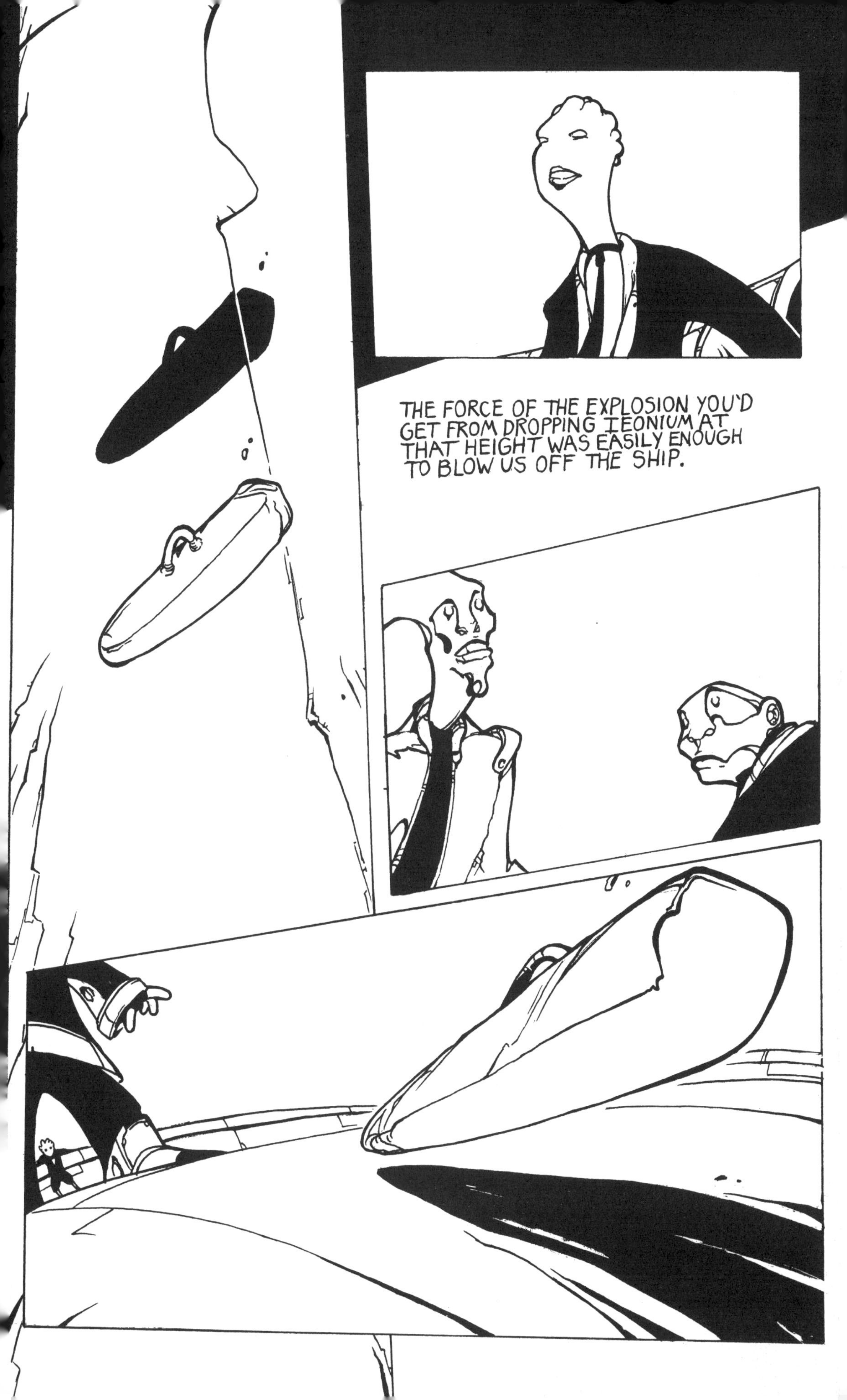
THE FORCE OF THE EXPLOSION YOU'D GET FROM DROPPING IEONIUM AT THAT HEIGHT WAS EASILY ENOUGH TO BLOW US OFF THE SHIP.

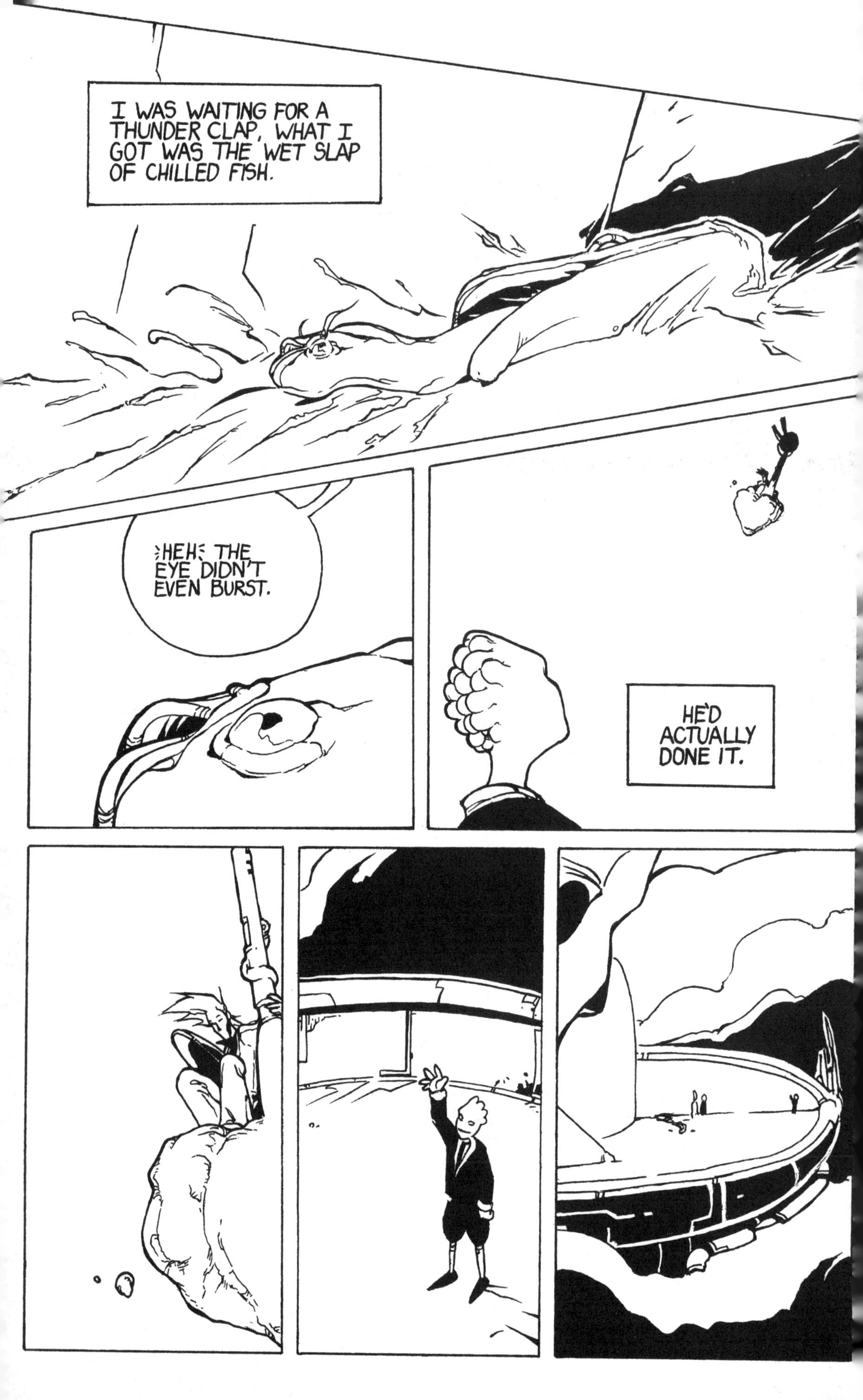
I WAS WAITING FOR A THUNDER CLAP, WHAT I GOT WAS THE WET SLAP OF CHILLED FISH.
HEH THE EYE DIDN'T EVEN BURST.
HE'D ACTUALLY DONE IT.

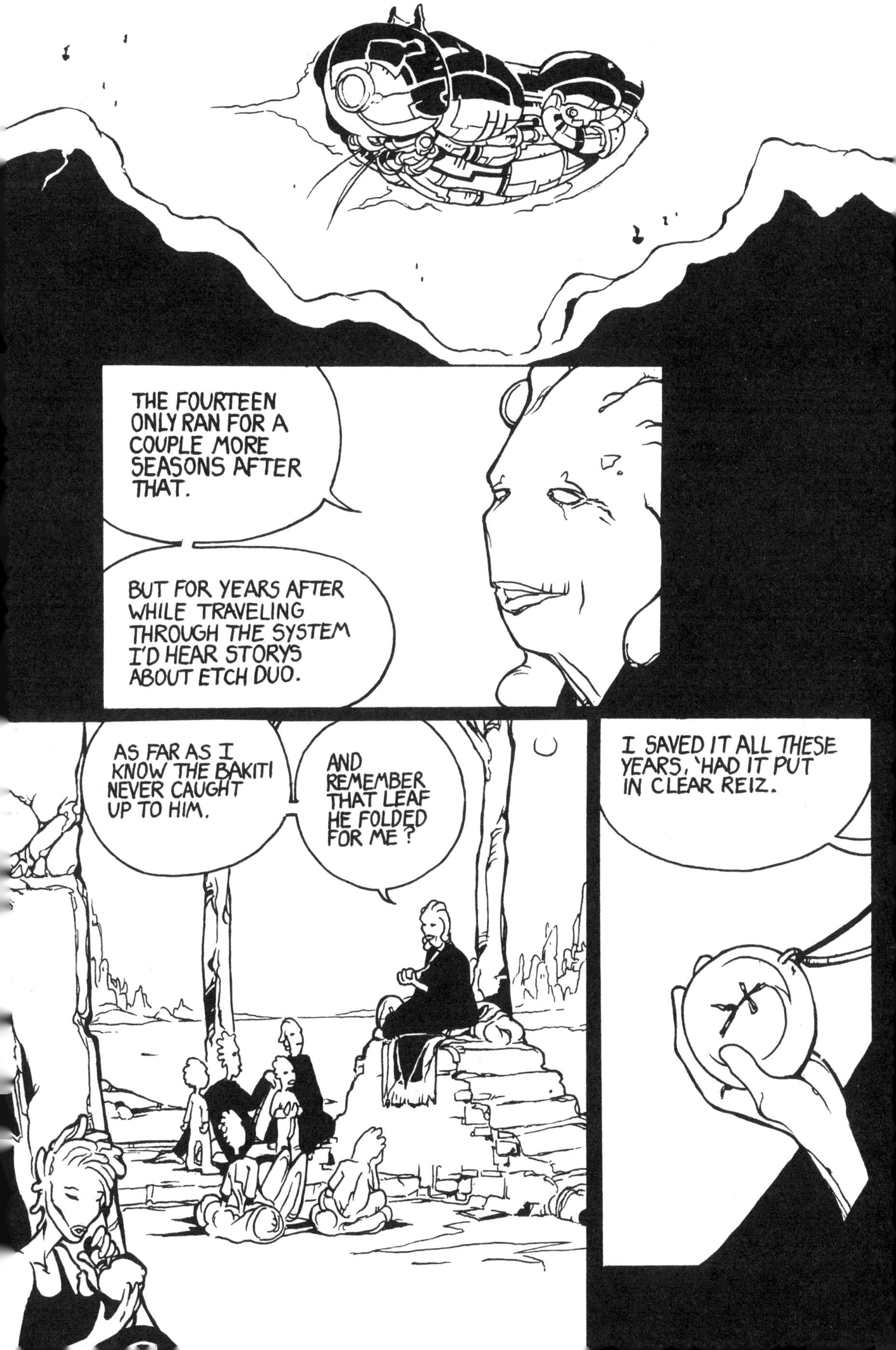
THE FOURTEEN ONLY RAN FOR A COUPLE MORE SEASONS AFTER THAT.
BUT FOR YEARS AFTER WHILE TRAVELING THROUGH THE SYSTEM I'D HEAR STORYS ABOUT ETCH DUO.
AS FAR AS I KNOW THE BAKITI NEVER CAUGHT UP TO HIM.
AND REMEMBER THAT LEAF HE FOLDED FOR ME?
I SAVED IT ALL THESE YEARS, 'HAD IT PUT IN CLEAR REIZ.

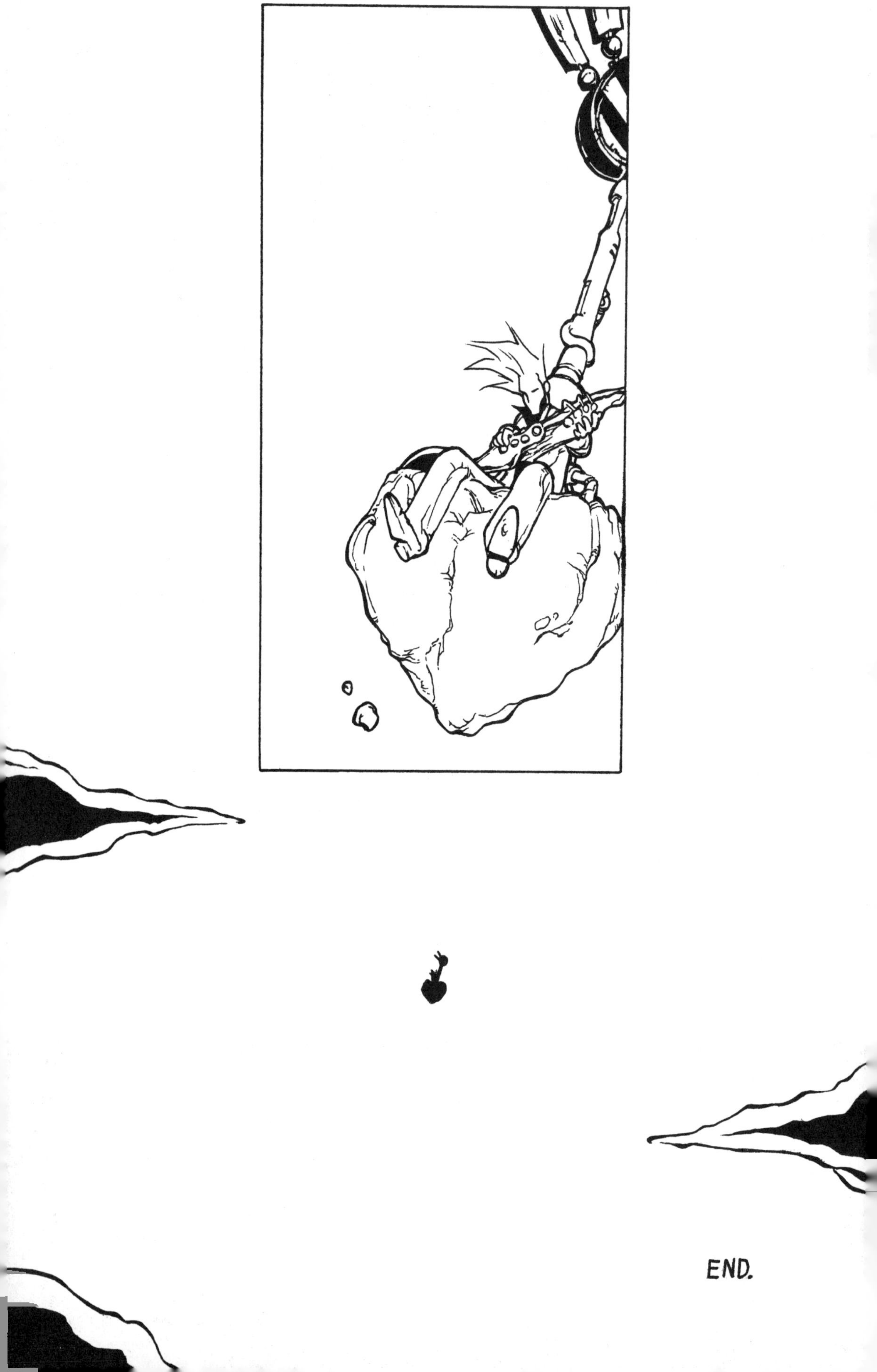
END.

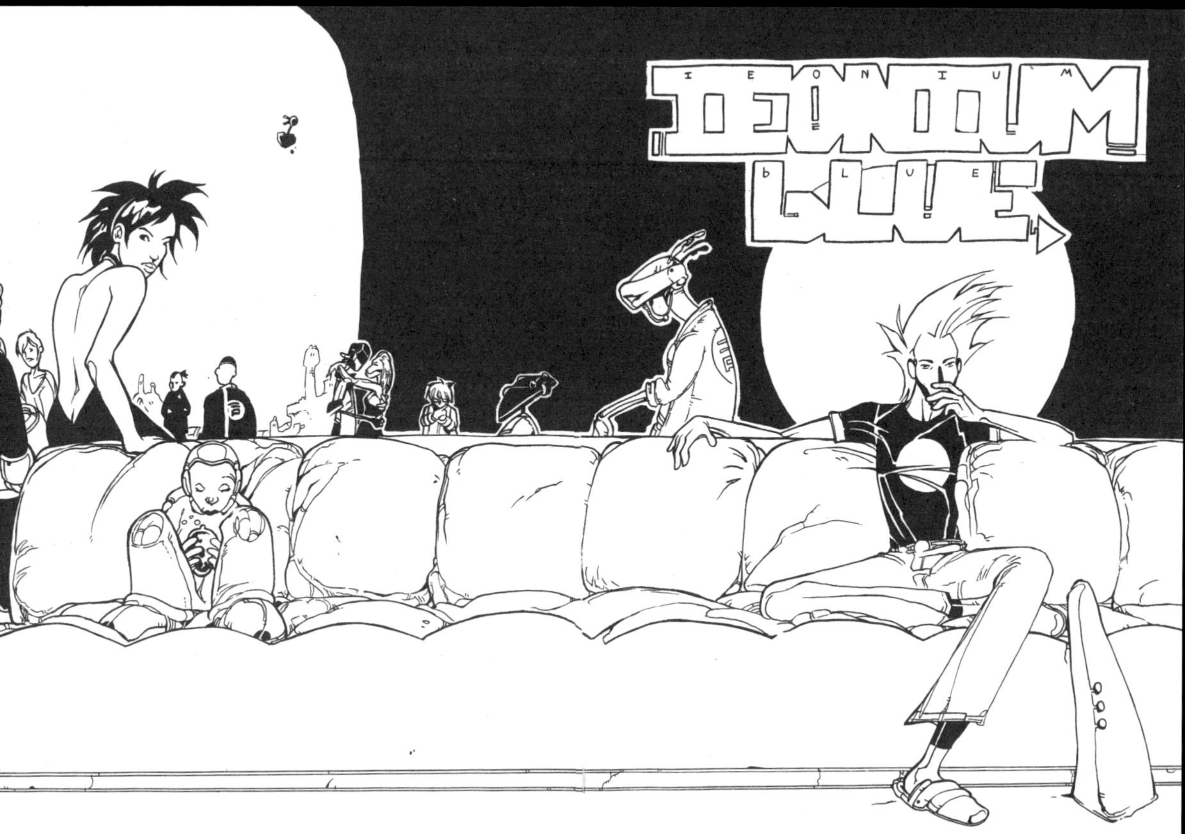
I E O N I U M
b l u e
IEONIUM BLUE

IEONIUM BLUE - I DID THIS IN '97, MOST OF IT WAS DRAWN ON THE BACKS OF 11X17 ADS I'D PULLED OUT OF NEWSPAPER BOXES. FREE PAPER. WHEN IT WAS DONE I MADE A BUNCH OF PHOTOCOPIED BOOKS WITH BROWN PAPER COVERS AND THREW A PARTY TO HAND THEM OUT TO MY FRIENDS. I SCAMMED FREE COPIES, BACK BEFORE KINKOS HAD PRE PAID CARDS YOU COULD PULL THE COPY KEY BEFORE IT COUNTED. WALK OUT WITH A BAG FULL OF BOOKS AFTER PAYING FOR JUST A FEW.

THIS IS OLD ENOUGH THAT IT ALMOST DOESN'T FEEL LIKE I DID IT. I WAS READING A LOT OF BANANA YOSHIMOTO'S WRITING SOME OF THE NARRATION SOUNDS TOO MUCH LIKE HER STUFF. THE NARRATOR WAS SUPPOSED TO BE SEXLESS BUT HE SPEAKS TOO MUCH LIKE A GUY. THERE'S AN OLD CHARACTER OF MINE IN THE CONCERT SCENE. A LIVING MACHINE NAMED BOB FROM A BOOK I DID CALLED "OCTOBER ¥EN."

ELEVATOR - THIS IS THE NEWEST STORY IN THIS BOOK. IT'S A FOLLOW UP TO A PORN COMIC I DID FOR NBM CALLED MULTIPLE WARHEADZ. IN IT THE GIRL, SEXICA SMUGGLES A WEREWOLF'S PENIS THROUGH A SECURITY CHECK AND SEWS IT ONTO HER BOYFRIEND. SO WHEN THEY HAVE SEX HE TURNS INTO A 2 DICKED WEREWOLF.

WHEN I MADE MULTIPLE WARHEADZ NYC WAS IN ITS POST 9-11 TERROR, SO THERE WAS A LOT OF THAT PUT IN. THE GUY WITH THE SWORD IN THE ELEVATOR IS THERE TO PROTECT IT FROM HIJACKERS. I DID THE 2 PAGE SPREAD AFTER READING AN OLD CONAN COMIC WITH A SPREAD OF CONAN FIGHTING SOME POOR SAP IN THE SNOW. "TASTE CIMMERIAN STEEL DOG"!"

I TRIED TO DESIGN THE CHARACTERS WITH STRONG BLACKS AND WHITES. YEARS AGO A GRAFFITI WRITER NAMED JABER TOLD ME THAT IF A DESIGN IS GOOD THEN THE DRAWING DOESN'T HAVE TO CARRY IT AS MUCH. SEXICA'S HAT IS A SKULL CAP THAT MY PAL FILTHY RICH MAKES. THE ELEVATOR OPERATORS' FIELD HAT IS SOMETHING A GUY NAMED ANGEL (I HAD THE HONOR OF WORKING WITH AT MY LAST DAY JOB IN A BOOK STORE.) WOULD WEAR INTO WORK.

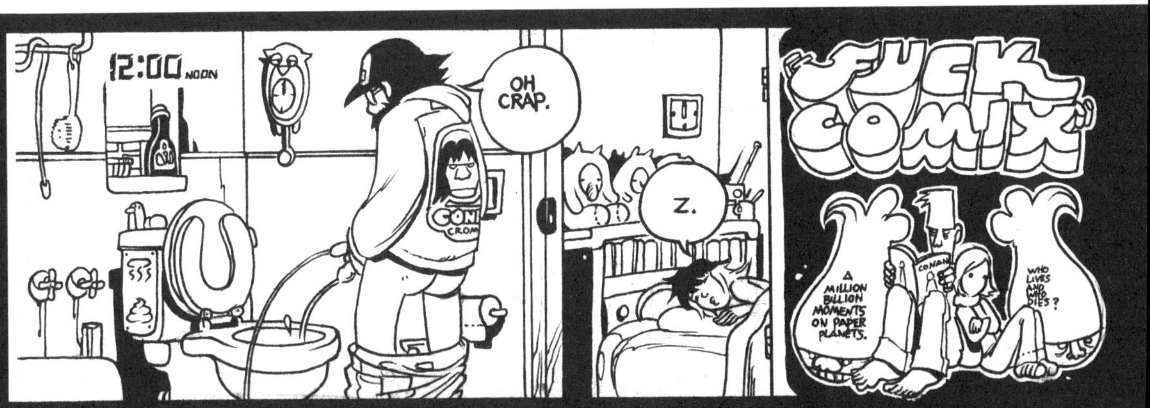
12:00 NOON
OH CRAP.
Z.
FUCK COMIX
CONAN
A MILLION BILLION MOMENTS ON PAPER PLANETS.
WHO LIVES AND WHO DIES?

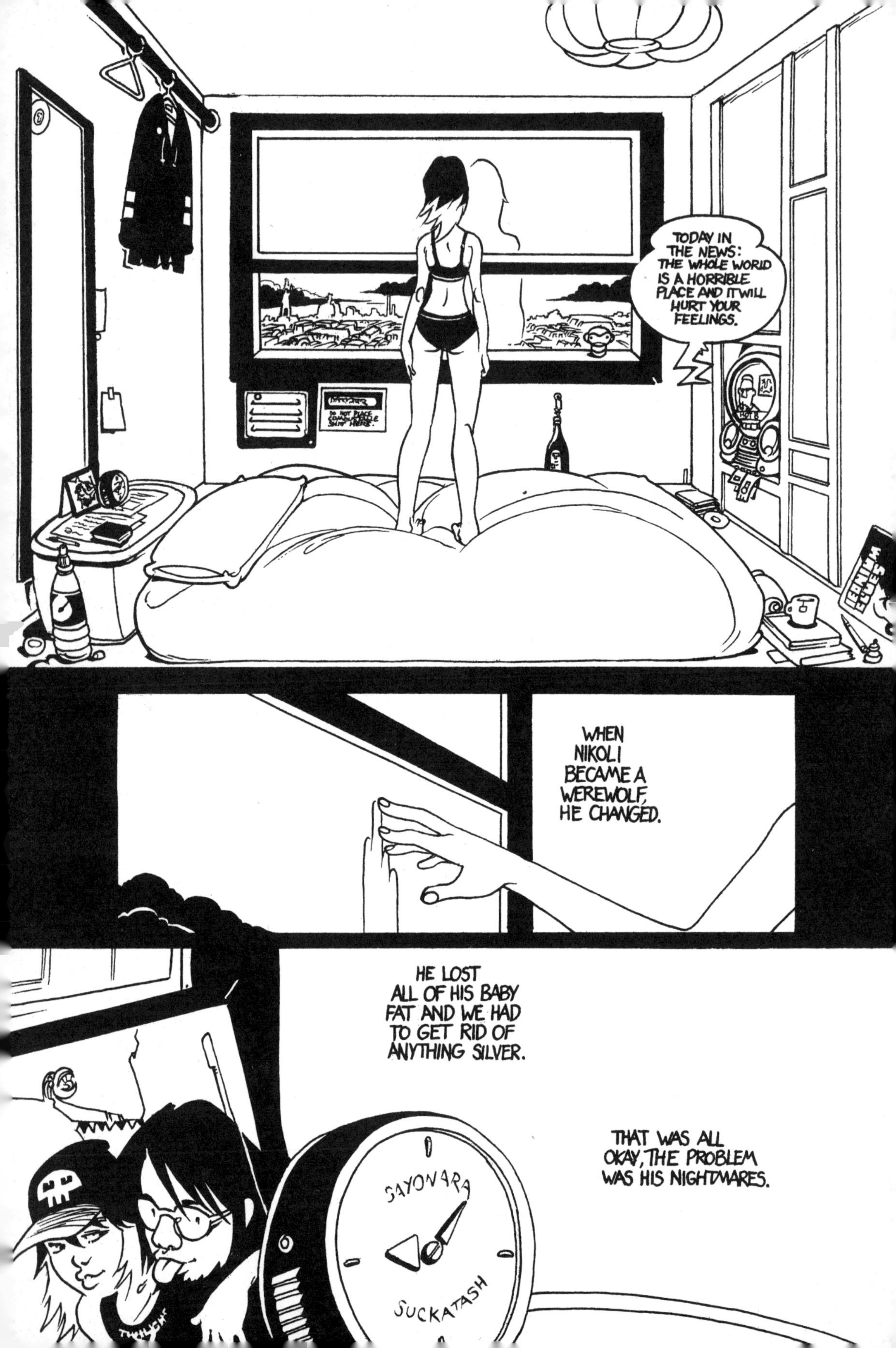
TODAY IN THE NEWS: THE WHOLE WORLD IS A HORRIBLE PLACE AND IT WILL HURT YOUR FEELINGS.
WHEN NIKOLI BECAME A WEREWOLF, HE CHANGED.
HE LOST ALL OF HIS BABY FAT AND WE HAD TO GET RID OF ANYTHING SILVER.
THAT WAS ALL OKAY, THE PROBLEM WAS HIS NIGHTMARES.
SAYONARA
SUCKATASH

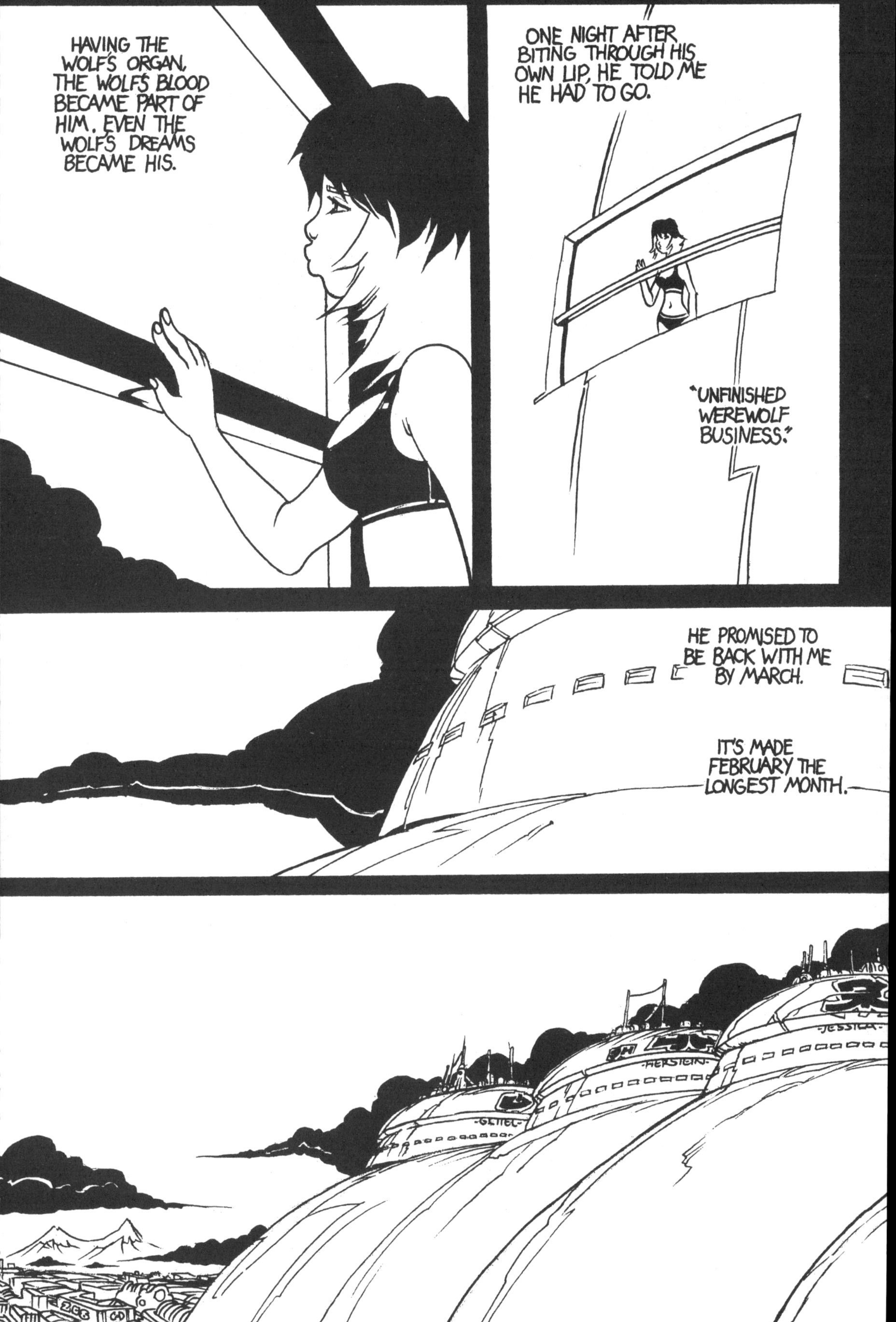
HAVING THE WOLF'S ORGAN, THE WOLF'S BLOOD BECAME PART OF HIM. EVEN THE WOLF'S DREAMS BECAME HIS.
ONE NIGHT AFTER BITING THROUGH HIS OWN LIP, HE TOLD ME HE HAD TO GO.
"UNFINISHED WEREWOLF BUSINESS."
HE PROMISED TO BE BACK WITH ME BY MARCH.
IT'S MADE FEBRUARY THE LONGEST MONTH.
-HERSTEIN-
-JESSICA-

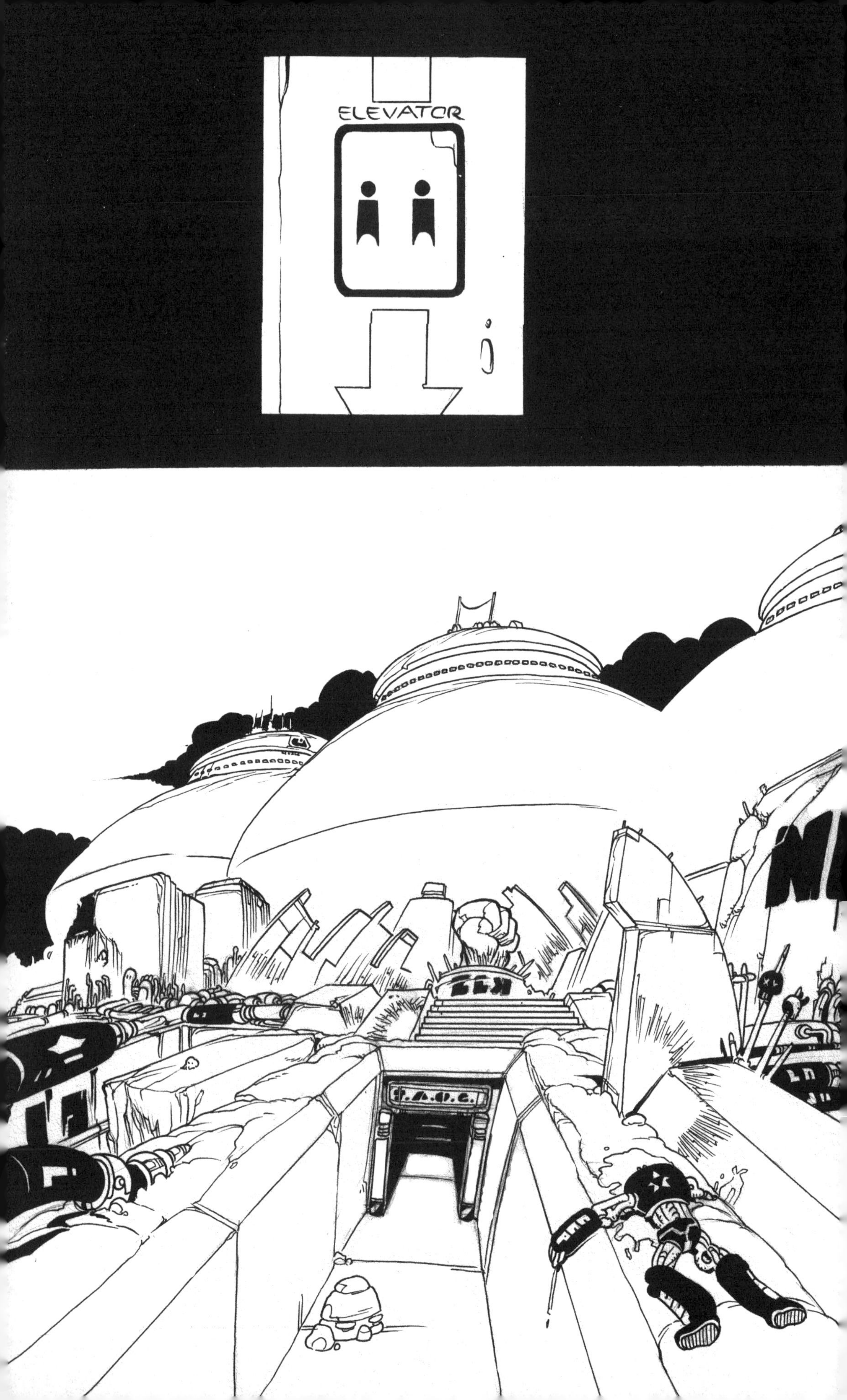
ELEVATOR

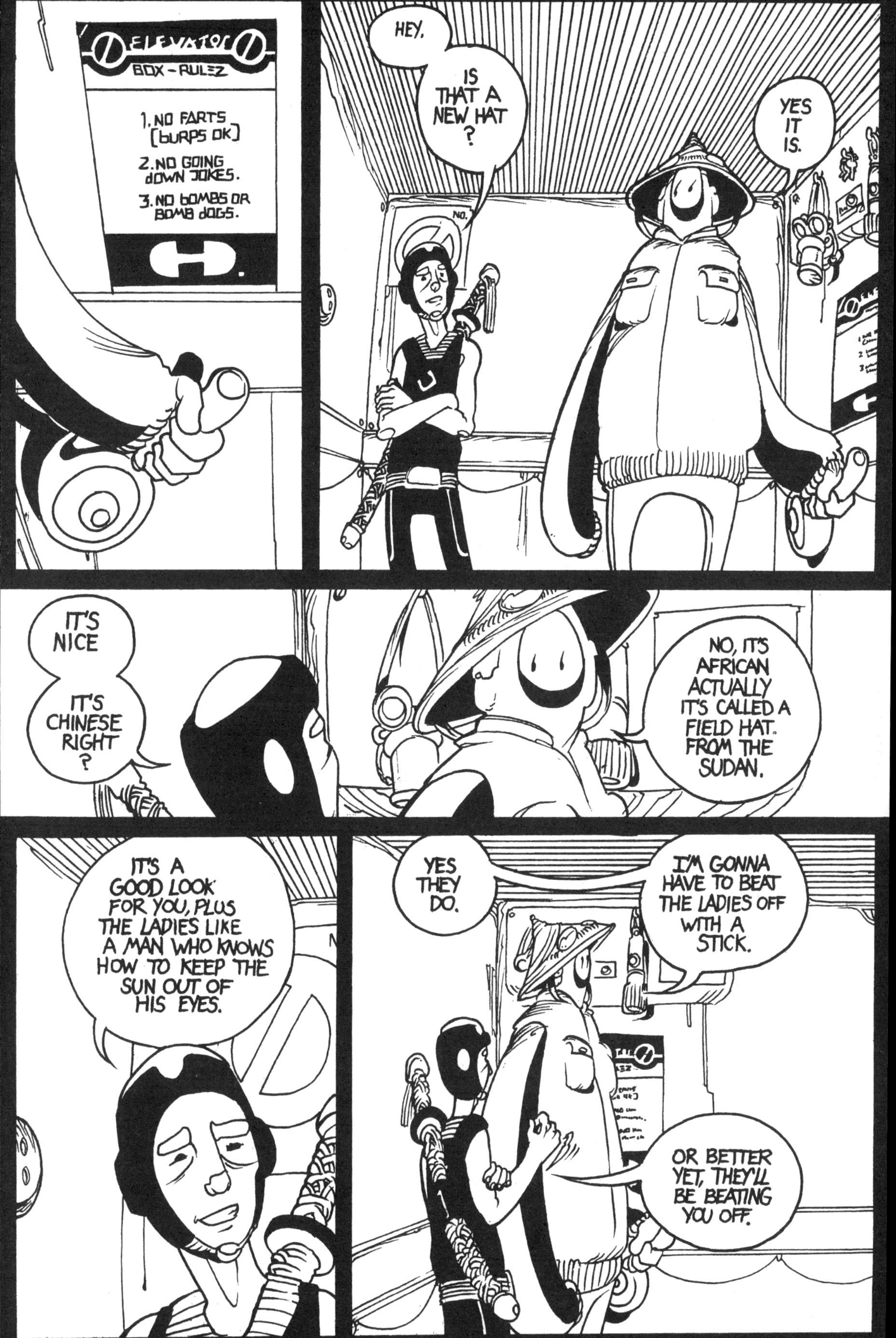
ELEVATOR
BOX-RULEZ
1. NO FARTS [BURPS OK]
2. NO GOING DOWN JOKES.
3. NO BOMBS OR BOMB DOGS.
HEY.
IS THAT A NEW HAT ?
YES IT IS.
NO.
IT'S NICE
IT'S CHINESE RIGHT ?
NO, IT'S AFRICAN ACTUALLY IT'S CALLED A FIELD HAT. FROM THE SUDAN.
IT'S A GOOD LOOK FOR YOU, PLUS THE LADIES LIKE A MAN WHO KNOWS HOW TO KEEP THE SUN OUT OF HIS EYES.
YES THEY DO.
I'M GONNA HAVE TO BEAT THE LADIES OFF WITH A STICK.
OR BETTER YET, THEY'LL BE BEATING YOU OFF.

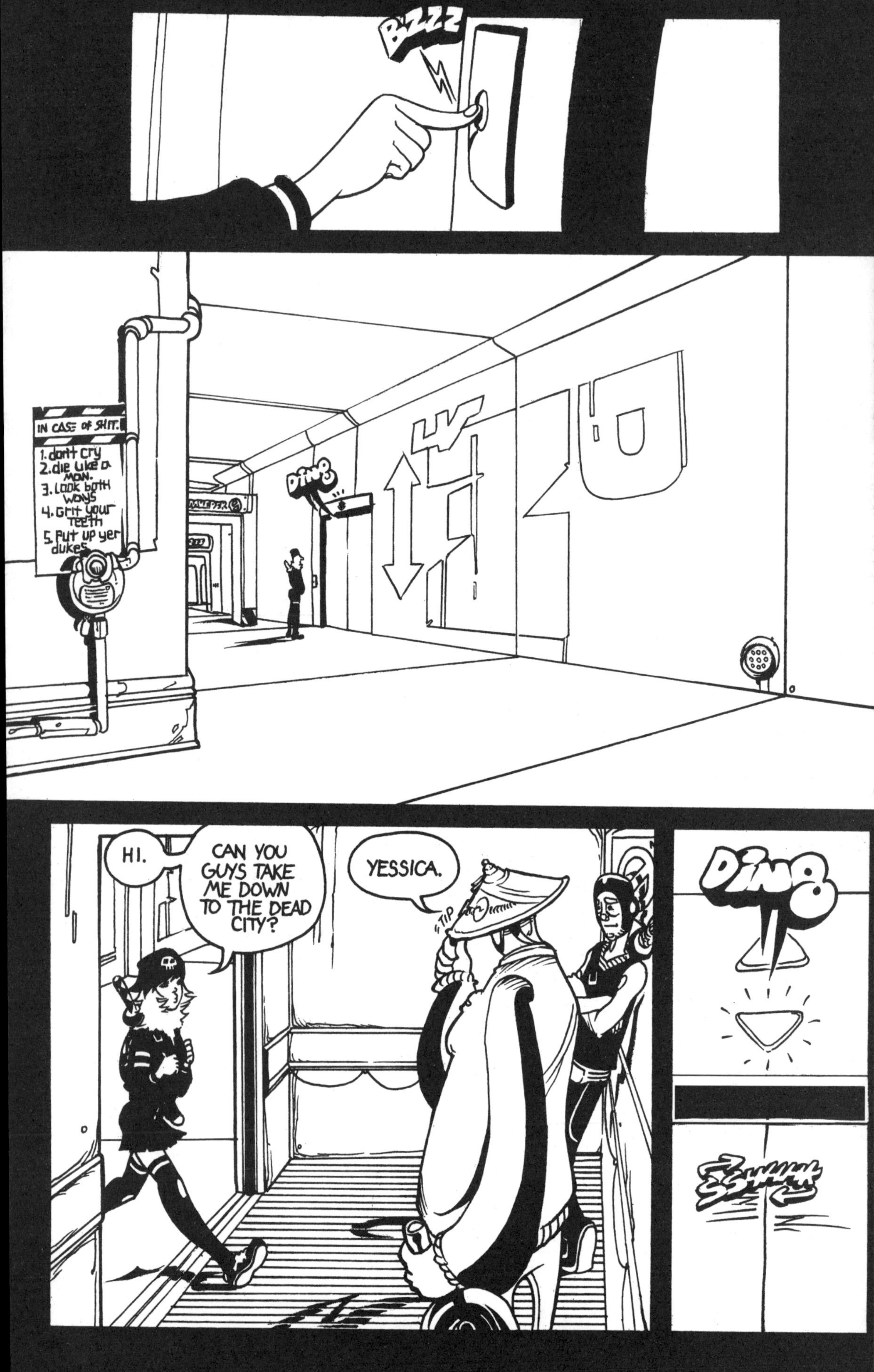
BZZZ
IN CASE OF SHIT.
1. dont cry
2. die like a man.
3. look both ways
4. Grit your teeth
5. Put up yer dukes
Ding
HI.
CAN YOU GUYS TAKE ME DOWN TO THE DEAD CITY?
YESSICA.
TIP
Ding

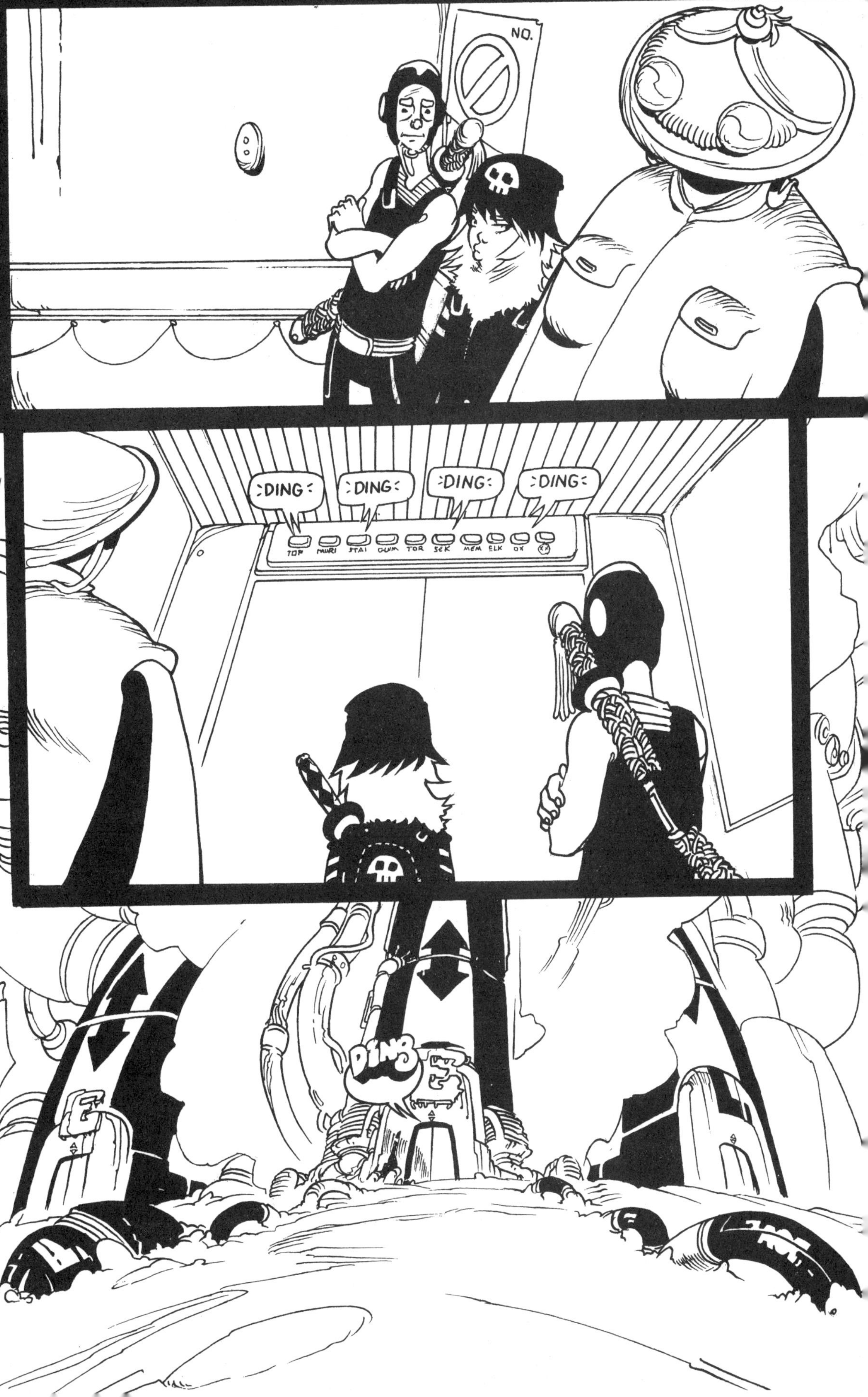
NO.
DING
DING
DING
DING
TOP
MURI
STAI
GUM
TOR
SEK
MEM
ELK
OX
DING

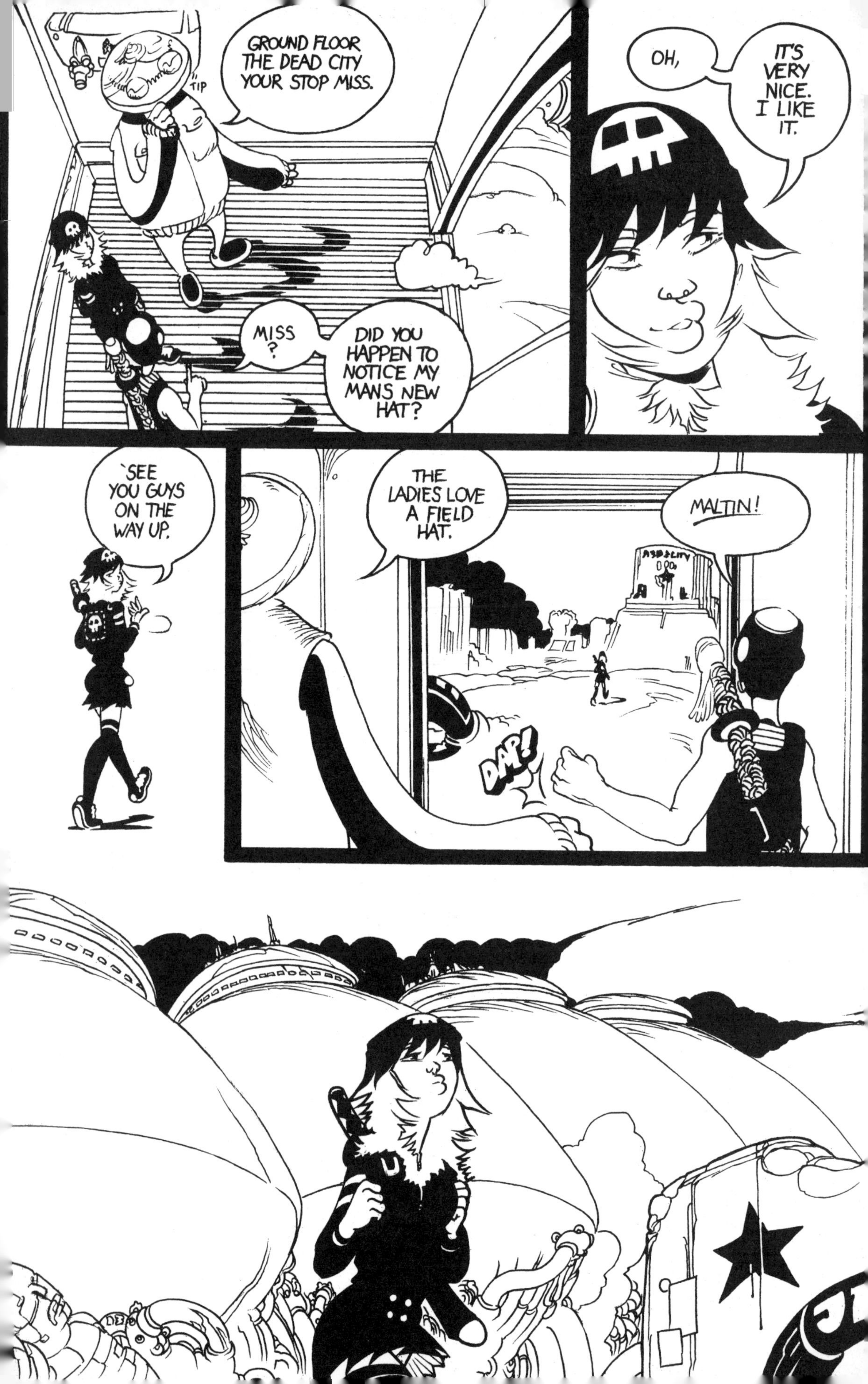
GROUND FLOOR THE DEAD CITY YOUR STOP MISS.
TIP
MISS ?
DID YOU HAPPEN TO NOTICE MY MANS NEW HAT?
OH,
IT'S VERY NICE. I LIKE IT.
`SEE YOU GUYS ON THE WAY UP.
THE LADIES LOVE A FIELD HAT.
MALTIN!
DAP!

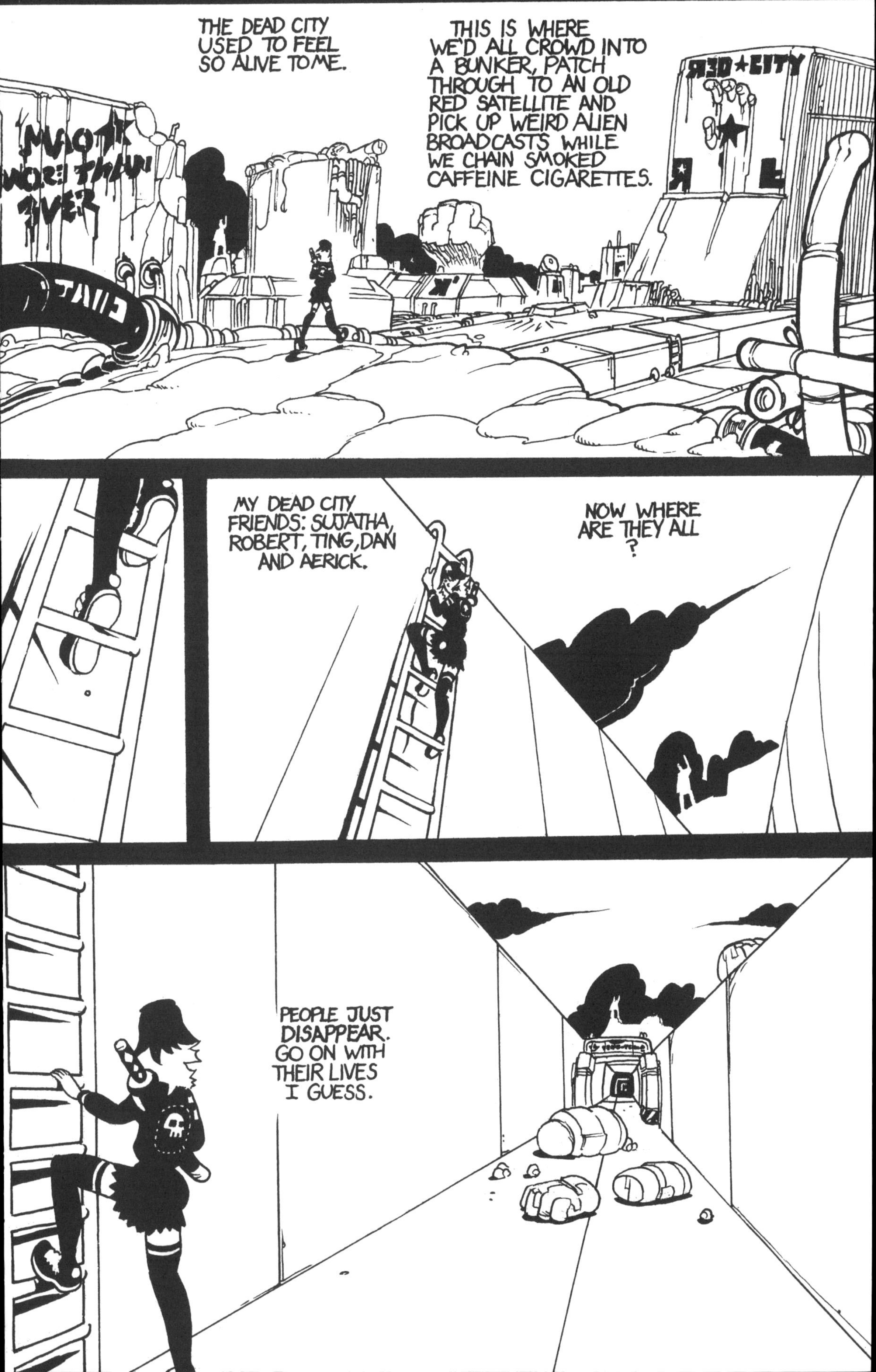
THE DEAD CITY USED TO FEEL SO ALIVE TO ME.
THIS IS WHERE WE'D ALL CROWD INTO A BUNKER, PATCH THROUGH TO AN OLD RED SATELLITE AND PICK UP WEIRD ALIEN BROADCASTS WHILE WE CHAIN SMOKED CAFFEINE CIGARETTES.
MY DEAD CITY FRIENDS: SUJATHA, ROBERT, TING, DAN AND AERICK.
NOW WHERE ARE THEY ALL ?
PEOPLE JUST DISAPPEAR. GO ON WITH THEIR LIVES I GUESS.

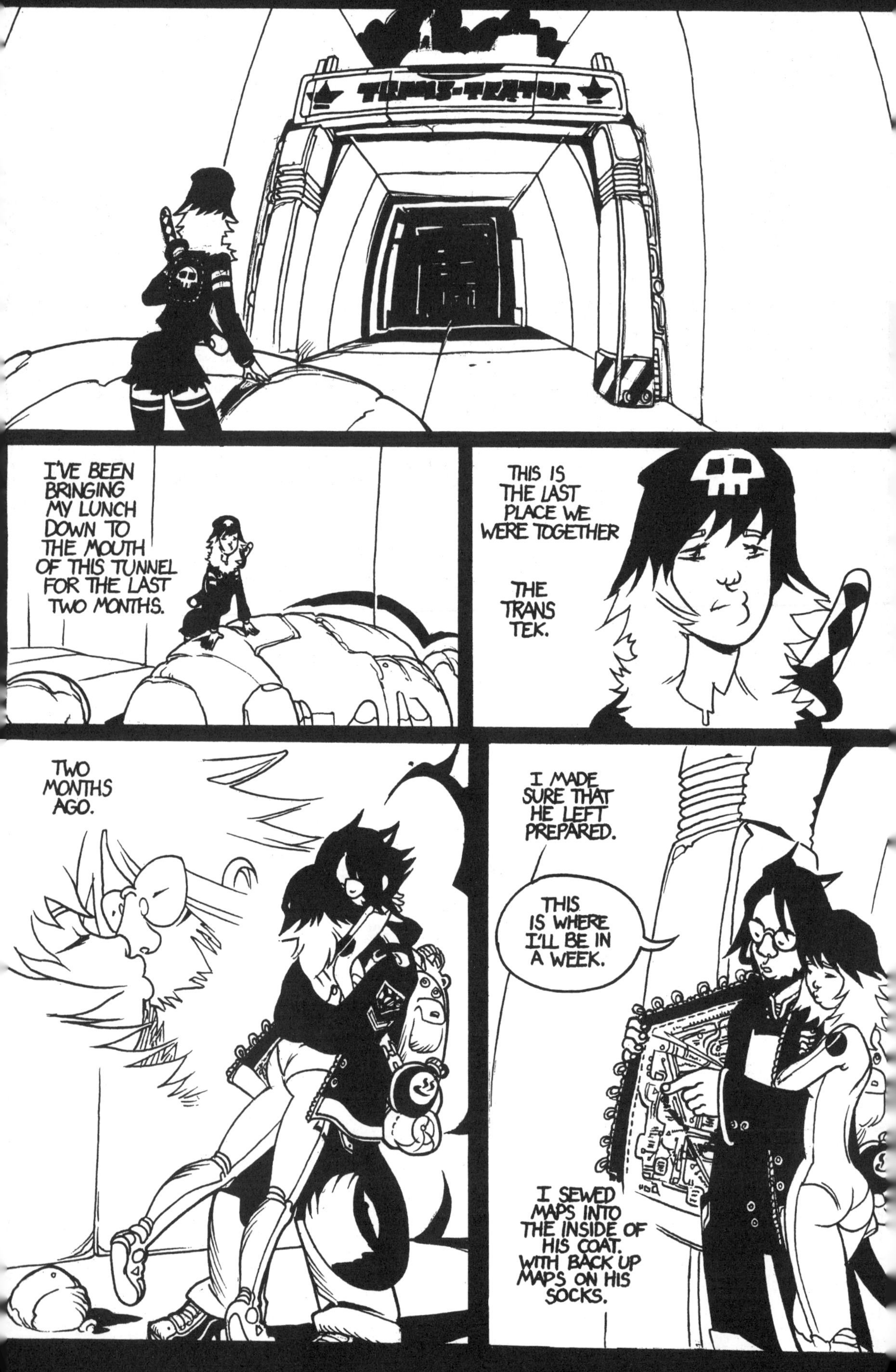
I'VE BEEN BRINGING MY LUNCH DOWN TO THE MOUTH OF THIS TUNNEL FOR THE LAST TWO MONTHS.
THIS IS THE LAST PLACE WE WERE TOGETHER
THE TRANS TEK.
TWO MONTHS AGO.
I MADE SURE THAT HE LEFT PREPARED.
THIS IS WHERE I'LL BE IN A WEEK.
I SEWED MAPS INTO THE INSIDE OF HIS COAT. WITH BACK UP MAPS ON HIS SOCKS.

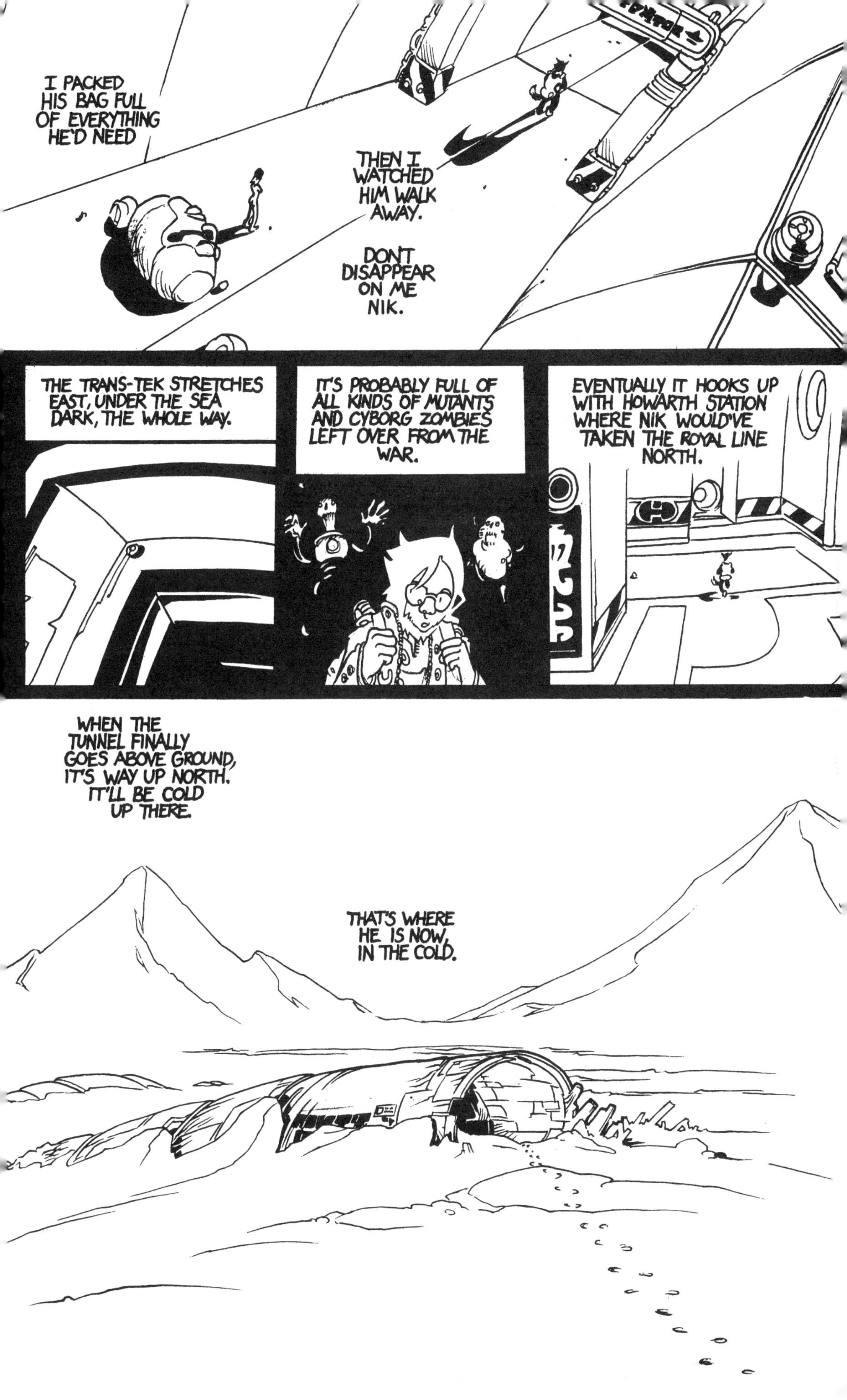

I PACKED HIS BAG FULL OF EVERYTHING HE'D NEED
THEN I WATCHED HIM WALK AWAY.
DON'T DISAPPEAR ON ME NIK.
THE TRANS-TEK STRETCHES EAST, UNDER THE SEA DARK, THE WHOLE WAY.
IT'S PROBABLY FULL OF ALL KINDS OF MUTANTS AND CYBORG ZOMBIES LEFT OVER FROM THE WAR.
EVENTUALLY IT HOOKS UP WITH HOWARTH STATION WHERE NIK WOULD'VE TAKEN THE ROYAL LINE NORTH.
WHEN THE TUNNEL FINALLY GOES ABOVE GROUND, IT'S WAY UP NORTH. IT'LL BE COLD UP THERE.
THAT'S WHERE HE IS NOW, IN THE COLD.

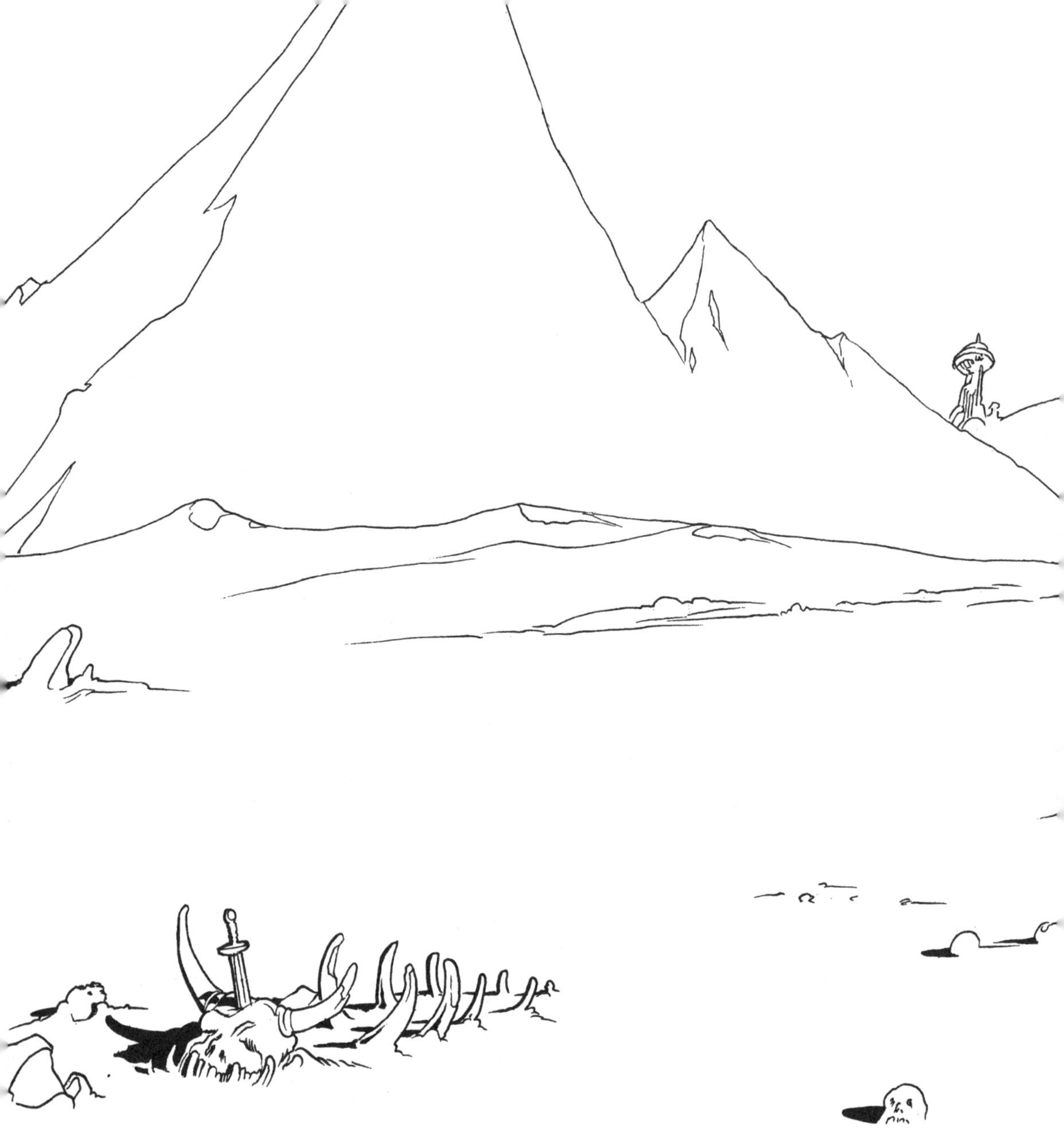

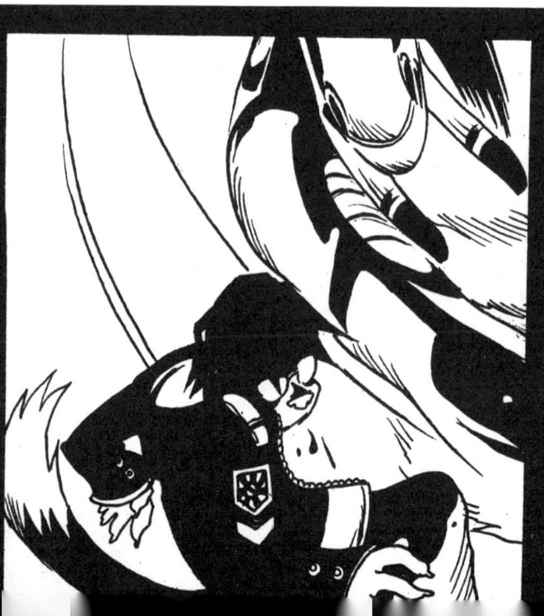

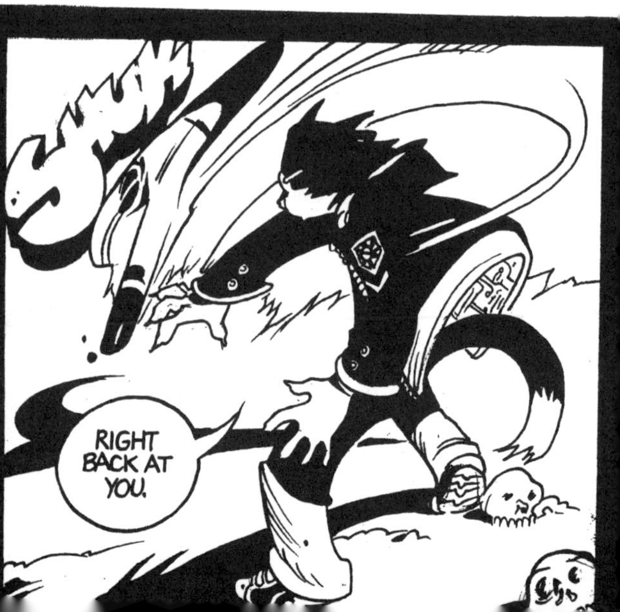
RIGHT BACK AT YOU.

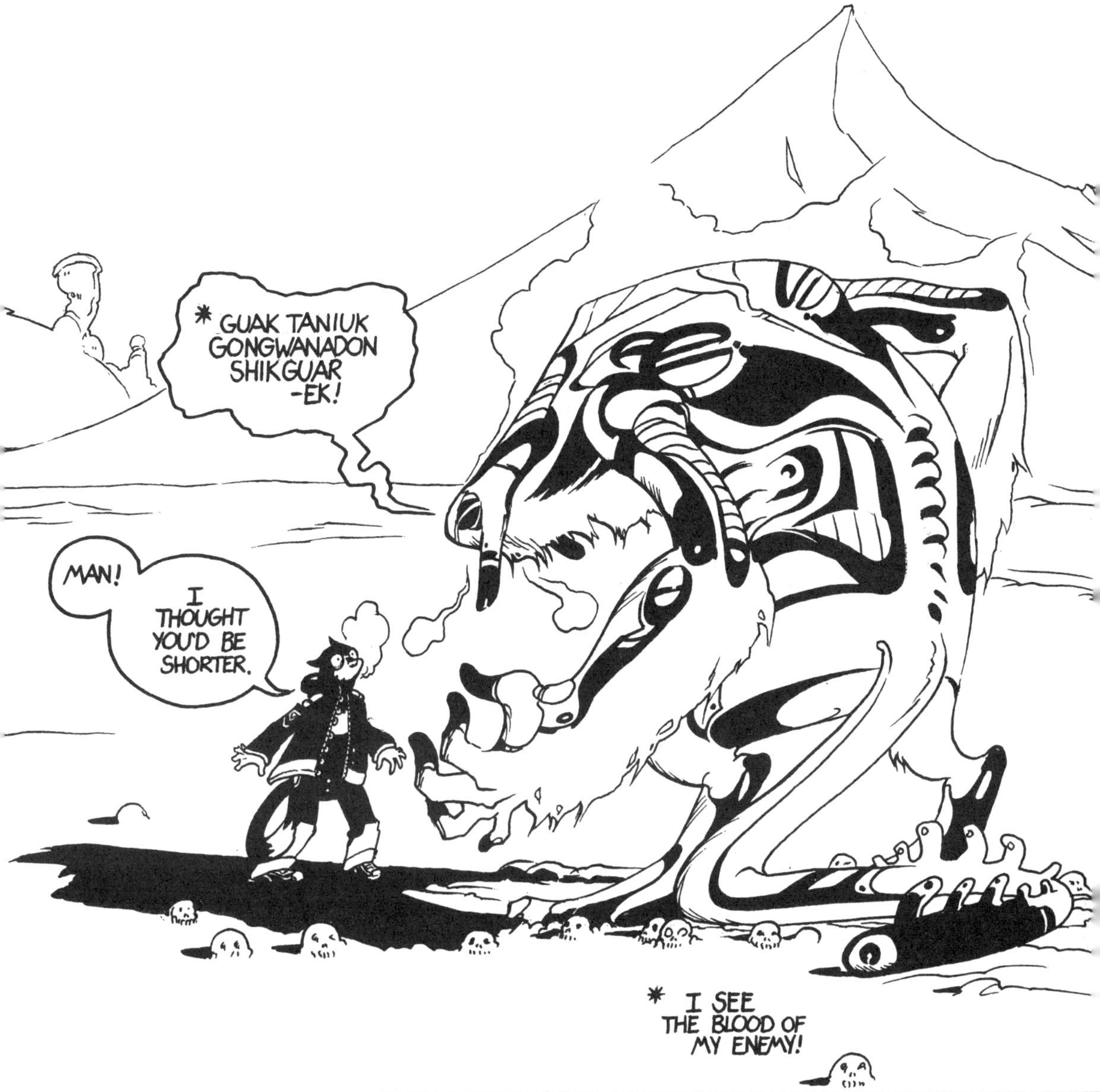
* GUAK TANIUK GONGWANADON SHIKGUAR -EK!
MAN! I THOUGHT YOU'D BE SHORTER.
* I SEE THE BLOOD OF MY ENEMY!

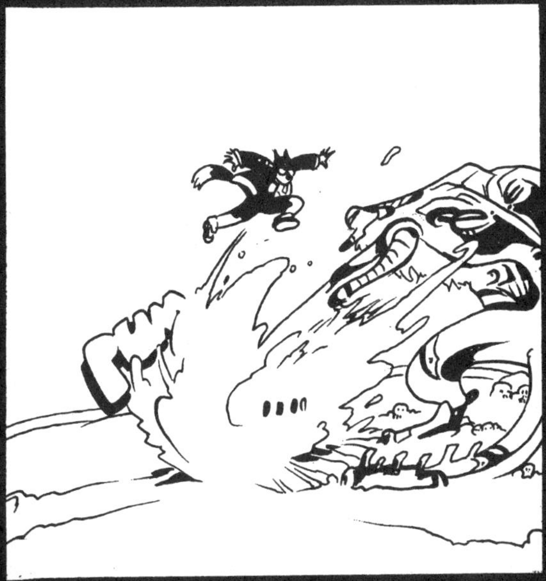

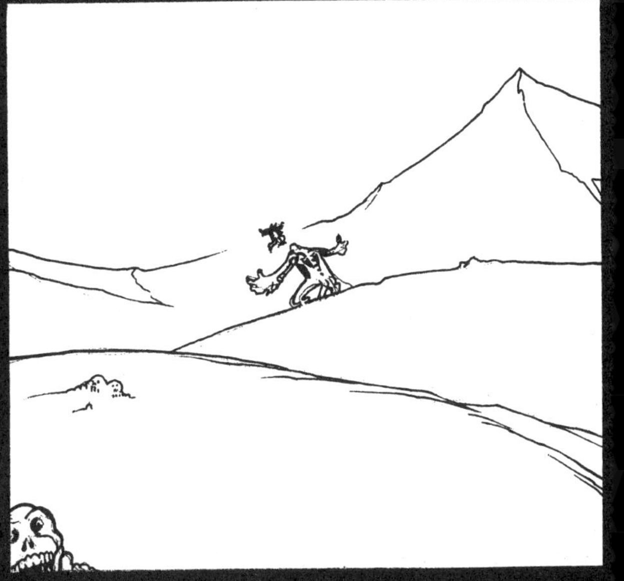

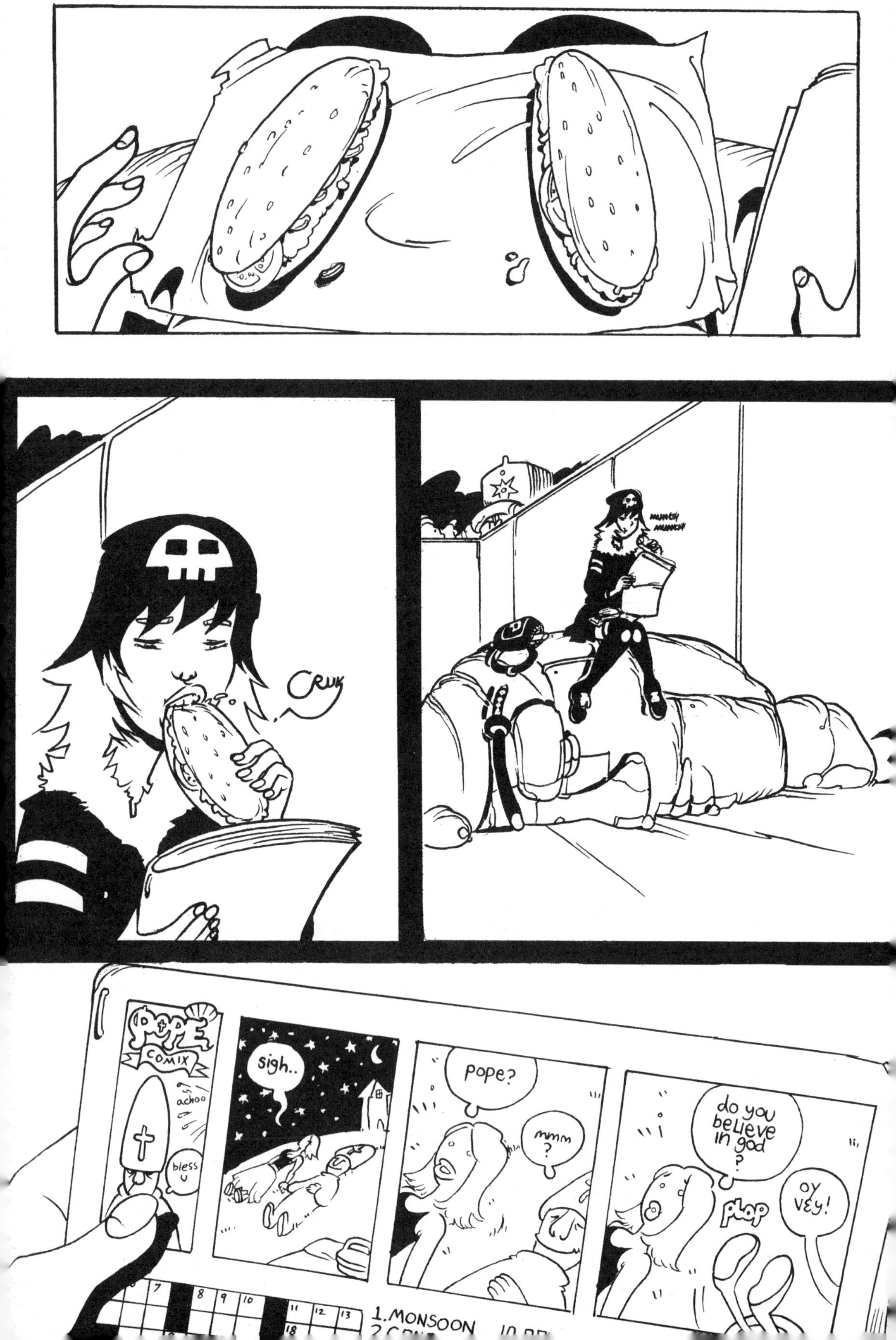
CRUK
POPE
COMIX
achoo
bless u
sigh..
pope?
mmm ?
do you believe in god ?
plop
oy vey!
1. MONSOON

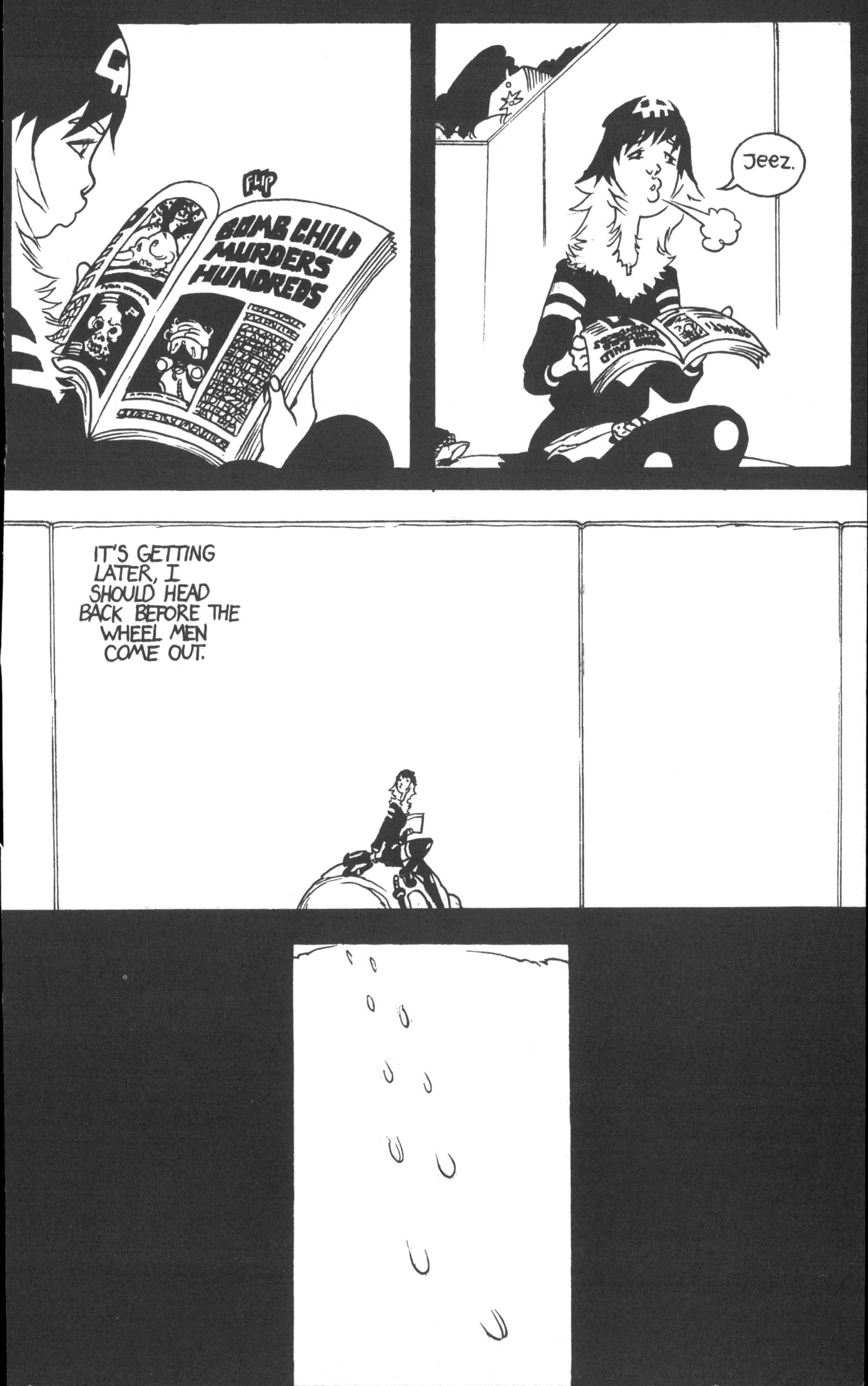
FLIP
BOMB CHILD MURDERS HUNDREDS
Jeez.
IT'S GETTING LATER, I SHOULD HEAD BACK BEFORE THE WHEEL MEN COME OUT.

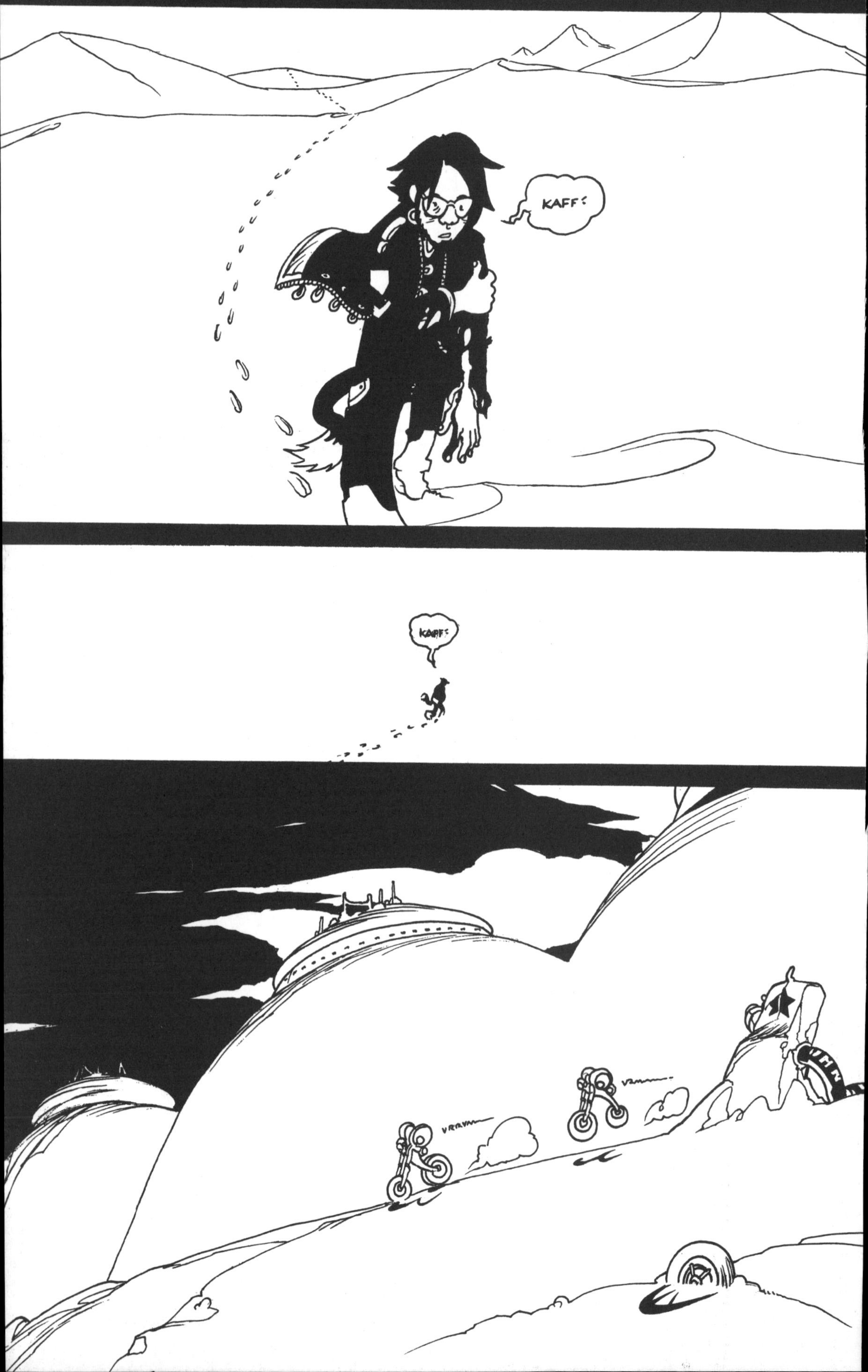
KAFF:
KAFF:
VRRVM

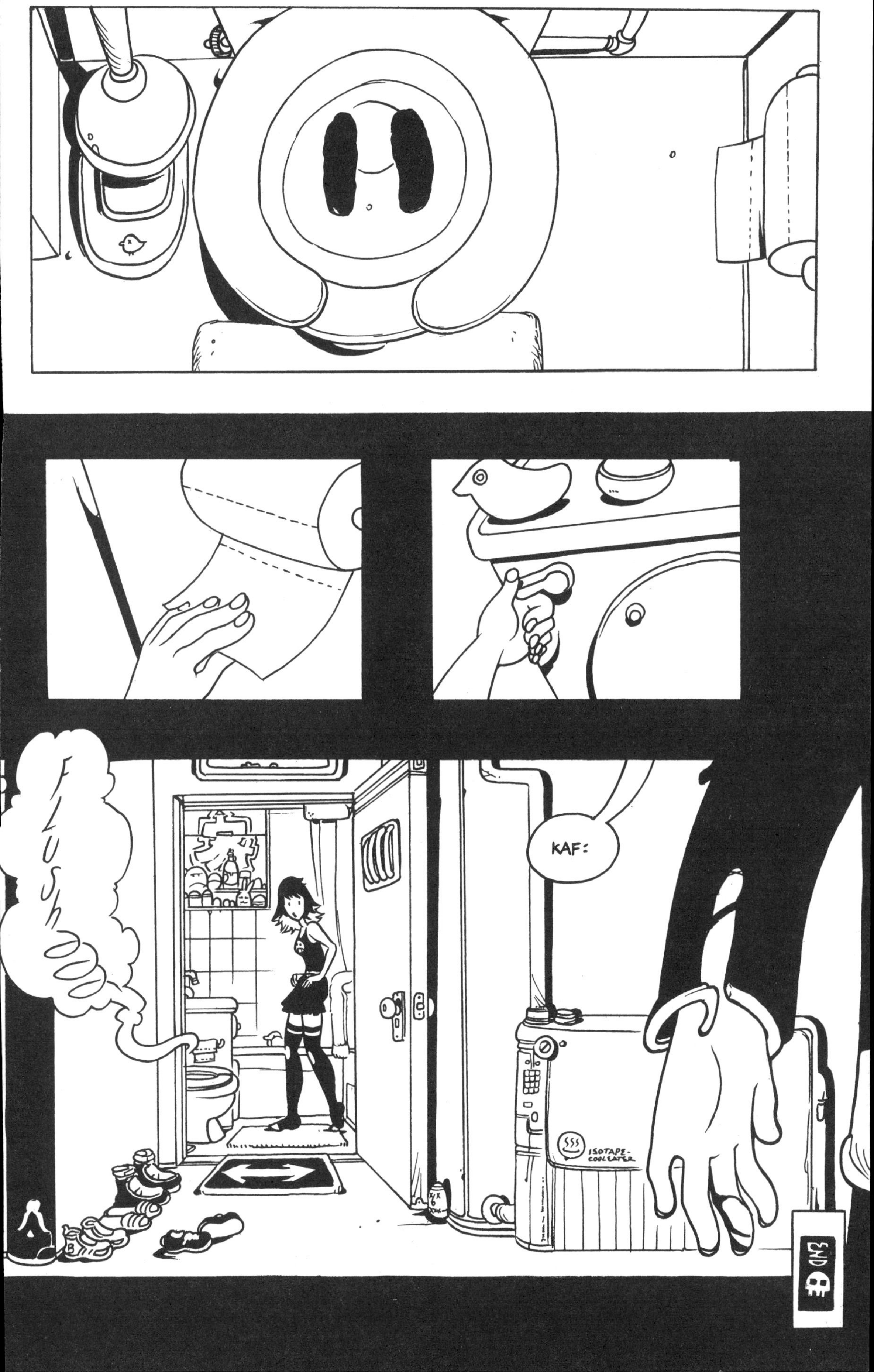
FLUSHOOO
KAF:
ISOTAPE-COOLEATER
END

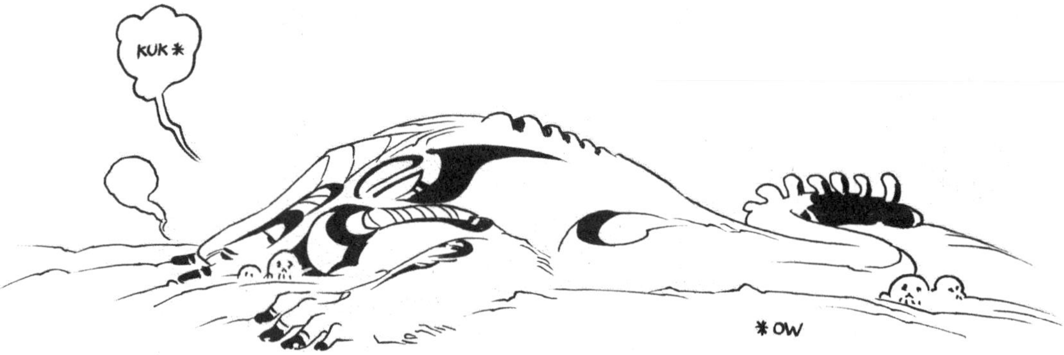
KUK *
* OW

I WANT TO THANK THE PEOPLE WHO HELPED AND INSPIRED ME TO PUT THIS BOOK TOGETHER.

JESSICA HERSTEIN-WHO MADE ME DO PUSH UPS TO GET HER NUMBER AND PUT UP WITH HUGE AMOUNTS OF MY CRAP JUST BECAUSE SHE LIKED MY NOSE.

TOM HERPICH-I SCANNED THE GUTS TO THIS AT HIS HOUSE. IT WOULD'VE BEEN IMPOSSIBLE TO PUT THIS TOGETHER WITHOUT HIS HELP. IT'S AN HONOR TO DRAW WHERE HE DRAWS.

DAVID LINDER-FOR HIS INTRODUCTION. HIS WORK HAS INSPIRED ME LIKE NOTHING ELSE. "-WHEN DID YOU GET SO MUCH OLDER THAN ME?"

FILTHY RICH MILLER-I COLORED THE COVERS ON HIS COMPUTER. WHEN ZOMBIES TAKE OVER I KNOW WHO'S GOT MY BACK.

TOMER HANUKA-HIS OPINION HAS MEANT SO MUCH TO ME, HIS DEADPAN HONESTY AND HIS SUPPORT.

JEFF MASON-FOR FUNDING AND PUSHING THIS BOOK, AND FOR PUTTING OUT A LINE OF COMICS I'M THRILLED TO BE AMONG.

ALSO THANKS TO MY BIG BROTHER KEITH, MY MOM, MY DAD, FAREL DALRYMPLE, CHRIS McD, MATT HOWARTH AND THE REST OF MY FRIENDS AND FAMILY, THANK YEW.

AS I WRITE THIS IT'S 4 IN THE MORNING IN MY TINY ROOM IN QUEENS. MY BED IS COVERED WITH DRAWINGS, PENS AND COMICS. I TURNED OFF THE RADIO SO I COULD THINK TO WRITE, NOW I CAN HEAR THE TRUCKS PASS OUT-SIDE. I REALLY DO LOVE MAKING THESE COMICS. I DON'T EVER WANT TO SLEEP.

BRANDON.

ROYALBOILER@HOTMAIL.COM
WWW.BROTHERSGRAHAM.COM

MW00805379

ARTIFACTS™

volume **2**

published by
Top Cow Productions, Inc.
Los Angeles

ARTIFACTS™

volume 2

For this edition Cover Art by:
Phil Noto

For this edition
Book Design and Layout by:
**Phil Smith &
Vincent Kukua**

Original editions edited by:
Filip Sablik & Phil Smith

Special Thanks to:
Marc Silvestri & Matt Hawkins

COMIC SHOP LOCATOR SERVICE
888-COMIC-BOOK
888-266-4226

to find the comic shop nearest
you call:
1-888-COMICBOOK

for Top Cow Productions Inc.
Marc Silvestri - CEO
Matt Hawkins - COO
Filip Sablik - Publisher
Bryan Rountree - Assistant to Publisher
Elena Salcedo - Sales Assistant
Betsy Gonia - Interns

Want more info? check out:
www.topcow.com
for news and exclusive Top Cow
merchandise!

IMAGE COMICS, INC

Robert Kirkman - chief operating officer
Erik Larsen - chief financial officer
Todd McFarlane - president
Marc Silvestri - chief executive officer
Jim Valentino - vice-president

Eric Stephenson - publisher
Todd Martinez - sales & licensing coordinator
Sarah deLaine - pr & marketing coordinator
Branwyn Bigglestone - accounts manager
Emily Miller - administrative assistant
Jamie Parreno - marketing assistant
Kevin Yuen - digital rights coordinator
Tyler Shainline - production manager
Drew Gill - art director
Jonathan Chan - senior production artist
Monica Garcia - production artist
Vincent Kukua - production artist
Jana Cook - production artist

www.imagecomics.com

ARTIFACTS Volume 2 Trade Paperback
AUGUST 2011. FIRST PRINTING. ISBN: 978-1-60706-211-0, $14.99 U.S.D..
Published by Image Comics Inc. Office of Publication: 2134 Allston Way, 2nd Floor Berkeley, CA 94704. Originally published in single magazine form as ARTIFACTS 5-8. ARTIFA
© 2011 Top Cow Productions, Inc. All rights reserved. "ARTIFACTS," the ARTIFACTS logos, and the likeness of all characters (human or otherwise) featured herein are regist
trademarks of Top Cow Productions, Inc. Image Comics and the Image Comics logo are trademarks of Image Comics, Inc. The characters, events, and stories in this publication
entirely fictional. Any resemblance to actual persons (living or dead), events, institutions, or locales, without satiric intent, is coincidental. No portion of this publication ma
reproduced or transmitted, in any form or by any means, without the express written permission of Top Cow Productions, Inc. PRINTED IN THE U.S.A. For information regarding
CPSIA on this printed material call: 203-595-3636 and provide reference # EAST – 381920

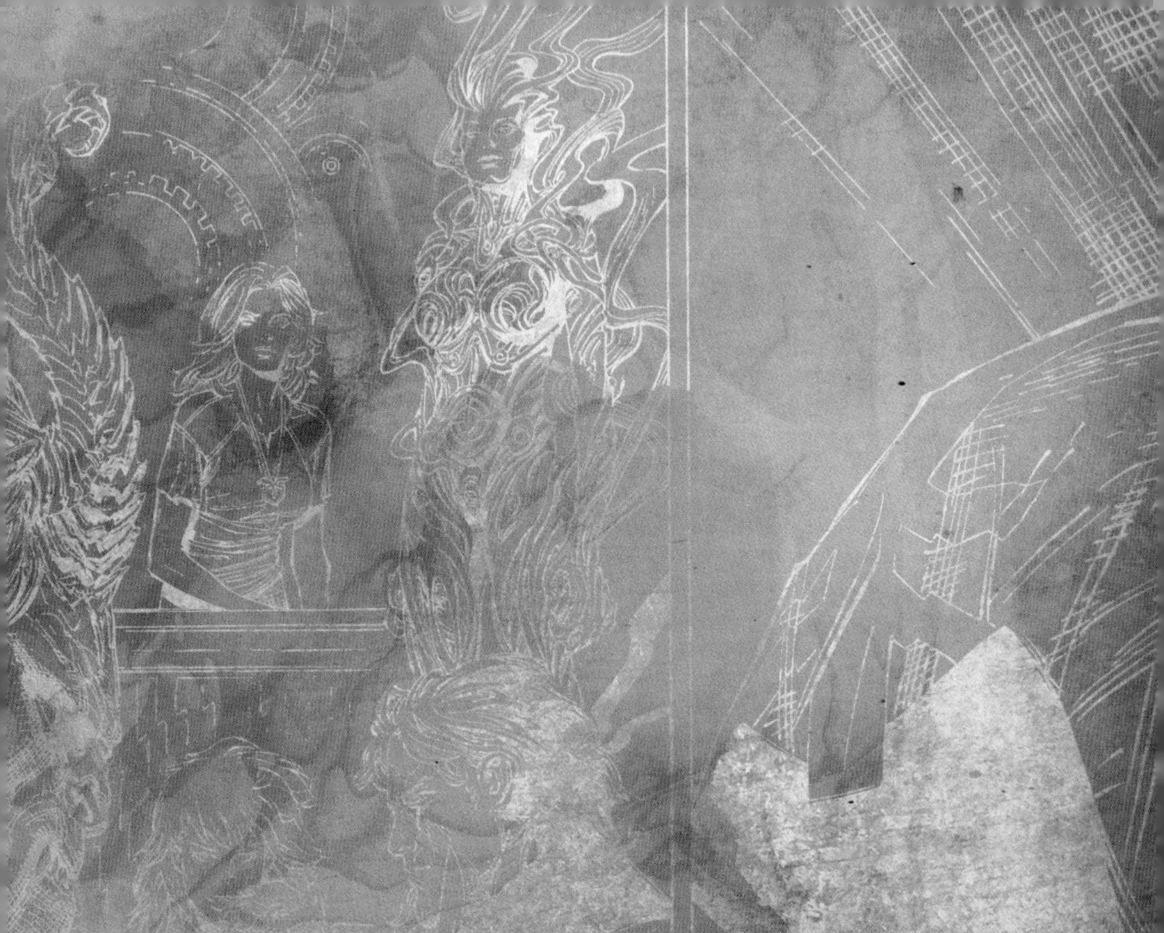

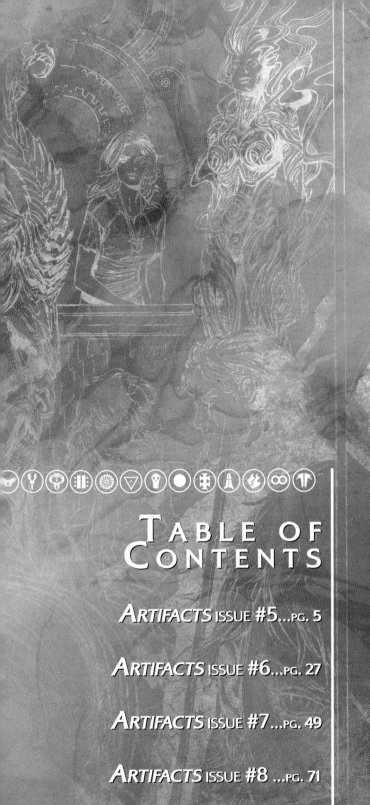

Table of Contents

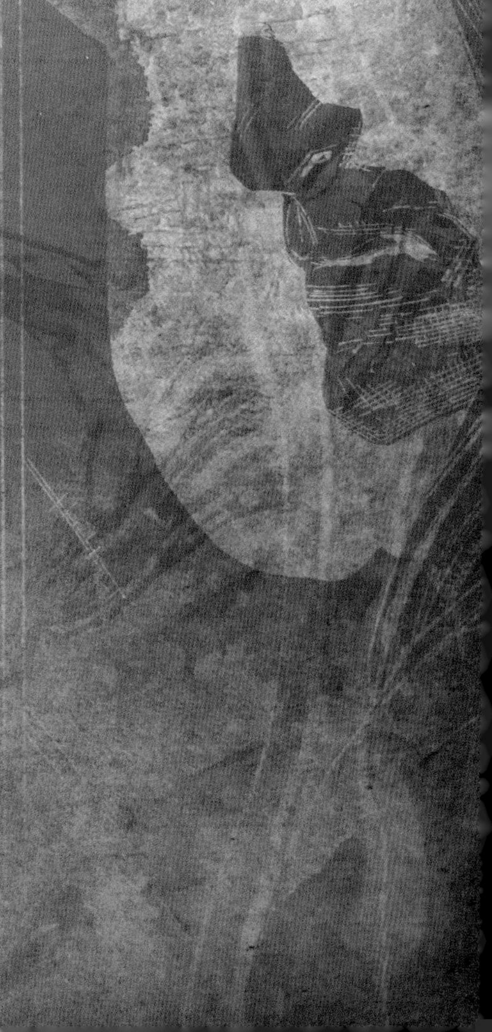

CREDITS

ARTIFACTS, ISSUE 5
WRITTEN BY: RON MARZ
PENCILS BY: WHILCE PORTACIO
INKS BY: JOE WEEMS & MARCO GALLI
INK ASSISTS BY: JARED LIFFREING
COLORS BY: SUNNY GHO & ARIF PRIANTO OF IFS
LETTERS BY: TROY PETERI

ARTIFACTS, ISSUE 6
WRITTEN BY: RON MARZ
PENCILS BY: WHILCE PORTACIO
INKS BY: JOE WEEMS
INK ASSISTS BY: TEAM WEEMS – MARCO GALLI,
JARED LIFFREING & RYAN WINN
COLORS BY: SUNNY GHO OF IFS
LETTERS BY: TROY PETERI

ARTIFACTS, ISSUE 7
WRITTEN BY: RON MARZ
PENCILS BY: WHILCE PORTACIO
INKS BY: JOE WEEMS
INK ASSISTS BY: MARCO GALLI & MIKE ODLE
COLORS BY: SUNNY GHO OF IFS
LETTERS BY: TROY PETERI

ARTIFACTS, ISSUE 8
WRITTEN BY: RON MARZ
PENCILS BY: WHILCE PORTACIO
INKS BY: JOE WEEMS
INK ASSISTS BY: MARCO GALLI & MIKE ODLE
COLORS BY: SUNNY GHO OF IFS
LETTERS BY: TROY PETERI

CHAPTER 5

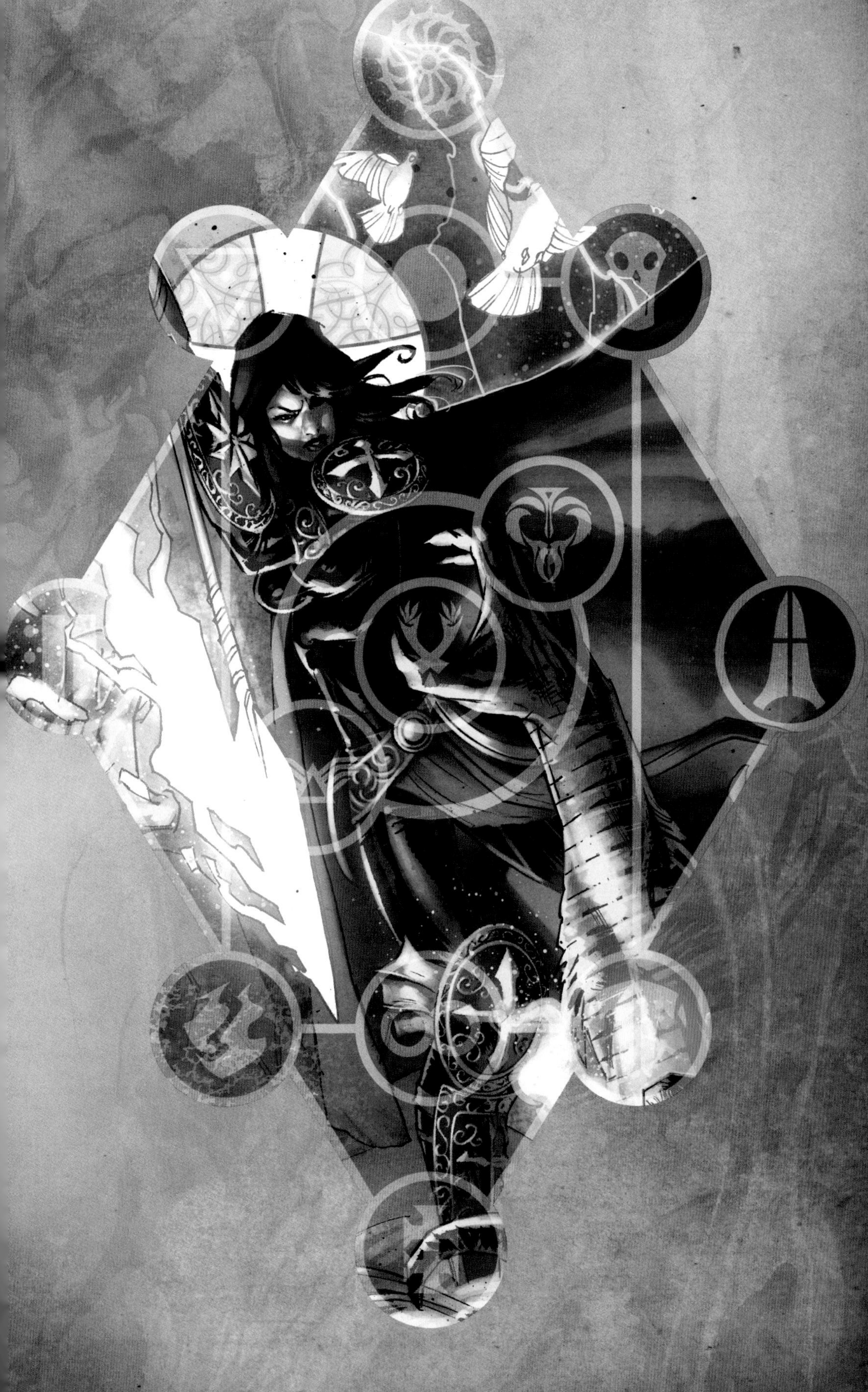

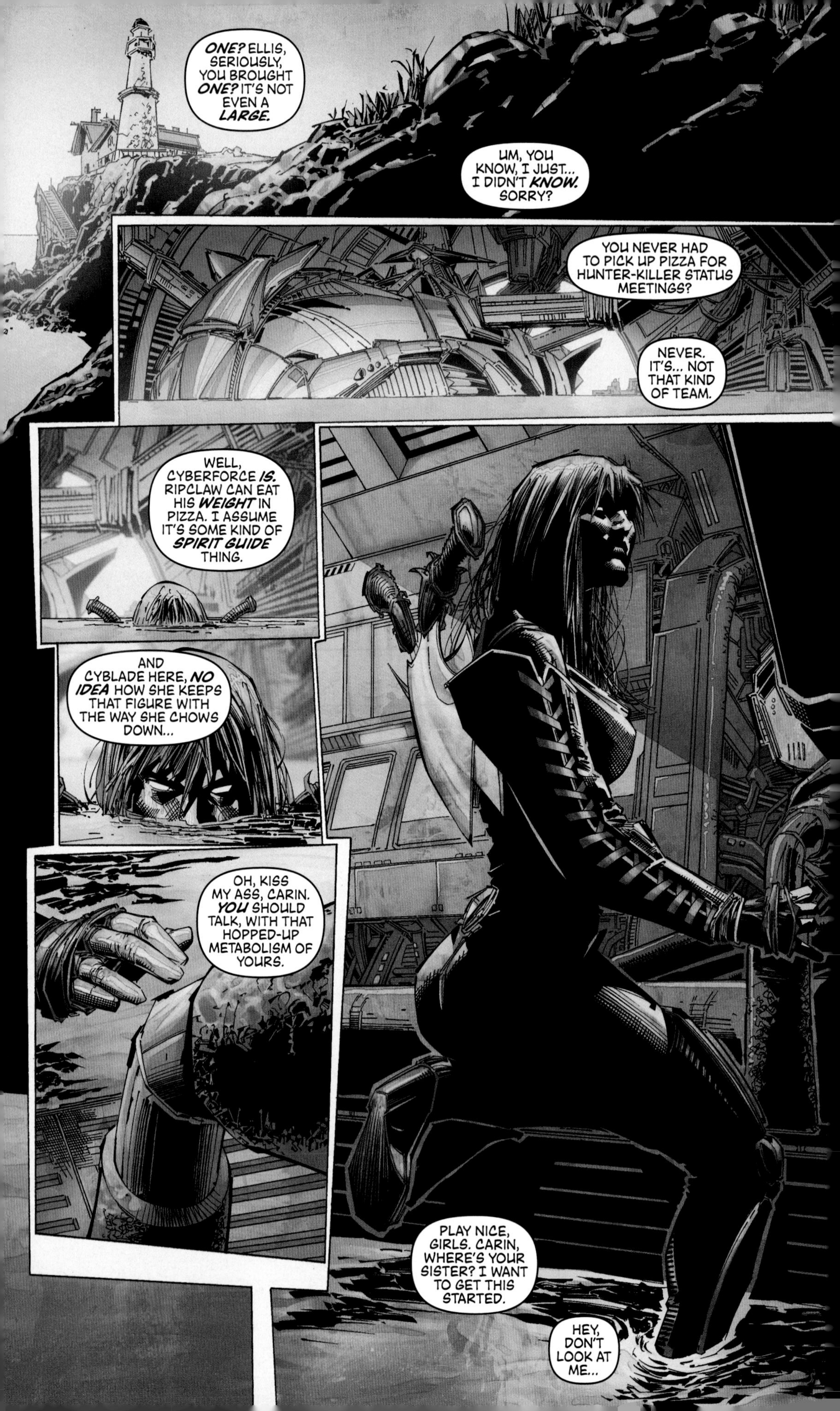
ONE? ELLIS, SERIOUSLY, YOU BROUGHT ONE? IT'S NOT EVEN A LARGE.
UM, YOU KNOW, I JUST... I DIDN'T KNOW. SORRY?
YOU NEVER HAD TO PICK UP PIZZA FOR HUNTER-KILLER STATUS MEETINGS?
NEVER. IT'S... NOT THAT KIND OF TEAM.
WELL, CYBERFORCE IS. RIPCLAW CAN EAT HIS WEIGHT IN PIZZA. I ASSUME IT'S SOME KIND OF SPIRIT GUIDE THING.
AND CYBLADE HERE, NO IDEA HOW SHE KEEPS THAT FIGURE WITH THE WAY SHE CHOWS DOWN...
OH, KISS MY ASS, CARIN. YOU SHOULD TALK, WITH THAT HOPPED-UP METABOLISM OF YOURS.
PLAY NICE, GIRLS. CARIN, WHERE'S YOUR SISTER? I WANT TO GET THIS STARTED.
HEY, DON'T LOOK AT ME...

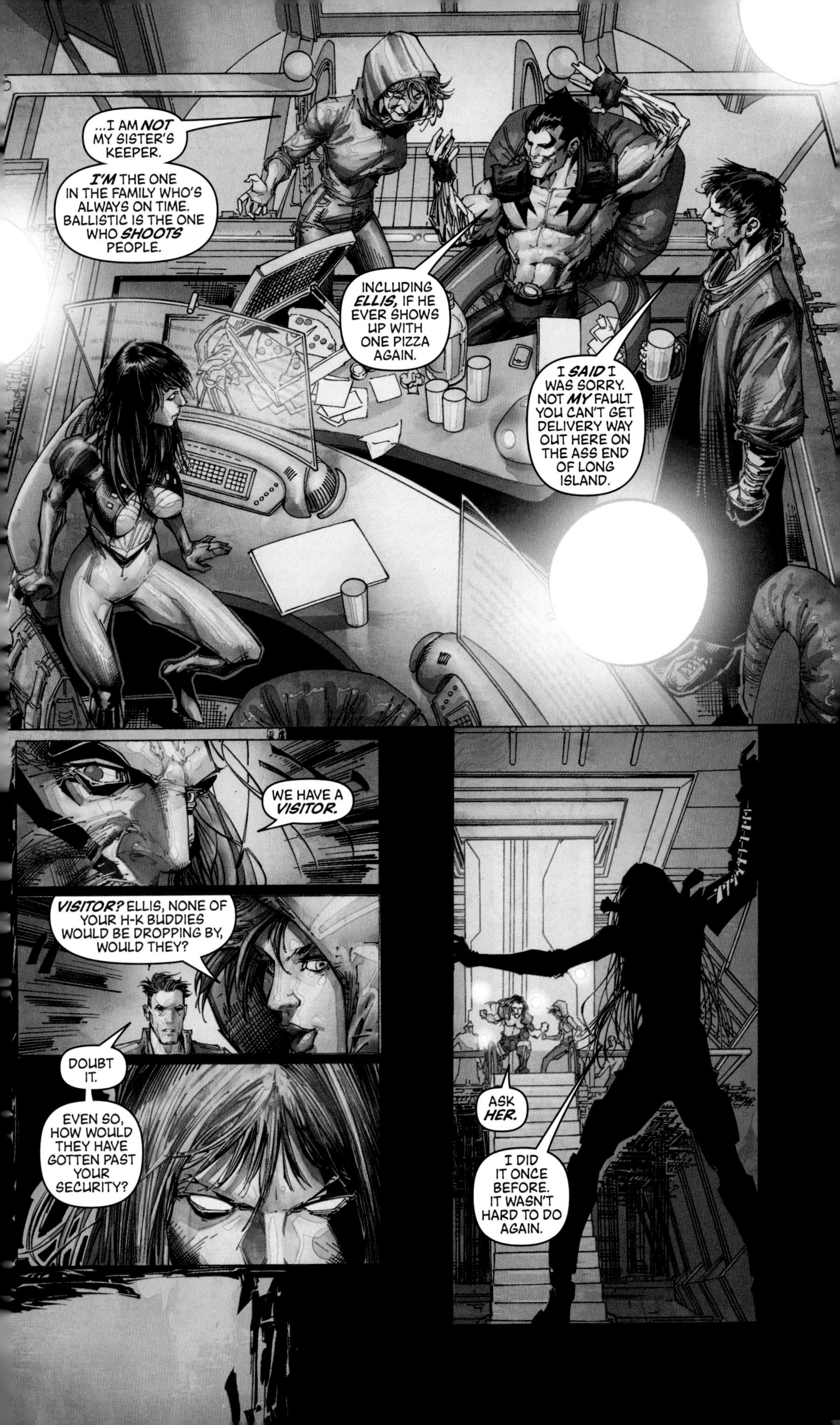
...I AM NOT MY SISTER'S KEEPER.
I'M THE ONE IN THE FAMILY WHO'S ALWAYS ON TIME. BALLISTIC IS THE ONE WHO SHOOTS PEOPLE.
INCLUDING ELLIS, IF HE EVER SHOWS UP WITH ONE PIZZA AGAIN.
I SAID I WAS SORRY. NOT MY FAULT YOU CAN'T GET DELIVERY WAY OUT HERE ON THE ASS END OF LONG ISLAND.
WE HAVE A VISITOR.
VISITOR? ELLIS, NONE OF YOUR H-K BUDDIES WOULD BE DROPPING BY, WOULD THEY?
DOUBT IT.
EVEN SO, HOW WOULD THEY HAVE GOTTEN PAST YOUR SECURITY?
ASK HER.
I DID IT ONCE BEFORE. IT WASN'T HARD TO DO AGAIN.

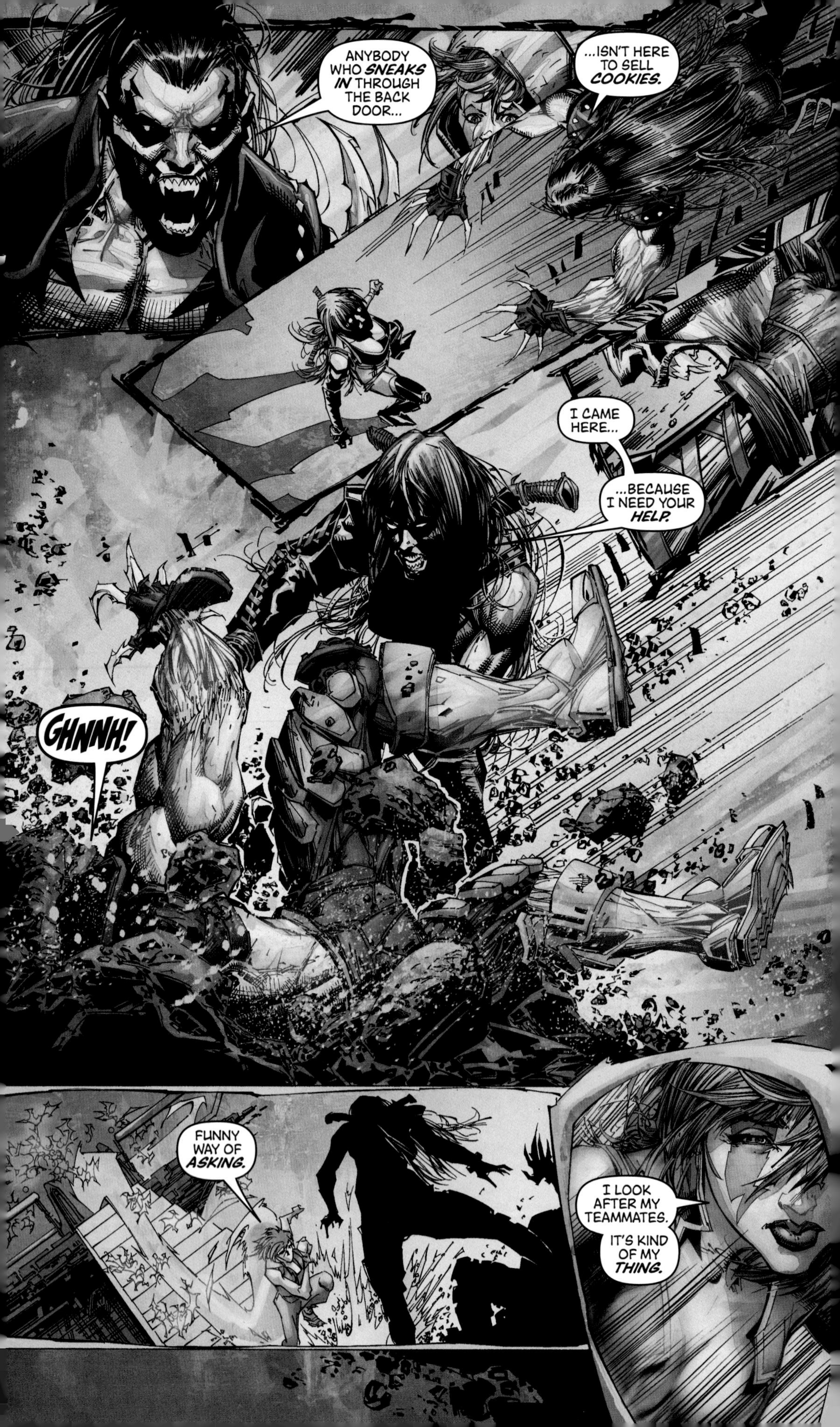
ANYBODY WHO SNEAKS IN THROUGH THE BACK DOOR...
...ISN'T HERE TO SELL COOKIES.
I CAME HERE...
...BECAUSE I NEED YOUR HELP.
GHNNH!
FUNNY WAY OF ASKING.
I LOOK AFTER MY TEAMMATES.
IT'S KIND OF MY THING.

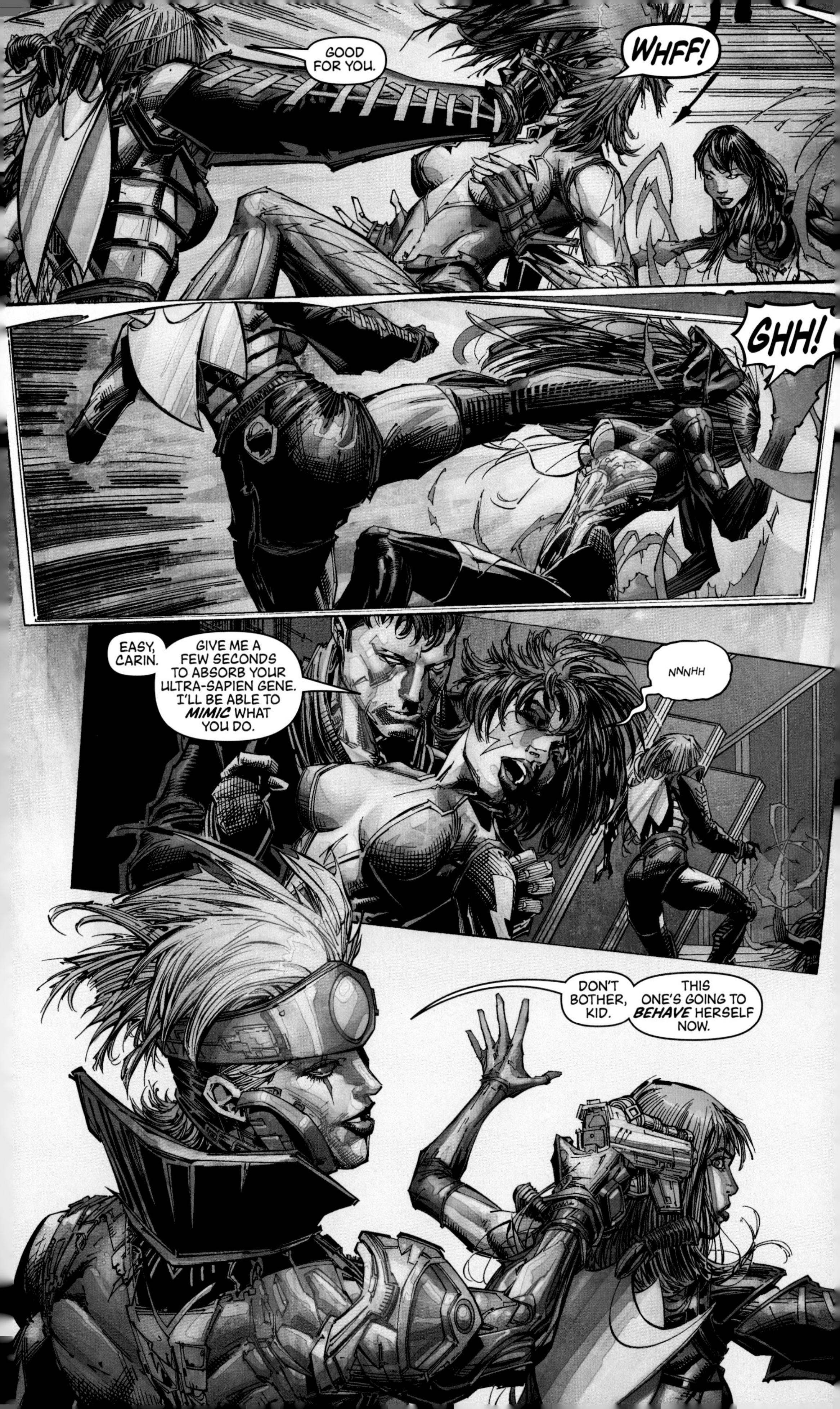
GOOD FOR YOU.
WHFF!
GHH!
EASY, CARIN.
GIVE ME A FEW SECONDS TO ABSORB YOUR ULTRA-SAPIEN GENE. I'LL BE ABLE TO MIMIC WHAT YOU DO.
NNNHH
DON'T BOTHER, KID.
THIS ONE'S GOING TO BEHAVE HERSELF NOW.

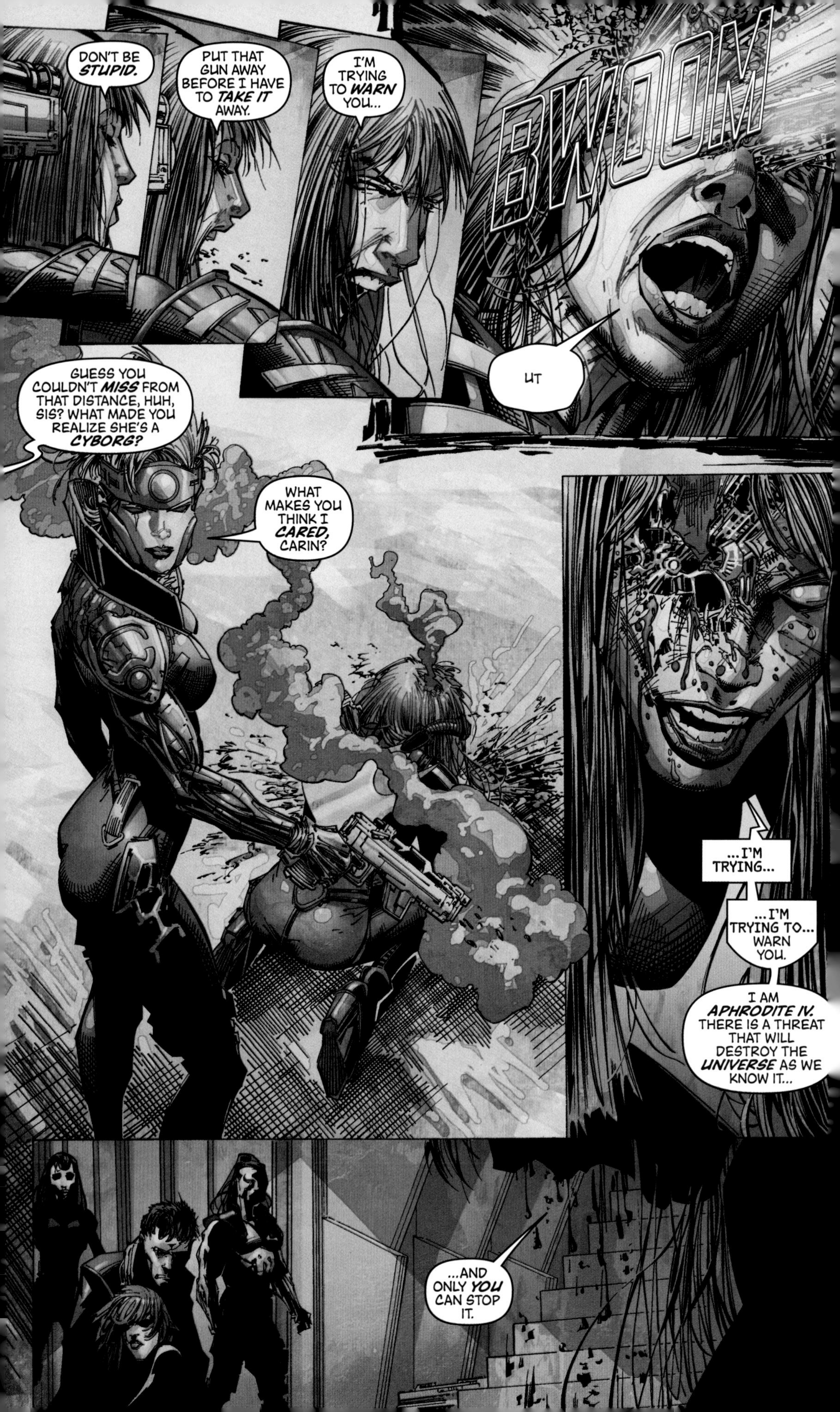
DON'T BE STUPID.
PUT THAT GUN AWAY BEFORE I HAVE TO TAKE IT AWAY.
I'M TRYING TO WARN YOU...
BWOOM
UT
GUESS YOU COULDN'T MISS FROM THAT DISTANCE, HUH, SIS? WHAT MADE YOU REALIZE SHE'S A CYBORG?
WHAT MAKES YOU THINK I CARED, CARIN?
...I'M TRYING...
...I'M TRYING TO... WARN YOU.
I AM APHRODITE IV. THERE IS A THREAT THAT WILL DESTROY THE UNIVERSE AS WE KNOW IT...
...AND ONLY YOU CAN STOP IT.

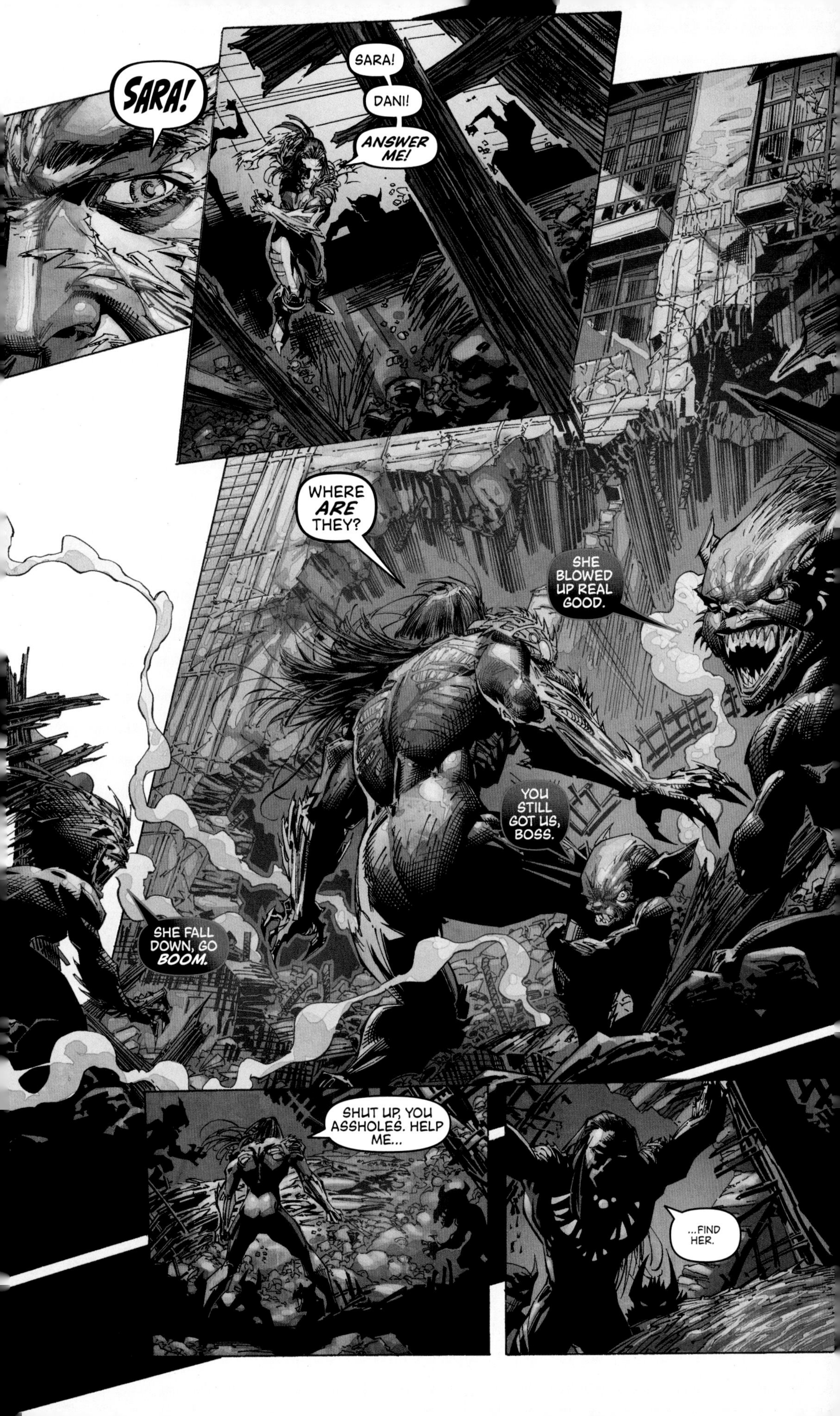

SARA!
SARA!
DANI!
ANSWER ME!
WHERE ARE THEY?
SHE BLOWED UP REAL GOOD.
YOU STILL GOT US, BOSS.
SHE FALL DOWN, GO BOOM.
SHUT UP, YOU ASSHOLES. HELP ME...
...FIND HER.

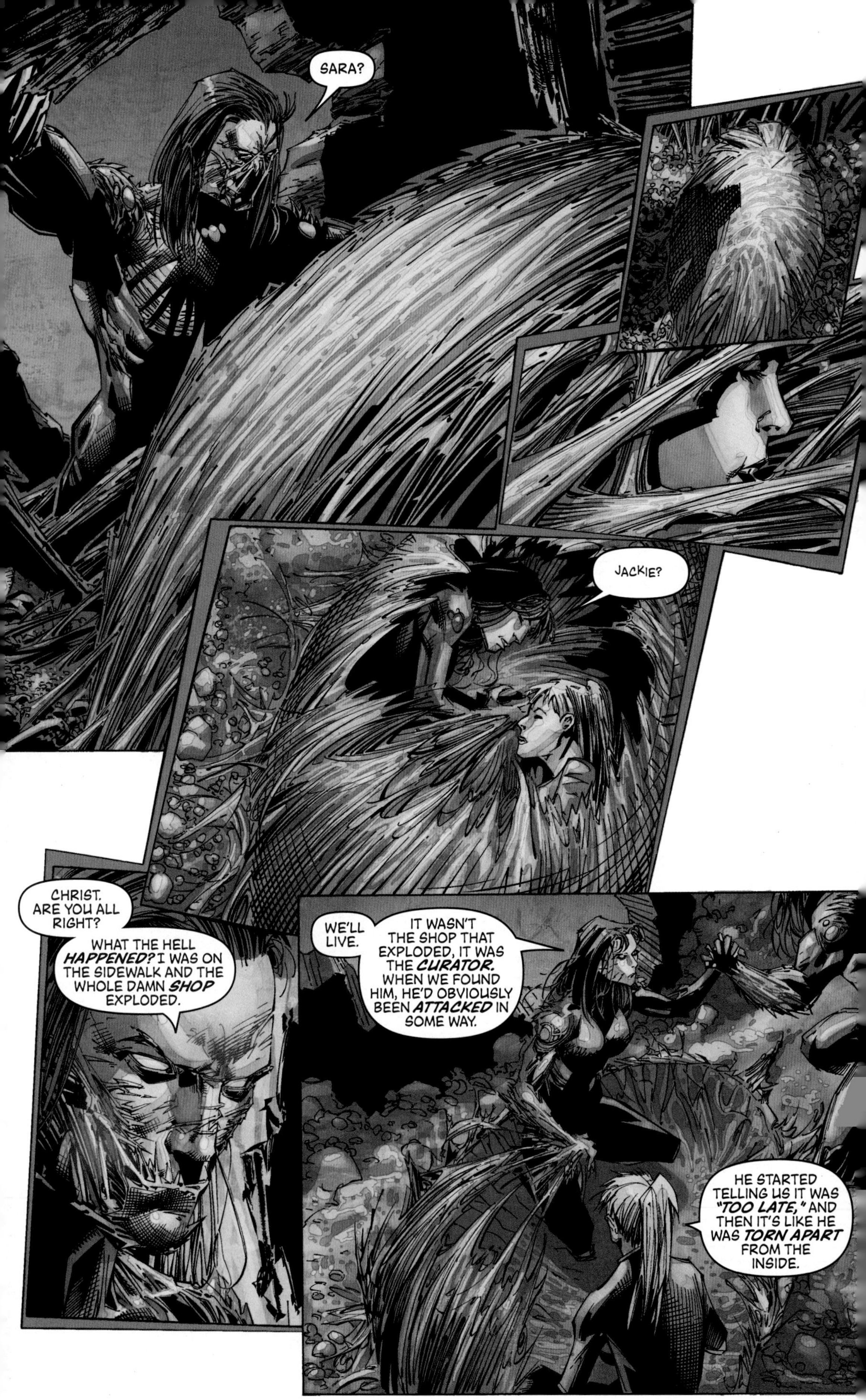
SARA?
JACKIE?
CHRIST. ARE YOU ALL RIGHT?
WHAT THE HELL *HAPPENED?* I WAS ON THE SIDEWALK AND THE WHOLE DAMN *SHOP* EXPLODED.
WE'LL LIVE.
IT WASN'T THE SHOP THAT EXPLODED, IT WAS THE *CURATOR.* WHEN WE FOUND HIM, HE'D OBVIOUSLY BEEN *ATTACKED* IN SOME WAY.
HE STARTED TELLING US IT WAS *"TOO LATE,"* AND THEN IT'S LIKE HE WAS *TORN APART* FROM THE INSIDE.

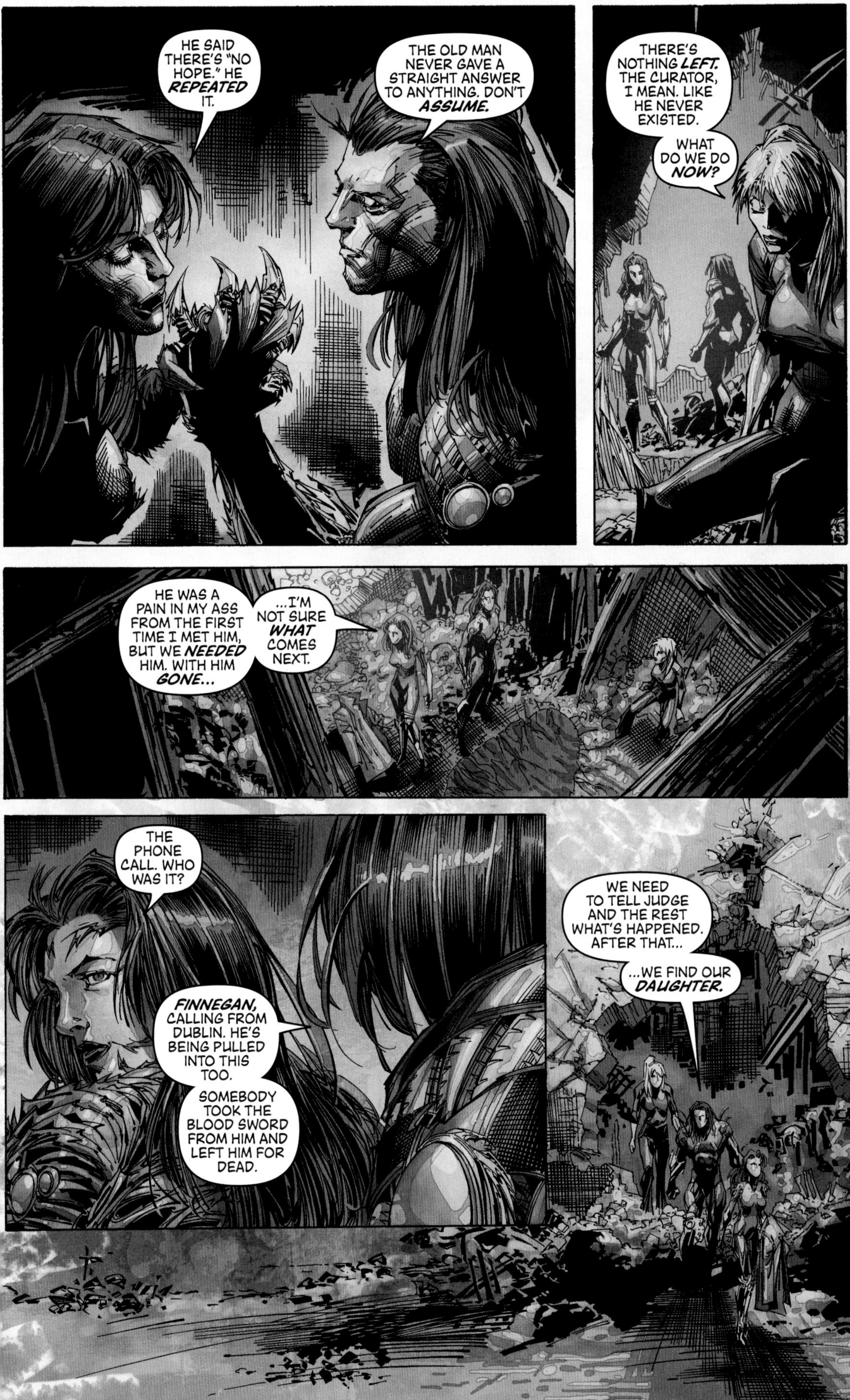
HE SAID THERE'S "NO HOPE." HE REPEATED IT.
THE OLD MAN NEVER GAVE A STRAIGHT ANSWER TO ANYTHING. DON'T ASSUME.
THERE'S NOTHING LEFT. THE CURATOR, I MEAN. LIKE HE NEVER EXISTED.
WHAT DO WE DO NOW?
HE WAS A PAIN IN MY ASS FROM THE FIRST TIME I MET HIM, BUT WE NEEDED HIM. WITH HIM GONE...
...I'M NOT SURE WHAT COMES NEXT.
THE PHONE CALL. WHO WAS IT?
FINNEGAN, CALLING FROM DUBLIN. HE'S BEING PULLED INTO THIS TOO.
SOMEBODY TOOK THE BLOOD SWORD FROM HIM AND LEFT HIM FOR DEAD.
WE NEED TO TELL JUDGE AND THE REST WHAT'S HAPPENED. AFTER THAT...
...WE FIND OUR DAUGHTER.

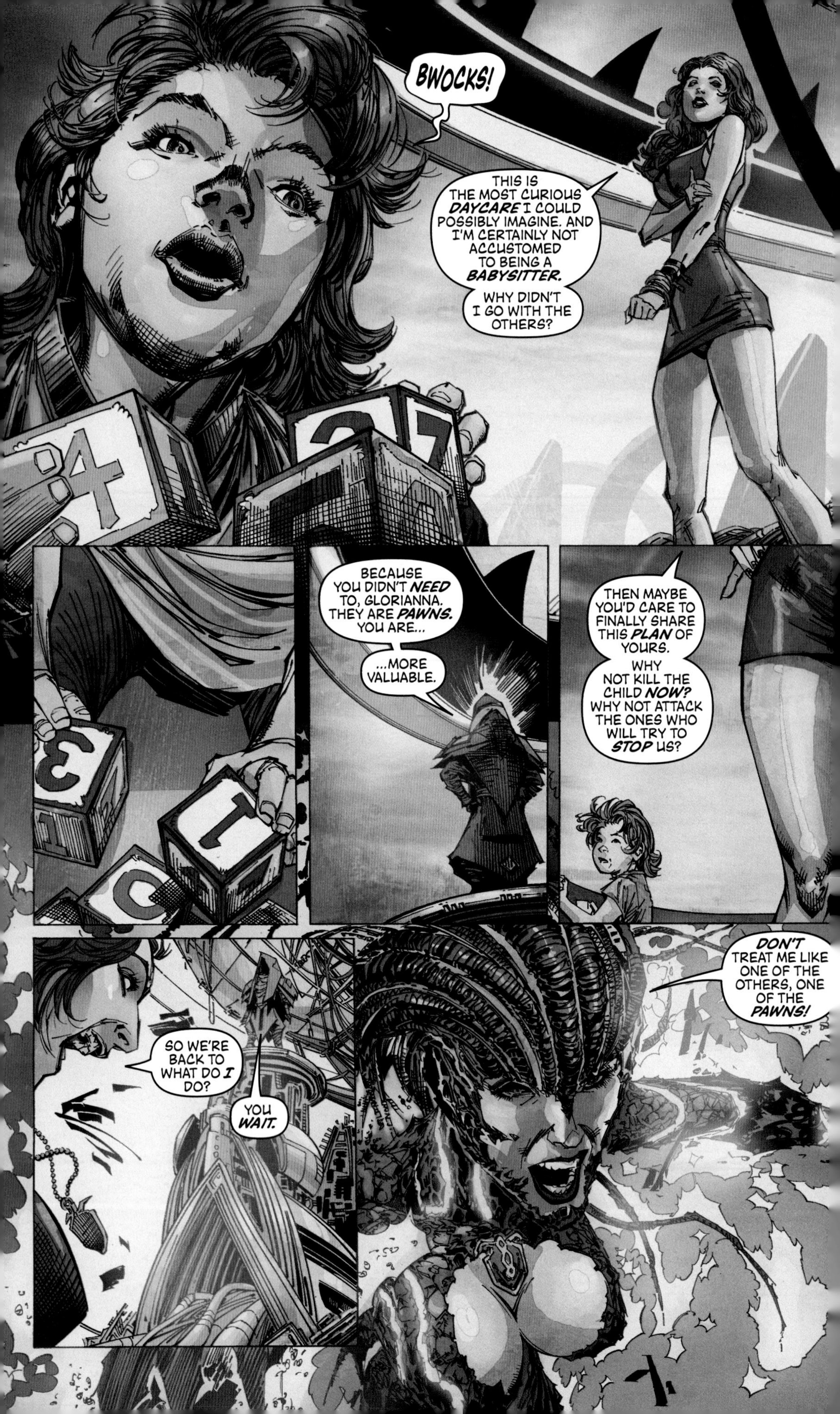
BWOCKS!
THIS IS THE MOST CURIOUS DAYCARE I COULD POSSIBLY IMAGINE. AND I'M CERTAINLY NOT ACCUSTOMED TO BEING A BABYSITTER.
WHY DIDN'T I GO WITH THE OTHERS?
BECAUSE YOU DIDN'T NEED TO, GLORIANNA. THEY ARE PAWNS. YOU ARE...
...MORE VALUABLE.
THEN MAYBE YOU'D CARE TO FINALLY SHARE THIS PLAN OF YOURS.
WHY NOT KILL THE CHILD NOW? WHY NOT ATTACK THE ONES WHO WILL TRY TO STOP US?
SO WE'RE BACK TO WHAT DO I DO?
YOU WAIT.
DON'T TREAT ME LIKE ONE OF THE OTHERS, ONE OF THE PAWNS!

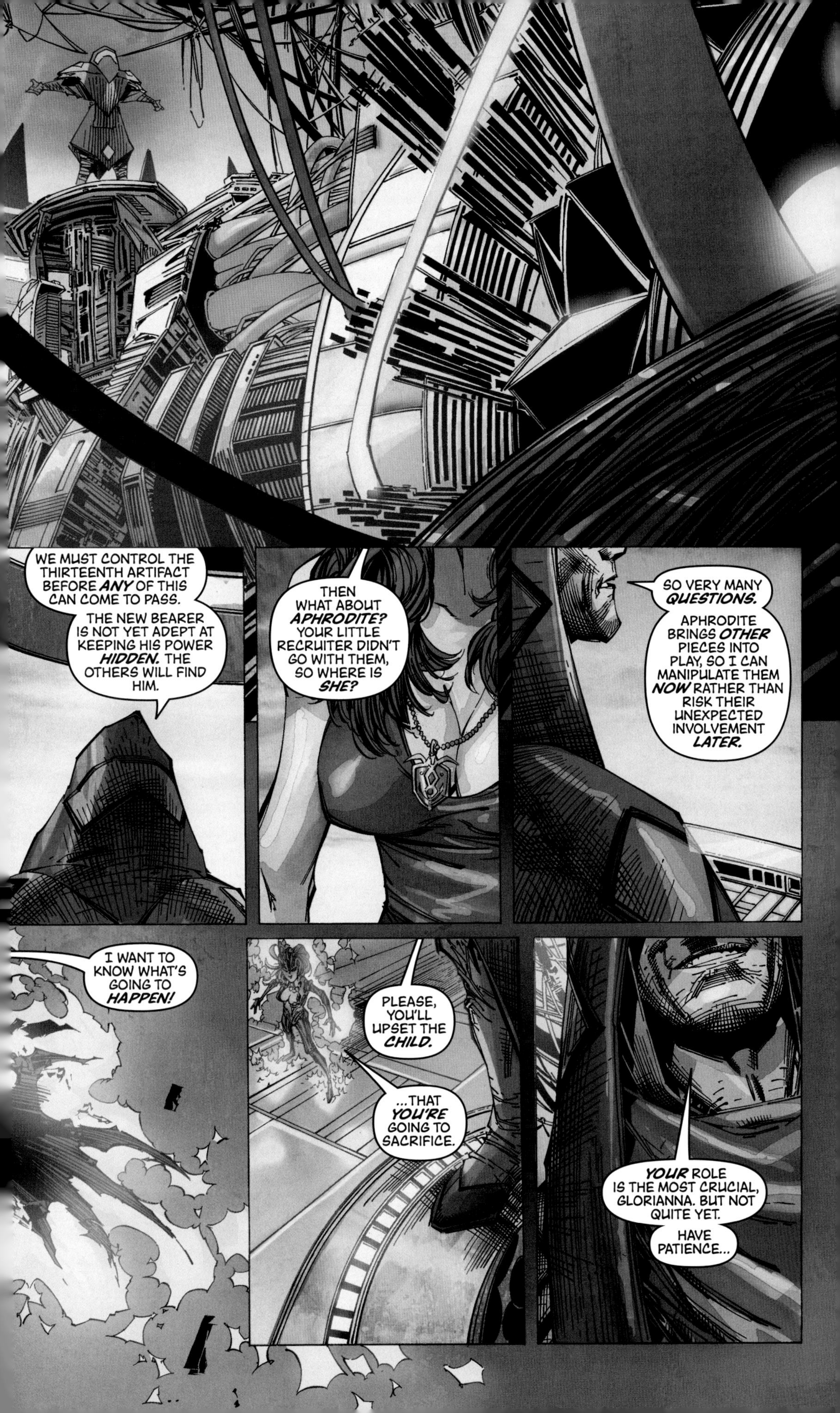
WE MUST CONTROL THE THIRTEENTH ARTIFACT BEFORE ANY OF THIS CAN COME TO PASS.
THE NEW BEARER IS NOT YET ADEPT AT KEEPING HIS POWER HIDDEN. THE OTHERS WILL FIND HIM.
THEN WHAT ABOUT APHRODITE? YOUR LITTLE RECRUITER DIDN'T GO WITH THEM, SO WHERE IS SHE?
SO VERY MANY QUESTIONS.
APHRODITE BRINGS OTHER PIECES INTO PLAY, SO I CAN MANIPULATE THEM NOW RATHER THAN RISK THEIR UNEXPECTED INVOLVEMENT LATER.
I WANT TO KNOW WHAT'S GOING TO HAPPEN!
PLEASE, YOU'LL UPSET THE CHILD.
...THAT YOU'RE GOING TO SACRIFICE.
YOUR ROLE IS THE MOST CRUCIAL, GLORIANNA. BUT NOT QUITE YET.
HAVE PATIENCE...

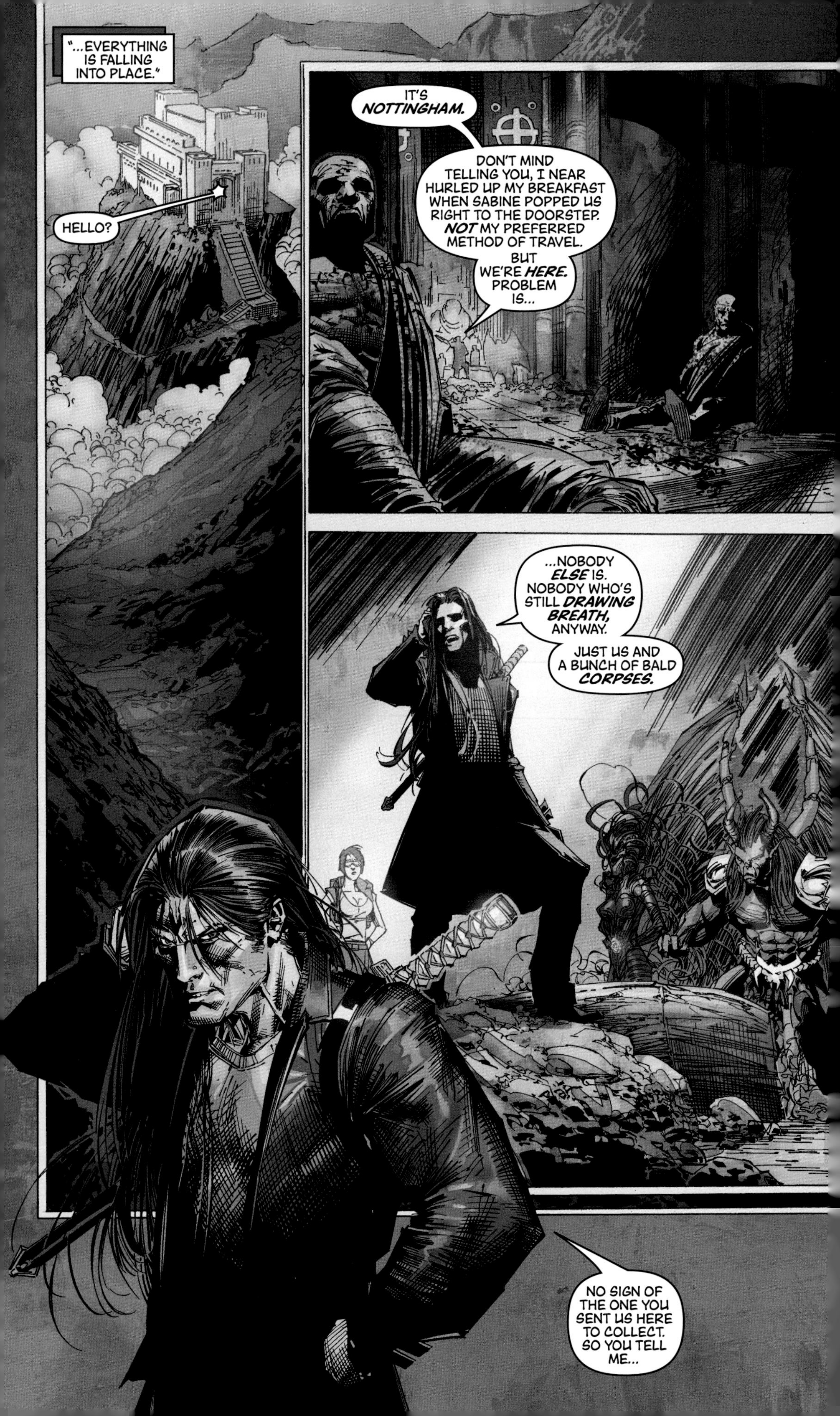
"...EVERYTHING IS FALLING INTO PLACE."
HELLO?
IT'S NOTTINGHAM.
DON'T MIND TELLING YOU, I NEAR HURLED UP MY BREAKFAST WHEN SABINE POPPED US RIGHT TO THE DOORSTEP. NOT MY PREFERRED METHOD OF TRAVEL.
BUT WE'RE HERE. PROBLEM IS...
...NOBODY ELSE IS. NOBODY WHO'S STILL DRAWING BREATH, ANYWAY.
JUST US AND A BUNCH OF BALD CORPSES.
NO SIGN OF THE ONE YOU SENT US HERE TO COLLECT. SO YOU TELL ME...

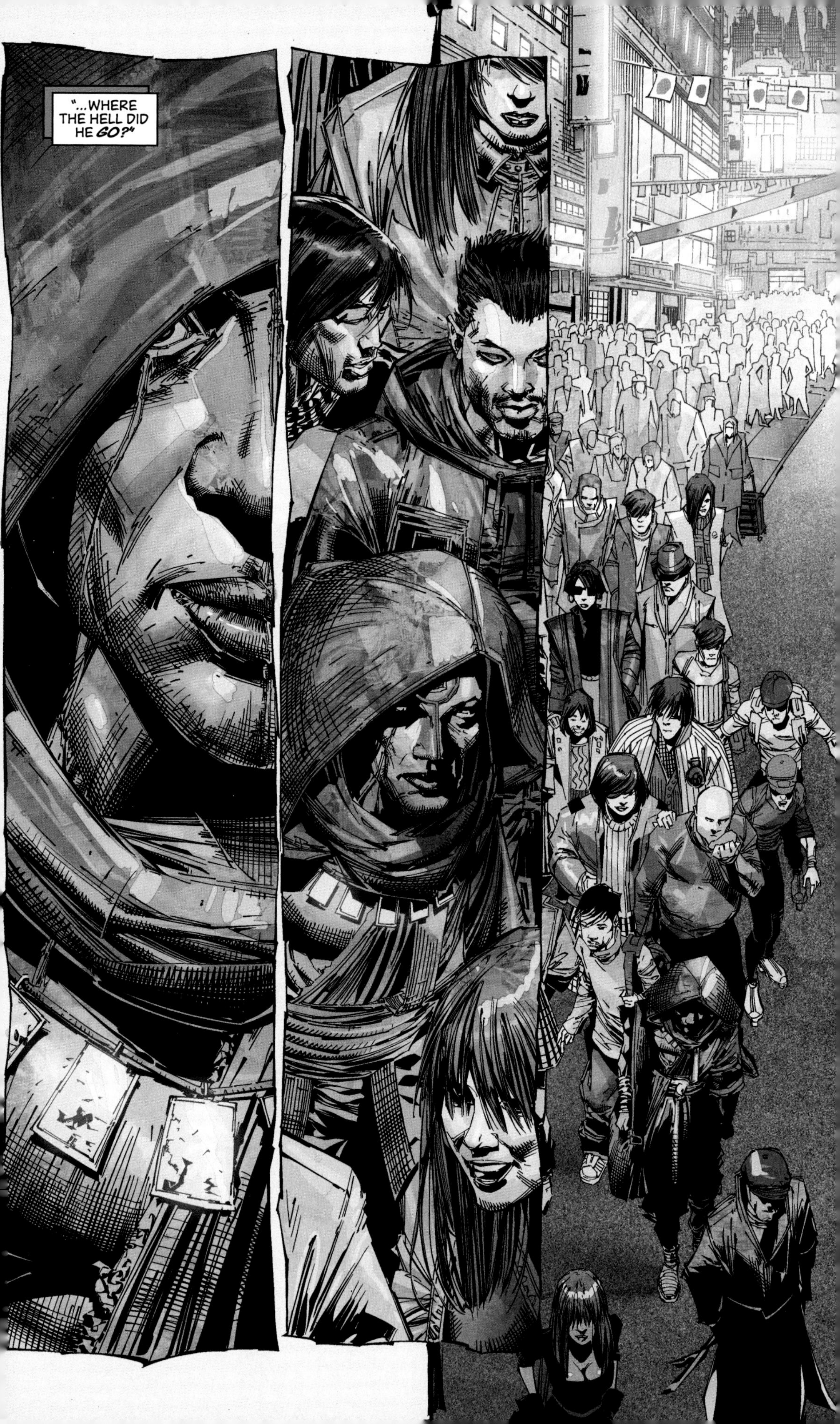
"...WHERE THE HELL DID HE GO?"

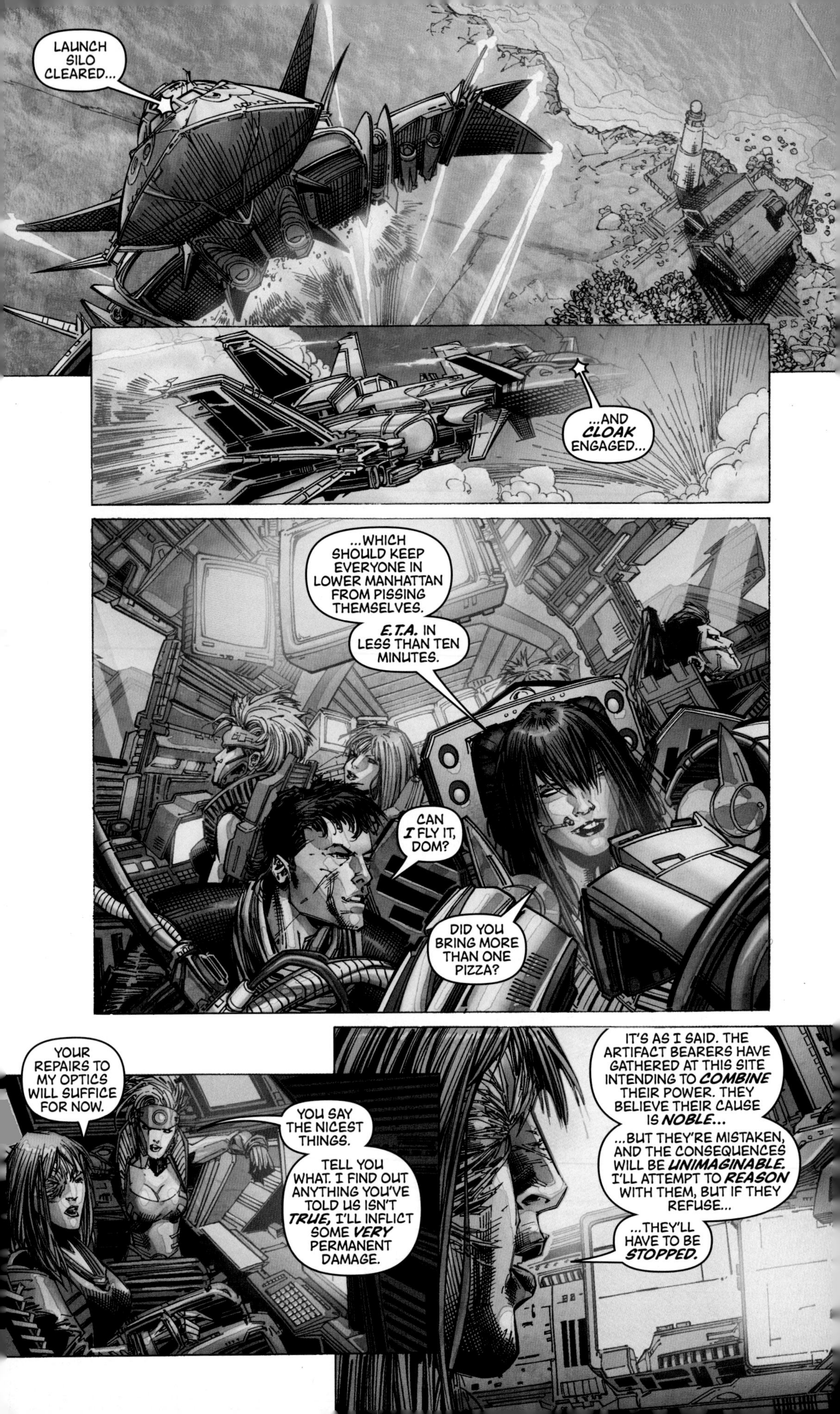
LAUNCH SILO CLEARED...
...AND CLOAK ENGAGED...
...WHICH SHOULD KEEP EVERYONE IN LOWER MANHATTAN FROM PISSING THEMSELVES.
E.T.A. IN LESS THAN TEN MINUTES.
CAN I FLY IT, DOM?
DID YOU BRING MORE THAN ONE PIZZA?
YOUR REPAIRS TO MY OPTICS WILL SUFFICE FOR NOW.
YOU SAY THE NICEST THINGS.
TELL YOU WHAT. I FIND OUT ANYTHING YOU'VE TOLD US ISN'T TRUE, I'LL INFLICT SOME VERY PERMANENT DAMAGE.
IT'S AS I SAID. THE ARTIFACT BEARERS HAVE GATHERED AT THIS SITE INTENDING TO COMBINE THEIR POWER. THEY BELIEVE THEIR CAUSE IS NOBLE...
...BUT THEY'RE MISTAKEN, AND THE CONSEQUENCES WILL BE UNIMAGINABLE. I'LL ATTEMPT TO REASON WITH THEM, BUT IF THEY REFUSE...
...THEY'LL HAVE TO BE STOPPED.

I AM *NOT* SACRIFICING MY DAUGHTER...

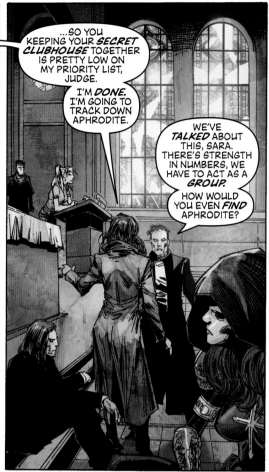

...SO YOU KEEPING YOUR *SECRET CLUBHOUSE* TOGETHER IS PRETTY LOW ON MY PRIORITY LIST, JUDGE.

I'M *DONE.* I'M GOING TO TRACK DOWN APHRODITE.

WE'VE *TALKED* ABOUT THIS, SARA. THERE'S STRENGTH IN NUMBERS, WE HAVE TO ACT AS A *GROUP.*

HOW WOULD YOU EVEN *FIND* APHRODITE?

YOU THINK I CAN'T *FIND* SOMEBODY? I'M A *POLICE DETECTIVE.*

I'LL FIND APHRODITE AND TAKE HER APART PIECE BY PIECE UNTIL SHE GIVES UP WHERE HOPE IS.

SARA, *PLEASE* RECONSIDER. YOU CAN'T JUST WALK OUT. YOU'RE *NEEDED.*

MY *DAUGHTER* NEEDS ME. NOW GET OUT OF MY WAY.

SOUNDS LIKE GOOD ADVICE, PREACHER MAN.

THIS IS A MISTAKE.

JACKIE?

YOU COMING?

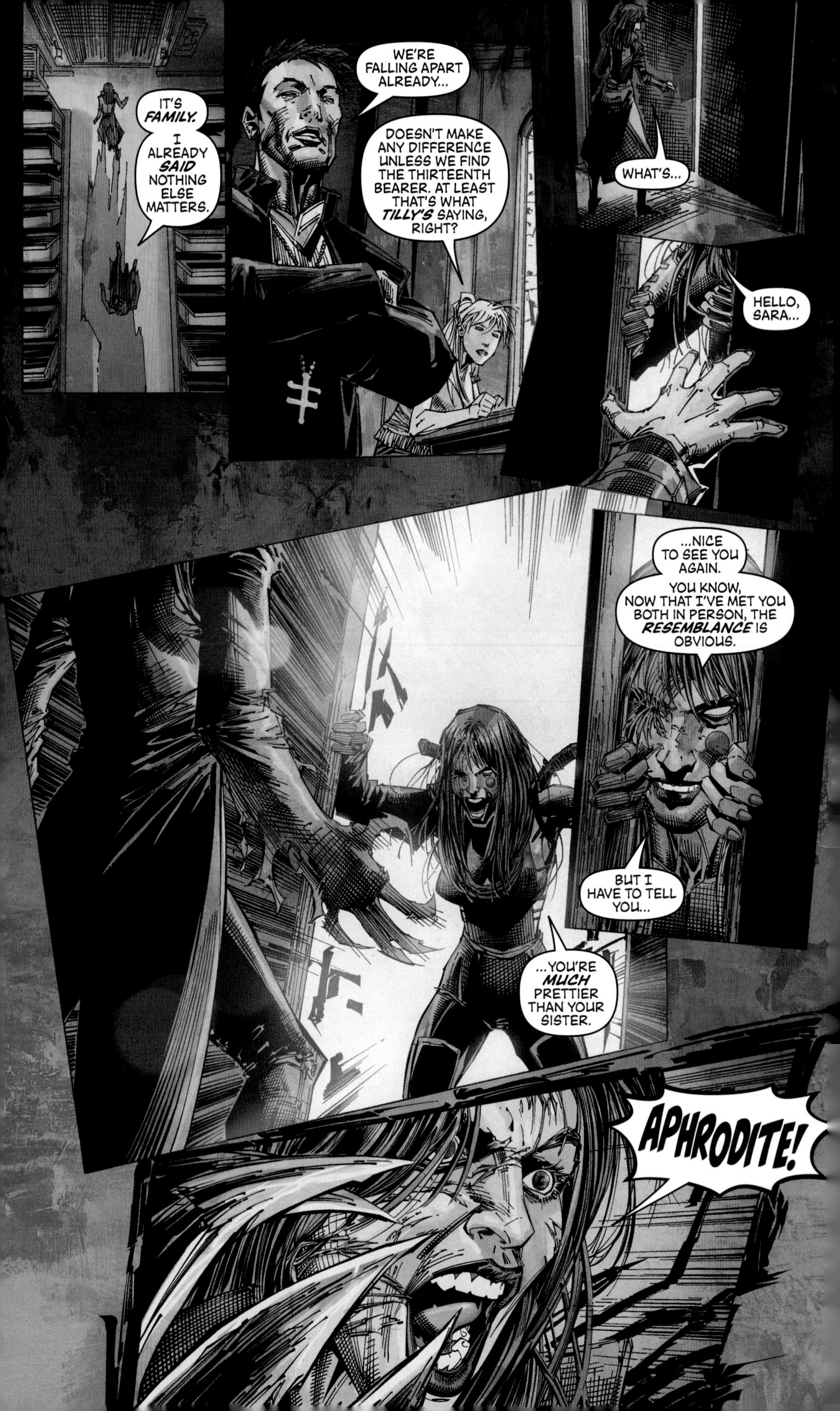
IT'S *FAMILY.*
I ALREADY *SAID* NOTHING ELSE MATTERS.
WE'RE FALLING APART ALREADY...
DOESN'T MAKE ANY DIFFERENCE UNLESS WE FIND THE THIRTEENTH BEARER. AT LEAST THAT'S WHAT *TILLY'S* SAYING, RIGHT?
WHAT'S...
HELLO, SARA...
...NICE TO SEE YOU AGAIN.
YOU KNOW, NOW THAT I'VE MET YOU BOTH IN PERSON, THE *RESEMBLANCE* IS OBVIOUS.
BUT I HAVE TO TELL YOU...
...YOU'RE *MUCH* PRETTIER THAN YOUR SISTER.
APHRODITE!

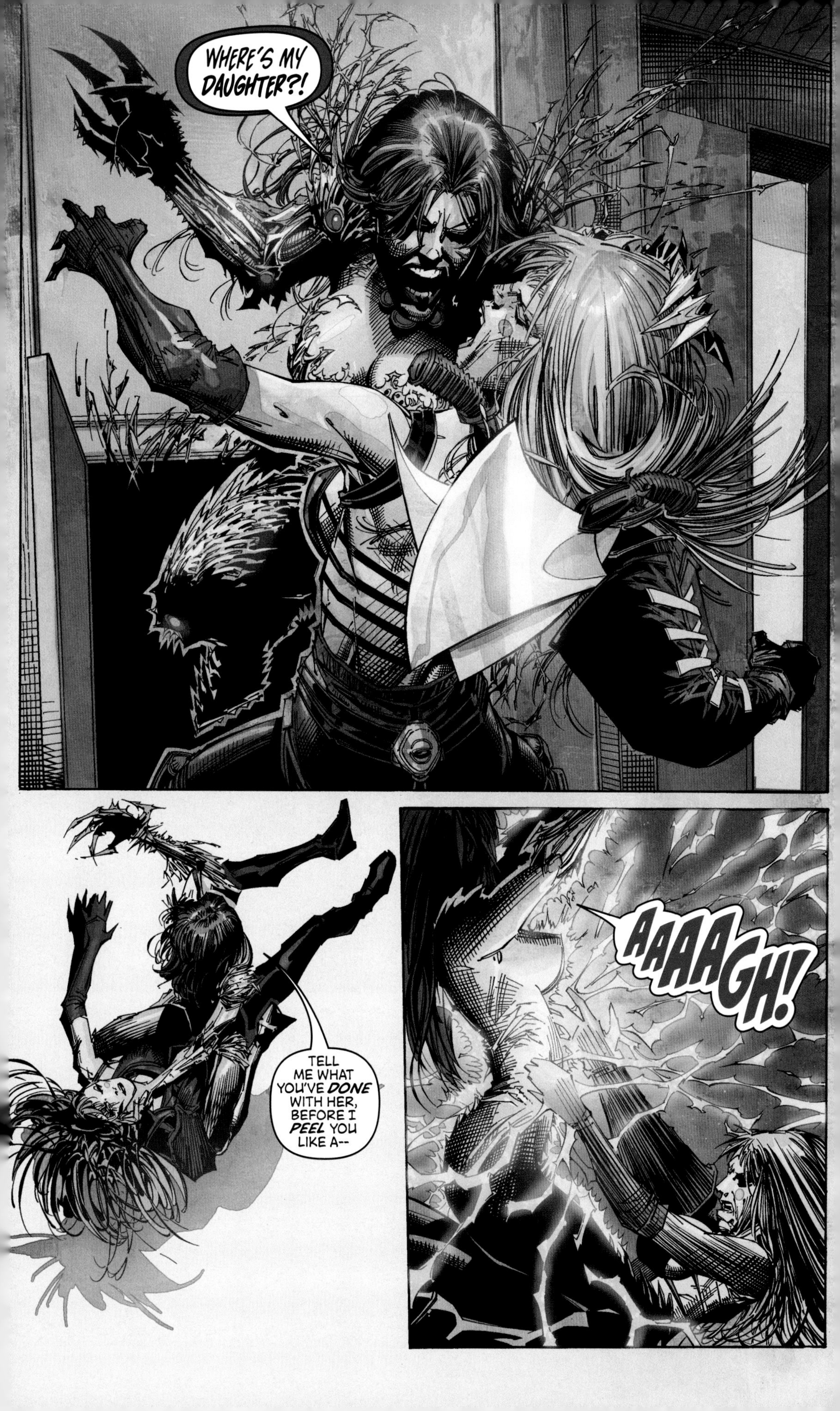
WHERE'S MY DAUGHTER?!
TELL ME WHAT YOU'VE DONE WITH HER, BEFORE I PEEL YOU LIKE A--
AAAAGH!

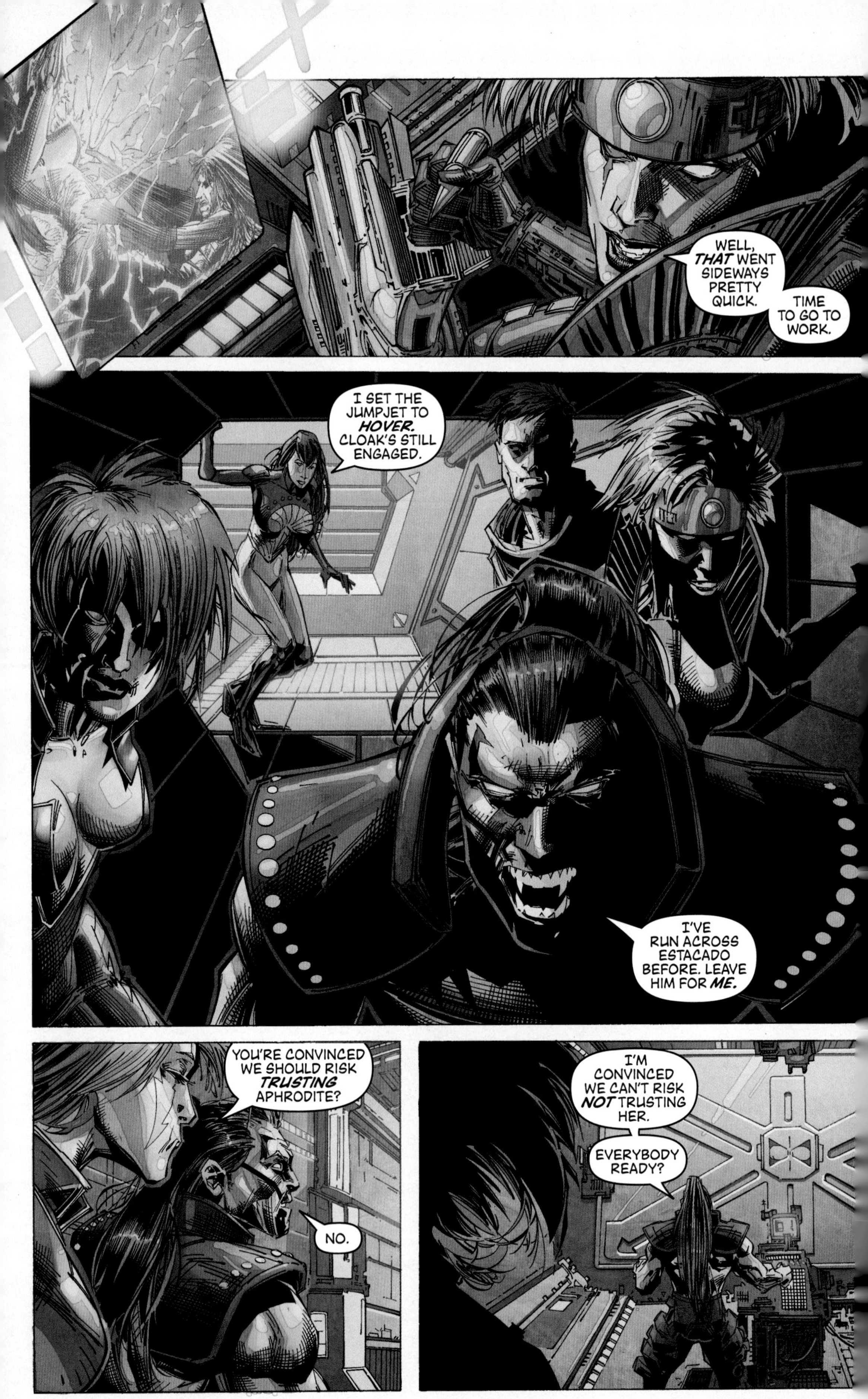

WELL, THAT WENT SIDEWAYS PRETTY QUICK.
TIME TO GO TO WORK.
I SET THE JUMPJET TO HOVER. CLOAK'S STILL ENGAGED.
I'VE RUN ACROSS ESTACADO BEFORE. LEAVE HIM FOR ME.
YOU'RE CONVINCED WE SHOULD RISK TRUSTING APHRODITE?
NO.
I'M CONVINCED WE CAN'T RISK NOT TRUSTING HER.
EVERYBODY READY?

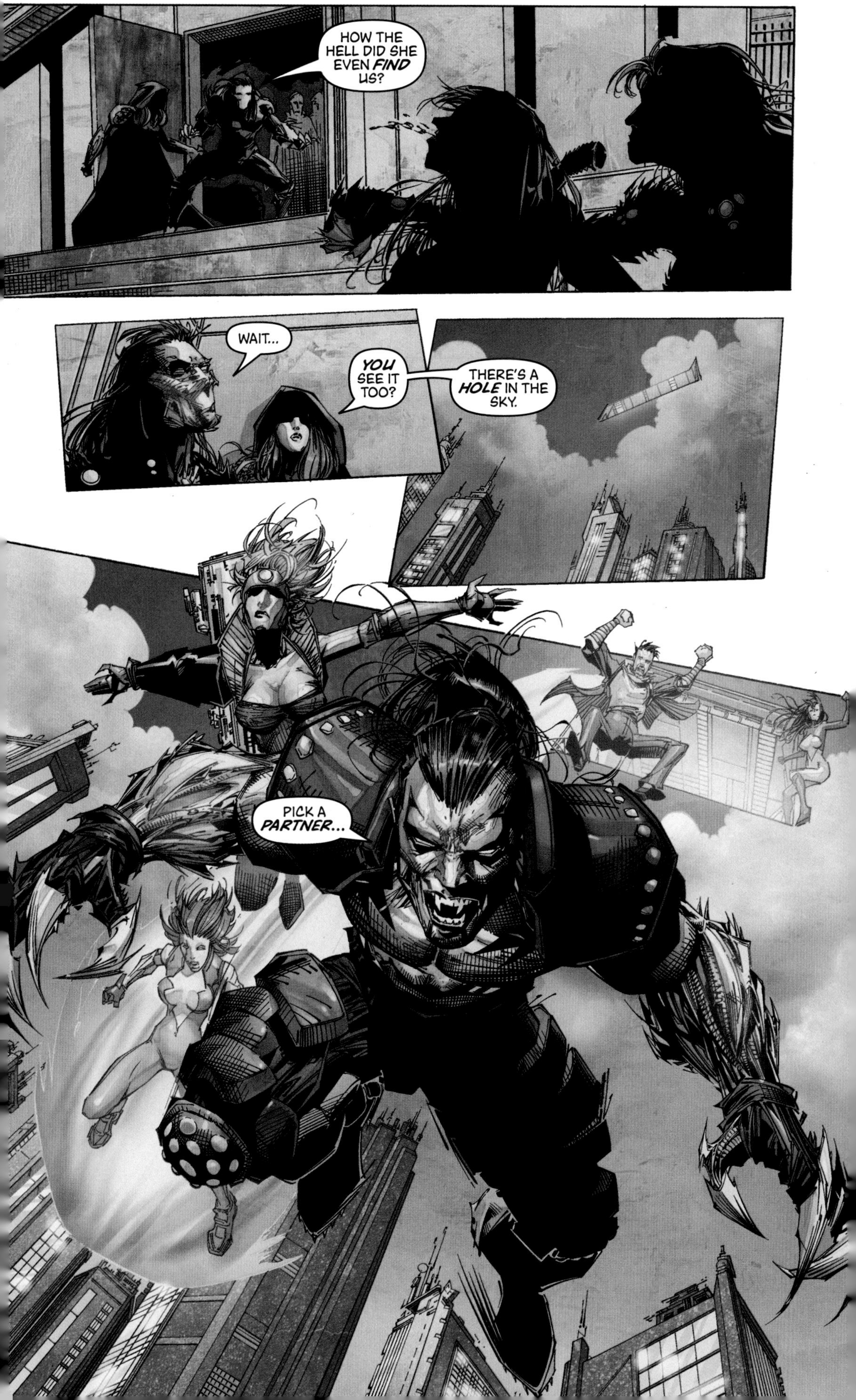

HOW THE HELL DID SHE EVEN FIND US?
WAIT...
YOU SEE IT TOO?
THERE'S A HOLE IN THE SKY.
PICK A PARTNER...

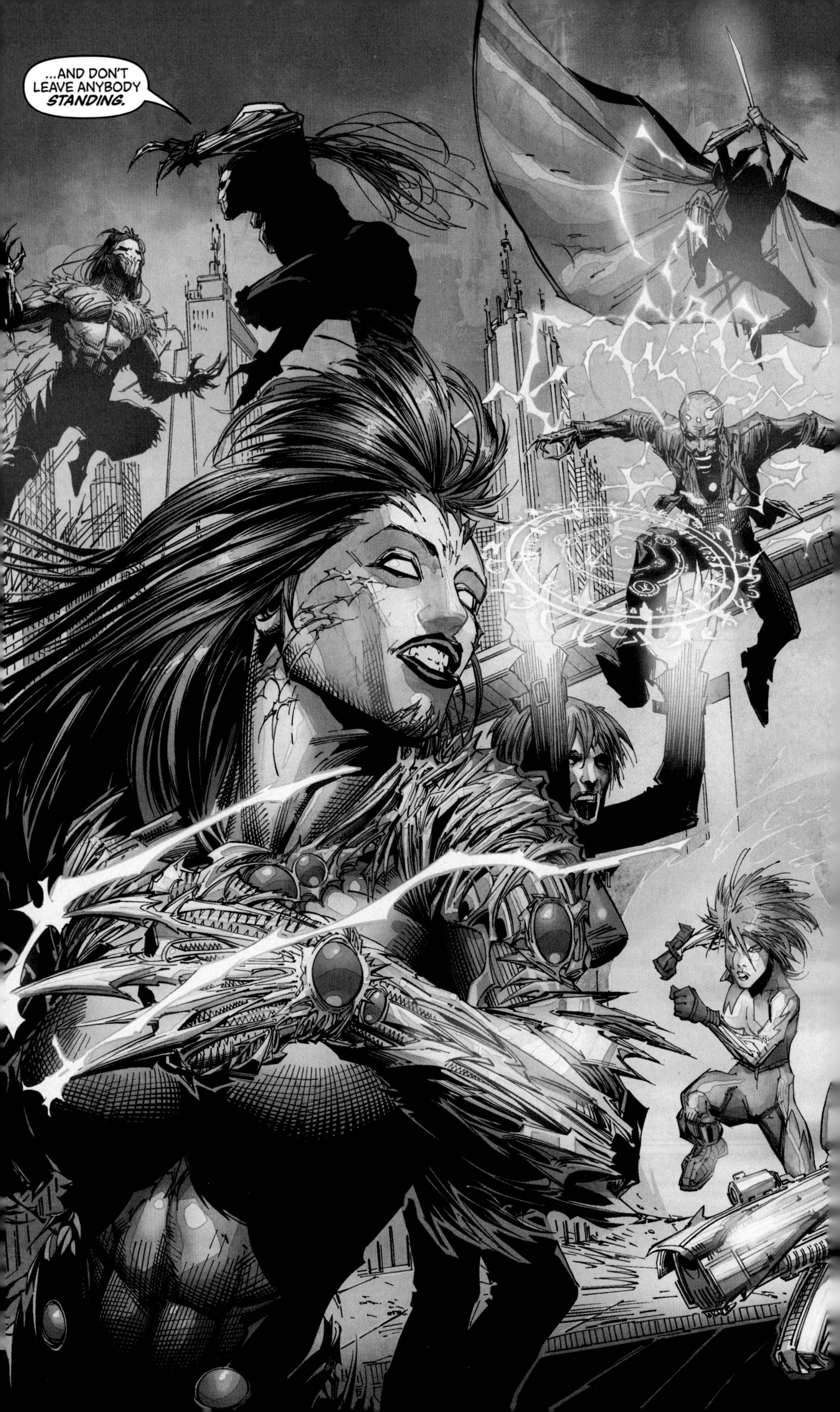
...AND DON'T LEAVE ANYBODY *STANDING.*

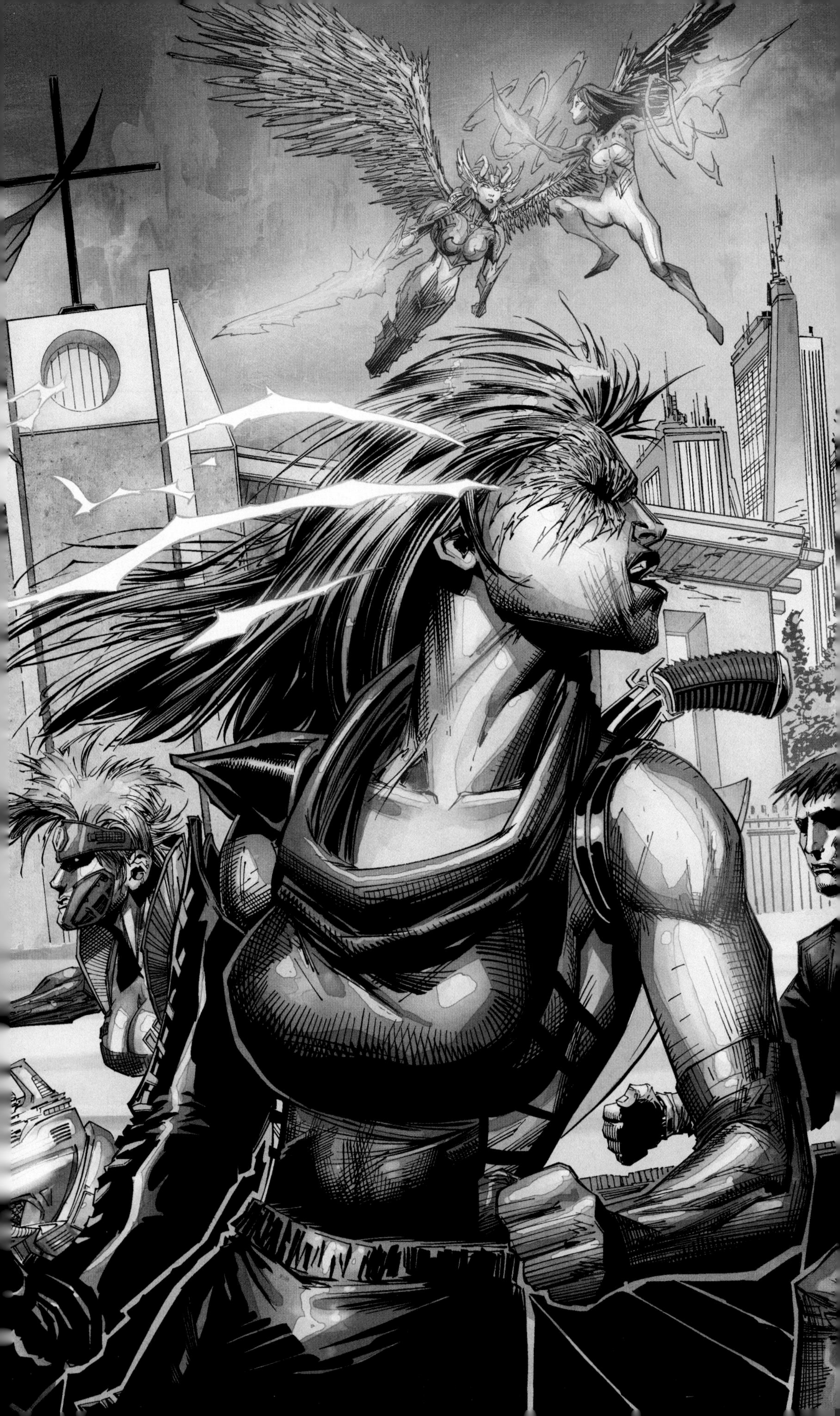

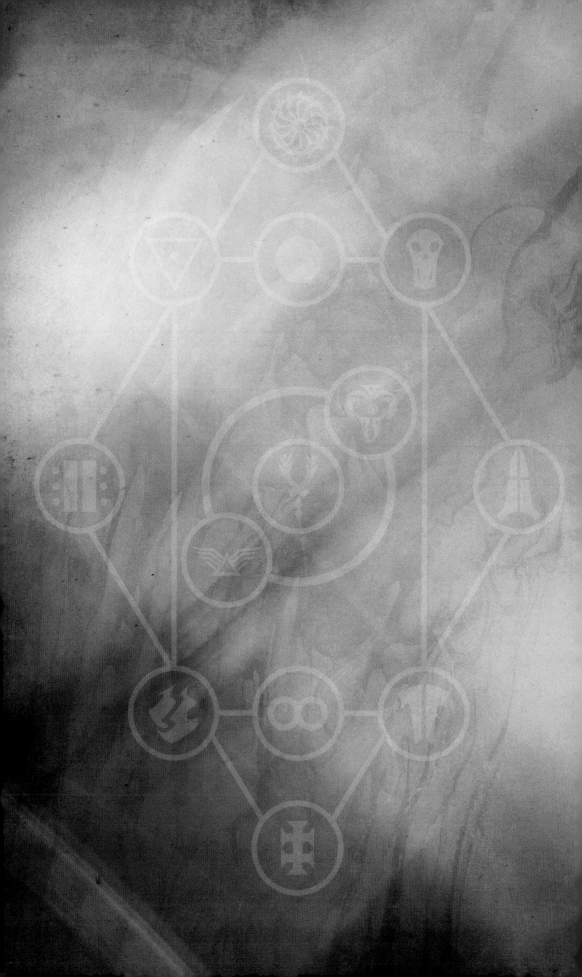

CHAPTER 6

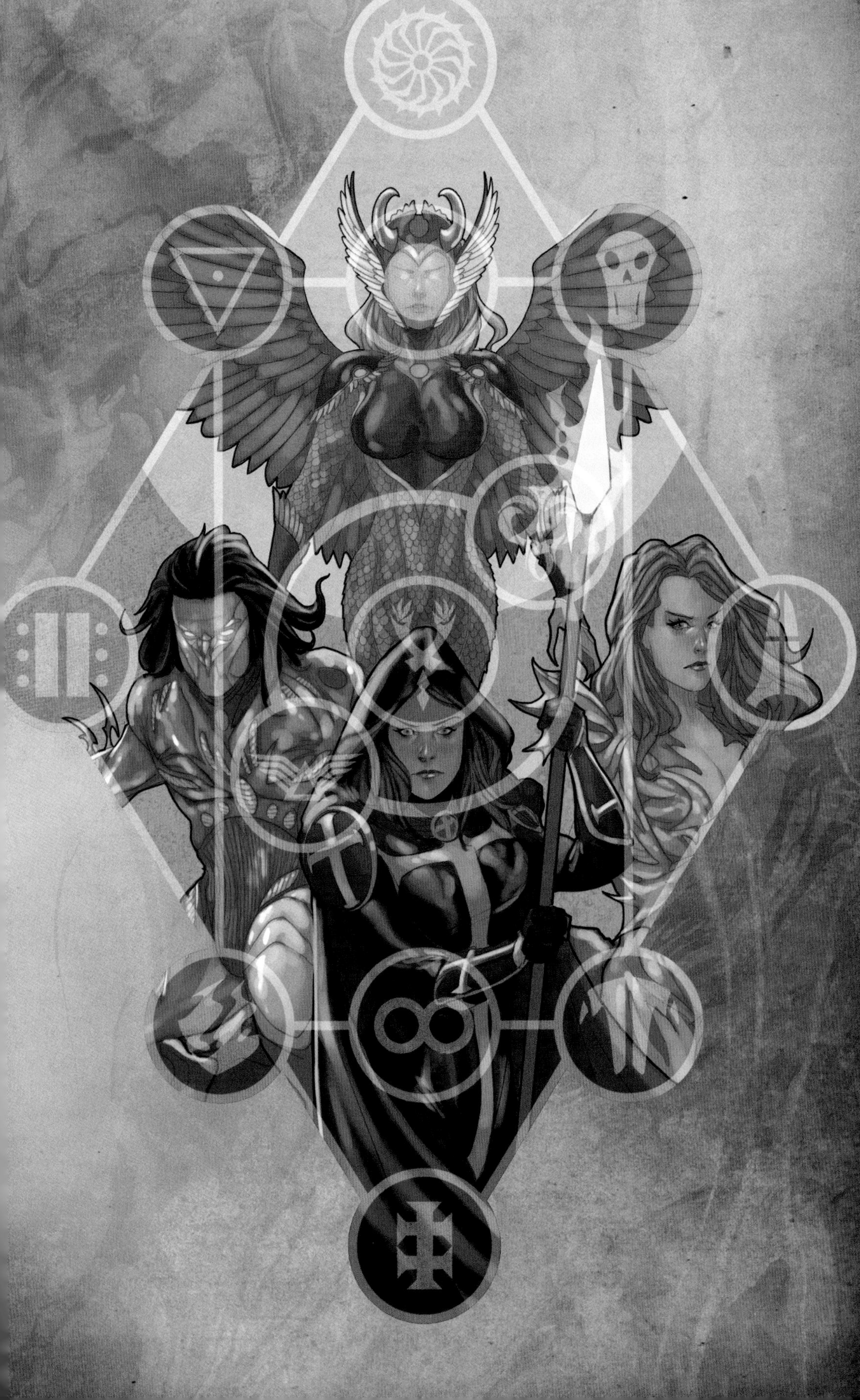

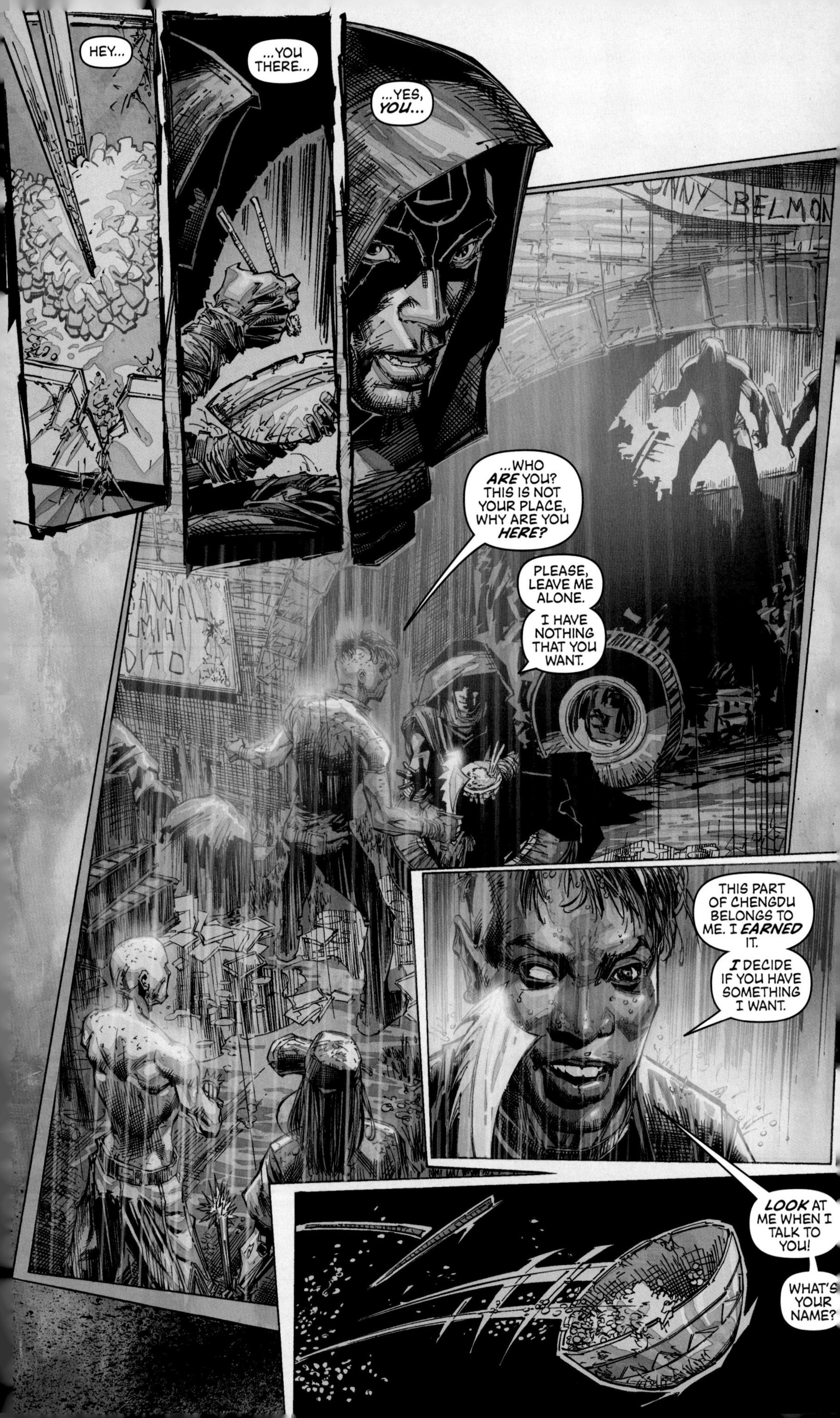
HEY...
...YOU THERE...
...YES, *YOU*...
...WHO *ARE* YOU? THIS IS NOT YOUR PLACE, WHY ARE YOU *HERE?*
PLEASE, LEAVE ME ALONE.
I HAVE NOTHING THAT YOU WANT.
THIS PART OF CHENGDU BELONGS TO ME. I *EARNED* IT.
I DECIDE IF YOU HAVE SOMETHING I WANT.
LOOK AT ME WHEN I TALK TO YOU!
WHAT'S YOUR NAME?

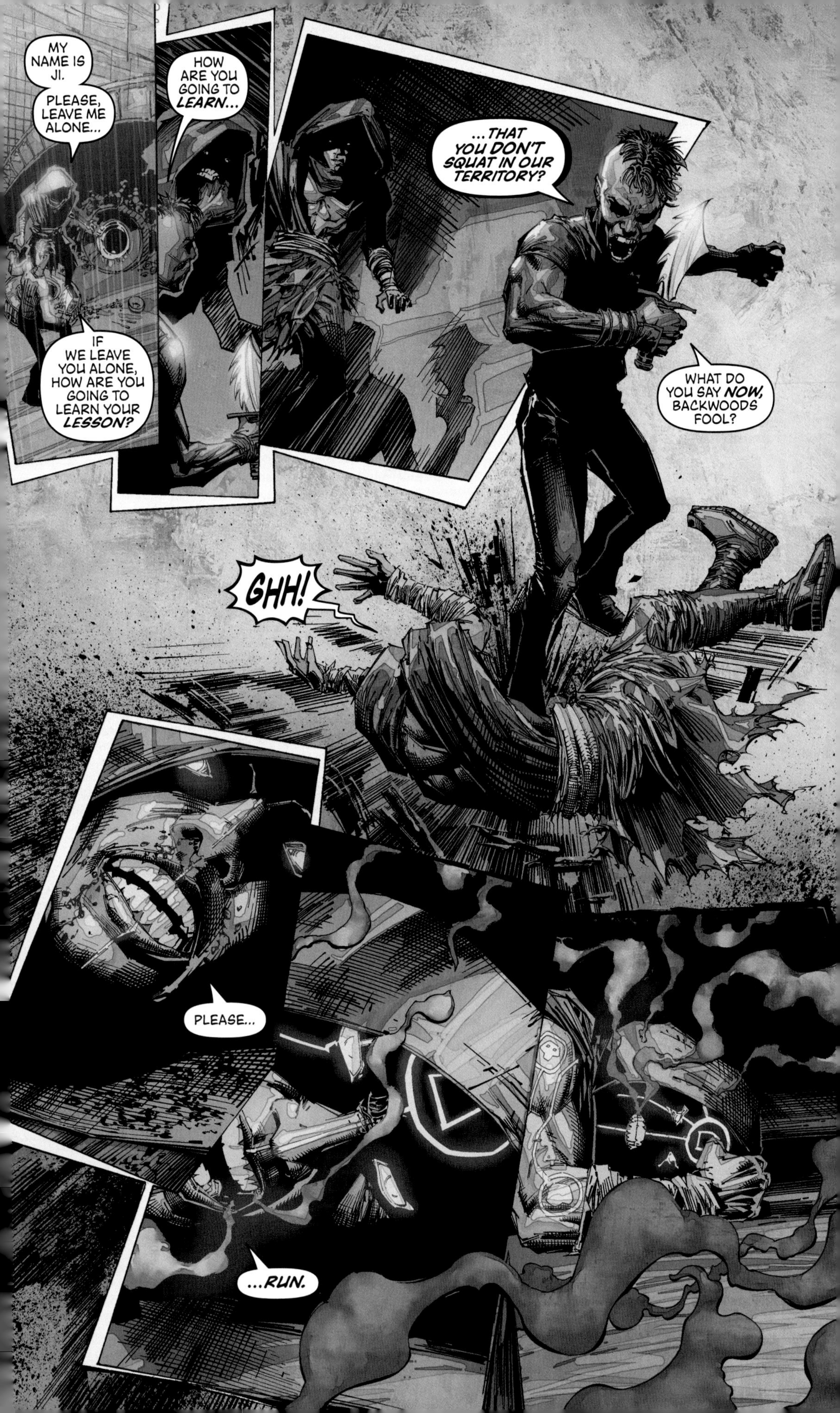
MY NAME IS JI.
PLEASE, LEAVE ME ALONE...
HOW ARE YOU GOING TO LEARN...
IF WE LEAVE YOU ALONE, HOW ARE YOU GOING TO LEARN YOUR LESSON?
...THAT YOU DON'T SQUAT IN OUR TERRITORY?
WHAT DO YOU SAY NOW, BACKWOODS FOOL?
GHH!
PLEASE...
...RUN.

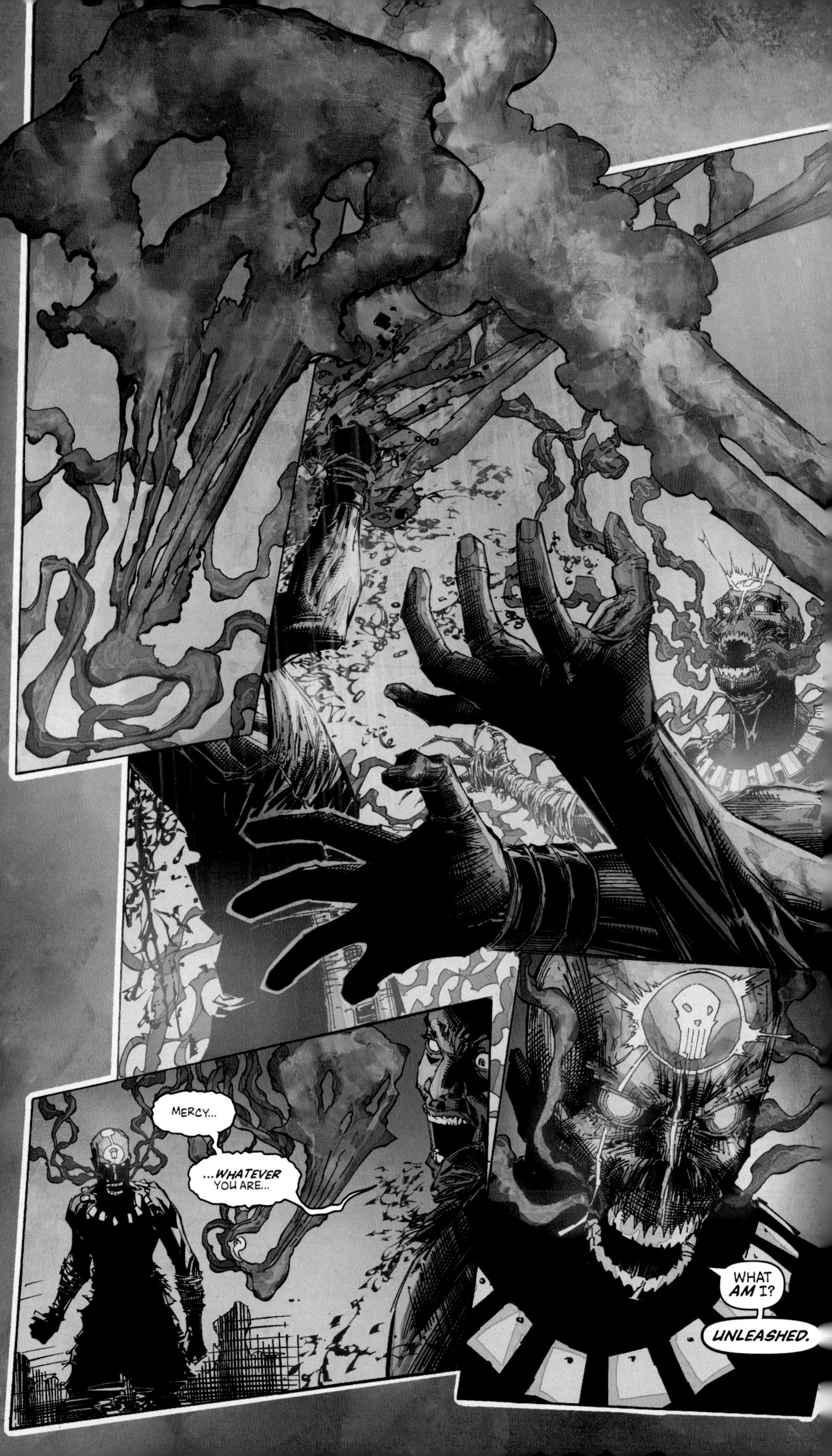
MERCY...
...WHATEVER YOU ARE...
WHAT AM I?
UNLEASHED.

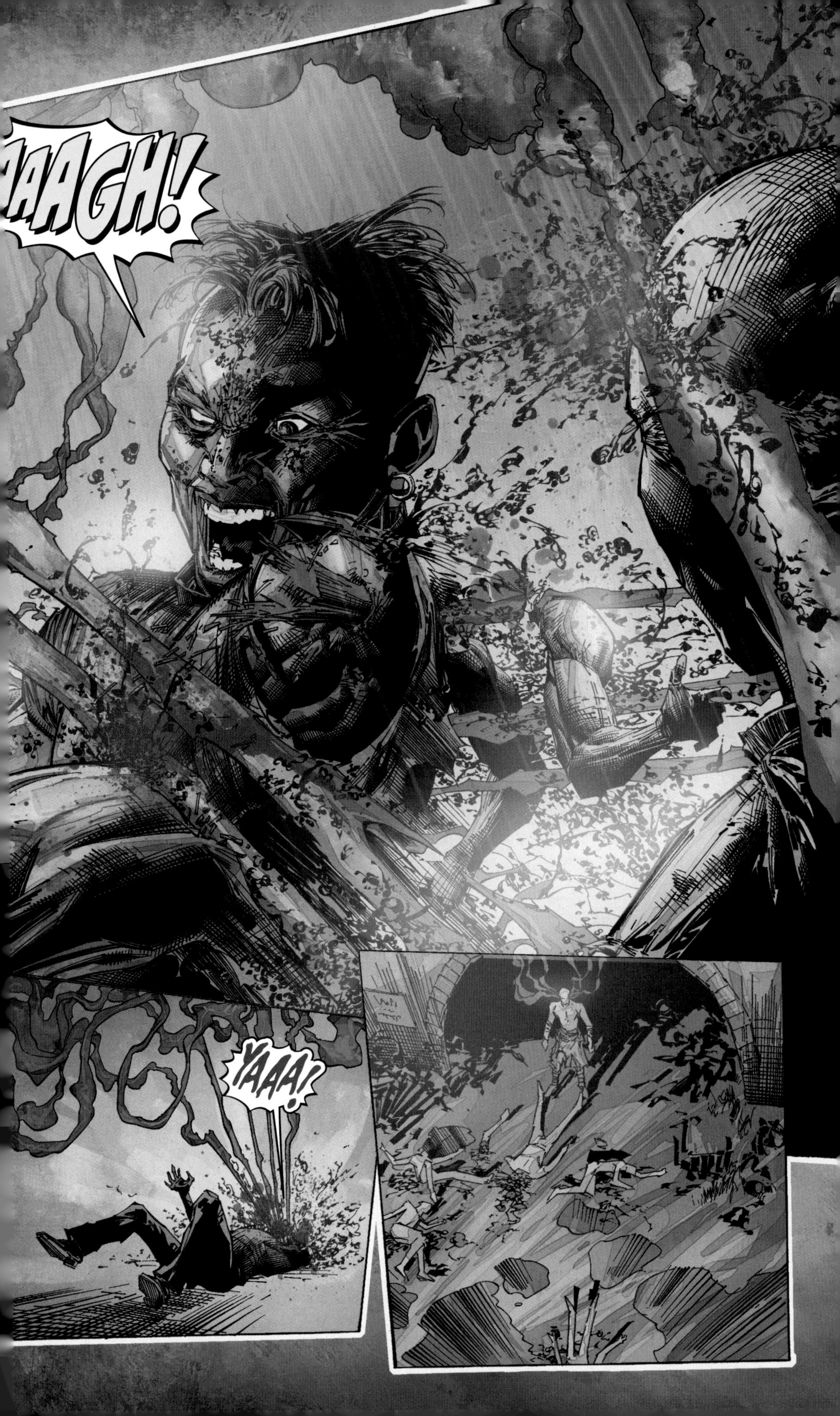
AAGH!
YAAA!

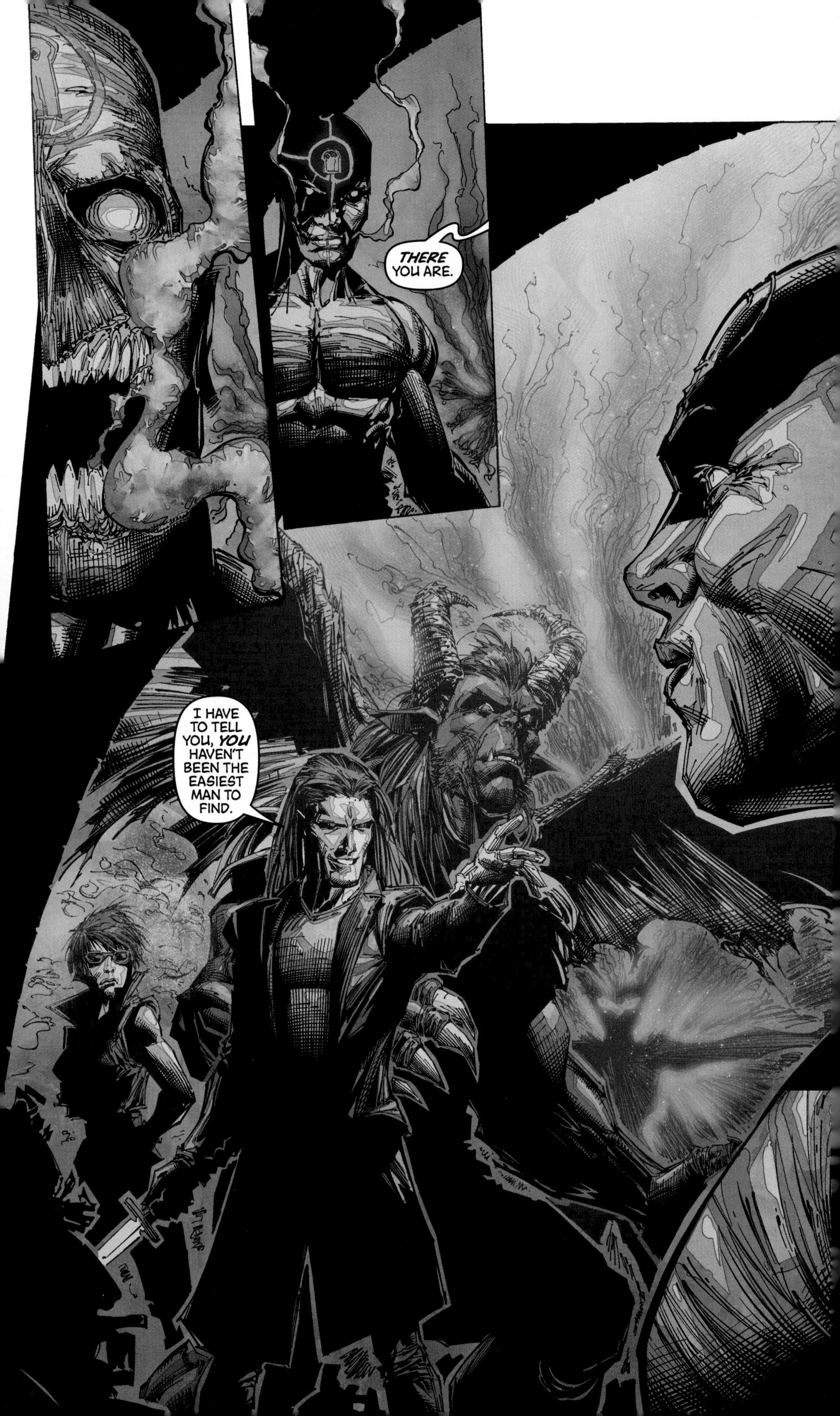
THERE YOU ARE.
I HAVE TO TELL YOU, YOU HAVEN'T BEEN THE EASIEST MAN TO FIND.

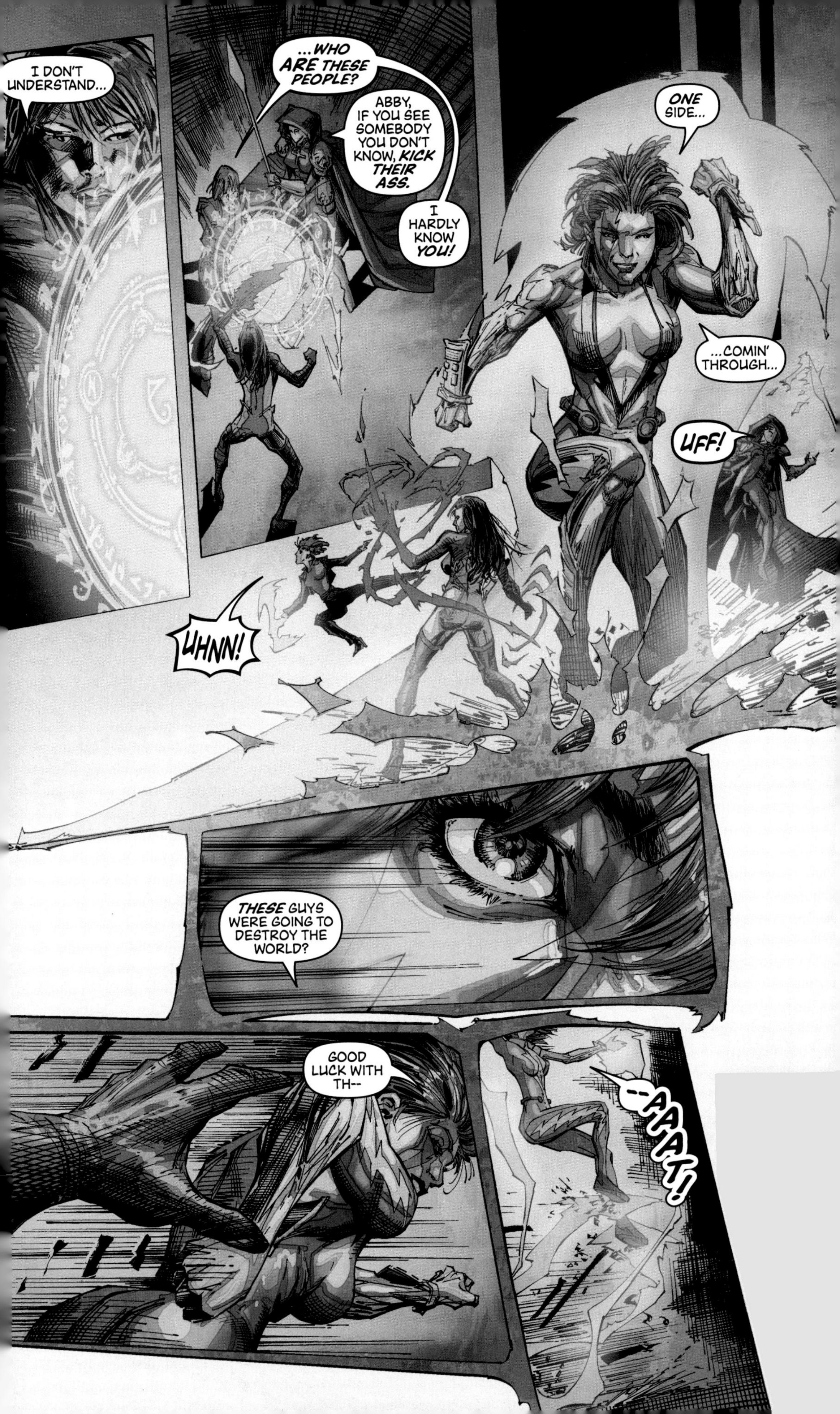
I DON'T UNDERSTAND...
...WHO ARE THESE PEOPLE?
ABBY, IF YOU SEE SOMEBODY YOU DON'T KNOW, KICK THEIR ASS.
I HARDLY KNOW YOU!
ONE SIDE...
...COMIN' THROUGH...
UFF!
UHNN!
THESE GUYS WERE GOING TO DESTROY THE WORLD?
GOOD LUCK WITH TH--
--AAAT!

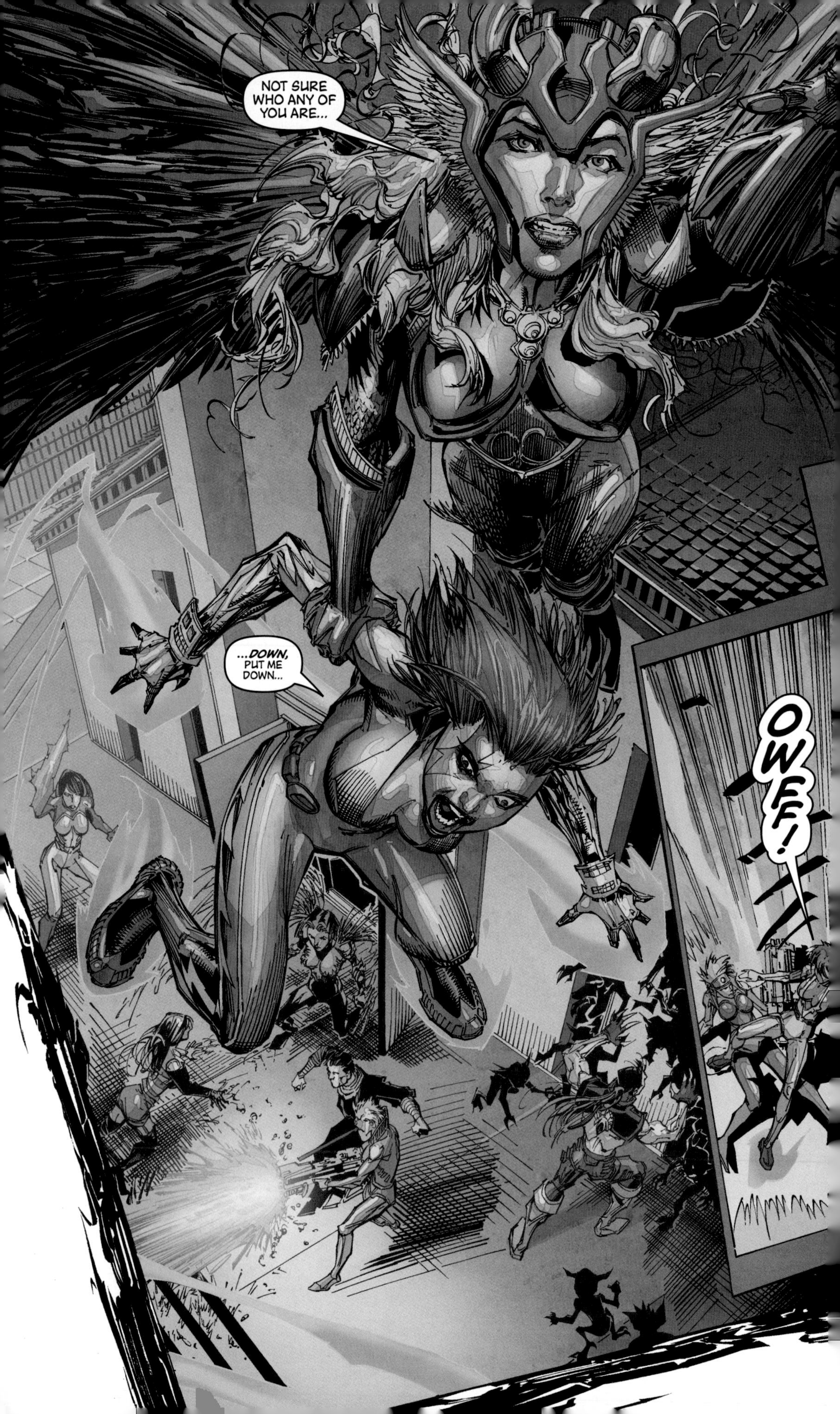
NOT SURE WHO ANY OF YOU ARE...
...DOWN, PUT ME DOWN...
OWFF!

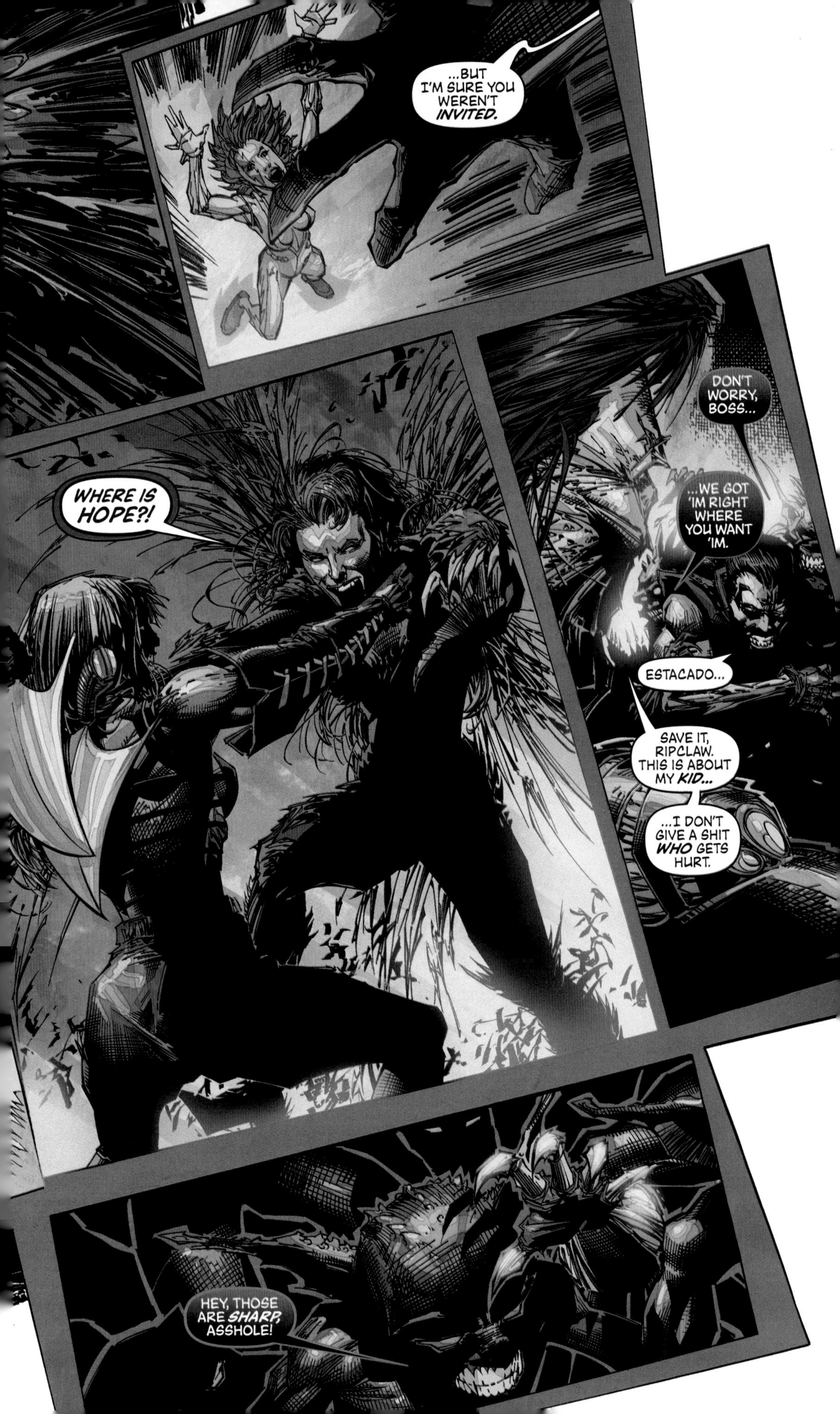
...BUT I'M SURE YOU WEREN'T *INVITED.*
WHERE IS HOPE?!
DON'T WORRY, BOSS...
...WE GOT 'IM RIGHT WHERE YOU WANT 'IM.
ESTACADO...
SAVE IT, RIPCLAW. THIS IS ABOUT MY *KID...*
...I DON'T GIVE A SHIT *WHO* GETS HURT.
HEY, THOSE ARE *SHARP,* ASSHOLE!

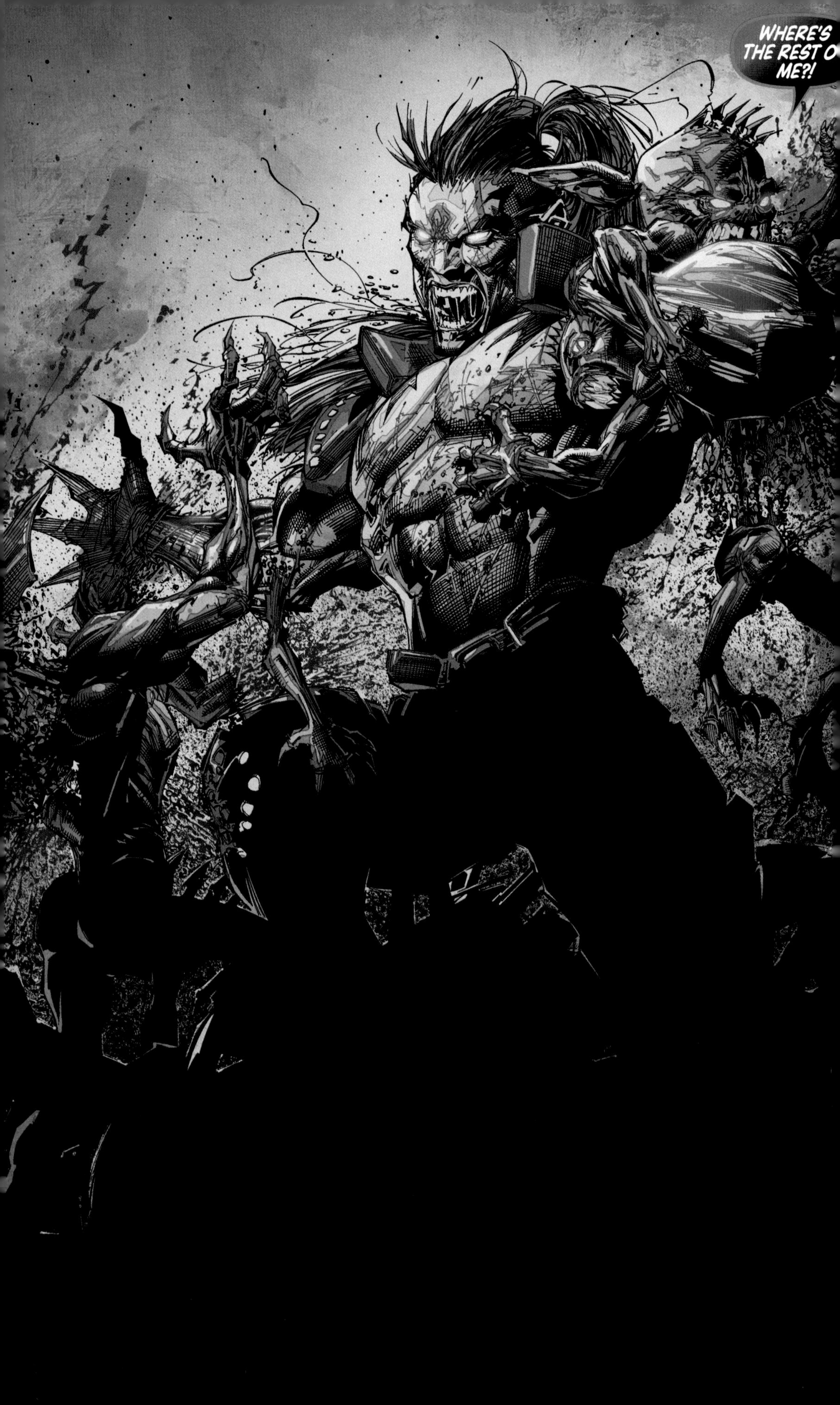
WHERE'S THE REST O ME?!

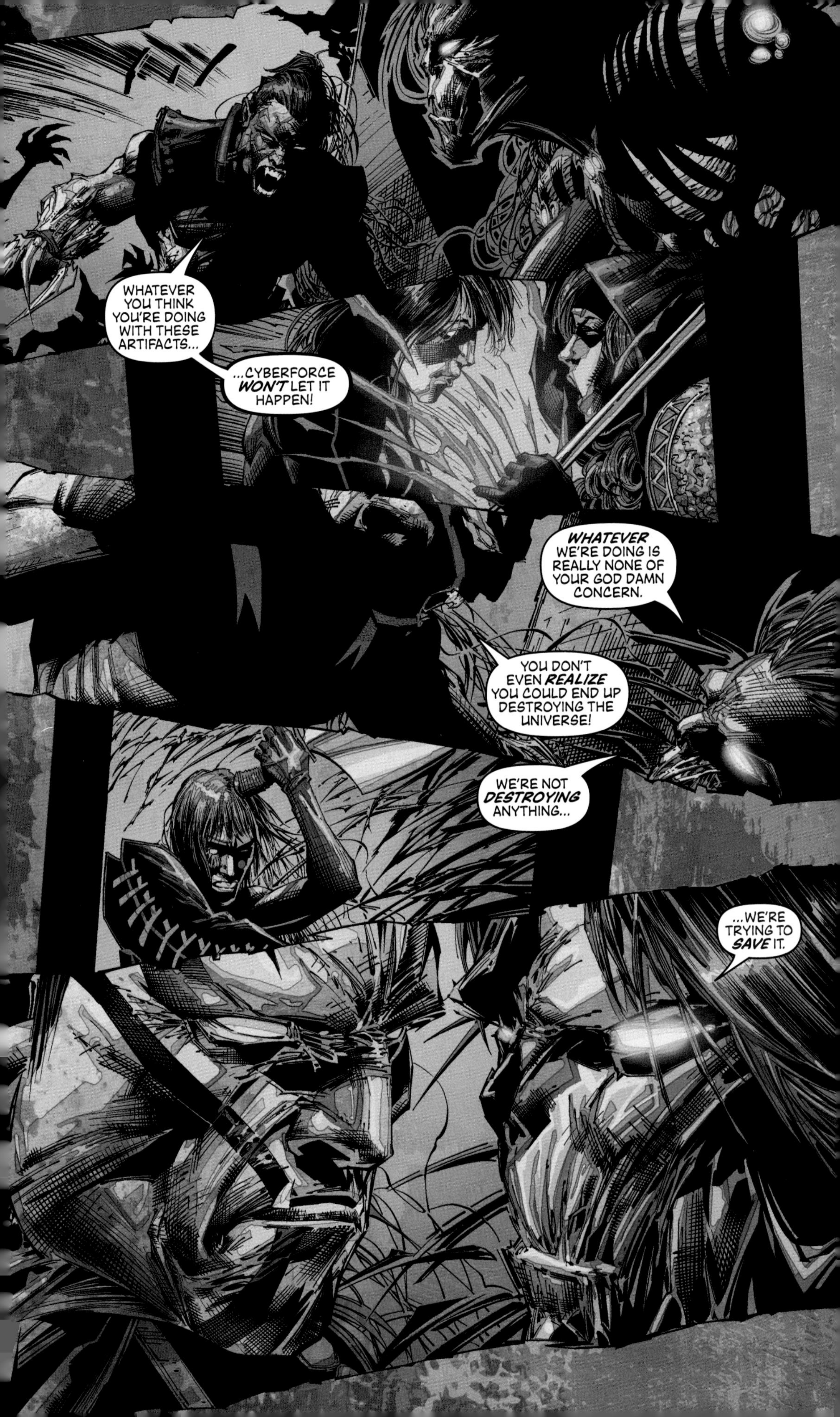

WHATEVER YOU THINK YOU'RE DOING WITH THESE ARTIFACTS...
...CYBERFORCE WON'T LET IT HAPPEN!
WHATEVER WE'RE DOING IS REALLY NONE OF YOUR GOD DAMN CONCERN.
YOU DON'T EVEN REALIZE YOU COULD END UP DESTROYING THE UNIVERSE!
WE'RE NOT DESTROYING ANYTHING...
...WE'RE TRYING TO SAVE IT.

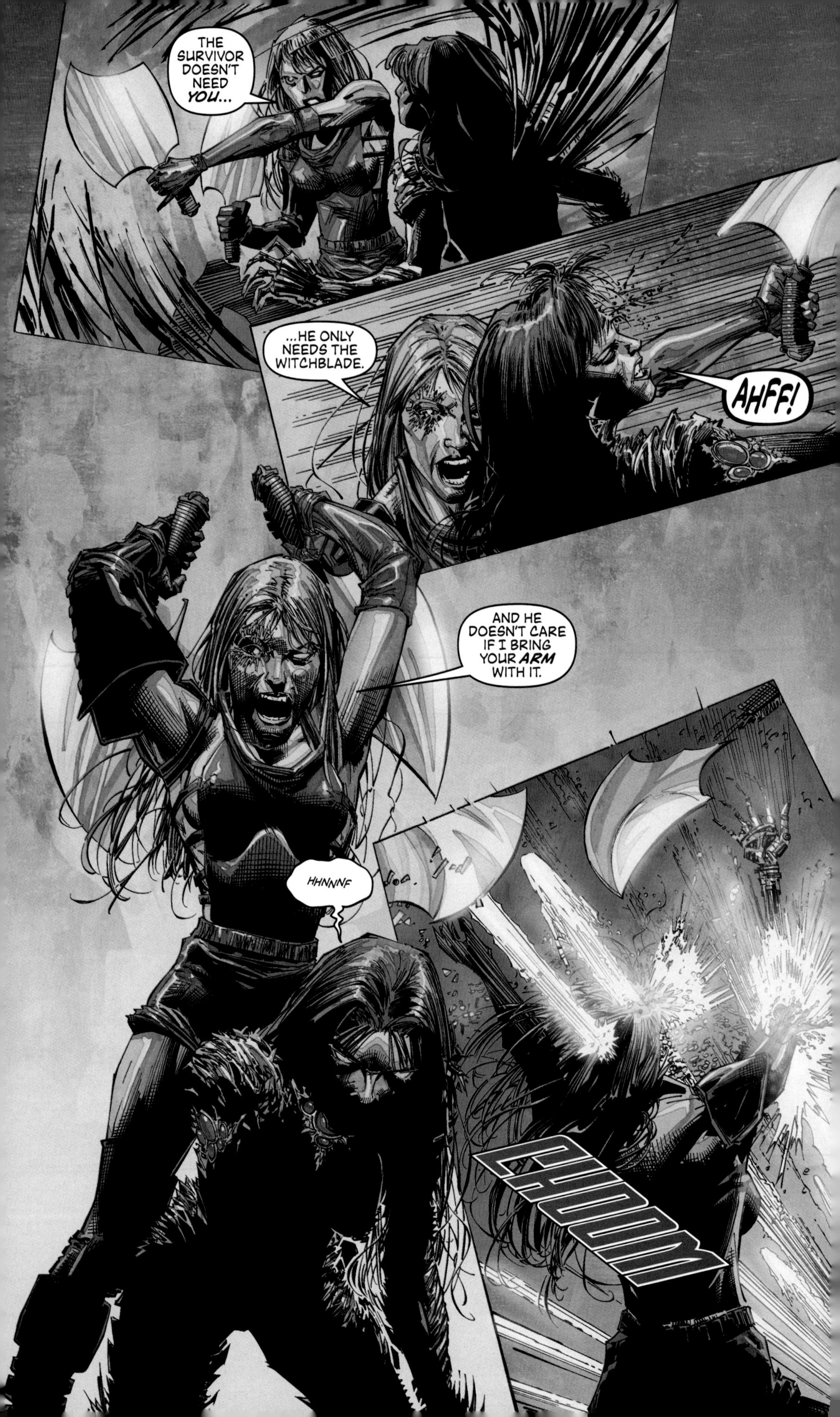
THE SURVIVOR DOESN'T NEED *YOU*...
...HE ONLY NEEDS THE WITCHBLADE.
AHFF!
AND HE DOESN'T CARE IF I BRING YOUR *ARM* WITH IT.
HHNNNF
CHOOM

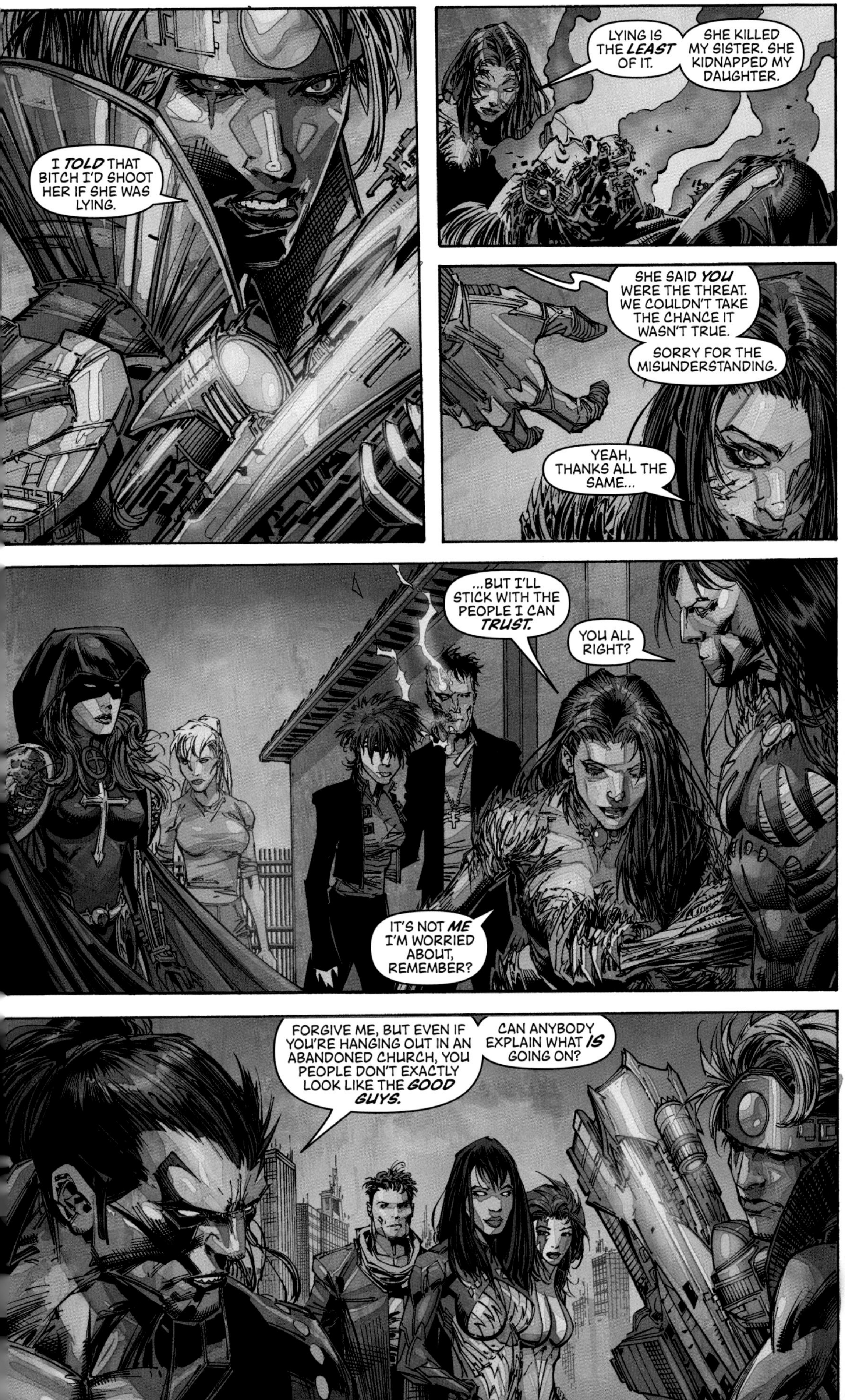

I *TOLD* THAT BITCH I'D SHOOT HER IF SHE WAS LYING.
LYING IS THE *LEAST* OF IT.
SHE KILLED MY SISTER. SHE KIDNAPPED MY DAUGHTER.
SHE SAID *YOU* WERE THE THREAT. WE COULDN'T TAKE THE CHANCE IT WASN'T TRUE.
SORRY FOR THE MISUNDERSTANDING.
YEAH, THANKS ALL THE SAME...
...BUT I'LL STICK WITH THE PEOPLE I CAN *TRUST.*
YOU ALL RIGHT?
IT'S NOT *ME* I'M WORRIED ABOUT, REMEMBER?
FORGIVE ME, BUT EVEN IF YOU'RE HANGING OUT IN AN ABANDONED CHURCH, YOU PEOPLE DON'T EXACTLY LOOK LIKE THE *GOOD GUYS.*
CAN ANYBODY EXPLAIN WHAT *IS* GOING ON?

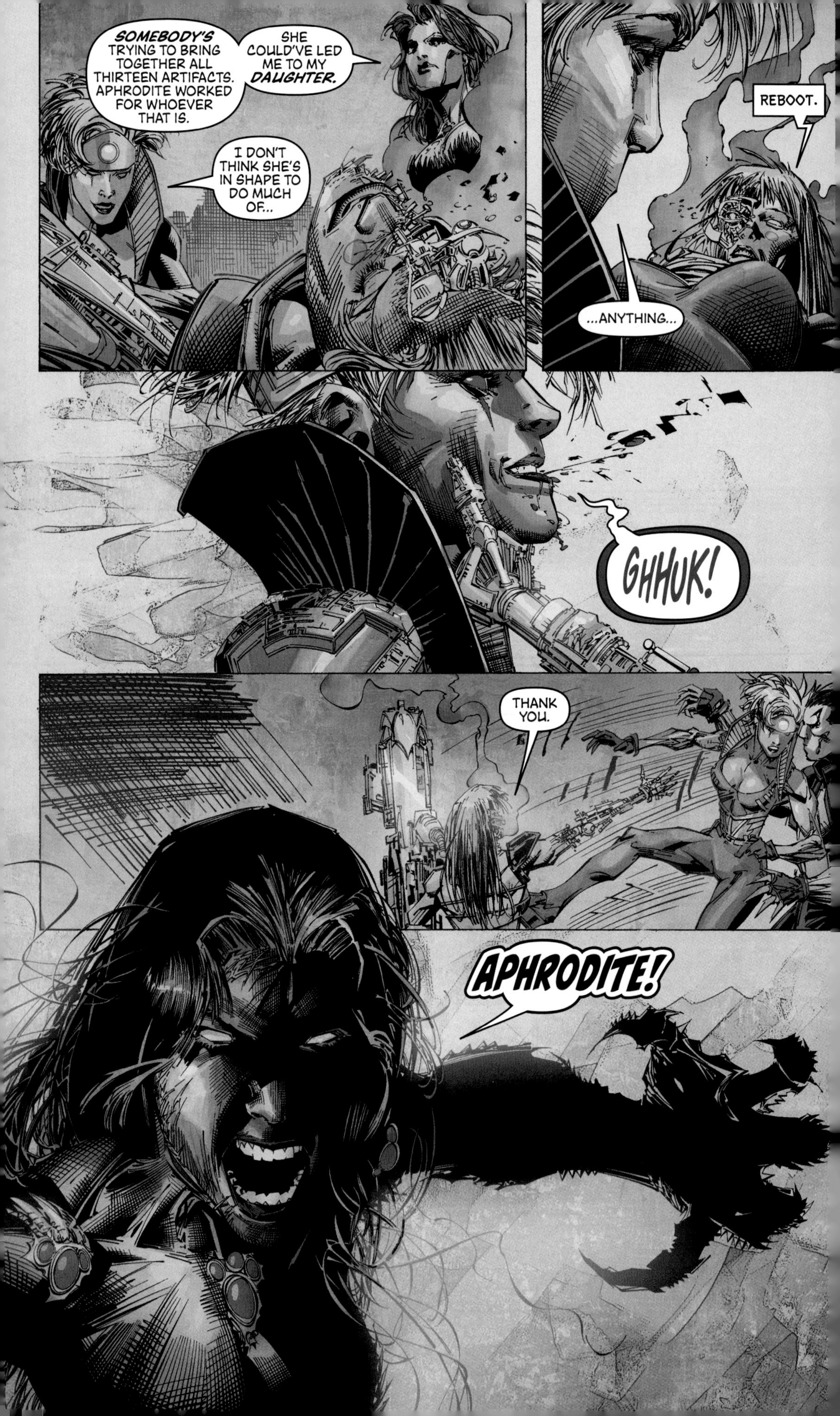
SOMEBODY'S TRYING TO BRING TOGETHER ALL THIRTEEN ARTIFACTS. APHRODITE WORKED FOR WHOEVER THAT IS.
SHE COULD'VE LED ME TO MY DAUGHTER.
I DON'T THINK SHE'S IN SHAPE TO DO MUCH OF...
...ANYTHING...
REBOOT.
GHHUK!
THANK YOU.
APHRODITE!

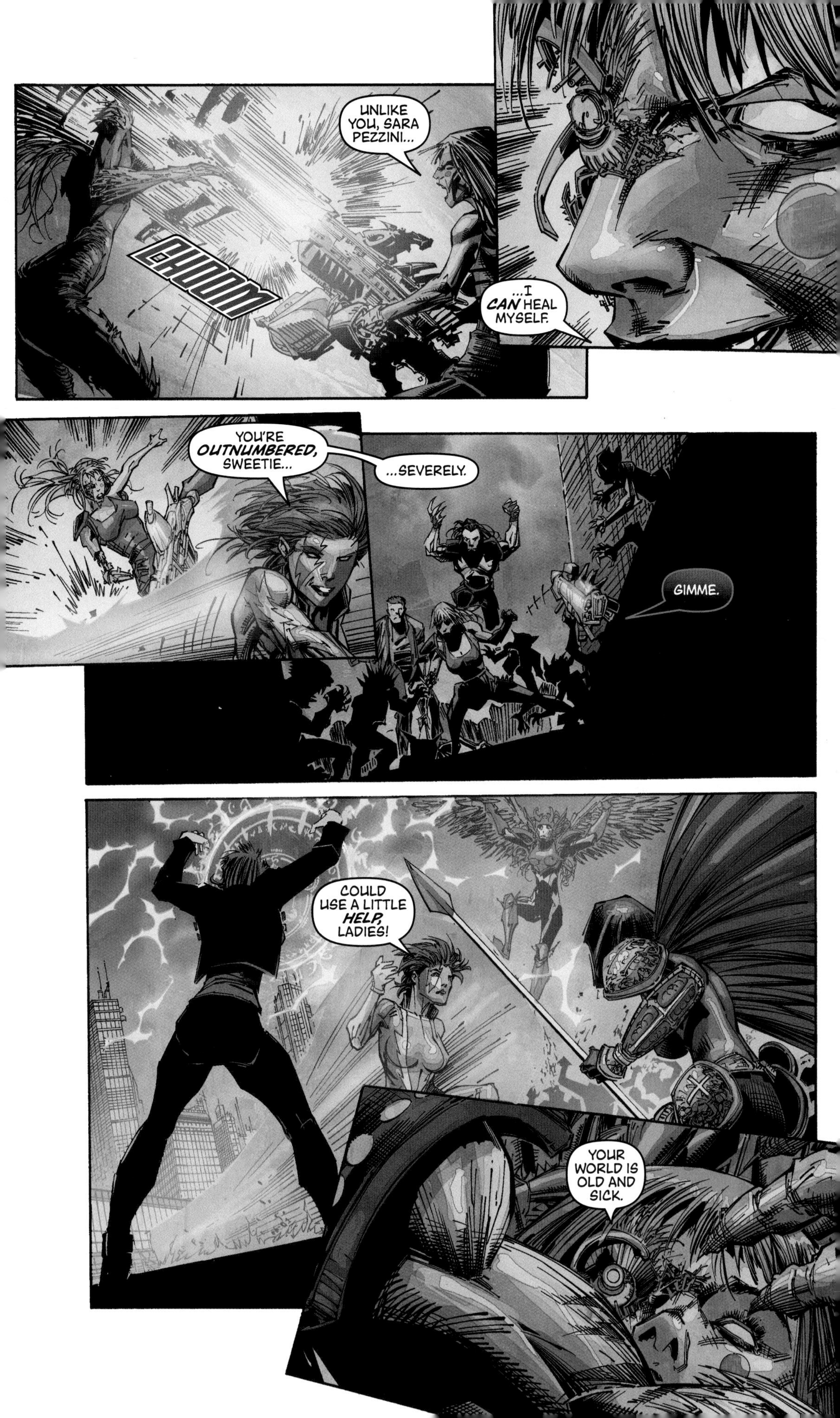
UNLIKE YOU, SARA PEZZINI...
CHOOM
...I CAN HEAL MYSELF.
YOU'RE OUTNUMBERED, SWEETIE...
...SEVERELY.
GIMME.
COULD USE A LITTLE HELP, LADIES!
YOUR WORLD IS OLD AND SICK.

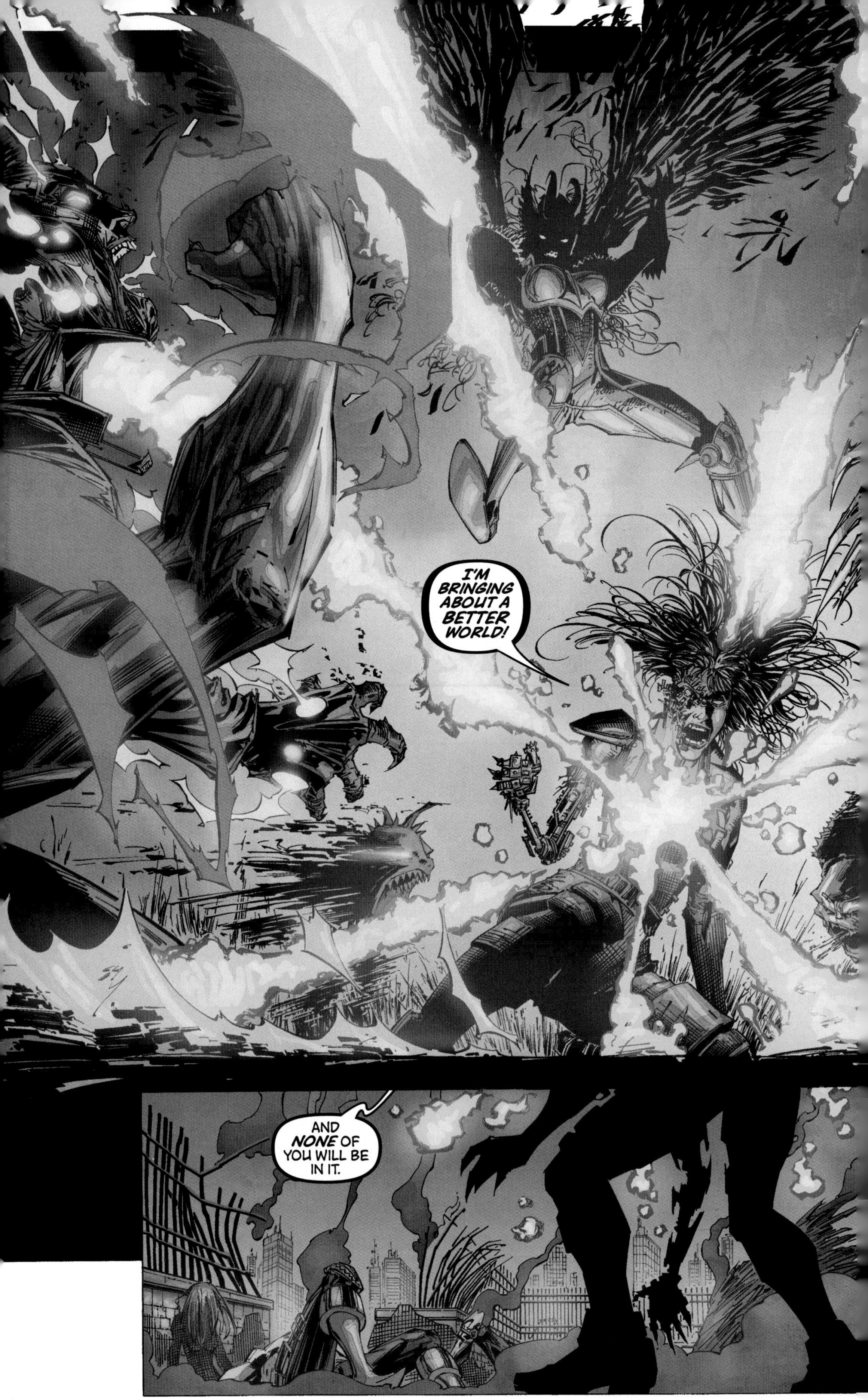
I'M BRINGING ABOUT A BETTER WORLD!
AND NONE OF YOU WILL BE IN IT.

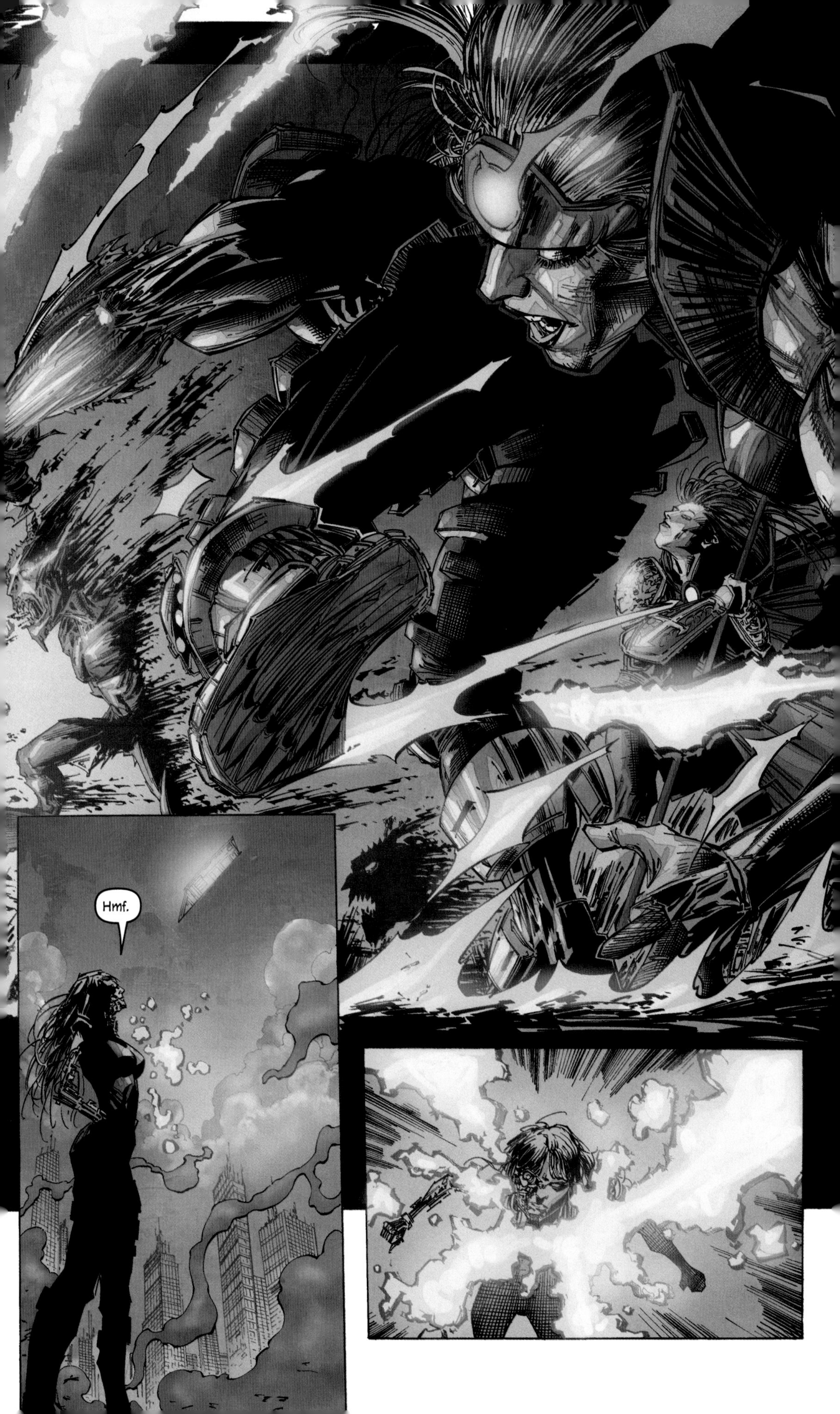
Hmf.

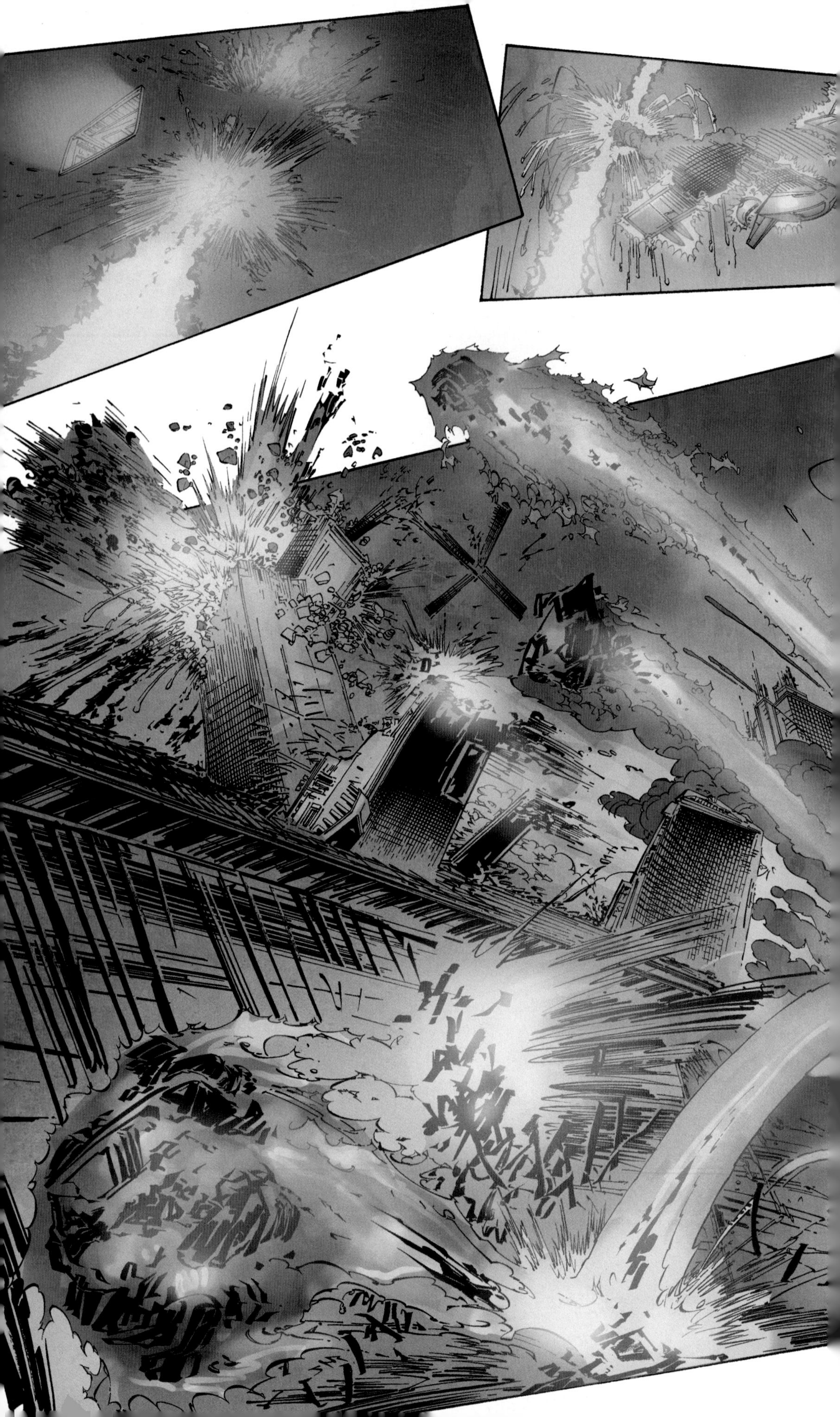

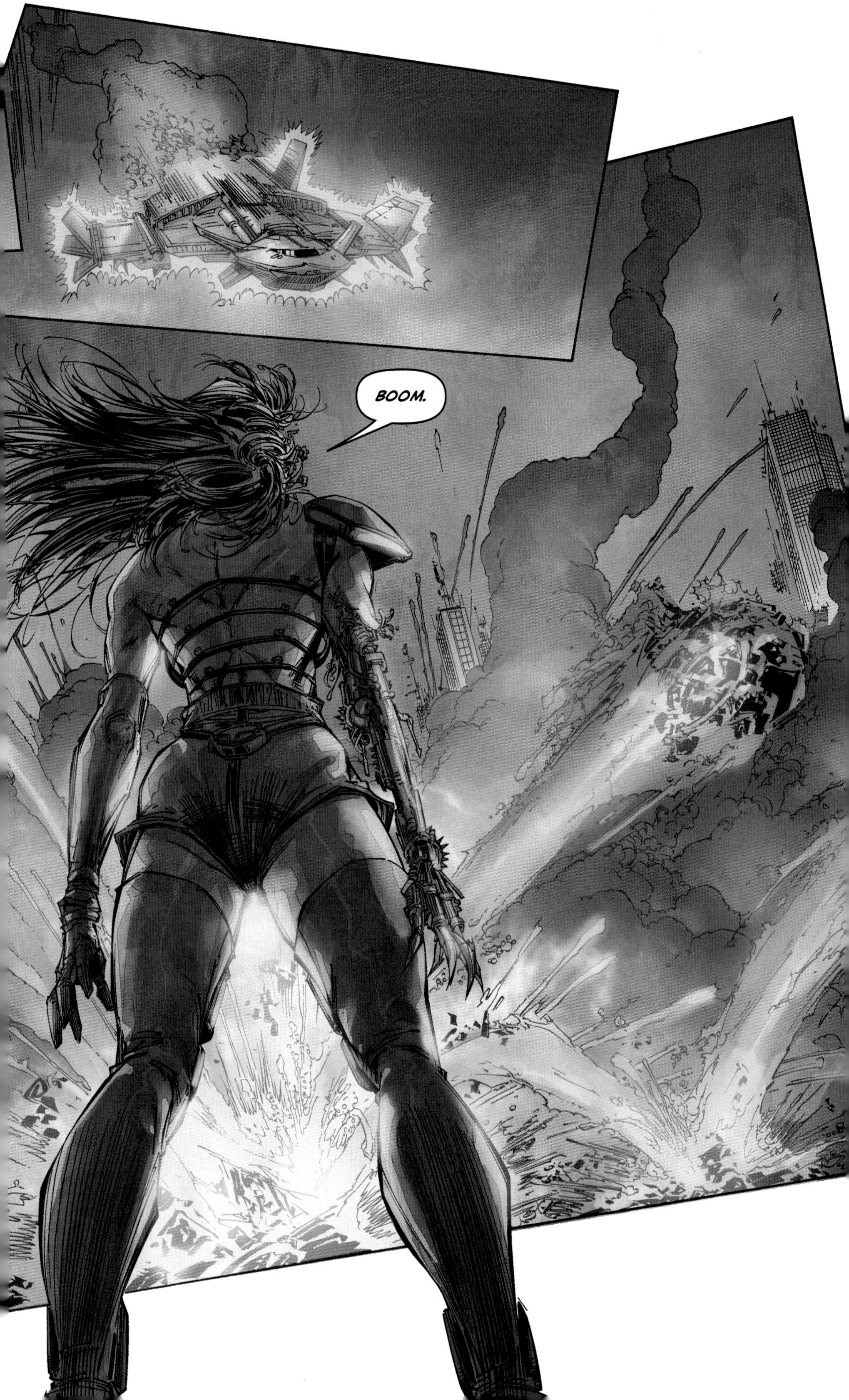
BOOM.

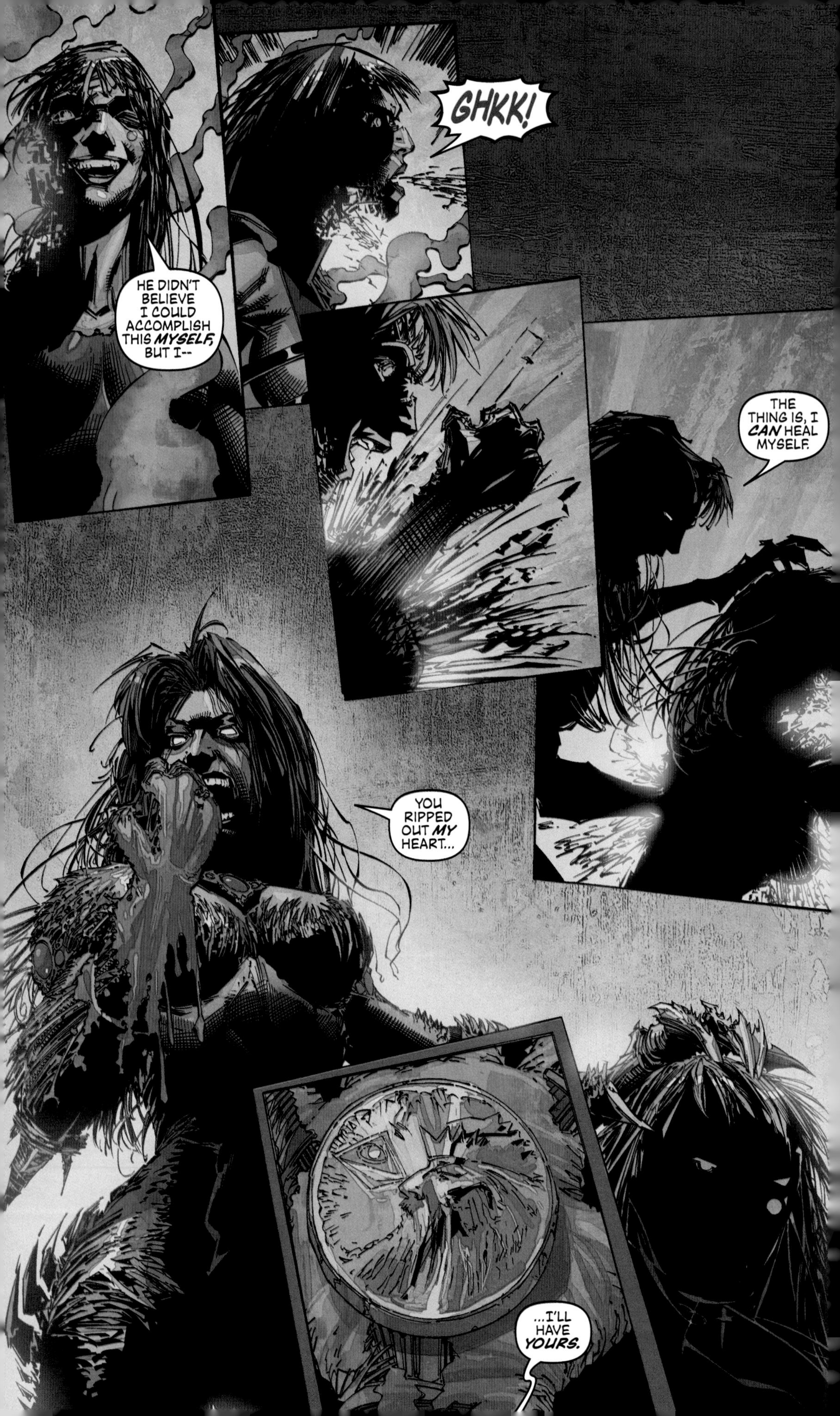
GHKK!
HE DIDN'T BELIEVE I COULD ACCOMPLISH THIS MYSELF, BUT I--
THE THING IS, I CAN HEAL MYSELF.
YOU RIPPED OUT MY HEART...
...I'LL HAVE YOURS.

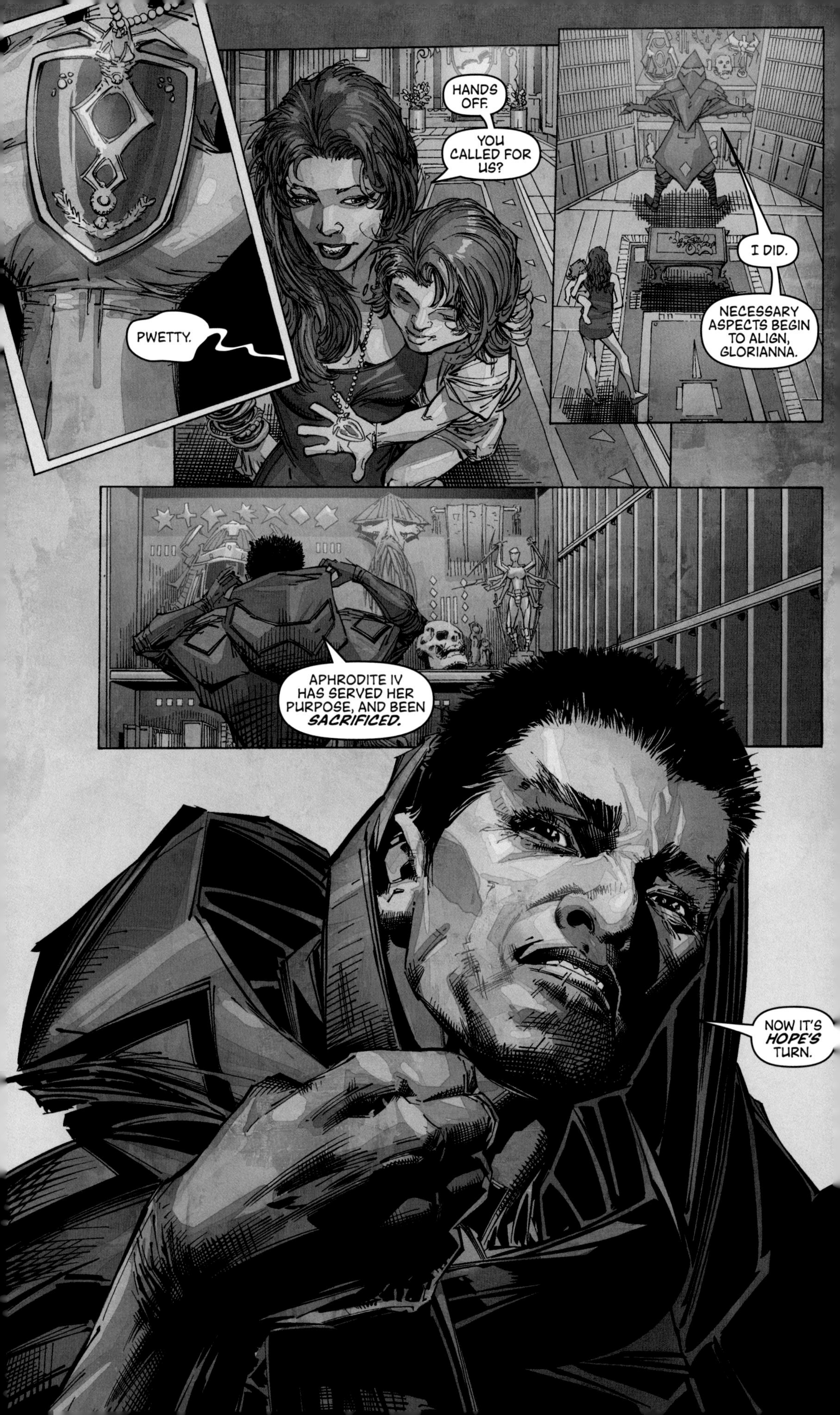

PWETTY.
HANDS OFF.
YOU CALLED FOR US?
I DID.
NECESSARY ASPECTS BEGIN TO ALIGN, GLORIANNA.
APHRODITE IV HAS SERVED HER PURPOSE, AND BEEN *SACRIFICED.*
NOW IT'S *HOPE'S* TURN.

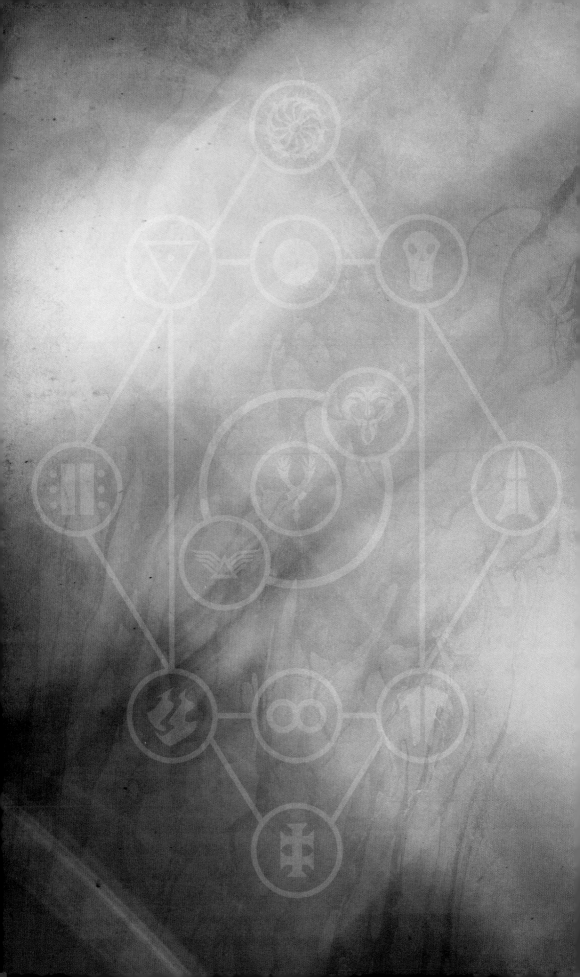

CHAPTER 7

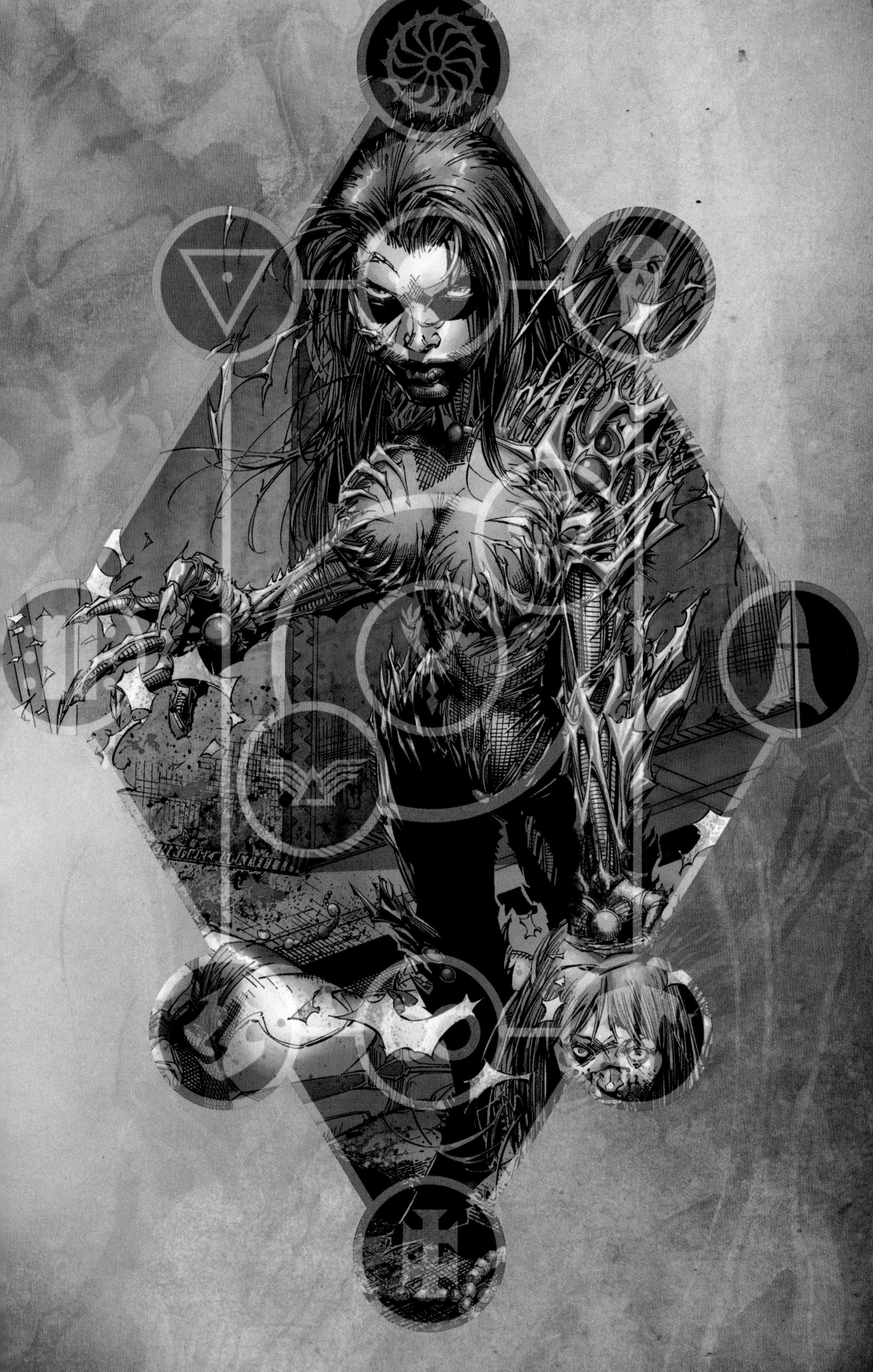

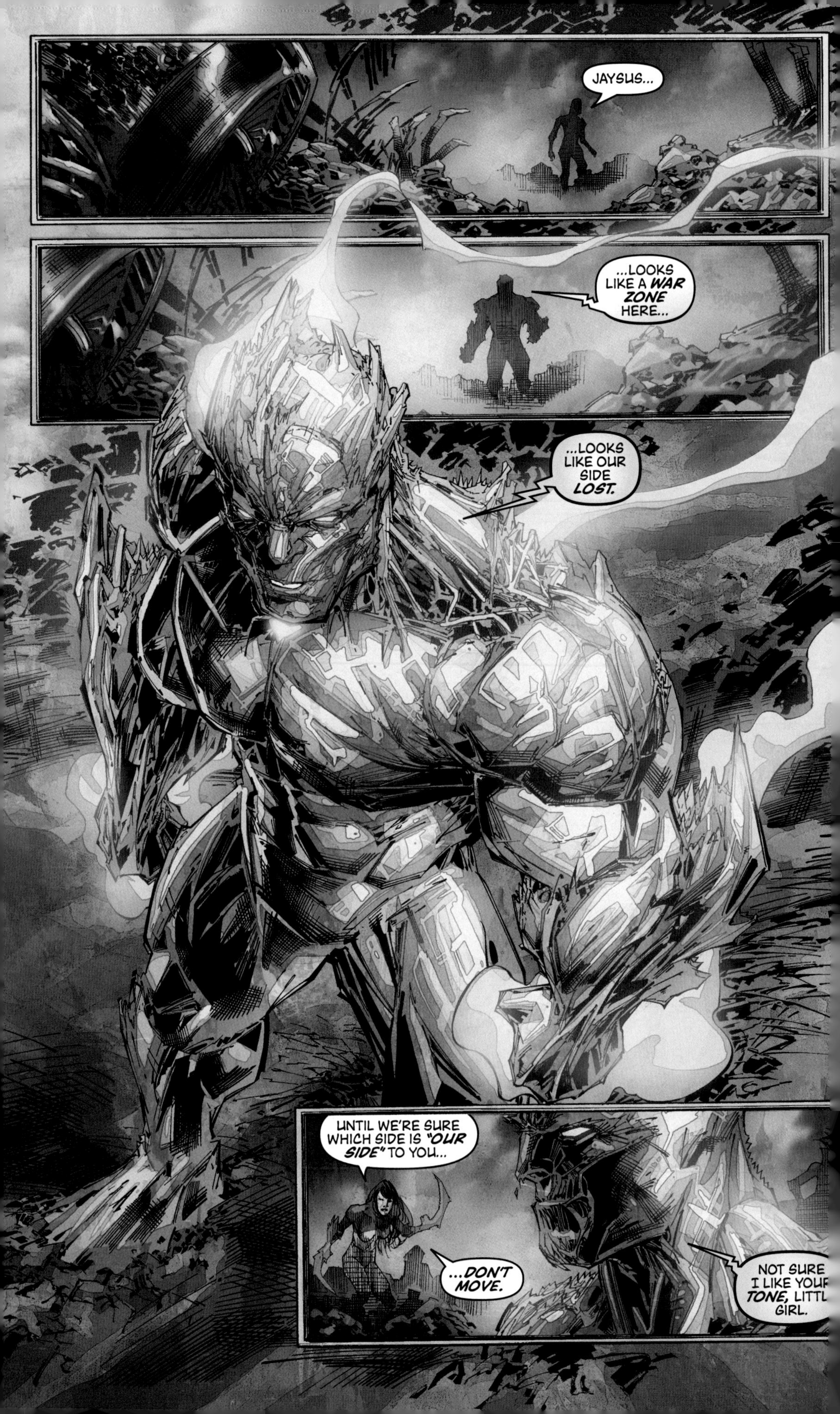
JAYSUS...
...LOOKS LIKE A WAR ZONE HERE...
...LOOKS LIKE OUR SIDE LOST.
UNTIL WE'RE SURE WHICH SIDE IS "OUR SIDE" TO YOU...
...DON'T MOVE.
NOT SURE I LIKE YOUR TONE, LITTL GIRL.

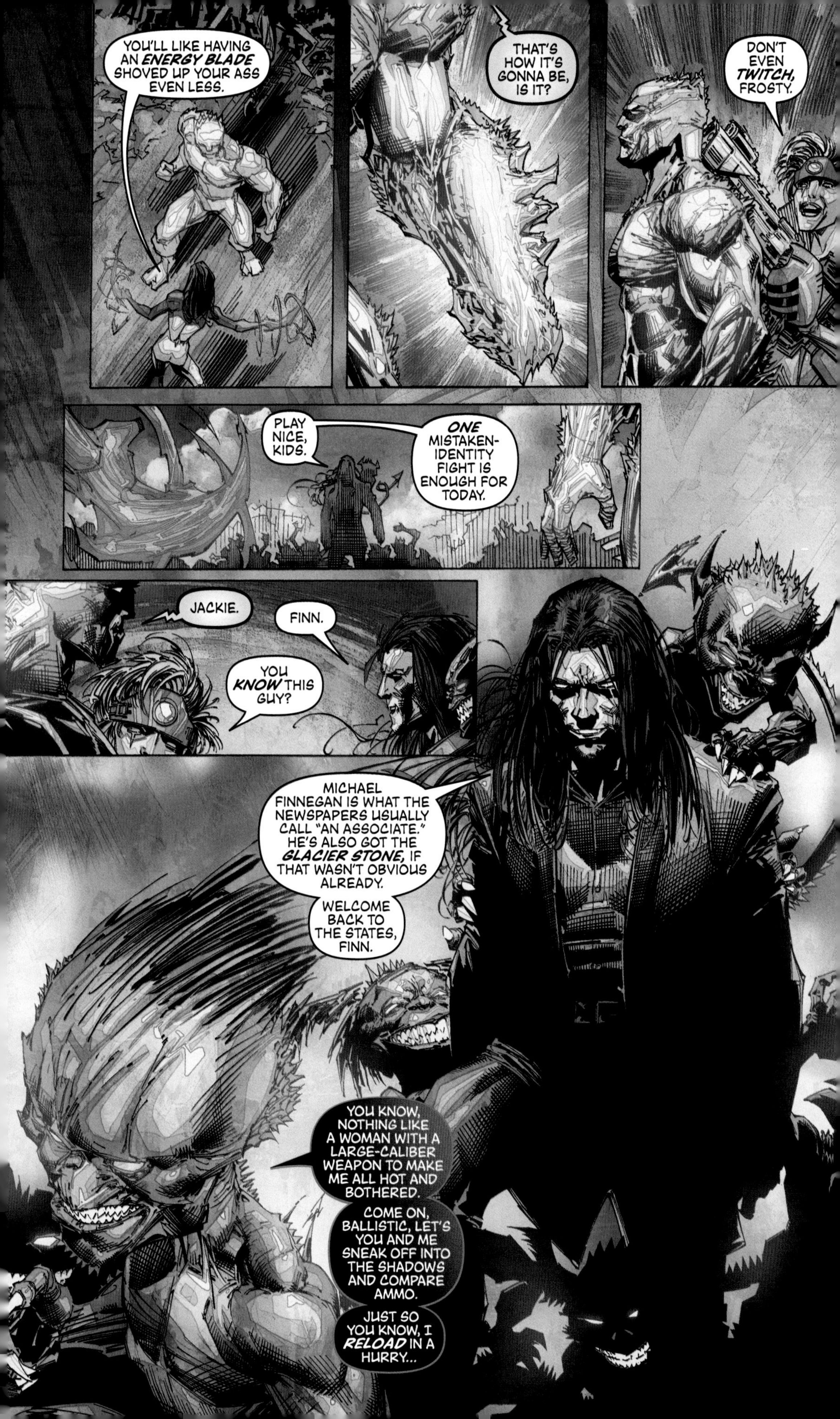

YOU'LL LIKE HAVING AN ***ENERGY BLADE*** SHOVED UP YOUR ASS EVEN LESS.
THAT'S HOW IT'S GONNA BE, IS IT?
DON'T EVEN ***TWITCH,*** FROSTY.
PLAY NICE, KIDS.
ONE MISTAKEN-IDENTITY FIGHT IS ENOUGH FOR TODAY.
JACKIE.
FINN.
YOU ***KNOW*** THIS GUY?
MICHAEL FINNEGAN IS WHAT THE NEWSPAPERS USUALLY CALL "AN ASSOCIATE." HE'S ALSO GOT THE ***GLACIER STONE,*** IF THAT WASN'T OBVIOUS ALREADY.
WELCOME BACK TO THE STATES, FINN.
YOU KNOW, NOTHING LIKE A WOMAN WITH A LARGE-CALIBER WEAPON TO MAKE ME ALL HOT AND BOTHERED.
COME ON, BALLISTIC, LET'S YOU AND ME SNEAK OFF INTO THE SHADOWS AND COMPARE AMMO.
JUST SO YOU KNOW, I ***RELOAD*** IN A HURRY...

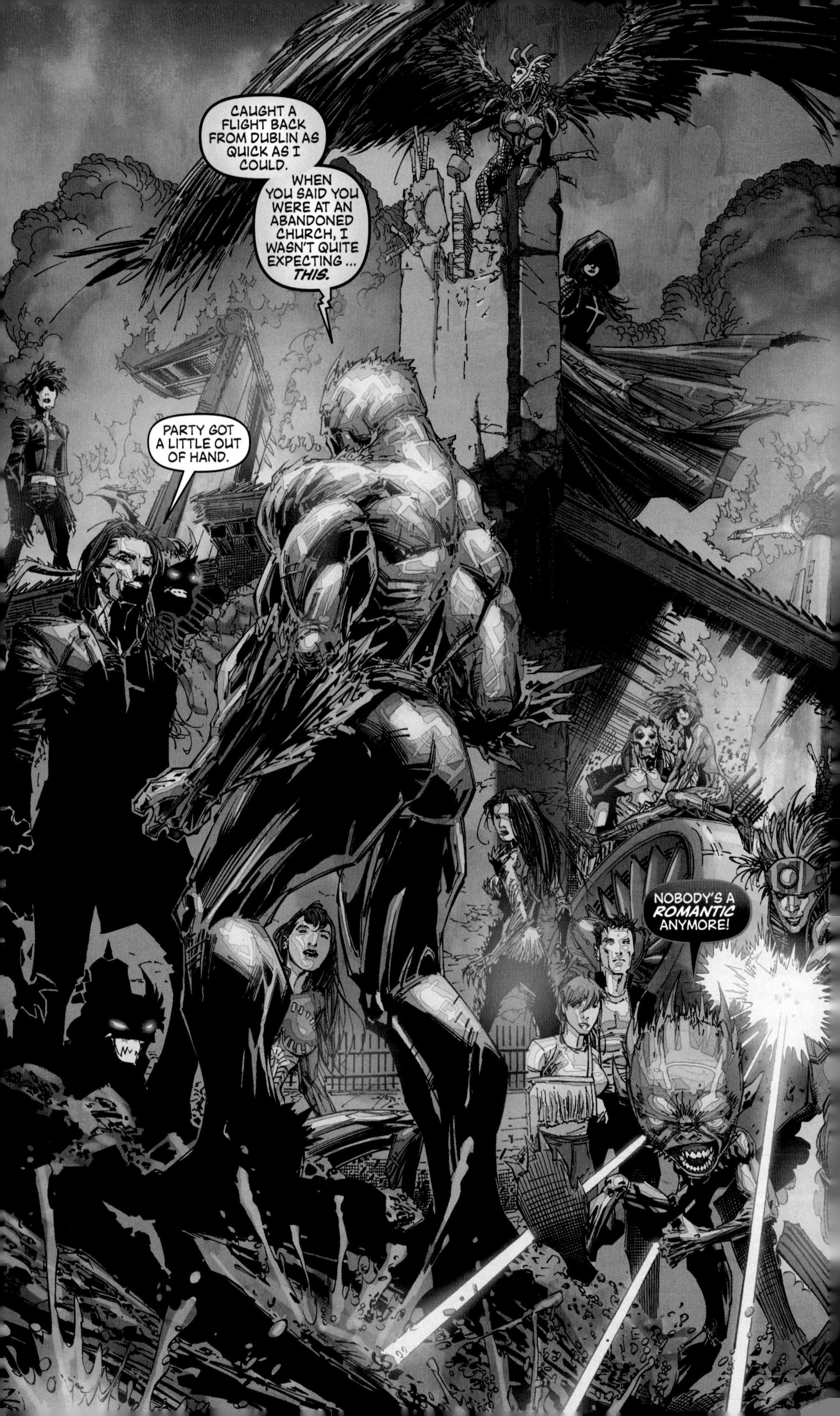
CAUGHT A FLIGHT BACK FROM DUBLIN AS QUICK AS I COULD.
WHEN YOU SAID YOU WERE AT AN ABANDONED CHURCH, I WASN'T QUITE EXPECTING ... THIS.
PARTY GOT A LITTLE OUT OF HAND.
NOBODY'S A ROMANTIC ANYMORE!

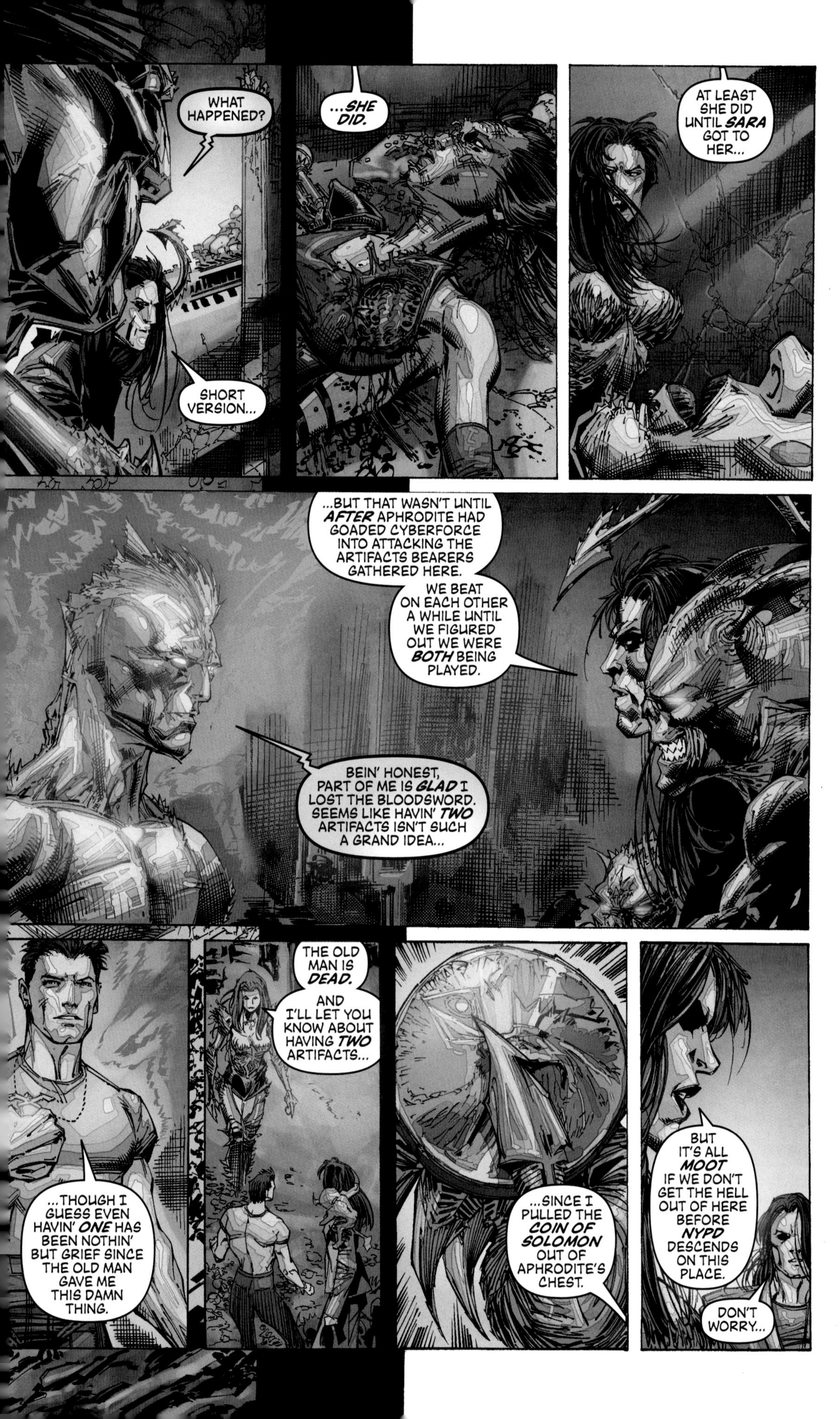
WHAT HAPPENED?
SHORT VERSION...
...SHE DID.
AT LEAST SHE DID UNTIL SARA GOT TO HER...
...BUT THAT WASN'T UNTIL AFTER APHRODITE HAD GOADED CYBERFORCE INTO ATTACKING THE ARTIFACTS BEARERS GATHERED HERE.
WE BEAT ON EACH OTHER A WHILE UNTIL WE FIGURED OUT WE WERE BOTH BEING PLAYED.
BEIN' HONEST, PART OF ME IS GLAD I LOST THE BLOODSWORD. SEEMS LIKE HAVIN' TWO ARTIFACTS ISN'T SUCH A GRAND IDEA...
...THOUGH I GUESS EVEN HAVIN' ONE HAS BEEN NOTHIN' BUT GRIEF SINCE THE OLD MAN GAVE ME THIS DAMN THING.
THE OLD MAN IS DEAD.
AND I'LL LET YOU KNOW ABOUT HAVING TWO ARTIFACTS...
...SINCE I PULLED THE COIN OF SOLOMON OUT OF APHRODITE'S CHEST.
BUT IT'S ALL MOOT IF WE DON'T GET THE HELL OUT OF HERE BEFORE NYPD DESCENDS ON THIS PLACE.
DON'T WORRY...

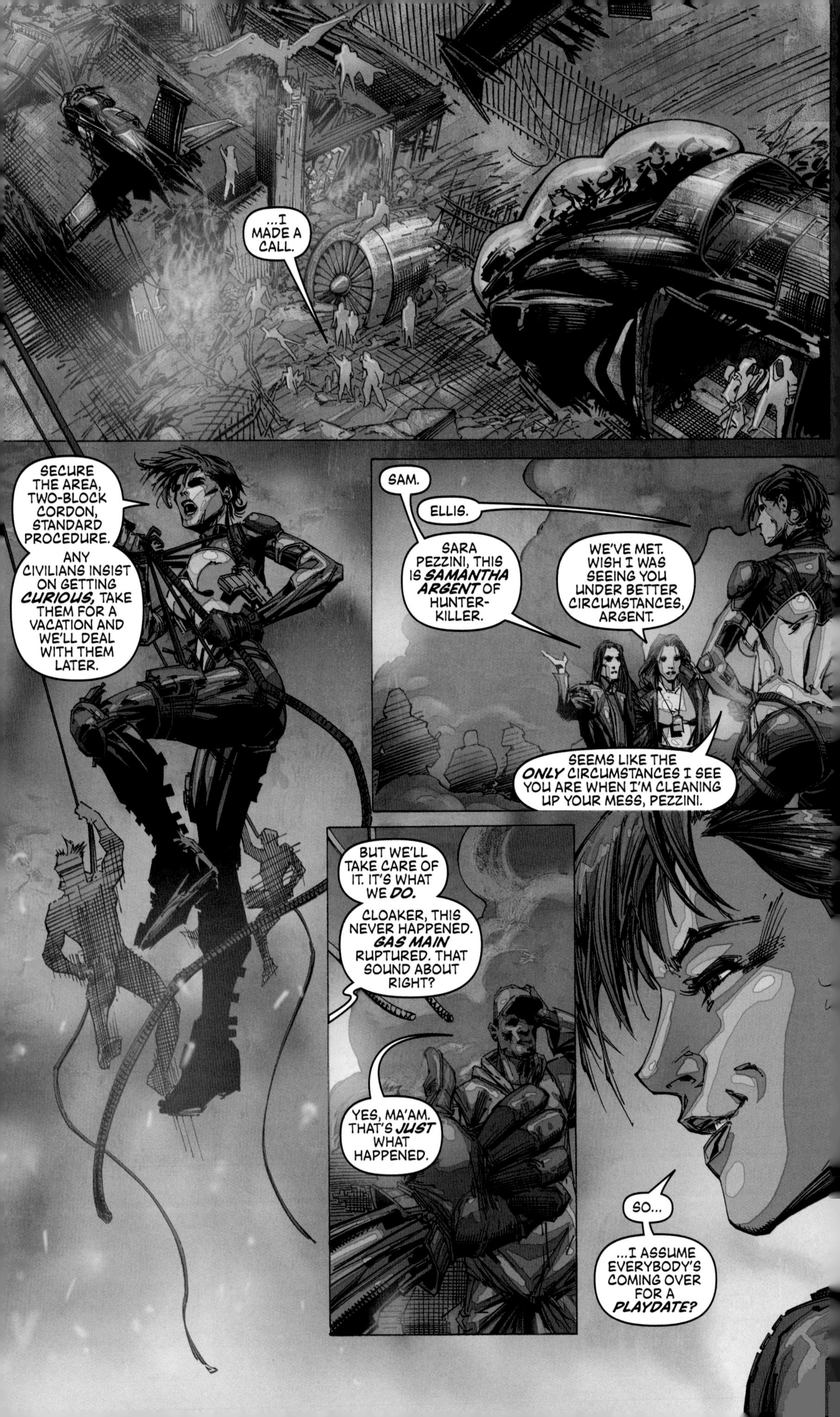
...I MADE A CALL.
SECURE THE AREA, TWO-BLOCK CORDON, STANDARD PROCEDURE.
ANY CIVILIANS INSIST ON GETTING *CURIOUS,* TAKE THEM FOR A VACATION AND WE'LL DEAL WITH THEM LATER.
SAM.
ELLIS.
SARA PEZZINI, THIS IS *SAMANTHA ARGENT* OF HUNTER-KILLER.
WE'VE MET. WISH I WAS SEEING YOU UNDER BETTER CIRCUMSTANCES, ARGENT.
SEEMS LIKE THE *ONLY* CIRCUMSTANCES I SEE YOU ARE WHEN I'M CLEANING UP YOUR MESS, PEZZINI.
BUT WE'LL TAKE CARE OF IT. IT'S WHAT WE *DO.*
CLOAKER, THIS NEVER HAPPENED. *GAS MAIN* RUPTURED. THAT SOUND ABOUT RIGHT?
YES, MA'AM. THAT'S *JUST* WHAT HAPPENED.
SO...
...I ASSUME EVERYBODY'S COMING OVER FOR A *PLAYDATE?*

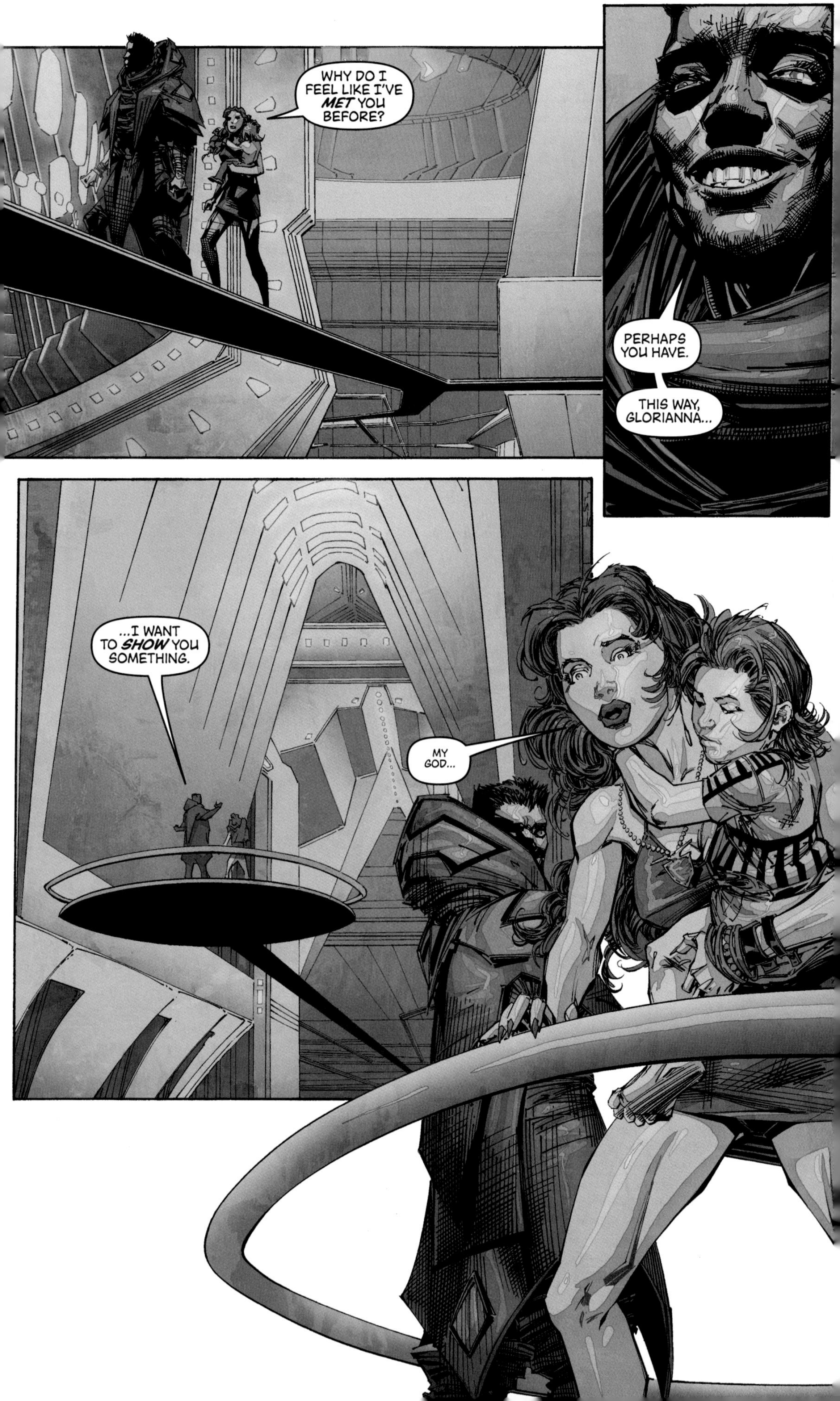
WHY DO I FEEL LIKE I'VE MET YOU BEFORE?
PERHAPS YOU HAVE.
THIS WAY, GLORIANNA...
...I WANT TO SHOW YOU SOMETHING.
MY GOD...

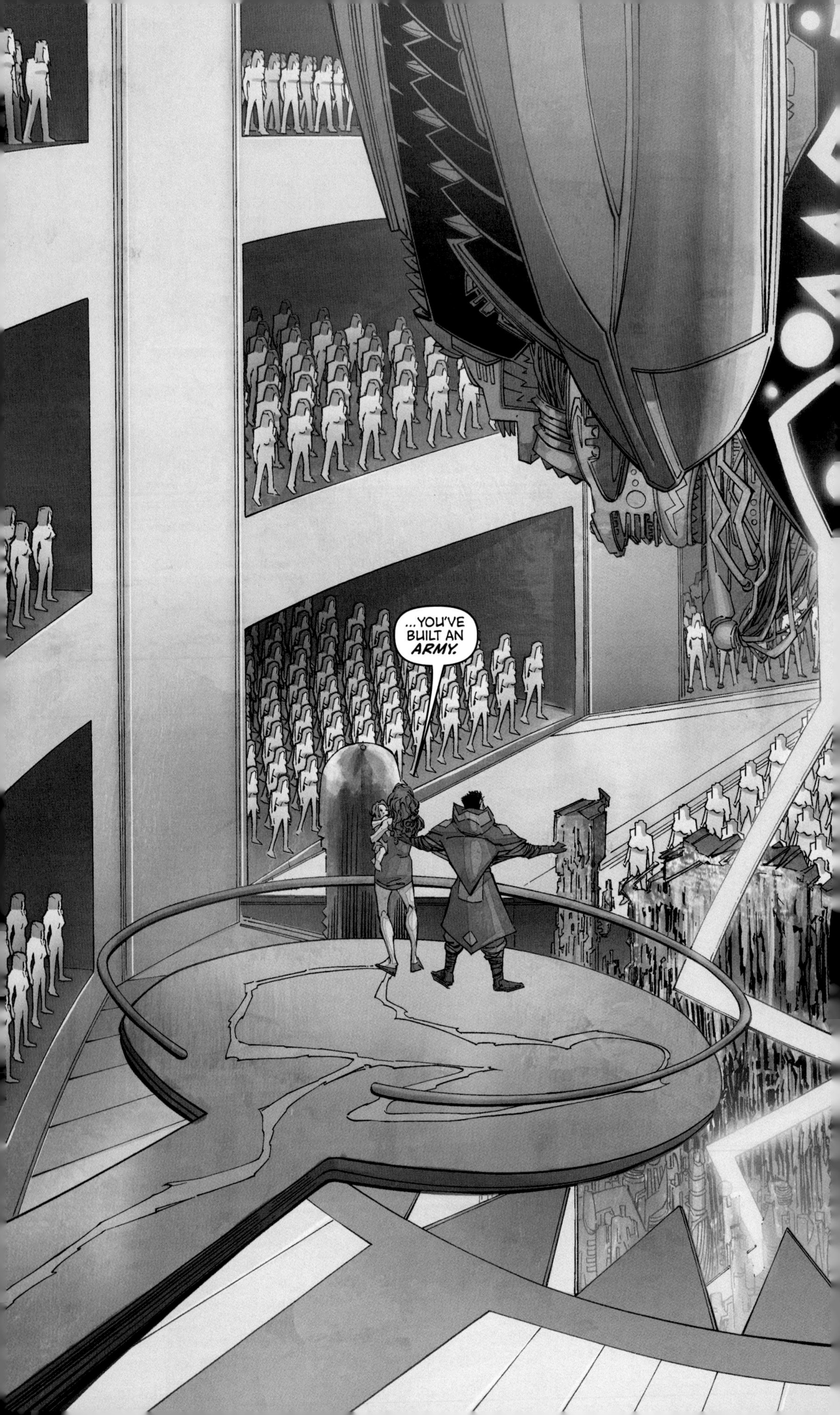
...YOU'VE BUILT AN ARMY.

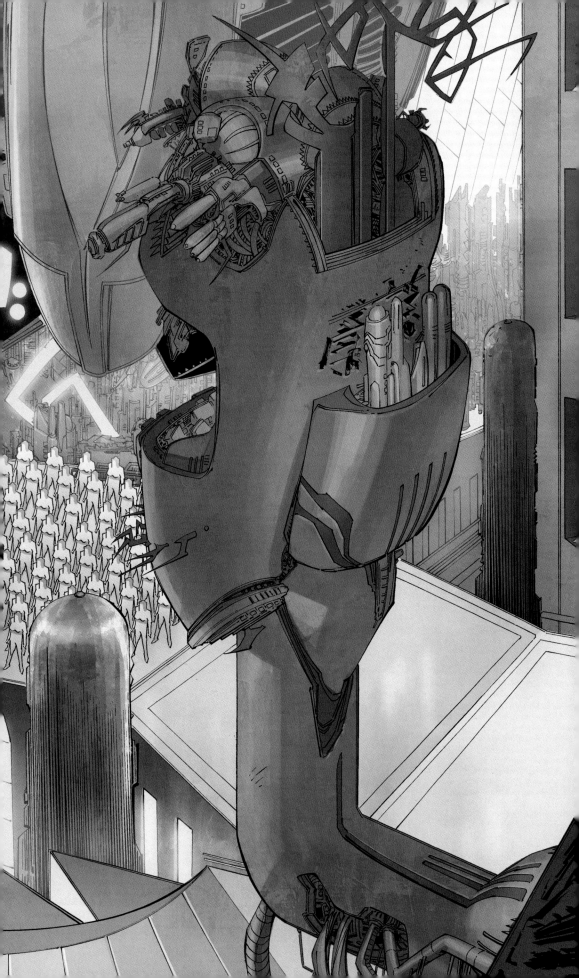

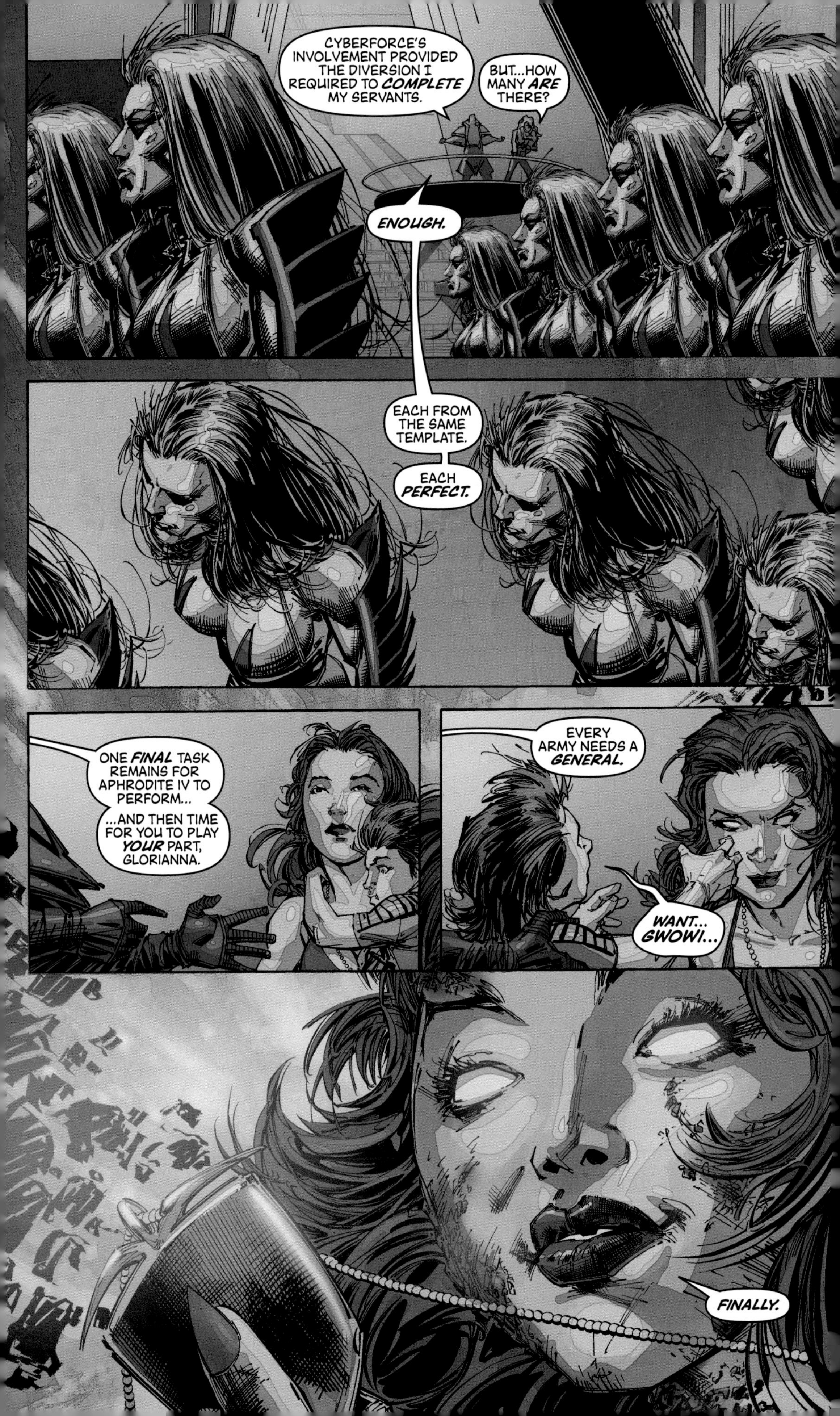
CYBERFORCE'S INVOLVEMENT PROVIDED THE DIVERSION I REQUIRED TO COMPLETE MY SERVANTS.
BUT...HOW MANY ARE THERE?
ENOUGH.
EACH FROM THE SAME TEMPLATE.
EACH PERFECT.
ONE FINAL TASK REMAINS FOR APHRODITE IV TO PERFORM...
...AND THEN TIME FOR YOU TO PLAY YOUR PART, GLORIANNA.
EVERY ARMY NEEDS A GENERAL.
WANT... GWOWI...
FINALLY.

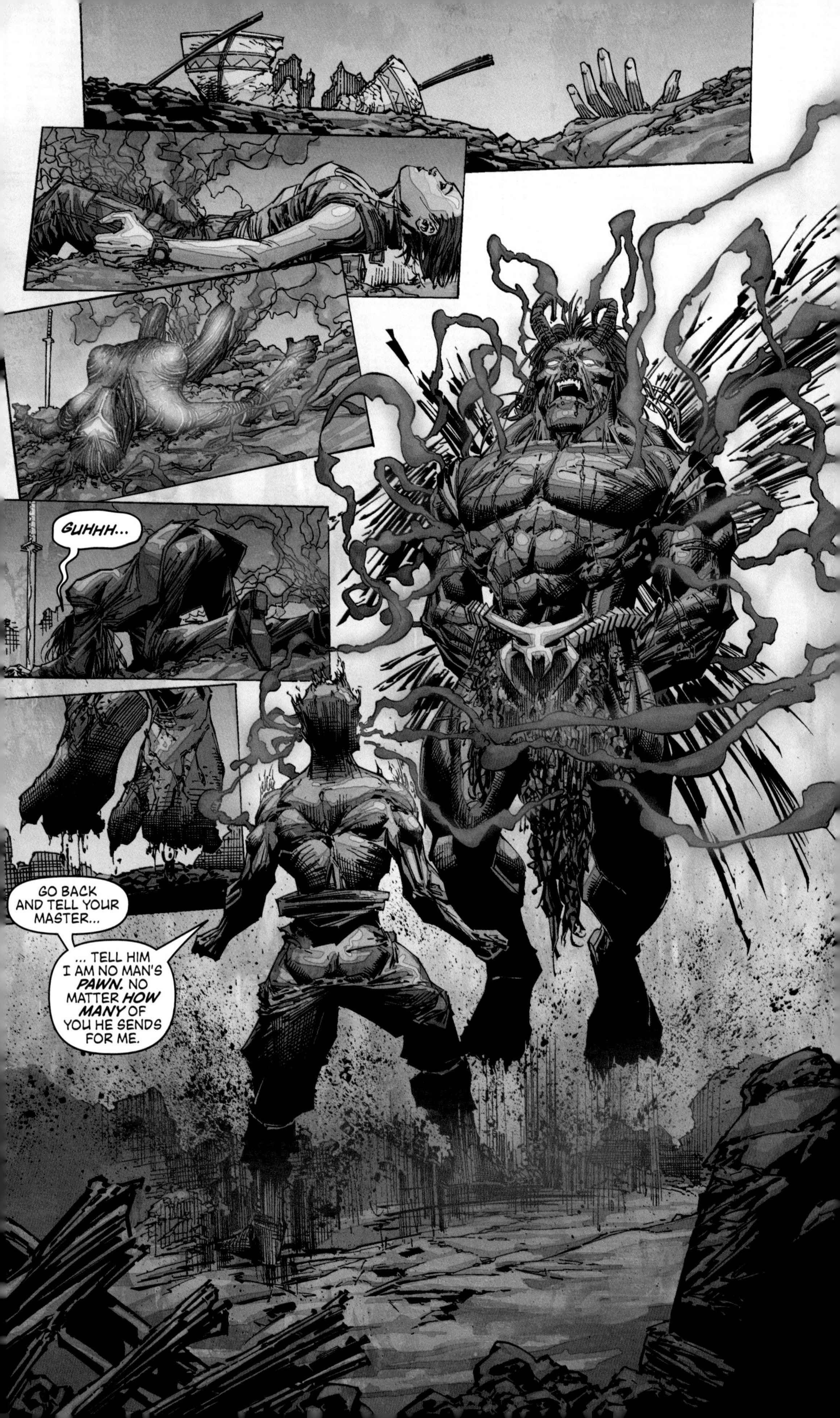
GUHHH...
GO BACK AND TELL YOUR MASTER...
... TELL HIM I AM NO MAN'S **PAWN.** NO MATTER ***HOW MANY*** OF YOU HE SENDS FOR ME.

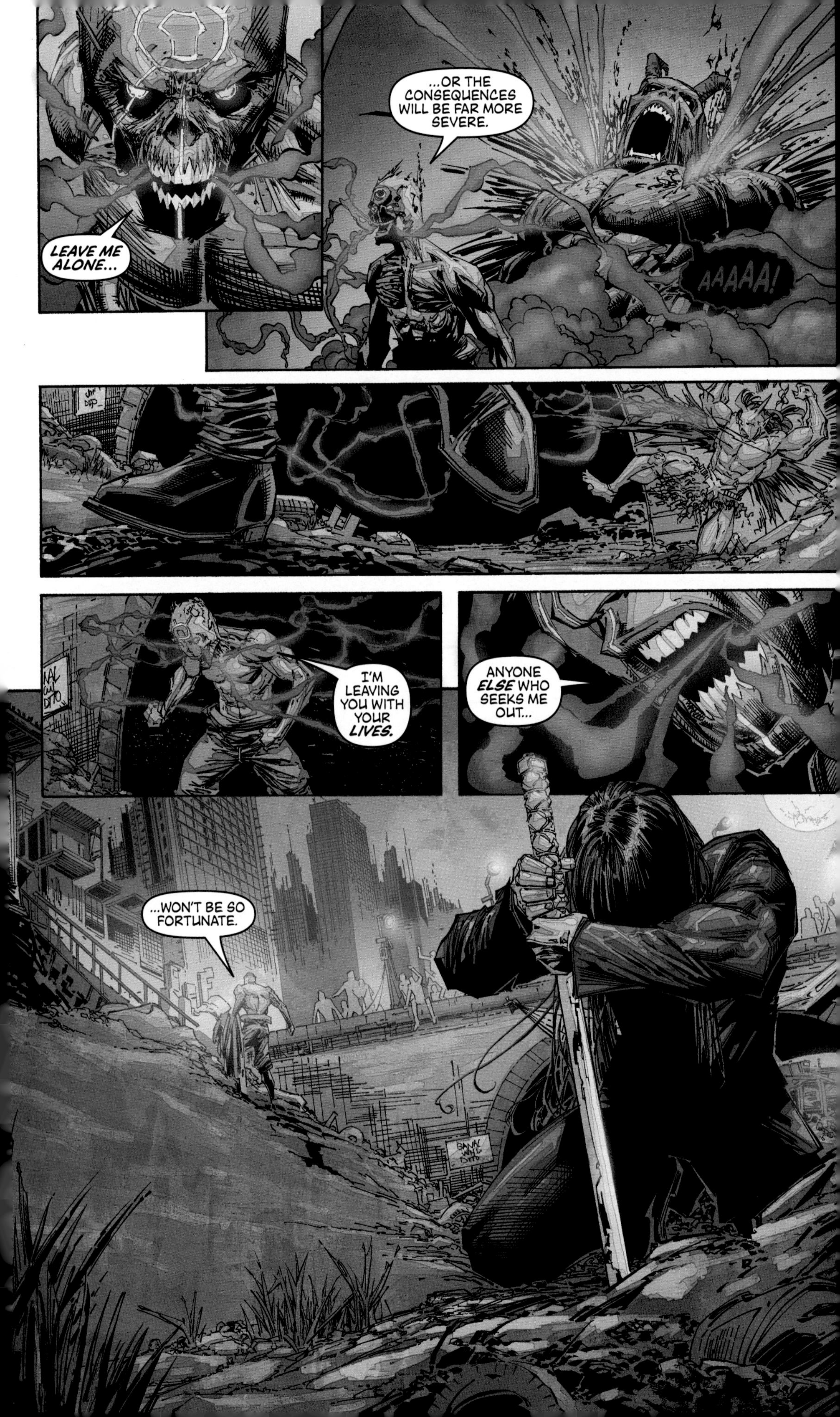
LEAVE ME ALONE...
...OR THE CONSEQUENCES WILL BE FAR MORE SEVERE.
AAAAA!
I'M LEAVING YOU WITH YOUR LIVES.
ANYONE ELSE WHO SEEKS ME OUT...
...WON'T BE SO FORTUNATE.

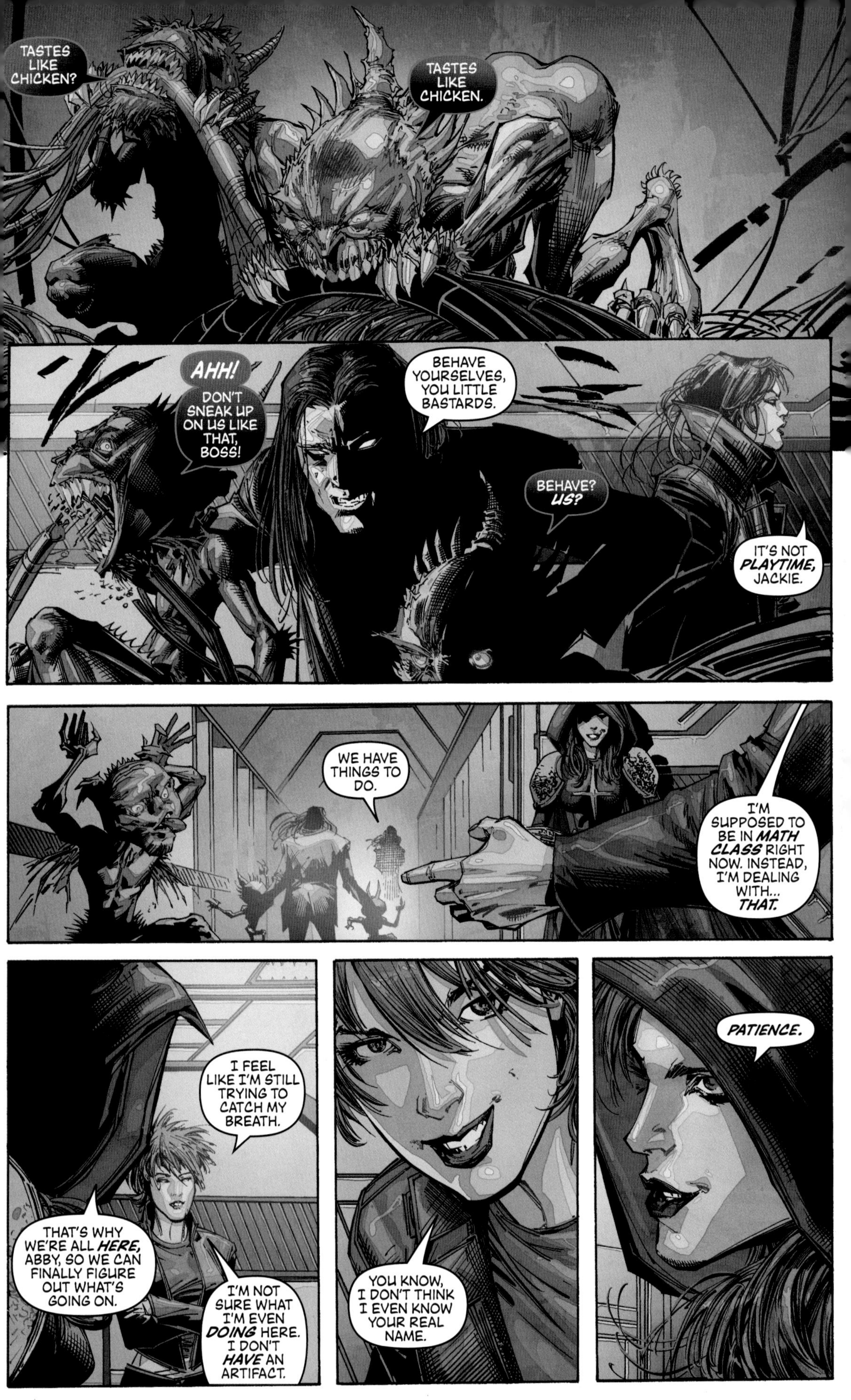
TASTES LIKE CHICKEN?
TASTES LIKE CHICKEN.
AHH!
DON'T SNEAK UP ON US LIKE THAT, BOSS!
BEHAVE YOURSELVES, YOU LITTLE BASTARDS.
BEHAVE? US?
IT'S NOT PLAYTIME, JACKIE.
WE HAVE THINGS TO DO.
I'M SUPPOSED TO BE IN MATH CLASS RIGHT NOW. INSTEAD, I'M DEALING WITH... THAT.
I FEEL LIKE I'M STILL TRYING TO CATCH MY BREATH.
THAT'S WHY WE'RE ALL HERE, ABBY, SO WE CAN FINALLY FIGURE OUT WHAT'S GOING ON.
I'M NOT SURE WHAT I'M EVEN DOING HERE. I DON'T HAVE AN ARTIFACT.
YOU KNOW, I DON'T THINK I EVEN KNOW YOUR REAL NAME.
PATIENCE.

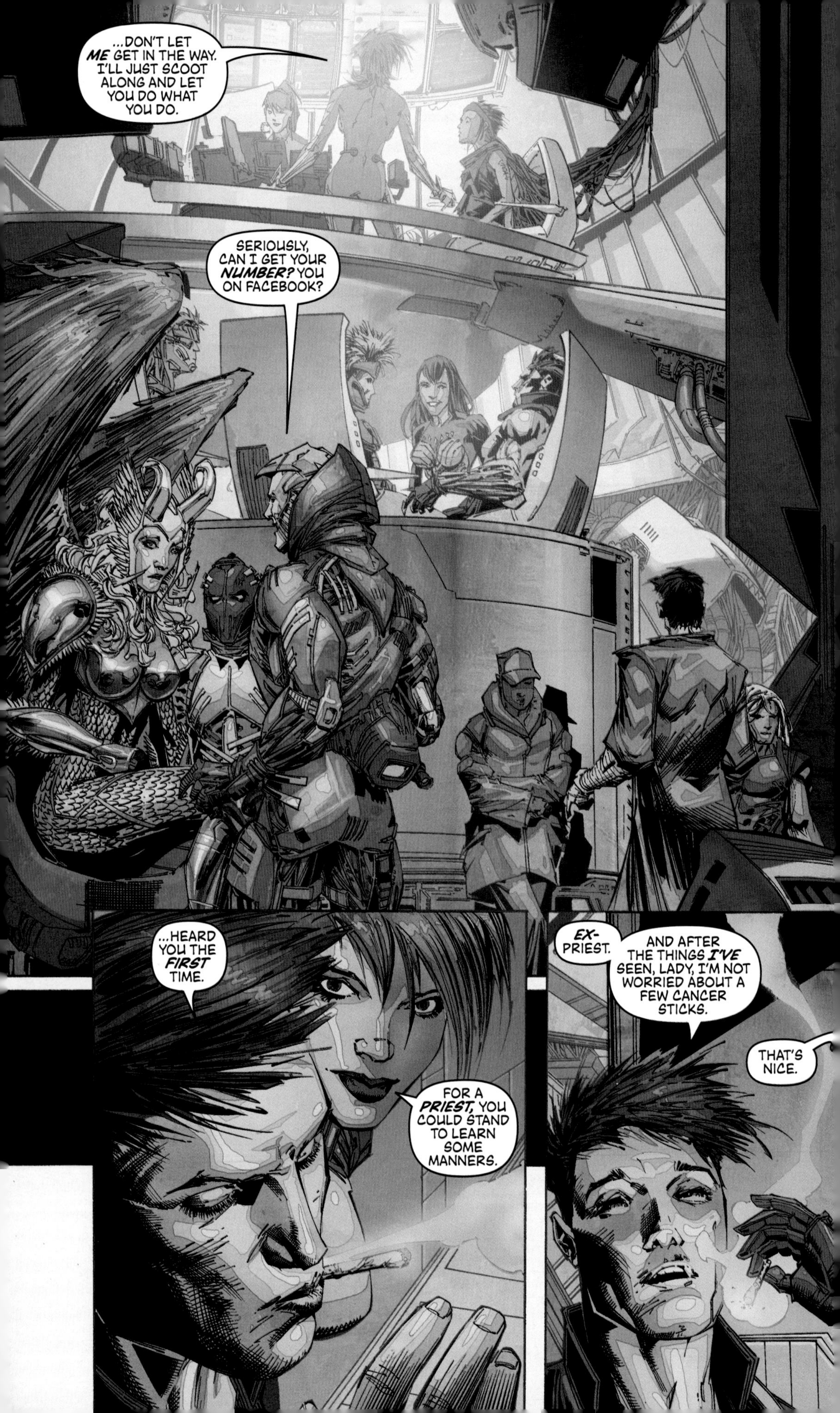
...DON'T LET ME GET IN THE WAY. I'LL JUST SCOOT ALONG AND LET YOU DO WHAT YOU DO.
SERIOUSLY, CAN I GET YOUR NUMBER? YOU ON FACEBOOK?
...HEARD YOU THE FIRST TIME.
FOR A PRIEST, YOU COULD STAND TO LEARN SOME MANNERS.
EX-PRIEST.
AND AFTER THE THINGS I'VE SEEN, LADY, I'M NOT WORRIED ABOUT A FEW CANCER STICKS.
THAT'S NICE.

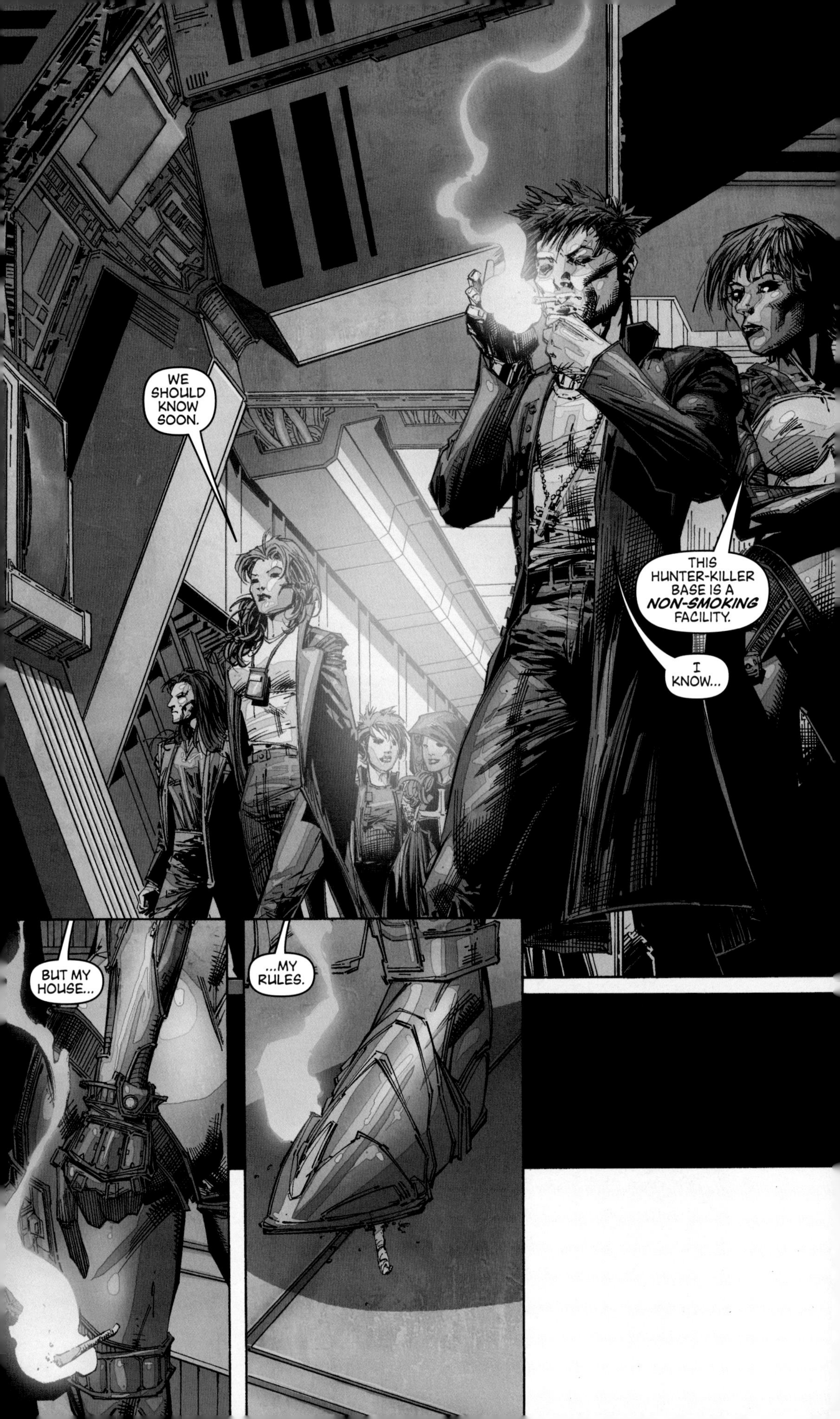

WE SHOULD KNOW SOON.
THIS HUNTER-KILLER BASE IS A *NON-SMOKING* FACILITY.
I KNOW...
BUT MY HOUSE...
...MY RULES.

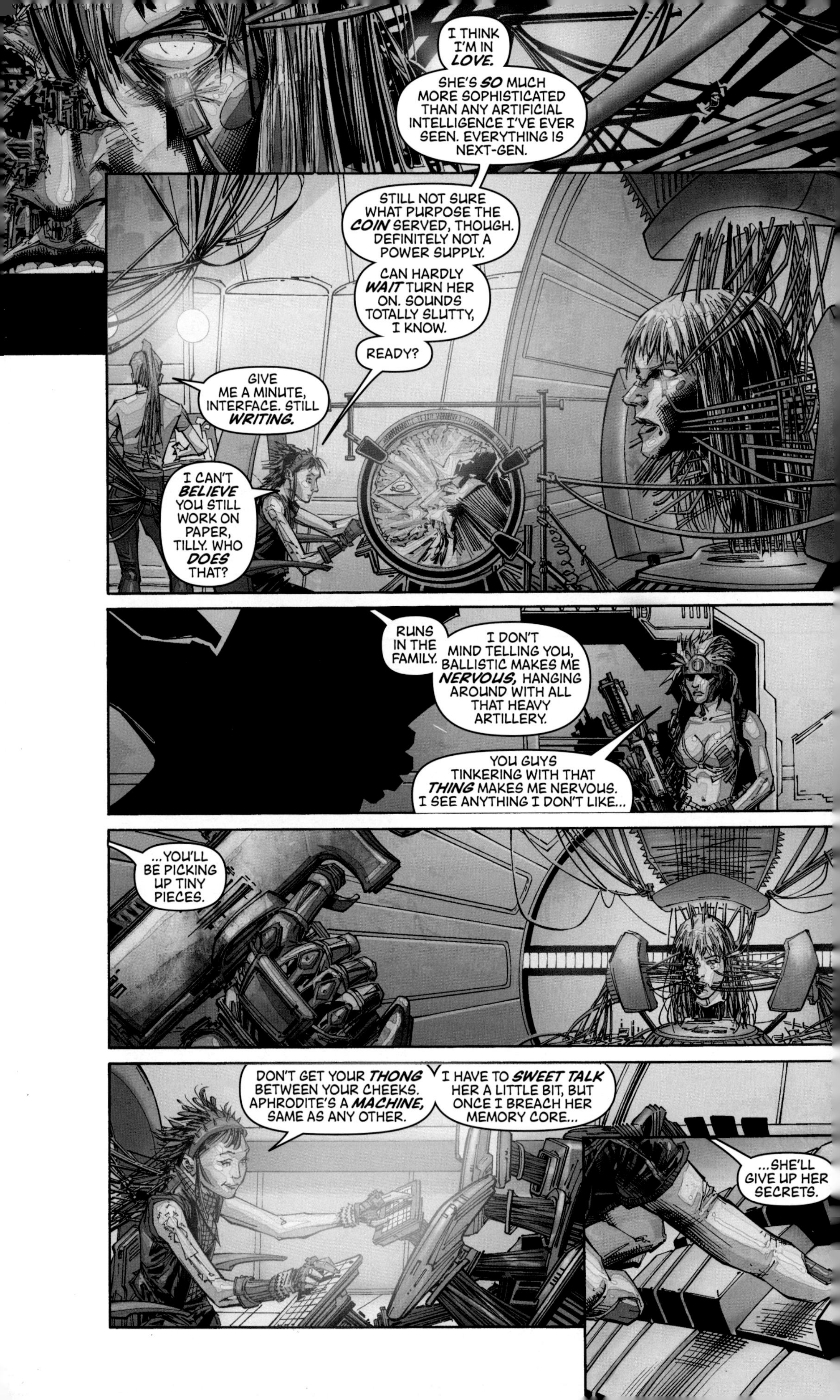
I THINK I'M IN LOVE.
SHE'S SO MUCH MORE SOPHISTICATED THAN ANY ARTIFICIAL INTELLIGENCE I'VE EVER SEEN. EVERYTHING IS NEXT-GEN.
STILL NOT SURE WHAT PURPOSE THE COIN SERVED, THOUGH. DEFINITELY NOT A POWER SUPPLY.
CAN HARDLY WAIT TURN HER ON. SOUNDS TOTALLY SLUTTY, I KNOW.
READY?
GIVE ME A MINUTE, INTERFACE. STILL WRITING.
I CAN'T BELIEVE YOU STILL WORK ON PAPER, TILLY. WHO DOES THAT?
RUNS IN THE FAMILY.
I DON'T MIND TELLING YOU, BALLISTIC MAKES ME NERVOUS, HANGING AROUND WITH ALL THAT HEAVY ARTILLERY.
YOU GUYS TINKERING WITH THAT THING MAKES ME NERVOUS. I SEE ANYTHING I DON'T LIKE...
...YOU'LL BE PICKING UP TINY PIECES.
DON'T GET YOUR THONG BETWEEN YOUR CHEEKS. APHRODITE'S A MACHINE, SAME AS ANY OTHER.
I HAVE TO SWEET TALK HER A LITTLE BIT, BUT ONCE I BREACH HER MEMORY CORE...
...SHE'LL GIVE UP HER SECRETS.

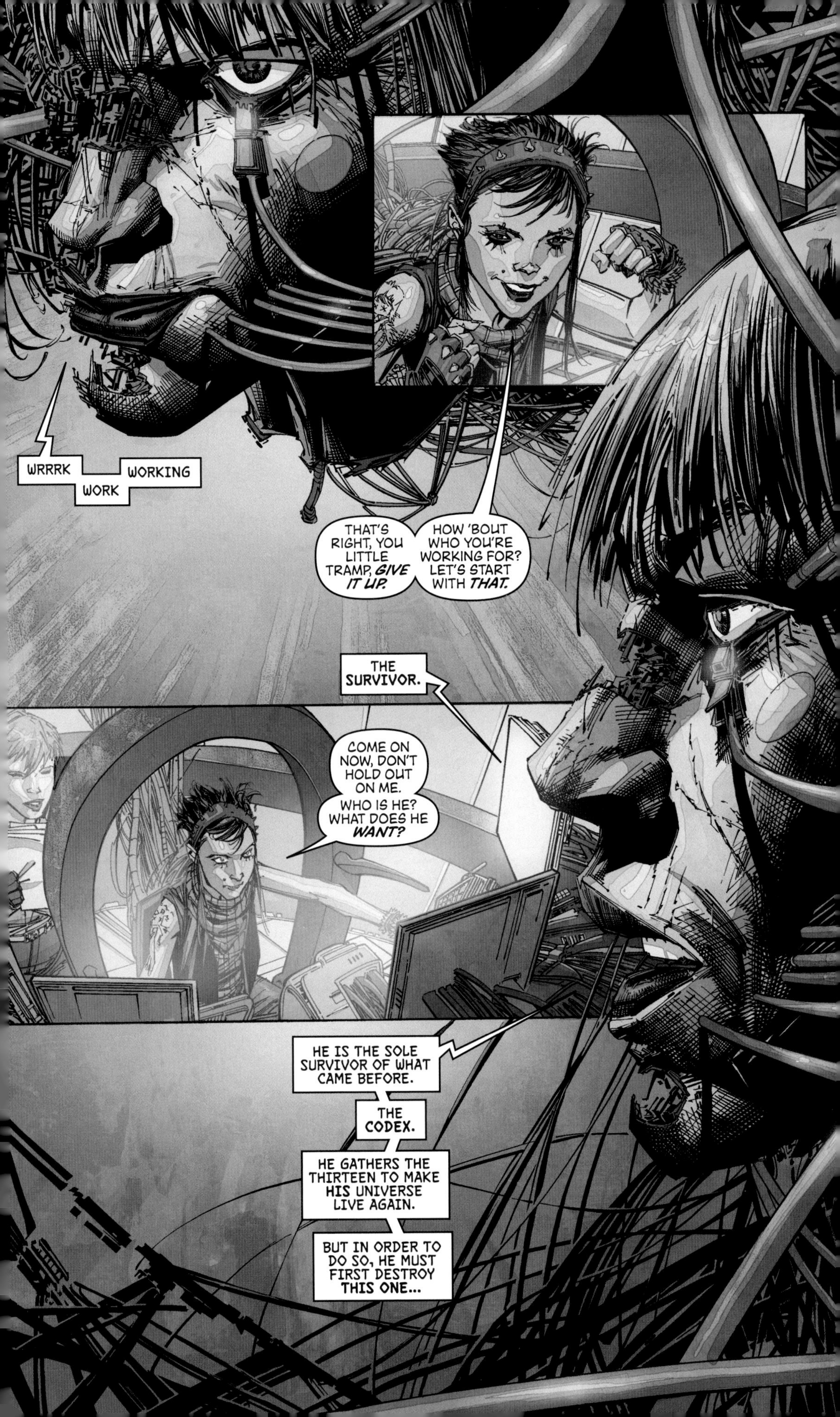

WRRRK WORK WORKING
THAT'S RIGHT, YOU LITTLE TRAMP, GIVE IT UP.
HOW 'BOUT WHO YOU'RE WORKING FOR? LET'S START WITH THAT.
THE SURVIVOR.
COME ON NOW, DON'T HOLD OUT ON ME.
WHO IS HE? WHAT DOES HE WANT?
HE IS THE SOLE SURVIVOR OF WHAT CAME BEFORE.
THE CODEX.
HE GATHERS THE THIRTEEN TO MAKE HIS UNIVERSE LIVE AGAIN.
BUT IN ORDER TO DO SO, HE MUST FIRST DESTROY THIS ONE...

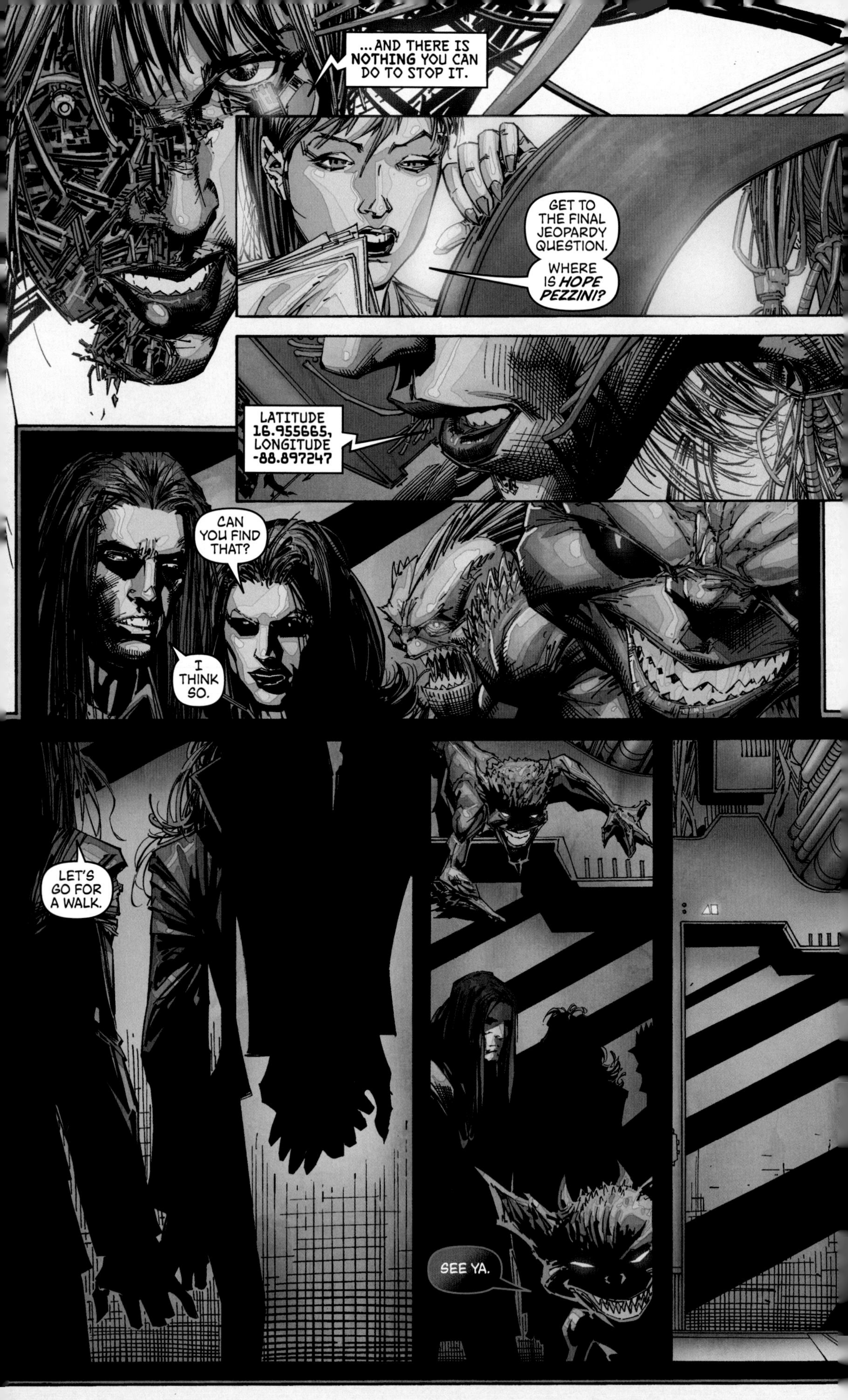
...AND THERE IS NOTHING YOU CAN DO TO STOP IT.
GET TO THE FINAL JEOPARDY QUESTION.
WHERE IS *HOPE PEZZINI!?*
LATITUDE 16.955665, LONGITUDE -88.897247
CAN YOU FIND THAT?
I THINK SO.
LET'S GO FOR A WALK.
SEE YA.

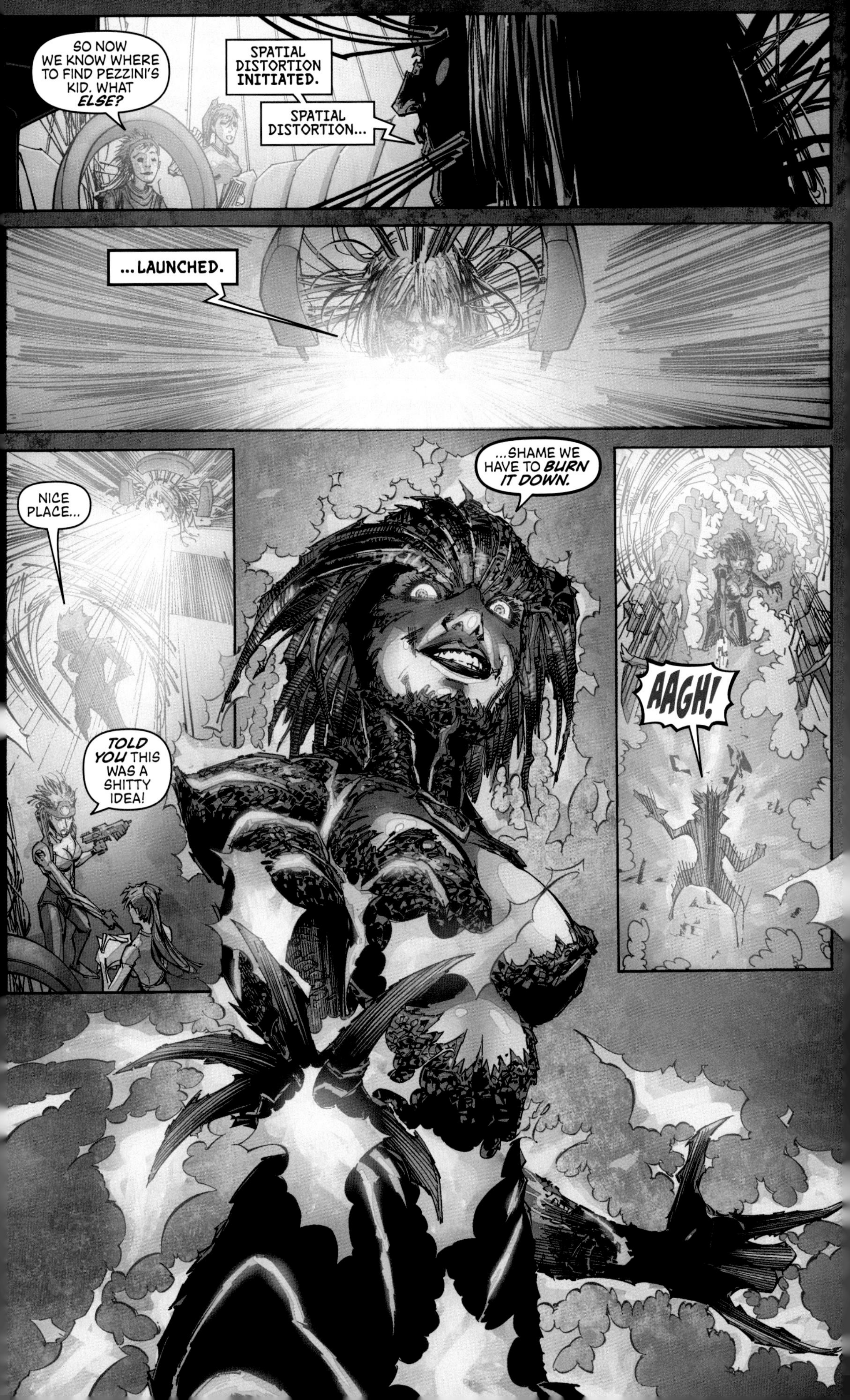
SO NOW WE KNOW WHERE TO FIND PEZZINI'S KID. WHAT *ELSE?*
SPATIAL DISTORTION **INITIATED.**
SPATIAL DISTORTION...
...LAUNCHED.
NICE PLACE...
...SHAME WE HAVE TO *BURN IT DOWN.*
TOLD YOU THIS WAS A SHITTY IDEA!
AAGH!

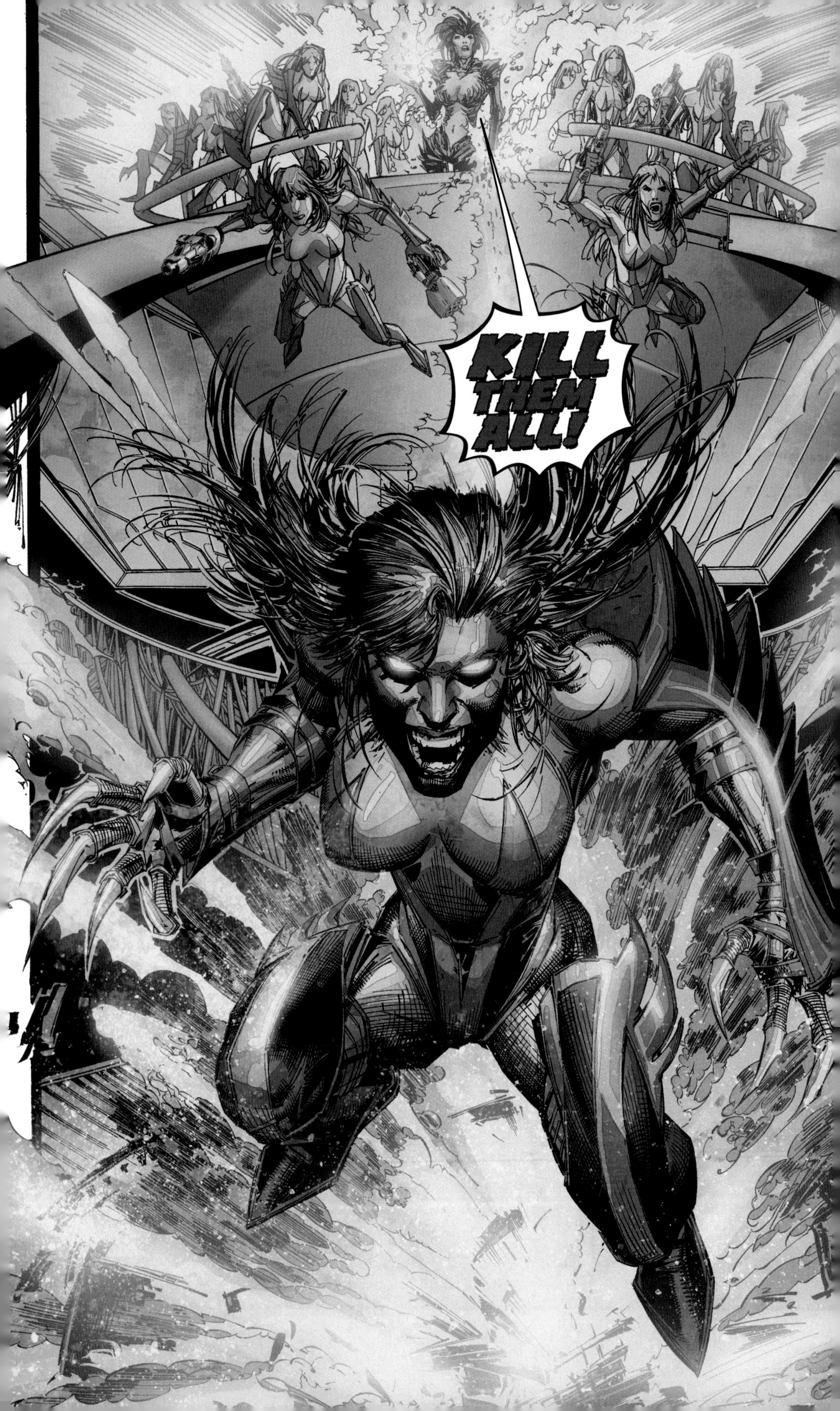
KILL THEM ALL!

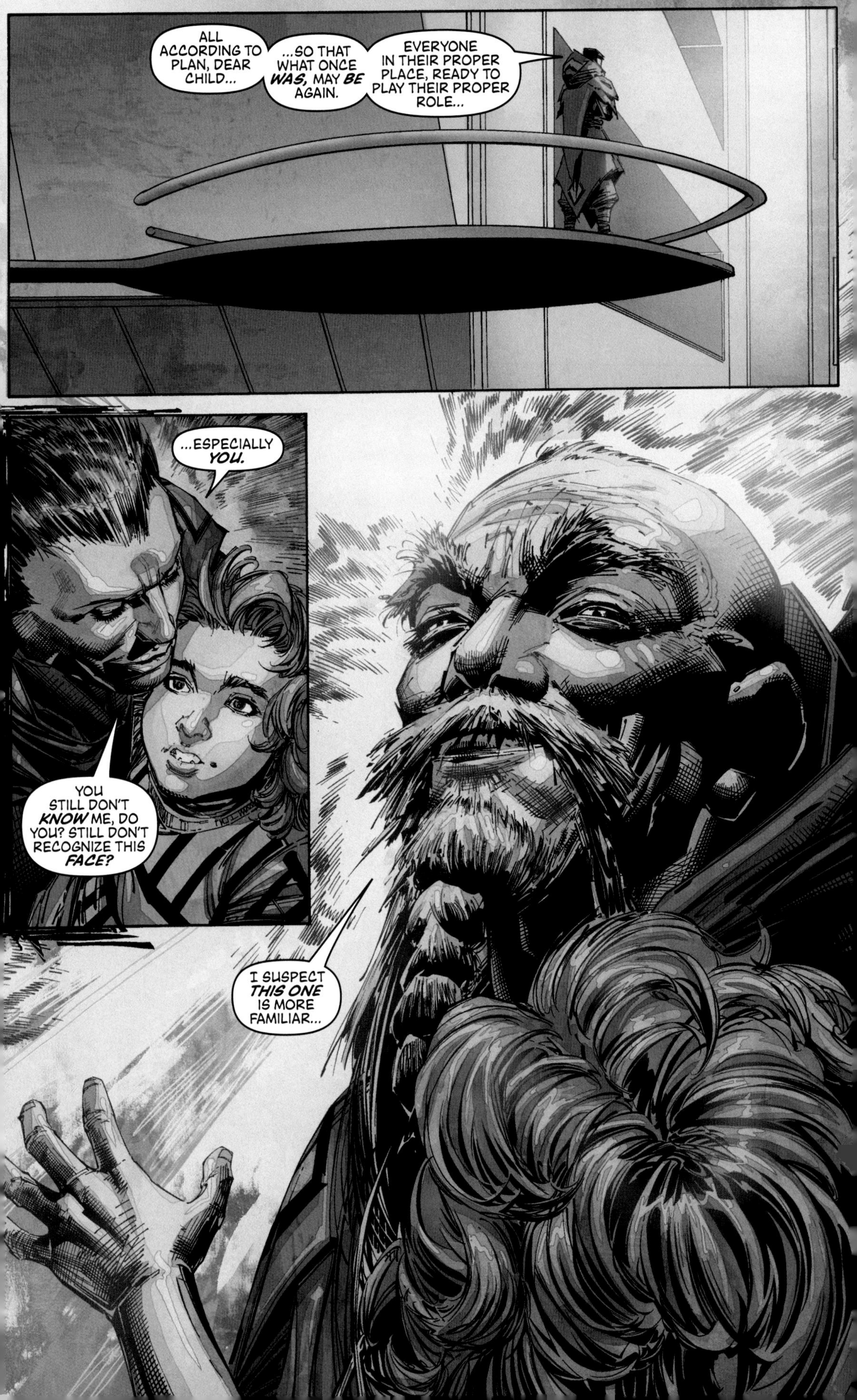
ALL ACCORDING TO PLAN, DEAR CHILD...
...SO THAT WHAT ONCE *WAS,* MAY *BE* AGAIN.
EVERYONE IN THEIR PROPER PLACE, READY TO PLAY THEIR PROPER ROLE...
...ESPECIALLY *YOU.*
YOU STILL DON'T *KNOW* ME, DO YOU? STILL DON'T RECOGNIZE THIS *FACE?*
I SUSPECT *THIS ONE* IS MORE FAMILIAR...

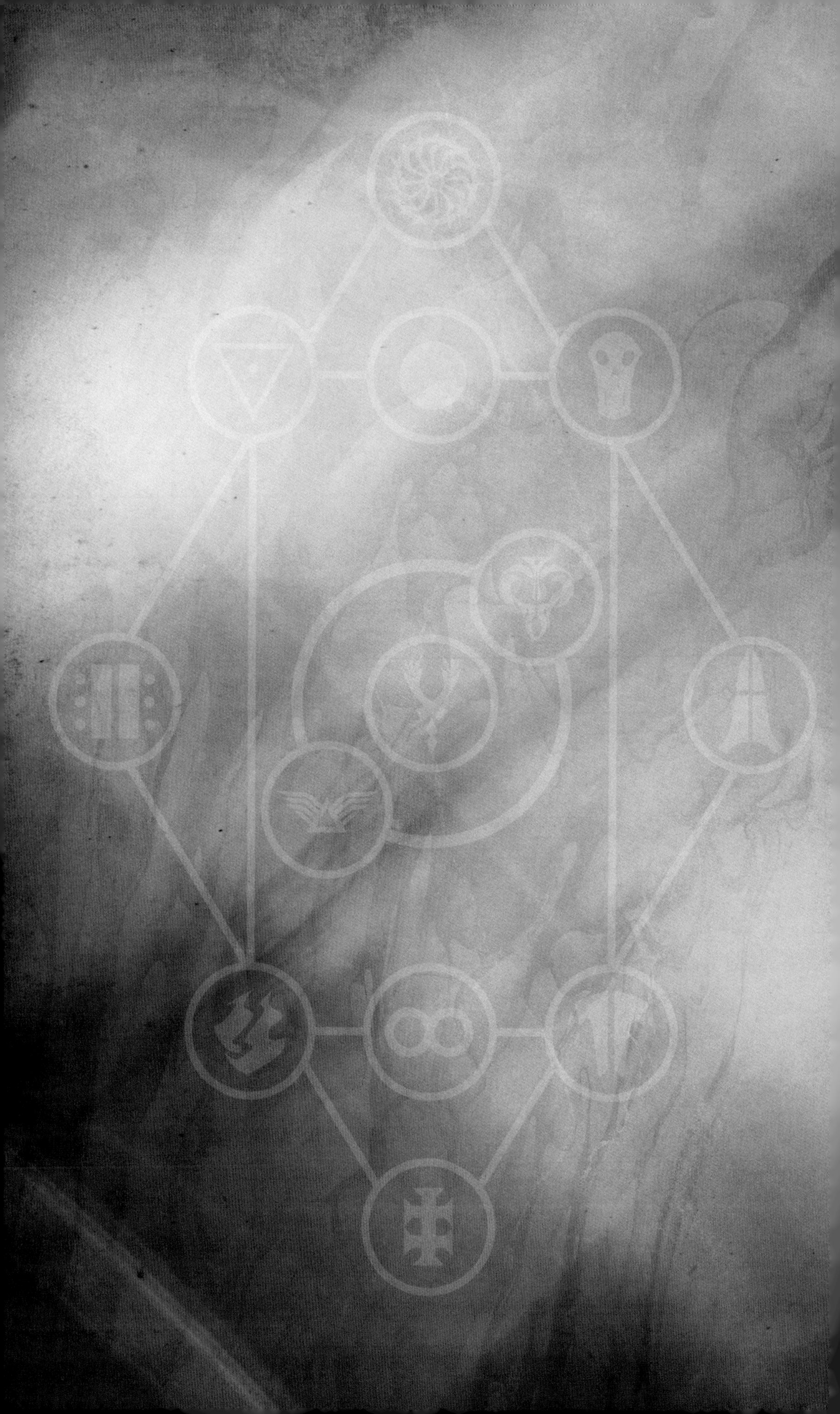

CHAPTER 8

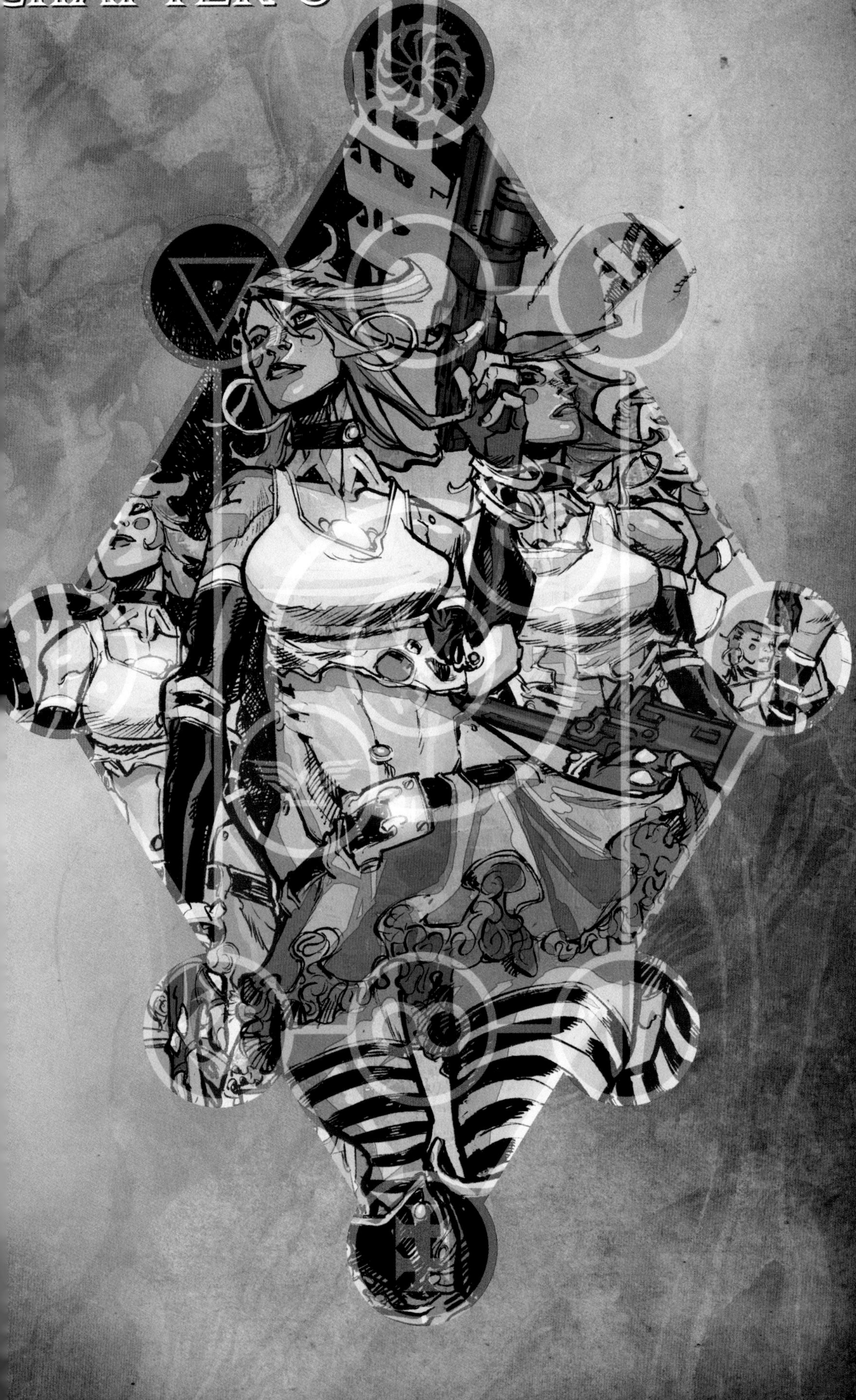

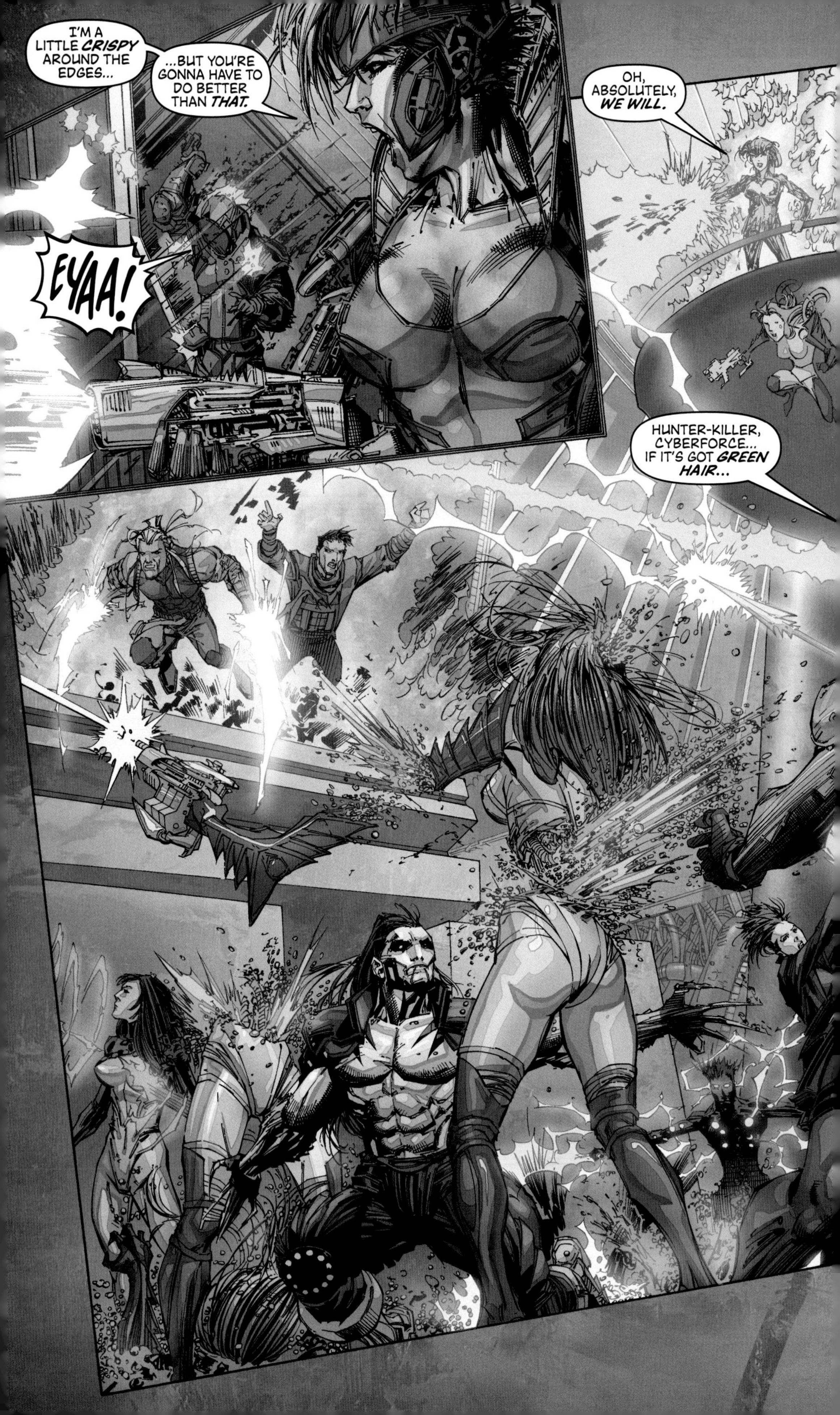
I'M A LITTLE CRISPY AROUND THE EDGES...
...BUT YOU'RE GONNA HAVE TO DO BETTER THAN THAT.
OH, ABSOLUTELY, WE WILL.
EYAA!
HUNTER-KILLER, CYBERFORCE... IF IT'S GOT GREEN HAIR...

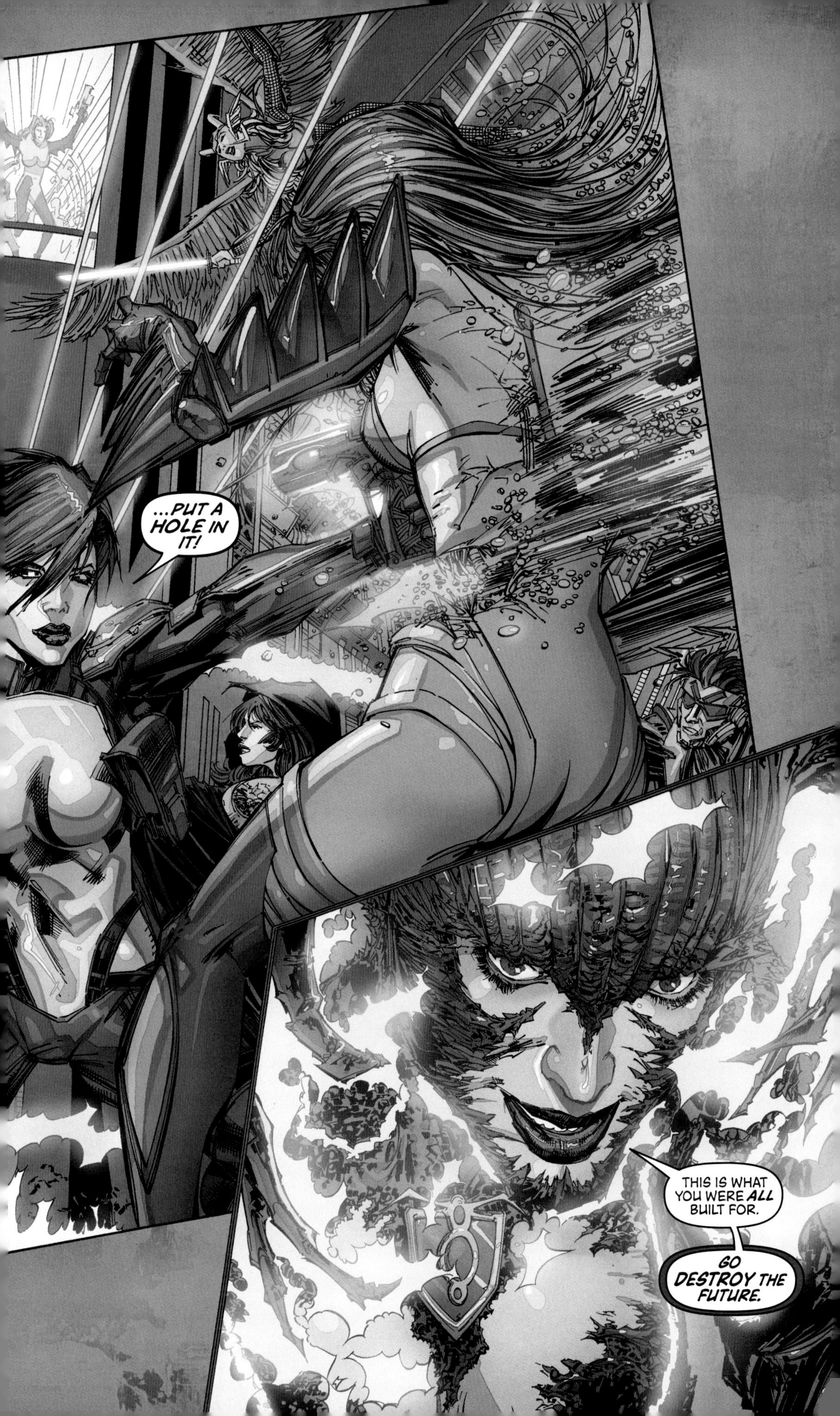
...PUT A HOLE IN IT!
THIS IS WHAT YOU WERE ALL BUILT FOR.
GO DESTROY THE FUTURE.

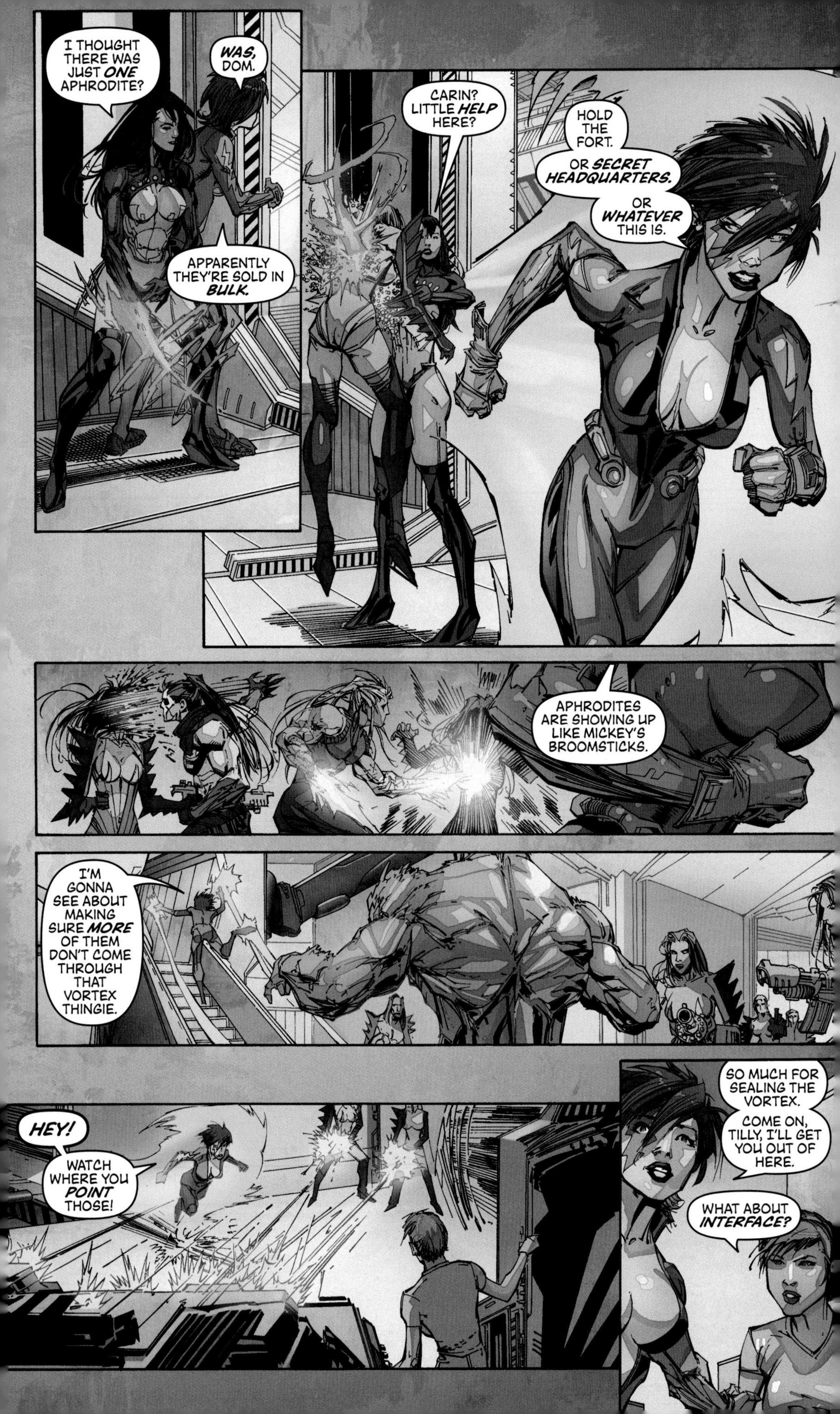
I THOUGHT THERE WAS JUST ONE APHRODITE?
WAS, DOM.
APPARENTLY THEY'RE SOLD IN BULK.
CARIN? LITTLE HELP HERE?
HOLD THE FORT.
OR SECRET HEADQUARTERS.
OR WHATEVER THIS IS.
APHRODITES ARE SHOWING UP LIKE MICKEY'S BROOMSTICKS.
I'M GONNA SEE ABOUT MAKING SURE MORE OF THEM DON'T COME THROUGH THAT VORTEX THINGIE.
HEY!
WATCH WHERE YOU POINT THOSE!
SO MUCH FOR SEALING THE VORTEX.
COME ON, TILLY, I'LL GET YOU OUT OF HERE.
WHAT ABOUT INTERFACE?

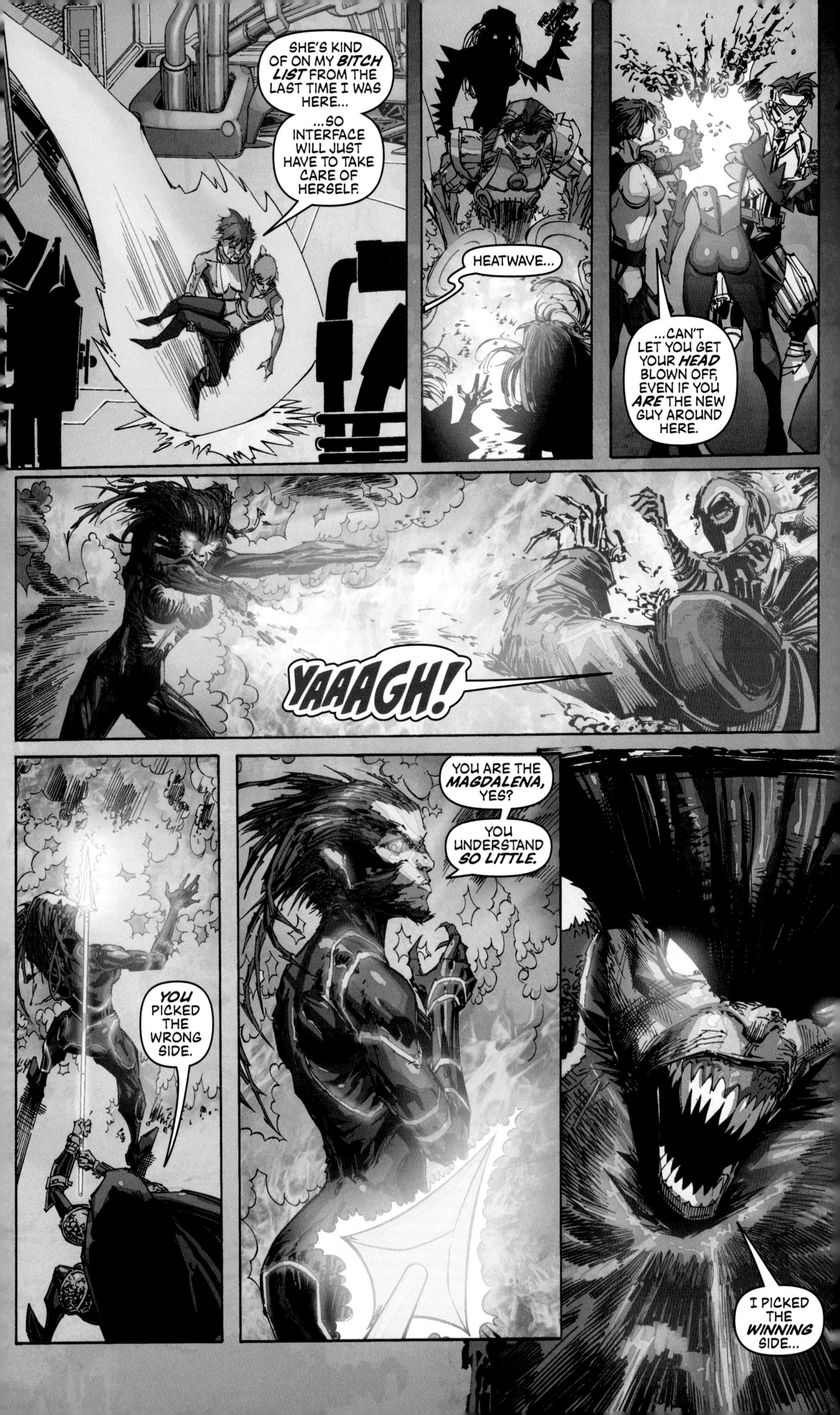

SHE'S KIND OF ON MY *BITCH LIST* FROM THE LAST TIME I WAS HERE...
...SO INTERFACE WILL JUST HAVE TO TAKE CARE OF HERSELF.
HEATWAVE...
...CAN'T LET YOU GET YOUR *HEAD* BLOWN OFF, EVEN IF YOU *ARE* THE NEW GUY AROUND HERE.
YAAAGH!
YOU PICKED THE WRONG SIDE.
YOU ARE THE *MAGDALENA,* YES?
YOU UNDERSTAND *SO LITTLE.*
I PICKED THE *WINNING* SIDE...

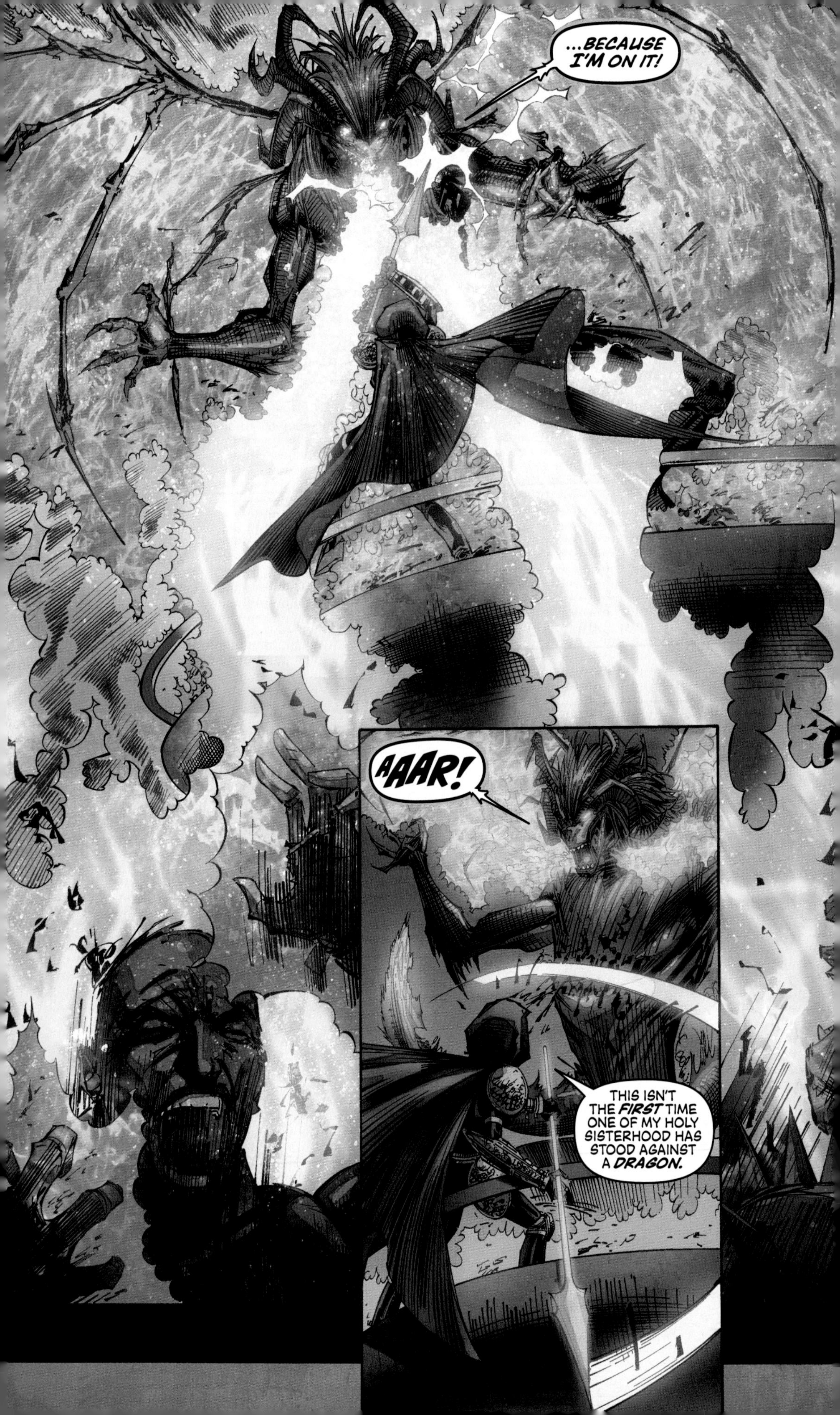
...BECAUSE I'M ON IT!
AAAR!
THIS ISN'T THE FIRST TIME ONE OF MY HOLY SISTERHOOD HAS STOOD AGAINST A DRAGON.

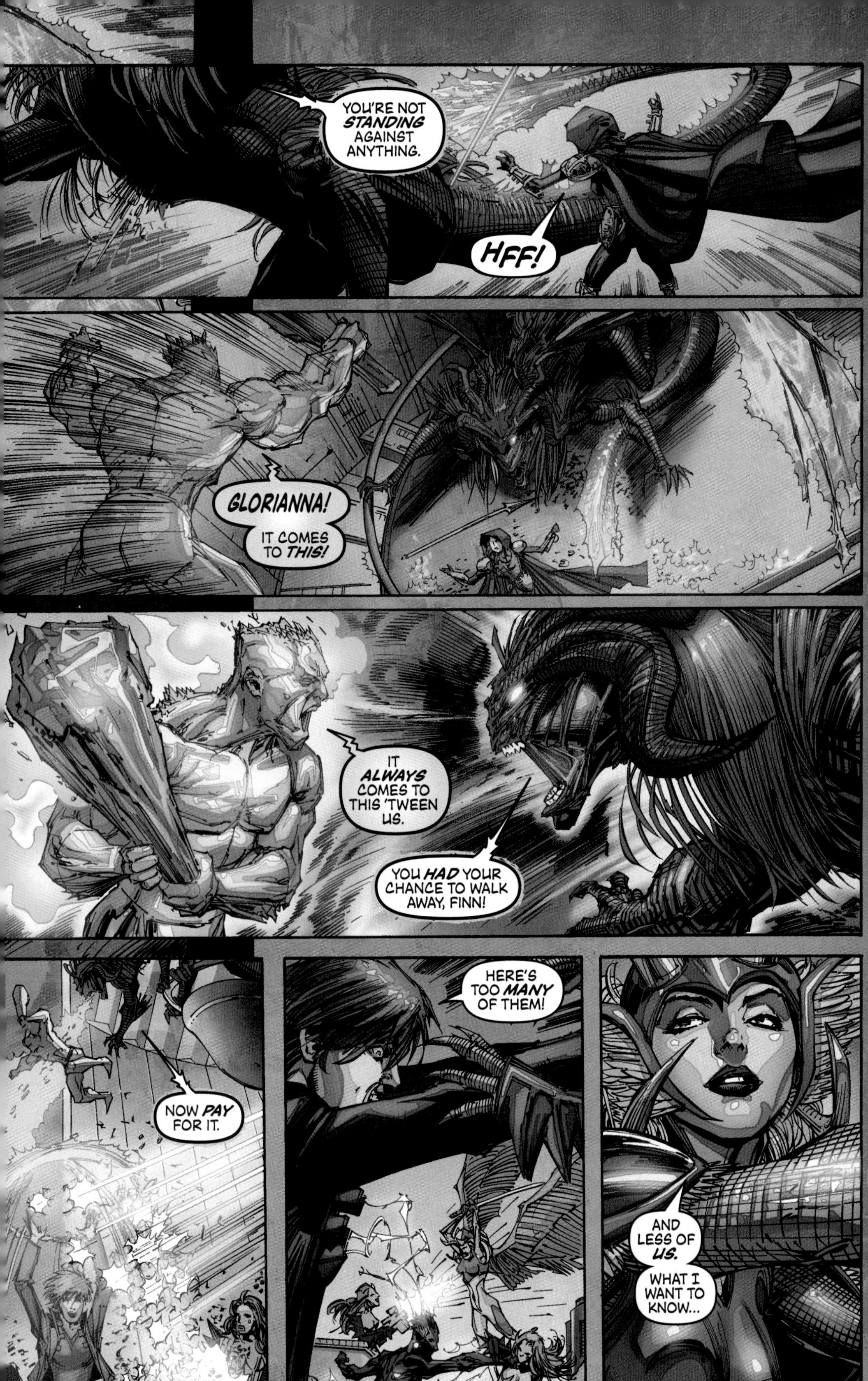
YOU'RE NOT STANDING AGAINST ANYTHING.
HFF!
GLORIANNA!
IT COMES TO THIS!
IT ALWAYS COMES TO THIS 'TWEEN US.
YOU HAD YOUR CHANCE TO WALK AWAY, FINN!
NOW PAY FOR IT.
HERE'S TOO MANY OF THEM!
AND LESS OF US.
WHAT I WANT TO KNOW...

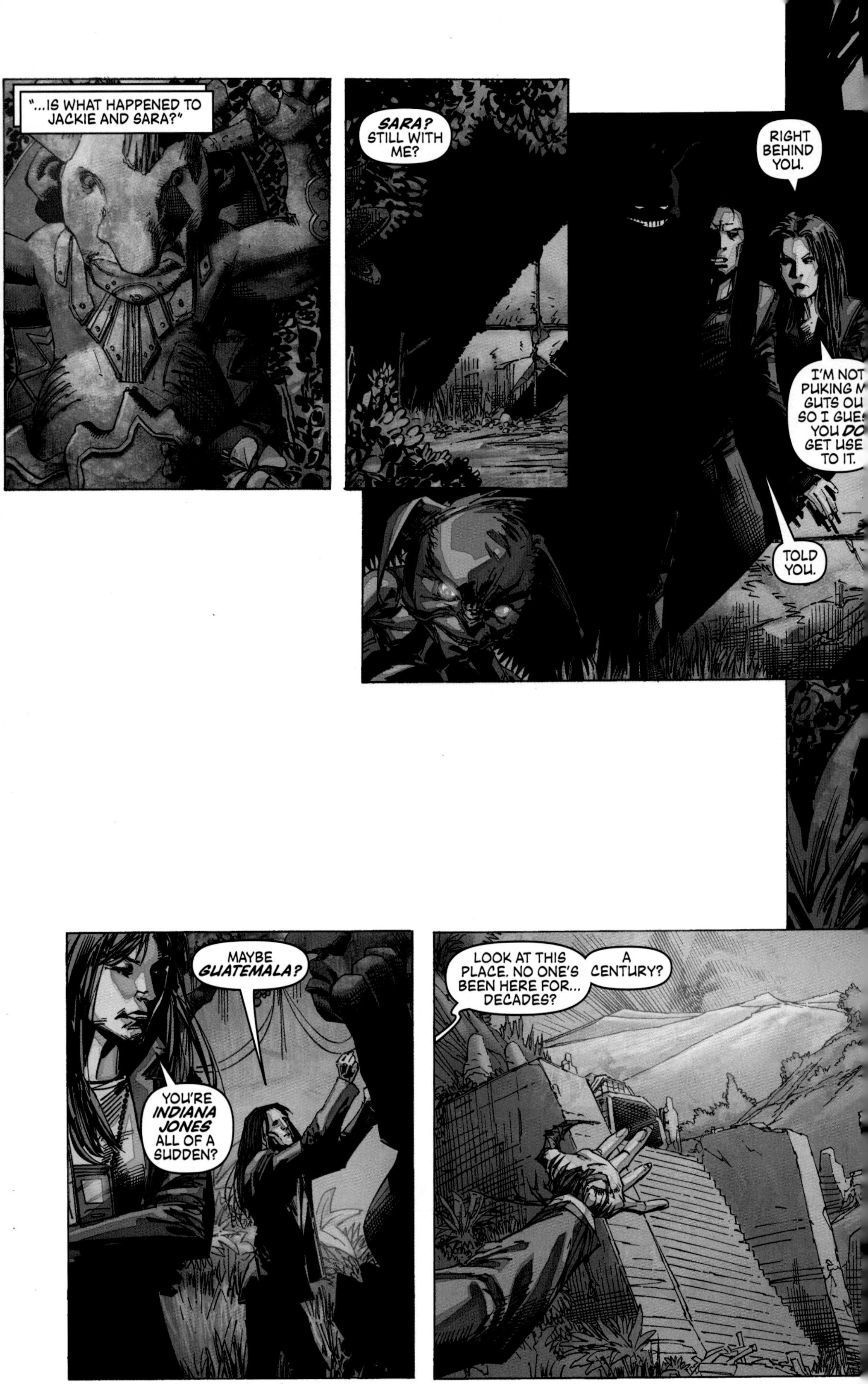

"...IS WHAT HAPPENED TO JACKIE AND SARA?"
SARA? STILL WITH ME?
RIGHT BEHIND YOU.
I'M NOT PUKING M GUTS OU SO I GUE YOU DO GET USE TO IT.
TOLD YOU.
MAYBE GUATEMALA?
YOU'RE INDIANA JONES ALL OF A SUDDEN?
LOOK AT THIS PLACE. NO ONE'S BEEN HERE FOR... DECADES?
A CENTURY?

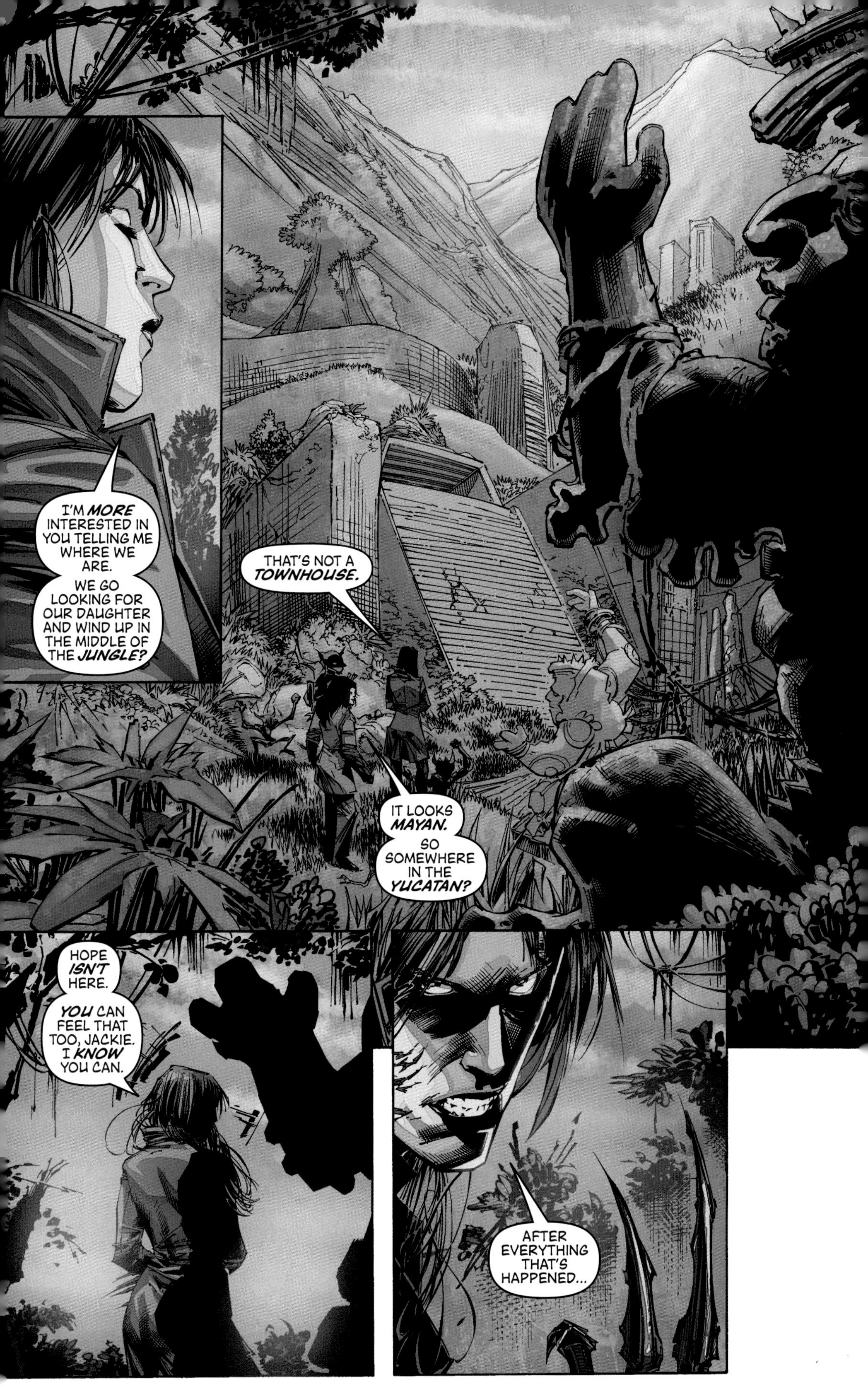
I'M MORE INTERESTED IN YOU TELLING ME WHERE WE ARE.
WE GO LOOKING FOR OUR DAUGHTER AND WIND UP IN THE MIDDLE OF THE JUNGLE?
THAT'S NOT A TOWNHOUSE.
IT LOOKS MAYAN.
SO SOMEWHERE IN THE YUCATAN?
HOPE ISN'T HERE.
YOU CAN FEEL THAT TOO, JACKIE. I KNOW YOU CAN.
AFTER EVERYTHING THAT'S HAPPENED...

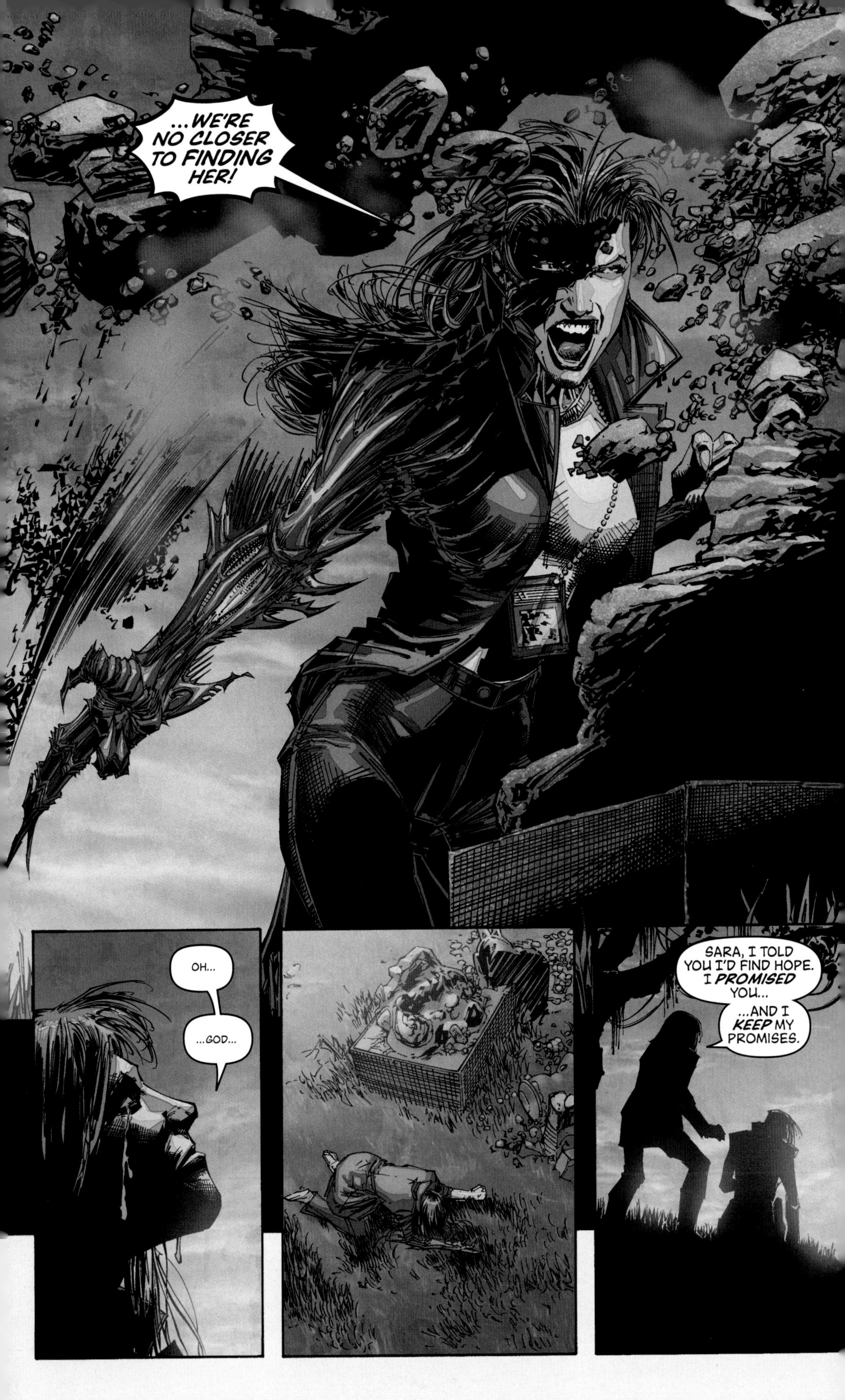
...WE'RE NO CLOSER TO FINDING HER!
OH...
...GOD...
SARA, I TOLD YOU I'D FIND HOPE. I PROMISED YOU...
...AND I KEEP MY PROMISES.

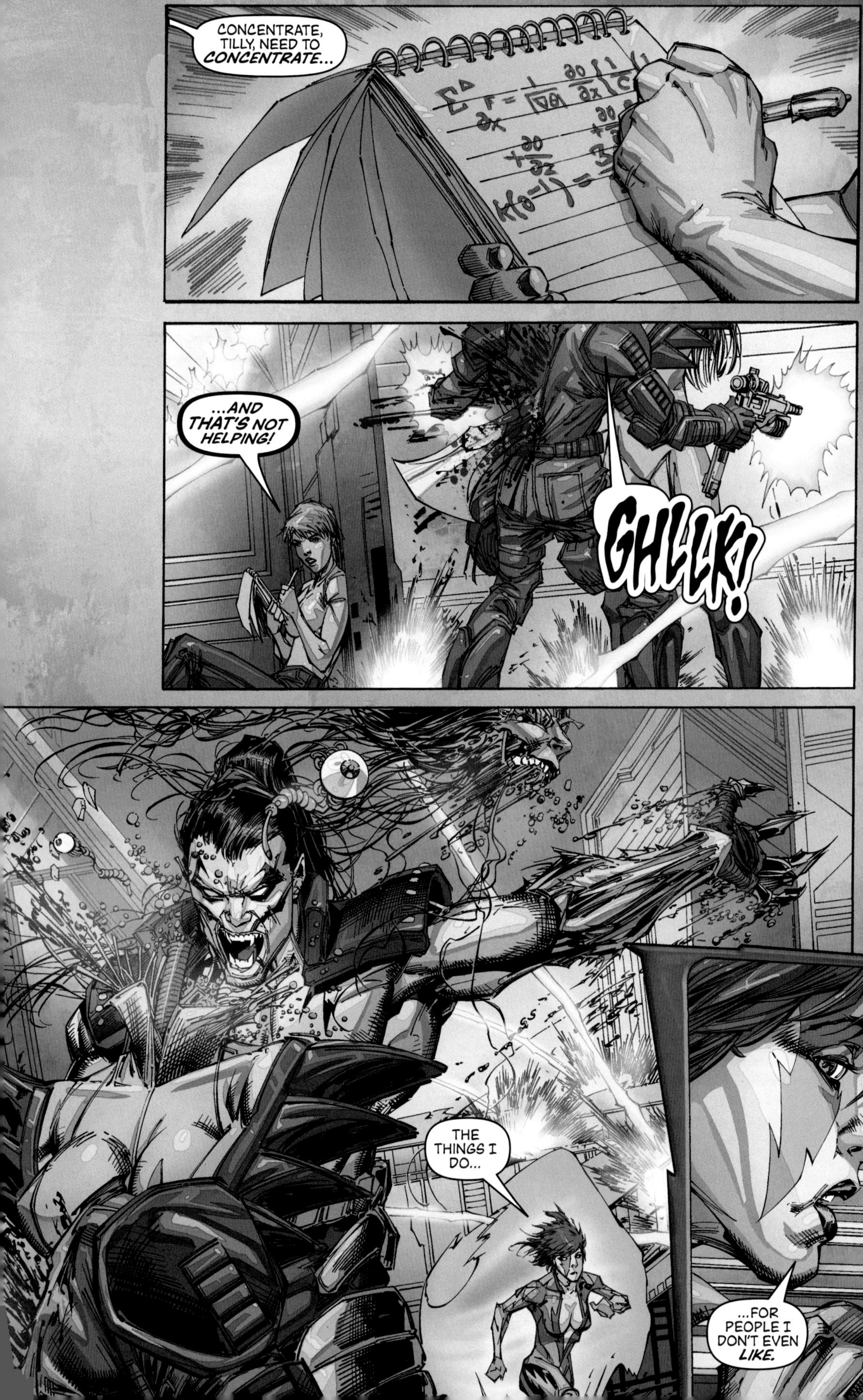
CONCENTRATE, TILLY, NEED TO CONCENTRATE...
...AND THAT'S NOT HELPING!
GHLLK!
THE THINGS I DO...
...FOR PEOPLE I DON'T EVEN LIKE.

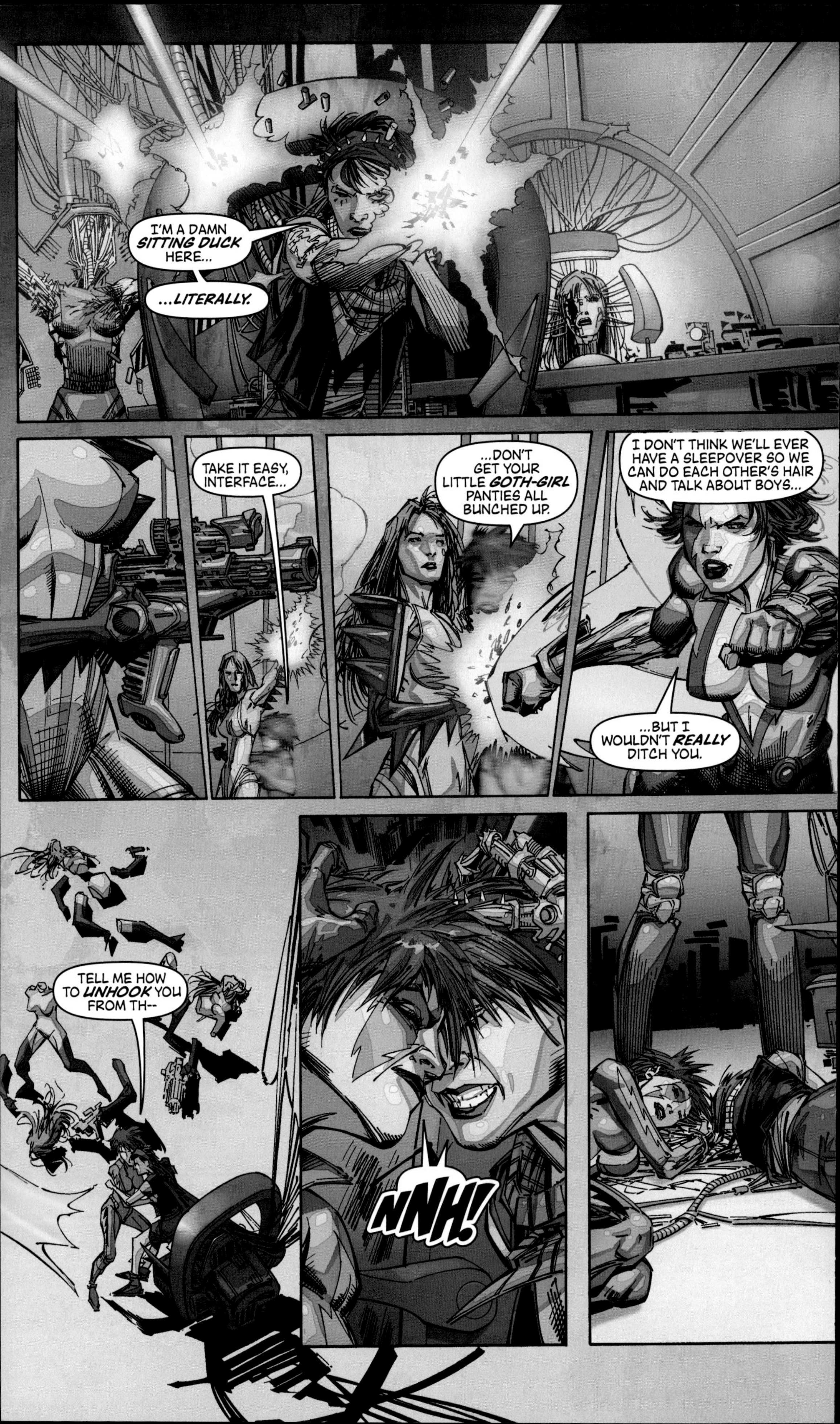
I'M A DAMN SITTING DUCK HERE...
...LITERALLY.
TAKE IT EASY, INTERFACE...
...DON'T GET YOUR LITTLE GOTH-GIRL PANTIES ALL BUNCHED UP.
I DON'T THINK WE'LL EVER HAVE A SLEEPOVER SO WE CAN DO EACH OTHER'S HAIR AND TALK ABOUT BOYS...
...BUT I WOULDN'T REALLY DITCH YOU.
TELL ME HOW TO UNHOOK YOU FROM TH--
NNH!

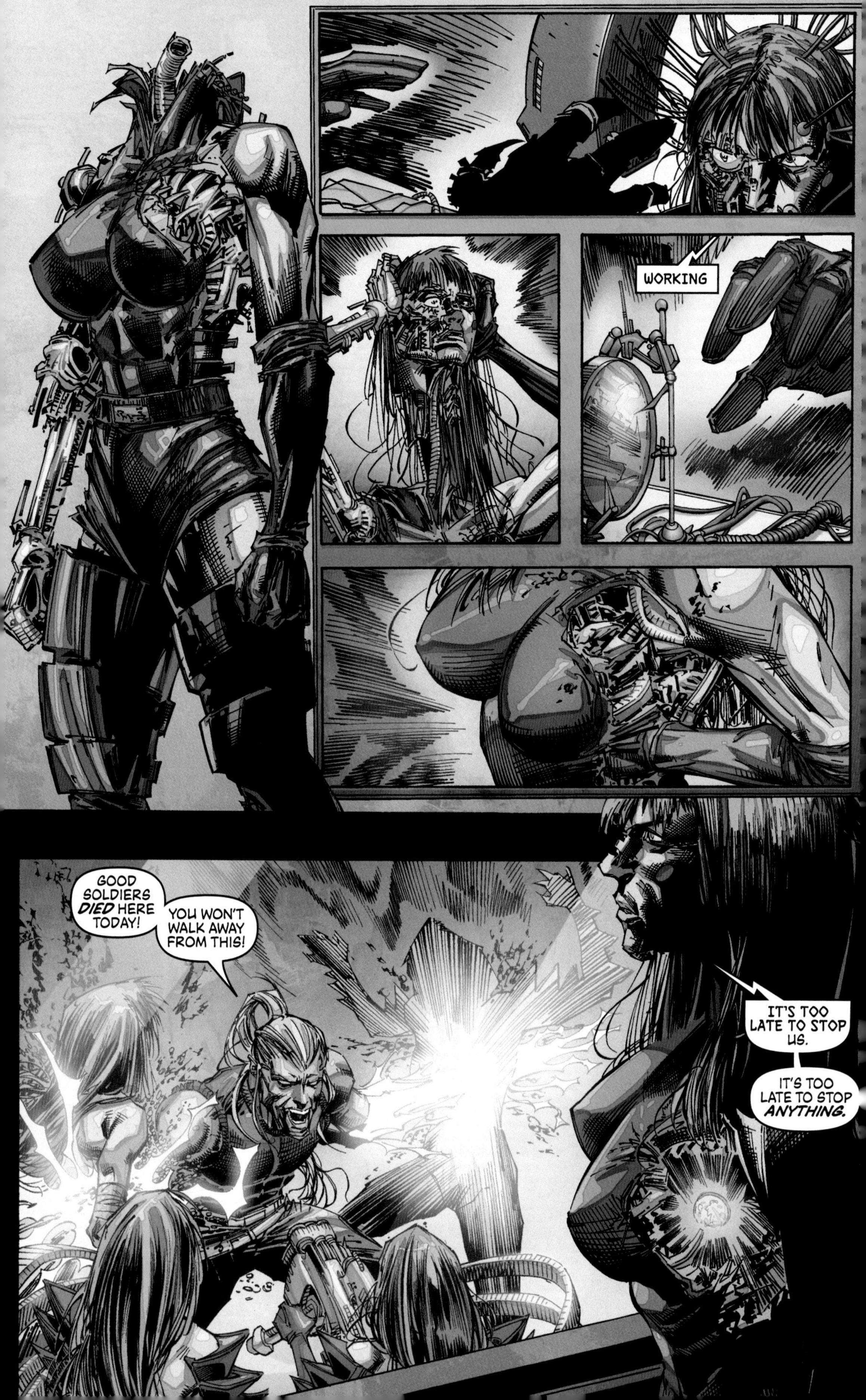
WORKING
GOOD SOLDIERS DIED HERE TODAY!
YOU WON'T WALK AWAY FROM THIS!
IT'S TOO LATE TO STOP US.
IT'S TOO LATE TO STOP ANYTHING.

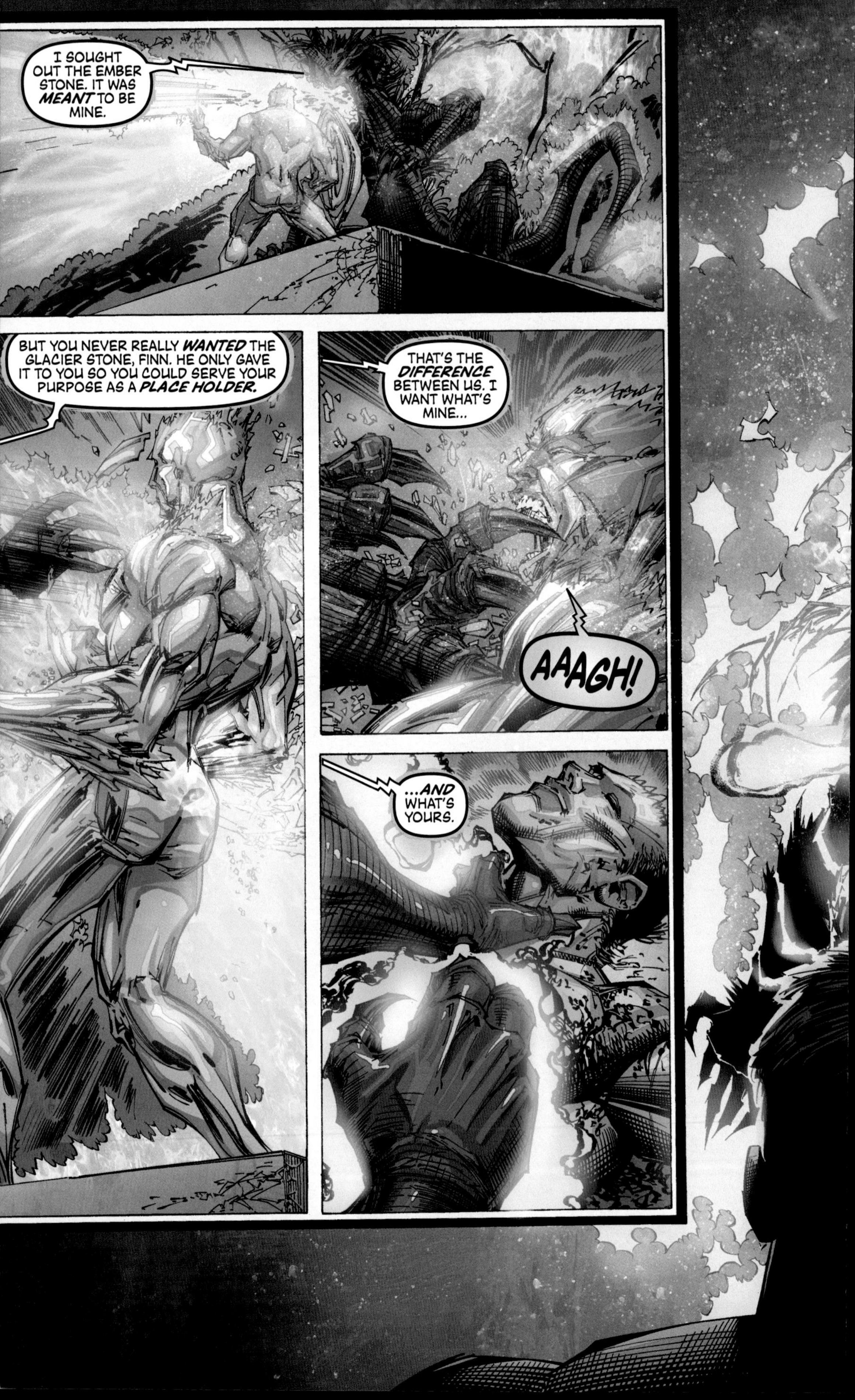
I SOUGHT OUT THE EMBER STONE. IT WAS MEANT TO BE MINE.
BUT YOU NEVER REALLY WANTED THE GLACIER STONE, FINN. HE ONLY GAVE IT TO YOU SO YOU COULD SERVE YOUR PURPOSE AS A PLACE HOLDER.
THAT'S THE DIFFERENCE BETWEEN US. I WANT WHAT'S MINE...
AAAGH!
...AND WHAT'S YOURS.

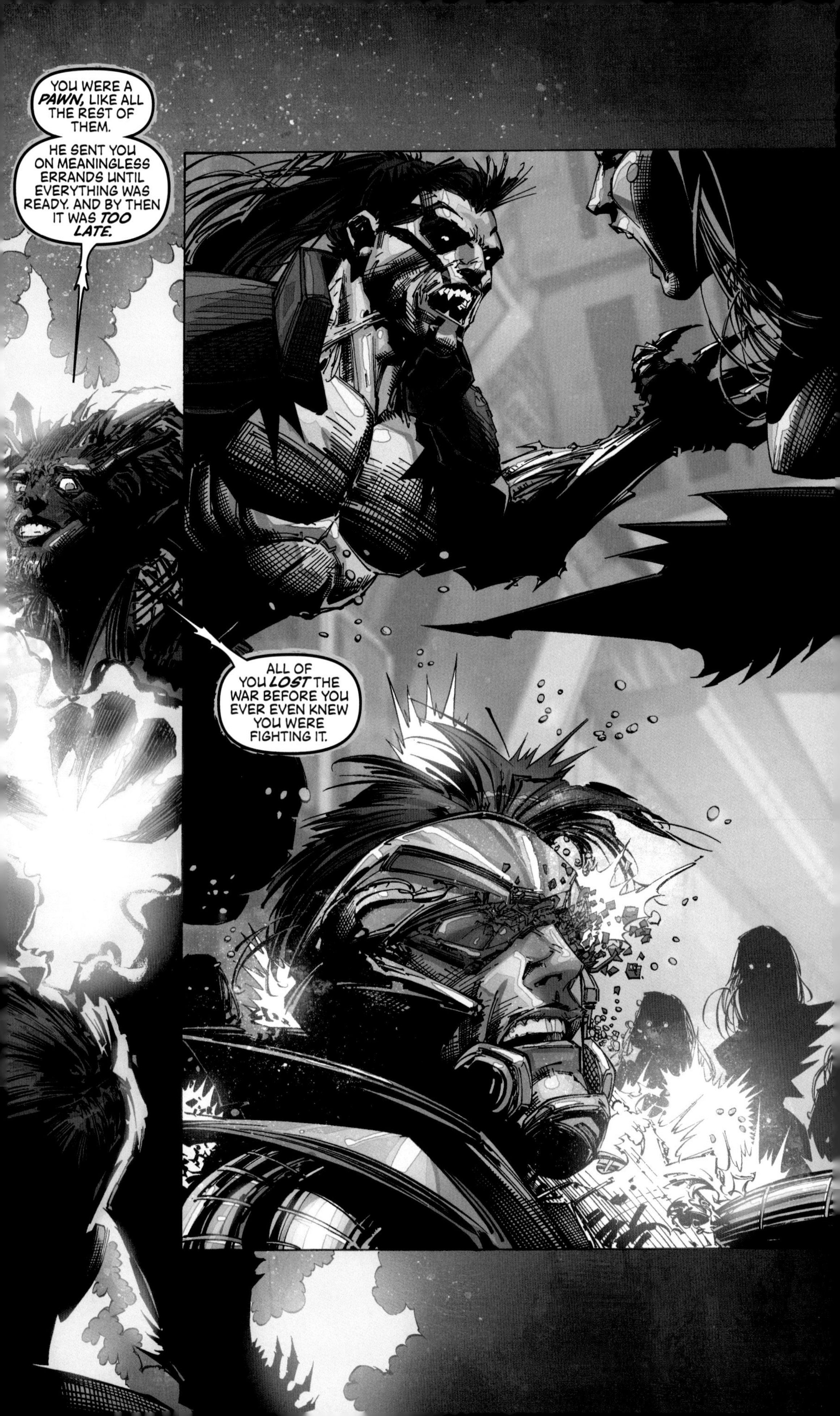
YOU WERE A PAWN, LIKE ALL THE REST OF THEM.
HE SENT YOU ON MEANINGLESS ERRANDS UNTIL EVERYTHING WAS READY. AND BY THEN IT WAS TOO LATE.
ALL OF YOU LOST THE WAR BEFORE YOU EVER EVEN KNEW YOU WERE FIGHTING IT.

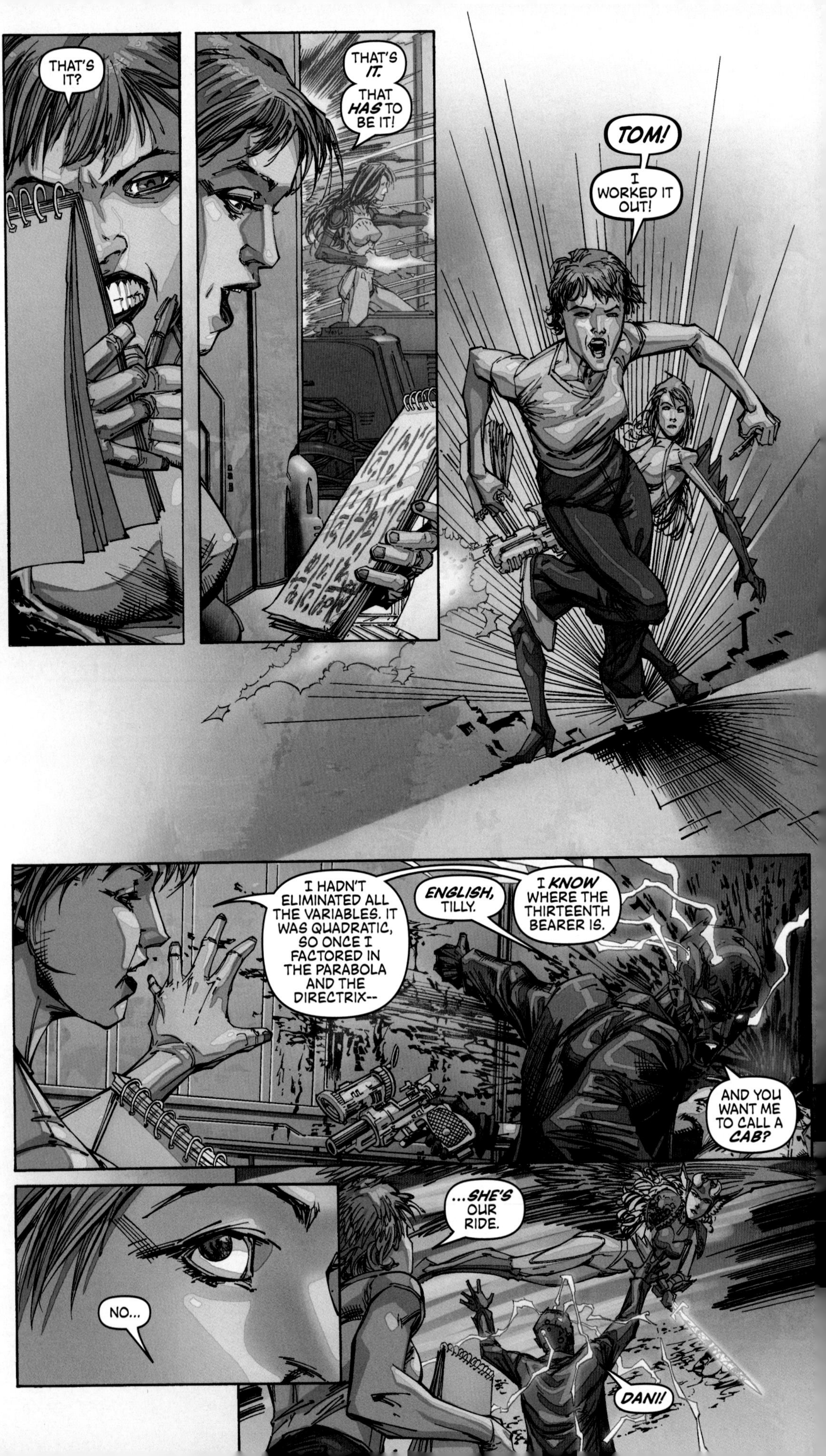
THAT'S IT?
THAT'S *IT.* THAT *HAS* TO BE IT!
TOM!
I WORKED IT OUT!
I HADN'T ELIMINATED ALL THE VARIABLES. IT WAS QUADRATIC, SO ONCE I FACTORED IN THE PARABOLA AND THE DIRECTRIX--
ENGLISH, TILLY.
I *KNOW* WHERE THE THIRTEENTH BEARER IS.
AND YOU WANT ME TO CALL A *CAB?*
NO...
...*SHE'S* OUR RIDE.
DANI!

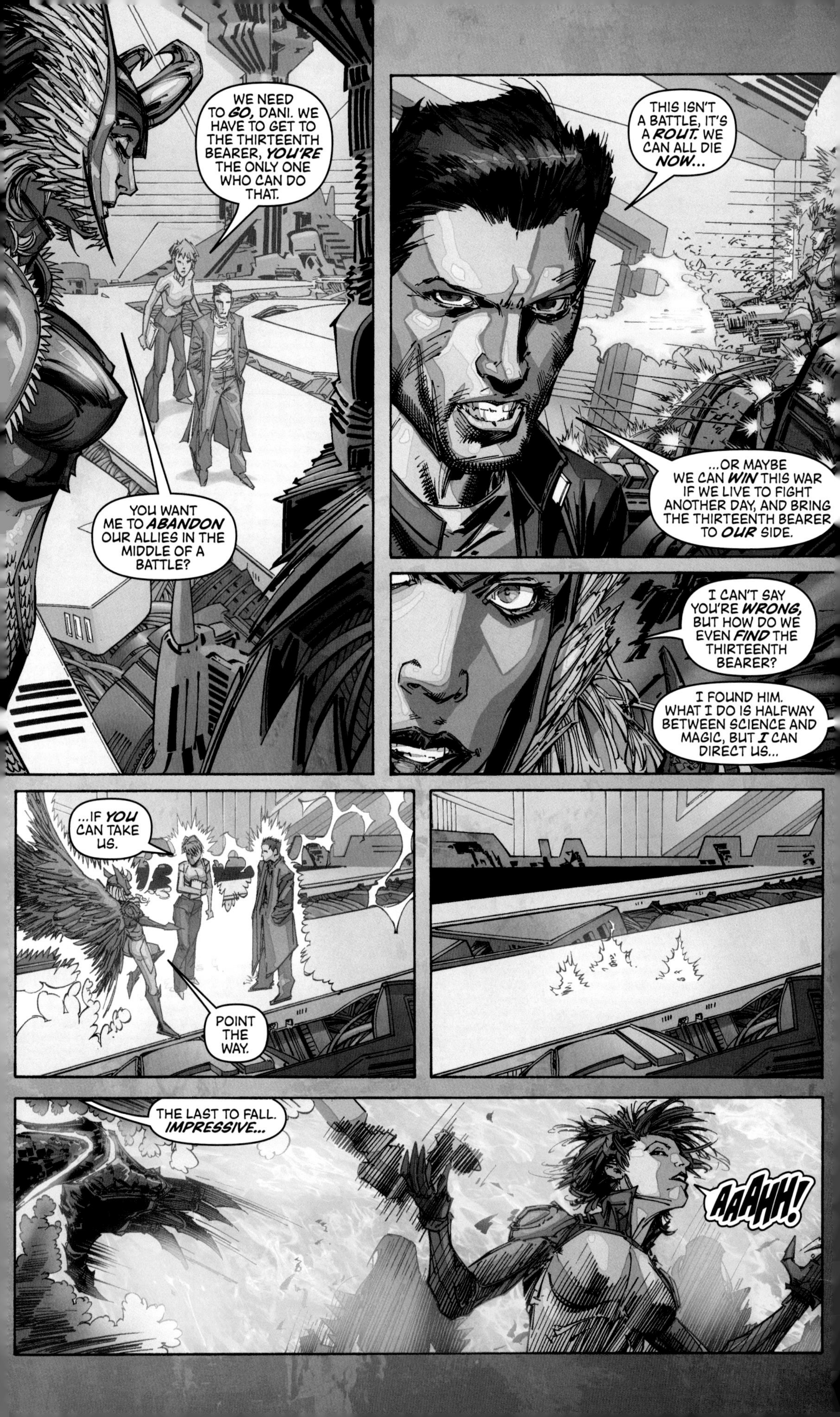
WE NEED TO GO, DANI. WE HAVE TO GET TO THE THIRTEENTH BEARER, YOU'RE THE ONLY ONE WHO CAN DO THAT.
YOU WANT ME TO ABANDON OUR ALLIES IN THE MIDDLE OF A BATTLE?
THIS ISN'T A BATTLE, IT'S A ROUT. WE CAN ALL DIE NOW...
...OR MAYBE WE CAN WIN THIS WAR IF WE LIVE TO FIGHT ANOTHER DAY, AND BRING THE THIRTEENTH BEARER TO OUR SIDE.
I CAN'T SAY YOU'RE WRONG, BUT HOW DO WE EVEN FIND THE THIRTEENTH BEARER?
I FOUND HIM. WHAT I DO IS HALFWAY BETWEEN SCIENCE AND MAGIC, BUT I CAN DIRECT US...
...IF YOU CAN TAKE US.
POINT THE WAY.
THE LAST TO FALL. IMPRESSIVE...
AAAHH!

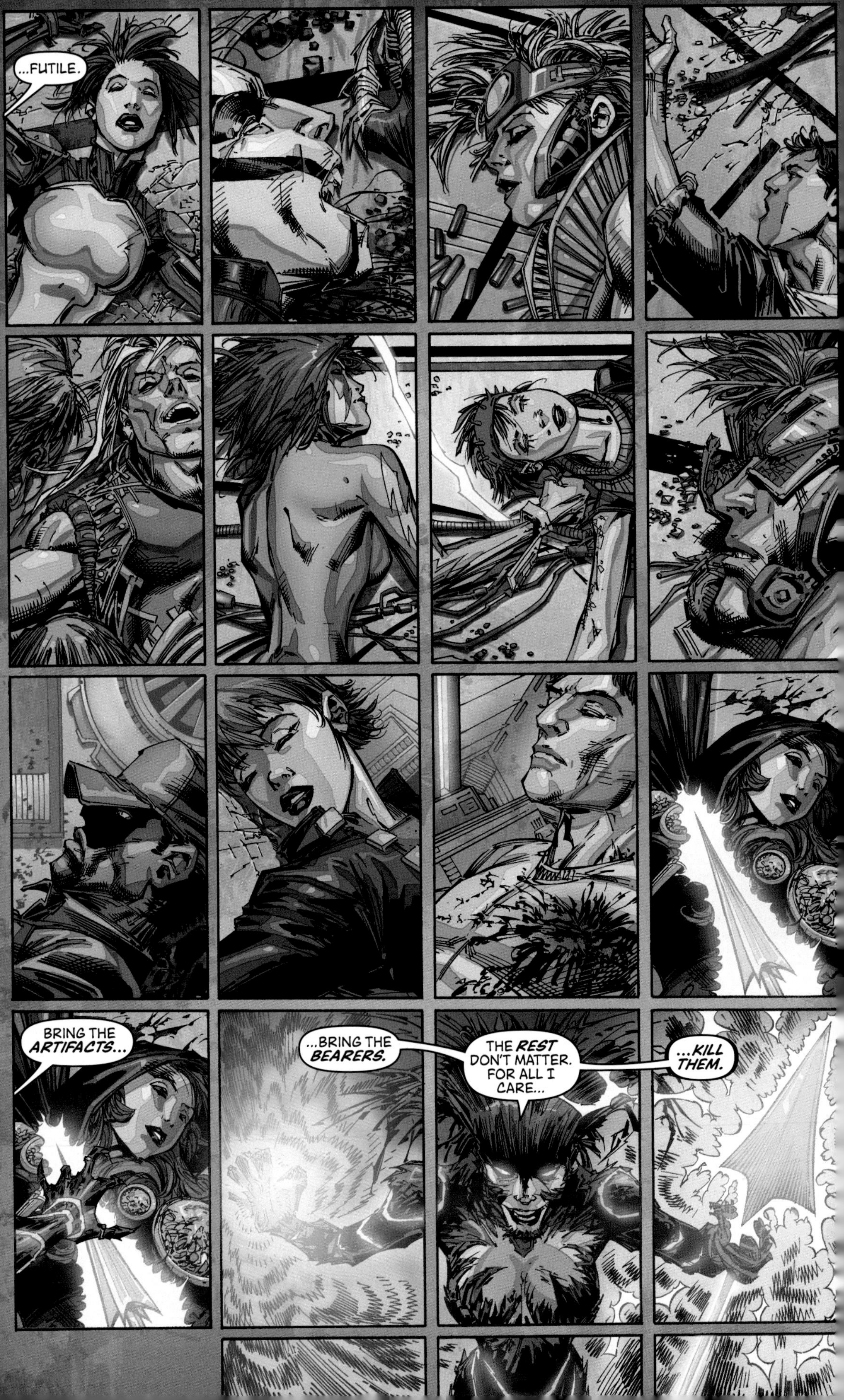
...FUTILE.
BRING THE ARTIFACTS...
...BRING THE BEARERS.
THE REST DON'T MATTER. FOR ALL I CARE...
...KILL THEM.

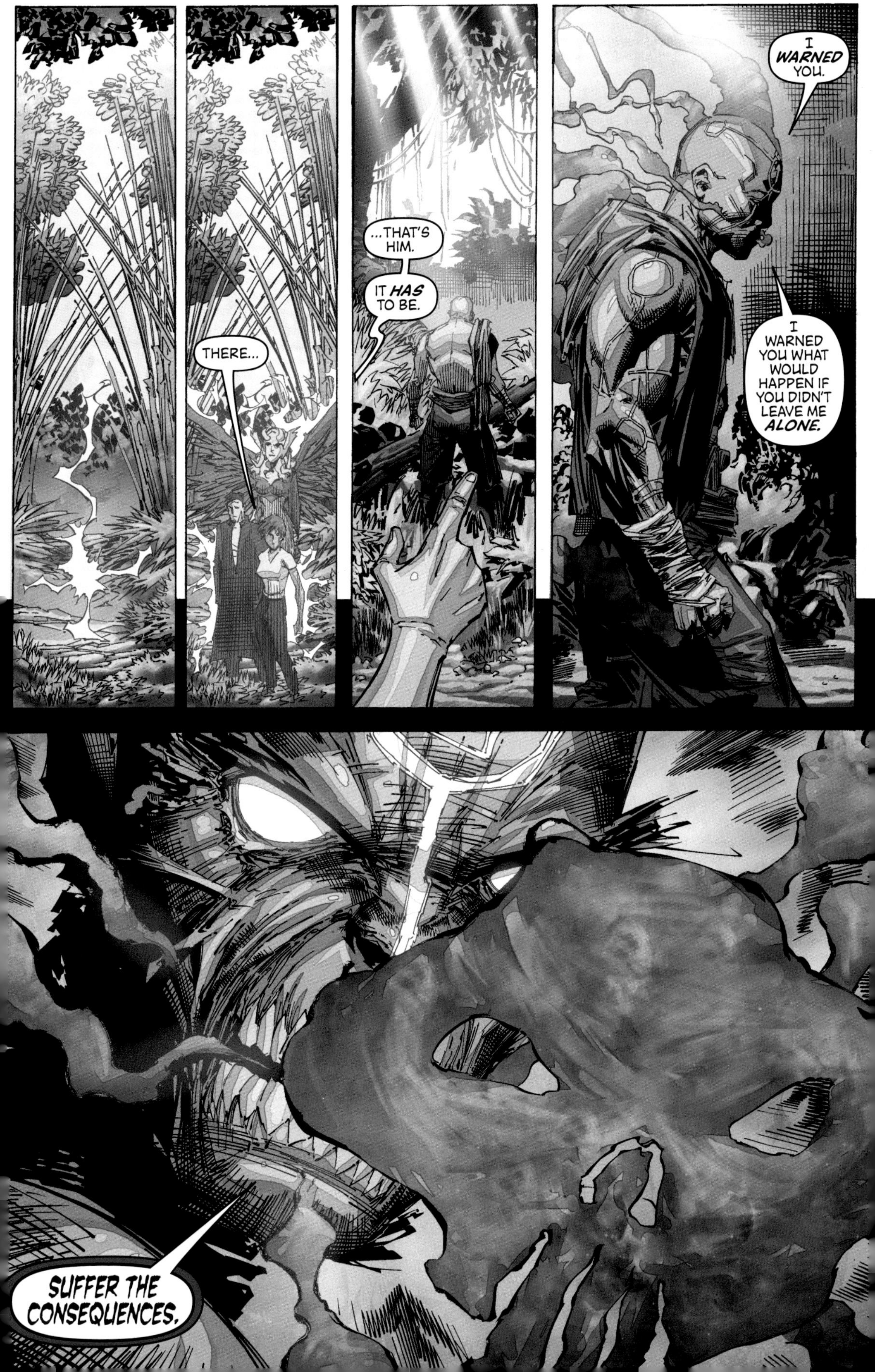
THERE...
...THAT'S HIM.
IT HAS TO BE.
I WARNED YOU.
I WARNED YOU WHAT WOULD HAPPEN IF YOU DIDN'T LEAVE ME ALONE.
SUFFER THE CONSEQUENCES.

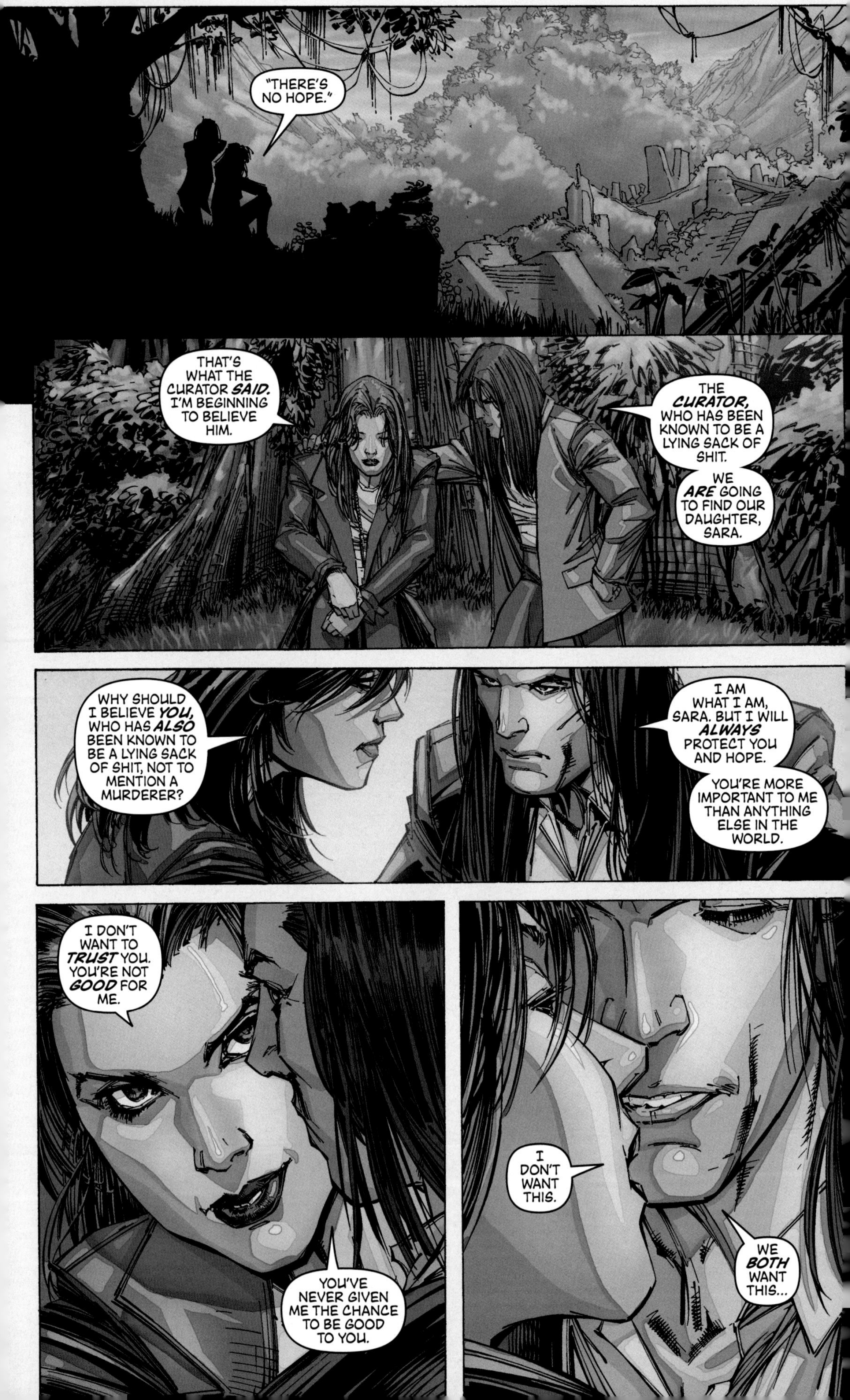
"THERE'S NO HOPE."
THAT'S WHAT THE CURATOR *SAID.* I'M BEGINNING TO BELIEVE HIM.
THE *CURATOR,* WHO HAS BEEN KNOWN TO BE A LYING SACK OF SHIT.
WE *ARE* GOING TO FIND OUR DAUGHTER, SARA.
WHY SHOULD I BELIEVE *YOU,* WHO HAS *ALSO* BEEN KNOWN TO BE A LYING SACK OF SHIT, NOT TO MENTION A MURDERER?
I AM WHAT I AM, SARA. BUT I WILL *ALWAYS* PROTECT YOU AND HOPE.
YOU'RE MORE IMPORTANT TO ME THAN ANYTHING ELSE IN THE WORLD.
I DON'T WANT TO *TRUST* YOU. YOU'RE NOT *GOOD* FOR ME.
YOU'VE NEVER GIVEN ME THE CHANCE TO BE GOOD TO YOU.
I DON'T WANT THIS.
WE *BOTH* WANT THIS...

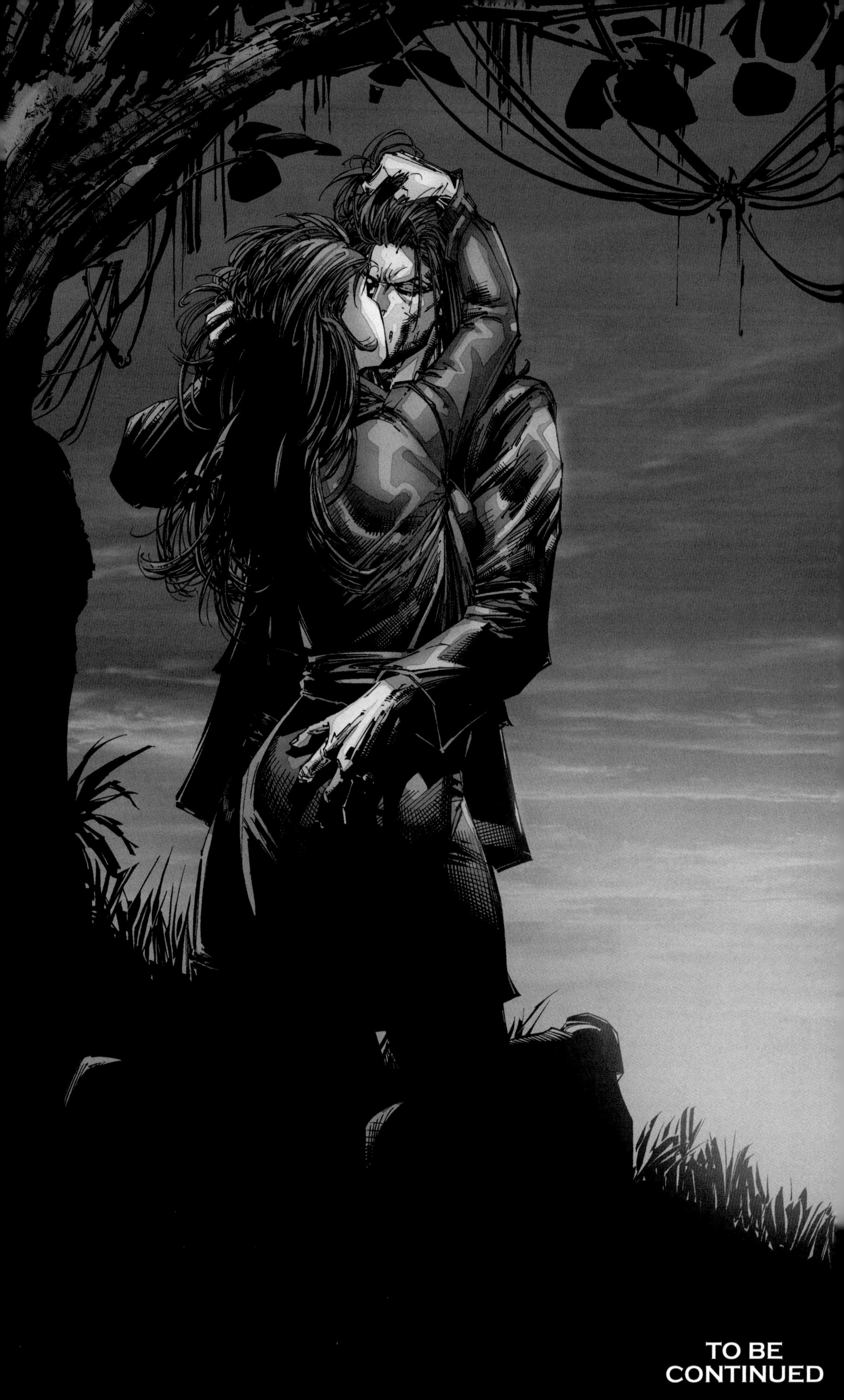
TO BE
CONTINUED

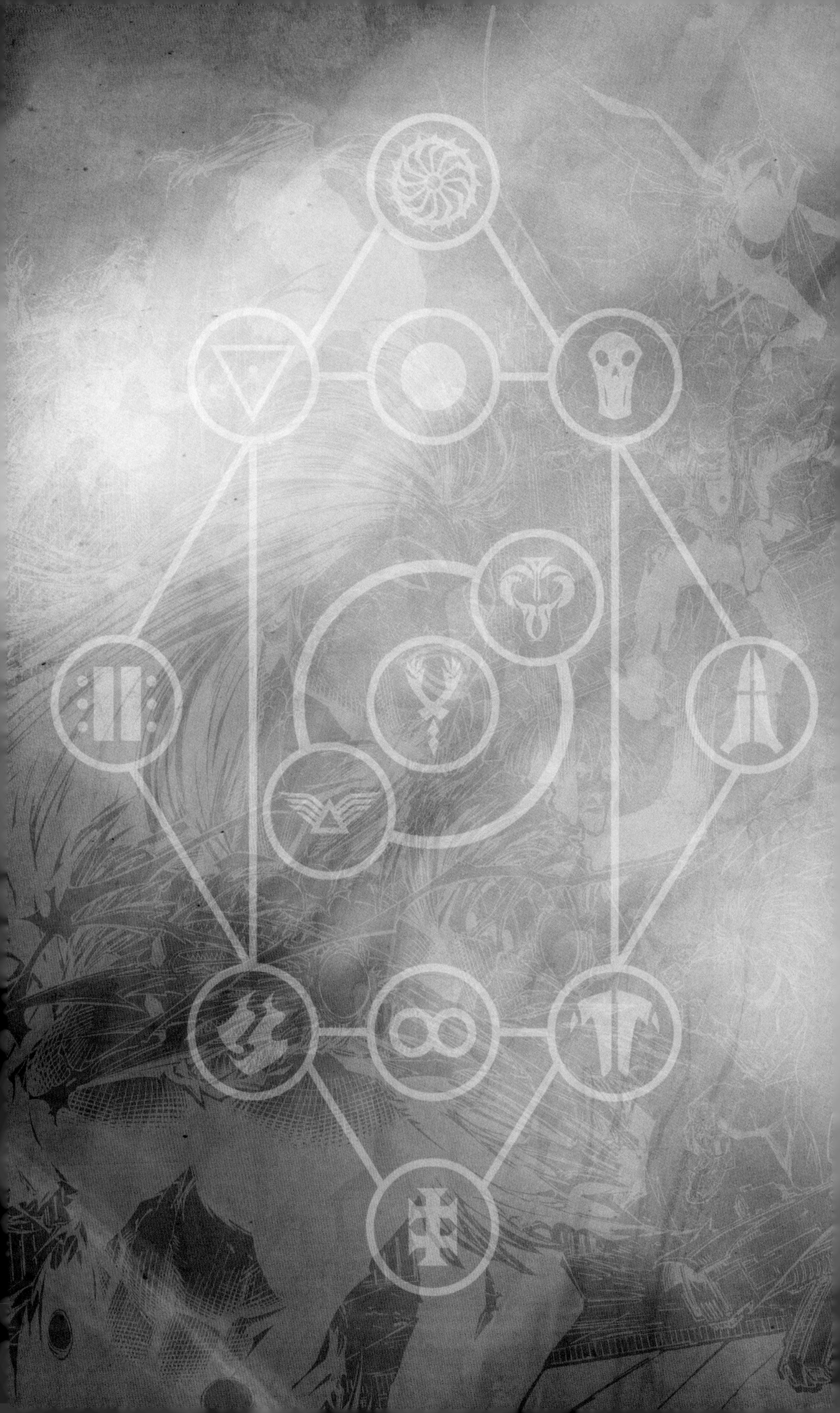

CHARACTER PROFILES

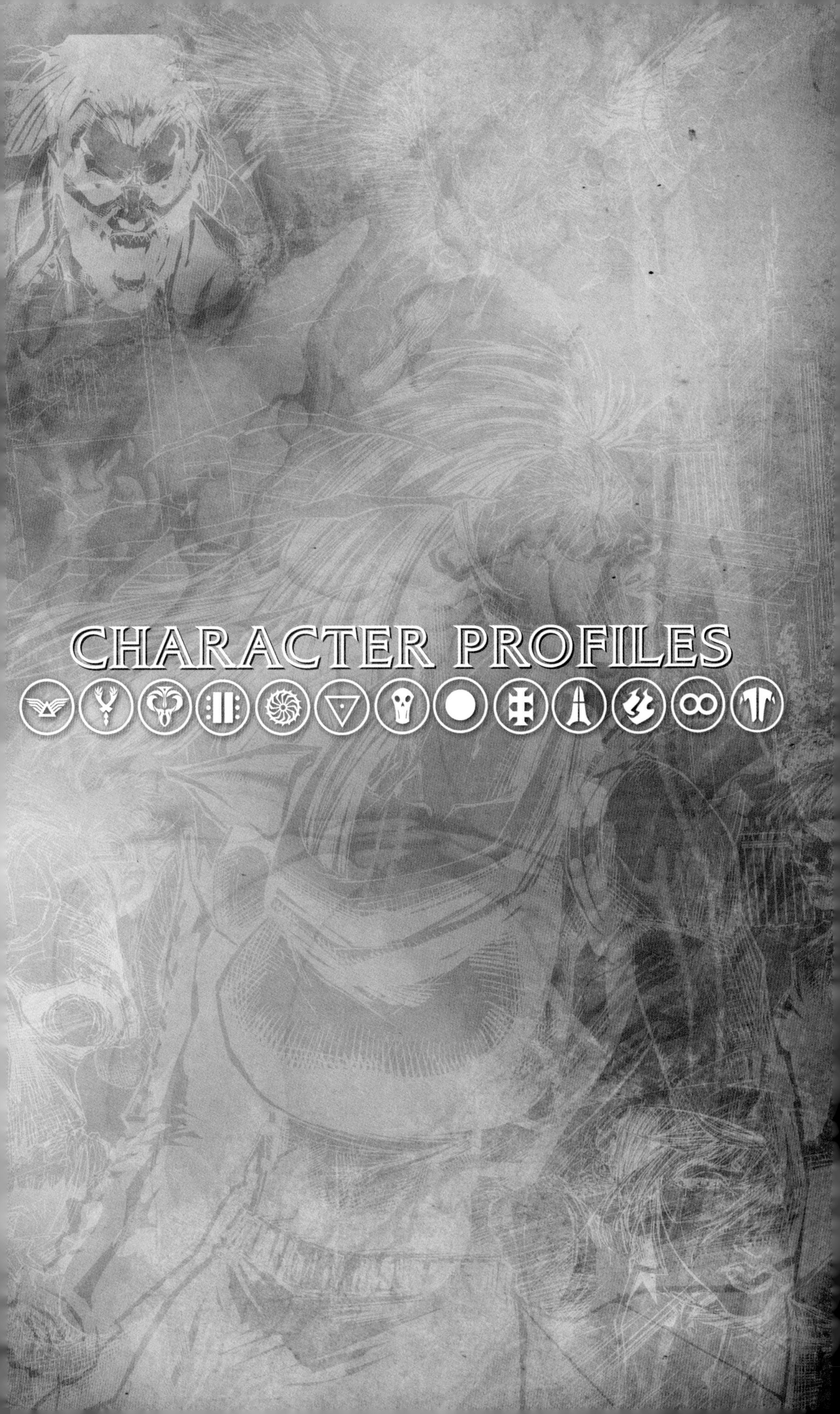

ARTIFACTS

House of Cards: The Players of Artifacts
By Bryan Rountree

Sara Pezzini – Bearer of the Witchblade – Sara is the consummate career New York Police Detective. Born into a cop family, Sara grew up believing that she would die standing with a .38 caliber clutched in her death grip.

Life has dealt Sara a child, an overly understanding boyfriend, and a mystical gauntlet known as the Witchblade. Sara loves Patrick Gleason, but as her professional partner in the Special Cases Division, she hates to think of the day being discreet is no longer enough and she has to choose between her job and a sweetheart. Wielding an ancient Artifact that acts less like an ornate Kevlar vest and more like a lightning rod for the supernatural doesn't make her dangerous job any safer. More and more the Witchblade proves itself a liability… and an indispensable too to protect her family.

Curator – When Manhattan tourists turn down the wrong street corner, they may stumble into a humble curio shop hot-boxed with incense and cluttered with ancient knick-knacks obscured under a film of dust and spider webs. This little store that millions of pedestrians blindly pass on their way to their morning coffee or the train is the epicenter of our universal conflict.

Owned and operated by an elderly Chinese man who refers to himself as only "The Curator," Artifacts older than our world itself are available for those who are meant to bear them, and occasionally to those who want to purchase them. Not much is known about the true identity and history of The Curator. Still he remains Sara Pezzini's only go-to source for information on the Witchblade and the other twelve Artifacts. But to visit the Curator in search of answers is to leave with more questions.

Aphrodite IV – For an artificial intelligence to transcend humanity, it must first absolutely despise human nature. There is nothing colder than the emerald eyes of Aphrodite IV. She desires no passion and feels no fear. She won't close her eyes and bite her upper lip unless she has been programmed to do so.

Accessorizing in side arms and hand grenades, Aphrodite was the perfection of a unique android by her designers. Cut off from her creators, she has received further modifications and upgrades to her build and programming from a mysterious benefactor to make her an even more effective killing machine. A machine, now armed with the most dangerous weapon of all – purpose.

Tom Judge – Bearer of The Rapture – Tom Judge can mark off every rock-bottom cliché there is on the list. Unshaven? Check. Alcoholic? Check. Lost his faith? Check. Spent the late '90s wearing a distressed black leather jacket with no shirt just to prove he was cognizant enough to remember to flick the burning cigarette ash off his stomach before it ignited his bellybutton lint? Check.

Tom wields The Rapture, one of the most powerful of the Thirteen Artifacts known to bring hope to some and take it away from others, and allowing its bearer to journey to and from Hell itself. Oh, and he can transform into a hulking creature who would make the Devil wet himself.

Do you really want this to be the guy who deems you worthy of eternal salvation? We thought so.

Julie Pezzini – Julie Pezzini used to be the girl who turned all the men's heads whenever she made an entrance. She vigorously enjoyed a fast-lane lifestyle, cutting past crowds at the hottest nightclubs, scoring the trendiest drugs, and joining the most fashionable religions. But this lifestyle came at a cost beyond what the inflated salaries of one of L.A.'s most in demand fashion models could afford.

Julie has recently been released from prison, where she served time for drug trafficking. But this has legitimately helped her shift gears and she has since thrust herself head first into playing "Auntie Julie" to Sara's daughter Hope. Whereas it used to be common for Sara to return to her apartment and find that Julie had picked the front door lock to raid the liquor cabinet, Julie now has copy of the key and a family to stay with while she gets back on her feet.

Patrick Gleason – Patrick Gleason is that ideal guy every young woman claims to want, but passes up for the next "bad boy" who passes by. Sure, he's sweet enough. He was raised an Irish mama's boy, trained to always call ahead to see if he needed to pick up the vindaloo before coming home. He's also a New York Police Detective. So even if he doesn't have the British accent, the long flowing hair, or rides a motorcycle with a katana strapped to his back, he's got enough street cred to make the average woman quiver at the knees.

Too bad Gleason's the type of guy who lusts after dangerous women. His relationship with Sara is just swell, but the Witchblade is a jealous lover. For now, Gleason has been considerate enough to ignore that sooner or later he may have to choose between Sara… and his life.

Hope Pezzini – Hope is the offspring of the bearer of the Balance and the eternal force of the Darkness, even if she seems like any other toddler. Biologically, she is the daughter of Sara and former Mafia hit man Jackie Estacado. Her mere existence, however, is a strategic move that threatens to shift the tides of power in the ongoing struggle between Dark and Light.

There is immense power within Hope. After she was born, she abolished an entire army of Angelus Warriors in a single strike. Since then, this power has laid dormant. Hope is not of the Angelus, nor is she completely of the Darkness. She is something else, making her a wildcard among powerful players.

House of Cards: The Players of Artifacts part 2
By Bryan Rountree

Jackie Estacado – Bearer of the Darkness – Mob enforcer. De facto dictator. Daddy. Jackie Estacado has done enough terrible things in his life that it's only fitting for him to embody the horror of his past. When Jackie inherited the power of the Darkness on his 21st birthday, his enemies discovered firsthand that he probably gave the beige smear of a cockroach bubbling out from under the heel of his Tanino Crisci more consideration.

Under city lights, the glow of Jackie's pale, greening skin barely masks the curse within him. In the pitch black, Jackie isn't your worst nightmare, he is nightmare manifest. When he's not seeking trouble, he's seeking retribution. The Darkness took his childhood love, his crime family – even the fulfillment of his libido – away from him. He has become Darkness and all he is burns away under daylight.

Jackie is a man exhausted of second chances. If he straps C-4 to his chest and hits the detonator, the Darkness will rebuild his body, burning nerve ending by burning nerve ending. But having a family changes a man. Even if Jackie doesn't understand the nature of evil too intimately to ever remove himself from a violent life, his daughter Hope keeps him strong.

Darklings – The Darklings are smirking, ugly wise-asses, pure a simple. As the army of other worldly hellions that Jackie Estaca conjures from the shadows to do his bidding, the Darklings are t creatures that go bump in the night.

They are hungry. They are vicious. Peer into the blackest shado at night and they will gnash their teeth and leap at your throat. Un the stark daylight banishes them to our nightmares, their vacant gre eyes betray their lust for carnage and terror. Jackie Estacado may be t current host to the Darkness, but what he knows about the power dwarfed by what he does not know. Without unleashing the Darklir periodically, he will become a victim of their chaos.

Danielle Baptiste – Bearer of the Angelus – New York attracts all the hopefuls and wannabes. Dani isn't quite ready to admit it, but her failure to succeed as a dancer thrusts her plum into that category. Failed classical dancer or not, Dani found more than she bargained for when she met Sara Pezzini. No longer a girl and not quite a woman, Dani is torn between returning to her roots in her flooded hometown of New Orleans and establishing an identity in her adoptive city.

Her ambivalence toward her ambition makes her mantle as the current host to the primal force of the Angelus tentative at best. Having briefly wielded the Witchblade, Dani maintains her independence from a power that generally prefers its human host to act as nothing more than a vessel with marionette strings tied on. This stark display of her individuality has led to the entropy of her control over her alliance of Angelus Warriors, created a bitter enemy from within her ranks, and furthered Dani's own conflict of identity.

Angelus Warriors – The Light is divine. The Light is order. The Light is all-consuming. The host warriors of the Angelus display the conceit of an unwavering allegiance to their mistress, but their true purpose is borne of their eternal obsession to destroy the curse of the Darkness.

They are a warrior race – light made into flesh and granted sentience by the Angelus. No room for weakness is permitted among their ranks. Should any warrior flicker or dim in their duty, they will be vanquished and returned into the Light – even if that warrior is the Angelus herself.

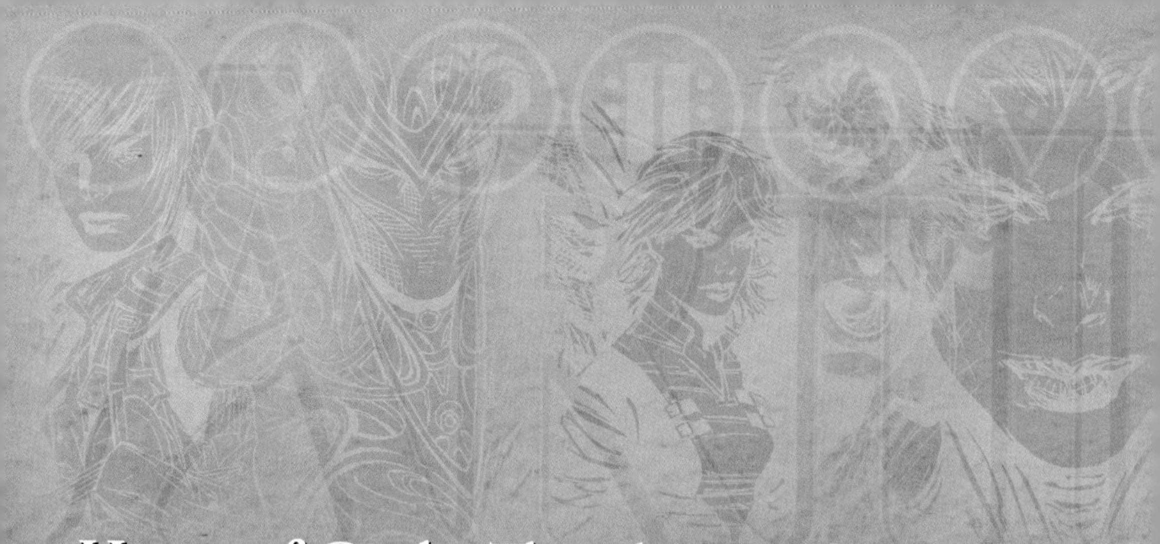

House of Cards: The Players of Artifacts part 3

By Bryan Rountree

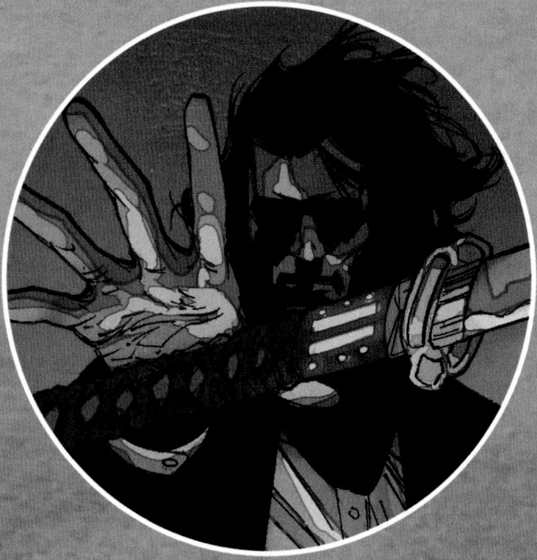

Ian Nottingham – **Bearer of the Blood Sword** – Sa
Pezzini has burned through more than her fair share
partners in her career as a New York Police Detecti
Between the late Michael Yee and Jake McCarthy,
seems that all of the nice boys with the puppy dog ey
who aren't scared off by the Witchblade are killed
by it.

There is, however, one man whose history with Sa
almost predates her introduction to the Witchblac
Ian Nottingham. Tall, dark, handsome – and Britis
to boot – Nottingham was trained to charm his w
into Sara's life. He was also trained to withstar
excruciating torture in preparation to strengthen h
constitution to become the first male to wield t
Witchblade. Though he is no longer confidant to t
possessive Kenneth Irons, a man who only sought t
Witchblade for his own selfish pursuits, he is no less
a threat to Sara and her world.

Gone rogue, he is nobody's assassin. He is nobod
servant. Nottingham lives to sate his own bloodlust.

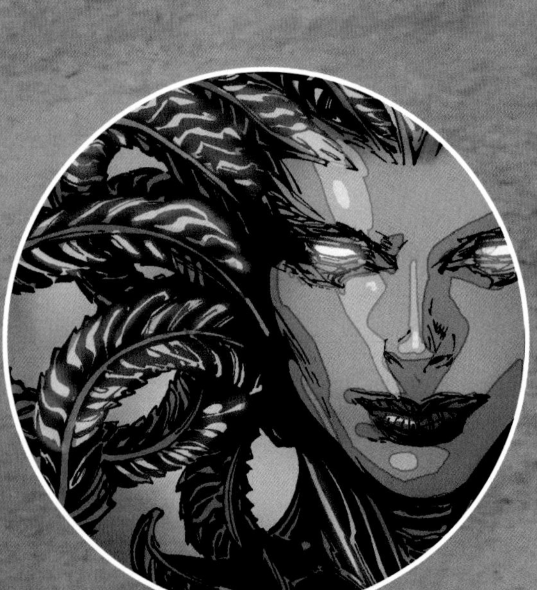

Glorianna Silver – **Bearer of the Ember Stone**
"Heart of ice, not so nice. Heart of fire, just as dir
For all her worth, billionaire industrialist Glorian
Silver has nothing. Orphaned at a young age, Gl
was adopted into the wealthy Olafsson family line a
raised believing her sole purpose was to find the Emb
Stone and wield its fiery power to gather all of t
Artifacts and unite the Trinity of Stones.

Like most children raised with an inherited weal
far beyond her understanding, Glori has embraced h
upbringing to the detriment of her individuality. H
life is a mission. One she lives to the point of obsessio
Without her mission to unite the Artifacts and rema
the world to her vision, she is the cold seven year-o
standing outside of a burning Norwegian farmhou
again.

For all her charities, political contacts, and glob
influence, Glori is discontent to being no closer
obtaining the twelve other Artifacts.

bine – Bearer of the Wheel of Shadows – Sabine s once the chief lieutenant to Angelus host Celestine ight and, in her mind, a proud candidate to one day come dissolved in an ecstasy of Light as she ascended the mantle of the Angelus herself. But the Angelus ce did not choose Sabine as it rushed from Celestine's ortally wounded host body. It chose another.

Sabine's service to Dani Baptiste became the bane of r existence. The authoritarian wrath of the Light and obsession to destroy the Darkness did not consume ni as it had for eons of previous hosts. Envious and sing a usurper in charge of her ranks, Sabine chose stave out her own purpose. She sent her warriors on nission to Hell to retrieve the Wheel of Shadows, a ol she deemed powerful enough to trump the reticent d inexperienced Baptiste.

Although the Wheel of Shadows has granted Sabine lities to accelerate the natural aging process as well control over time-space, its transformative powers nded the Artifact to her. No longer a creature of ght, Sabine is forever barred from what she covets ost.

lina Enstrom – Bearer of Pandora's Box – When na removes her mirrored Aviators, it's usually to peer wn the scope of her Heckler & Koch MP5. The rest the time, the sleek reflection off her frames conceals weight her life of violence bears upon her. No man, r woman, can solely function as a machine of death.

Alina once followed a prophet named Elias Legion, o believed he could remake the world in the name of avior he called Adam. But Elias's New Eden did not wn, and how his faithful lieutenant bonded with ndora's Box is still a mystery.

To possess Pandora's Box – otherwise known as the osidian Stone – is to be more victim than victor. bridled chaos is at Alina's fingertips. Her gravitas demeanor of sadness. Surrounded by black market apons manufacturers and religious cults, Alina's lection proves her to be the pure and the righteous. e rest of the world? Sinners.

ali – Elder Demon Lord – There is magic erywhere and its influence is neither completely nevolent nor malicious. The demon known as Mali a manifestation of evil, but for three hundred years influence over the world has been drowned by a entless stream of Holy Water.

Without their warrior demon, the Church of Mali came nothing more than neutered Satanists awaiting arrival of the child transcendental who would bring out his freedom. Mali's "earthly vessel" may have en trapped under a gentle stream, but his power was t. When the teenager Abby van Alstine read from the crenegrum as a joke during one of her Bible Study sions, Mali obtained possession over her dreams and ghtmares. The mage's tongue is the language of a ckster.

For a time Mali, was trapped within Abby herself, t thanks to an ancient dagger held in New York's etropolitan Museum the demon lord is once again e.

House of Cards: The Players of Artifacts part 4
By Bryan Rountree

Michael Finnegan – Bearer of t
Glacier Stone – Michael Finnegan has be
down on his luck so long that a slap to t
face would seem like the nicest way anyor
said hello to him lately. Before comi
into possession of the Glacier Stone, Fi
bounced between stints as a black mark
gunrunner and a mob errand boy. Unl
you think a bullet to the back of your he
is the fastest way to ascend beyond the gl
ceiling, neither of those vocations offer mu
in the way of professional growth.

If you listen to Finn's side of the story, one c
he is tailing Sara Pezzini under the empl
of Jackie Estacado, the next, he is a bu
frost giant, smashing through doorw
and bumping into things. Born into a l
of violence but not a life of mysticism, Fi
hardly seems like the ideal candidate to
the first bearer of the Glacier Stone in o
a millennium.

In a firefight, his knack for violence a
charm has kept him mostly unscathed. I
war that has waged for ages, however, Fin
myopic habit of following orders preve
him from recognizing the gravitas of t
bigger picture. But after years of being pushed around, Finn's made a resolution to stick to his gut and do wh
he believes is right. Too bad that no matter what he does or which side he fights for, there is always a blade pois
for attack, waiting behind each street corner in anticipation to slice into his back.

Patience – The Magdalena – Bearer of t
Spear of Destiny – Descending from a Sacr
Order within the Catholic Church, t
Magdalena is tasked to protect the Chur
and its relics at all costs. The Magdalena i
legacy of Holy Defenders, her duties passi
to each ascendant through the lineage
Christ himself. Each woman who bears t
burden of the Magdalena wields the Spear
Destiny – the Artifact that pierced the si
of Christ – in her battle against the evils
the world. A battle that has historically be
short and met with a violent end.

The current Magdalena was nam
Patience, proof that God does indeed hav
sense of irony, according the nuns at Sincl
Abbey. As an orphan raised in a cloister
convent in rural Quebec, Patience used
long for the day she might escape to t
outside world. As the current defender
the Church battling in the trenches agair
all threats political or supernatural, Patier
has grown weary of the careless evil creat
by mankind – especially those men of t
Cloth who deem themselves her superiors

Personal experience has made her
wildcard to rogue Cardinals and Bishops who would deploy her for their own personal profit. While Patier
is a true inheritor of the Holy Bloodline, the ambitions of men with ambiguous morals does not register amo
her concerns. Trusting herself more than the administrative structures of the Church, Patience serves her man
on the basis of faith rather than order.

She is one of the most independent women to bear the title of Magdalena, but this has also kept her mos
alone and with limited resources in her bullish struggle against evil.

Abigail van Alstine – Necromancer – Abigail van Alstine used to wear the façade of middle-American perfection. She was a blonde cheerleader, a bubbly model student, and an absolute bitch between organizing Bible-study sessions at Manitou High – red, white, and blue incarnate. Slather her with apple pie and there is no girl better to bring home and show off to mom.

The only problem – she sees dead people. And if the recently deceased could just stay buried, then maybe the desire to read from the Necrenegrum wouldn't have itched her teenage curiosity. Instead, she inadvertently conjured the demon Mali, who slaughtered her family and friends and everything she thought her life to be burned down with them.

Sometimes second chances give us the opportunity to realize we aren't being the person we know ourselves to be. Since fleeing to Southern California with Locke, her mentor and guardian in all things magic, Abby's busted out the black leather corset and let her natural hair color shine through. After all, when you're a transcendental prodigy with cults and demons on the lookout for you, what better place there than Los Angeles to blend into the crowd?

A recent encounter with Witchblade bearer Sara Pezzini in New York City resulted in the demon Mali being leased from his prison, which as it turned out was Abby herself. New abilities have begun to manifest themselves thin Abby leaving her to wonder with Mali gone from her life, what did he leave behind?

Tilly Grimes – Clairvoyant – Her name is Tilly and she can predict the future. No, it's not a special power she's got, wise guy, it's plain ole' smarts mixed with an observational sensitivity to the minutia of all the signs the universe already presents to us. "That's cow-pucky!" you say, right? Well, by analyzing the mathematical implications of the randomly generated barcode on an ordinary can of baked beans and triangulating it against the expiration date of that jar of boysenberry jelly in your refrigerator, she knew you were going to say that.

She worked with the government spooks at the Pentagon to develop artificial gateways to Hell, even though she foresaw herself stealing the plans. She organized workgroup camping retreats when she knew one of her employees was destined to die. And she sought out Tom Judge so he might claim the Artifact known as the Rapture, even though that same damn can of beans pointed to the outcome of Tom being doomed to Hell.

The only problem for Tilly is that she gets ahead of herself. Just because she intuitively sees all the invisible connections of cause-ect in the universe when she steps in bubblegum doesn't mean she's resigned herself to allowing the End of ays to come to fruition. But it is mighty bothersome that right now, all of her equations are leading to the same utcome. Because in her notebook, that means we're screwed.

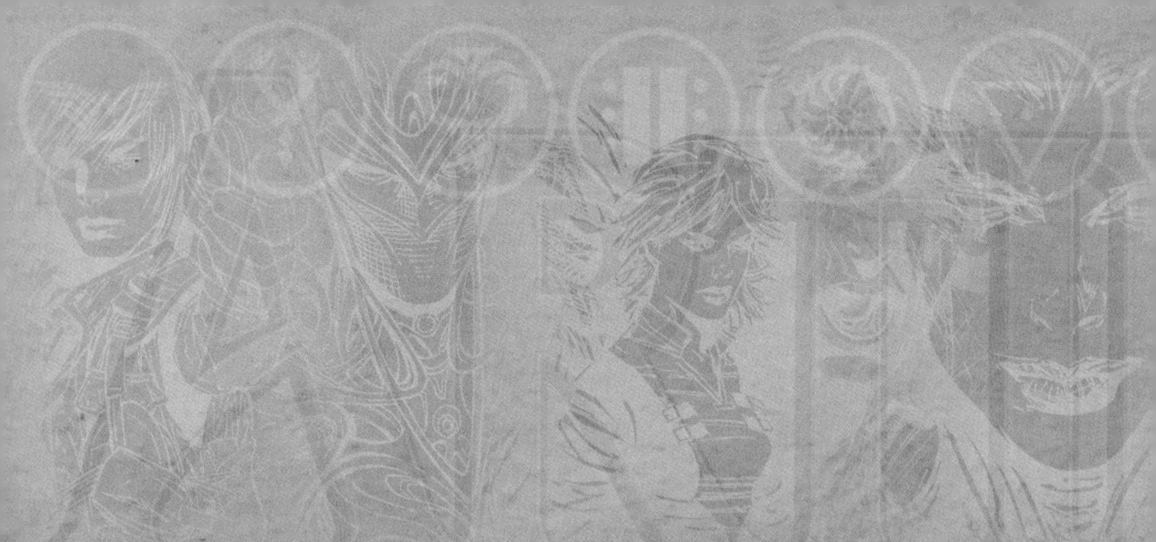

House of Cards: The Players of Artifacts part 5

By Bryan Rountree

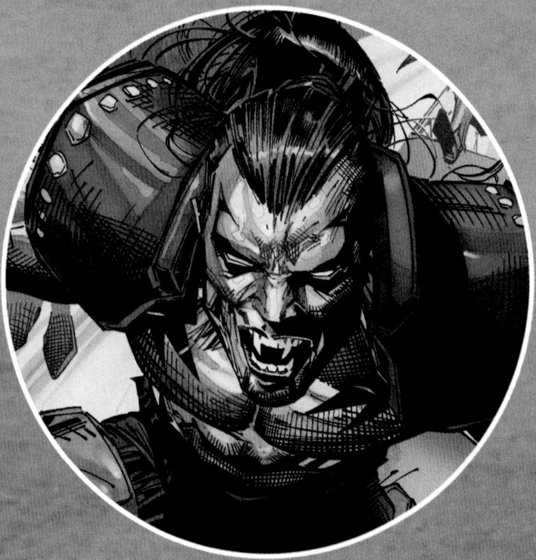

Robert Bearclaw – **Ripclaw** – As the spiritual cent that balances and motivates the other members Cyberforce, Robert Bearclaw bears the arduous task juggling the humanist mission of his team against t implications of their technological implants.

There was a point in time when none of the membe of Cy berforce bore cybernetic limbs. It was a simpl time before the transnational Cyberdata Corporatic abducted their unwilling subjects and erased the memories. He was freed by insurgent Cyberda handlers to fight the good fight, but it's not mu personal consolation against all the prior harm committed under Cyberdata's control.

Since the inception of Cyberforce, Ripclaw has struggl with his alienation from his Native American roots a Shaman and the connection it gave him to the natur world. But he can never return to his natural state. a modern world where technology advances with tl blink of an eye, his previously cutting-edge cyberne implants are growing increasingly obsolete in contra to the universal surveillance and global control of h enemies. It's claw forth or die.

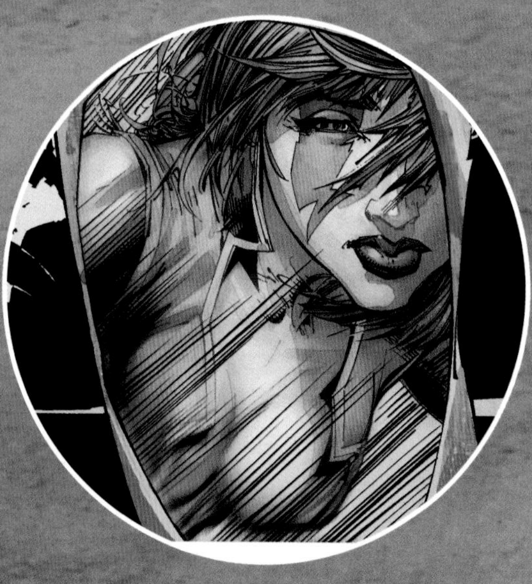

Carin Taylor – **Velocity** – Carin Taylor embodi her codename: Velocity. Fast enough to appear in Ne York and Prairie View, Texas at virtually the same tim she's the resident wisecracking, redheaded speedst of Cyberforce. But a lifetime of running fast is also lifetime of running away from the people and plac she wish she were closer to.

It's as if every technological upgrade performed improve her has also isolated her. The eerie pale moc glow of her skin? That's the experimental form Kevlar that's bonded with her skin so her face doesn melt off when she approaches the sound barric Beyond supersonic speeds, radio waves become visib and sprinting across the Pacific is like jogging on a sa flat. But no one is quick enough to catch up and sha this splendor with her.

Dominique Thiebaut – Cyblade – Dominique can lick her lips and still taste the best material luxuries and cultural refinement the world has to afford. It's one of two side effects of being born into European royalty. The other? Other people make it their business to ensure her safety. Not long after Dominique was abducted by the malicious Cyberdata Corporation to serve as one of their most valuable S.H.O.C. troops, Dominique became the first of Cyberdata's S.H.O.C. troops to be freed by insurgent handlers working within the company.

Just because this hiccup of privilege makes her the original founding member of Cyberforce doesn't mean she's a stuck up bitch. No, her myopic preference for French wine and an obnoxious obsession with gourmet cheese does. Even though she's a rich girl, she is a calculating and deadly adversary who would never give an opponent the cold shoulder. After all, Dominique reveals her best self in combat at close-quarters. The bright pink flash of the electromagnetic energy blades she can generate with the snap of her fingers is a dazzling sight capable of cutting both flesh and steel.

Cassandra Lane – Ballistic – If she can see you, she can kill you. It is something Cassandra's teammates will never forget.

Cassandra's cybernetic arm and eye have effectively eliminated the margin of error in her aim. Those who stare down the barrel of a gun Cassandra points at them have never seen a more perfect example of concentric circles. It's a vicious harmony that blocks out the days before Cassandra's mind was wiped away by a Cyberdata Brain Box, when a violent ex-boyfriend nearly crippled her with a baseball bat.

Before she fought alongside Cyberforce, she hunted them. As the final member of Cyberforce to defect from Cyberdata, Cassandra struggles to trust her adoptive team who cannot forget the firepower she put in their way. She's one of the good guys, but she'll blow your head off if she even thinks you'll mention that her hairstyle hasn't been in fashion since Belinda Carlisle sang for the Go-Go's.

Ellis Baker – Hunter-Killer – A prior conflict between the members of Cyberforce and the members of Hunter-Killer has placed Ellis in the crosshairs of the uneasy truce between the two teams. Just because Hunter-Killer is united by a distrust of the government and Cyberforce is united by a distrust of mega-corporations doesn't mean everyone wants to enjoy each other's company and play fair.

Before the Hunter-Killer task force "traded" Ellis to Cyberforce in a game of checks and balances, he was a second-generation Ultra-Sapien who was the living codex to the subjects of Project: USA. Anticipating the collapse of Project: USA, Ellis was born to be the government's tool to fight fire with fire. The problem: rogue Ultra-Sapiens dispersed and took Ellis into hiding once he was born. For the entirety of his picturesque childhood of Montana seclusion, Ellis had no idea of his ability to mirror the powers of other Ultra-Sapiens in close proximity.

Ellis is looking for an understanding of the world and of himself. It has led to his current limbo between being neither a Hunter-Killer nor a member of Cyberforce.

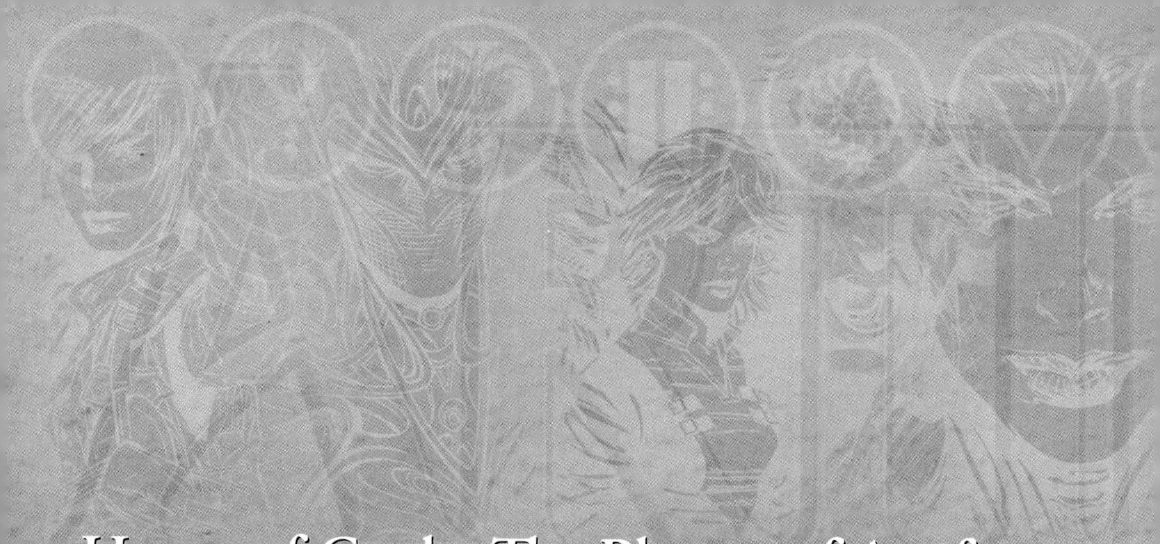

House of Cards: The Players of Artifacts part 6
By Bryan Rountree

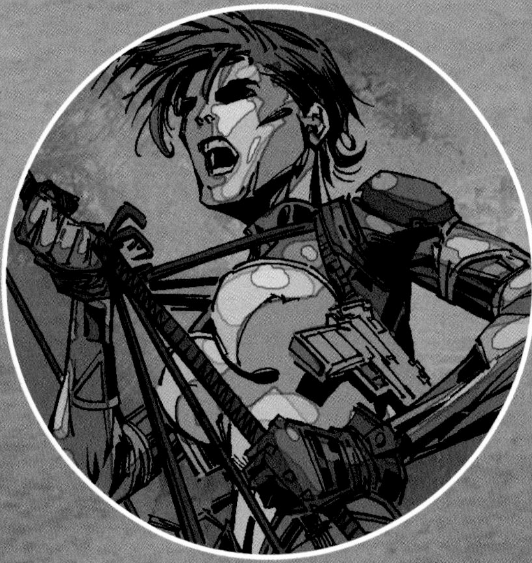

Samantha Argent – Hunter-Killer – In the l 1940s, government scientists developed a gene codi process that could grant ordinary men and women wi exceptional powers and abilities through a tattoo-li "technoderm" graft branded on their skin. The proj participants were dubbed "Ultra-Sapiens," and althou their mere creation sparked the conflicts of the C War, their existence was not public knowledge.

Sam herself is among the latest generation Ultra-Sapiens, but her circumstances are not the same her predecessors. Today, rogue Ultra-Sapiens disconte with manipulative shadow governments exploiting th abilities for profit hide among ordinary citizens. B many Ultra-Sapiens are walking atom bombs with frag emotions and a flawed control over their abilities. I rogue Ultra-Sapien's out-of-control telepathic abilit threaten to melt the brains of the entire population Tehran, Sam's duty is capture, containment, control. S is a professional, accomplishing her missions no mat the cost, no matter who must die. She is a Hunter-Kill

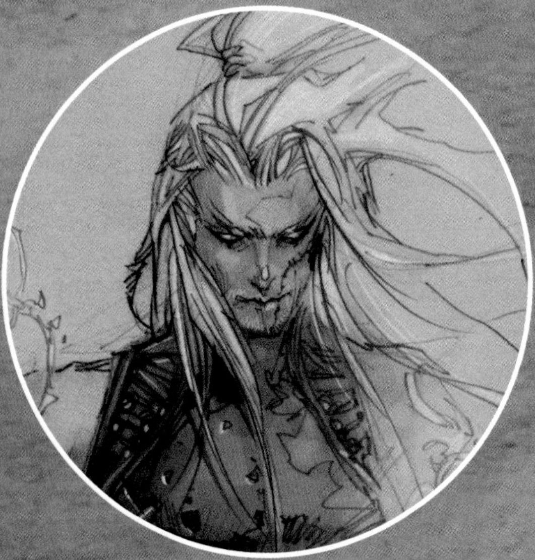

Wolf – Hunter-Killer – The razor's edge, the thin r line… these are quaint dance steps to the mysteri Ultra-Sapien known only by his codename: Wolf. Bo and bred within the Hunter-Killer program and train to hunt his own kind, Wolf is a legend in his own rig His flawless tracking and containment prowess ma him feared by those he hunts. His silent autonomy fro the confines of the Hunter-Killer program keeps h feared by those with whom he works.

Even on the battlefield, at the very mome Wolf is in position to pounce on a target, it's unclear wh side he's on. At one point, he defected yet continued hunt rogue Ultra-Sapiens on his own initiative. Ma of his personal missions paralleled the path taken by t taskforce led by Samatha Argent. Although he's no long shadowing Hunter-Killer and is currently a member their roster, Wolf's ultimate intentions remain, as alwa a mystery.

Dylan Cruise – Heatwave – Hunter-Killer – Dylan is a man who can harness the power of the sun, but can't even keep his own life in order. Able to absorb and retain ambient solar energy, the rest of the world is just lucky enough that he's a nice enough guy to not feel compelled to stand over the world like a seven-year-old focusing a magnifying glass to burn ants.

He is a team player – mostly because he needs to be. His suit is not designed solely for suave aesthetics; he needs it to mitigate his own power, lest he wants his excess energy to disintegrate his body. When Cyberforce was temporarily disbanded, it was Heatwave who maintained the Cyberforce safehouse off Long Island Sound and transformed it into a new headquarters. Yet ever since his presumed death, this former team leader hasn't fully regained the trust of his home team. Heatwave recently assigned himself to Hunter-Killer in a "checks and balances" agreement when Ellis Baker posted himself to Cyberforce. Although neither team fully trusts the other, Heatwave hopes he will regain Cyberforce's faith in him by proving himself on the side of the other team.

Interface – Hunter-Killer – The fallout from the initial clash between the Cyberforce and Hunter-Killer team resulted in many casualties among Hunter-Killer's ranks. The harshest blow was the team's loss of Jay Kennedy – aka Network – the walking, talking, electro-neural computer. Lower ranking Hunter-Killer soldiers feared that when Network would fall, the whole world would crash down with him.

Enter: Interface. Deep within the bowels of the Hunter-Killer complex, children who can barely be considered adolescents are preemptively trained to replace their predecessors. Interface may still be a snarky little scamp who dresses like the lovechild of Marilyn Manson and Amanda Palmer, but the entire Hunter-Killer network runs through her now. As for team commander Argent, she can only hope that Interface will grow out of being a sarcastic, know-it-all before her ego bests her ability to perform her duty.

Cloaker – Hunter-Killer – He is the master of disguise, the man of a million and one faces. He is the reason the Hunter-Killer program is able to stay out of sight while they operate in plain sight.

Born John Bradley Seals, the Ultra-Sapien codenamed Cloaker is a telepath with limited control over the visual cortex. When a group of heavily armed Hunter-Killer troops parade down the street in pursuit of a rogue Ultra-Sapien, why doesn't anyone give them a second look? Because thanks to Cloaker's ability to cast illusions into the brains of anyone in sight, they all look like a group of third graders on a field trip to the Natural History Museum.

Unfortunately, Cloaker can't maintain control over all perceived reality. The greater the illusion, the greater the stress. And after he was recently wounded in a battle alongside Cyberforce, Cloaker is less confident in his ability to slip by unnoticed.

House of Cards: Orbits of Confluence

By Bryan Rountree

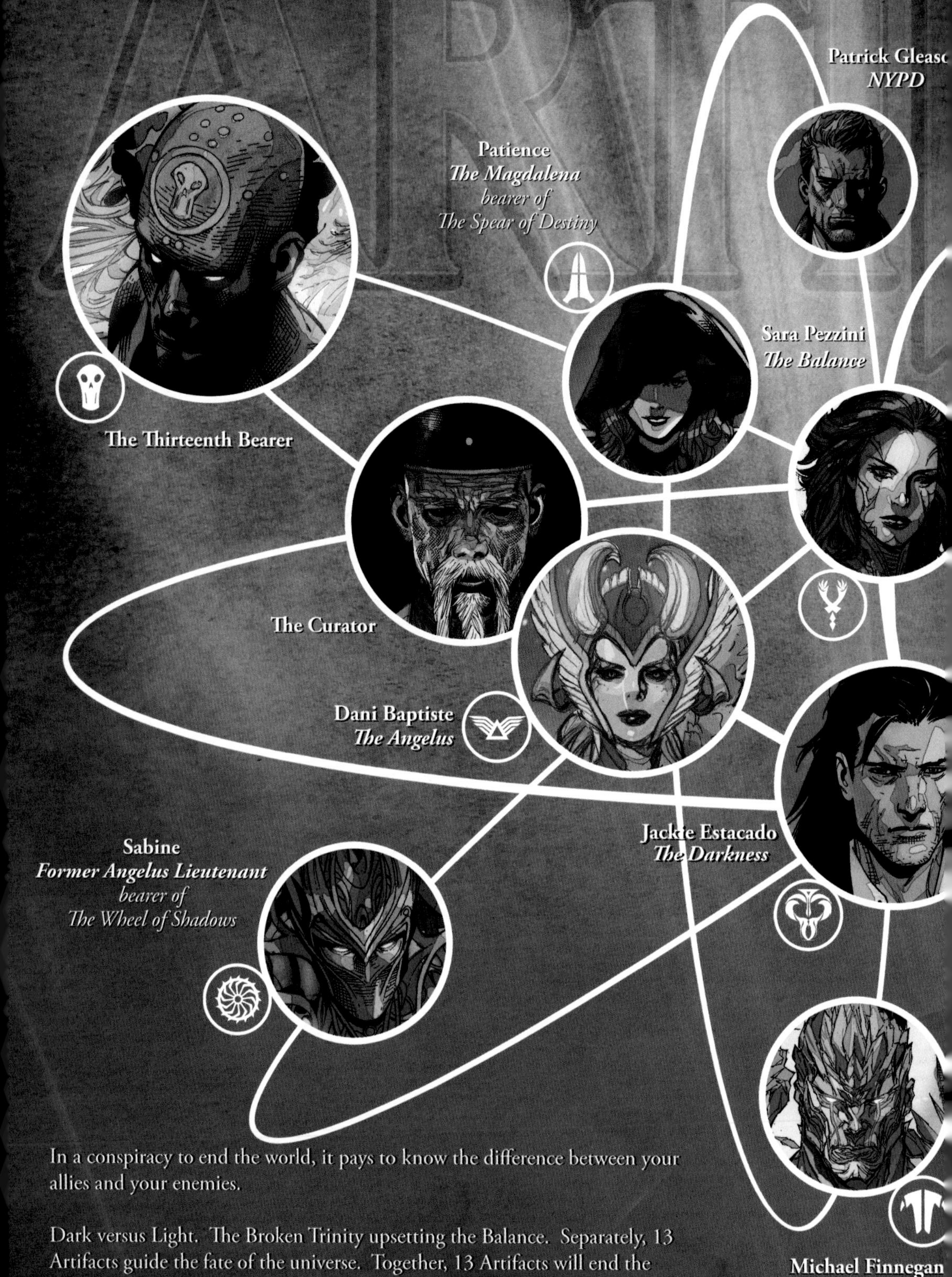
Patrick Gleas
NYPD
Patience
The Magdalena
bearer of
The Spear of Destiny
Sara Pezzini
The Balance
The Thirteenth Bearer
The Curator
Dani Baptiste
The Angelus
Sabine
Former Angelus Lieutenant
bearer of
The Wheel of Shadows
Jackie Estacado
The Darkness
Michael Finnegan
bearer of
The Glacier Stone

In a conspiracy to end the world, it pays to know the difference between your allies and your enemies.

Dark versus Light. The Broken Trinity upsetting the Balance. Separately, 13 Artifacts guide the fate of the universe. Together, 13 Artifacts will end the universe. But that does not mean it is the endeavor of the Artifact bearers to bring about the End of Days. There are other forces at work. The involvement of Cyberforce in this conflict barely scratches at the surface at who's playing whom, and who's getting played...

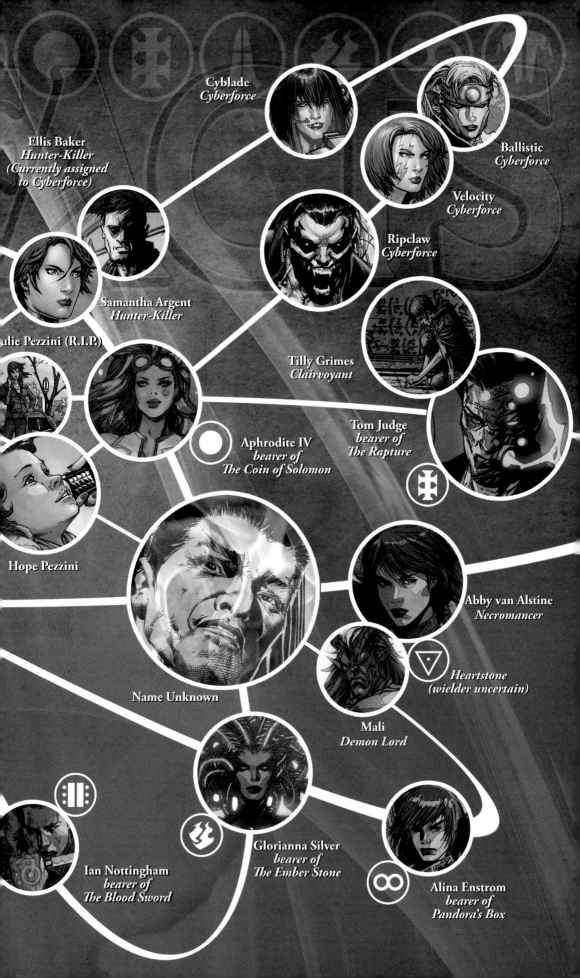

Cyblade
Cyberforce

Ballistic
Cyberforce

Velocity
Cyberforce

Ellis Baker
*Hunter-Killer
(Currently assigned
to Cyberforce)*

Ripclaw
Cyberforce

Samantha Argent
Hunter-Killer

Tilly Grimes
Clairvoyant

Julie Pezzini (R.I.P.)

Tom Judge
*bearer of
The Rapture*

Aphrodite IV
*bearer of
The Coin of Solomon*

Hope Pezzini

Abby van Alstine
Necromancer

Heartstone
(wielder uncertain)

Name Unknown

Mali
Demon Lord

Ian Nottingham
*bearer of
The Blood Sword*

Glorianna Silver
*bearer of
The Ember Stone*

Alina Enstrom
*bearer of
Pandora's Box*

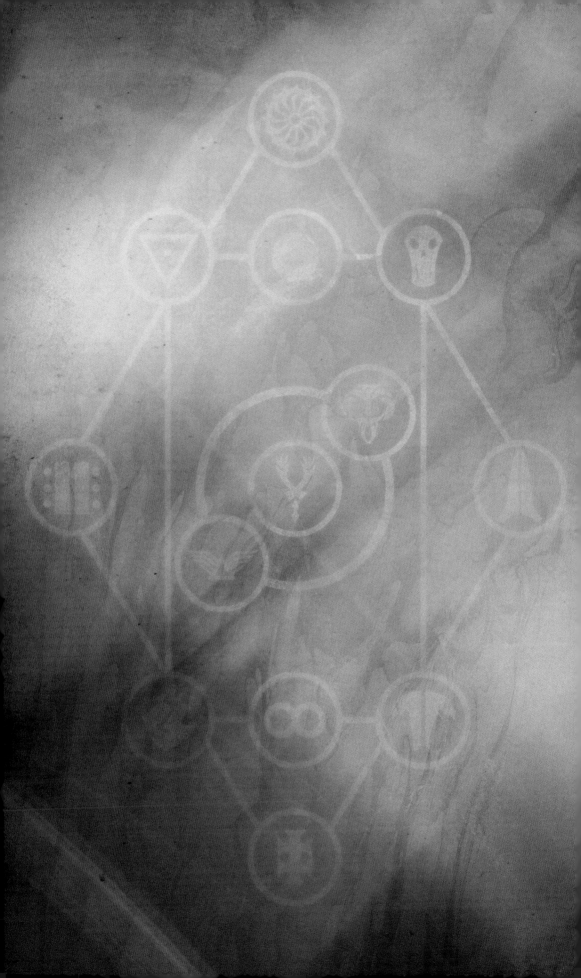

ARTIFACTS

COVER GALLERY

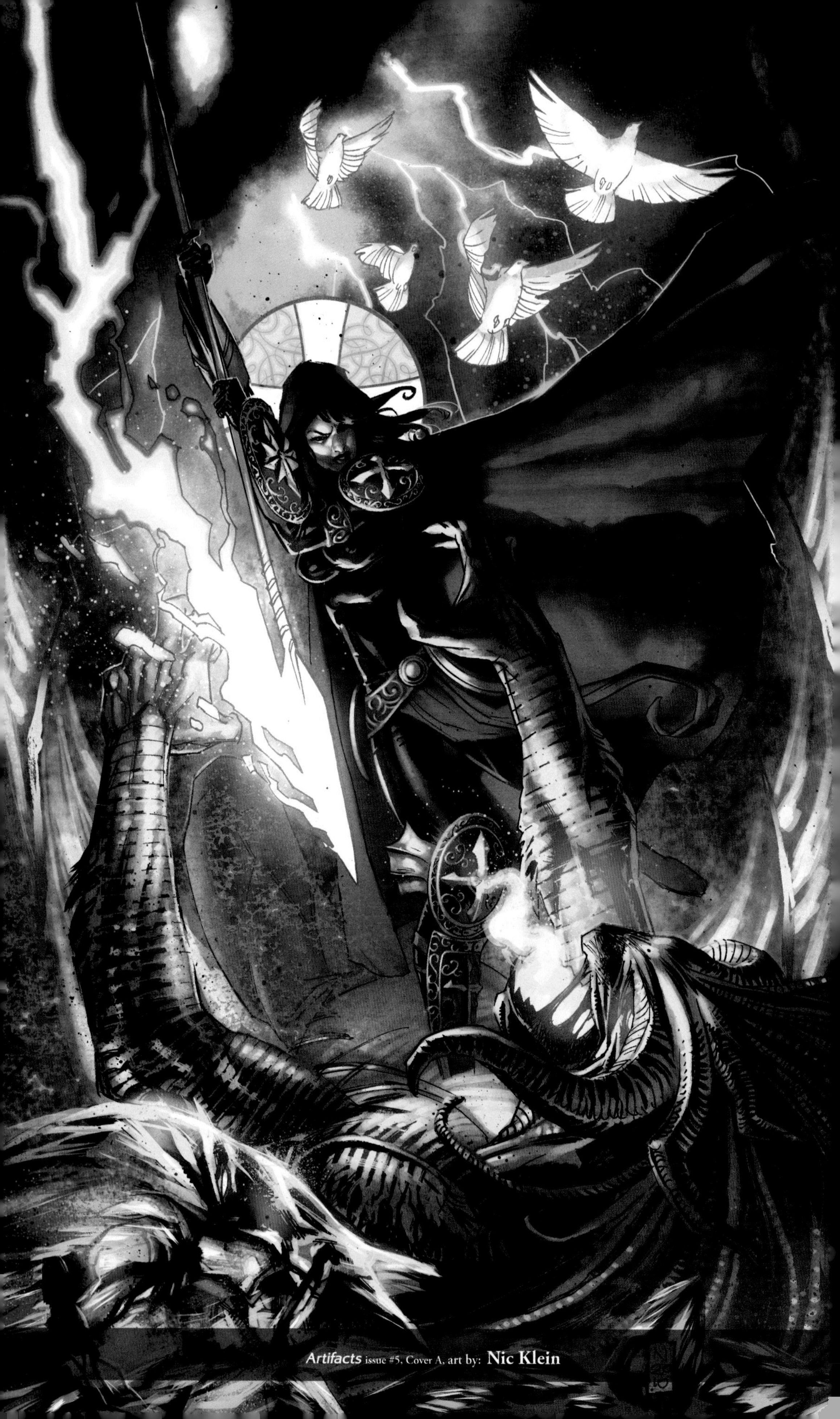

Artifacts issue #5, Cover A, art by: **Nic Klein**

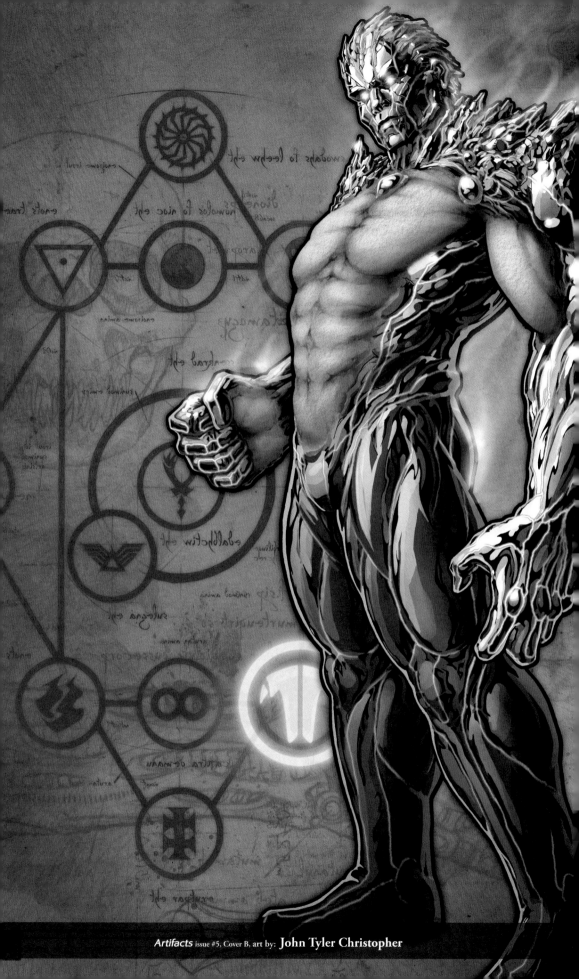

Artifacts issue #5, Cover B, art by: **John Tyler Christopher**

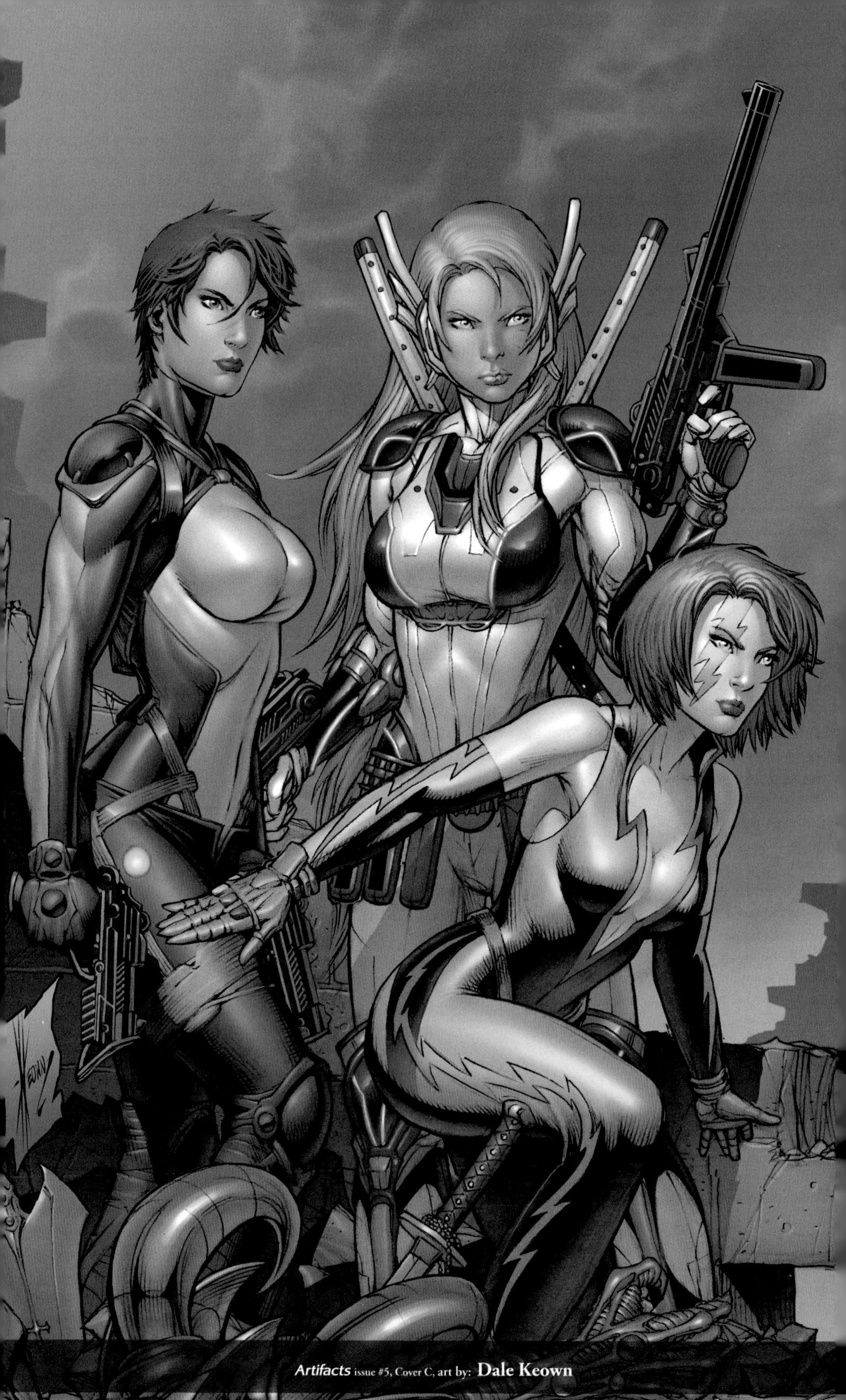

Artifacts issue #5, Cover C, art by: **Dale Keown**

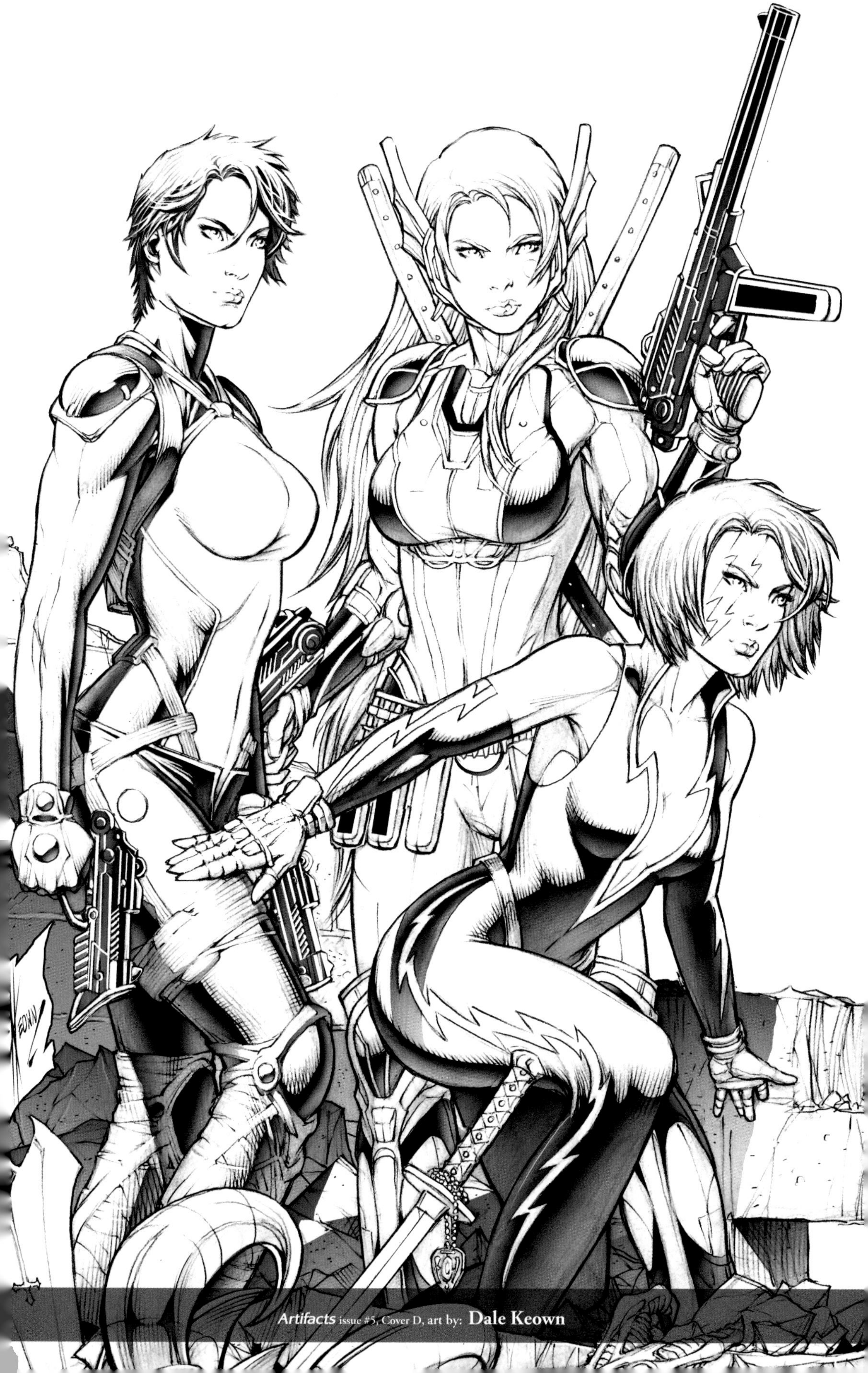

Artifacts issue #5, Cover D, art by: **Dale Keown**

Artifacts issue #5, Cover E, Retailer Incentive Foil Edition

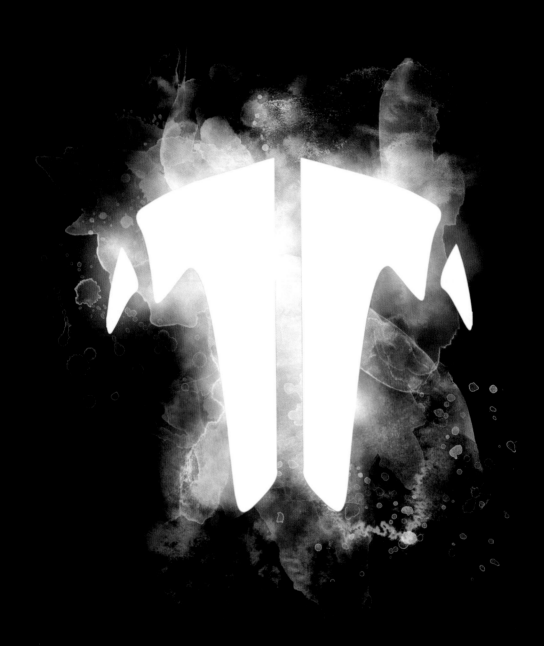

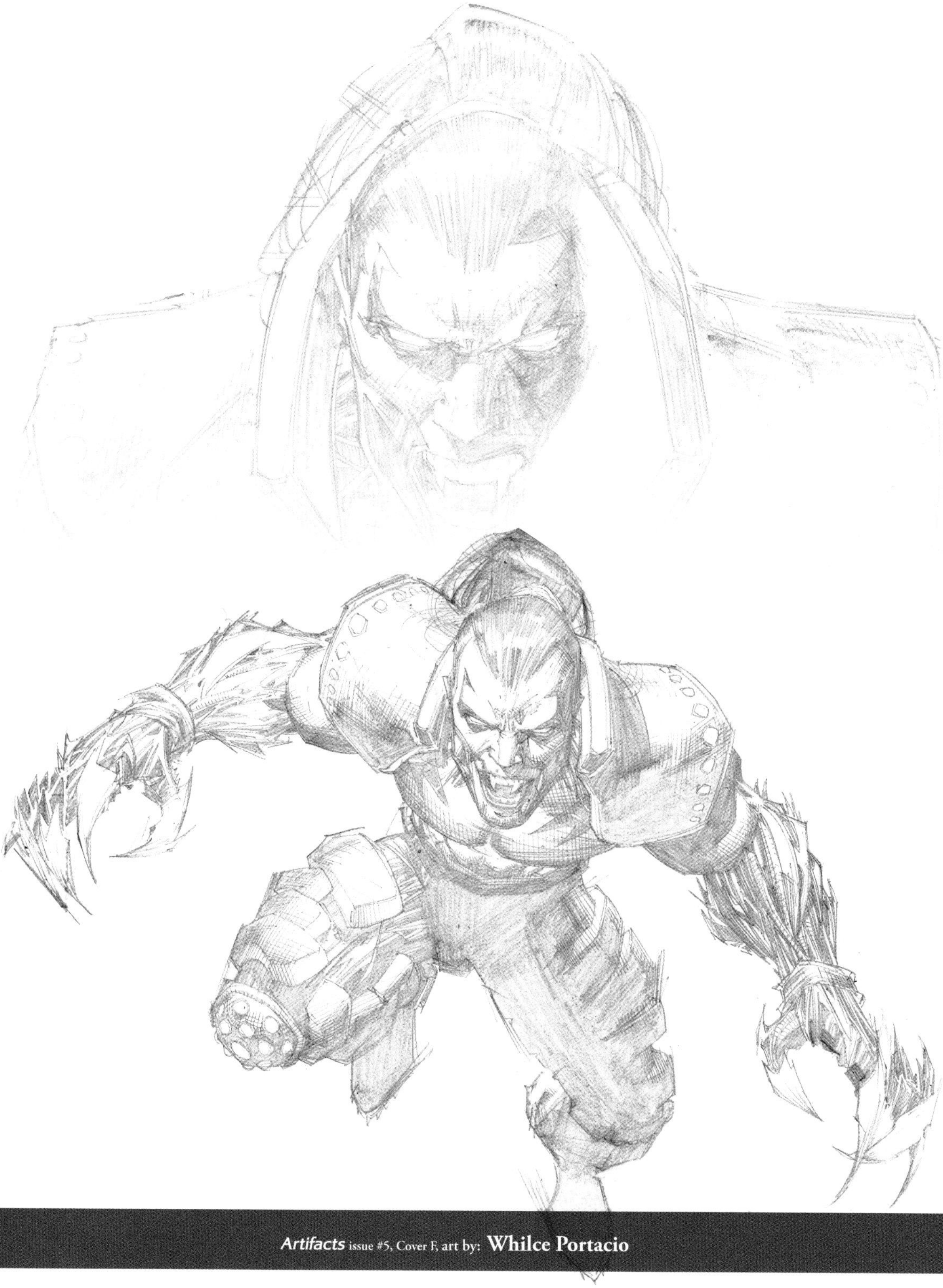

Artifacts issue #5, Cover F, art by: **Whilce Portacio**

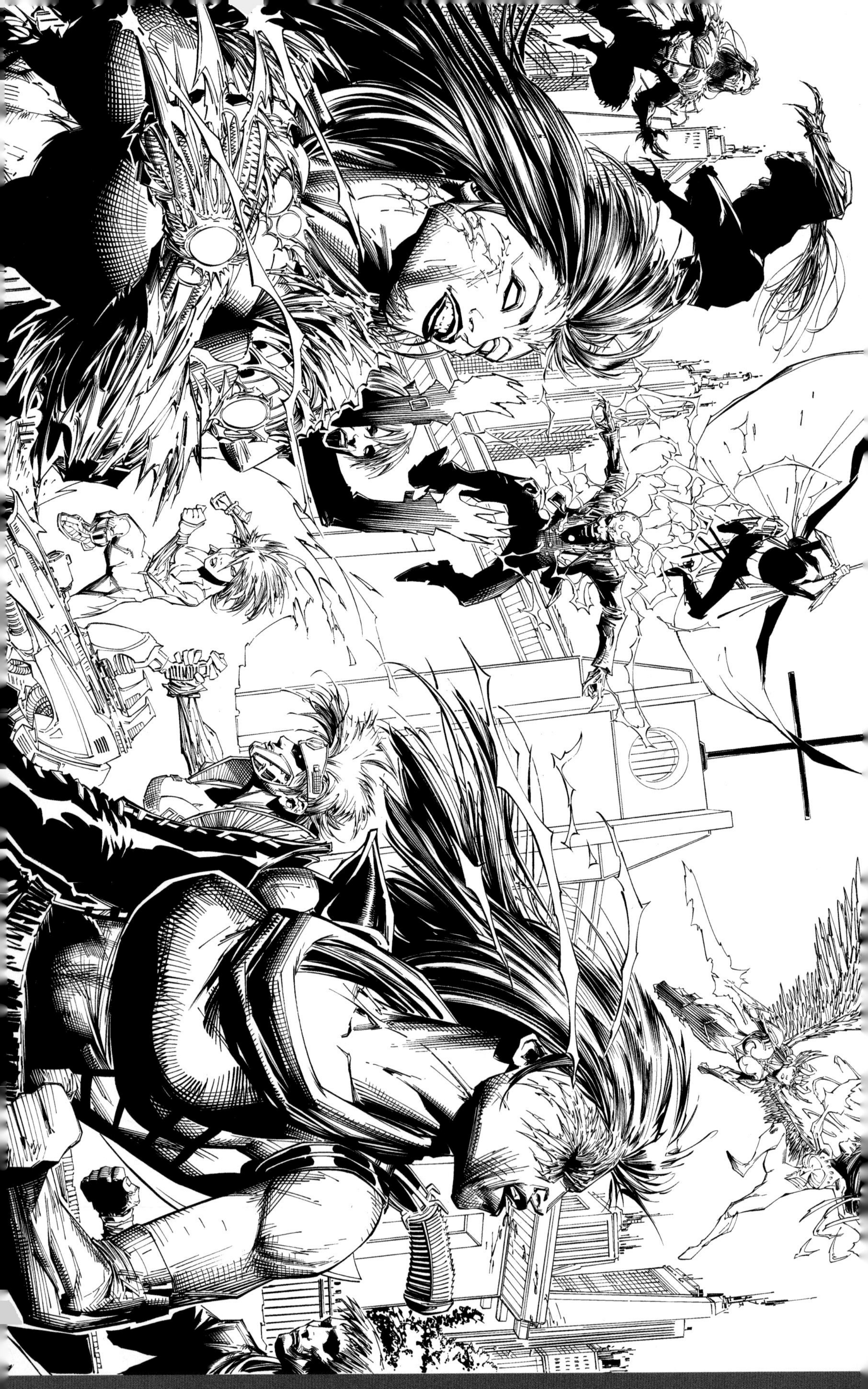

Artifacts issue #5, Cover G, art by: **Whilce Portacio**

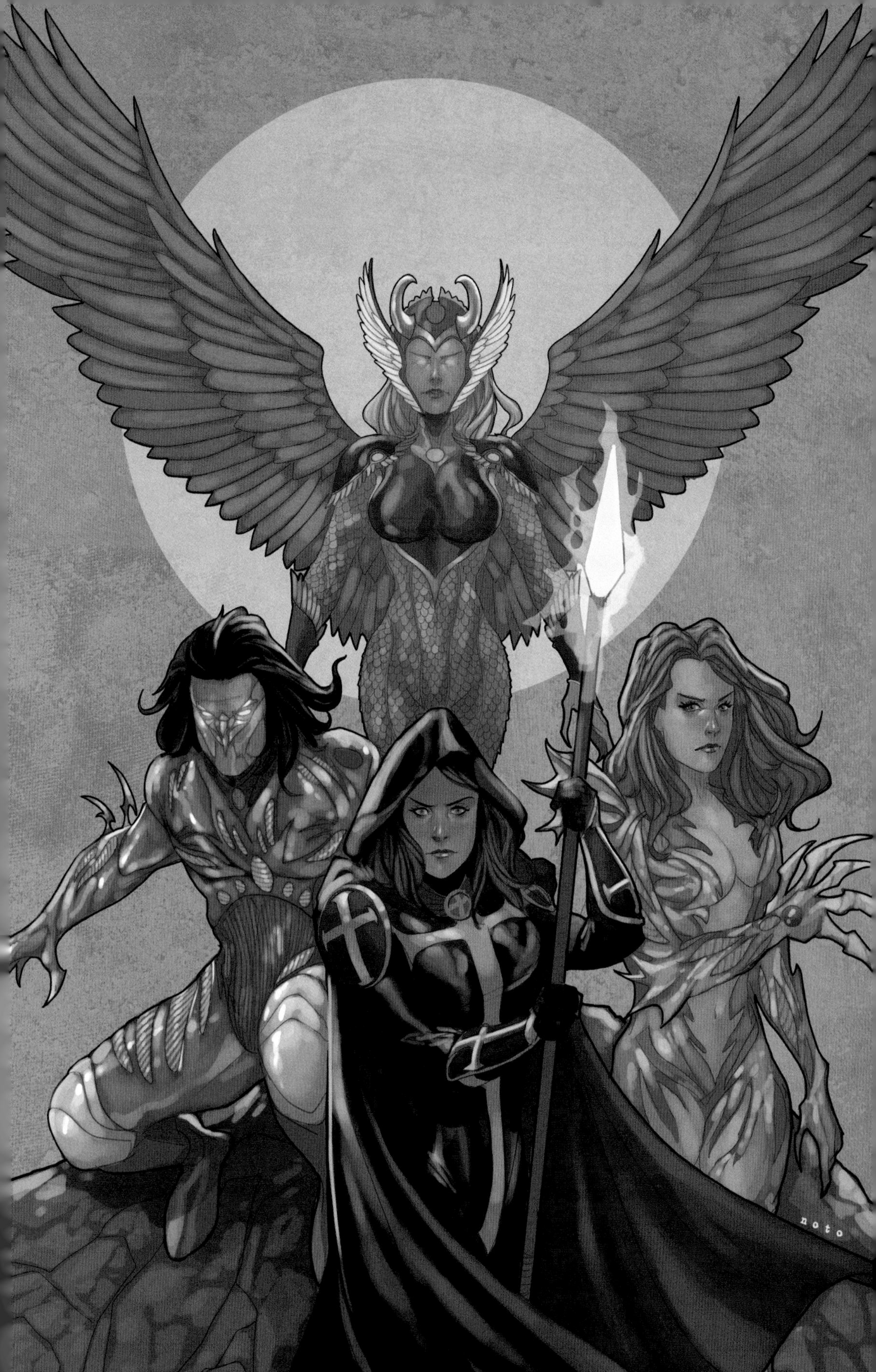
noto

Artifacts issue #6, Cover A, art by: **Phil Noto**

Artifacts issue #6, Cover B, art by: **John Tyler Christopher**

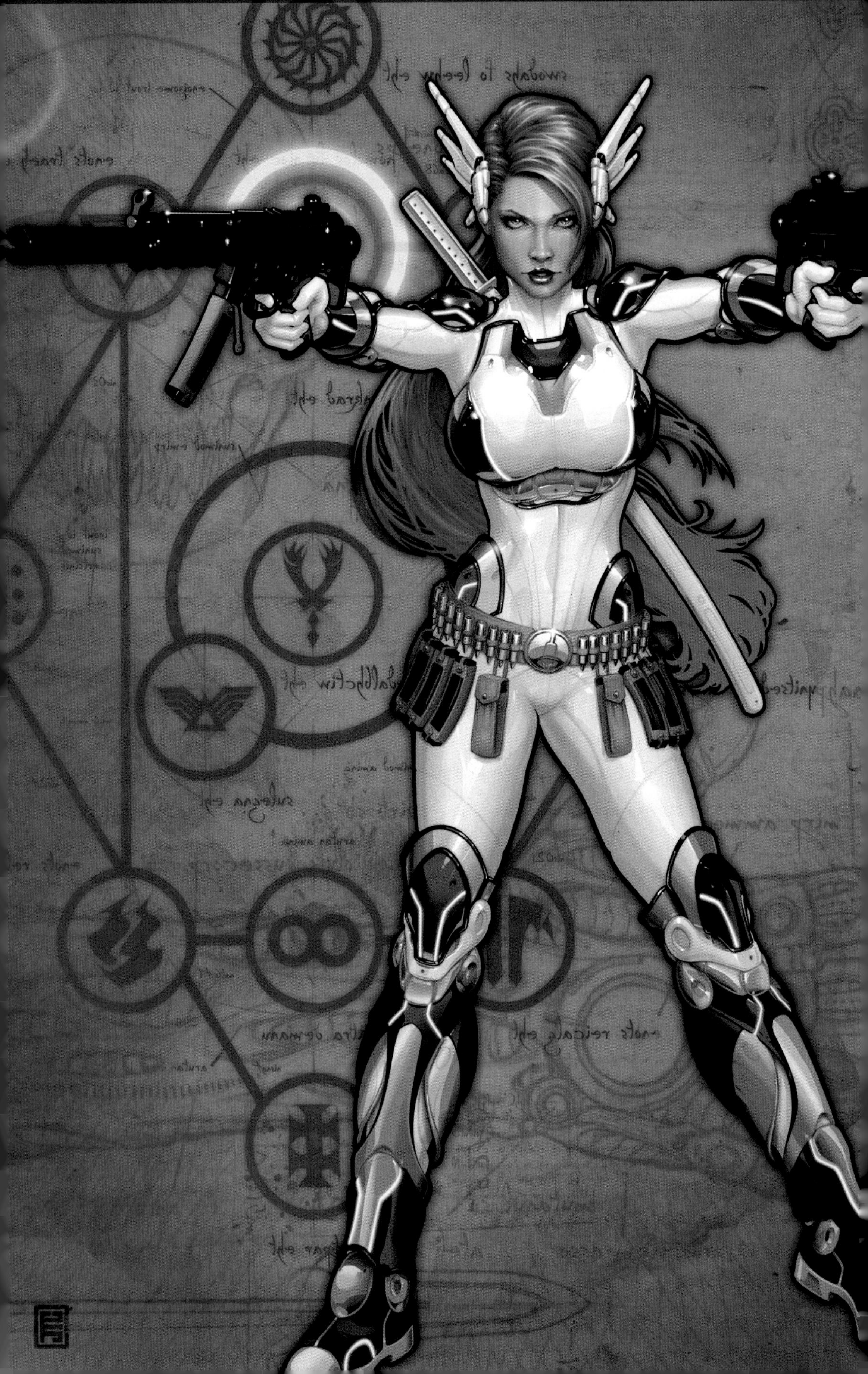

Artifacts issue #6, Cover C, Retailer Incentive cover, art by: **Michael Broussard**

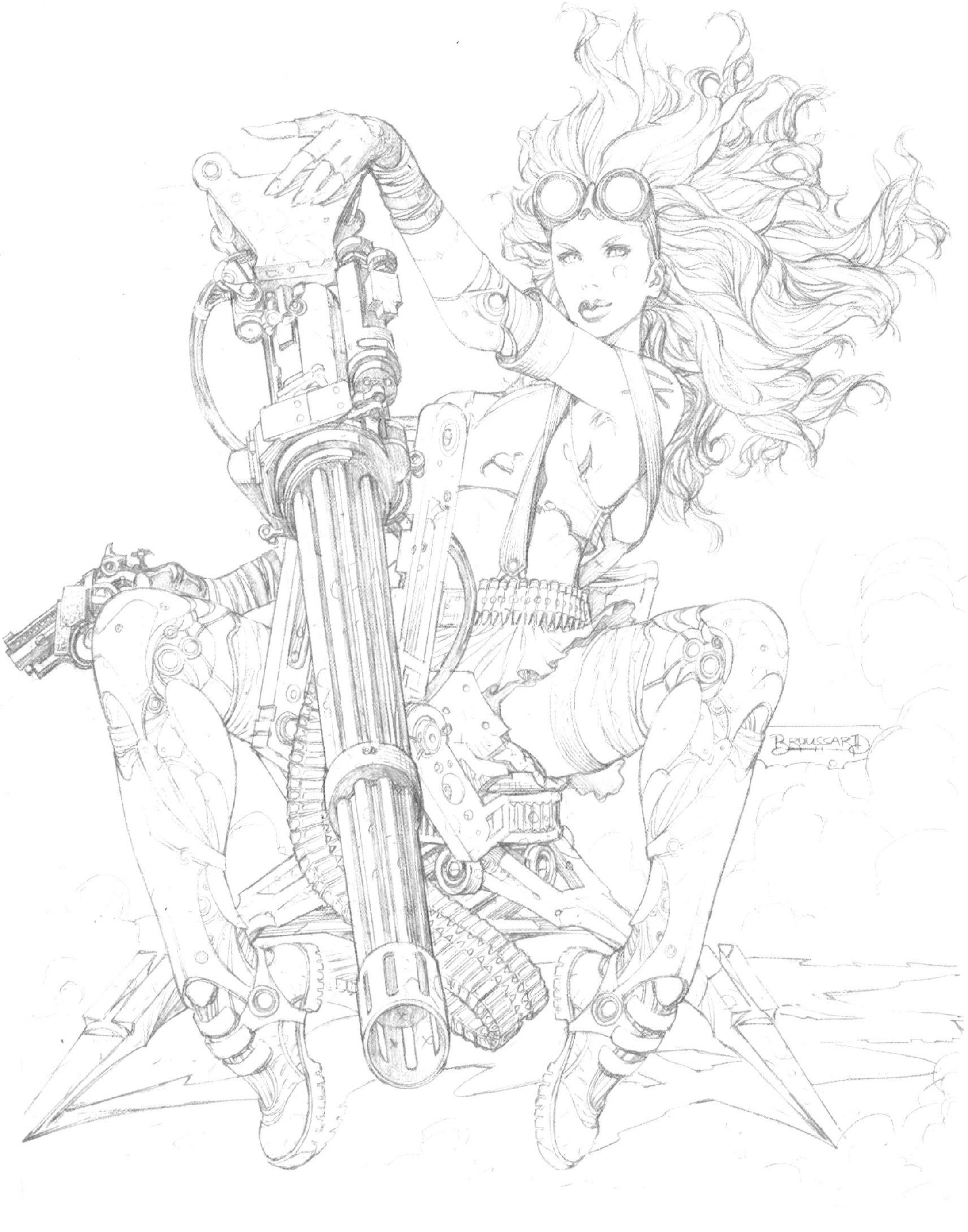
BROUSSARD

Artifacts issue #6, Cover D, Retailer Incentive Foil Edition

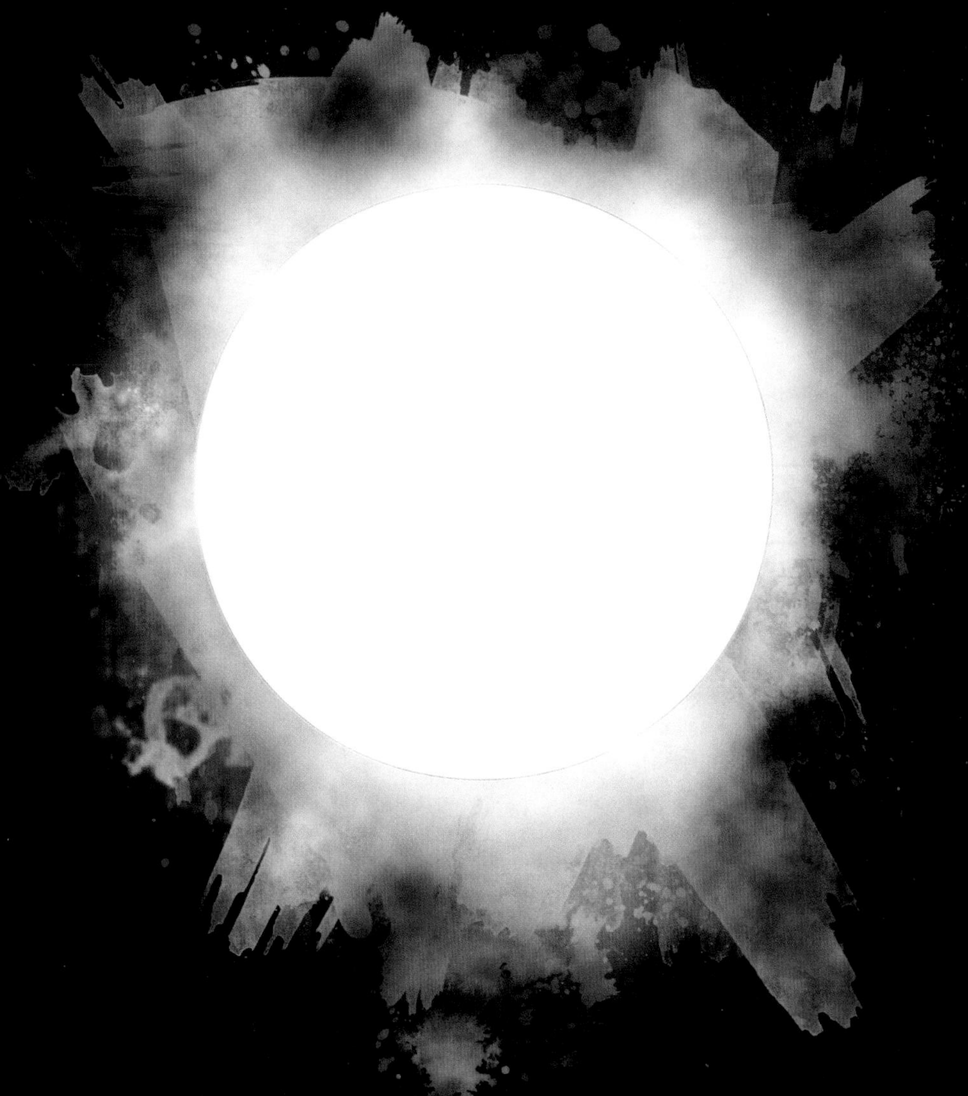

Artifacts issue #6, Cover E, C2E2 Edition, art by: **Michael Broussard & Sunny Gho of IFS**

Artifacts issue #7, Cover A, art by: Whilce Portacio, Joe Weems, & Sunny Gho of IFS

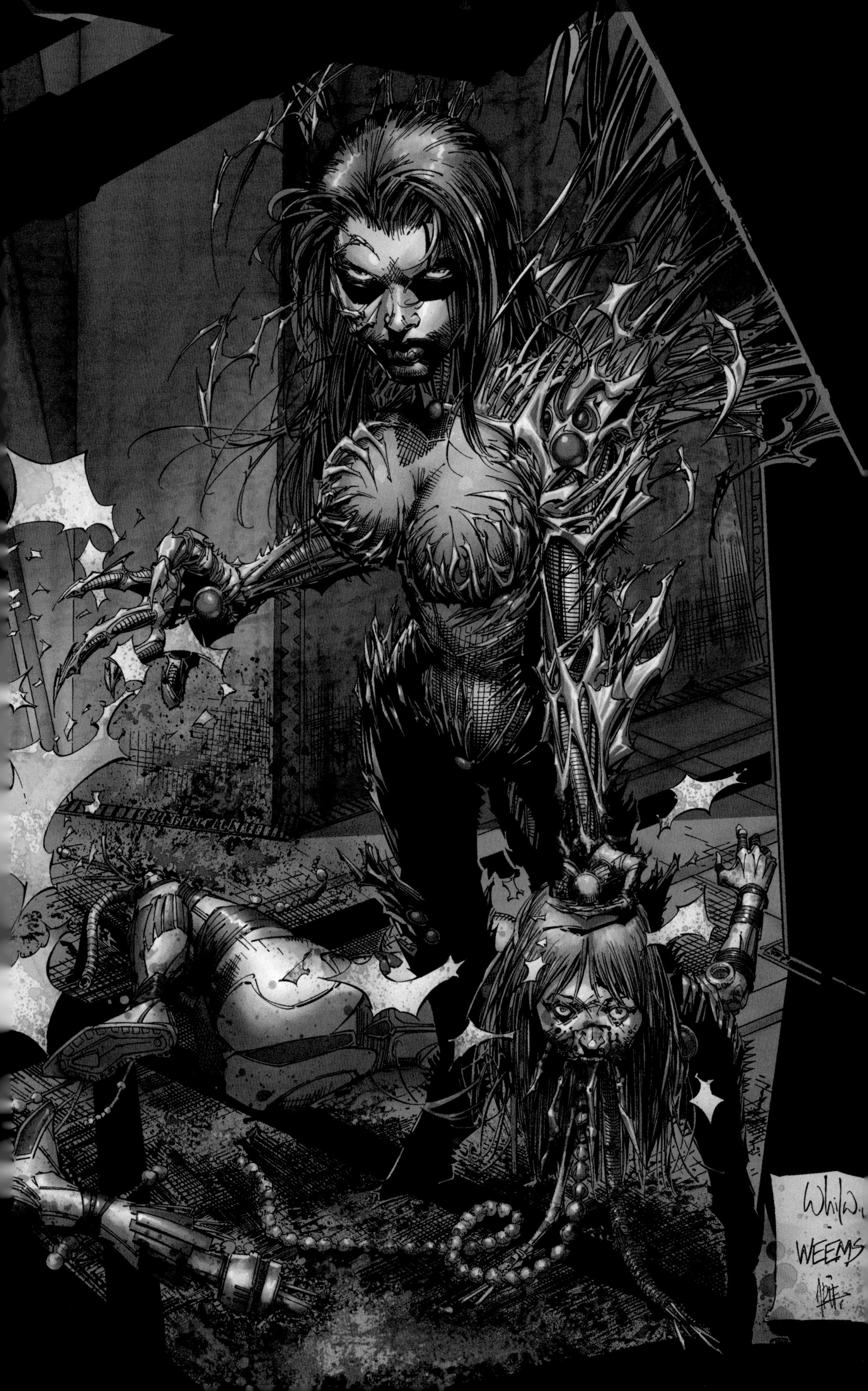
Whilce
WEEMS

Artifacts issue #7, Cover B, art by: **John Tyler Christopher**

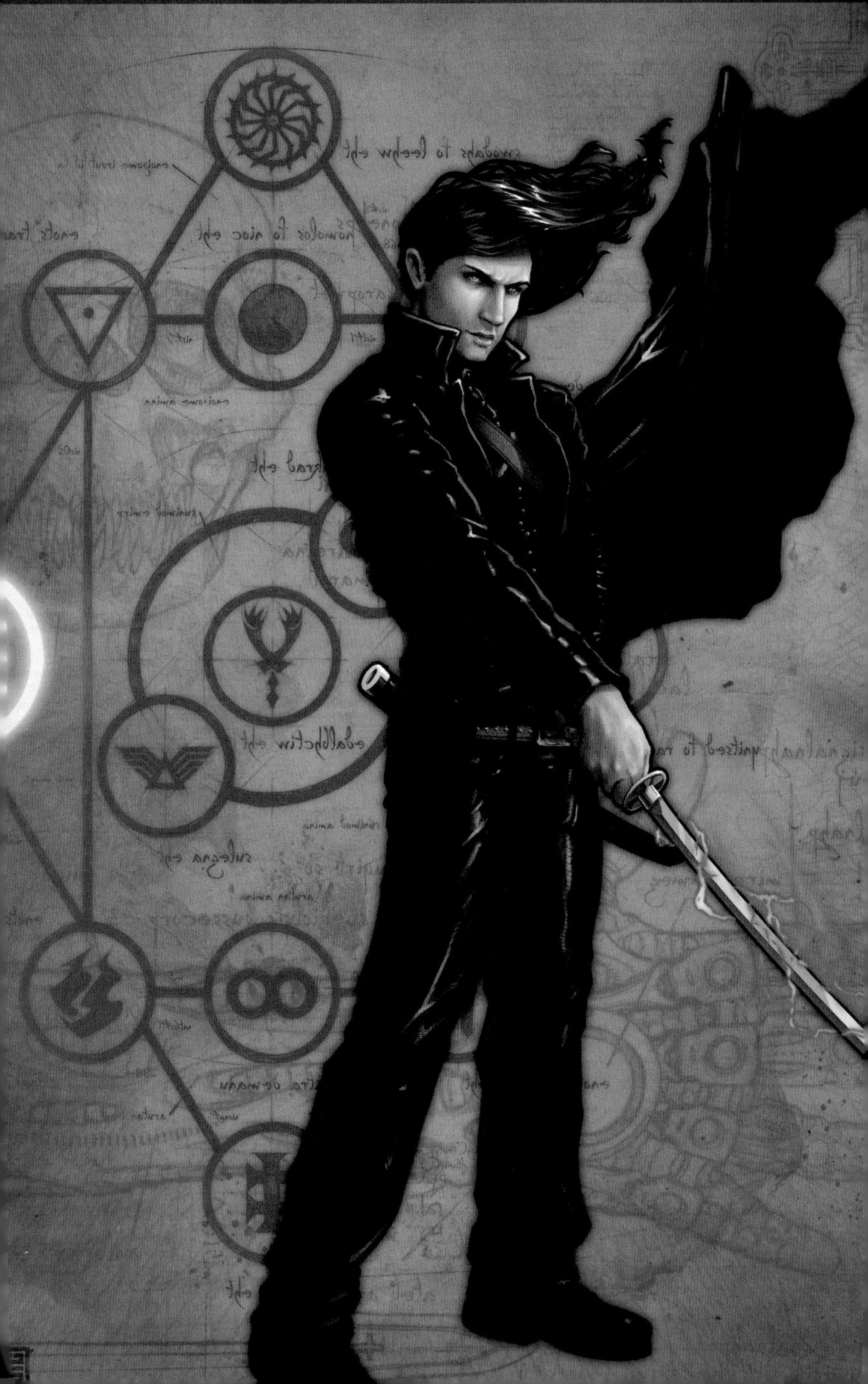

Artifacts issue #7, Cover C, Retailer Incentive, art by: **Whilce Portacio & Joe Weems**

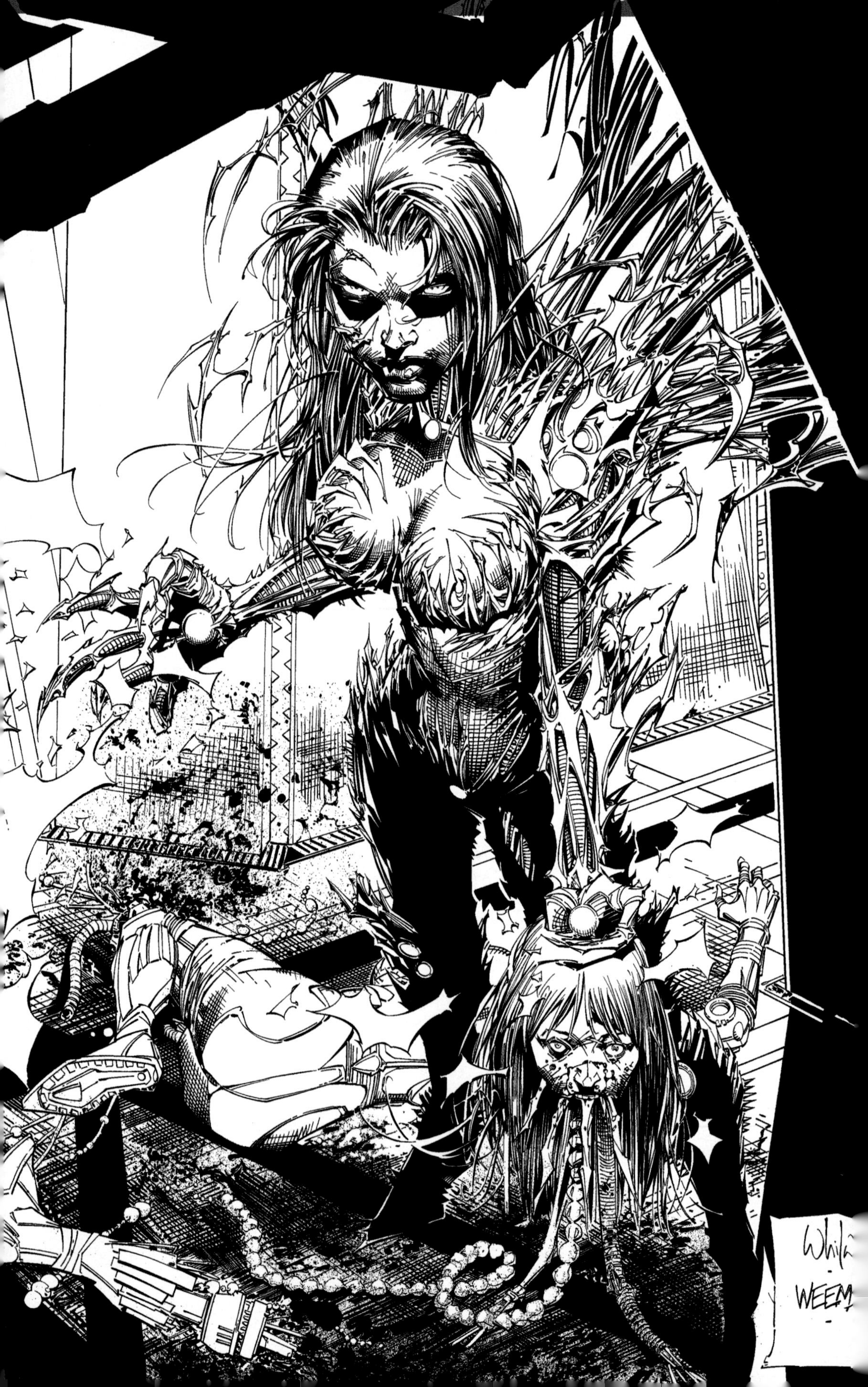

Artifacts issue #7, Cover D, Retailer Incentive Foil Edition

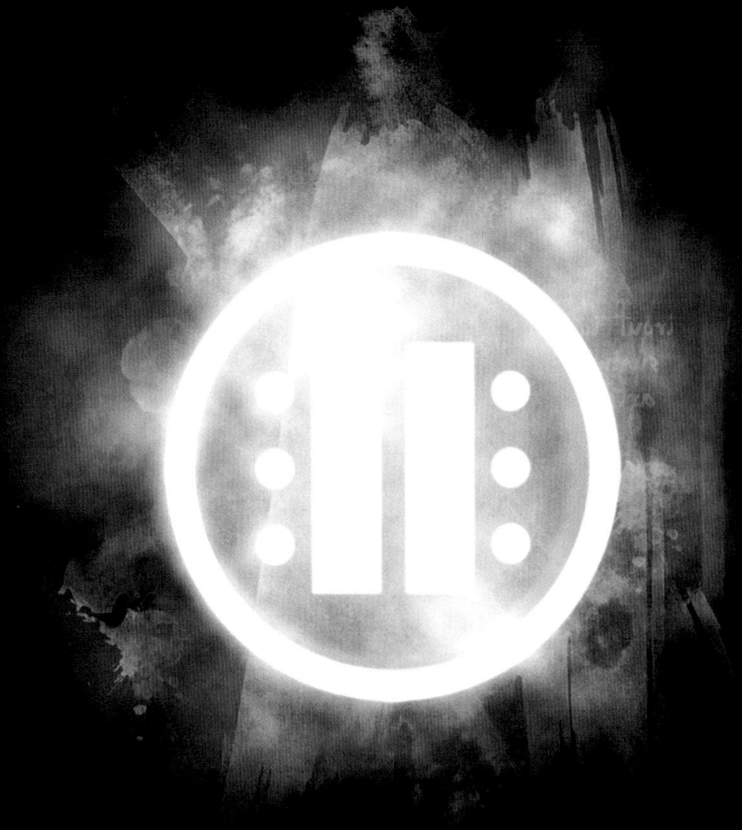

Artifacts issue #7, Cover E, Top Cow Store Edition, art by: **Paolo Pantalena & Jorge Fares**

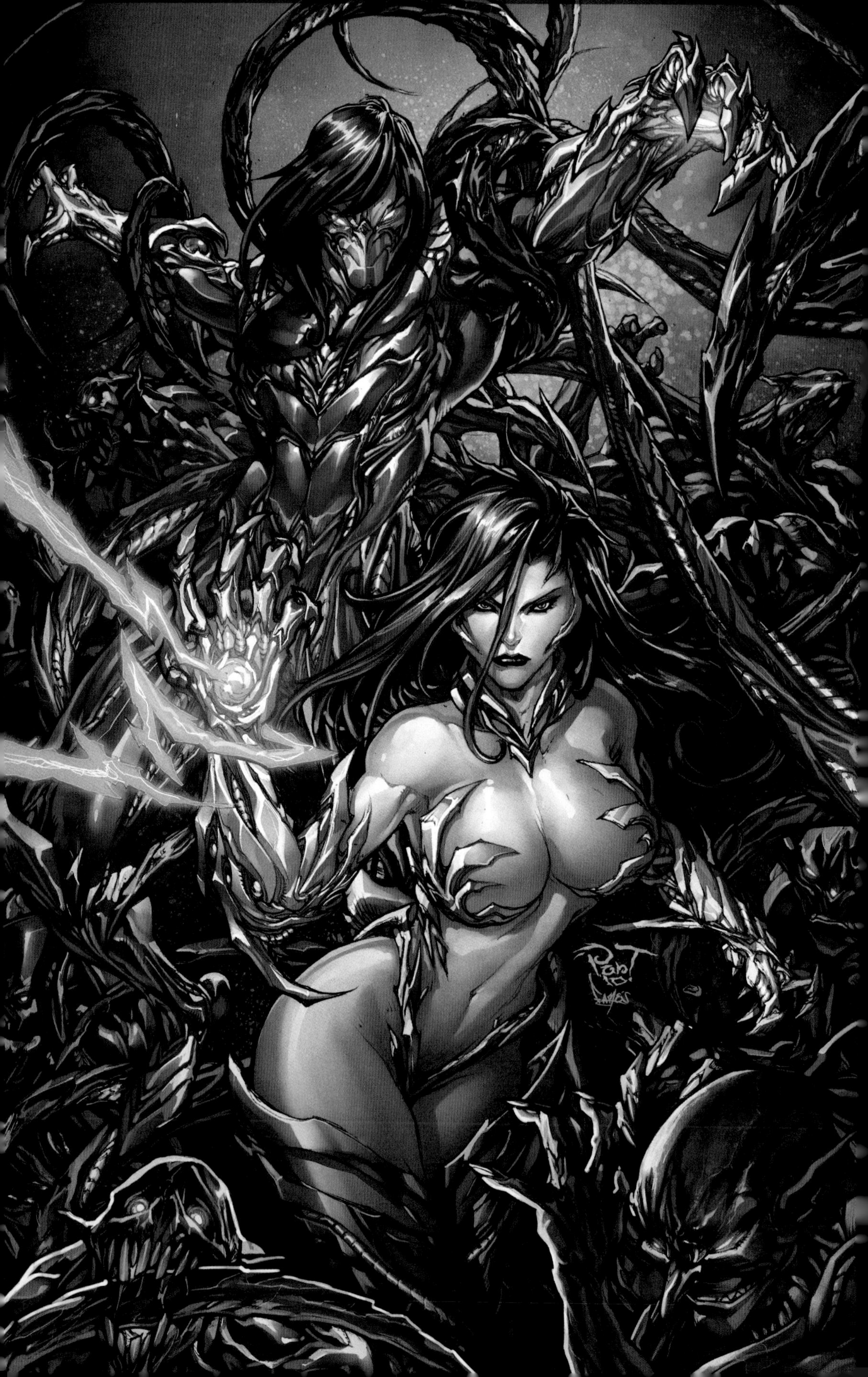

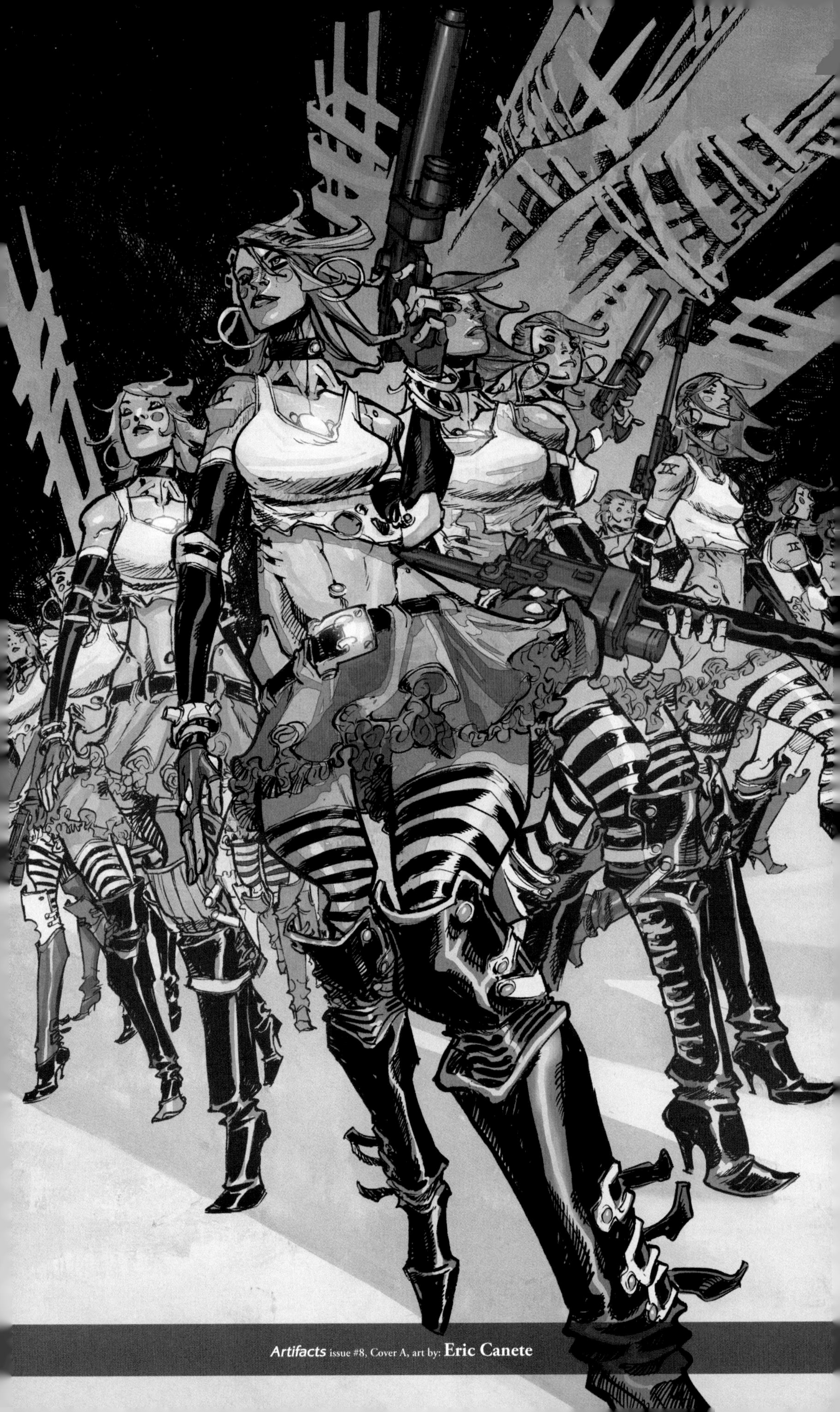

Artifacts issue #8, Cover A, art by: **Eric Canete**

Artifacts issue #8, Cover B, art by: **John Tyler Christopher**

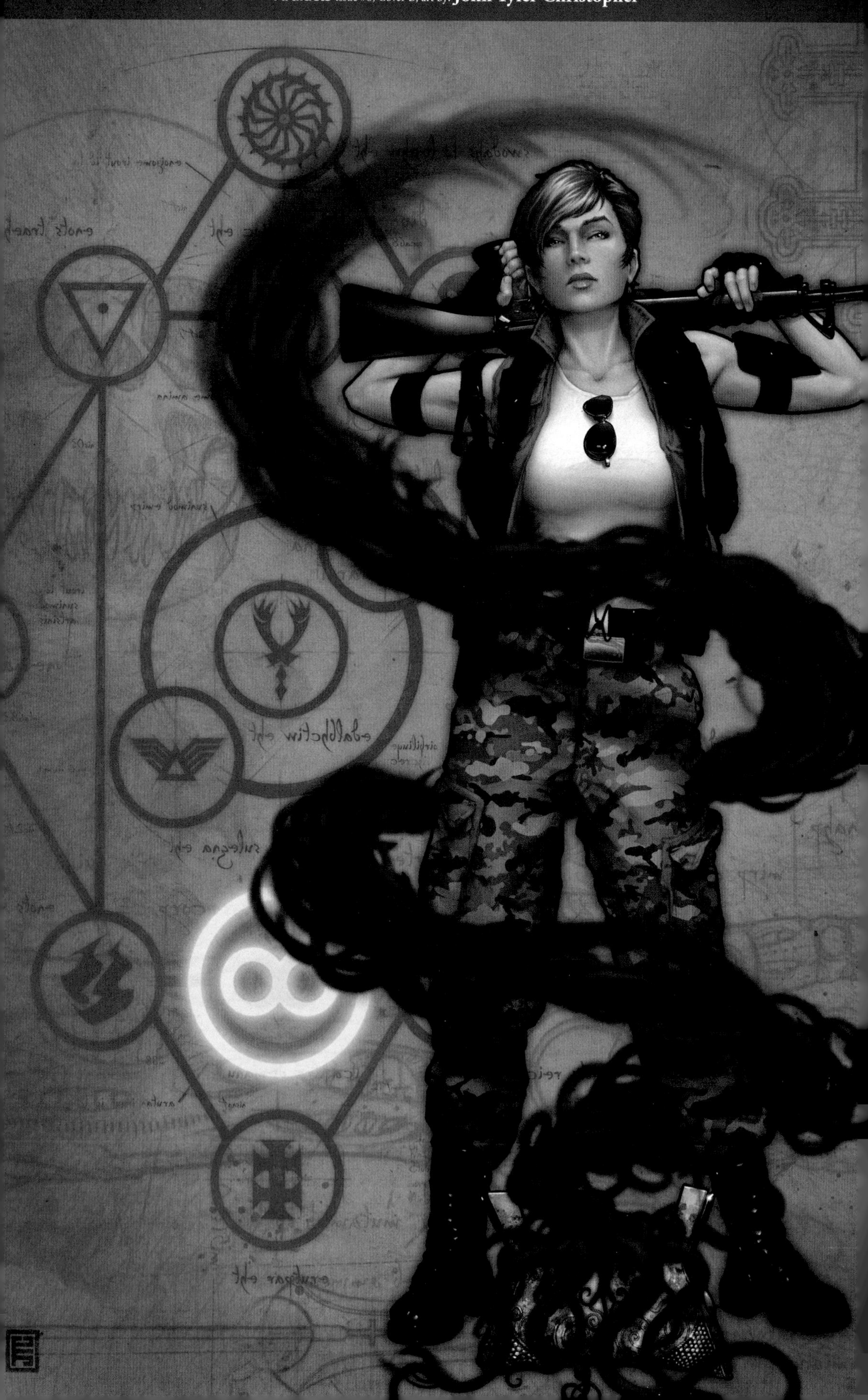

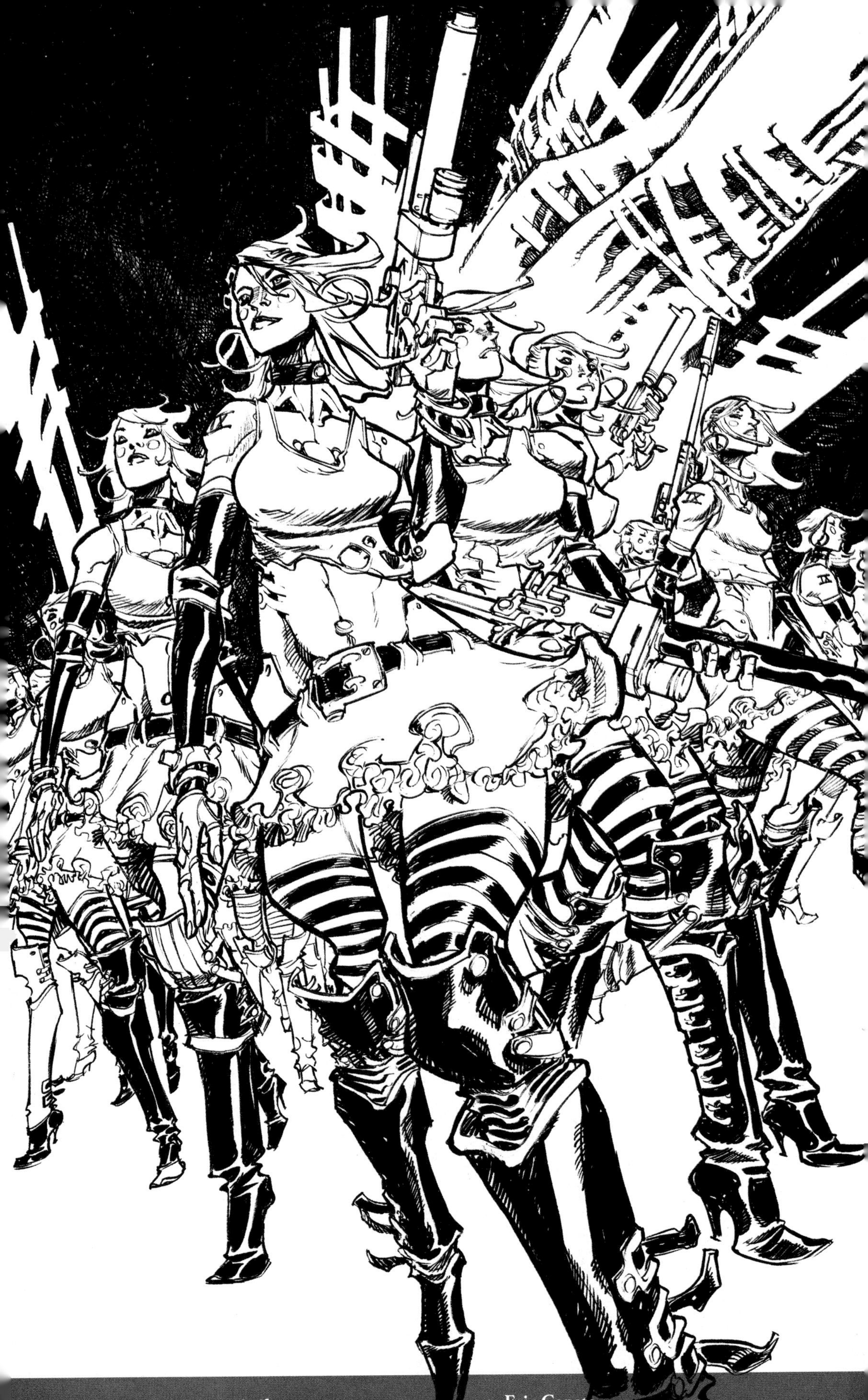

Artifacts issue #8, Cover C, Retailer Incentive, art by: **Eric Canete**

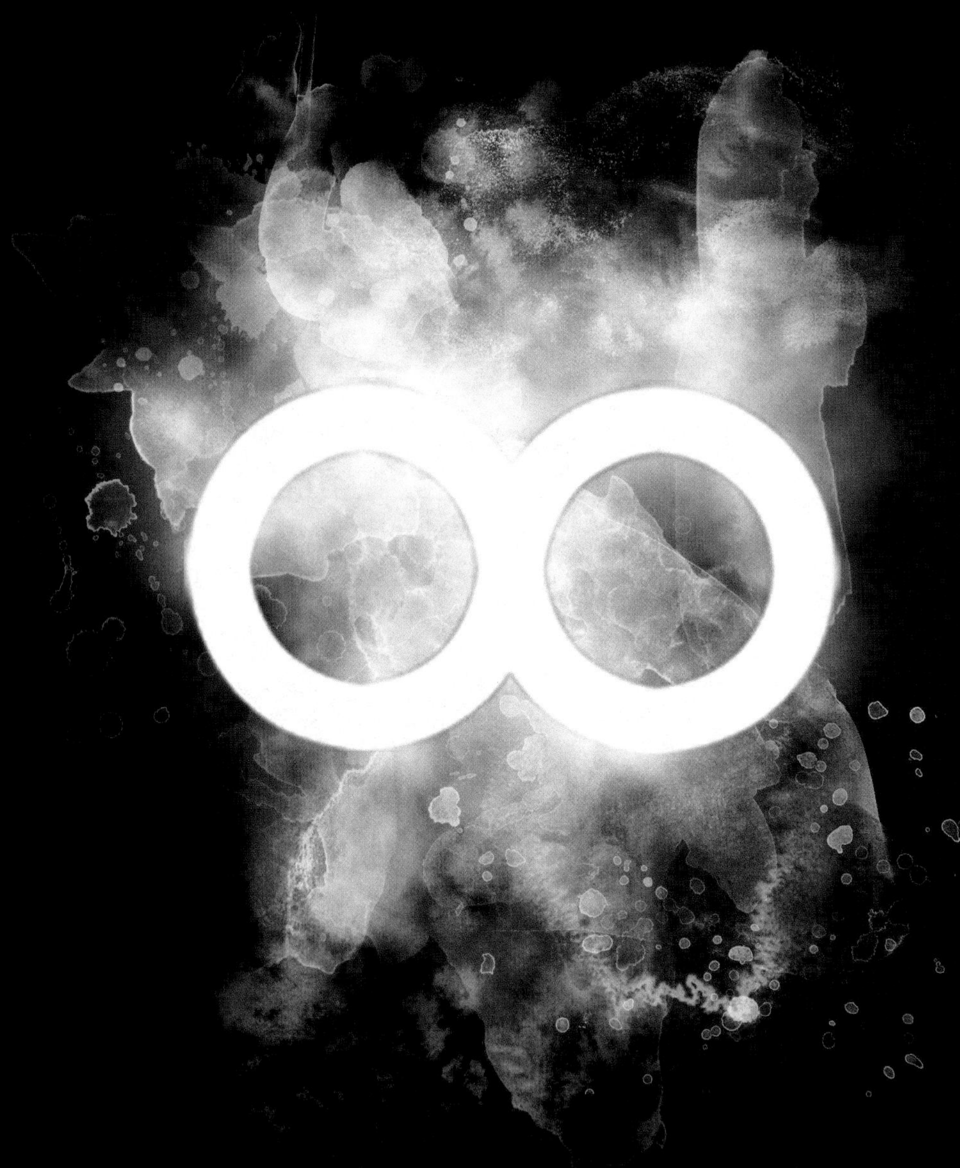

Artifacts issue #8, Cover D, Retail Incentive Foil Edition

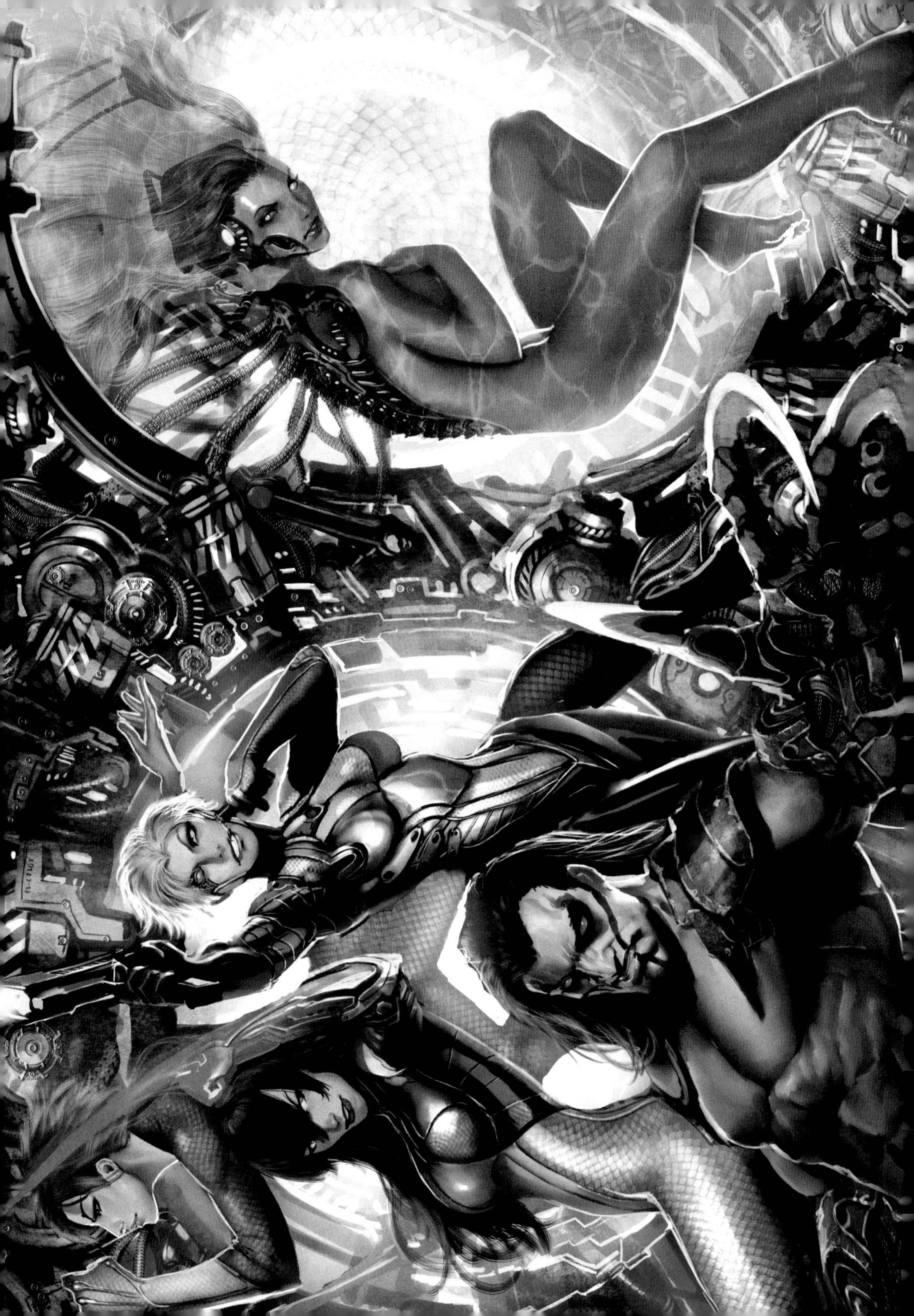

SPECIAL BONUS

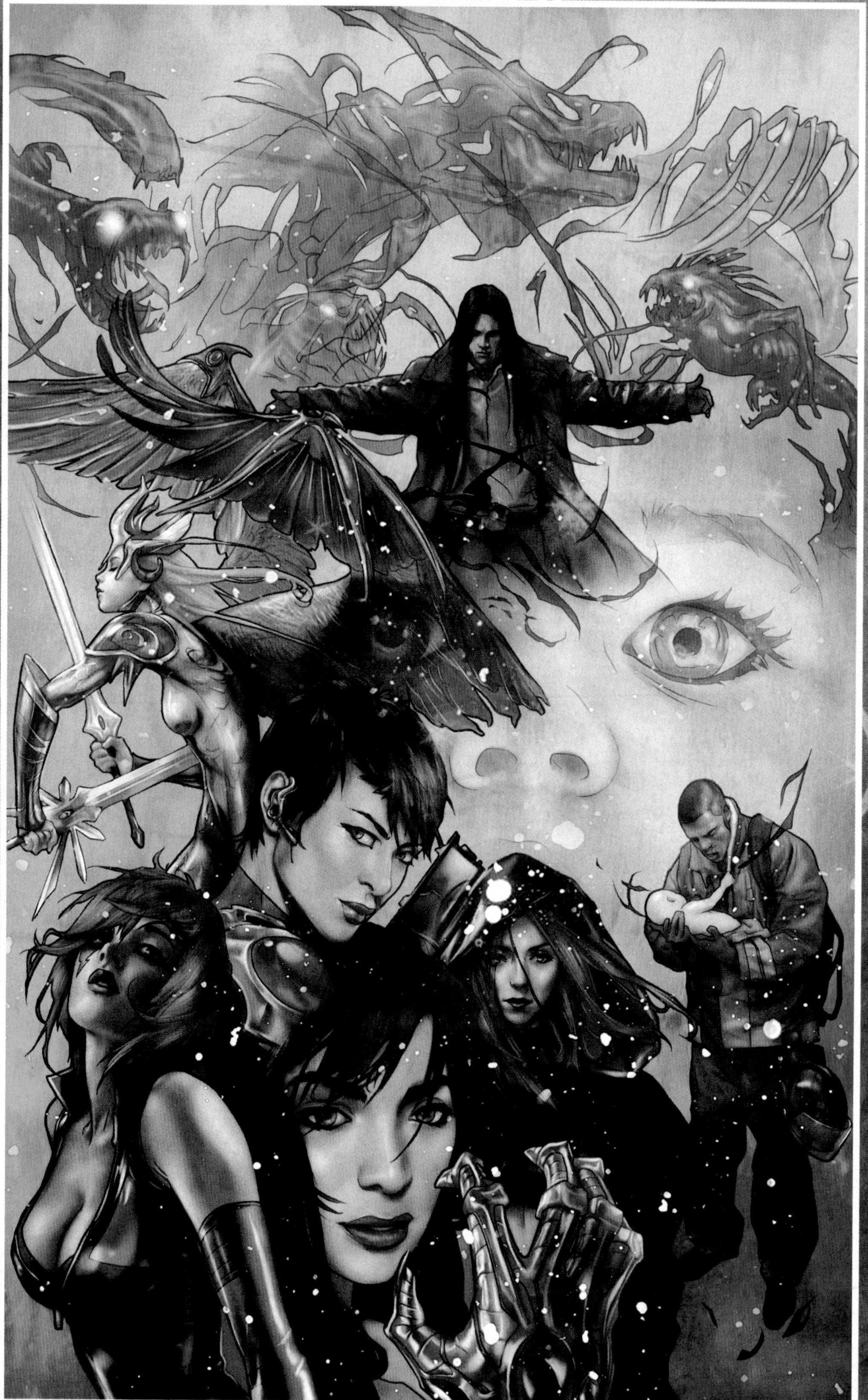

TOP COW HOLIDAY SPECIAL

WRITTEN BY: PHIL SMITH
ART BY: ALINA URUSOV
COLORS BY: SCOTT FORBES & ALINA URUSOV
LETTERS BY: TROY PETERI
ORIGINAL EDITION EDITED BY: FILIP SABLIK & PHIL SMITH

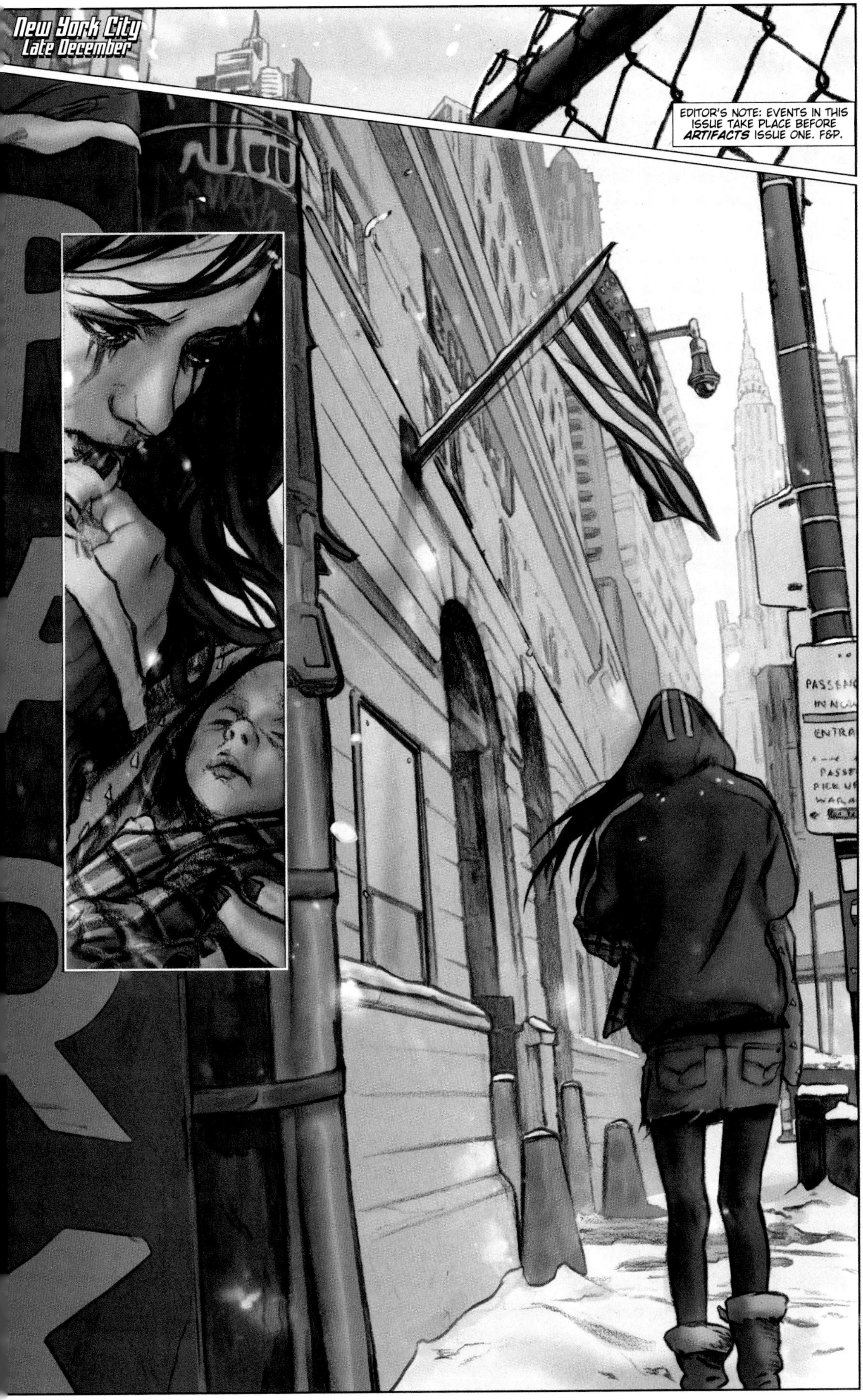
New York City
Late December
EDITOR'S NOTE: EVENTS IN THIS ISSUE TAKE PLACE BEFORE *ARTIFACTS* ISSUE ONE. F&P.

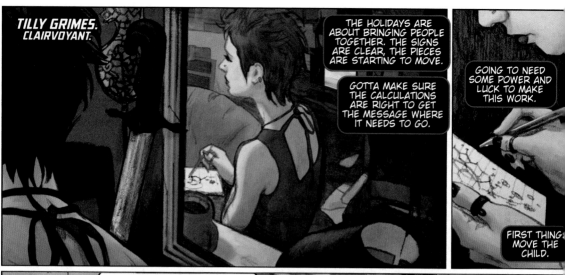

TILLY GRIMES.
CLAIRVOYANT.

THE HOLIDAYS ARE ABOUT BRINGING PEOPLE TOGETHER. THE SIGNS ARE CLEAR, THE PIECES ARE STARTING TO MOVE.

GOTTA MAKE SURE THE CALCULATIONS ARE RIGHT TO GET THE MESSAGE WHERE IT NEEDS TO GO.

GOING TO NEED SOME POWER AND LUCK TO MAKE THIS WORK.

FIRST THING: MOVE THE CHILD.

SO AFTER TWENTY MINUTES OF WORKING IT ALL SHE HAS TO SAY IS THE CEILING NEEDS TO BE REPAINTED.

THAT'S JUST SAD, JIMMY.

ALRIGHT, GUYS, WE JUST GOT A HEADS UP THAT FROM BRIGHTON TO MIDTOWN THE CITY'S BEEN HAVING WHAT THEY ARE DESCRIBING AS EARTHQUAKES...

...WE'VE BEEN PUT ON AN ALERT. GET YOUR GEAR READY, LOOKS LIKE WE MIGHT HAVE SOME WORK TODAY.

EXCUSE ME.

AM NEEDING HELP. WAS TOLD THIS WAS "SAFE HEAVEN?"

HELLO, MA'AM. YOU MEAN "SAFE HAVEN."

WELL... SURE, THIS IS, UH...

...ONE OF THOSE... SURE.

PLEASE HELP.

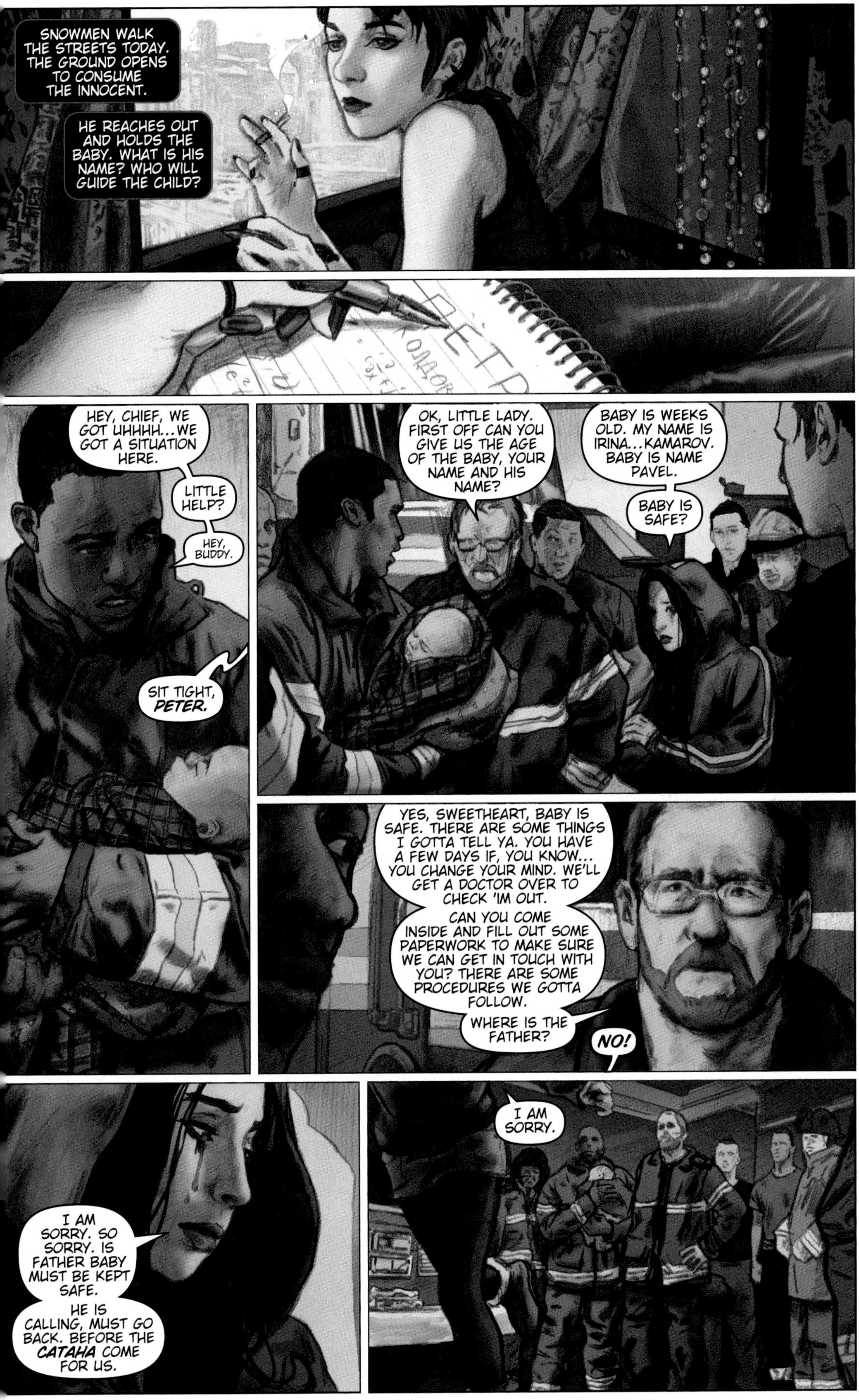
SNOWMEN WALK THE STREETS TODAY. THE GROUND OPENS TO CONSUME THE INNOCENT.
HE REACHES OUT AND HOLDS THE BABY. WHAT IS HIS NAME? WHO WILL GUIDE THE CHILD?
HEY, CHIEF, WE GOT UHHHH...WE GOT A SITUATION HERE.
LITTLE HELP?
HEY, BUDDY.
SIT TIGHT, PETER.
OK, LITTLE LADY. FIRST OFF CAN YOU GIVE US THE AGE OF THE BABY, YOUR NAME AND HIS NAME?
BABY IS WEEKS OLD. MY NAME IS IRINA...KAMAROV. BABY IS NAME PAVEL.
BABY IS SAFE?
YES, SWEETHEART, BABY IS SAFE. THERE ARE SOME THINGS I GOTTA TELL YA. YOU HAVE A FEW DAYS IF, YOU KNOW... YOU CHANGE YOUR MIND. WE'LL GET A DOCTOR OVER TO CHECK 'IM OUT.
CAN YOU COME INSIDE AND FILL OUT SOME PAPERWORK TO MAKE SURE WE CAN GET IN TOUCH WITH YOU? THERE ARE SOME PROCEDURES WE GOTTA FOLLOW.
WHERE IS THE FATHER?
NO!
I AM SORRY. SO SORRY. IS FATHER BABY MUST BE KEPT SAFE.
HE IS CALLING, MUST GO BACK. BEFORE THE CATAHA COME FOR US.
I AM SORRY.

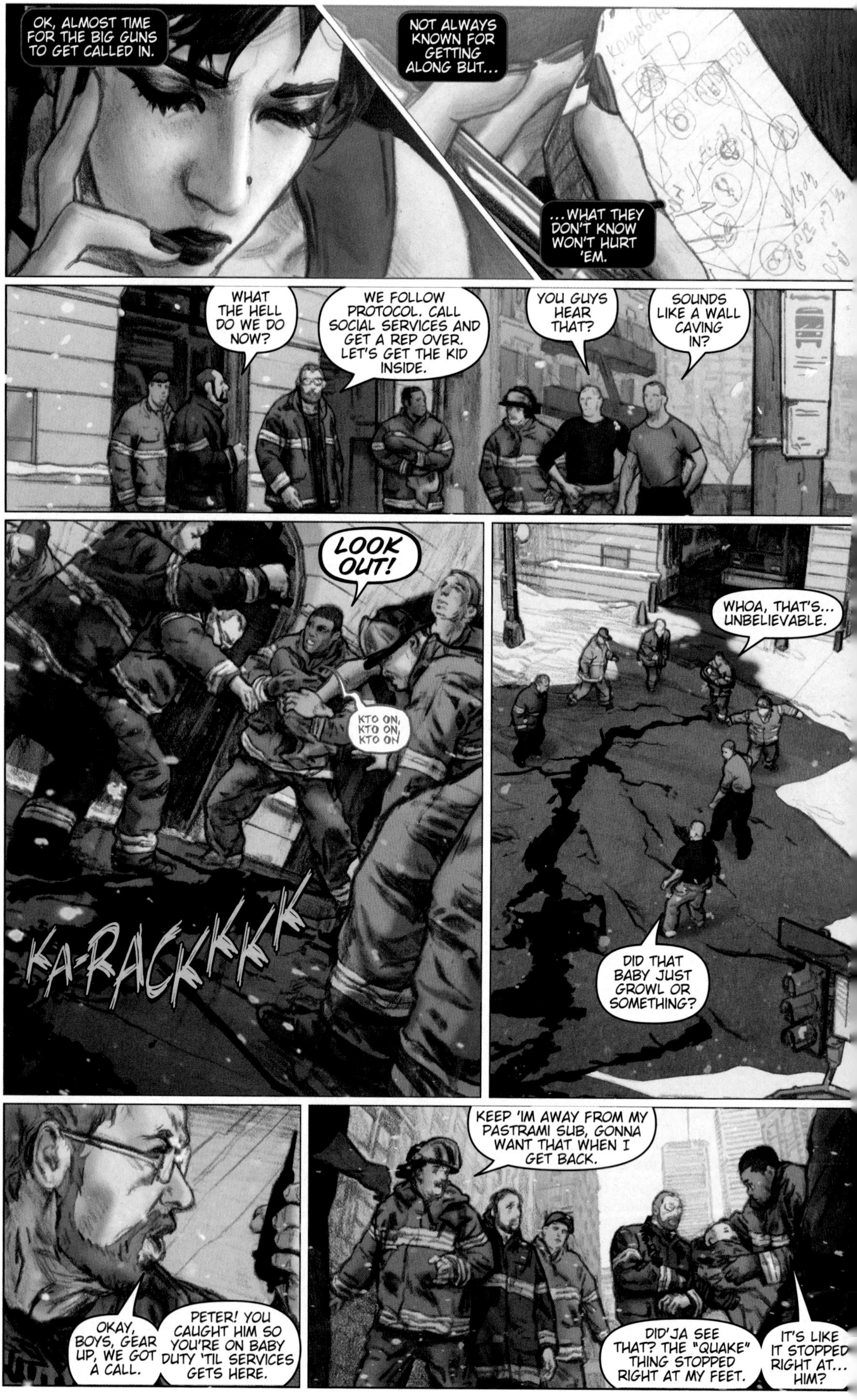
OK, ALMOST TIME FOR THE BIG GUNS TO GET CALLED IN.
NOT ALWAYS KNOWN FOR GETTING ALONG BUT...
...WHAT THEY DON'T KNOW WON'T HURT 'EM.
WHAT THE HELL DO WE DO NOW?
WE FOLLOW PROTOCOL. CALL SOCIAL SERVICES AND GET A REP OVER. LET'S GET THE KID INSIDE.
YOU GUYS HEAR THAT?
SOUNDS LIKE A WALL CAVING IN?
LOOK OUT!
KTO ON, KTO ON, KTO ON
KA-RACKKKK
WHOA, THAT'S... UNBELIEVABLE.
DID THAT BABY JUST GROWL OR SOMETHING?
OKAY, BOYS, GEAR UP, WE GOT A CALL.
PETER! YOU CAUGHT HIM SO YOU'RE ON BABY DUTY 'TIL SERVICES GETS HERE.
KEEP 'IM AWAY FROM MY PASTRAMI SUB, GONNA WANT THAT WHEN I GET BACK.
DID'JA SEE THAT? THE "QUAKE" THING STOPPED RIGHT AT MY FEET.
IT'S LIKE IT STOPPED RIGHT AT... HIM?

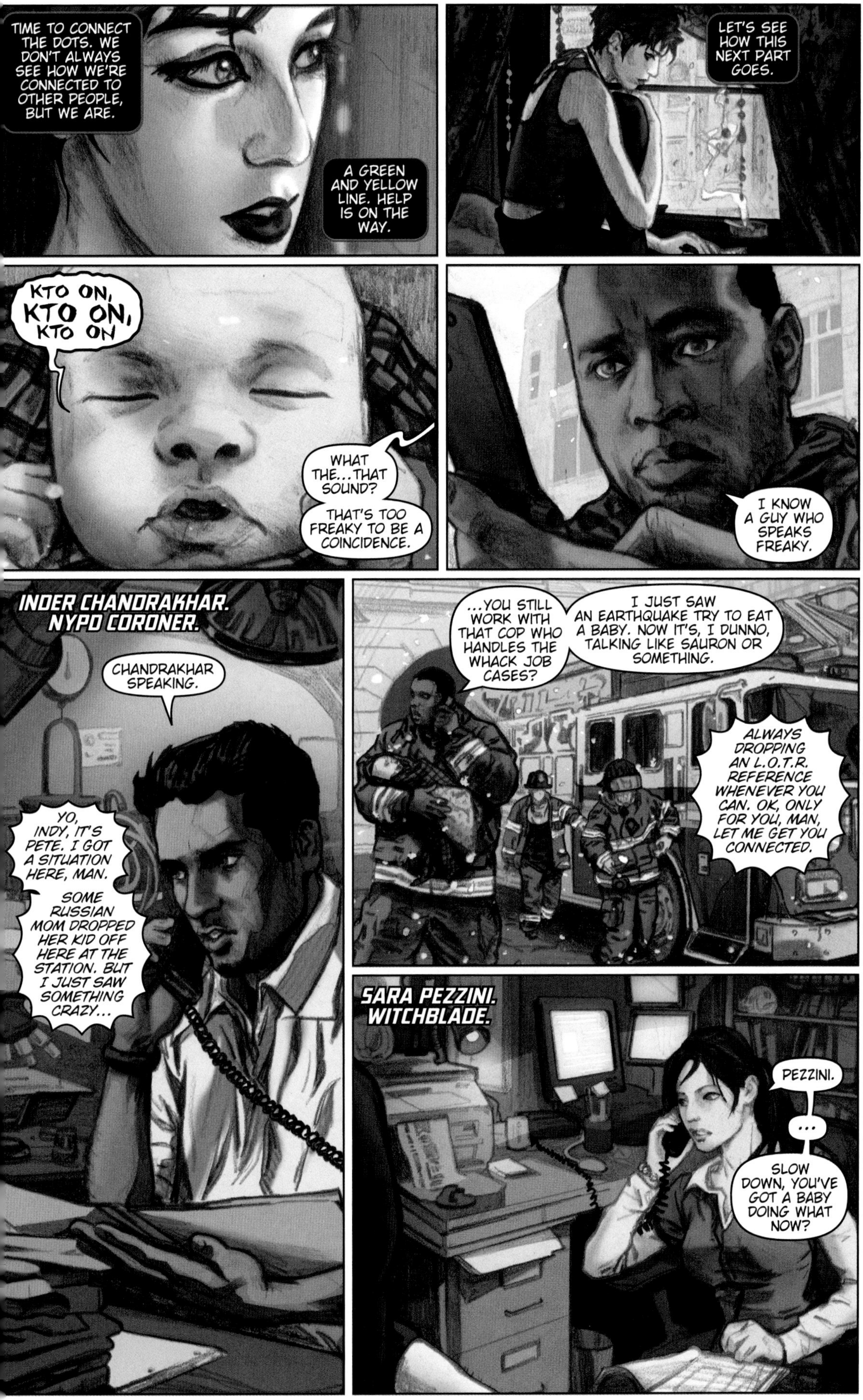
TIME TO CONNECT THE DOTS. WE DON'T ALWAYS SEE HOW WE'RE CONNECTED TO OTHER PEOPLE, BUT WE ARE.
A GREEN AND YELLOW LINE. HELP IS ON THE WAY.
LET'S SEE HOW THIS NEXT PART GOES.
KTO ON, KTO ON, KTO ON
WHAT THE...THAT SOUND?
THAT'S TOO FREAKY TO BE A COINCIDENCE.
I KNOW A GUY WHO SPEAKS FREAKY.
INDER CHANDRAKHAR. NYPD CORONER.
CHANDRAKHAR SPEAKING.
YO, INDY, IT'S PETE. I GOT A SITUATION HERE, MAN.
SOME RUSSIAN MOM DROPPED HER KID OFF HERE AT THE STATION. BUT I JUST SAW SOMETHING CRAZY...
...YOU STILL WORK WITH THAT COP WHO HANDLES THE WHACK JOB CASES?
I JUST SAW AN EARTHQUAKE TRY TO EAT A BABY. NOW IT'S, I DUNNO, TALKING LIKE SAURON OR SOMETHING.
ALWAYS DROPPING AN L.O.T.R. REFERENCE WHENEVER YOU CAN. OK, ONLY FOR YOU, MAN, LET ME GET YOU CONNECTED.
SARA PEZZINI. WITCHBLADE.
PEZZINI.
...
SLOW DOWN, YOU'VE GOT A BABY DOING WHAT NOW?

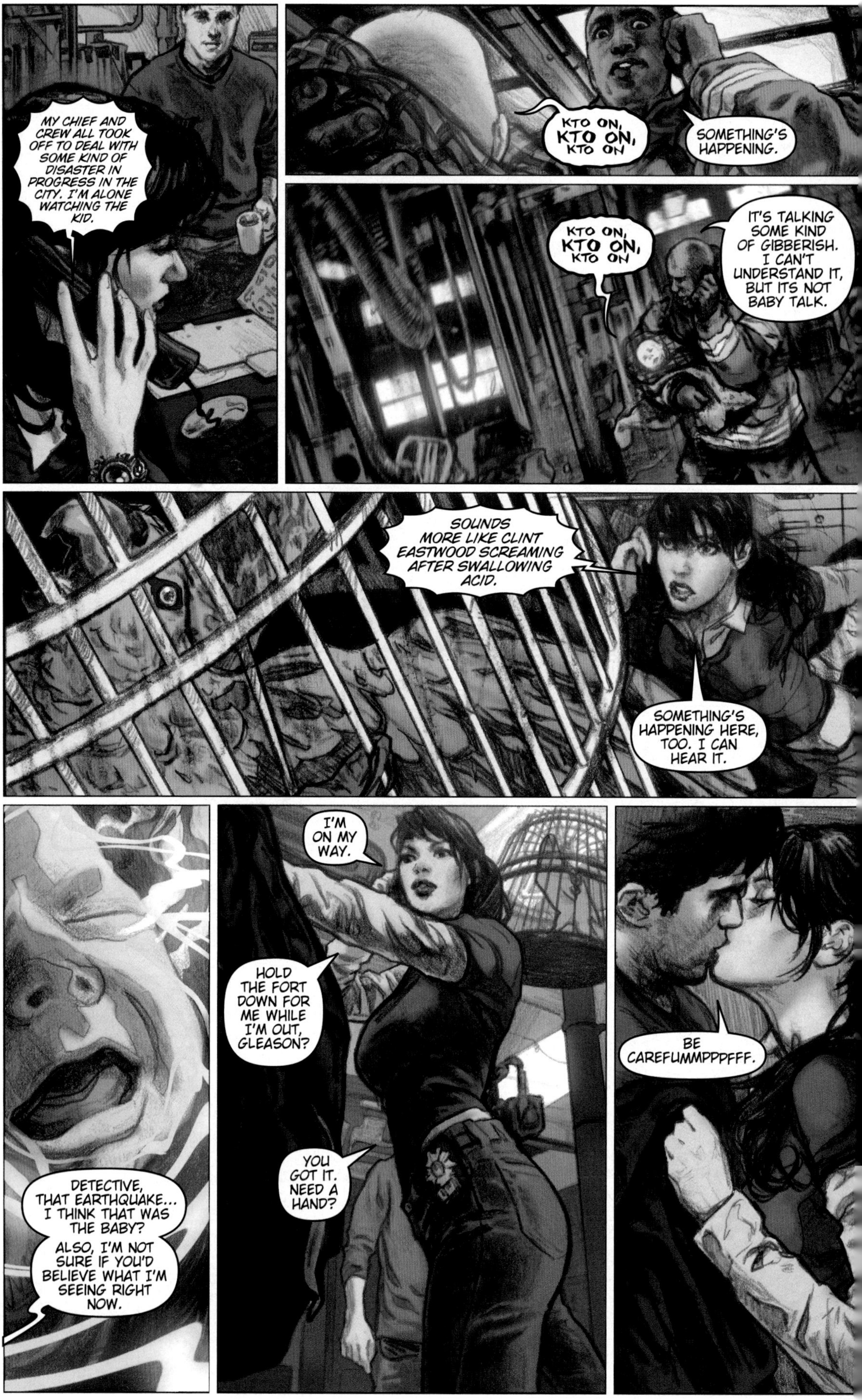
MY CHIEF AND CREW ALL TOOK OFF TO DEAL WITH SOME KIND OF DISASTER IN PROGRESS IN THE CITY. I'M ALONE WATCHING THE KID.
KTO ON, KTO ON, KTO ON
SOMETHING'S HAPPENING.
KTO ON, KTO ON, KTO ON
IT'S TALKING SOME KIND OF GIBBERISH. I CAN'T UNDERSTAND IT, BUT ITS NOT BABY TALK.
SOUNDS MORE LIKE CLINT EASTWOOD SCREAMING AFTER SWALLOWING ACID.
SOMETHING'S HAPPENING HERE, TOO. I CAN HEAR IT.
DETECTIVE, THAT EARTHQUAKE... I THINK THAT WAS THE BABY?
ALSO, I'M NOT SURE IF YOU'D BELIEVE WHAT I'M SEEING RIGHT NOW.
I'M ON MY WAY.
HOLD THE FORT DOWN FOR ME WHILE I'M OUT, GLEASON?
YOU GOT IT. NEED A HAND?
BE CAREFUMMPPPFFF.

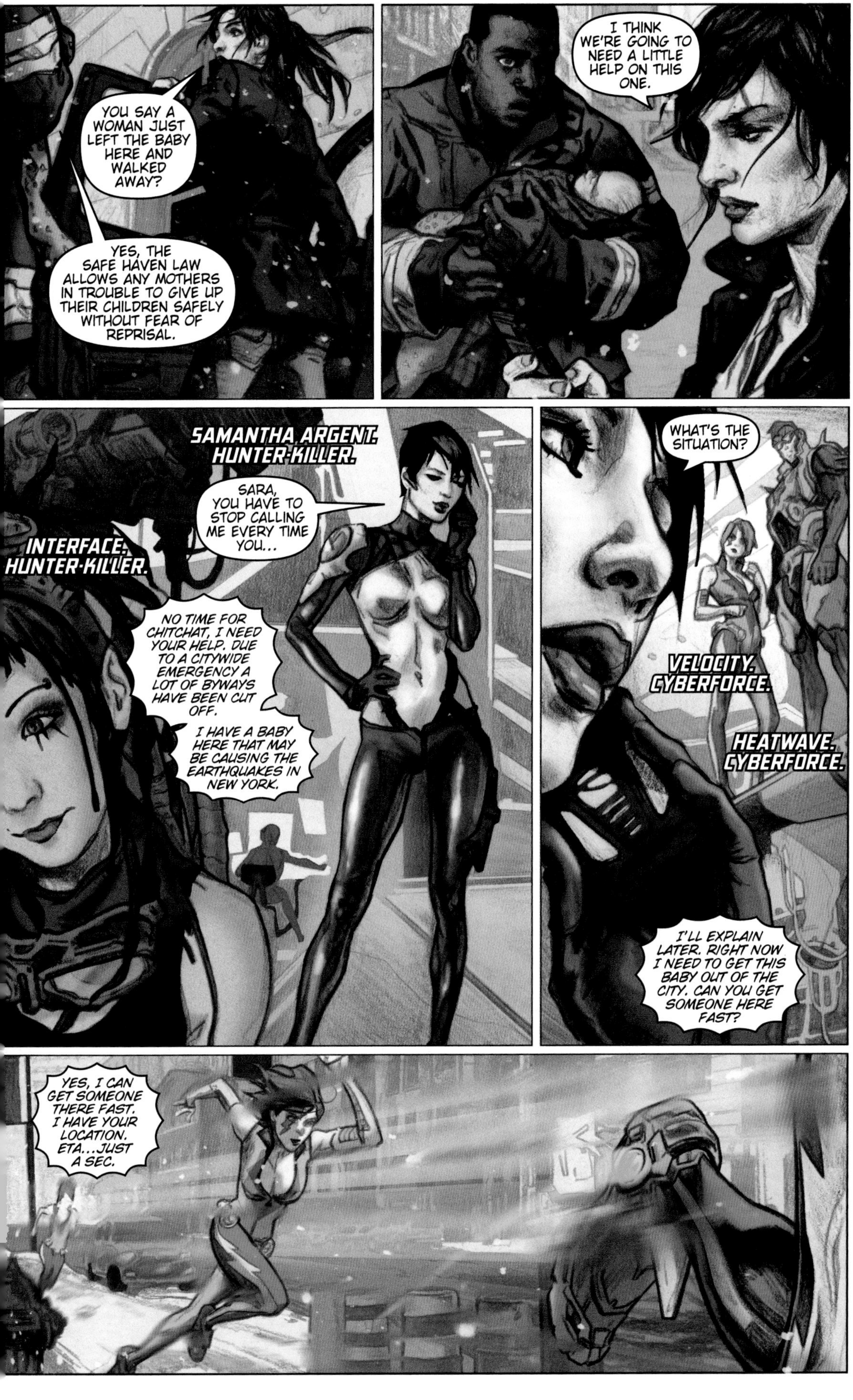
YOU SAY A WOMAN JUST LEFT THE BABY HERE AND WALKED AWAY?
YES, THE SAFE HAVEN LAW ALLOWS ANY MOTHERS IN TROUBLE TO GIVE UP THEIR CHILDREN SAFELY WITHOUT FEAR OF REPRISAL.
I THINK WE'RE GOING TO NEED A LITTLE HELP ON THIS ONE.
SAMANTHA ARGENT. HUNTER-KILLER.
INTERFACE. HUNTER-KILLER.
SARA, YOU HAVE TO STOP CALLING ME EVERY TIME YOU...
NO TIME FOR CHITCHAT, I NEED YOUR HELP. DUE TO A CITYWIDE EMERGENCY A LOT OF BYWAYS HAVE BEEN CUT OFF.
I HAVE A BABY HERE THAT MAY BE CAUSING THE EARTHQUAKES IN NEW YORK.
WHAT'S THE SITUATION?
VELOCITY. CYBERFORCE.
HEATWAVE. CYBERFORCE.
I'LL EXPLAIN LATER. RIGHT NOW I NEED TO GET THIS BABY OUT OF THE CITY. CAN YOU GET SOMEONE HERE FAST?
YES, I CAN GET SOMEONE THERE FAST. I HAVE YOUR LOCATION. ETA...JUST A SEC.

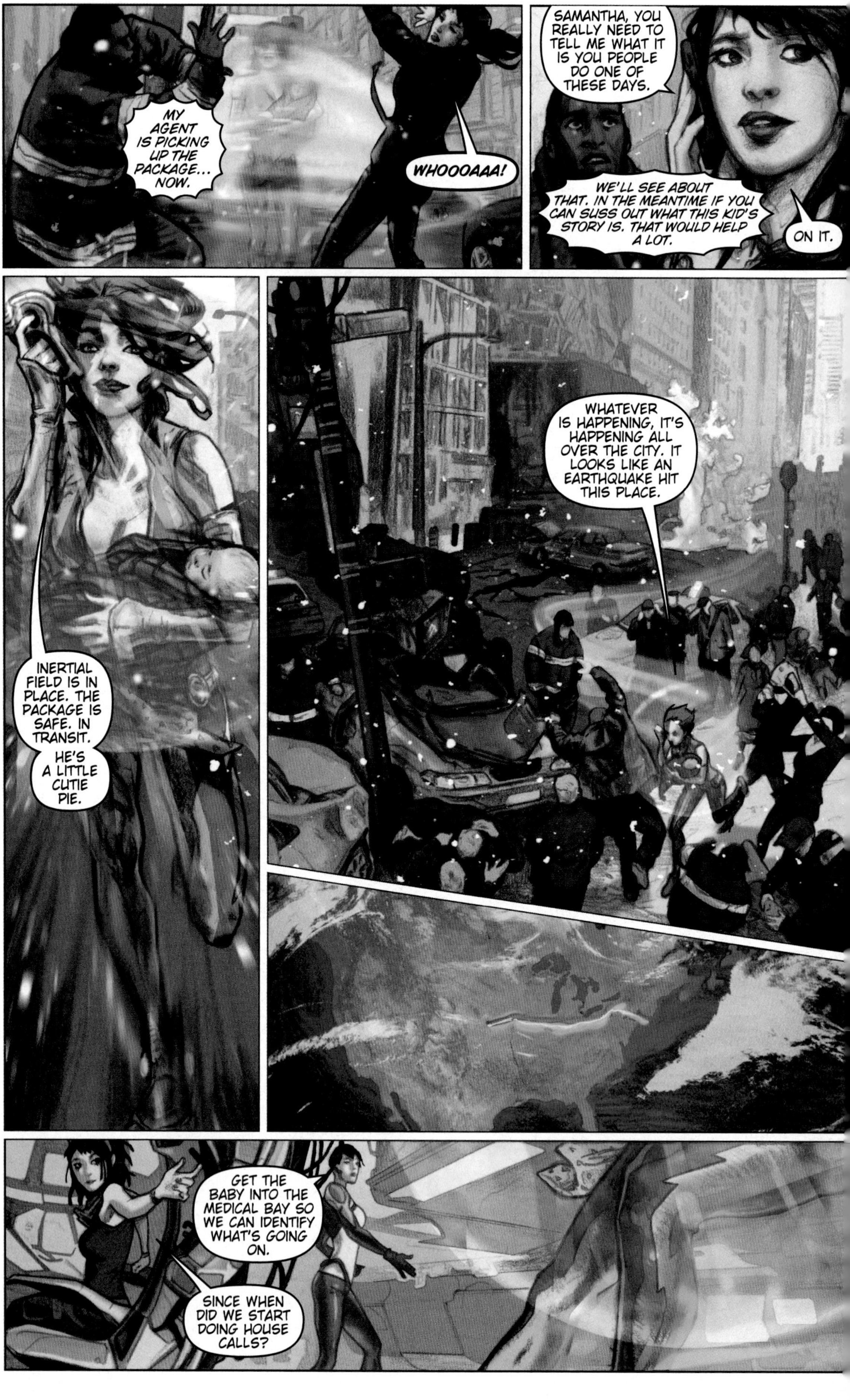
MY AGENT IS PICKING UP THE PACKAGE... NOW.
WHOOOAAA!
SAMANTHA, YOU REALLY NEED TO TELL ME WHAT IT IS YOU PEOPLE DO ONE OF THESE DAYS.
WE'LL SEE ABOUT THAT. IN THE MEANTIME IF YOU CAN SUSS OUT WHAT THIS KID'S STORY IS. THAT WOULD HELP A LOT.
ON IT.
INERTIAL FIELD IS IN PLACE. THE PACKAGE IS SAFE. IN TRANSIT.
HE'S A LITTLE CUTIE PIE.
WHATEVER IS HAPPENING, IT'S HAPPENING ALL OVER THE CITY. IT LOOKS LIKE AN EARTHQUAKE HIT THIS PLACE.
GET THE BABY INTO THE MEDICAL BAY SO WE CAN IDENTIFY WHAT'S GOING ON.
SINCE WHEN DID WE START DOING HOUSE CALLS?

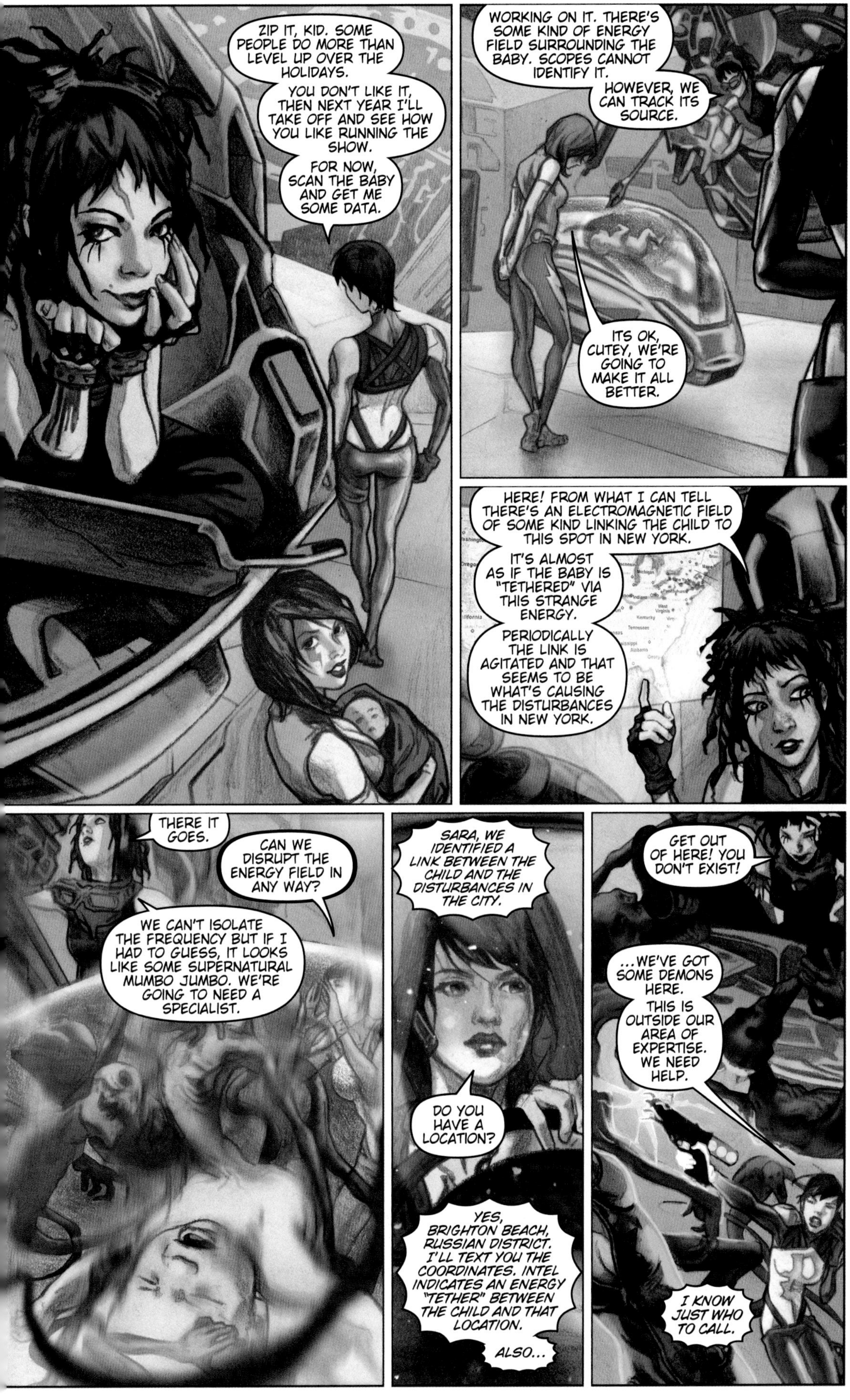
ZIP IT, KID. SOME PEOPLE DO MORE THAN LEVEL UP OVER THE HOLIDAYS.
YOU DON'T LIKE IT, THEN NEXT YEAR I'LL TAKE OFF AND SEE HOW YOU LIKE RUNNING THE SHOW.
FOR NOW, SCAN THE BABY AND GET ME SOME DATA.
WORKING ON IT. THERE'S SOME KIND OF ENERGY FIELD SURROUNDING THE BABY. SCOPES CANNOT IDENTIFY IT.
HOWEVER, WE CAN TRACK ITS SOURCE.
ITS OK, CUTEY, WE'RE GOING TO MAKE IT ALL BETTER.
HERE! FROM WHAT I CAN TELL THERE'S AN ELECTROMAGNETIC FIELD OF SOME KIND LINKING THE CHILD TO THIS SPOT IN NEW YORK.
IT'S ALMOST AS IF THE BABY IS "TETHERED" VIA THIS STRANGE ENERGY.
PERIODICALLY THE LINK IS AGITATED AND THAT SEEMS TO BE WHAT'S CAUSING THE DISTURBANCES IN NEW YORK.
THERE IT GOES.
CAN WE DISRUPT THE ENERGY FIELD IN ANY WAY?
WE CAN'T ISOLATE THE FREQUENCY BUT IF I HAD TO GUESS, IT LOOKS LIKE SOME SUPERNATURAL MUMBO JUMBO. WE'RE GOING TO NEED A SPECIALIST.
SARA, WE IDENTIFIED A LINK BETWEEN THE CHILD AND THE DISTURBANCES IN THE CITY.
DO YOU HAVE A LOCATION?
YES, BRIGHTON BEACH, RUSSIAN DISTRICT. I'LL TEXT YOU THE COORDINATES. INTEL INDICATES AN ENERGY "TETHER" BETWEEN THE CHILD AND THAT LOCATION.
ALSO...
GET OUT OF HERE! YOU DON'T EXIST!
...WE'VE GOT SOME DEMONS HERE.
THIS IS OUTSIDE OUR AREA OF EXPERTISE. WE NEED HELP.
I KNOW JUST WHO TO CALL.

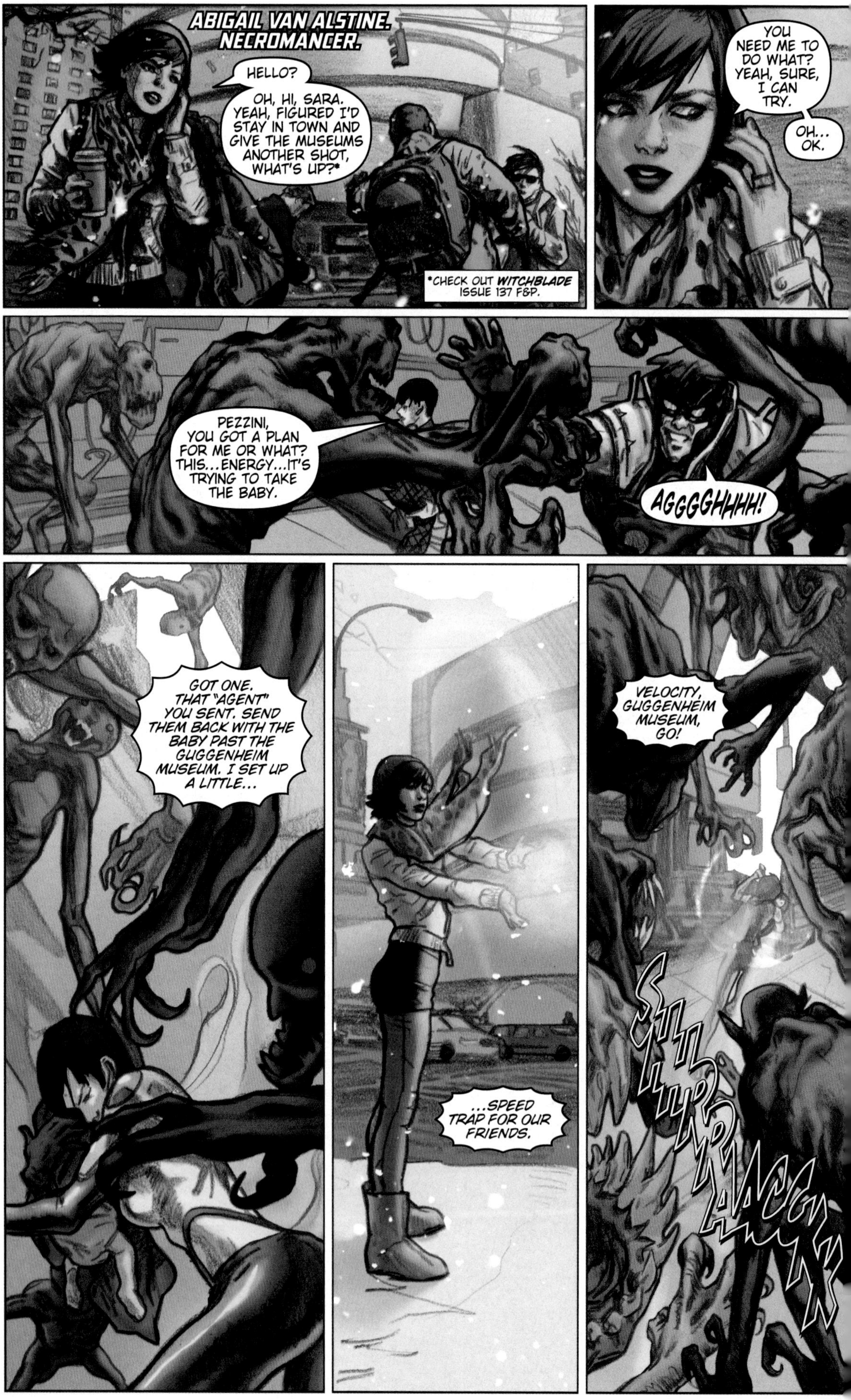
ABIGAIL VAN ALSTINE. NECROMANCER.
HELLO?
OH, HI, SARA. YEAH, FIGURED I'D STAY IN TOWN AND GIVE THE MUSEUMS ANOTHER SHOT, WHAT'S UP?*
*CHECK OUT WITCHBLADE ISSUE 137 F&P.
YOU NEED ME TO DO WHAT? YEAH, SURE, I CAN TRY.
OH... OK.
PEZZINI, YOU GOT A PLAN FOR ME OR WHAT? THIS...ENERGY...IT'S TRYING TO TAKE THE BABY.
AGGGGHHHH!
GOT ONE. THAT "AGENT" YOU SENT. SEND THEM BACK WITH THE BABY PAST THE GUGGENHEIM MUSEUM. I SET UP A LITTLE...
...SPEED TRAP FOR OUR FRIENDS.
VELOCITY, GUGGENHEIM MUSEUM, GO!
SHHRRAACCKK

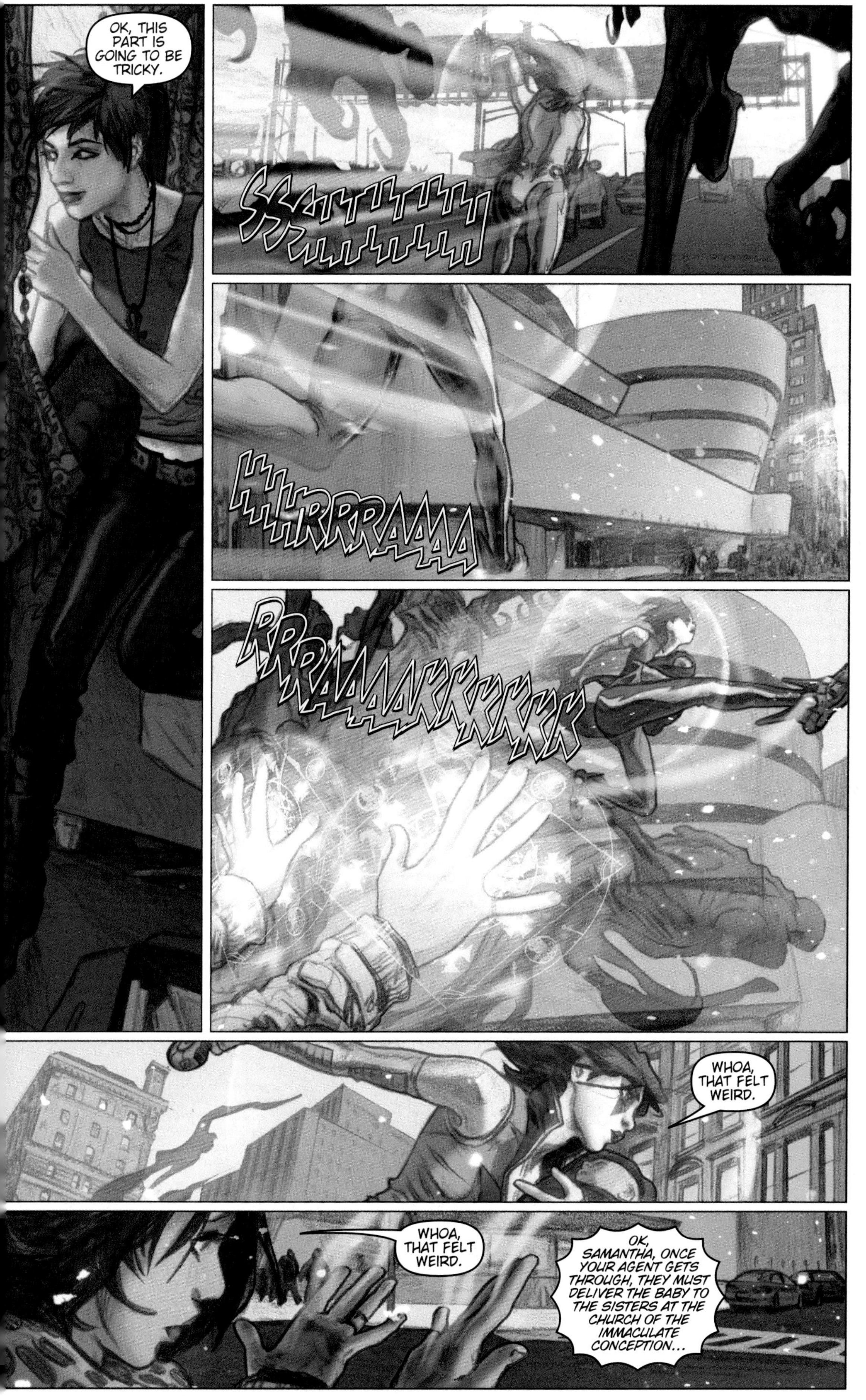
OK, THIS PART IS GOING TO BE TRICKY.
SSSHHHHHHH
HHHRRRAAAA
RRRAAAKKKKK
WHOA, THAT FELT WEIRD.
WHOA, THAT FELT WEIRD.
OK, SAMANTHA, ONCE YOUR AGENT GETS THROUGH, THEY MUST DELIVER THE BABY TO THE SISTERS AT THE CHURCH OF THE IMMACULATE CONCEPTION...

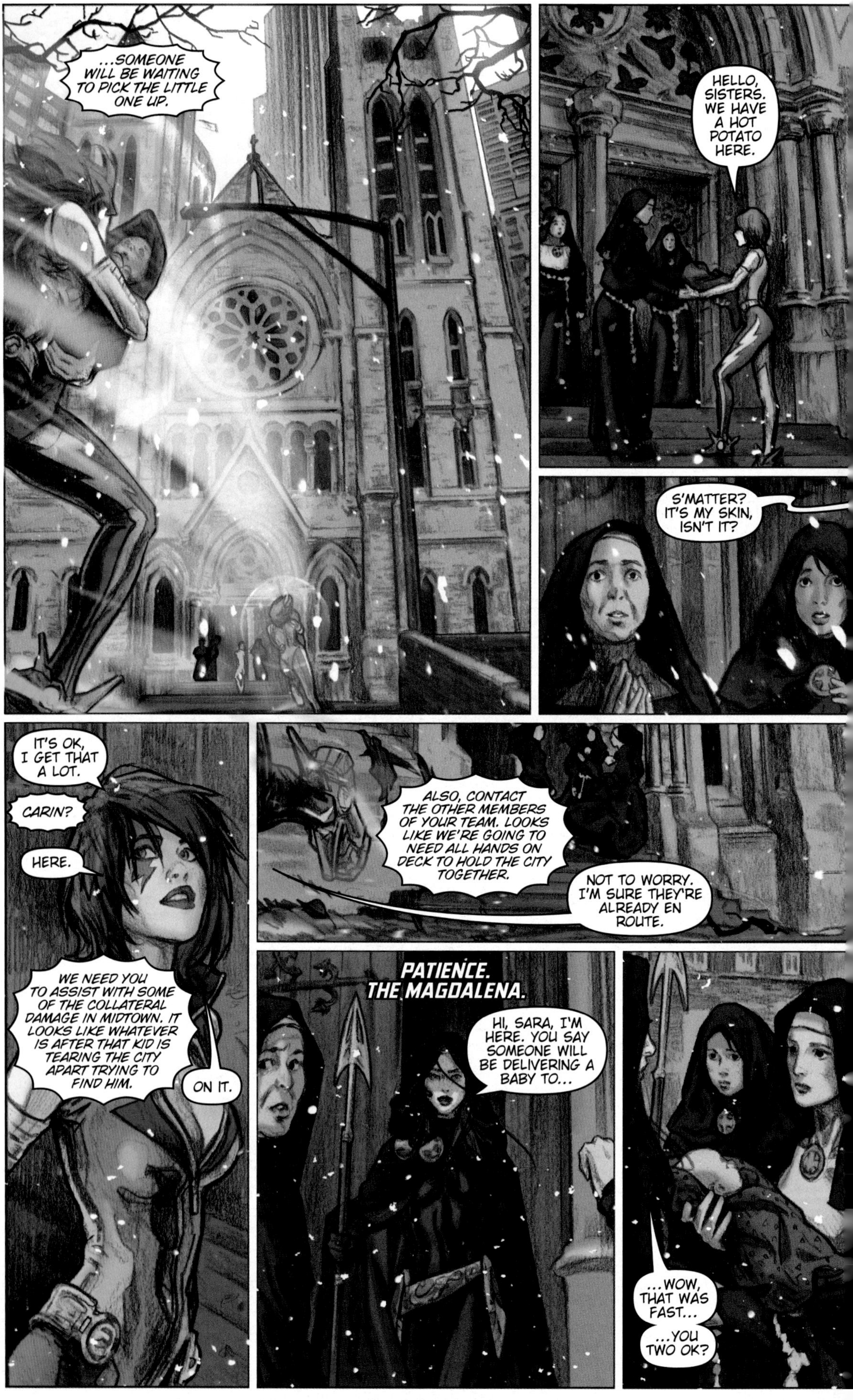
...SOMEONE WILL BE WAITING TO PICK THE LITTLE ONE UP.
HELLO, SISTERS. WE HAVE A HOT POTATO HERE.
S'MATTER? IT'S MY SKIN, ISN'T IT?
IT'S OK, I GET THAT A LOT.
CARIN?
HERE.
WE NEED YOU TO ASSIST WITH SOME OF THE COLLATERAL DAMAGE IN MIDTOWN. IT LOOKS LIKE WHATEVER IS AFTER THAT KID IS TEARING THE CITY APART TRYING TO FIND HIM.
ON IT.
ALSO, CONTACT THE OTHER MEMBERS OF YOUR TEAM. LOOKS LIKE WE'RE GOING TO NEED ALL HANDS ON DECK TO HOLD THE CITY TOGETHER.
NOT TO WORRY. I'M SURE THEY'RE ALREADY EN ROUTE.
PATIENCE. THE MAGDALENA.
HI, SARA, I'M HERE. YOU SAY SOMEONE WILL BE DELIVERING A BABY TO...
...WOW, THAT WAS FAST...
...YOU TWO OK?

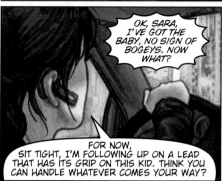

OK, SARA, I'VE GOT THE BABY, NO SIGN OF BOGEYS. NOW WHAT?

FOR NOW, SIT TIGHT, I'M FOLLOWING UP ON A LEAD THAT HAS ITS GRIP ON THIS KID. THINK YOU CAN HANDLE WHATEVER COMES YOUR WAY?

I CAN HANDLE A FEW DEMONS. THE CHILD IS SAFE WITH ME.

GOOD... OH, CRAP!

SARA, WHAT'S WRONG?

SSSCCRRRREEEECCCHHH

MY MISTRESS APOLOGIZES FOR NOT HAVING ANSWERED SOONER. SHE SENDS HER REGRETS, HOWEVER...

I THINK THE CAVALRY JUST ARRIVED.

...SHE BIDS YOU REST ASSURED SHE IS SEEING TO THE NEEDS OF THOSE TO WHOM SHE CAN.

DANIELLE BAPTISTE. ANGELUS.

FIRST WING, SHORE UP THAT HOSPITAL AND GET THOSE PEOPLE OUT OF THERE.

SECOND WING, WITH ME!

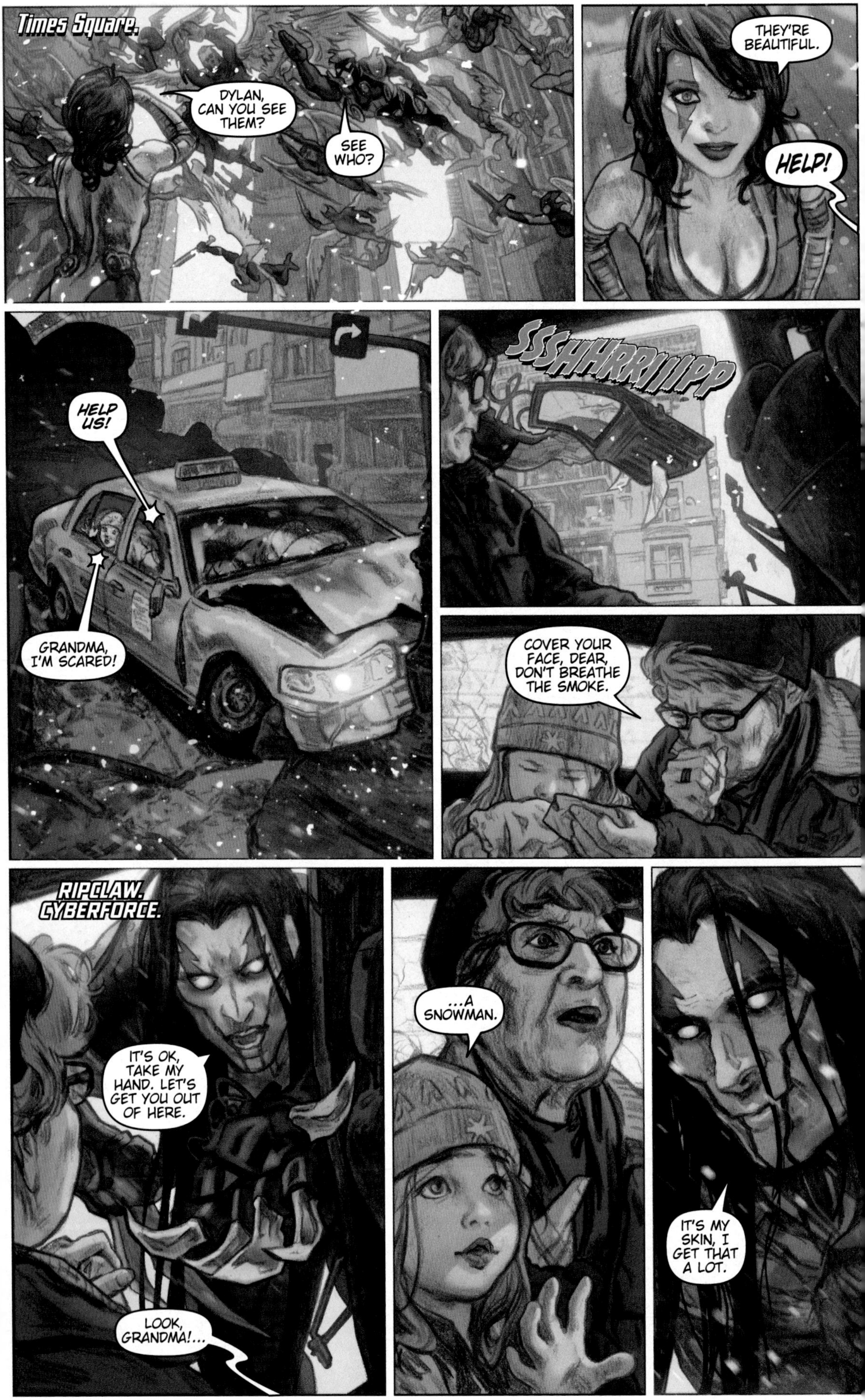
Times Square.
DYLAN, CAN YOU SEE THEM?
SEE WHO?
THEY'RE BEAUTIFUL.
HELP!
HELP US!
GRANDMA, I'M SCARED!
SSSHHRRIIIPP
COVER YOUR FACE, DEAR, DON'T BREATHE THE SMOKE.
RIPCLAW. CYBERFORCE.
IT'S OK, TAKE MY HAND. LET'S GET YOU OUT OF HERE.
LOOK, GRANDMA!...
...A SNOWMAN.
IT'S MY SKIN, I GET THAT A LOT.

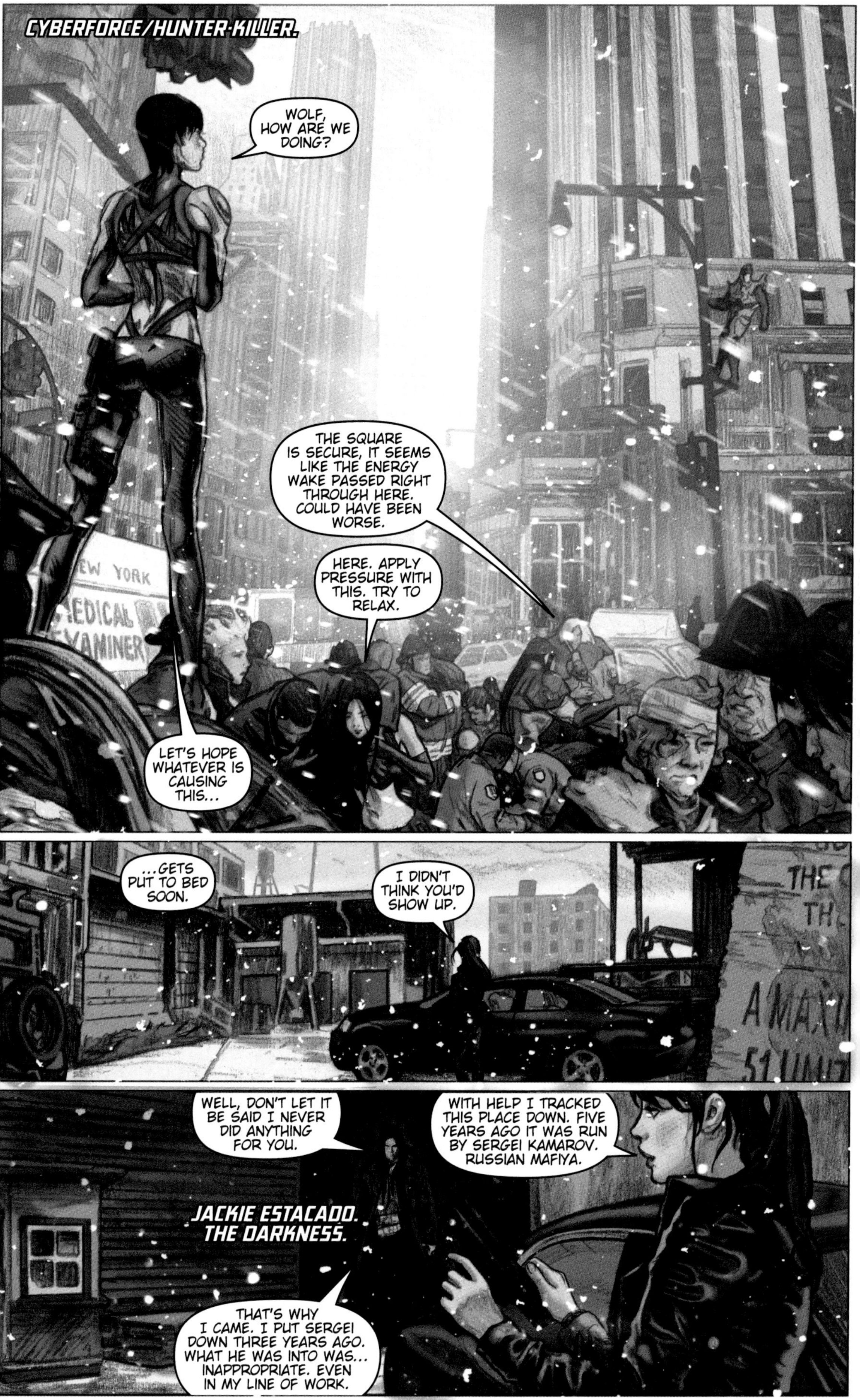
CYBERFORCE/HUNTER-KILLER.
WOLF, HOW ARE WE DOING?
THE SQUARE IS SECURE, IT SEEMS LIKE THE ENERGY WAKE PASSED RIGHT THROUGH HERE. COULD HAVE BEEN WORSE.
HERE. APPLY PRESSURE WITH THIS. TRY TO RELAX.
LET'S HOPE WHATEVER IS CAUSING THIS...
...GETS PUT TO BED SOON.
I DIDN'T THINK YOU'D SHOW UP.
WELL, DON'T LET IT BE SAID I NEVER DID ANYTHING FOR YOU.
WITH HELP I TRACKED THIS PLACE DOWN. FIVE YEARS AGO IT WAS RUN BY SERGEI KAMAROV. RUSSIAN MAFIYA.
JACKIE ESTACADO. THE DARKNESS.
THAT'S WHY I CAME. I PUT SERGEI DOWN THREE YEARS AGO. WHAT HE WAS INTO WAS... INAPPROPRIATE. EVEN IN MY LINE OF WORK.

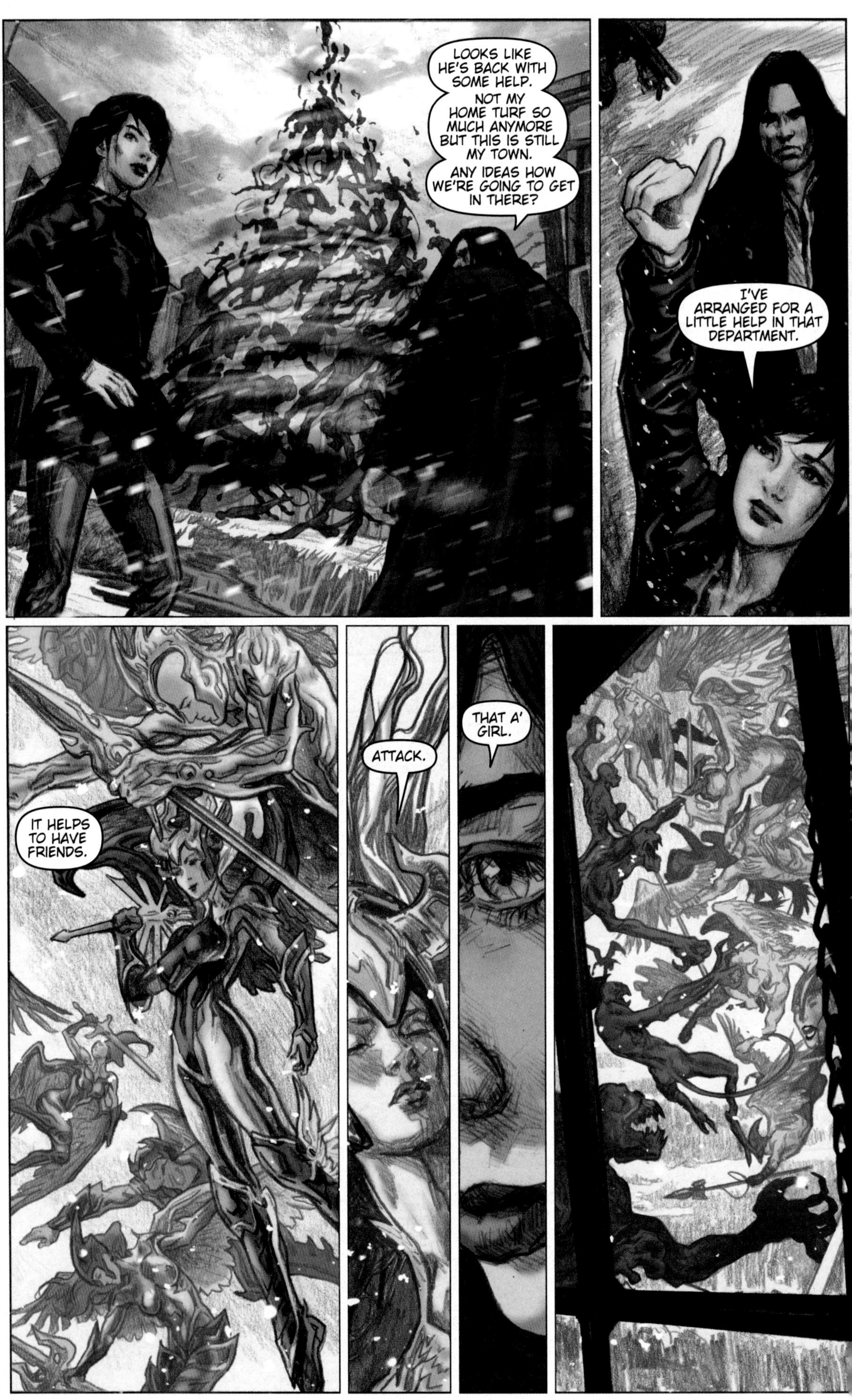
LOOKS LIKE HE'S BACK WITH SOME HELP.
NOT MY HOME TURF SO MUCH ANYMORE BUT THIS IS STILL MY TOWN.
ANY IDEAS HOW WE'RE GOING TO GET IN THERE?
I'VE ARRANGED FOR A LITTLE HELP IN THAT DEPARTMENT.
IT HELPS TO HAVE FRIENDS.
ATTACK.
THAT A' GIRL.

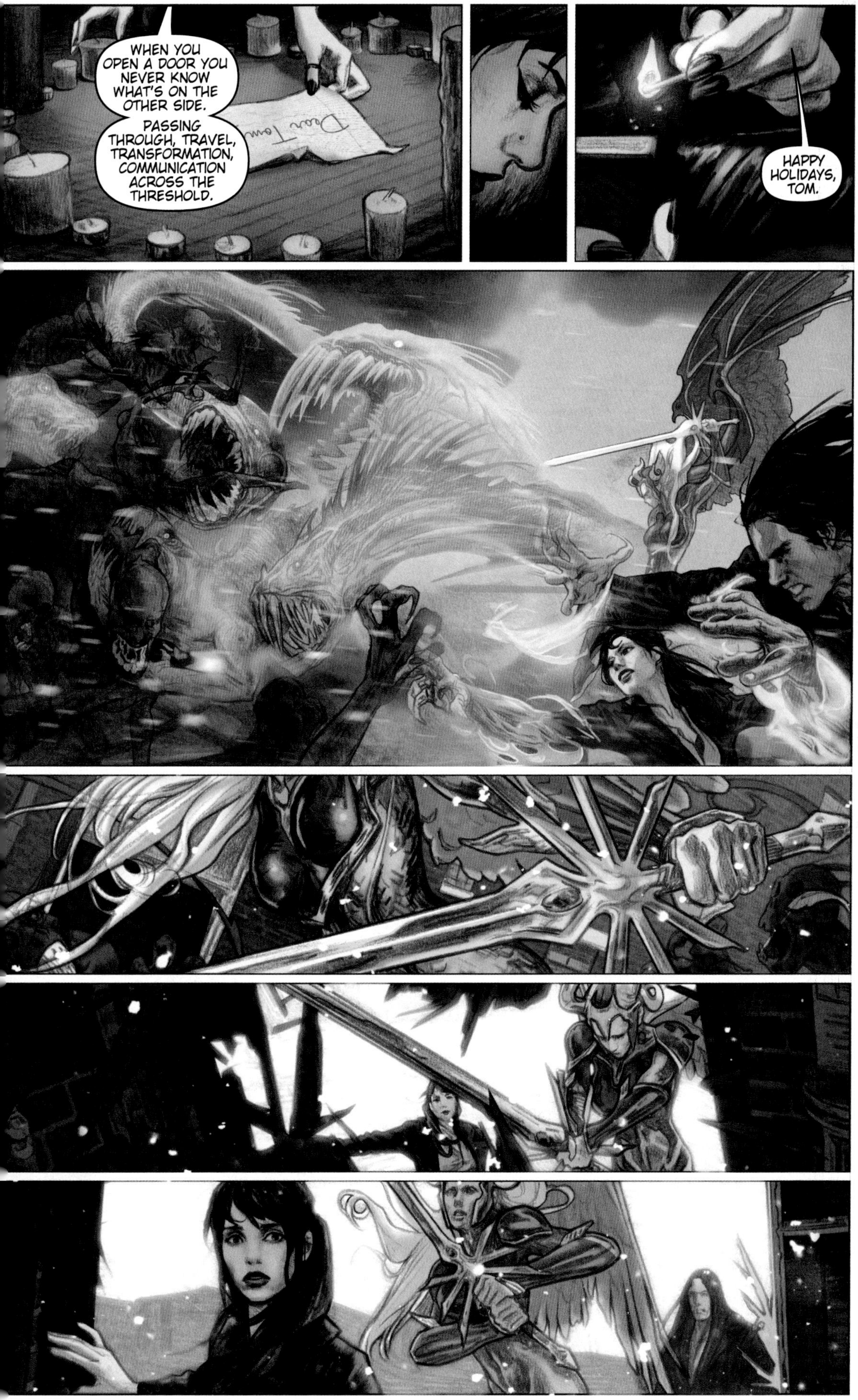
WHEN YOU OPEN A DOOR YOU NEVER KNOW WHAT'S ON THE OTHER SIDE.
PASSING THROUGH, TRAVEL, TRANSFORMATION, COMMUNICATION ACROSS THE THRESHOLD.
HAPPY HOLIDAYS, TOM.

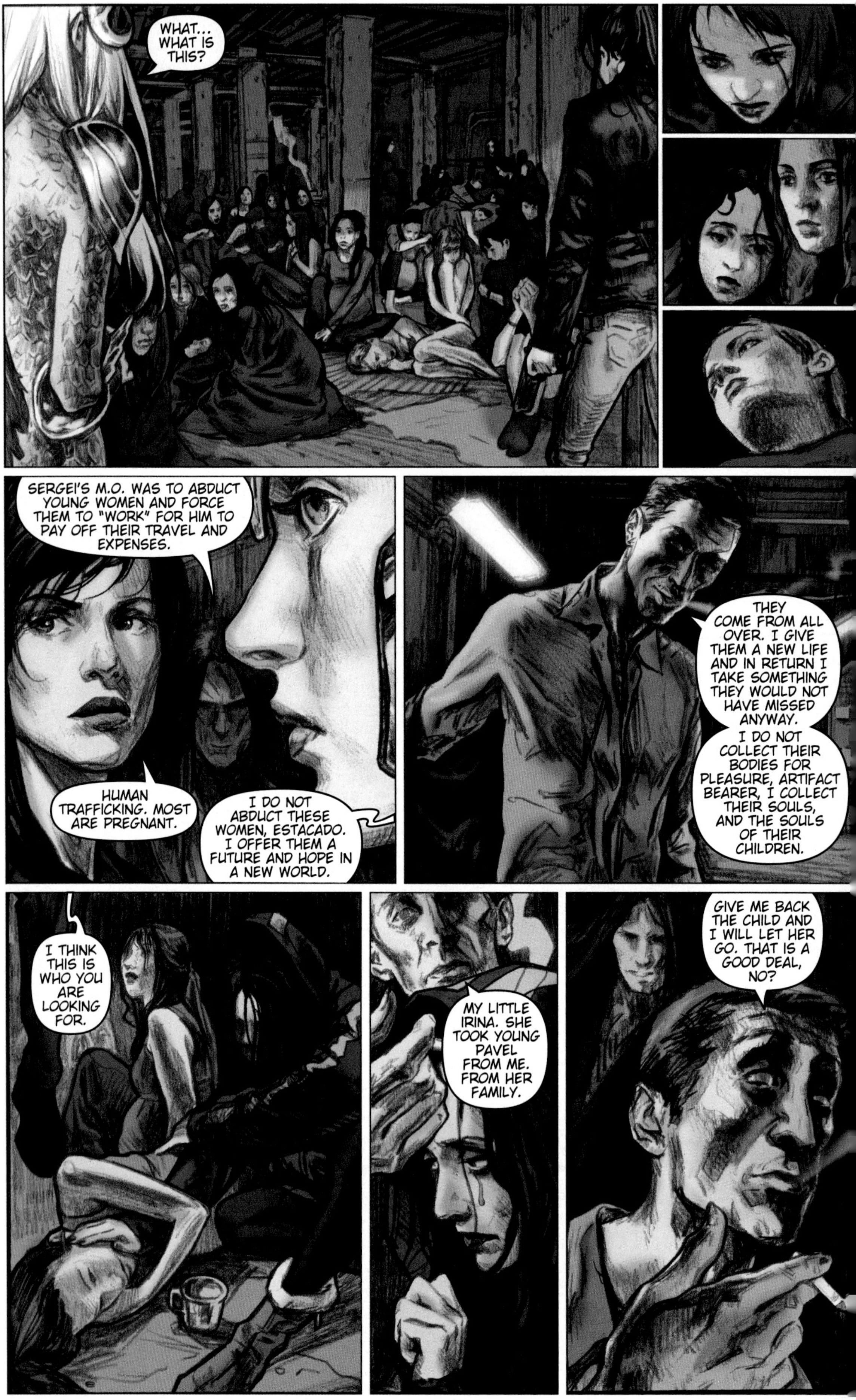
WHAT... WHAT IS THIS?
SERGEI'S M.O. WAS TO ABDUCT YOUNG WOMEN AND FORCE THEM TO "WORK" FOR HIM TO PAY OFF THEIR TRAVEL AND EXPENSES.
HUMAN TRAFFICKING. MOST ARE PREGNANT.
I DO NOT ABDUCT THESE WOMEN, ESTACADO. I OFFER THEM A FUTURE AND HOPE IN A NEW WORLD.
THEY COME FROM ALL OVER. I GIVE THEM A NEW LIFE AND IN RETURN I TAKE SOMETHING THEY WOULD NOT HAVE MISSED ANYWAY.
I DO NOT COLLECT THEIR BODIES FOR PLEASURE, ARTIFACT BEARER, I COLLECT THEIR SOULS, AND THE SOULS OF THEIR CHILDREN.
I THINK THIS IS WHO YOU ARE LOOKING FOR.
MY LITTLE IRINA. SHE TOOK YOUNG PAVEL FROM ME. FROM HER FAMILY.
GIVE ME BACK THE CHILD AND I WILL LET HER GO. THAT IS A GOOD DEAL, NO?

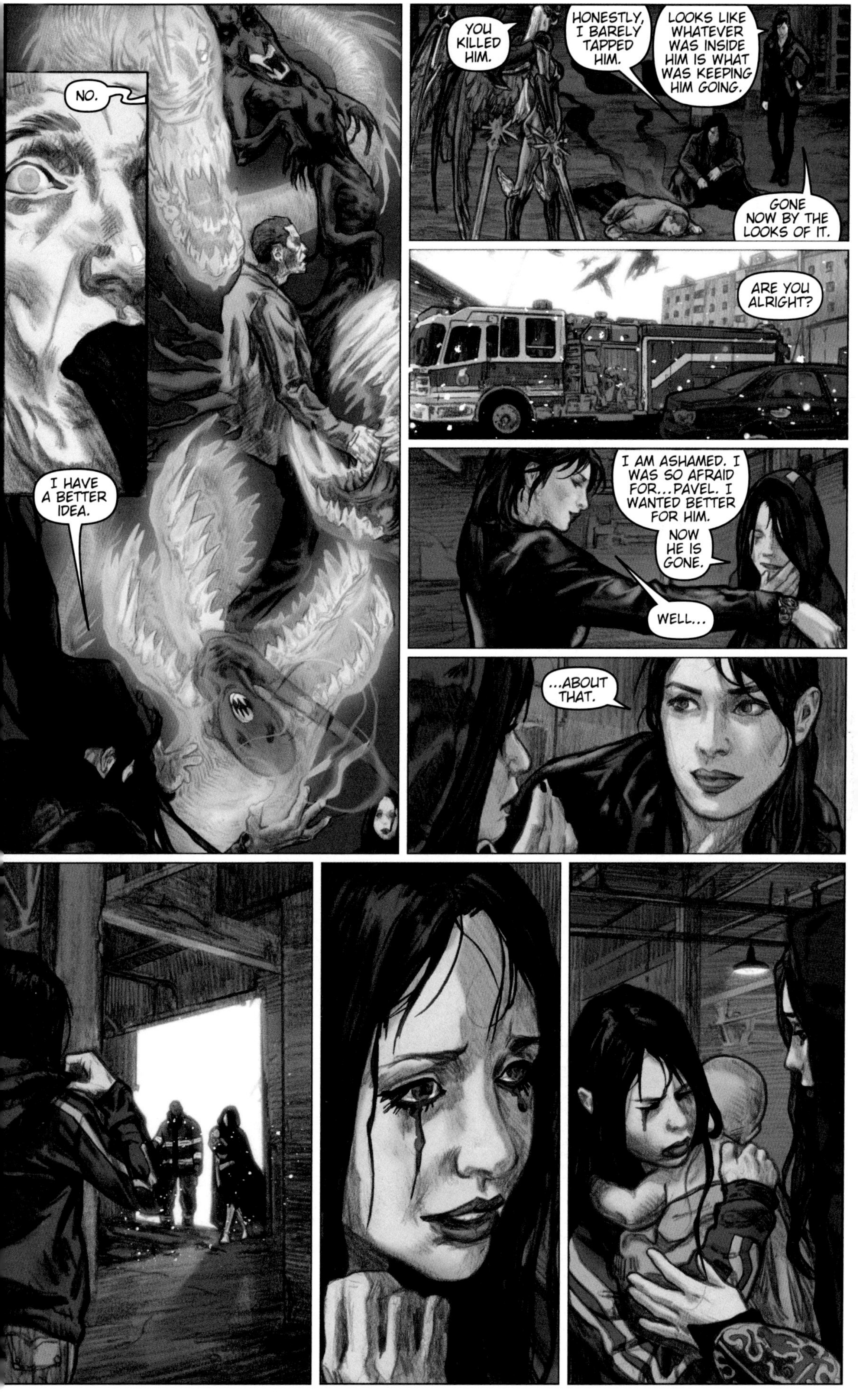
NO.
I HAVE A BETTER IDEA.
YOU KILLED HIM.
HONESTLY, I BARELY TAPPED HIM.
LOOKS LIKE WHATEVER WAS INSIDE HIM IS WHAT WAS KEEPING HIM GOING.
GONE NOW BY THE LOOKS OF IT.
ARE YOU ALRIGHT?
I AM ASHAMED. I WAS SO AFRAID FOR...PAVEL. I WANTED BETTER FOR HIM.
NOW HE IS GONE.
WELL...
...ABOUT THAT.

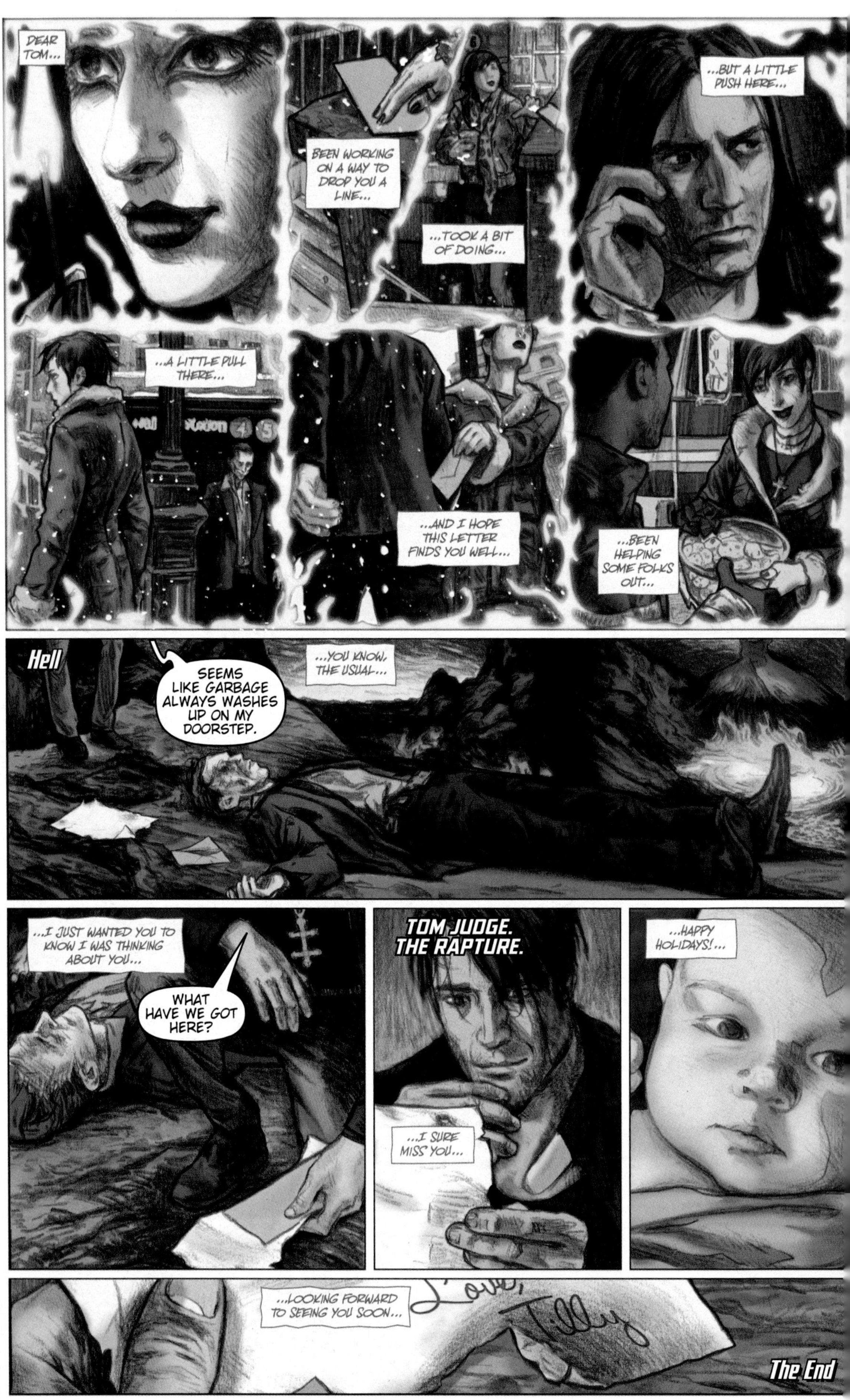
DEAR TOM...
BEEN WORKING ON A WAY TO DROP YOU A LINE...
...TOOK A BIT OF DOING...
...BUT A LITTLE PUSH HERE...
...A LITTLE PULL THERE...
...AND I HOPE THIS LETTER FINDS YOU WELL...
...BEEN HELPING SOME FOLKS OUT...
Hell
SEEMS LIKE GARBAGE ALWAYS WASHES UP ON MY DOORSTEP.
...YOU KNOW, THE USUAL...
...I JUST WANTED YOU TO KNOW I WAS THINKING ABOUT YOU...
WHAT HAVE WE GOT HERE?
TOM JUDGE. THE RAPTURE.
...I SURE MISS YOU...
...HAPPY HOLIDAYS!...
...LOOKING FORWARD TO SEEING YOU SOON...
Love, Tilly
The End

SNEAK PREVIEW

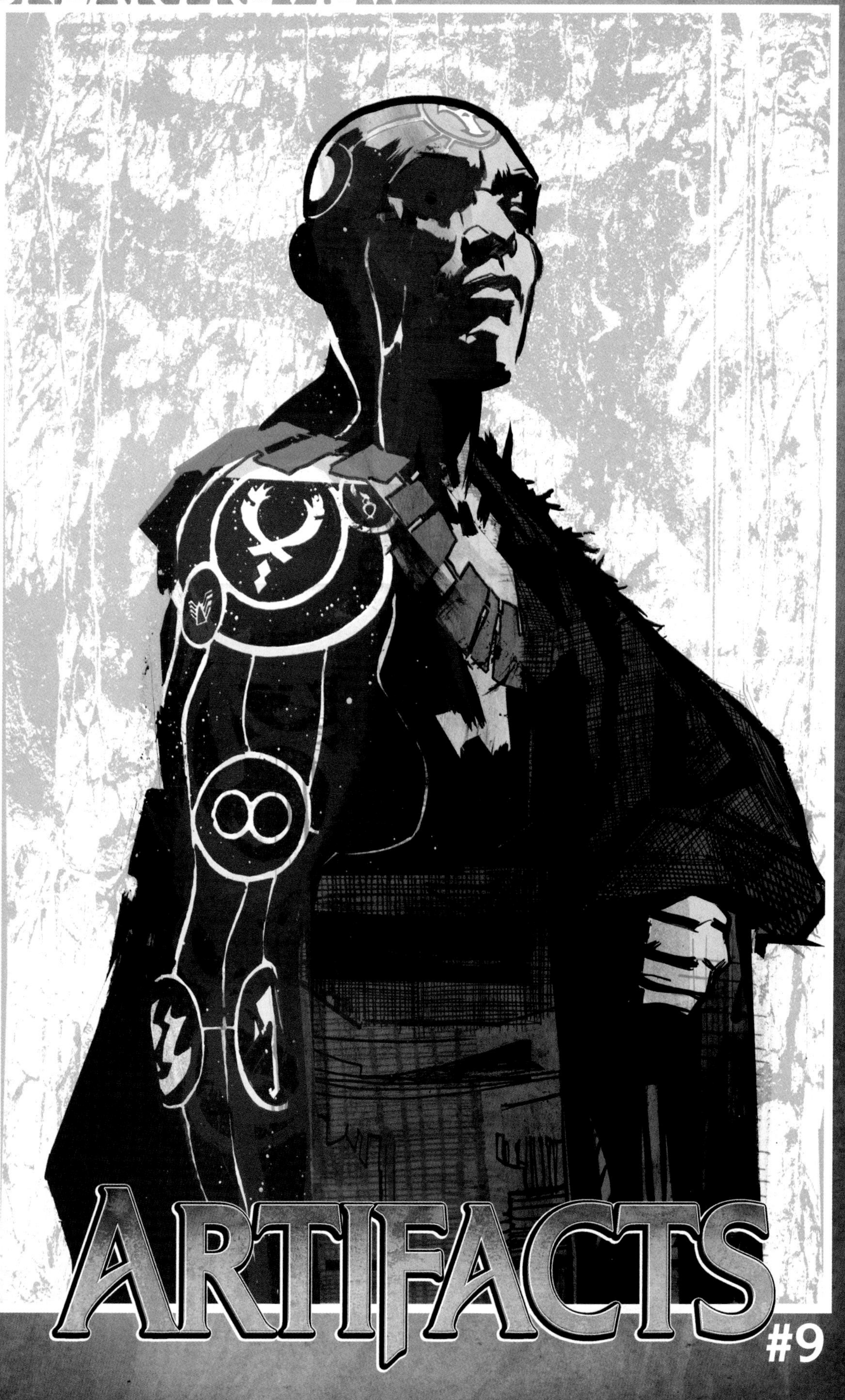
ARTIFACTS
#9

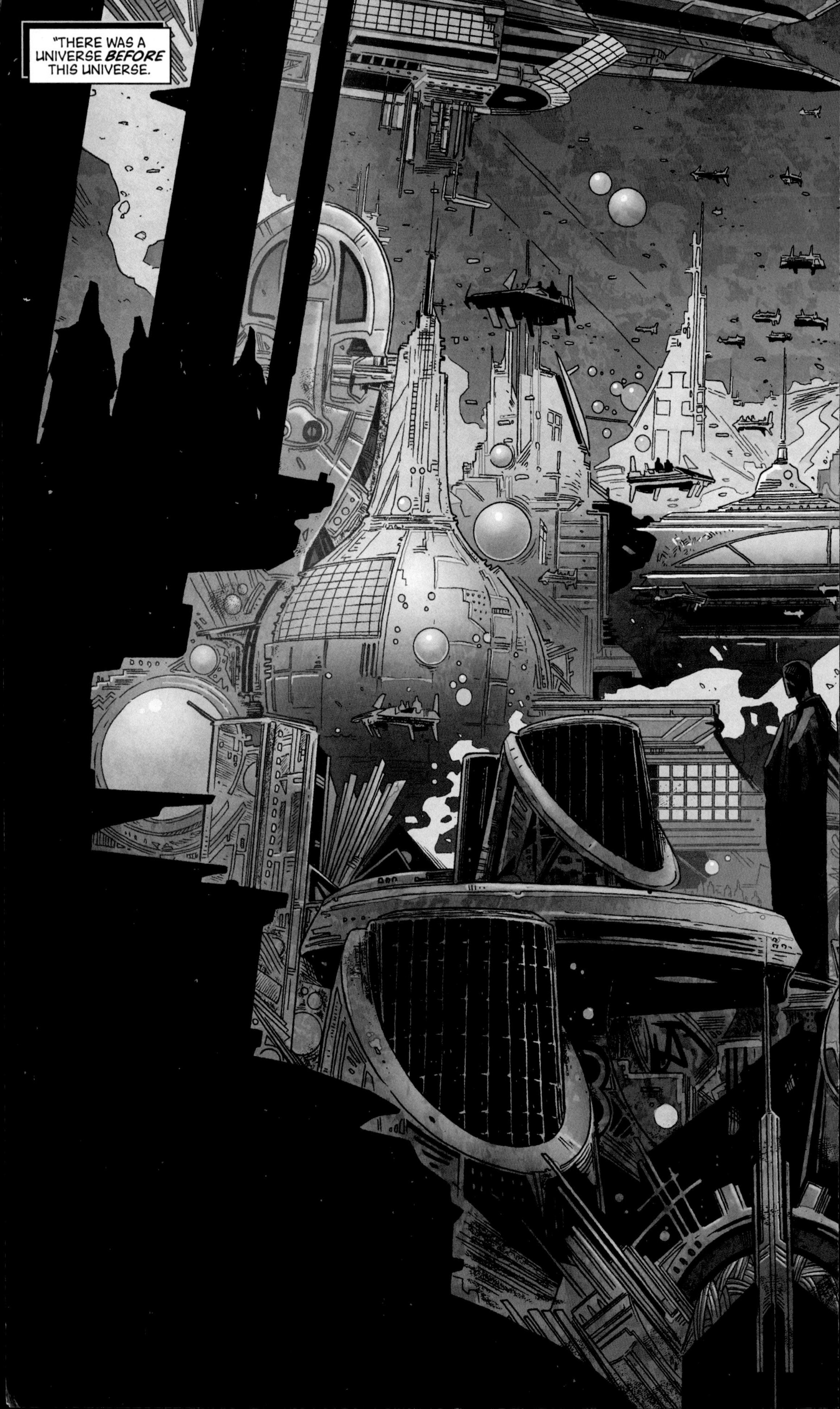
"THERE WAS A UNIVERSE *BEFORE* THIS UNIVERSE.

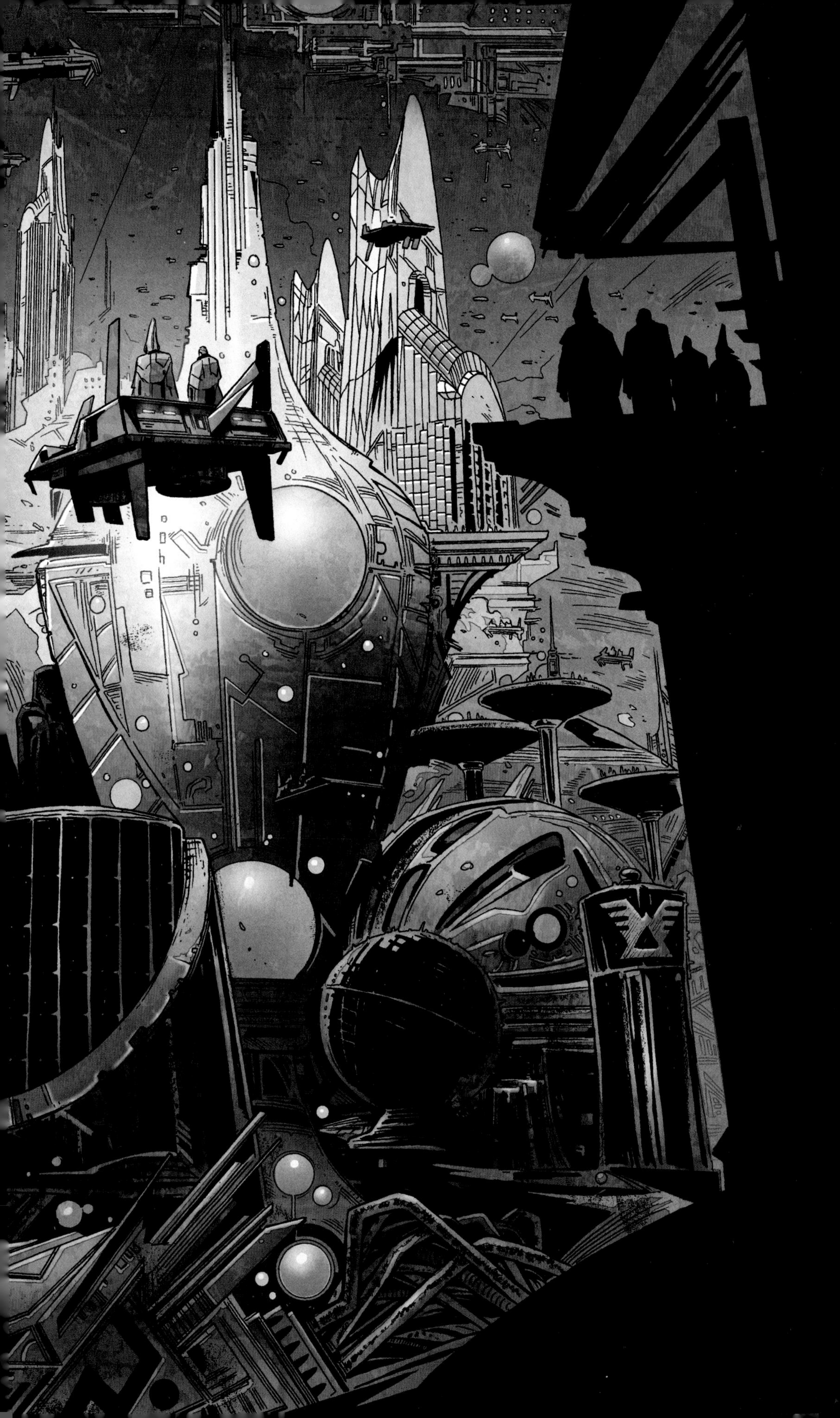

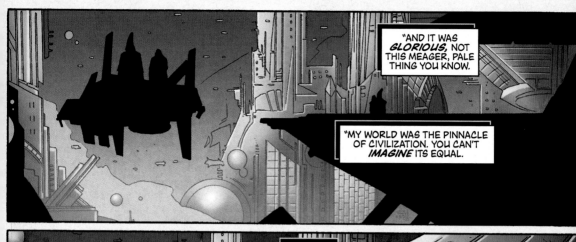

"AND IT WAS *GLORIOUS,* NOT THIS MEAGER, PALE THING YOU KNOW.

"MY WORLD WAS THE PINNACLE OF CIVILIZATION. YOU CAN'T *IMAGINE* ITS EQUAL.

"WE KNEW PEACE.

"WE KNEW PROSPERITY.

"AND *I* KNEW LOVE.

"MY WIFE AND SON WERE MORE PRECIOUS TO ME THAN THE *ENTIRETY* OF YOUR WORLD, A THOUSAND TIMES OVER.

"MY PEOPLE *REVELED* IN ALL THAT WE HAD CREATED. AND WHY NOT?

"WE BENT THE UNIVERSE ITSELF TO OUR WILL.

"OR SO WE BELIEVED.

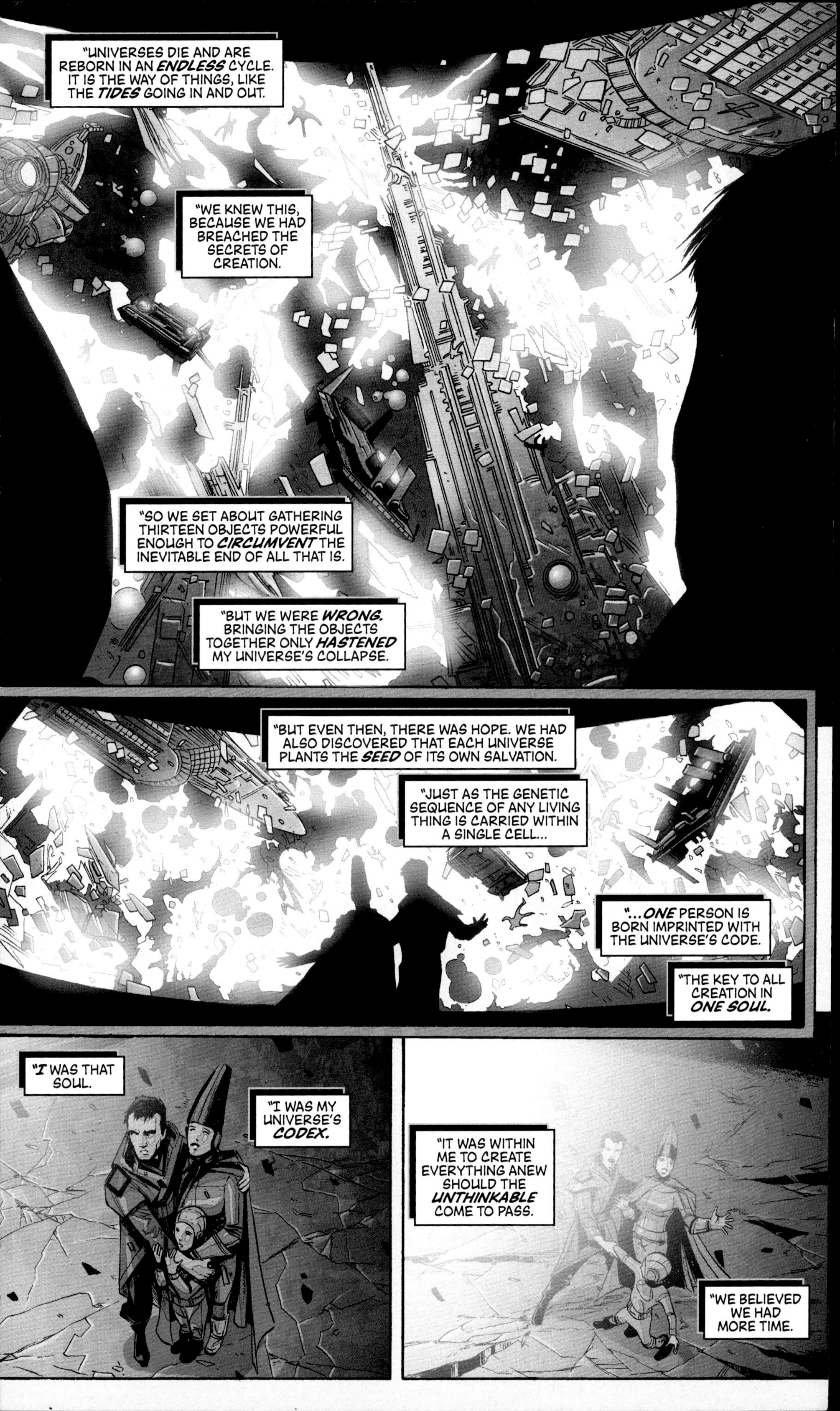
"UNIVERSES DIE AND ARE REBORN IN AN ENDLESS CYCLE. IT IS THE WAY OF THINGS, LIKE THE TIDES GOING IN AND OUT.
"WE KNEW THIS, BECAUSE WE HAD BREACHED THE SECRETS OF CREATION.
"SO WE SET ABOUT GATHERING THIRTEEN OBJECTS POWERFUL ENOUGH TO CIRCUMVENT THE INEVITABLE END OF ALL THAT IS.
"BUT WE WERE WRONG. BRINGING THE OBJECTS TOGETHER ONLY HASTENED MY UNIVERSE'S COLLAPSE.
"BUT EVEN THEN, THERE WAS HOPE. WE HAD ALSO DISCOVERED THAT EACH UNIVERSE PLANTS THE SEED OF ITS OWN SALVATION.
"JUST AS THE GENETIC SEQUENCE OF ANY LIVING THING IS CARRIED WITHIN A SINGLE CELL...
"...ONE PERSON IS BORN IMPRINTED WITH THE UNIVERSE'S CODE.
"THE KEY TO ALL CREATION IN ONE SOUL.
"I WAS THAT SOUL.
"I WAS MY UNIVERSE'S CODEX.
"IT WAS WITHIN ME TO CREATE EVERYTHING ANEW SHOULD THE UNTHINKABLE COME TO PASS.
"WE BELIEVED WE HAD MORE TIME.

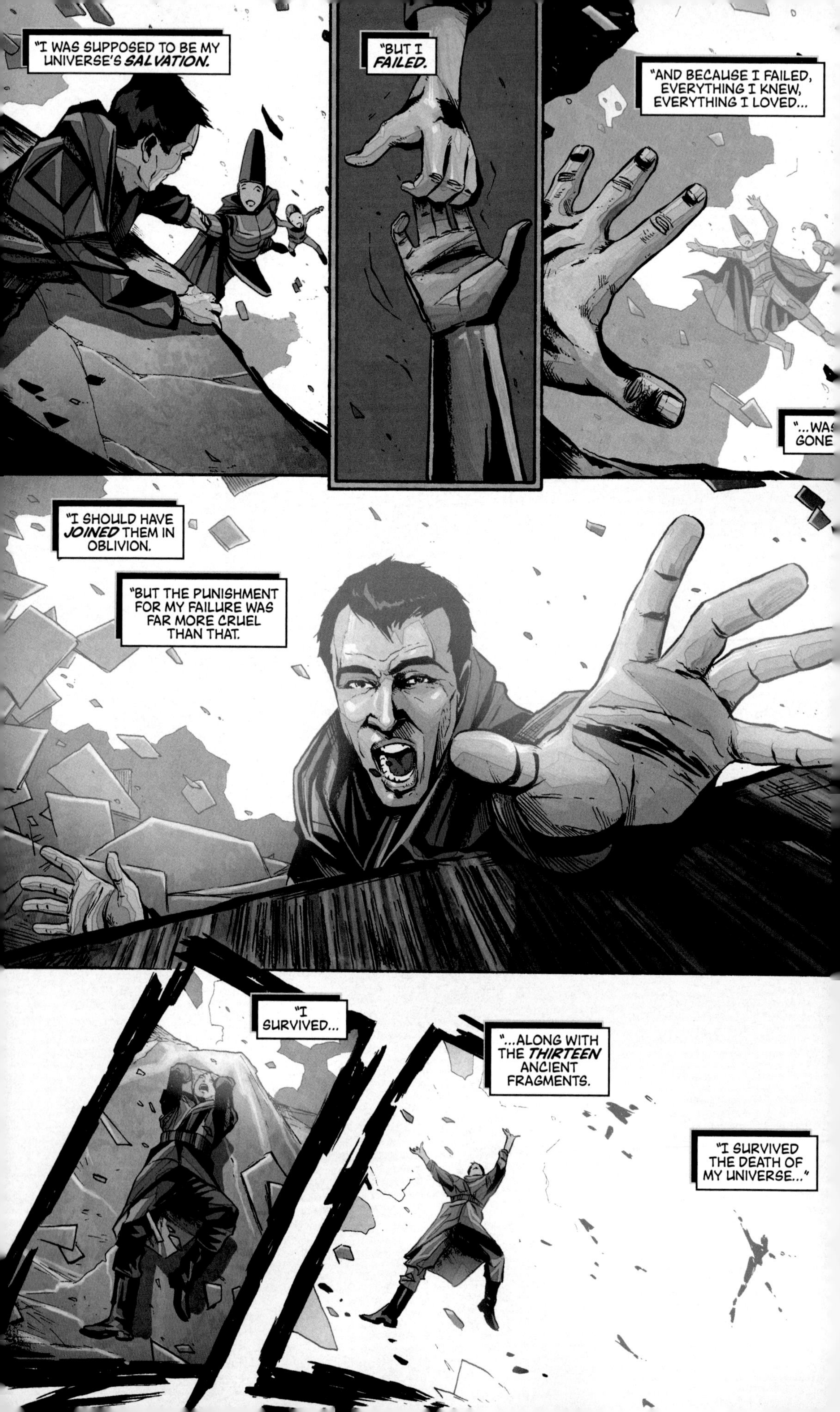
"I WAS SUPPOSED TO BE MY UNIVERSE'S *SALVATION.*
"BUT I *FAILED.*
"AND BECAUSE I FAILED, EVERYTHING I KNEW, EVERYTHING I LOVED...
"...WAS GONE
"I SHOULD HAVE *JOINED* THEM IN OBLIVION.
"BUT THE PUNISHMENT FOR MY FAILURE WAS FAR MORE CRUEL THAN THAT.
"I SURVIVED...
"...ALONG WITH THE *THIRTEEN* ANCIENT FRAGMENTS.
"I SURVIVED THE DEATH OF MY UNIVERSE..."

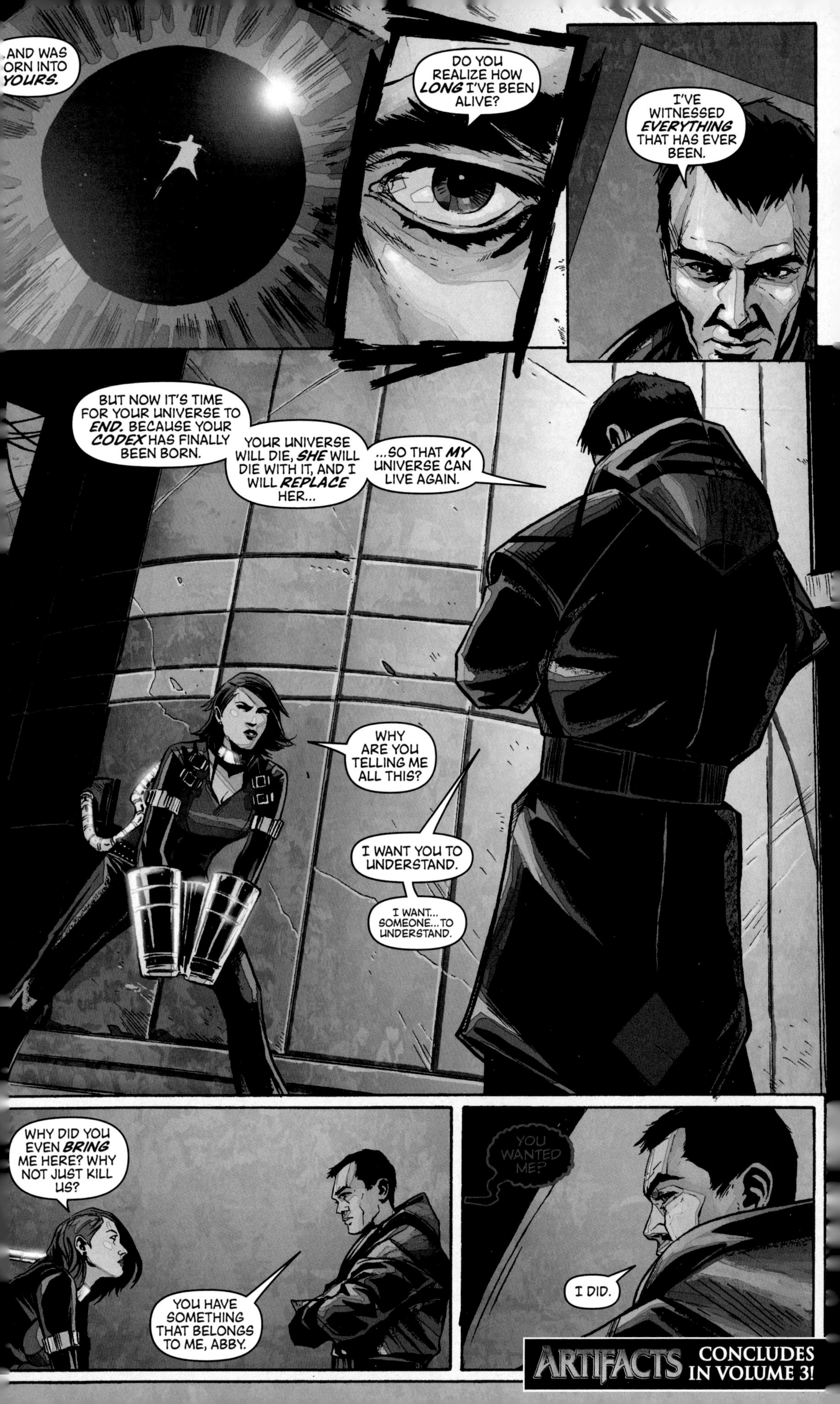

...AND WAS
...ORN INTO
YOURS.
DO YOU REALIZE HOW LONG I'VE BEEN ALIVE?
I'VE WITNESSED EVERYTHING THAT HAS EVER BEEN.
BUT NOW IT'S TIME FOR YOUR UNIVERSE TO END. BECAUSE YOUR CODEX HAS FINALLY BEEN BORN.
YOUR UNIVERSE WILL DIE, SHE WILL DIE WITH IT, AND I WILL REPLACE HER...
...SO THAT MY UNIVERSE CAN LIVE AGAIN.
WHY ARE YOU TELLING ME ALL THIS?
I WANT YOU TO UNDERSTAND.
I WANT... SOMEONE... TO UNDERSTAND.
WHY DID YOU EVEN BRING ME HERE? WHY NOT JUST KILL US?
YOU HAVE SOMETHING THAT BELONGS TO ME, ABBY.
YOU WANTED ME?
I DID.
ARTIFACTS CONCLUDES IN VOLUME 3!

Explore more about The Artifacts within the Top Cow Universe!

Ron Marz • Michael Broussard
ARTIFACTS
volume 1
FEATURING AN INTRODUCTION BY
MARC SILVESTRI

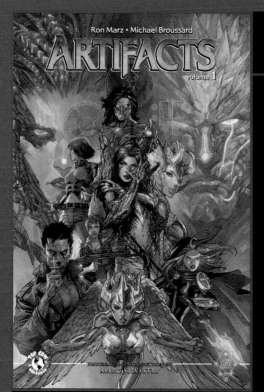

Artifacts
Volume 1

written by:
Ron Marz
pencils by:
Michael Broussard &
Stjepan Sejic

When a mysterious antagonist kidnaps Hope, the daughter of Sara Pezzini and Jackie Estacado, Armageddon is set in motion. Featuring virtually every character in the Top Cow Universe, Artifacts is an epic story for longtime fans and new readers alike.

Collects issues #0-4

(ISBN 978-1-60706-201-1)

ANGELUS

RON MARZ • STJEPAN SEJIC
BROKEN TRINITY

Angelus
Volume 1
written by:
Ron Marz
art by:
Stjepan Sejic

Collects issues #1-6

ISBN#
978-1-60706-198-4

First Born
Volume 1
written by:
Ron Marz
art by:
Stjepan Sejic

Collects First Born issues #0-3
& Witchblade issues #110-112

ISBN#
978-1-58240-864-5

Broken Trinity
Volume 1
written by:
Ron Marz with Phil Hester
& Bryan Edward Hill
art by:
Stjepan Sejic & more

Collects issues #1-3, Broken Trinity: The Darkness #1, Broken Trinity: Witchblade #1, Broken Trinity: The Angelus #1 & Broken Trinity: Aftermath #1

ISBN#
978-1-60706-198-4